Corporate Governance

Mechanisms and Systems

Corporate Governance

Mechanisms and Systems

Steen Thomsen and Martin Conyon

McGraw-Hill
Higher Education

London   Boston   Burr Ridge, IL   Dubuque, IA   Madison, WI   New York   San Francisco
St. Louis   Bangkok   Bogotá   Caracas   Kuala Lumpur   Lisbon   Madrid   Mexico City
Milan   Montreal   New Delhi   Santiago   Seoul   Singapore   Sydney   Taipei   Toronto

Corporate Governance: Mechanisms and Systems
Steen Thomsen and Martin Conyon
ISBN-13 9780077132590
ISBN-10 0077132599

Published by McGraw-Hill Education
Shoppenhangers Road
Maidenhead
Berkshire
SL6 2QL
Telephone: 44 (0) 1628 502 500
Fax: 44 (0) 1628 770 224
Website: www.mcgraw-hill.co.uk

British Library Cataloguing in Publication Data
A catalogue record for this book is available from the British Library

Library of Congress Cataloguing in Publication Data
The Library of Congress data for this book has been applied for from the Library of Congress

Acquisitions Editor: Tom Hill
Production Editor: Alison Davis
Marketing Manager: Vanessa Boddington

Text Design by HL Studios
Cover design by Adam Renvoize
Printed and bound by CPI Group (UK) Ltd, Croydon, CR0 4YY

Published by McGraw-Hill Education (UK) Limited, an imprint of The McGraw-Hill Companies, Inc., 1221 Avenue of the Americas, New York, NY 10020. © 2012, worldwide rights owned by McGraw-Hill International (UK) Limited England, Danish distribution rights granted to DJØF Publishing.

ISBN-13 9780077132590
ISBN-10 0077132599

The *McGraw·Hill* Companies

Dedication

To my wife Annette for her love and support,
and to my sons Nicolai and Michael for
making this world a much more interesting place.

Steen Thomsen

To Lina for all her love and support.

Martin Conyon

Brief Table of Contents

Detailed Table of Contents

About the Authors

Professor Steen Thomsen is director of the Center for Corporate Governance at Copenhagen Business School. He specializes in corporate governance as a teacher, researcher, consultant, commentator and practitioner. His academic publications include 25 international journal articles on corporate governance as well as several papers on other issues. He is currently researching industrial foundations – charitable foundations which own business firms. Steen has taught corporate governance courses since 1993 and has developed courses in international corporate governance, and corporate governance and finance. He has previously written the textbook *An introduction to Corporate Governance*. Steen has served as a board member in several business companies and is currently a non-executive chairman of two consulting firms. He writes regular newspaper columns, and has served as a consultant lecturer to several large companies and government organizations, including the EU, the UN, the Copenhagen Stock Exchange, the Danish Central Bank and the Danish Venture Capital Association. He has also contributed to the Danish corporate governance code and other best practice codes. He is married to Annette Blegvad, lives in Charlottenlund, north of Copenhagen, Denmark and is the proud father of two grown-up red-haired boys.

Martin Conyon is a Senior Fellow and Lecturer at the Wharton School, University of Pennsylvania. He also holds a Chair in Corporate Governance at the University of Lancaster, UK. In addition, he is a Research Fellow at the Institute of Compensation Studies at Cornell University.

Martin has published over 75 articles and has made contributions to the fields of management and economics especially in the areas of boards of directors and the leadership of organizations. He has contributed to major economics and finance journals including the *Review of Financial Studies*, *International Journal of Industrial Organization*, and *Journal of Industrial Economics*.

He is an editorial board member of the *Strategic Management Journal*, *Strategic Organization* and *Corporate Governance: An International Review*.

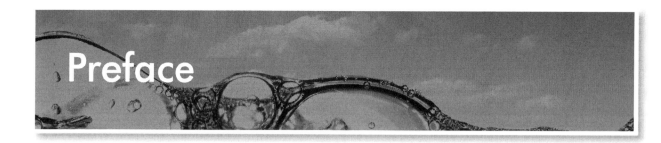
Preface

This book about corporate governance can be read independently or be used for a semester course in corporate governance. When you have read and understood it, you can congratulate yourself that you are now at the master's level! We have tried to write in an engaging manner, so the determined reader should have no problem digesting it. The book is divided in four parts:

I. Introduction (Chapters 1–4). Here we define the topic, discuss various relevant theories including a formal analysis of agency problems, present the many different governance mechanisms, large owners, boards, incentives, company law etc. and show how countries combine governance mechanisms to governance systems.

II. Mechanisms (Chapters 5–10). Here we study some of the most important governance mechanisms in detail: social norms, CSR, ownership, boards and incentives.

III. International Systems (Chapters 11–17). Here we study governance systems (country models): the US–UK market model, the traditional German bank model, Japanese relational capitalism, Chinese state ownership, the Scandinavian stakeholder model and family business in East Asia.

IV. Practice (Chapter 18). Here we conclude with a brief discussion of governance practices.

The structure is modular and can therefore be used in different types of courses. The first four chapters form the common core which most courses will probably use. From then on, governance and finance courses may want to focus on ownership, institutional investors, managerial incentives and Chapter 11 on the market model (US/UK). International business courses will typically use the country Chapters 11–17. Management courses will want to focus on board work and practice (Chapters 8, 9, 18) and pay (Chapter 10). Courses in business ethics will (we hope) make use of the chapters on informal governance, CSR and the stakeholder model (Chapters 5, 6, 16).

The book is a sequel to Steen's earlier book *An Introduction to Corporate Governance: Mechanisms and Systems*, which we draw from, but all chapters have been rewritten and many completely new chapters have been added.

We try to combine a theoretical, evidence-based approach with an informal style and attention to practice. Thus, the book is probably more theoretical and research-intensive than standard management textbooks, but less so than textbooks in finance and economics. Readers familiar with the topic will hopefully also recognize a few new ideas.

Martin wrote the appendix to Chapter 2, as well as the chapters on CSR (6), executive compensation (10), the US and the UK (11) and China (15). Chapter 12 was co-authored and Steen wrote the rest (Chapters 1, 2, 3, 4, 5, 7, 8, 9, 13, 14, 16, 17 and 18).

March 2012

Steen Thomsen
Center for Corporate Governance
Copenhagen Business School

Martin Conyon
Lancaster University
& The Wharton School

Acknowledgements

We are grateful to Christa Børsting and Annette Blegvad for research assistance and proofreading. Thank you to Therese Strand for her work on the Online Learning Centre. Martin has benefited from comments and discussions with many people. His thanks are extended to Rocio Bonet, Bert Cannella, Peter Cappelli, John Core, Gina Dokko, Paul Gregg, Wayne Guay, Don Hambrick, Lerong He, Bill Judge, David Larker, Steve Machin, Kevin Murphy, Graham Sadler, Steve Thompson, as well as many other colleagues and friends.

Our thanks go to the following reviewers for their comments at various stages in the text's development:

Tom Aabo, Aarhus University
Sanjay Banejee, University of Essex
Edel Barnes, University College Cork
Tom Berglund, Hanken School of Economics
Catherine H. Chen, Middlesex University
Jean Chen, University of Surrey
Derek Condon, Warwick Business School
Robert Day, Bournemouth University
Roy Edwards, University of Southampton
Sean Elder, University of Hertfordshire
Oliver Marnet, University of Exeter
Rob Melville, City University
Donald Nordberg, London Metropolitan University
Trond Randøy, University of Agder
Eleni Sophocleous, University of Durham
Konstantinos Stathopoulos, University of Manchester
Claes Svensson, Lund University

Finally, Steen and Martin would like to thank Thomas Hill at McGraw-Hill for his help and expert guidance during this project.

Every effort has been made to trace and acknowledge ownership of copyright and to clear permission for material reproduced in this book. The publishers will be pleased to make suitable arrangements to clear permission with any copyright holders whom it has not been possible to contact.

Guided Tour

Figures and Tables

Each chapter provides a number of tables and figures to help you to visualise key theories and studies.

Figure 3.1 *Declining marginal productivity*

Company performance
(or social performance)

Governance by factor X

shareholders to make better choices. Beyond this point, which is difficult to define and varies from mechanism to mechanism and from firm to firm, the costs start to kick in. From that point increasing use of this governance mechanism will destroy the value.

In other words, corporate governance is about finding the golden mean, that is, how a particular set of mechanisms create most value in a particular situation. Note that this could be a corner solution: it may be that some companies are better off without large owners or even without a board. We will go through the different mechanisms of corporate governance and will point to some of their costs and their benefits.

3.2 Social norms

At the most basic level corporate governance depends on social norms or what we call morality. Suppose a manager gets an opportunity to steal shareholder funds and knows it will never be detected. Will he do it? Economic man would. Would you? Suppose that it was a lot of money, so much that you could live on it comfortably for the rest of your life. Maybe the temptation is stronger

Minicase

This feature uses real-life situations to illustrate and expand on the concepts and ideas covered in the chapter.

iz **viewpoint** is that the different approaches to corporate governance are complementary than contradictory. Rather than negating the role of incentives of information asymmetries, ology and law and a host of other factors shape how they are perceived and handled in ular companies. Corporate governance students can examine to what extent the governance articular company is shaped by the factors and understand more of what is going on. The risk theory is of course that we end up with a lot of 'hand waving' and little value added. We ore recommend that students start with agency theory and introduce alternative perspectives they are in fact believed to add significantly to understanding the problem at hand.

Minicase

Bankers' pay 2010

According to the Financial Times of June 15, 2011, bankers' pay started to rise again in 2010 - just a year after the financial crisis. Loyd Blankenfein, CEO of Goldman Sachs took a pay increase of 15.45% from $862,657 in 2009 to $14,114,980 in 2010. Jamie Dimon, CEO of JPMorgan Chase got $20,776,324 in 2010, up by 15419% from $1,265,708 in 2009. James Gorman CEO of Morgan Stanley, hired in 2010, got $14,854,049. These figures do not include capital gains on equity awards granted in earlier years. These gains can be significant, for example in the case of Jamie Dimon they are estimated at $35 million dollars in 2010. The pay increase reflects both increases in share prices for equity-linked pay and increases in fixed salaries.

Critics are outraged that the same people who nearly destroyed the world's financial system are now again paid so much. Banks retort that the CEOs got much more before the crisis. For example Loyd Blankenfein took home $70 million in 2007.

Bankers' pay also rose in the UK. Stephen Hester of Royal Bank of Scotland got $11,537,346, up 15% from 2009. The British Government had to take over 83% of RBS during the crisis. Eric Daniels of Lloyds Banking Group got $8,367,953 in 2010, up 68% from 2009. Eric Daniels is criticized for a disastrous tie-up between Lloyds and HBOS during the crisis. John Varley of Barclays got $5,945,946 in 2010, up 239% from 2009. Barclays bought the failed investment bank Lehman's US business cheaply and did not have to get government aid.

The trend was less expansive in continental Europe. Brady Dougan of Credit Suisse had to take a pay cut of 33% to $11,807,725. The Swiss media was outraged that he got $83 million in 2010 under a long-term incentive plan. Joseph Ackerman of Deutsche Bank got $8,548,380 in 2010 down 19%. Fransisco Gonsalez of Banco Bilbao got $8,070,985 in 2010, down 10%. Badouin Prot of BNP Paribas got $3,530,624, up 3% from 2009.

Discussion Questions

These questions get you to think in more detail about the Minicase and explore the subject area further.

Discussion questions

1 What are the key governance differences between US and German firms?
2 What problems could this create for the merged company?
3 What do you think about 'the merger of equals'?
4 Did governance become stronger or weaker after the merger?
5 Why do you think share prices fell during the talks with Nissan?
6 Was DaimlerChrysler doomed to failure?
7 Do you think Fiat-Chrysler will work?

Summary (learning points)

■ Countries tend to have distinctive governance systems conditioned by history, politics and interdependencies among governance mechanisms.
■ The UK and the USA broadly conform to the market model: they have large liquid stock markets, dispersed ownership, high investor protection, and widespread use of incentive pay and independent one-tier boards.
■ Germany, in contrast, has a much smaller stock market, more concentrated ownership, two-tier boards with employee representation and influential banks. The system can be described as a stakeholder model.
■ Japan is characterized by powerful banks, ownership ties between business firms, insider-dominated boards and limited use of performance pay. We describe it as a network system.
■ France has medium ownership concentration, primarily one-tier boards with a powerful President Directeur General and a tradition for government intervention. We therefore characterize the French model as 'public governance'.
■ Scandinavia has strong elements of the stakeholder model, which are taken even further by specific features such as strong welfare states, a gender quota (in Norway) and industrial foundations (in Denmark).
■ Governance systems are not constant and we see some signs of convergence over time.

Summary

Every chapter concludes with a number of bullet points, highlighting the most important points to take away from the chapter.

Would the company's long-term progress be served by dispersed ownership?
What would be the costs and benefits of foreign ownership?
What might a private equity firm do to the company?
How about a domestic blockholder taking a large share? Would that work?
What would you advise the government to do?

Summary (learning points)

■ Ownership is a set of rights to use, control, profit from and transfer assets.
■ Shareholders usually have rights to control (vote), profit (dividend) and transfer (sell) shares.
■ Ownership matters most when ownership is concentrated.
■ Ownership identity matters because different owners (individuals, institutions, companies, governments, non-profits) have different goals, competences and resources.
■ Each ownership structure has its costs and benefits which makes it appropriate for certain firms.
■ A higher ownership share can lead to positive incentive effects and negative entrenchment effects.
■ Private equity funds specialize in buying, owning and selling firms. They typically target mature firms with a high cash flow.
■ Cooperatives are associations which may own business firms. They are particularly common in farm-related businesses.

References and further reading

Acharya, V.V., C. Kehoe and M. Reyner (2009) Private Equity vs. PLC Boards in the U.K. A Comparison of Practices and Effectiveness, Journal of Applied Corporate Finance, Vol. 21, No. 1, pp. 45-56.
Alchian, A.A. and H. Demsetz (1972) Production

Vol. 1, U.S. Joint Economic Committee, 91st Congress, 1st Session, US Print Office, Washington DC.
Arrow, K.J. (1975) Vertical Integration and Communication, Bell Journal of Economics, Vol. 6, pp. 173-183.

References

An extensive list of references can be found at the end of each chapter.

References and further reading

Acharya, V.V., Kehoe, C. and Reyner, M. (2009) Private Equity vs. PLC Boards in the U.K. A Comparison of Practices and Effectiveness, Journal of Applied Corporate Finance, 21 (1), 45-56.
Alchian, A.A. and Demsetz, H. (1972) Production, Information Costs, and Economic Organization, American Economic Review, 62 (5), 777-795.
Amihud, Y. and Lev, B. (1981) Risk reduction as a managerial motive for conglomerate mergers, Bell Journal of Economics, 12 (2), 605-617.
Arrow, K.J. (1969) The organization of economic activity: issues pertinent to the choice of market versus nonmarket allocation, in The Analysis and Evaluation of Public Expenditure: The PPB System, Vol. 1, U.S. Joint Economic Committee, 91st Congress, 1st Session, US Print Office, Washington DC.

Arrow, K.J. (1975) Vertical Integration and Communication, Bell Journal of Economics, 6, 173-183.
Bergh, D.D. (1995) Size and relatedness of units sold: an agency theory and resource-based perspective, Strategic Management Journal, 16 (3).
Bergström, C. and Rydqvist, K. (1990) The Determinants of Corporate Ownership. An Empirical Study on Swedish Data, Journal of Banking and Finance, 14 (2), 237-253.
Berle, A. and Means, C. (1932) The Modern Corporation and Private Property, Macmillan: New York.
Bethel, J.E. and Liebeskind, J. (1993) The effects of ownership structure on corporate restructuring, Strategic Management Journal, 14 (Summer Special Issue), 15-31.

Online Learning Centre

www.mcgraw-hill.co.uk/textbooks/thomsen

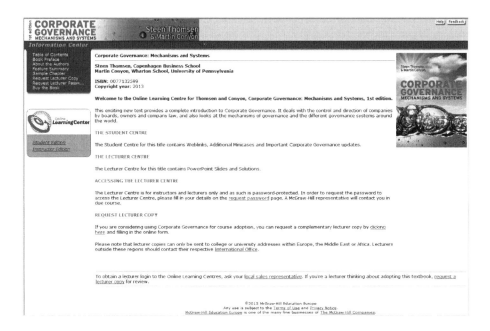

Lecturer support – Helping you to help your students

The Online Learning Centre offers lecturers adopting this book a range of resources designed to offer:

- **Faster course preparation** – time-saving support for your module
- **High-calibre content to support your students** – resources written by your academic peers, who understand your need for rigorous and reliable content
- **Flexibility** – edit, adapt or repurpose; test in EZ Test or your department's Course Management System. The choice is yours.

The materials created specifically for lecturers adopting this textbook include:

- *PowerPoint Slides*
- *Solutions Manual.*

Students get access to:

- *Website Links*
- *Additional Case Studies*
- *Important Corporate Governance Updates*

To request your password to access these resources, contact your McGraw-Hill representative or visit **www.mcgraw-hill.co.uk/textbooks/thomsen**.

Let us help make our **content** your **solution**

At McGraw-Hill Education our aim is to help lecturers to find the most suitable content for their needs delivered to their students in the most appropriate way. Our **custom publishing solutions** offer the ideal combination of content delivered in the way which best suits lecturer and students.

Our custom publishing programme offers lecturers the opportunity to select just the chapters or sections of material they wish to deliver to their students from a database called CREATE™ at

www.mcgrawhillcreate.co.uk

CREATE™ contains over two million pages of content from:
- textbooks
- professional books
- case books – Harvard Articles, Insead, Ivey, Darden, Thunderbird and BusinessWeek
- Taking Sides – debate materials

Across the following imprints:
- McGraw-Hill Education
- Open University Press
- Harvard Business Publishing
- US and European material

There is also the option to include additional material authored by lecturers in the custom product – this does not necessarily have to be in English.

We will take care of everything from start to finish in the process of developing and delivering a custom product to ensure that lecturers and students receive exactly the material needed in the most suitable way.

With a Custom Publishing Solution, students enjoy the best selection of material deemed to be the most suitable for learning everything they need for their courses – something of real value to support their learning. Teachers are able to use exactly the material they want, in the way they want, to support their teaching on the course.

Please contact your local McGraw-Hill representative with any questions or alternatively contact Warren Eels **e: warren_eels@mcgraw-hill.com.**

PART **1**

Introduction

Part contents

Chapter 1

What is Corporate Governance?

Chapter contents

1.1   Introduction

We define corporate governance as the control and direction of companies by ownership, boards, incentives, company law, and other mechanisms. This follows the widely-used definition by Cadbury (1992) as *'the system by which companies are directed and controlled'*. It means setting the direction in which the company is going, its goals and objectives, as well as controlling the implementation of these goals.

There are many other definitions in the literature. To business people and in the management literature corporate governance is all about boards: what boards do, how they are composed, and so on. This is reflected in best practice corporate governance codes such as the UK corporate governance code or the NYSE code. Among investors and in the finance literature there is a tendency to focus on the relations between the company and its shareholders. This includes specifying what rights shareholders have, whether the firm is protected against takeover by various defences, etc. Legal scholars and professionals focus on company and securities law as the primary corporate governance issue. Accounting scholars and professionals focus on how companies are held accountable to outside stakeholders through annual reports. Politicians and the media tend to focus on business ethics and corporate social responsibility, including financial scandals, fraud, and the possibility of corrupt practices. Sociologists focus on networks, socialization, and values. Psychologists focus on motivation, for example the intrinsic utility of 'good stewardship'. As is evident, different communities view corporate governance in different ways.

It is natural that there should be different perspectives on this important subject. The views of various stakeholders may be expected to reflect their fields of experience and, to some extent, their vested interests. It is not surprising, for example, that financial investors try to make shareholder value the central objective in corporate governance.

In the *Journal of Finance*, Shleifer and Vishny (1997) defined corporate governance as 'the ways in which suppliers of finance assure themselves of getting a return on their investment'. This definition is focused on the financial aspects of governance and may be useful for many purposes, but it can be too narrow in other cases. For example, business efficiency might be more important than investor relations. Note, however, that suppliers of finance include both shareholders and creditors such as banks. These suppliers provide the firm with funding and are, of course, concerned with the payback. Cadbury's (1992) definition (above) is somewhat broader. For example, it does not exclude stakeholder concerns or corporate governance issues in privately held companies that do not attract outside funding.

An even broader definition was given by Charkham (1994): 'The way companies are run'. This is perhaps too broad because it includes everything that companies do. And a definition that includes everything is meaningless. But one thing is clear: corporate governance is influenced by national history, culture and institutions. German or Japanese corporate governance is very different from what is found in the USA or the UK. Charkham's (1994) book had the title *'Keeping Good Company'* to underline the social aspects. Monks and Minow (2001) also adopt a broader view of governance as 'the relationship between various participants in determining the direction and performance of corporations' with shareholders, management and boards as the primary participants.

A key distinction in governance definitions is to what extent the company is seen as accountable to shareholders or to a broader set of stakeholders. There is little doubt that Non-Government Agencies (NGOs), ethical investors, and managers themselves have broadened the corporate governance agenda in recent years. Many now see companies as responsible for issues such as child labour or climate change, which were previously not debated in boardrooms. Corporate social responsibility issues are now addressed in British company law. Since these trends do influence the direction and control of companies they are effectively part of corporate governance whether or not they ought to be.

Much of this book will be concerned with publicly traded companies, but corporate governance is very relevant for other organizational forms such as state-owned enterprises, family businesses, cooperatives and not-for-profit firms. Management needs to be held accountable to somebody or other. In addition these types of organizational forms have special governance challenges that need to be addressed. How much and how should politicians be involved in the actual running of state-owned enterprises? How do not-for-profit firms elect new board members if there is no annual general meeting? How are management and board succession problems in family firms best managed? Dealing with such issues in non-publicly traded firms is as important as corporate governance arrangements in large publicly quoted companies. Often, though, it is the large public companies that attract media attention.

1.2   What corporate governance is not

A definition must also be clear about what it excludes. If it does not exclude anything, it's not a definition.

For example, there is an important difference between corporate governance and corporate management. Although corporate governance is concerned with good management, it is not about management as such. Rather, corporate governance is about the control and direction of managers. Operationally, this means that important business functions like marketing, human resource management or financial management are not normally part of corporate governance. To be sure, managers can be controlled and directed by other more senior managers within the firm. Hiring managers to control managers just moves the control problem one level up; who will then control the managers who control the managers? It follows that top managers must necessarily be controlled by some other mechanism than management: in other words, by some governance mechanism. Juvenal's classic question 'Quis custodiet ipsos custodes?' – Who is to guard the guardians? – captures the essence of the problem.

Moreover, corporate governance is not a religion. It is a field of practice and study. After all, if it was a religion, it could not be studied in business schools. We are concerned with corporate governance because we want companies to perform well and to create value for society. Good management and good investments are clearly essential conditions for good performance, and corporate governance aims to ensure good management and good investment. There is no inherently 'right' kind of corporate governance since what works well in one firm does not necessarily work well in another. In practice, good corporate governance is about finding appropriate solutions – tailor-made, if you like – for the individual firm.

Finally, corporate governance is not synonymous with governance codes or Sarbanes–Oxley-like regulation. Family firms or state-owned enterprises have their own kind of governance, for better or for worse. Whenever there are companies there is governance of some kind. In extreme examples where managers run companies without any kind of control we can talk about managerialism.

1.3   The basic governance problem

Corporate governance problems are not new. Economists have long recognized that conflicts of interest can arise in the direction and control of companies. Adam Smith (1776) in the *Wealth of Nations* knew all too well the central governance problem and wrote: 'The directors of such companies, however, being the managers rather of other people's money than of their own, it cannot well be expected that they should watch over it with the same anxious vigilance with which the partners in a private copartnery frequently watch over their own. Like the stewards of a rich man, they are apt to consider attention to small matters as not for their master's honour, and very easily

give themselves a dispensation from having it. Negligence and profusion, therefore, must always prevail, more or less, in the management of the affairs of such a company'.[1]

The basic problem of corporate governance, from a theoretical perspective, then, is the so-called 'agency problem' which occurs because of the separation between ownership and management. This is termed 'the separation of ownership and control' by Berle and Means (1932).

The idea is that owners (shareholders) hire executives to manage companies on their behalf. In agency theory, we say that the agent (i.e. managers) acts on behalf of the principal (i.e. shareholders). The shareholders leave their money and other assets in the custody of the managers. The basic question to address is how to ensure that managers will manage the assets well. For example, what keeps them from taking the money and running away with it? Clearly, the law has some bearing on this and is, therefore, perhaps the most fundamental governance mechanism. It is worth noting however that stock markets have historically been able to flourish with little legal support. Thus informal mechanisms like reputation and trust may be even more basic control factors. Vigilant owners, for example owner-managers or large shareholders, represent another powerful control mechanism; self-interested owners will monitor what goes on in the firm and replace bad or opportunistic managers. Managers may be motivated to create more value for the shareholders through incentive systems (i.e. bonuses or stock options). The threat of being fired by an alert board could also be enough to make them work hard. Agency theory, by far the most important approach to corporate governance, is specifically concerned with devising efficient solutions to the agency problem when both owners and managers are rational and self-interested.

There are more theories about corporate governance than agency theory, of course. As previously mentioned, corporate governance is a multidisciplinary subject which draws on economics, law, sociology, psychology and political science. Within business studies it draws on management and organizational behaviour, finance, accounting, international business, and other topics. Economic theories of corporate governance include agency, transaction cost and incomplete contract theory. The focus within these economic theories is, likewise, on relatively rational, selfish and sometimes opportunistic decision makers who interact with and create organizational mechanisms to further their own interests. This 'model of man' has been challenged by sociologists and psychologists who emphasize that human beings are not always rational and may not be motivated by self-interest.

In this book we subscribe to what we call 'enlightened agency theory', which takes agency theory as a starting point, but borrows from psychology, sociology, political science, law and other fields where appropriate. This creates a more complicated but richer understanding of governance issues without losing track of the central governance issues. For example, not all managers or shareholders are selfishly rational, but this does not mean that we can forget incentive problems. Agency problems are shaped by regulation and social context, but they do not become irrelevant.

1.4   The extended agency problem

In the real world, of course, there are more than two actors (principal and agent), so the picture becomes much more complicated (Figure 1.1).

Between owners and managers there is a board elected by the owners. Not all types of firms are required to have a board, but for most large firms this is a legal requirement. Boards are the straightforward solution to the corporate governance problem. A group of people are elected to the board to sanction major decisions and to monitor that managers are doing their jobs well. Boards usually meet regularly (e.g. five times a year, sometimes as often as 10 times a year).

The owners of a firm do not necessarily comprise a homogeneous group. There may be many or few owners. Some owners may be private individuals (i.e. 'mom and pop' investors). Some may be founders or members of the founding family. Owners may be institutional investors, mutual funds or hedge funds. There might be some owners who are actively concerned with corporate governance.

---

[1] Adam Smith, 1776, Book V, Part III article 1: http://www.econlib.org/library/Smith/smWN20.html#anchor_j65

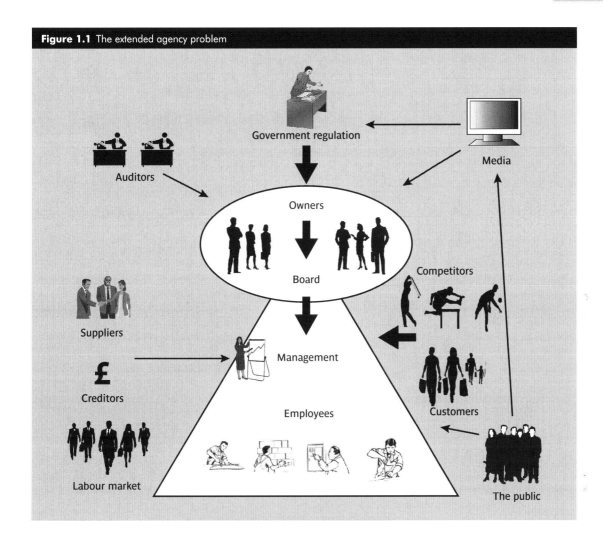

Figure 1.1 The extended agency problem

Others may be passive investors who never vote and who mechanically match their portfolio to an index and choose to leave it to others to be active owners.

Moreover, most firms have stakeholders with whom they do business and who can directly and indirectly influence their corporate governance.

Banks and other creditors can play a powerful role in corporate governance for firms in need of external finance because they can sanction or veto investment projects, make demands on the composition of the board, and write debt contracts that include conditions (covenants) about what the firm should and should not do. In some countries, banks are so powerful that we talk about a bank-based corporate governance model. Banks may own large stakes in companies if the law permits.

Employees can also play a role in corporate governance. In some countries, employees are entitled to elect board members (e.g. Germany, Austria, and in Scandinavia). If labour unions are strong, they influence the strategic direction of the company since many decisions must be negotiated with them. Employees can also be owners: in owner-managed firms or in professional partnerships, for example, which are common structures for law firms, accounting firms and management consulting firms. Employees may acquire shares as part of employee-ownership policies.

Suppliers can play a role in corporate governance as owners of firms: for example in cooperatives, where farmers jointly own the slaughterhouses or dairies to which they sell their product. A subsidiary relationship is another structure: for example, as when IBM USA owns a sales subsidiary in France. In joint ventures, the participating companies will often share ownership and will appoint their own representatives to the board.

Customers can also own the companies from which they buy (e.g. retail cooperatives, investment funds) or they can influence them in other ways. The futurist Alvin Toffler once suggested that companies should appoint advisory boards composed partly of customers and through which the customers could get a formal channel of communication to the company. Many companies work hard to build customer relationships and to endorse the marketing concept according to which the customers should have priority over other stakeholder groups.

The most direct way in which customers exercise their influence, however, is through competition. In very competitive markets the job of controlling managers is effectively 'taken over' by the competition since the managers must continuously work hard to stay ahead of their competition. If there are many competitors in a market, shareholders can more easily evaluate the performance of their managers. They can compare their performance with other firms and owners can more easily replace their managers with those from competing firms.

Governments influence corporate governance by making the rules (i.e. laws and regulation). For example, should banks be allowed to own firms? How much should family ownership be taxed by inheritance and wealth taxes? Should pension fund ownership be subsidized by tax benefits? Governments in different parts of the world address these questions in different ways.

Governments can also play a direct role as owners of business enterprises. This used to be quite common, particularly in the former socialist countries, but until recently the trend was to privatize. However, with the financial crisis the pendulum swung back. Banks, insurance companies and even automakers were nationalized.

In addition to the direct stakeholders, the media and various kinds of special interest organizations (NGOs, etc.) can influence corporate governance. Managers and shareholders fear public exposure and act to avoid scandal, sometimes by changing their policies to accommodate grassroots organizations like Greenpeace.

There are several other actors. Auditors, analysts and stock exchanges play a special role by providing information to shareholders and to other stakeholders. Lawyers, stockbrokers, consultants, insurance companies and others also have their role to play.

In all this complexity, the primary focal point in corporate governance is the relationship between owners and companies, with particular focus on the board.

1.5 Why governance?

A third approach to the definition of the subject is to examine why people are interested in it.

At the most general level, good management is obviously crucial to economic efficiency, productivity, firm performance and social welfare. According to Bengt Holmström, 'corporate governance is about mechanisms by which scarce decision making resources are allocated in society'. Corporate governance aims to ensure good decision making – meaning hiring the right managers, motivating them well through reward systems, giving them sufficient freedom to act and combining this freedom with a system of checks and balances to prevent the abuse of power. In this sense, good corporate governance has always been essential for good economic performance.

It is not difficult to find examples of good and bad corporate governance at many levels. Many boards are known to rubber stamp proposals put forward by the executives and so fail to take their control role seriously. Others act in time and replace the CEO or veto dubious acquisitions. Many owners do not take their ownership seriously and do not even bother to show up at shareholder meetings. Others actively seek to influence the direction of companies through dialogue or board representation. The executives of some banks now in government custody live well because they

cashed in their stock options in time. Others co-invest in their companies and align their future with the stockholders.

One way of thinking about governance is that it has the same functions as a safety switch which will turn off your electricity or gas before the accident happens. Some people even compare it to a national defence which is intended to avoid war. Hopefully you will not need it at all. In normal times you will not be able to see any benefits from it, but it can still be a good idea to have one. The safety belt metaphor captures some of the same ideas but ideally we want it to work before the accident happens!

But there is another, more obvious, reason which can explain why corporate governance has become such a fashionable topic in the past few decades. An unprecedented amount of savings is currently flowing from pension schemes into the global economy. This money must be used as well as possible since its investment will directly influence the living standards of future pensioners. In 1936, Keynes declared the coordination of savings and investment to be the Achilles heel of the capitalist economies. Keynes was concerned with the short-term macroeconomic impact of these imbalances. But there are also important microeconomic problems associated with them. How can we make sure that our pension money is put to good use? It is therefore no coincidence that pension funds have led the corporate governance debate around the world.

Recent scandals – such as Madoff or Lehman in 2008 or before that Enron, WorldCom, Tyco, Parmalat after the dot.com bubble or before that Maxwell and BCGI – are vivid examples that our pension money is not always being put to good use. Shareholders and debt holders suddenly realized they had lost a significant amount of money, in some cases because they had been deliberately misled by fraudulent managers. Stunning examples of mismanagement often inspire action: for example, the implementation of new laws or codes of best practice to prevent a repeat of these errors.

Long before Keynes, another economist, Adam Smith (1776), discovered that government intervention is not always the best way to create wealth. For example, corporate governance structures that invite scandals may, over time, be replaced by more efficient structures, if the rules and regulations allow it. Although most corporate governance regulation is based on the 'latest' scandal, it is doubtful whether the avoidance of scandals should be the overriding goal of corporate governance. Other famous economists, Frank Knight and Joseph Schumpeter, for example, have discovered that economic growth is to a large extent created by risk taking. Thus there are serious costs to regulation which makes firms more bureaucratic and more risk adverse. It may be better, in fact it probably is better, to tolerate a few scandals now and again than to slow down the capitalist engine of innovation and growth.

It is therefore important to find governance structures which on the one hand allow managers and entrepreneurs to do what they do best and on the other hand hold them accountable to investors if they also invest other people's money. Avoiding overregulation is another good reason to be interested in corporate governance.

1.6   Discussion

At the most general level corporate governance is concerned with how to devise institutions (i.e. governance mechanisms) that lead to wealth-creating decisions in businesses. It should come as no surprise that there are different opinions about what mechanisms are most effective and about how to define wealth generation. This diversity of views may in itself be productive, since it allows for various solutions to compete in the marketplace. In many other business disciplines – including business strategy, innovation studies and marketing – differentiation is considered to be an asset. Thus, it could also be argued that differentiation in corporate governance mechanisms at the firm level can be a source of advantage, since this enlarges the menu of choices available to investors and to other stakeholders.

However, it is important to remember that some of the most pertinent problems of corporate governance are associated with finance: in particular with how best to utilize the huge savings which are currently being accumulated in pension funds around the world.

The financial crisis: A wake-up call for corporate governance

The financial crisis of 2007–2009 was an economic disaster. It was the world's longest economic crisis since the great depression began in 1929. Warren Buffet called it an 'economic Pearl Harbor'. Even today few people realize how close the world was to economic meltdown – to a situation when ATMs would stop working, shops would close and economic activity would cease. The financial system was saved by quick, strong and untraditional countermeasures by central bankers and governments. Nevertheless, the crisis has left lasting scars in the form of an overwhelming debt burden, mass unemployment and a heavy burden of regulation.

How could this happen? While monetary and financial regulations were obviously part of the picture, the current consensus view is that the crisis was at least partly attributable to bad corporate governance. For example, the OECD Steering Committee on Corporate Governance argued that 'the financial crisis can to an important extent be attributed to failures and weaknesses in corporate governance' (Kirkpatrick, 2009). If you consider that the global stock MSCI index fell by more than 50% during the crisis and conservatively estimate that perhaps 1% of this was attributable to bad corporate governance, bad corporate governance cost the world $200–300 billion!

Most commentators focus on failing incentive systems. For example Barack Obama (2009) announced: 'We're going to examine the ways in which the means and manner of executive compensation have contributed to a reckless culture and quarter-by-quarter mentality that in turn have wrought havoc in our financial system.' A common theme is that short-term incentives like bonuses induced managers to take more and more risks. Given the familiar trade-off between risk and returns, managers can increase returns by taking on more risks, and this is what the bankers did. So it is suggested that bonuses should be stretched over longer periods of time, e.g. 3–5 years, so that they capture potential negative effects of risk taking. Instead of a 'bonus' (good) there may in some years be a 'malus' (bad), which is deducted from your bonus account. Another idea is to risk-adjust management compensation, for example by letting it depend on spreads which reveal the market's risk assessment. A third suggested solution is to rely more on share ownership and less on stock options, because shares are more sensitive to downside risk.

Some also direct attention to the role of boards, for example board competencies. After all, boards were responsible for hiring bank managers and negotiating their pay. So boards must take responsibility for incentive failures. One idea is that bank boards were not sufficiently competent in modern finance, and the recommended cure is then to upgrade competencies. For example the economist Willem Buiter (2009) suggested that 'All new board members should take a written test, set by the regulator and marked by independent experts, on the products, services and instruments traded and managed by their financial institutions. Existing board members should be tested every other year. Unless a passing grade is achieved, the would-be board member cannot serve. The graded test will be in the public domain.' With the recommendations of the UK Walker review, practice has actually moved in that direction. Another idea is that boards were insufficiently informed, and this has led to rules demanding that a much wider set of issues in risk management and management pay are put to bank boards.

It is possible to probe even deeper. Boards are elected by the shareholders, so where were the shareholders? If risk taking was excessive, management pay was over-incentivized and boards were too incompetent to do anything about it, why didn't the shareholders revolt? After all, it was their money which was first to go during the crisis. One answer is that many banks had highly diversified ownership without majority owners. This gives rise to free-rider problems and passivity among the shareholders who do little to control the agency problems between shareholders and managers. Many banks reinforced their managerial hegemony by voting caps and other takeover defences. It is interesting that the most leveraged financial institutions – the US investment banks which formed the vanguard of the financial crisis – were historically organized as partnerships where partners had equity at stake and therefore some in-built aversion to downside risk. Converting them to ordinary joint stock companies may have shifted their preferences towards risk taking. It is also interesting that many financially conservative institutions like mutuals were converted to stock companies before the crisis.

It is even possible that the crisis was ultimately attributable to culture. There have been numerous popular references to a culture of greed, perhaps spreading from Wall Street to the rest of the world. For example, Dr Rowan Williams, the Archbishop of Canterbury, has blamed the financial crisis on human greed (*The Telegraph*, 2011). Investment bankers and house owners got used to rising assets prices during the boom years preceding the crisis and expected prices to continue to rise in the future. This may have encouraged them to borrow and invest, thus blowing the bubble.

Sorting out these issues is a monumental task for corporate governance. Certainly the times have changed, and many practices are being changed. There is much more willingness to regulate, for example.

The crisis ended with a massive global bailout. Governments took over failing banks and businesses, and provided guarantees and rescue packages as well as volumes of credit at historically low interest rates. Ultimately, taxpayers had to pick up the bill. Many observers see this as an extreme case of 'moral hazard'. If banks and financial institutions know that they will be bailed out by the government, should they fail, they have much more of an incentive to take excessive risk. The knowledge that governments would save them may have contributed to the build up to the current crisis. With unchanged incentive structure the same could happen again in the not too distant future. Already in 2011 it was rumoured that bank bonuses were back to their pre-crisis levels. Thus the relevant agency problem may no longer be between owners and managers, but between managers and taxpayers.

Whatever the outcome of all these discussions, corporate governance has never been so topical as it is today, and it has never been more necessary to understand it in order it to manoeuvre in today's business environment.

Discussion questions

1 In rough terms the value of global stocks fell from US$60 trillion to US$30 trillion from top 28 September 2007 to bottom 27 February 2009. Global unemployment hit record levels (6.6%). Do you think this crisis could have been avoided if corporate governance had been optimal around the world?
2 How do you see the links between corporate governance and the crisis?
3 Is it correct to lay most responsibility on banks?
4 What do you think of the popular notion that the financial crisis was caused by greed? Does it contain a grain of truth? Does greed have anything to do with corporate governance?

Summary (learning points)

- We define corporate governance as 'the control and direction of companies'.
- Corporate governance is not company management – and not a religion!
- The basic governance problem is the agency problem: how do owners control managers?

- The extended agency problem includes governments, banks, employees and other stakeholders, who also influence corporate governance.
- One good reason to care about corporate governance is that it will influence the value of your future pension.
- The financial crisis has been (at least partly) attributed to bad corporate governance.

 ## References and further reading

Beckford, M. (2008) Archbishop of Canterbury: Greed has caused global financial crisis, *The Telegraph*. (15 October 2008).

Berle, A. and Means, G. (1932) *The Modern Corporation and Private Property*, Harcourt, Brace and World: New York [1932] 1968.

Buiter, W. (2009) Lessons from the Global Financial Crisis for Regulators and Supervisors, *Financial Times* Blog (accessed 26 May 2009).

Cadbury Commission (1992) *Code of Best Practice: Report of the Committee on the Financial Aspects of Corporate Governance*, Gee and Co.: London.

Charkham, J.P. (1994) *Keeping Good Company – A Study of Corporate Governance in Five Countries*, Oxford University Press Inc: New York.

Keynes, J.M. (1936) *The General Theory of Employment, Interest and Money*, Harcourt, Brace & World: New York.

Kirkpatrick, G. (2009) *The Corporate Governance Lessons from the Financial Crises*, OECD.

Knight, F. (1921) *Risk, Uncertainty and Profit*, Houghton Mifflin: Boston.

Monks, R.A. and Minow, N. (2001) *Corporate Governance*, Blackwell: Oxford.

Monks, R.A.G. and Minow, N. (2008) *Corporate Governance*, 4th edition, Wiley-Blackwell: Chichester.

Moore, M. (2008) Religious Leaders Blame Bankers' Greed for Financial Crisis, *The Telegraph* (accessed 25 December 2008).

Obama, B. (2009) Speech on Executive Compensation. http://www.cnbc.com/id/29014485/ CNBC.com (accessed 04 February 2009)

Schumpeter, J.A. (1934) *The Theory of Economic Development*, 2nd edition. Harvard University Press: New York.

Shleifer, A. and Vishny, R.W. (1997) A Survey of Corporate Governance, *Journal of Finance*, **52** (2), 737–83.

Smith, A. (1776) *An Inquiry into the Nature and Causes of the Wealth of Nations*, 1st edition. Liberty Classics: Indianapolis.

Chapter 2

Theories of Corporate Governance

Chapter contents

2.1 Introduction

In this chapter we review corporate governance theories beginning with the market model of standard microeconomics, which essentially rules out agency problems because of full information and competition. We go on to agency theory, which is in a sense just applied microeconomics based on the idea that people will respond rationally to incentives under asymmetric information. We also discuss other economic theories based on the same assumptions including transaction cost and incomplete contract theory.

While agency theory appears to lead to many insights about real world behaviour, and while it is unquestionably the single most important theory in corporate governance, it cannot explain all human behaviour. For a better understanding of corporate governance we also need to draw on other theories within the fields of economics, psychology, law, political science and sociology. An intelligent user will apply agency theory, but take into consideration, for example, that soft variables like ethics or prestige are sometimes more important to people than monetary gain.

We therefore also summarize relevant theories from related disciplines. For example, psychology offers more nuanced theories of human motivation and cognition, group behaviour and personality which can enrich our understanding of governance issues like design of incentive systems, board composition and board behaviour. Political science and what has come to be known as the political theory of governance allows a deeper understanding of how politics creates law and regulation which have an enormous independent influence on corporate governance. Sociology tends to emphasize the importance of social context, particularly social networks and social norms. Finally, management research has produced influential theories like stewardship, resource dependency and stakeholder theory.

Most of these are not strictly speaking theories of corporate governance, but more general theories which have applications in corporate governance. Together they form the basis for what we call 'enlightened agency theory', which takes its point of departure in mainstream economic agency theory, but allows the analysis to be modified by the psychological, political and sociological issues which come up in particular situations.

2.2 The market model

In abstract microeconomic theory the firm is a black box characterized by a technology (a set of production possibilities) and profit maximization. The theory abstracts from what actually goes on inside firms (e.g. whether, why and how they maximize profits). For a theoretical exposition see Debreu (1959).

In this model all resource allocation is handled by the price mechanism. Firms maximize profits by choosing what to produce while taking market prices for given and do not have to expend resources on solving information or incentive problems. In jargon, there are no transaction costs in the neoclassical economy.

The standard assumptions for this model to work optimally are:

- many firms (sellers) who compete prices down
- many buyers (no buyer power)
- centralized exchange (market clearing)
- full information
- complete markets (a complete set of forward markets)
- no transaction costs.

Under these and other assumptions it's possible to show that the price mechanism may lead to a market equilibrium (i.e. a set of prices for which supply equals demand). Moreover, it can be shown that this equilibrium is efficient in the sense that it will not be possible to find a universally better resource allocation. Nor will it be possible for individual agents to do better by changing their production or consumption plans.

The concept of market efficiency has been further developed in financial economics to characterize an asset market in which it will not be possible for individual investors to make above-average returns by reallocating their portfolios. This implies that the prices are unpredictable (if they were predictable investors could make money by trading) and that they already incorporate all relevant information (i.e. all publicly available or perhaps even in the strong form all accessible information).

The seamless working of the price system implies that there is no rationale for other institutions such as governments or companies. By default such institutions must be justified by 'market failure', which must again depend on breach of one or more of the basic assumptions mentioned above. For example, with perfectly informed competitive stock markets there would be no need for governance mechanisms like shareholder monitoring, boards or performance-based pay.

If we accept that not just markets, but other institutions like governments, boards or firms can fail as well, the relevant benchmark for comparison becomes the opportunity costs of using a particular institution, or more abstractly its *transaction costs*. *Institutional economics* is the sub-discipline concerned with assessing the relative costs and benefits of alternative institutions. Since corporate governance is concerned with the institutions which regulate company behaviour, it may therefore be regarded as a sub-discipline of institutional economics. Institutional economics also works to explain other institutions like money, families or property rights, which will not be addressed in this book. The core institutions of concern in corporate governance are legal forms (companies, cooperatives etc.), ownership structure, boards, incentive systems, information systems (accounting) and government regulation hereof.

As general as the market model may be, it informs much of the corporate governance discussion. For example, policymakers often attempt to increase transparency in the belief that more information will lead to a better resource allocation. The EU is trying to harmonize standards in the belief that a common European capital market would benefit the competitiveness of European companies. The large liquid stock markets in the US and UK provide quite a good fit with the market model.

One reason for this is that the market model is relatively robust. Competition works. The price system can survive substantial transaction costs and some degree of monopoly and still produce excellent results compared with systemic alternatives like centrally planned economies. Market actors can contract around incomplete markets and find second-best alternatives to hedging risk. Non-market institutions like firms, joint ventures, organizations, standards and even ethics may emerge more or less spontaneously to fill gaps in the market mechanism.

In the perfect market model ownership is just a parameter which determines income distribution: O_{ij} = consumer i's ownership share of firm j, where ownership shares must sum to 1 for each firm, and an individual consumer can own a share of the firm anywhere between 0 and 1. Ownership in this case means dividend rights; it does not matter to overall resource allocation (except by influencing the demand for goods and services), since firms maximize profits no matter who owns them, and since ownership does not influence technology.

The fact that firms are owned by consumers goes some way towards explaining profit maximization. Since consumers are assumed to be insatiable, they want as high profits as possible. Moreover, on the assumption of a complete set of forward markets, consumers can insure against all future contingencies and do not have to be risk adverse.

The idea that ownership is irrelevant to resource allocation (for example firm behaviour) was formalized in the Coase theorem (Coase, 1960), which states that ownership does not matter to resource allocation in the absence of transaction costs. This is trivial when there are no interdependencies (externalities) between economic activities, but even when there are, rational actors will manage to find an optimal solution. Imagine for example a train that causes sparks which may set fire to an adjacent field. If the railroad company owns the field, it has an incentive to take steps to prevent fire, e.g. make the train travel more slowly or put up a fence. A farmer who owns the railroad will have exactly the same incentive to maximize joint profits. More surprisingly, the same cost-effective measures will be taken if the farmer and the railroad company bargain rationally as

independent owners. The farmer will put up a fence to protect his land, or force the railroad company to do so by a court order. Alternatively he can pay to have the trains run slower if that is cheaper. In other words, in the absence of transaction costs an efficient solution may be found.

This means that efficient ownership depends on transaction costs. It may for example be optimal for the railroad company to buy the adjacent land in order to save on transaction costs (bargaining with stubborn farmers). Alternatively we may ask whether it makes sense to assume that firm managers (producers) maximize profits regardless of whether they or others own the firm.

2.3   Agency theory

How can we be sure that firms maximize profits, if individuals maximize their utility? This is perhaps (or perhaps not) intuitive in an owner-managed firm, but remember that ownership in the market model was a parameter which could in principle be fixed arbitrarily. If owner-management was generally optimal, we would have a strong theoretical prediction (good governance = owner management), but perhaps there is more to it than that? More generally we need to think about whether a manager acting as an agent for an anonymous owner will maximize profits.

Agency problems arise whenever someone does something for somebody else. This somebody else we designate 'the principal' and the actor we denote the 'agent':

> *… an agency relationship has arisen between two (or more) parties when one,*
> *designated as the agent, acts for, or on behalf of, or as a representative for the other,*
> *designated the principal, in a particular domain of decision problems.*[1]

Agency relationships lead to costly incentive problems. There are many examples of agency relationships, apart from the relationship between owners and managers, which comprise the core problem in corporate governance.

For example, there is an agency relationship between a boss and his employees. The boss would like the employees to work hard or to do certain tasks which he believes to be beneficial (although these tasks may not be beneficial to anyone else). In contrast, the employees will have their own ideas about what they would like to do. Only in rare cases (i.e. by luck) will these tasks coincide with what the manager would like them to do. For example, the employees may like to relax rather than to work hard, or they may prefer to hold meetings among themselves rather than talk to the customers. The boss will therefore want to induce them to 'behave': for example she will tell them what to do and will threaten to fire them if they do not obey. Or she may be a more modern type of manager who prefers to motivate employees by more subtle means: for example through offering a bonus scheme or through psychological tricks. A hierarchical organization can be defined as a chain of such boss–employee relationships from top management to middle managers to workers on the shop floor.

Another example of an agency relationship is the affiliation between a house seller and a real estate agent (Posner, 2000). In this case, the house seller is the principal and the real estate agent acts on her behalf. The house seller would like the real estate agent to contact as many prospective buyers as possible, to bargain hard on her behalf to get a high price, and so on. But the real estate agent may prefer to take it easy and wait until the customers come along, or he may prefer to concentrate his energy on selling other people's houses. It may be difficult for the seller to verify whether the agent in fact devotes a reasonable amount of effort to the task, so this is a case of asymmetric information (the real estate agent is better informed than the house seller). In general, all relationships between firms and sales agents involve similar incentive problems.

More general problems with agency relationships include the relationships between citizens and their governments, where the citizens want the government to act on their behalf. In this

---

[1] Ross (1973).

light democracy can be seen as a (political) governance mechanism which allows the voters to replace inefficient politicians. In the absence of democracy, politicians become dictators who govern according to their own ideas (and very likely for their own benefit). Thus the citizens, much like shareholders in a firm, must organize a system to ensure that their interests are served.

Finally, the relationship between a patient and a doctor is a classical principal–agent problem (Arrow, 1963). The doctor is better informed than the patient about medicine and sickness; that is why the patient seeks his advice. So we again have a case of asymmetric information. And with that comes the incentive problem: the doctor could prescribe useless, expensive treatments and medicines (especially since many patients get better without treatment and since some patients get worse even with the best possible treatment). So how are the patients to know whether the doctor is fooling them? One solution to this asymmetry would be for the government to step in and require all practising doctors to have a university degree in medicine. Another solution would be the invention within the medical profession of a 'medical ethic' (Arrow, 1963), e.g. the Hippocratic Oath, which is enforced through internalization (i.e. doctors identify with it) and through strong collegial pressure. The pressures may be so strong that doctors who are criticized by their peers have been known to commit suicide and they certainly can lose their licence to practise. Note that the doctors have an economic interest in this medical ethic; if they did not have it, they would get far fewer patients, since the patients would rationally fear being taken advantage of. The medical profession up to the 19th century is a vivid example.

We find similar social sanctions in corporate governance; for example, when an opportunistic manager gets a bad reputation this makes it more difficult for him to find a new job or to do business in the future. We note that law, reputation and ethics can all function as governance mechanisms.

So how about the relationship between sellers and buyers? This also involves a conflict of interest. When buying an apple from a grocer, a consumer would like to get as good an apple as possible and to pay as little as possible for it. The grocer, however, would like to charge as much as possible. But we would not usually talk of an agency relationship in this case. We assume that the customer knows what she is buying, and the grocer knows what he sells. So there is no asymmetric information here, and conflicting interests as such are not enough to create an agency problem. To be sure there is always some asymmetric information in any transaction, but unless it is significant, we tend to disregard it. However, under certain circumstances, there are significant information asymmetries even in standard transactions. For example, if I buy an organic apple, I may not be able to tell whether it is really organic, whereas the grocer may know very well. Here a standard solution is to have a declaration of contents (a label) which is guaranteed by the government or some other body that can punish the grocer if he cheats people. Note that this kind of control may be in the grocer's own interest because it will encourage people to buy more. Similar guarantees, like product labels, are found in corporate governance. We call them 'corporate governance codes'.

In summary, agency problems are universal. There are many different solutions to them: monitoring and sanctions, bonus systems, laws, and even ethical codes can be regarded as governance mechanisms. In Chapter 11 we will see how these different mechanisms can be applied to corporate governance. For now we would like to take a closer look at the agency problems which these governance mechanisms intend to solve.

2.4 The owner-manager problem

The owner-management agency problem begins with the separation of ownership and management or, as it is sometimes (confusingly) called, the separation of ownership and control (Berle and Means, 1932). Without this separation, in owned-managed firms, the basic agency problem disappears.

Owner-managers have a natural incentive to work hard and to employ somebody else if they are not the best managers. If they choose to use company funds for private expenditure (on-the-job consumption), they will only do so if consuming on the job is more beneficial to them than

consuming at home[2] (taxes and other complications aside). From the viewpoint of professional managers, the incentives look different since it is not their money which they manage. Their incentives may be to spend money on things that they like without thinking too much of the costs, and they may also have an interest in maintaining their jobs because they need the money.

A CEO once described to us how his view of corporate expenditure changed after he bought 15% of the company's stock. Every time he authorized the payment of a bill by using his signature, he questioned immediately whether this expense was really necessary.

By separation of ownership and management we get a specialization of resources where the principal/owner/investor is a supplier of finance, whereas the agent/manager supplies human capital. The idea is that managers act on behalf of the shareholders and the agency problem is to find ways in which shareholders can ensure that the manager will act in their interest, for example how they can make sure that she maximizes the stock price (value) of the firm.

From the viewpoint of the shareholders, a value-maximizing manager is an entrepreneurial and creative leader, who is able to implement her ideas in the organization. She is hard working and economical with the shareholders' money and she delivers results (we could easily extend the list). In reality, we expect the average manager to be more ordinary, but normally a very decent and conscientious person. But unfortunately, there are also many examples of managers who do not live up to this ideal.

The following are generic agency problems: some managers act criminally and embezzle (steal) shareholders' funds. In a way, that is easy for the shareholder: it is a criminal act and the police will come after them. Some managers are known to undertake 'self dealing', i.e. they use company money for transactions which benefit themselves, for example with a company which they own themselves. This was apparently the case in Parmalat, a publicly listed Italian dairy controlled by a founding family. Parmalat transferred money to a company which was 100% owned by the family. This type of transaction is illegal in most countries but the police will typically be unable to uncover such problems on their own accord, so shareholders must be on their toes and monitor company activities.

Another classical agency problem is excess expenditure. The question here is when an expense is business motivated and when it is really private consumption for the manager. Paper and pencils will typically not be much of a problem, but how about a company jet? The managers may argue that they need a company jet so as not to waste precious managerial time in the airport and, if the board approves, they can buy one. So one jet might be OK, or perhaps it is not. But how about two? Or three? At some point, this expense seems difficult to justify from a company viewpoint. Similar uncertainties apply to meals in expensive restaurants, luxurious headquarters, expensive thick carpets, and very good-looking secretaries (i.e. do we really need a Playmate secretary?). One American manager was known to let the company plane fly around with his dog. The problem with excess expenditure is that it is a grey area. It will usually be possible for the manager to make a case that this was necessary or beneficial from a business point of view; a nice-looking secretary may charm business relations, it may be easier to close important deals over a meal, and the company jet saves time. Remember that a court must prove beyond reasonable doubt that this was harmful to shareholders in order to send him to jail, and this is very difficult. Courts will be reluctant to do this because of the *business judgement rule:* a legal principle according to which managers are assumed to be in the right, unless proven otherwise. The underlying argument seems to be that if the shareholders do not like what the manager does, they can fire him. But we want managers to be dynamic and to do things: that is, to take risks, since that is part of their job. Sometimes this means that they make mistakes. If we sent them to jail every time they made a mistake, it would soon be difficult to fill CEO positions. Or, even worse, the CEOs would only think about how not to make mistakes and all activity would cease.

Empire building, particularly through mergers and acquisitions, is another example of a conflict of interest between shareholders and managers. Usually managers like growth and size. It is more fun to lead a growth company, it is more prestigious to lead a large company, and managerial pay

---

[2] This point was forcefully made by Harold Demsetz (1983).

is positively correlated with company size. The risk of being taken over by another company also declines with firm size. So managers like to build their own little empires. But it is well known that many mergers and acquisitions fail to create value for the acquiring company, so shareholders often have a different view, particularly if the acquisitions are outside the company's core business. Usually, hidden private consumption is not what takes a company down; private consumption is trifling compared with other business expenses. But there are many examples of acquisitions which cost a company dearly, so in a way this is a more serious problem for shareholders, and they will typically be considered to be a normal part of doing business. Thus, courts would not accept a case against a manager because the company made an acquisition. After all, there *are* examples of good acquisitions which create value.

Overinvestment falls into the same category as empire building. Oil companies are known to have overinvested in finding new sources of oil when it would have been much cheaper to buy it on the market (Shleifer and Vishny, 1997).

Entrenchment – when managers create barriers which make it difficult to fire them and they then stay on for too long – can also be regarded as an agency problem. The CEO likes his job, the prestige and the money. But shareholders may prefer to have a new, more dynamic profile to head the company. This may be why some studies found that share prices actually rise when entrenched CEOs suddenly die. A 5% increase in share prices would then indicate that the old manager cost the company 5% of its value.

Finally, the inventor of 'shareholder value' Alfred Rappaport (and later, Jensen 1993) found that many, if not most, US companies did not cover their costs of capital during the 1970s and 1980s. In other words, they lost money for their shareholders. Jensen calculated that General Motors (GM) lost 100 billion dollars during the 1980s. Obviously, at the time, many managers could have done better in terms of maximizing shareholder value, and it is difficult to argue that they were unlucky over such a long period of time. So whatever else they did could, in principle, be attributed to agency problems.

2.5 Assumptions in agency theory

Theoretically, the key elements of the agency problem are:

- Separation between principal and agent;
- Conflicting interests (selfishness), since principal and agent each have their own utility functions;
- Rationality: both principal and agent are rational and rationally further their own interests;
- Asymmetric information: the agent is better informed about his own abilities, his own activities and what is going on in the firm than is the principal;
- Uncertainty (risk): the existence of 'other factors' – weather, bad luck and unforeseen changes of any kind – means there is no one-to-one relationship between the activities of the agent and the outcome. If the information asymmetry problem disappeared, then the agency problem itself would disappear, since the principal would be able to deduce the behaviour of the agent by monitoring his performance;
- Risk aversion: performance pay will usually involve some kind of risk for the agent (either over- or underpay), and the risk averse will demand compensation for this. If the agent is sufficiently risk averse, he will only want to work for a fixed pay to avoid economic uncertainty altogether. The risk will then be carried by the principal who, like entrepreneur capitalists, gets a variable profit while his employees are paid a fixed salary.

The appendix to this chapter provides a formal treatment of the optimal compensation contract between principal and agent. In the basic model the 'principal delegates decision-making authority to an agent whose behaviour influences the welfare of the principal'. The goal of the principal is to find an optimal contract that makes the agent maximize her utility or value function.

2.6 Types of agency problems

Type 1 agency problems (owner-manager problems) arise between shareholders (the principals) and managers (agents). They arise because the agents (managers) do not always act in the interests of the shareholders.

Type 2 agency problems between majority and minority investors occur if there are conflicts of interests between the two groups. A founding family in control of the firm may have different views from those of minority investors. The family in charge effectively acts on behalf of the other investors, so in this case the family is the agent, while the minority investors are the principals.

Type 3 agency problems between shareholders and stakeholders occur when shareholders make self-interested decisions which influence the welfare of stakeholders. For example, shareholders may decide to pay out high dividends or to pursue a risky strategy, both of which increase the risk of bankruptcy and reduce the welfare of creditors. In the same way shareholders may decide to close down a factory and this can harm the welfare of the employees, the suppliers, the local government, and perhaps the customers. Type 3 agency problems fall under the broad heading of corporate social responsibility.

The three types of generic problems can be regarded as an expression of increasing responsibility. In the first instance, managers and the firm are responsible to the controlling owners, who decide whether they are hired or fired. In the second instance, the responsibility is extended to all shareholders, not just the controlling shareholders. In the third instance, the responsibility is extended further to cover all stakeholders, not just shareholders.

2.7 Information problems

There are two particularly important types of information asymmetry: moral hazard (i.e. hidden action) and adverse selection (i.e. hidden knowledge), which will be discussed in greater detail in the following sections.

To distinguish between moral hazard and adverse selection, it is useful to draw a timeline (Figure 2.1). Adverse selection problems tend to occur before the principal is to make a decision. Moral hazard problems tend to occur after the decision.

For example, to ensure good management of the company is perhaps the most important task in corporate governance. This task involves:

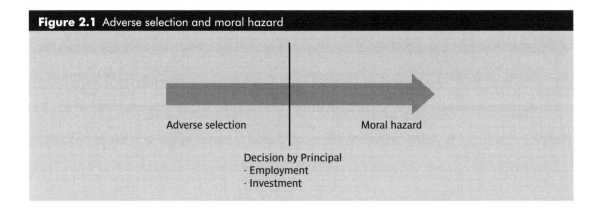

Figure 2.1 Adverse selection and moral hazard

Adverse selection   Moral hazard

Decision by Principal
· Employment
· Investment

1 Selection: hire the right managers and replace bad ones, if necessary. The key problem here is 'adverse selection'.
2 Motivation: encourage management to do their best through incentives and monitoring. The key problem here is 'moral hazard'.

Since the moral hazard problem is easier to understand, we begin with that.

2.8 Moral hazard

Moral hazard (also known as hidden action) occurs when the activity of the agent cannot be observed by the principal. For example, as shareholders we do not know what managers are doing. We can observe some indicators, but most of their behaviour remains hidden. For all we know they could spend their time playing golf or checkers all day, eating expensive lunches with their friends at the company's expense while demanding sky-high salaries.

The term 'moral hazard' originates in the insurance literature. Insurers found that when people have fire insurance, the probability of fire increases. This can to some extent be attributed to direct fraud; some people may set their shop on fire in the hope of getting a new one financed with insurance money. But it is also possible that people become more careless when they know they are insured. For example, when you leave your house you may ask yourself if you forgot a burning candle or if you forgot to turn off the stove. If you are not insured, agency theory would predict that you are more likely to go back and check an extra time. Thus, on top of the usual risk of fire, there is an additional element – a moral hazard – which insurance companies must take into account.

The moral hazard case illustrates a general principle: there is a trade-off between risk and incentives. If you insure people against risk they also lose the incentive to do something about it. For example, insurers will routinely ask people to pay a minimum amount (deductible) when their car is insured and there is an accident. The argument for this is that the insured person will then share some of the risk and will therefore not lose all of the incentive.

In the case of shareholders and managers, managers can be given incentives: for example, a bonus if profits are high or a stock option scheme so that the manager benefits if the stock price increases. In this case, the manager shares some of the shareholders' risk and receives an incentive to act in our interest as stockholders.

Monitoring is another strategy. Insurance companies may examine whether there is any indication of fraud or negligence before they pay out the insurance premium. When there is even a small chance of detection, or a small chance that one will not receive an insurance claim, people will be much more careful about negligence and fraud.

In the case of company managers, shareholders commission auditors to inform them annually (in the annual report) about the company's performance and management's performance. Although there are many examples of non-performance which auditors do not detect, at least some checks are probably better than no checks.

2.9 Adverse selection

Adverse selection, or hidden knowledge, occurs when there is some element in the situation which is known to the agent but not known to the principal. For example, when the shareholders (via the board) hire a new manager for the company, they may not know how capable she is. She may be more or less intelligent, more or less hard-working, but she may also be an alcoholic or a sex offender. Prior to appointment, shareholders can scan some signs of performance – her grades from business school or her references, for example – but they cannot measure what they really want to know:

how will she actually perform in the new job? The agent, of course, knows herself much better than principals do. Therefore, she has some hidden knowledge.

For the sake of the argument imagine that an agent, Susan, knows she is worth €40,000 a month but she gets an offer of only €20,000. In this case, Susan may decide not to take the offer. Instead, she could choose to become self-employed and make €40,000 per month plus incur a risk premium. In contrast, if she knows that she is worth only €10,000, she might want to take the job, because it is an attractive bargain from her viewpoint.

This means that the company will have selected the wrong employee, or rather that the wrong employees were self-selected to work for the company. This is 'adverse selection'; the term was suggested by George Akerlof who received the Nobel Prize in economics for identifying this problem (and many other contributions to economic theory).

The now classic example is the market for bad cars, so-called 'lemons'. As the story goes, auto workers in the old days would not work on Sundays and they would take this opportunity to drink. When they returned to work on Mondays, the auto workers had hangovers. The result was that the cars produced that day would be full of errors. It would be referred to as a 'Monday car' or 'lemon' which was lower quality than cars produced on the other five workdays. It would be impossible for a new buyer to tell the difference between Monday and Tuesday cars before they made their purchase. Post-purchase, however, there would be constant problems with Monday cars. They would need constant repairs. So let us say that a Monday car is worth 0 and that a normal workday car is worth 100 000. People would then only be willing to pay 83 333 for the new cars because they knew there was a 16,666% chance of buying a lemon.[3]

A customer who bought a new car would quickly discover it was a Monday car and might want to sell it to buy another one. Used car buyers would consider that the fraction of Monday cars for sale in the used car market would be substantially higher than 1:6, since many more owners of Monday cars would want to sell their cars than owners of Tuesday cars. Since some cars are worth 100 000 minus usage and some cars are worth 0, what could one expect the price of used cars would be? 0!

If the price was 50 000, the owners of good cars would not want to sell. Thus only Monday cars (lemons) would be on the market. The same is true for any price < 100 000 minus a little. Now suppose that the price was 100 000. All the Monday cars would then be put up for sale. For the sake of the argument, let us assume that the other cars would also be put up for sale because the price was slightly higher than what the cars were worth. The problem is, however, that nobody would want to buy at that price. Rational buyers would certainly not pay more than the 83 333 that they would pay for a new car, given that the probability of a lemon car was around the same for new and used cars. But at a price of 83 333, none of the good-car owners would want to sell. Thus there would be only lemons, worth 0, on the market. Buyers would recognize this and not buy. Ultimately, the sellers would have to offer a lower price; in fact they would have to lower the price to 0 before anyone would buy.

It is possible to make this example more realistic (and more complicated) by assuming that there would also be sellers of good cars at lower prices, for example because some of them had changed their mind and wanted to buy a new car or because they found that they could afford a better car because of increased income or wealth. Without going too much into detail, suppose that half of all car owners had good cars, but they would sell at a price of 60. But the lemon owners would of course also offer their cars for sale. This means that $\frac{1}{2} + \frac{1}{6} = \frac{4}{6}$ of the cars would be up for sale, and 25% of them would be lemons. Buyers would have to consider that the cars would not be worth 60 to them, but only 45, since $\frac{1}{4}$ of the used cars for sale would turn out to be lemons. So they would offer 45. But at that price, perhaps only $\frac{1}{3}$ would be willing to sell. The lemon owners would still offer their cars, so now there would be $\frac{1}{3} + \frac{1}{6} = \frac{1}{2}$ of the cars up for sale of which $\frac{1}{3}$ would be lemons. So the cars on sale would on average only be worth 30 to the buyers, which would encourage even fewer good car owners to sell. The number of lemons on the market would increase and demand would fall. You can see where this leads. The market will collapse.

---

[3] We assume that one out of six cars is a lemon because one out of six workdays is a Monday.

In the real world, of course, there is a market for used cars. In part this is because very few cars have no value at all, so prices will not fall to zero. Moreover, it is possible to examine cars to reduce the information asymmetry.

In corporate governance we would call this monitoring. Owners of good cars or the intermediaries (dealers) may signal to buyers that they are good – by offering a guarantee, for example. The law may also help the process by punishing cheaters. Nevertheless, used car dealers still have a bad name, and the prices for used cars are substantially lower than for new cars.

We can apply the same logic to the job market. Suppose that ⅙ of the applicants for a new job are no good (value 0), while the rest have a value of 100 to the firm. In order that the appointment creates value for the firm, the company cannot offer more than a salary of 83.3. But at that salary level, all the 'good applicants' might decide to start their own businesses or find another job offer. So the value of the new hires to the firm would be 0, and the firm would lose money if it offered them more. Alternatively, half of the good applicants might want to work for 60, since that was what they could make on their own. But there would still be ⅙ 'good-for-nothings'. Thus the firm could only offer 45. You can work the rest out for yourself.

One solution to this problem is to screen, or monitor, incoming applicants. For example a human resource function can screen applicants prior to appointment. Another solution to this problem is incentives. If the firm offers performance-based pay, the good-for-nothings will not want to risk it, but the high-performers will.

Example 1: The IPO market

Adverse selection also occurs among firms that want to go public: an Initial Public Offering (IPO). Some firms go public because they need new capital. Others go public because the owners want to cash out. A third group wants to go public to sell out because the business is bad. It is difficult for investors to tell the difference. As a result, there is a discount on IPOs. In some cases, owners are better off to keep their ownership and live off the dividends which profitable businesses can generate. One of the solutions is that owners can signal to the market that they believe in the firm by retaining a high ownership share. During the dot.com boom, investors were apparently unable to tell the difference between good and bad. In hindsight, it might have been a good rule-of-thumb for investors to only buy stock in companies where the incumbent owners also had some money at stake rather than to buy stock in those companies where the owners ran away as fast as they could.

Example 2: Banking

The same problem occurs in banking. Some loans are bad and bankers try to sort the good from the bad, but they cannot perfectly do so *ex ante* (i.e. beforehand). Some of the bad borrowers have unrealistic expectations, some are gamblers, and some want to use the money for their own consumption. So banks have to charge a risk premium on their loans over the risk-free rate of interest (e.g. treasury bills). This will make the 'good' borrowers less likely to borrow, but the bad borrowers will not be discouraged. So there can be adverse selection. In fact, one theory is that banks exist because they can specialize in handling adverse selection and moral hazard problems in the market for loans.

2.10　Extensions to agency theory

The simple agency model can be extended in many ways. For example, many shareholders are agents (employees) rather than ultimate owners. Thus we get *agents watching agents*. Since fund managers do not have their own money at stake, this creates a new set of incentive problems. They may for example be satisfied with normal performance compared with other investors, but averse to underperformance. Investors may therefore tend to herd.

Another extension is to recognize that there may be not just one single principal but many, and they may have conflicting objectives. For example there may be many owners with different preferences, or the firm may be accountable to multiple constituencies. From an agency-theoretical viewpoint this implies that firm behaviour should be modelled as a *common agency problem* (Bernheim and Whinston, 1986) in which the agent (management) faces not just one but a set of principals whose objectives (preferences) differ and may even conflict sufficiently to constitute a zero-sum game between them. If the firm is seen as a nexus of contracts (Jensen and Meckling, 1976), the principals are the buyers and sellers of its products and services plus stakeholders whose welfare is affected by external effects produced by the firm.

A third extension is that agency problems often have a time dimension or in other words we have a *repeated game* (Kreps, 1986). An agent who misbehaves will see her reputation suffer, and she will find it more difficult to get a new job or attract funds from investors or banks. Knowing this the agent has incentives to behave better so reputation may reduce agency problems.

2.11 Incomplete contracts

As relevant as agency theory is, it misses one important point (which we will return to in the chapter on ownership): there is more to ownership than dividends or monetary incentives. Ownership also implies control which is a valuable asset in all those situations which are not contracted for in advance (Grossman and Hart, 1986). Since economic actors have access to different information it seems natural to allocate ownership to agents which have the most important information. According to agency theory, it would be possible to achieve the same outcome by a pay-for-performance contract, but since such a contract could not possibly specify all future contingencies, agents only get the full incentive when they acquire ownership.

In incomplete contracts theory (Grossman and Hart, 1986; Hart, 1988, 1995a, 1995b), whoever has asset ownership possesses the residual rights of control, i.e. control rights in all those situations which are not covered by formal contracts between the parties. The allocation of ownership influences incentives to invest and value creation. Unlike in neoclassical theory or the zero transaction cost benchmark proposed by Coase (1960), the identity of the owner therefore becomes important. This provides the theoretical foundation for a theory of 'best owner'. Moreover, the theory shows that it may be preferable to integrate ownership under the same owner. It therefore also provides the theoretical foundation for a theory of firm size and scope, including mergers and acquisitions.

For example, incomplete contracts theory explains why it is not possible for large organizations to replicate the incentives of entrepreneurial firms even with full profit sharing (i.e. letting an employee have all the profits). Since an employee does not have the residual rights of control she has less incentive to make an effort and to invest in the job because the employer can act in his own interest in all those cases not covered by the incomplete contract. Thus there is a strong rationale for owner management. However, when two firms need to work together, joint ownership may be more efficient because they do not have to fear 'hold up' (the risk that one party exploits their mutual dependence to her own benefit) to the same extent.

2.12 Transaction costs

Like information asymmetry in agency theory, transaction costs are at the root of many deviations from the market model. Coase (1960) showed that ownership is irrelevant to resource allocation in the absence of transaction costs. In an earlier paper, Coase (1937) had demonstrated how firms sometimes internalize market transactions (conduct the same activities internally in the firm) and that the decision of whether or not to do so will depend mainly on transaction costs, which he defined as the costs of using the price system (relative to internal governance in firms). Subsequently, Oliver Williamson (1975) found that transaction costs could be attributed to general human characteristics under conditions of asset specificity, uncertainty and high transaction frequency.

Applied to corporate governance, transaction costs are relevant because it can explain vertical integration, i.e. why two possibly independent firms doing business with each other might save costs by joint ownership. In particular, asset specificity can create interdependencies which one firm may use to extract benefits from the other (e.g. hold-up problems).

The classical example in transaction cost economics is vertical integration, sometimes known as the make-or-buy decision: should a company produce a product or service itself or outsource it to independent suppliers? Effectively this is a choice between market (outsourcing) and hierarchy (insourcing). Transaction cost theory tells us that insourcing is more efficient if the relationship between buyer and seller is characterized by asset specificity, uncertainty and a high transaction frequency. Asset specificity gives rise to monopolistic or monopsonistic problems which are particularly difficult to handle when there is high uncertainty about business conditions. For one or two transactions insourcing may be overdoing it because of higher fixed administration costs, but for a continuing relationship it may be the optimal solution. Thus transaction costs economics predicts that there will be more hierarchy, i.e. larger and more integrated firms, under such conditions.

Transaction costs theory is also relevant for pointing to more complex human behaviour than the rational and selfish, but law-abiding, agents in the market model. Opportunism, defined as self-interest seeking with guile, seems quite consistent with some types of managerial behaviour such as distorting information, fraud, internal political games and so on. Bounded rationality – that humans are in Herbert Simon's words (1958) intendedly rational but only limitedly so – may be a more realistic description of owners, managers, board members and other important agents that we find in the neoclassical model. In fact, because bounded rationality implies costs of information collection, it can explain why there will usually be information asymmetries in corporate governance.

2.13   Psychology

In recent years it has become generally accepted in economics that human beings are not completely rational or completely selfish. The neoclassical model is an approximation which leaves room for improvement. A body of research in behavioural economics or behavioural finance has emerged, and this research also has implications for corporate governance. Behavioural economics has drawn primarily on cognitive psychology so we start by considering that, but psychology is also important to corporate governance in other respects and we go on to discuss many of these possible applications. For reference we refer to Hayes (2000).

Cognitive psychology is full of so-called biases or deviations from rationality. Here is a list of the most well-established ones.

Confirmation bias (Wason, 1968) means that decision makers look for information which confirms their own ideas and past decisions. They may therefore persist in erroneous judgements for a long time. For example, CEOs and boards will continue to hold on to bad strategies and bad practices for a long time because they selectively look for (and find) confirmation of their own ideas. This implies that external control mechanisms such as active owners or vigilant boards can be useful to get managers to change direction. *Entrapment bias* – aversion to admitting a mistake – only makes this bias stronger and often leads to throwing good money after bad.

Small sample bias implies that decision makers will often make decisions based on small samples (one or two observations). For example, a board member once argued against foreign board members because the board had already had one and this was not a success (he tended to doze off during the board meetings). More generally, they tend to underestimate or ignore statistical information (base

rates bias). A related visibility bias makes people tend to put more stock in data which is highly visible to them. For example, bankers may learn from their own past experience with bad loans or those of other domestic banks, whereas information from other sectors or countries is neglected.

Illusory patterns and correlations biases imply that decision makers see patterns even when there are none (like tea leaves on the bottom of a tea cup). Moreover, from Gestalt theory we know that they tend to prefer certain patterns over others, e.g. symmetrical, well-defined shapes. Such biases will not necessarily disappear over time as decision makers learn. In fact, when people are misled by stochastic feedback, misunderstandings and spurious correlations may reinforce superstition rather than learning so that 'superstitious learning' takes place (Skinner, 1938).

The fundamental attribution error implies that people tend to see their own failures as a result of bad luck or external causes, while they attribute their successes to their own performance and ability. Thus (using popular, non-scientific jargon) the egos of successful CEOs and chairs will tend to inflate over time. In contrast, when assessing others people tend to ascribe success to external causes or luck to a much greater degree. This will, for example, influence the way CEOs assess their employees or competitors.

Anchoring bias implies that people tend to use reference points when assessing situations. In a famous experiment Kahnemann and Tversky (1973) spun a wheel to generate a random number and then asked participants a quantity question, e.g. 'What is the population of Nigeria?' The higher the random numbers the higher these estimates were. More generally, human judgement and decision will depend very much on how decisions are framed (*framing bias*). Skilful managers and chairs are experts in framing proposals to the board or to shareholders to get their way. According to prospect theory (Kahneman and Tversky, 1979) preferences will depend critically on the reference point (e.g. the status quo). Decision makers will be strongly averse to small losses, but much less strongly pleased by small gains.

Simple mechanisms like memory loss probably aggravate cognitive biases, because they create distortions when information is passed up and down hierarchical levels (Bartlett, 1932; Williamson, 1967). Boards or top management may have little idea of what happens on the shop floor, and shop floor workers may be imperfectly informed about what the board wants. Generally, these biases will exacerbate agency problems.

Emotional stress can lead to even more biased decision making in times of crisis. In the short term, the 'fight-or-flight response' leads some decision makers to become aggressive when their position is threatened. Challenged leaders may react irrationally with denial, threats and distortion. In the long term, when there is time to cool down and reflect, they may be able to respond more rationally, however.

Hindsight bias is another source of bias which matters in corporate governance. They say that hindsight is the most exact of all sciences. Everybody always knew what would happen, 5 minutes after. This is important when shareholders or boards find fault with the performance of managers who should (in their opinion) have known better. In the same way successful decisions tend to be obvious afterwards.

All of this means that people (economic actors) are far from perfectly rational, but it does not entirely dispense with rationality. Experienced business people are often aware of biases and try to correct for them in ways which are not available in laboratory experiments; for example they continuously experiment, i.e. try out ideas and reject those that do not work. To some extent governance mechanisms like boards or auditing may even function as checks or balances to reduce some of the biases. However, it would be an exaggeration to say that psychological biases have been eliminated by corporate governance.

Personality may also have a bearing on corporate governance. This is particularly true of the personal characteristics of CEOs who may influence an entire organization as well as corporate governance.

Leaders have different capabilities, e.g. analytical or interpersonal intelligence (Gardner, 1983). The personalities of board chairs or large owners may also influence governance.

Summarizing many personality studies, Norman (1963) found that people (and leaders) differ in terms of extroversion (or introversion), stability (or neuroticism), agreeableness (or criticalness), conscientiousness (or disorganization) and openness (or closedness). Generally we expect leaders to be extrovert, emotionally stable, conscientious and open (Judge et al., 2002), but there are also many exceptions. For example, Collins (2001) argued that great leaders tend to be introvert and to subordinate their own personality to organizational goals. Moreover, many well-known leaders have been known to have neurotic tendencies (e.g. to be prone to fits of anger).

Neuroticism, in particular, can create serious problems in governance. Eric Fromm (1994) identified three negative personality orientations which are easily recognizable from corporate governance cases:

- *exploitative (sadistic) and dominant characters*, who derive satisfaction from controlling and outsmarting others, have little empathy for their equals and contempt for their inferiors;
- *hoarding characters*, who try to protect what they have and resist change;
- *marketing characters*, who are concerned with image, appearances and style and derive satisfaction from admiration and social success.

In addition, there are *receptive (masochistic) characters*, who are self-effacing and loyal, but pass responsibilities to others. These traits could be characteristic of 'useful idiots' who may have insufficient personal integrity to stand up to despotic CEOs or corrupt corporate culture. *Authoritarian characters* (Adorno et al., 1950), who are deferential to authority, intolerant to deviations, dominating and hard-liners, may also play a role both as leaders and followers in corporate governance.

Group psychology matters to board behaviour since boards are in essence small groups. This means, for example, that board work is highly influenced by social roles and subject to pathologies such as groupthink.

In an effective team there is room for a division of labour between team roles (Belbin, 1993; Hayes, 2000). Some group members contribute ideas, other make contacts to the outside world, coordinate group activities or give support to whatever is happening. For a non-exhaustive list, see Table 2.1. At a more mundane level, it seems important that the psychological characteristics of board members complement rather than substitute each other. A creative board which is unable to finish on time or implement its ideas is worthless.

Groupthink (Janis, 1972) is a pathological uniformity of group behaviour which prevents the group from understanding its environment and invites bad decisions. It consists of defending and rationalizing the group's own decisions, brushing away criticism by stereotyping critics ('theoretists', 'radicals'), preserving an illusion of moral superiority, pressuring members to conformity and

Table 2.1 A sketch of Belbin's team roles (after Hayes, 2000)

Shaper	Pushes towards agreement
Plant	Ideas, proposals and suggestions
Monitor	Analyses problems and contributions
Implementer	Gets on with the job, puts into practice
Team worker	Gives support and help
Resource investigator	Negotiates with outsiders to locate resources
Completer	Pushes to meet schedules and targets
Coordinator	Clarifies goals, allocates tasks and expresses the conclusions of the group

suppressing disagreements. Organizations with a long successful history and a strong leader are particularly likely to fall into this trap.

A rationale for groupthink may be found in studies of conformity (Sherif, 1936), which show that groups often tend to establish group norms to which the minority tends to conform even in cases when this is obviously wrong. However, subsequent studies indicated that minority dissent (Moscovici et al., 1969) may be effective in making group members change their mind and see the situation more correctly. Such studies provide a rationale for independent board members.

In a famous experiment, Milgram (1963) showed how people could be manipulated to give electroshocks to others in what they believed to be a learning experiment. While designed to reveal authoritarian behaviour more generally, this study may also be helpful to understand how employees and other insiders may effectively connive in fraud and other scandalous behaviour. Milgram's explanation of this was an alternative agency theory according to which individuals acting in an official capacity come to act in an agentic state in which they lose moral conscience and the sense of responsibility for their own actions. They tend to redefine the situation in ways which make it easier to accept, i.e. to deny how serious it is, avoid contact with victims or try to compensate somewhat by helping them. In contrast, the same people in an autonomous state would act much more morally and rationally. Note that this agency theory is quite the reverse of economic agency theory.

2.14   Sociology

Sociology, the science of society, is obviously also relevant to corporate governance, although many branches of sociology – sociology of religion, secularization, science, medicine – are not (or are only indirectly) concerned with corporate governance. However, some branches of sociology explicitly study corporate governance.

Social network theory is used to describe connections between companies through board membership (interlocking directorates) and ownership (cross-ownership). The contention that there is more to governance than formal institutions is captured by Kogut and Walker (2003): '... governance and control operate through the constitution of relationships that bind economic organizations and individual actors. The ultimate source of governance is society rather than the rule of formal law or even boards of directors narrowly defined'. It is also possible to put this a bit more radically: 'People and organizations are not the source of action so much as they are the vehicles for structurally induced action' (Burt, 1982). This implies a view of governance which is different from the methodological individualism of economics and agency theory. Depending on their constellations (i.e. network structure) rather than their individual characteristics, carbon atoms may yield soft graphite or hard diamonds (Parkhe et al., 2006). In the same way, network theory postulates that network structure rather than individual agent attributes determine behaviour and performance. However, network theory does not exclude the study of individual actors or rule out that they influence behaviour, it just focuses on the network relations. Network theory may thus be complementary to rather than competing with the more individualistic agency models of economic theory.

Quantitative measures can be used to describe and compare the density and other properties of such networks. Most have been found to be 'small worlds' in the sense that although they cluster locally there are 'weak ties' which make the entire system interconnected. As shown by Mark Granovetter (1973), weak ties can be important even though they are less intense because they can supply information from outside the immediate neighbourhood. Such information will probably be different and is more likely to be new than information supplied by one's immediate neighbourhood. The idea of 'six degrees of separation' implies that most actors are connected through no more than six steps.

Formally, a social network can be defined as a set of agents (firms, board members, owners ... also called vertices) connected by a set of ties (ownership, board interlocks ... also called nodes). The neighbourhood of an agent is defined as its immediately connected neighbours (agents). The degree of an agent is the number of other agents in its neighbourhood.

The clustering coefficient for an agent is the proportion of links between the agents within its neighbourhood divided by the number of links that could possibly exist between them. This measure is 1 if every neighbour connected to the agent is also connected to every other agent within the neighbourhood, and 0 if no agent that is connected to the agent connects to any other agent connected to the agent. The clustering coefficient for the whole system is given by Watts and Strogatz (1998) as the average of the clustering coefficient for each agent.

Given a social network, the path length between two agents is the number of connections in the shortest path connecting the two agents. The average path length is the average of the path length for all agents in the network.

We say that a network is a 'small world' if the clustering coefficient (cc) is high and the average path length (apl) is low, in other words if the small world statistic (sws = apl/cc) is large and particularly > 1. We measure the small world statistics only for connected firms since in particular the average path length is not defined for firms that are not connected.

Network theory has been applied to the study of business groups (Granovetter, 1994), but can also inform the study of board diversity. Board members around the world tend to belong to the business elite (Wright Mills, 1956) and to be homogeneous in terms of gender (men), education (economists, lawyers, engineers), nationality (national rather than international citizenship), age (50+) and other characteristics such as club memberships, residential area, political views etc. This may create a uniformity which on the one hand can facilitate decision making on boards, but on the other hand may also lead to groupthink problems. It may also be that board members come to identify too much with the CEO because they belong to the same social class. To break this conformity it has been argued that boards need to become more diverse, e.g. to include more international or female members.

The study of social norms, values and cultures is another aspect of sociology which has an obvious bearing on corporate governance. Attitudes towards honesty and fairness directly influence the magnitude of agency problems. Cultures vary across nations and can influence corporate governance, for example the degree of control which owners need to have to counter opportunistic behaviour or the degree to which managers can be motivated by performance-based pay. Thus it may be that board oversight or monetary incentives are less effective and less necessary in cultures governed by strong social norms. It is also conceivable that social norms can change over time, for example weaken, which would then necessitate more control and/or stronger economic incentives. Informal stories about growing greed might in principle be explained in this way.

2.15 Political science

Politics is clearly important because it shapes the law, because policymakers influence corporations through taxation and other policies, and because governments often own companies.

Political theory is also important because there are parallels between corporate governance and political democracy. Activists may advocate greater shareholder democracy in order to make companies more responsive to shareholders. This may imply one share–one vote (e.g. eliminating shares with different voting rights or secret voting (secret ballot). It is worth noting, however, that democracy is only a metaphor which has already been abandoned since shareholders tend to vote according to number of shares rather than one person–one vote.

Shareholder democracy is subject to some of the failures observed in political systems. For example, because of free-rider effects it may not be economically advantageous for small shareholders to be active in monitoring and influencing managers because they have to share the gains with all other shareholders. So shareholders (like voters) may rationally decide to be passive which creates a power vacuum that favours managers. Furthermore, if there are serious disagreements between shareholders it may be difficult to reach a decision which reflects their overall views in a meaningful way (Arrow, 1951). Voting may be subject to agenda effects such that manipulating the agenda may change the decision outcome. This implies that shareholder heterogeneity may be an important source of transaction costs. A key advantage of listed companies in this respect may be the ability of shareholders to sell their shares and leave. Public choice theory and political economy try to model the politics of governance in the sense that special interest groups influence the political process. For example, crony capitalism may enable strong interest groups like family dynasties to protect their interest at the expense of the general public.

Finally, political ideology is not infrequently closely linked to governance. There have been many political conflicts between adherents of different styles of corporate governance, for example between government ownership (socialism, communism) and capitalism (private property and free markets). Around 1900, cooperatives and friendly societies (mutuals) were regarded by many as a way to address inequality in society.

2.16 Law

Law influences corporate governance in a myriad of ways, for example through company and securities law. Law can be defined as a set of rules for society enforced by institutions such as courts, the police and public administration. Both rules and enforcement are crucial to governance. For example, capitalism presupposes private property. When the basic institutions fail, e.g. when governments or criminals can freely steal from citizens or companies, when judges and public officials are corrupt, the system ceases to function as is the case to various degrees in some 'failed states' in developing countries. Thus the rule of law is an important determinant of economic efficiency.

We follow Armour, Hansmann and Kraakman (2009a) in regarding company law as a response to agency problems including both type 1 agency problems between shareholders and managers, type 2 conflicts between shareholders and type 3 conflicts between shareholders and other stakeholders (Armour, Hansmann and Kraakman, 2009a, p. 2). Company law can be seen as a set of legal strategies to mitigate such agency problems (Armour, Hansmann and Kraakman, 2009b).

These legal strategies can be divided into regulation and governance. Regulation consists for example of rules which require or prohibit certain kinds of behaviour (e.g. minimum capital requirements or dividend restrictions) or more open-ended standards such as the duty of loyalty to the company or the duty of fair dealing. Governance rules regulate who has the right to decide what, such as the right of the shareholders to elect the board.

Across jurisdictions, five core characteristics common to most business corporations have emerged (Armour, Hansmann and Kraakman, 2009a): 1) legal personality, 2) limited liability, 3) transferable shares, 4) centralized management, and 5) shared ownership by investors.

Legal personality is useful for the firm as a nexus for contracting, i.e. an entity which is independent of its owners as a 'separate patrimony' with its own asset base and management. The managers can pledge the firm's capital and other resources in transactions with third parties, and separate rules are necessary to determine who has the ability to do this. Moreover, companies can be sued directly, irrespectively of who owns them. Legal personality serves to shield the company from the personal creditors of the owners and vice versa to shield the owners from the creditors of the company. The company's creditors have priority over the creditors of the owners. This necessitates a certain liquidation protection, i.e. the shareholders cannot at will withdraw their share of the company's capital.

Limited liability is a strong form of shielding the owners from the company. Risk can be shared with creditors who have no recourse to the shareholders. The security which limited liability gives shareholders is regarded as a condition for the emergence of modern stock markets.

Transferable shares allow the firm to do business continuously independently of ownership changes. For owners this implies a convenience in yield in the form of liquidity and the ability to diversify investments.

Centralized management implies the company is run by the board that is formally separate from both the management and the shareholders. While some corporate decisions can be made by the

management, others must be made by the board and some even by the shareholders. The board is invariably a group and is invariably elected by shareholders.

Investor ownership implies that the investors have the right to control the firm (including electing the board members) and the right to profits.

2.17 Management

Management researchers have developed their own toolbox. Concepts like corporate strategy, core competences, resource dependency, business ethics and corporate social responsibility are useful to better understand corporate governance. We deal with these important issues in subsequent chapters.

Here we just want to mention that there is a connection between leadership style and governance. A classic study by Lewin, Lippitt and White (1939) distinguished between authoritarian and democratic leaders. An authoritarian leader would typically want to centralize decision making and avoid intervention by the board or sharing power with employees. This obviously creates a different kind of corporate governance than would a more open consultative decision style, where the board can have greater influence.

2.18 Philosophy

Philosophy has a bearing on corporate governance primarily when it is applied to business, such as for example business ethics. A particularly influential branch is stakeholder theory (Freeman, 1984), which emphasizes that the purpose of the corporation is to create value for all its primary stakeholders, i.e. suppliers, customers, employees etc. and not just its stockholders. Stakeholder theory is normative, instrumental and descriptive (Donaldson and Preston, 1995). Many studies have normatively defended stakeholder theory on moral grounds (Evan and Freeman, 1983), because paying attention to stakeholders is the right thing to do. The theory is therefore perhaps at heart philosophical (the seminal contribution was by Freeman, who is a philosopher).

However, others argue instrumentally that corporate profits are served best by paying attention to stakeholders (Jones, 1995). To maximize shareholder value you need to nurture your employees and be close to your customers, the argument goes. This effectively makes stakeholder theory a management theory. It may in fact be a bit of both philosophy and management as in the following definition of stakeholder theory (Dunham et al., 2006; Stieb, 2009).

> *We hypothesize that a firm ought to interact with other communities that it affects or is affected by, seeking to understand their perspectives, listen to their preferences, and evaluate the impact of actions on them. Such interaction is best characterized as ... cooperation ... it ought to be in closer community with those upon whom it relies for support – employees, suppliers and customers. Such interaction requires a deeper commitment than that necessary for the first set of communities. It requires a more active pursuit ... – sharing interest, actions, and values. The firm's interaction with these groups must be ... collaboration.*[4]

It is even possible to see stakeholder theory as a branch of social science, for example sociology or economics. Descriptive stakeholder theory emphasizes that managers do in fact spend their time managing stakeholders and seeks to understand their relative influence (Mitchell et al., 1997; Jones and Wicks, 1999; Jawahar and McLaughlin, 2001). Hill and Jones (1992) propose to integrate stakeholder and agency theory in a 'stakeholder-agency theory', which holds managers accountable not just to stockholders but to stakeholders more generally. Descriptive agency theory can help identify which

---

[4] Dunham et al., 2006, p. 38.

stakeholders are particularly influential. Thomsen (2004, 2005) shows how stakeholder influence is internalized in companies through ownership structures, board composition and market pressures. For example, cooperative ownership of a dairy by a group of farmers assures these suppliers of having a say over the company. Mandatory employee representation on company boards is intended to have the same effect. Likewise, firms in highly competitive industries may come to identify with their customers.

2.19   Enlightened agency theory

The many theories in corporate governance can be seen as a toolkit for use in specific situations. However, the richness of theoretical frameworks also poses challenges because it can create confusion and allow for conflicting interpretations.

The approach we advocate to handle this complexity is to start with the basic agency problem and to nuance the analysis with attention to the institutional context, the psychology of the individuals concerned and so on. We call this approach 'enlightened agency theory'.

For example, the egos of alpha male imperial CEOs may sometimes drive them to actions which are difficult to imagine in dry mathematical agency theory. Families may value control of the business to the point of madness. Investors may herd to buy fashionable stocks, blind to the underlying businesses. Laws may require companies to do things which conflict with their business judgement.

We will argue that taking such things into consideration often makes agency theory more powerful. For example, the imperial CEO may need more discipline than a self-interest in stock options. Control preferences in families make the type 2 agency problem between majority and minority investors even more acute. Investor irrationality may foster a rethink of accountability to shareholders.

To be sure, there are also instances in which psychology or sociology make agency problems less acute. For example, as emphasized in stewardship theory some managers appear to be motivated by an unselfish need to do a good job. In such cases we would argue that agency theory should 'back off' in the same way that a safety belt is for the most part not very useful, but can still come in very handy in extreme situations. Moreover we maintain that the many scandals and failures in recent years have shown that selfishness and opportunism are not pure fiction. Investors or boards can seldom know for sure what kind of person they are dealing with. Most people tend to lock their cars!

The approach we advocate is to identify the key decision makers and the key social and psychological constraints facing them. Given this understanding, it will be easier to understand how corporate governance mechanisms work and how they could be changed for the better.

2.20   Discussion

Agency theory remains the most influential theory of corporate governance, but has been challenged and enriched in recent years by alternative perspectives from economics, law, psychology, sociology, political science and even philosophy. Given our definition of governance as the control and direction of companies, agency issues like control, information and incentives are clearly of paramount importance. Moreover, people do appear to respond to economic incentives in ways which make agency theory useful to understanding corporate governance. However, the assumptions of selfishness and rationality are clearly simplifications which can be nuanced by a deeper understanding of human psychology, law and other influential factors. For example, we know from cognitive psychology that human beings are not perfectly rational, but are subject to biases. We also know that motivation is not just a question of money. Furthermore we know that the goals and aspirations of managers or shareholders are shaped by social context and the way they perceive their situation. Because of this the way they act changes over time and varies across countries.

Our viewpoint is that the different approaches to corporate governance are complementary rather than contradictory. Rather than negating the role of incentives of information asymmetries, psychology and law and a host of other factors shape how they are perceived and handled in particular companies. Corporate governance students can examine to what extent the governance of a particular company is shaped by the factors and understand more of what is going on. The risk of rich theory is of course that we end up with a lot of 'hand waving' and little value added. We therefore recommend that students start with agency theory and introduce alternative perspectives when they are in fact believed to add significantly to understanding the problem at hand.

Minicase

Bankers' pay 2010

According to the *Financial Times* of 15 June 2011, bankers' pay started to rise again in 2010 – just a year after the financial crisis. Loyd Blankenfein, CEO of Goldman Sachs, took a pay increase of 1535% from $862,657 in 2009 to $14,114,080 in 2010. Jamie Dimon, CEO of JPMorgan Chase, got $20,776,324 in 2010, up by 1541% from $1,265,708 in 2009. James Gorman, CEO of Morgan Stanley, hired in 2010, got $14,854,049. These figures do not include capital gains on equity awards granted in earlier years. These gains can be significant; for example in the case of Jamie Dimon they are estimated at $35 million dollars in 2010. The pay increase reflects both increases in share prices for equity-linked pay and increases in fixed salaries.

Critics are outraged that the same people who nearly destroyed the world's financial system are now again paid so much. Banks retort that the CEOs got much more before the crisis. For example Loyd Blankenfein took home $70 million in 2007.

Bankers' pay also rose in the UK. Stephen Hester of Royal Bank of Scotland got $11,537,346, up 15% from 2009. The British Government had to take over 83% of RBS during the crisis. Eric Daniels of Lloyds Banking Group got $8,367,953 in 2010, up 68% from 2009. Eric Daniels is criticized for a disastrous tie-up between Lloyds and HBOS during the crisis. John Varley of Barclays got $5,945,946 in 2010, up 239% from 2009. Barclays bought the failed investment bank Lehman's US business cheaply and did not have to get government aid.

The trend was less expansive in continental Europe. Brady Dougan of Credit Suisse had to take a pay cut of 33% to $11,807,725. The Swiss media was outraged that he got $83 million in 2010 under a long-term incentive plan. Joseph Ackerman of Deutsche Bank got $8,548,380 in 2010, down 19%. Fransisco Gonsalez of Banco Bilbao got $8,070,985 in 2010, down 10%. Badouin Prot of BNP Paribas got $3,530,624, up 3% from 2009.

Source: *Bank chiefs ditch the hair shirts* by Megan Murphy, 15 June 2011 © The Financial Times Ltd 2012.

Discussion questions

1 What would be the agency-theoretic view of bankers' pay?
2 Does equity-linked compensation make bank managers behave like owners? What would be the incomplete contract view of this?
3 a Is it possible to argue from an agency-theoretic viewpoint that bankers are overpaid?
   b What might a sociologist say to this discussion?
   c What might a psychologist say?
   d What could a philosopher say?
   e What do you think?
4 a Why might European bank CEOs get less and face a different trend?
   b What would a political scientist say to this?

Summary (learning points)

- Agency theories assume rational selfish agents and principals.

- Agents (e.g. managers) are assumed to be better informed than principals (e.g. shareholders). The information asymmetry creates incentive problems (also known as agency problems).

- There are two generic information asymmetries which give rise to two different agency problems: moral hazard (hidden action) and adverse selection (hidden knowledge).

- There are three generic agency problems: type 1: owner vs. managers, type 2: majority vs. minority owners, type 3: shareholders vs. stakeholders (aka CSR issues).

- Psychology can modify agency theory because it demonstrates that agents are not always rational or self-interested.

- The political theory of corporate governance stresses that governance is fundamentally shaped by politics, primarily through law, which leads to international differences in corporate governance.

- Sociology emphasizes social context such as networks and norms, i.e. not just formal but also informal institutions, which influence governance.

- Philosophy has given rise to stakeholder theory which emphasizes that companies should pay heed not just to stakeholders, but also to stockholders.

Appendix: Optimal contracts and agency problems

2.21 Introduction

Principal agent theory is frequently used to understand executive compensation and corporate governance issues. Agency theory helps understand how to motivate managers in the presence of asymmetric information. Importantly, it gives important predictions on the optimal design of executive compensation contracts. It contrasts to sociological pay models that assert that CEO behaviour stems from the use of power (i.e. rent-extraction). In these alternative power models of pay determination, CEOs extract greater than necessary pay because shareholders are weak. In contrast, the economics of executive pay literature has used agency theory to outline central features of empirically observed CEO pay contracts. The usefulness of such models is a) they make clear the assumptions that are in play when thinking about and designing the optimal CEO pay contract, and b) a parsimonious model may lead to significant insights about contract design (Laffont and Martimort, 2002; Bolton and Dewatripont, 2005). In particular, the canonical agency model helps understand why performance related elements (such as stock options and annual incentive pay based on earnings) are important in CEO pay contracts. Our goal is to describe the main elements of this model. The basic principal–agent model has the following features. There are two parties. The 'principal' delegates decision-making authority to an 'agent' who takes actions that materially affect the welfare of the principal. The classic principal–agent problem is the shareholder and CEO–manager relation. The shareholders are assumed to want to optimize the firm's profits but are not involved in the strategic decisions of the firm directly. Usually, the principal cannot monitor or observe at zero cost the actions that the agent takes. This asymmetric information is termed a moral hazard. Moral hazard arises from the fact that one party (the agent) can take actions that cannot be completely monitored by the other party (the principal) at zero cost. In the economics of information literature, this means that information is asymmetrically distributed. In this case the agent's actions are hidden from the principal. The agent knows 'more' than the principal. Specifically, the agent knows with certainty whether he worked hard or not, or tried to take the most beneficial course of action for the principal or not. This information is 'hidden' from the principal, who has to figure out what contract elicits efficient behaviour from the CEO.

2.22 Moral hazards

The agency problem gives rise to a complex set of contracting problems. How does the principal (shareholder) guarantee that the agent (CEO) takes the right action to optimize the principal's welfare? There is a vast economics literature that deals with this (Laffont and Martimort, 2002). The principal's objective is to find an optimal or efficient contract that induces the agent to take the 'right' action of his own free will, without coercion from shareholders. The solution to this agency problem, though, depends critically on the underlying structure of the model, and it is not easy to arrive at general predictions or easy answers. The answers typically depend on the payoff (or utility) functions for each party, the distribution of information between the principal and agent, and the number of times the parties interact with each other.

Moral hazards are everywhere in the ownership and control of firms. Thinking carefully about them is important. Tirole (2006) lists four types of moral hazard. First is *insufficient effort*. This does not mean the number of hours worked by CEOs, but instead it refers to the allocation of their time to the right type of tasks. For example, CEOs may not lay off workers when it is an economic necessity to do so because firing workers is an unpleasant task to perform. The second moral hazard is the tendency to *engage in extravagant investments*. These include pet projects that the CEO is interested in, or activities that build empires, but do not increase shareholder value. For example, CEOs might engage in diversifying merger and acquisition activities that increase the size of the firm (and the CEO's pay packet) but do not necessarily increase the firm's value, as they do not focus on core competencies. The third moral hazard is *entrenchment strategies*. CEOs may take actions that secure their own tenure and position within the firm, at the expense of shareholder value. First, CEOs might invest in shareholder value-destroying related diversifications because this increases their power in the combined organization. Second, CEOs might resist a hostile takeover, perhaps by adopting a poison pill strategy. The takeover might benefit incumbent shareholders but will result in the loss of the CEO's job. Other examples undoubtedly exist. The fourth moral hazard is *self-dealing*. Self-dealing increases the private benefits enjoyed by the CEO, possibly at the expense of shareholders. Self-dealing activities lie on a continuum from the benign to the prohibited. CEOs might use corporate jets or have country club memberships. It is important to recognize that these are legal benefits that might also increase shareholder welfare as well as being enjoyed by the CEO. Some activities are illegal. Robert Maxwell stole from the employees' pension fund, and Bernard Madoff stole from investors in a sophisticated Ponzi scheme. Corporate scandals are a very public (and obvious) form of moral hazard. Controlling moral hazards (arising from insufficient effort, extravagant investments, entrenchment strategies and self-dealing) is an important issue in corporate governance.

Agency costs can arise in many areas of corporate life. One is the field of corporate finance and especially the capital structure decision that the firm makes. What are some of the agency costs associated with the capital structure decision? First, there is an asset substitution effect. As the debt to equity ratio increases within the firm, management has an increased incentive to undertake risky and possibly negative net present value projects. Why is this? If the project is successful, shareholders will get all the upside from that success. Conversely, if the project fails the risks are shared with debt holders. The shareholder can lose up to the maximum of his investment. If the project is undertaken, there is a chance of firm value decreasing and a wealth transfer from debtholders to shareholders. An optimal contract from a bondholder perspective will use covenants to restrict excessively risky management behaviour. Second, there is a free cash flow problem. Suppose the firm generates earnings greater than is currently necessary to fund positive present value projects. Management may not return this free cash flow to investors. In consequence, management has an incentive to destroy firm value through activities such as empire building and perks which do not contribute to firm value.

2.23   The standard model

Define the following variables: V is the output of the firm; e is the effort of the employee; α is the agent's salary. This is 'insurance' from the perspective of the agent since it does not vary with the performance of the enterprise, or agent effort. The term βv is the proportion of the firm's output V that is to be paid to the CEO or employee. It is the division of the pie, or so-called 'sharing-rate'; W is the CEO wage; w_0 is the exogenous wage that prevails in the market place. The CEO's payoff function (or 'utility') is denoted by U. The payoff for the firm is the net profit (or surplus) given by the function S. We define $c(e)$ as the agent's cost of effort function. The cost of effect is convex ($c'(e) > 0$, $c''(e) > 0$). These are the basic necessary ingredients. The additional ε term imparts randomness to the outcome of firm output. We assume that firm performance is subject to stochastic shocks (luck), such that $\varepsilon \sim N(0, \sigma_e^2)$, and is independent and identically distributed ('iid'). The term r is the CEO's coefficient of absolute risk aversion. With this notation, we are in a position to determine the optimal linear compensation contract that solves the moral hazard problem.

Following the standard literature we consider a linear compensation contract (Milgrom and Roberts, 1992, Chapter 7). We find the agent's wage that is made up of a fixed part and an element that varies linearly with observable variables such as output (which in turn depends on agent effort and a stochastic component). The logic of this is that such contracts are often observable in practice, but not always so. For example, the optimal compensation contract might depend in a complex way on observable effort and other signals of agent effort. However, as discussed in Holmström and Milgrom (1987) various assumptions are necessary to make the linear contract optimal, such as exponential agent utility and normal distributions. The general case is given in Holmström (1979).

The principal (shareholders) must take into account two binding constraints. The first is the incentive compatibility constraint. The agent (CEO) must take the costly actions of his own volition. Since effort adversely affects agent welfare, the tendency is towards low rather than high effort that the principal wants the agent to take. The contract must make it worthwhile for the CEO to work hard in the presence of the moral hazard, rather than not. The second concern is the participation constraint. This means the agent must receive at least what can be received by not accepting the contract (i.e. the market alternative).

We posit that the CEO is risk averse, and that production (firm output, $V = e + \varepsilon$) is non-separable in both effort and luck (e and ε). We find the efficient linear contract such that $W = \alpha + \beta v V$ and that the employee's simple convex cost of effort function is $c(e) = e^2/2$. First, consider the employee's optimal effort response to a given linear contract.

The employee optimizes expected utility E[U], with respect to own effort:

$$\max_e E[U] = \max_e \left\{ E[W] - c(e) - \frac{r}{2} \text{var}(W) \right\}$$

where E[W] is the expected wage, and $(r/2)\text{var}(W)$ is a term reflecting the loss to the agent's utility associated with accepting the risky contract. Statistical decision theory tells us that:

$$\text{var}(W) = \text{var}\{\alpha + \beta_v(e + \varepsilon)\}$$
$$= \beta_v^2 \sigma_\varepsilon^2$$

so that the CEO's objective function can be rewritten as:

$$\max_e E[U] = \max_e \left\{ \alpha + \beta_v e - \frac{e^2}{2} - \frac{r}{2} \beta_v^2 \sigma_\varepsilon^2 \right\}$$

The agent's first order labour supply condition (which gives us the incentive compatibility condition) is:

$$\frac{\partial E[U]}{\partial e} = \beta_v - e$$

In consequence, optimal CEO effort / labour supply is simply $e^* = \beta_v$. This is the incentive compatibility constraint. It ensures that the CEO takes the right action of his own volition. The agent sets the marginal returns to effort equal to the marginal costs of effort. In addition, the CEO will only accept the contract if the expected utility is at least as good as the expected utility he would expect elsewhere (i.e. w_0). This is the participation constraint (P.C.).

$$E[U] = w_0 = \alpha + \beta_v e - \frac{e^2}{2} - \frac{r}{2} \beta_v^2 \sigma_\varepsilon^2$$

Knowing the optimal labour supply actions of the agent we next consider the principal's (or shareholder's) problem. The investor would like to maximize their expected surplus, i.e. E[firm output] – E[wages]. Namely investors maximize

$$\max_{\alpha, \beta v} E[S] = \max_{\alpha, \beta v} \{E[V] - E[W]\}$$

subject to the constraint that the CEO chooses the optimal effort level (I.C.) and that compensation is sufficiently high to meet the participation constraint (P.C.). Other solutions are not enforceable in an open market. Given that the employee uses effort e^*, the expected output of the firm will be e^*, the expected wages paid to the employee will be $\alpha + \beta v e^\star$ and the employer will maximize $e^\star - (\alpha + \beta v e^\star)$:

$$\frac{\partial E[S^\star]}{\partial \beta_v} = \frac{\partial}{\partial \beta_v} \{e^\star - \alpha - \beta_v e^\star\}$$

$$= \frac{\partial}{\partial \beta_v} \left\{ \beta_v - \frac{\beta_v^2}{2} - \frac{r}{2} \beta_v^2 \sigma_\varepsilon^2 \right\} \quad \text{(using I.C. and P.C.)}$$

$$= 1 - \beta_v - r\beta_v \sigma_\varepsilon^2$$

At the expected level firm profit, $E[S^\star]$, the optimal sharing rate (that is the intensity of the CEO's incentives) is given as

$$\beta v^\star = \frac{1}{1 + r\sigma_e^2}$$

This is the well-known result showing an inverse relation between incentives and risk. The optimal output of α can be found by simply substituting this output of βv into the participation constraint:

$$w_0 = \alpha + \beta_v e - \frac{e^2}{2} - \frac{r}{2} \beta_2^v \sigma_2^\varepsilon$$

$$\alpha^\star = w_0 - \frac{1 - r\sigma_\varepsilon^2}{2(1 + r\sigma_\varepsilon^2)^2}$$

From this simplified model we get a number of important predictions. First, the optimal sharing rate between the principal (shareholder) and the agent (CEO) is less than 100%. This arises because the employee is risk averse and the shareholder is risk neutral, and firm production function is subject to a stochastic component.

Second, the optimal sharing rate is equal to 100% if the CEO is risk neutral ($r = 0$). This is because the CEO is willing to accept the risky gamble. In effect, the moral hazard externality has been internalized and the enterprise is sold to the CEO. Liquidity constraints are assumed to be non-binding in the model. This is equivalent to assuming the CEO can borrow sufficient funds to buy the expected income stream from the principal.

Third, as CEO risk-aversion increases, the optimal sharing rate declines. The optimal contract does not impose 'too much' risk on a risk-averse agent.

Fourth, the more noise there is in firm output, the lower is the sharing rate. Intuitively, the less that output is due to the CEO and the more it is due to luck, the less high-powered should be the incentive function. The more the CEO is responsible for the fortunes of the firm, the greater is the incentive rate. Finally, the model predicts the presence of risky pay in the CEO's contract. Such 'pay at risk' can include bonuses that depend on earnings or accounting profits, or equity contracts such as restricted stock, stock options, or stock appreciation rights.

The model described here provides fundamental insights into the optimal design of CEO contracts. However, it is necessarily simplified. We have imposed structure on it, and this helps derive tractable solutions. In more complex models this is not the case. Holmström (1979) describes a model where any performance metric that provides a signal of the CEO's effort may be (optimally) contracted on. This is the 'informativeness' principle in contract theory. In summary, although formal models may be abstract, they do give insight into rational behaviour, incentives and risk preferences. In addition, in developing models the underlying objective functions and core assumptions need to be made explicit, which helps in evaluating the realism of the model for empirical purposes.

2.24 Relative performance evaluation

The standard model can be extended in a number of ways. One important area is so-called relative performance evaluation. The basic idea here is that although shareholders cannot observe at zero cost CEO effort, they can receive a signal of it by comparing CEO output with the output of others in similar situations. Shareholders can benchmark CEO performance against the performance of similarly situated CEOs and improve upon the contract.

Consider a CEO of a publicly traded firm that operates in a fairly standardized and homogeneous industry. This means that the firms in the same industry are good candidates to compare our CEO against. Suppose now that stock returns in the focal firm increased by 10% over a given interval. At first sight this looks like good news for shareholders. However, if the stock market performance of all the other similar firms has increased by 20% then our CEO would appear to have underperformed relative to the market. Analogously, suppose that stock returns in the focal firm declined by 10% over a given interval. At first sight this looks like bad news for shareholders. However, if the stock market performance of all the other similar firms has decreased by 20% then our CEO would appear to have outperformed relative to the market. Benchmarking, or relative performance, is an informative signal for shareholders. Filtering out common shocks (namely the performance of similarly situated firms) can improve the contracting environment.

2.25 A simple model

The standard model described above can be extended. We ask what happens if $E[\varepsilon] = k \neq 0$? In this case the mathematical expectation is $E[V] = E[e] + E[\varepsilon] = E[e] + k$. Therefore, expected output $E[V]$ contains one component due to the effort of the employee and another component due to other (relative) factors. Now, the CEO's expected wage is

$$E[W] = \alpha + \beta E[V] = \alpha + \beta(\bar{e} + k) \text{ where } \bar{e} = E[e]$$

$$\text{So } \alpha = E[W] - \beta(\bar{e} + k)$$

If the firm assumes that $k = 0$ but $k > 0$ then the firm will pay a salary which is too high – they will pay the CEO for output which is not due to his effort. This will lead to happy employees but the firm will not be maximizing profits. On the other hand, if the firm assumes that $k > 0$ but $k = 0$, the firm will pay a salary which is too low – they will assume that some of the output is due to favourable conditions rather than worker effort. This will lead to disgruntled CEOs who may quit. The firm wants to reward the employee's efforts but not reward favourable conditions. If the firm knew k with certainty they could simply factor it into the wage equation. However, k is difficult to measure. A performance standard is used instead; there are three suitable standards: 1) a suitable peer group of individuals or firms, 2) a standard that is determined subjectively by an evaluator, 3) the firm can use employee performance from a previous period.

Suppose that firm production is as before: $V = e + \varepsilon$. Now we suppose that a performance standard is defined as $P = \bar{e} - E[\varepsilon] = \bar{e} + k$. Wages are paid to the CEO net of the performance standard $W = \alpha + \beta v(V - P)$. As before the convex cost of effort function is: $c(e) = e^2/2$. We first determine the employees' labour supply (the incentive constraint). The CEO optimizes expected utility:

$$\max_e E[U] = \max_e \left\{ E[W] - c(e) - \frac{r}{2} \text{var}(W) \right\}$$

$$\max_e E[U] = \max_e \left\{ \alpha + \beta_v (e + k - \bar{e} - k) - \frac{e^2}{2} - \frac{r}{2} \beta_v^2 \sigma_\varepsilon^2 \right\}$$

$$\frac{\partial E[U]}{\partial e} = \beta_v - e$$

$$\text{So } e^* = \beta_v$$

The optimal labour supply condition is unchanged compared with the standard model, but rewards relative performance. The participation constraint requires expected utility from taking this job is at least as good as the expected utility from the next best alternative: w_0.

$$E[U] = w_0 = \alpha + \beta_v (e - \bar{e}) - \frac{e^2}{2} - \frac{r}{2}\beta_2^v \sigma_2^\varepsilon$$

From the firm's perspective, the employer would like to maximize their expected surplus, i.e. E[firm production] – E[wages]:

$$\max_{\alpha,\beta_v} E[S] = \max_{\alpha,\beta_v} \{E[V] - E[W]\}$$

subject to the constraint that the employee will choose their optimal effort level (I.C.) and the pay is high enough for participation by the employee (P.C.). So, given that the employee uses effort e^*, the expected production of the firm will be $e^* + k$, the expected wages paid to the employee will be $\alpha + \beta v(e^* - \bar{e})$ and the employer will maximize $e^* + k - (\alpha + \beta_v(e^* - \bar{e}))$

$$\frac{\partial E[S^*]}{\partial \beta_v} = \frac{\partial}{\partial \beta_v} \left\{ e^* + k - \alpha - \beta_v (e^* - \bar{e}) \right\}$$

$$= \frac{\partial}{\partial \beta_v} \left\{ \beta_v - \frac{\beta_v^2}{2} - \frac{r}{2}\beta_v^2\sigma_\varepsilon^2 \right\} \quad \text{(using I.C. and P.C.)}$$

$$= 1 - \beta_v - r\beta_v\sigma_\varepsilon^2$$

So, at the optimal value E[S*], the efficient contract is the same as the standard model: $\beta v^* = 1/1 + r\sigma_\varepsilon^2$ The optimal value of α can be found by substituting this value of βv into P.C.:

$$w_0 = a^* + \beta_v (e^* - \bar{e}) - \frac{e^{*2}}{2} - \frac{r}{2} \beta_v^2\sigma_\varepsilon^2$$

$$\alpha^* = w_0 - \frac{1 - r\sigma_\varepsilon^2}{2(1 + r\sigma_\varepsilon^2)^2} + \frac{1}{(1 + r\sigma_\varepsilon^2)}\bar{e}$$

The relative performance evaluation model shows that if $P = E[\varepsilon] = k$, i.e. k can be estimated, then α^* in this case would be exactly the same as in the standard model where $E[\varepsilon] = 0$. However, if a relative performance measure is used, the incentive payment will reflect any improvements over the standard – the average performance of the peer group, a subjective standard or a previous period performance. However, the salary component of the wage will increase from that in the standard model to the point where the employee is performing at the standard.

2.26 Discussion

This appendix has considered the optimal contract approach to CEO compensation. The firm defines an efficient contract in the presence of moral hazard. Moral hazards are ubiquitous in firms, so agency models are central to understanding the control of organizations. Conditions for the optimal contract in the presence of moral hazard were outlined. We have shown the results of the standard model. We have shown the importance of relative performance evaluation. These ideas are central in the economics of corporate governance.

Minicase

Safelite Auto

Getting the structure of incentives right in a firm is critical if agents are to be properly motivated. Professor Edward Lazear at Stanford University studied the Safelite Auto Glass Company. Safelite is an auto glass repair company. Its business is to replace broken windshields. Professor Lazear showed that Safelite faced a big problem. Although windshields took a little over an hour to install, the average installation rate per worker was a little over three per day. Even accounting for travel time etc. this was a low rate of productivity. The company decided to move from a fixed salary compensation scheme for its workers to a piece rate system. That is, windshield installers would now be paid on the basis of the number of windshields that they installed, and not simply a fixed salary per day.

Professor Lazear, and other labour economists, predicted a number of effects from the switch from salaries to piece rates. First, and fundamentally, it was predicated that productivity would increase. Why? Now instead of working to the minimum standard, installers would receive more compensation the more windshields they installed. In the language of this chapter, it solved a moral hazard problem and provided the worker with more pay tied to performance. Second, they predicted that there would be a sorting effect. This means that workers who did not like the new compensation arrangements would leave the firm. In addition, workers who heard about the new programme and thought they could install a lot of windshields would join the company. Naturally, workers were therefore sorted and matched differently according to their preferences and abilities. In the language of this chapter, an adverse selection problem was solved with the new optimal contract. Finally, there were unanticipated (but predictable) consequences of the new pay scheme. Workers would rush to complete jobs and the quality of the windshield installation would suffer.

What happened? Professor Lazear showed that productivity increased by about 30%: a dramatic amount. Approximately half of the increase was attributed to the incentive effects of the new pay-for-performance scheme. Approximately half the increase in productivity was attributed to changes in personnel. As predicted, negative reports of failed windshield installations increased, but the company instituted steps to address this.

Discussion questions

1 How can the compensation scheme at Safelite solve the productivity problem?
2 Contrast the effects of these two schemes. Scheme 1 is a fixed salary that does not vary with performance or output. Scheme 2 pays a salary proportional to performance or output. What is the effect on a) incentives, b) personnel recruitment?
3 Why is the optimal contract not likely to reward the employee with 100% of his or her performance?
4 Is a compensation scheme that does not relate pay to performance likely to be optimal?

Summary (learning points)

■ An optimal compensation contract is one that solves a manager and shareholder objective optimization problem subject to the binding constraints imposed by limited information sets.
■ To motivate the agent CEO, the contract must get the agent to engage in effort of his or her own volition (incentive compatibility constraint) and make sure that the contract is attractive to the CEO (participation constraint).
■ Moral hazards are unobserved effort. They include insufficient effort, extravagant investments, entrenchment and self-dealing.
■ The informativeness principle says that any performance measure that provides information to

the owner about level of effort expended by the agent is a good candidate variable to include in the compensation contract.

■ Evaluating the performance of one individual relative to the performance of suitable peers is useful in the optimal contract. It reduces the noise in the contract and tells the principal something about the amount of 'luck' that the employee faced in the production process.

 ## References and further reading

Adorno, T.W., Frenkel-Brunswik, E., Levinson, D.J. and Sanford, R.N. (1950) *The Authoritarian Personality*, Harper and Row: New York.

Akerlof, G.A. (1970) The Market for 'Lemons': Quality Uncertainty and the Market Mechanism, *Quarterly Journal of Economics*, **84** (3), 488–500.

Armour, J., Hansmann, H. and Kraakman, R. (2009a) What is Corporate Law? in *The Anatomy of Corporate Law: A Comparative and Functional Approach*, H. Reinier et al. (eds), Oxford University Press: Oxford.

Armour, J., Hansmann, H. and Kraakman, R. (2009b) Agency Problems and Legal Strategies, in *The Anatomy of Corporate Law: A Comparative and Functional Approach*, 2nd edition, H. Reinier et al. (eds), Oxford University Press: Oxford.

Arrow, K.J. (1951) *Social Choice and Individual Values*, John Wiley & Sons: New York.

Arrow, K.J. (1963) Uncertainty and the Welfare Economics of Medical Care, *American Economic Review*, **53** (5), 941–973.

Arrow, K.J. (1973) Social Responsibility and Economic Efficiency, *Public Policy*, **21**, 303–318.

Bartlett, F. (1932) *Remembering*, Cambridge University Press: Cambridge.

Belbin, R.M. (1993) *Team Roles at Work*, Butterworth-Heinemann: Oxford

Berle, A. and Means G. (1932) *The Modern Corporation and Private Property*, Macmillan: New York.

Bernheim, D.B. and Whinston, M.D. (1986) Common Agency, *Econometrica*, **54** (4), 923–942.

Bolton, P. and Dewatripont, M. (2005) *Contract Theory*, MIT Press: Massachusetts.

Burt, R.S. (1982) *Toward a Structural Theory of Action: Network Models of Social Structure, Perception and Action*, Academic Press: New York.

Cannon, W.B. (1915) *Bodily Changes in Pain, Hunger, Fear and Rage: An Account of Recent Researches into the Function of Emotional Excitement*, D. Appleton and Co.: New York.

Coase, R.H. (1937) The Nature of the Firm, *Economica*, **4** (16), 386–405.

Coase, R.H. (1960) The Problem of Social Cost, *Journal of Law and Economics*, **3** (1), 1–44.

Collins, J. (2001) *Good to Great: Why Some Companies Make the Leap...and Others Don't*, Harper Collins: New York.

Debreu, G. (1959) *The Theory of Value: An Axiomatic Analysis of Economic Equilibrium*, Yale University Press: New Haven.

Demsetz, H. (1983) The Structure of Ownership and the Theory of the Firm, *Journal of Law and Economics*, **26** (2), 375–390.

Donaldson, T. and Preston, L.E. (1995) The Stakeholder Theory of the Corporation: Concepts, Evidence, and Implications, *Academy of Management Review*, **20** (1), 65–91.

Dunham, L., Freeman, R.E and Liedtka, J. (2006) Enhancing Stakeholder Practice: A Particularized Exploration of Community, *Business Ethics Quarterly*, **16** (1), 23–42.

Evan, W. and Freeman, R.E. (1983) A Stakeholder Theory of the Modern Corporation: Kantian Capitalism, in *Ethical Theory and Business*, Beauchamps, T., Bowie, N. and Arnold, D. (eds), Prentice Hall: Englewood Cliffs, NJ.

Freeman, R.E. (1984) *Strategic Management: A Stakeholder Approach*, Pitman: Marshfield, MA.

Fromm, E. (1994 [1941]) *Escape from Freedom*, Henry Holt: NY.

Gardner, H. (1983) *Frames of Mind: The Theory of Multiple Intelligences*, Basic Books: New York.

Granovetter, M.S. (1973) The Strength of Weak Ties, *American Journal of Sociology*, **78** (6), 1360–1380.

Granovetter, M.S. (1994) *Business Groups, Handbook of Economic Sociology*, Princeton University Press: Princeton, NJ.

Grossman, S.J. and Hart, O.D. (1986) The Costs and Benefits of Ownership: A Theory of Vertical and Lateral Integration, *Journal of Political Economy*, **94** (4), 691–719.

Hart, O.D. (1988) Incomplete Contracts and the Theory of the Firm, *Journal of Law, Economics, and Organization*, **4** (1), 119–139.

Hart, O.D. (1995a) Corporate Governance: Some Theory and Implications, *Economic Journal*, **105** (430), 678–689.

Hart, O.D. (1995b) *Firms, Contracts, and Financial Structure*, Oxford University Press: New York.

Hayes, N. (2000) *Foundations of Psychology: An Introductory Text*, London: Thomson Learning.

Hill, C.W. and Jones, T.M. (1992) Stakeholder-Agency

Theory, *Journal of Management Studies*, **29** (2), 131–154.

Holmström, B. (1979) Moral Hazard and Observability, *Bell Journal of Economics*, **10** (1), 4–91.

Holmström, B. (1982) Moral Hazard in Teams, *Bell Journal of Economics*, **13** (2), 324–340.

Holmström, B. and Milgrom, P. (1987) Aggregation and Linearity in the Provision of Intertemporal Incentives, *Econometrica*, **55** (2), 303–328.

Janis, I.L. (1972) *Victims of groupthink: A psychological study of foreign-policy decisions and fiascoes*, Houghton Mifflin: Oxford.

Jawahar, I.M. and McLaughlin, G.L. (2001) Toward a Descriptive Stakeholder Theory: an Organizational Life Cycle Approach, *Academy of Management Review*, **26** (3), 397–414.

Jensen, M.C. (1993) The Modern Industrial Revolution, Exit and the Failure of Internal Control Systems, *Journal of Finance*, **48** (3), 830–879.

Jensen, M.C. and Meckling, W.H. (1976) Theory of the Firm: Managerial Behaviour, Agency Costs and Ownership Structure, *Journal of Financial Economics*, **3** (4), 305–360.

Jones, T.M. (1995) Instrumental Stakeholder Theory: A Synthesis of Ethics and Economics, *Academy of Management Review*, **20** (2), 404–437.

Jones, T.M. and Wicks, A.C. (1999) Convergent Stakeholder Theory, *Academy of Management Review*, **24** (2), 206–221.

Judge, T.A., Bono, J.E., Ilies, R. and Gerhardt, M. (2002) Personality and leadership: A Qualitative and Quantitative Review, *Journal of Applied Psychology*, **87** (4), 765–780.

Kahneman, D. and Tversky, A. (1973) On the Psychology of Prediction, *Psychological Review*, **80** (4), 237–251.

Kahneman, D. and Tversky, A. (1979) Prospect Theory: An Analysis of Decisions under Risk, *Econometrica*, **47** (2), 263–292.

Kogut, B. and Walker, G. (2003) Restructuring or Disintegration of the German Corporate Network: Globalization as a Fifth Column, *Gérer et Comprendre*, **74**, 14–24.

Kraakman, R.H. et al. (eds) (2009) *The Anatomy of Corporate Law: A Comparative and Functional Approach*, Oxford University Press: Oxford.

Kreps, D.M. (1986) Corporate Culture and Economic Theory, in *Perspectives on Positive Political Economy*, Alt, J.E. and Shepsle, K.A. (eds), Cambridge University Press: Cambridge.

Kreps, D.M. and Wilson, R. (1982) Reputation and imperfect information, *Journal of Economic Theory*, **27** (2), 253–279

Laffont, J. And Martimort, D. (2002) *The Theory of Incentives: The Principal-Agent Model*, Princeton University Press: Princeton.

Lewin, K., Lippitt, R. and White, R.K (1939) Patterns of Aggressive Behavior in Experimentally Created "Social Climates", *Journal of Social Psychology*, **10** (2), 271–299.

March, J.G. and Simon, H.A. (1958) *Organizations*, Wiley: Oxford, England.

Milgram, S. (1963) Behavioral Study of Obedience, *Journal of Abnormal Social Psychology*, **67** (4), 371–378.

Milgrom, P. and Roberts, J. (1992) *Economics, Organizations and Management*, Prentice Hall:

Mitchell, R.K., Agle, B.R. and Wood, D.J. (1997) Toward a Theory of Stakeholder Identification and Salience: Defining the Principle of Who and What Really Counts, *Academy of Management Review*, **22** (40), 853–886.

Moscovici, S., Lage, E. and Naffrechoux, M. (1969) Influence of a Consistent Minority on the Response of a Majority in Color Perception Task, *Sociometry*, **32** (4), 365–380.

Norman, W.T. (1963) Toward an Adequate Taxonomy of Personality Attributes: Replicated Factor Structure in Peer Nomination Personality ratings, *Journal of Abnormal and Social Psychology*, **66** (6), 574–583.

Parkhe, A., Wasserman, S. and Ralston, D.A. (2006) New Frontiers in Network Theory Development, *Academy of Management Review*, **31** (3), 560–568.

Posner, E.A. (2000) Agency Models in Law and Economics, in *Chicago Lectures in Law and Economics*, Posner, E. (ed.), Foundation Press.

Rappaport, A. (1981) Selecting Strategies That Create Shareholder Value, *Harvard Business Review*, **59** (3), 139–149.

Rappaport, A. (1986) *Creating Shareholder Value: The New Standard for Business Performance*, Free Press: New York.

Ross, S.A. (1973) The Economic Theory of Agency: The Principal's Problem, *American Economic Review*, **63** (2).

Sherif, M. (1936) *The Psychology of Social Norms*, Harper: New York.

Shleifer, A. and Vishny, R.W. (1997) The Proper Scope of Government: Theory and an Application to Prisons, *Quarterly Journal of Economics*, **112** (4), 1127–1161.

Skinner, B.F. (1938) *The Behavior of Organisms: an Experimental Analysis*, Appleton-Century: Oxford.

Stieb, J.A. (2009) Assessing Freeman's Stakeholder Theory, *Journal of Business Ethics*, **87** (3), 401–414.

Thomsen, S. (2004) Corporate Values and Corporate Governance, *Corporate Governance*, **4** (4), 29–46.

Thomsen, S. (2005) Corporate Governance as a Determinant of Corporate Values, *Corporate Governance*, **5** (4), 10–27.

Tirole, J. (2006) *The Theory of Corporate Finance*, Princeton University Press.

Wason, P.C. (1968) Reasoning about a rule, *Quarterly Journal of Experimental Psychology*, **20** (3), 273–281.

Watts, D.J. and Strogatz, S.H. (1998) Collective dynamics of 'small-world' networks, *Nature,* **393** (6684), 440–442.

Williamson, O.E. (1967) Hierarchical control and optimum firm size, *Journal of Political Economy*, **75** (2), 123–138.

Williamson, O.E. (1973) Markets and hierarchies: Some Elementary Considerations, *American Economic Review*, **63** (2), 316–325.

Williamson, O.E. (1975) *Markets and Hierarchies*, Free Press: New York.

Wright Mills, C. (1956) *The Power Elite*, Oxford University Press: Oxford.

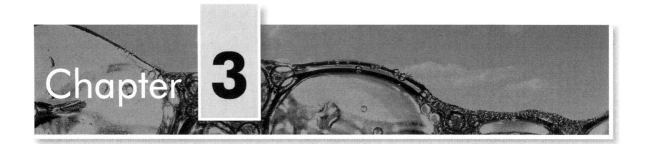

Chapter 3

The Mechanisms of Governance: An Introduction

Chapter contents

3.1   Introduction

Given agency problems, the central governance problem is how they are solved. How do the shareholders ensure that managers or large blockholders act in their best interest? There are several mechanisms of governance, all of which serve to mitigate agency problems. We list some of them in Table 3.1.

As you can see, there are many corporate governance mechanisms. Some are clearly more important than others, and some are logically prior to others. For example, you can argue that the owners elect the board and that the board hires/fires the CEO and sets his pay, so ownership is logically prior to board structure and board structure is logically prior to incentives. All this take place within a regulatory framework which the market participants have to take for granted, at least in the short run. So regulation is logically prior to ownership. And law is shaped by social forces such as culture, although in this case it is less clear what comes first.

In Table 3.1 we have grouped the mechanisms in categories, which we use to structure this chapter. We begin with the soft factors under the heading of 'culture', e.g. social norms, reputation and the like (media pressure). Next we have law and regulation, including company law and best practice codes (soft law), which border on culture. Then we have ownership: the role of large owners, takeovers and shareholder activism. We go on to the board, a huge topic in corporate governance, of course, and to the role of incentives (executive pay). Finally, a large group of mechanisms have to do with pressure exerted on managers by external stakeholders like banks, auditors, analysts and competition.

In this chapter we argue that each of these mechanisms has its costs and benefits. Therefore, good corporate governance essentially consists of tailoring these mechanisms to the individual firm. The general logic is that of the Aristotelian golden mean (Figure 3.1) or, in the wording of neoclassical economics, declining marginal productivity.

Up to a point, most corporate governance mechanisms will improve company economic performance, for example because the mechanisms press managers to work harder or enable the

Table 3.1 Mechanisms

Informal governance
Social norms
Reputation and trust
Codes
Regulation
Company law
Ownership
Large owners
Shareholder activism
Takeovers
Boards
Incentive systems (pay)
Stakeholder pressure
Creditor monitoring
Auditors
Analysts
Competition

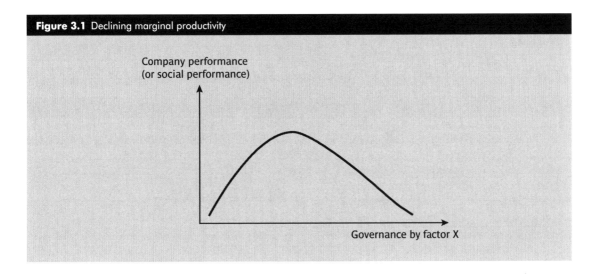

Figure 3.1 Declining marginal productivity

shareholders to make better choices. Beyond this point, which is difficult to define and varies from mechanism to mechanism and from firm to firm, the costs start to kick in. From that point increasing use of this governance mechanism will destroy the value.

In other words, corporate governance is about finding the golden mean, that is, how a particular set of mechanisms create most value in a particular situation. Note that this could be a corner solution: it may be that some companies are better off without large owners or even without a board. We will go through the different mechanisms of corporate governance and will point to some of their costs and their benefits.

3.2 Social norms

At the most basic level corporate governance depends on social norms or what we call morality. Suppose a manager gets an opportunity to steal shareholder funds and knows it will never be detected. Will he do it? Economic man would. Would you? Suppose that it was a lot of money, so much that you could live on it comfortably for the rest of your life. Maybe the temptation is stronger in that case. There is a good chance that many people would, so morality is an imperfect solution to governance problems. On the other hand, there are many examples of people who would not steal and many cases in which most people would not steal. It would be difficult to run a modern society if people were completely amoral; the same applies to corporate governance. Corporate governance scandals from Maxwell to Enron, Parmalat and Lehman are often regarded as expressions of immorality.

To see that morality plays a role in governance, think of the market for blood. Some people voluntarily give blood, but you can also buy it on the professional market or order others to give blood, as in the military. When people voluntarily give blood, there is less need for a market or for authority. This substitution between markets and other institutions led Nobel prize laureate Kenneth Arrow to propose that social norms may arise to compensate for market failure: '... when the market fails to achieve an optimal state, society will, to some extent at least, recognize the gap and nonmarket institutions will arise attempting to bridge it' (Arrow, 1962, p. 21). As an illustration of this principle Arrow (1963) argued that a medical ethic among doctors is a way to overcome failures in the market for medical services due to information asymmetries between doctors and patients. Because patients generally lack information about the nature of their illness and the effectiveness of

alternative treatments, doctors could manipulate them in their own interest. A medical ethic among doctors, enforced by powerful collective sanctions, helps to overcome this problem (Arrow, 1973, p. 139). The Hippocratic oath which doctors still take is a prime expression of the ethics. Indirectly, the medical ethic also serves the interests of the doctors because more patients will use doctors if they do not suspect them of being quacks. Other professions have their own ethical codes and Harvard Business School students recently proposed a code and an oath for managers.

Morality is related to what management researchers call 'stewardship', 'citizenship' or corporate social responsibility (CSR), which we will talk more about in this book. To the extent that managers act morally, as good stewards, there is a tendency for agency problems to disappear. However, they do not disappear entirely. As a manager, you may feel a moral duty to be an equal opportunity employer or help people in need, but your shareholders may not agree. Moreover, while some managers have high moral standards, others do not, and there are many who would be willing to compromise on their standards if the incentives were right. This can happen if the rewards are very high, but it may also happen if they are very low. For example, few managers hesitate to 'borrow' a pen at the office. Consider the classic story about Bernard Shaw:

> *George Bernard Shaw once found himself at a dinner party, seated beside an attractive woman. 'Madam,' he asked, 'would you go to bed with me for a thousand pounds?' The woman blushed and rather indignantly shook her head. 'For ten thousand pounds?' he asked. 'No. I would not.' 'Then how about fifty thousand pounds?' he continued. The colossal sum gave the woman pause, and after further reflection, she coyly replied: 'Perhaps.' 'And if I were to offer you five pounds?' Shaw asked. 'Mr. Shaw!' the woman exclaimed. 'What do you take me for?' 'We have already established what you are,' Shaw calmly replied. 'Now we are merely haggling over the price.'[1]*

Although shareholders cannot usually raise the moral standards of their employees, morality matters in corporate governance because moral standards differ between nations and may change over time. Some observers claim that corporate governance in the USA has become more of an issue because moral standards have fallen. Moreover, there may have to be more monitoring in countries where moral standards are low (or different). For example, corruption is more of a problem in some countries than it is in others. Finally, it is possible to influence morality among managers by carefully selecting who is hired (and fired) and by crafting corporate policies for what is and what is not acceptable behaviour.

It is clear, therefore, that good morals can increase company and social performance. Is it conversely true that moral standards can be too high? It is easy to think of examples of people who become so dogmatic that they are unable to act. From a strictly moral viewpoint we should perhaps give all our money to the poor, should only do business with the poorest countries, or should only employ people who have difficulties in finding a job. Perhaps there is a limit to morality, after all. Many academics would then argue that true morals would take all the constraints into account, but this is no different from saying that there is a limit even to morality.

3.3   Trust and reputation

Informal governance mechanisms like trust and reputation are also important. Managers who cheat investors will not find it easy to obtain more money or to get a new job. This means they have an incentive to protect their reputations. Thus, reputation may be a powerful deterrent to both adverse selection and moral hazard problems. In past centuries huge investment projects like the railroads were financed without much corporate governance or company law. Apparently, entrepreneurs and financiers asked the general public for money in good faith based on their reputation. However, a history of financial scandals testifies that the system was far from perfect.

---

[1] Jensen (1998).

Following Kreps (1990) and the ensuing literature, it can be shown formally that reputation can under certain circumstances help companies overcome opportunism in dealing with other market participants (buyers, sellers, employees and investors). The standard argument uses the prisoners' dilemma from game theory in which two players must both decide whether to cooperate or be opportunistic. If one prisoner decides to tell on the other he may get a lower penalty at the other's expense. But if both prisoners tell on the other, they will both get high penalties. Depending on how the players view their gains or losses in the different outcome each player may seem to be better off by acting opportunistically: she may get a slightly better deal if the other chooses to cooperate and avoids losses of trying to cooperate and being let down by the other. As a result opportunism prevails and both parties end up in the worst case equilibrium. The same logic can apply to a company manager dealing with a stakeholder (e.g. an outside investor). In so-called extended form the game is depicted in Table 3.2.

For example, the investor may choose to invest in the company, and the manager may take the money and run (opportunism) instead of putting it to good use in the company (cooperation). Expecting this, the investor may choose not to invest, so the company goes bankrupt. There are many other situations like it. Managers may decide to sell a bad product at a high price, breaching consumer trust. Employees who have committed their lives to a company in the assurance of life-time employment may suddenly be fired. And so on. Even the manager himself may suffer: shareholders may fire a manager who has done a good job before she is properly rewarded. The worst case opportunistic equilibrium appears inevitable.

However, the bad spell may be broken in repeated games. If one player decides to play opportunistic, the other player will not play cooperation in the next round and she will be punished. In contrast if she consistently cooperates, she will get a reputation for cooperation, and other players will be far more likely to cooperate with her. In the same way a company with a reputation for being ethical will find it much easier to attract finance and do business. In the long term the ethical company will therefore outcompete its less ethical rival. A good reputation becomes a valuable asset which the company manager and owners have a self-interest in protecting and investing in. Social norms, corporate culture and business ethics may arise and be sustainable for the same reasons.

Kreps argues that a company needs to be consistent to maintain its reputation. For example, opportunism in one market may damage its reputation in other markets. It also needs to be consistent over time. This may translate into a corporate culture which reinforces patterns of behaviour (values, principles, ethics, …) that may not be profitable in the short run but may sustain the company in the long term.

As Dyck and Zingales (2002) emphasize, the media can influence corporate governance through the reputation mechanism. Bad corporate governance and bad company performance can lead to media exposure, which is unpleasant for the managers and which may induce them to change their ways. Media exposure seems to work for both listed and unlisted companies regardless of ownership structure. Media exposure may have a more pervasive effect than the other mechanisms mentioned. However, there is little doubt that media exposure is a very blunt instrument which often targets the wrong cases and which overlooks other cases which should have been addressed.

Table 3.2 Extended form of the prisoners' dilemma

		PLAYER 2: The stakeholder	
		Cooperation	Opportunism
PLAYER 1: The manager	Cooperation	Joint optimum Both players win	Player 2 wins at player 1's expense
	Opportunism	Player 1 wins at player 2's expense	Worst case Both players lose

Personal reputations also matter. Managers have an interest in maintaining a good track record if they want to advance in their careers (Fama, 1980). Even if the top managers do not care, perhaps because they plan to retire after their present job, their mid-level managers may be concerned. Moreover, a good track record will be helpful to managers who would like to have post-executive careers as board members after they retire. Therefore, the managerial labour market can also be regarded as a corporate governance mechanism. One of the correction mechanisms available to mid-level managers is 'whistle blowing'. They can leak information to the press so that shareholders or government organizations can take action before a scandal takes the whole company down (and the employee loses his job). Sarbanes–Oxley, an American corporate governance law enacted in 2002, specifically recognizes the social value of whistleblowers and tries to protect them against reprisals.

It would no doubt be impossible to sustain effective corporate governance without trust, but reputation is no panacea. It does not work in end-game situation where the game is not continued after a certain point in time. If a mature company does not need more external finance, it has less of an incentive to please investors.

Moreover, trust and reputation are difficult to sustain in large societies with impersonal exchange. Tadelis (1999) shows that a market for reputation, for example, when new owners unknown to the business partners acquire the reputations of other firms by acquisitions, gives rise to adverse selection problems and market failure. The reputation mechanism works better in small societies where everybody knows everybody else and information flows easily. It cannot work if market participants are anonymous, as they may be in large markets or large countries. Globalization will, therefore, tend to attenuate reputation mechanisms. Franks, Mayer and Rossi (2004) document that the industrial revolution in the UK was financed to a large extent by informal governance, e.g. gentlemen's agreements within the 'old boys' networks'. Specialized stock exchanges, like the textile exchange in Manchester, were places where everybody knew everybody else and it was more difficult to get away with bad behaviour.

Finally, reputation is not a fine-tuned instrument. Suppose that a Russian manager forgets to pay dividends to some Italian investors. He may not care very much about his reputation in Italy. And if there is disagreement among the parties, it may be unclear to what side public opinion will lean. One of the advantages of the law is that the courts are able to take large amounts of information into consideration which could not realistically and accurately be handled by reputation.

3.4   Company law

Legal protection of shareholder rights is clearly very important. For example, managers can be sent to jail if they steal from stockholders. Moreover, the law obligates companies to many practices which protect the interests of investors. For example, there must be a shareholder meeting at least once a year. All shareholders must be duly informed about the meeting. Boards are elected by shareholders. The decisions made at the shareholder meetings are binding for the company. In between meetings all major decisions, including the choice of manager, must be ratified by the board. Managers must respect whatever shareholders decide to write into the bylaws and so on.

The law stipulates duties for officers and directors in the corporation. Directors have a duty of loyalty (to shareholders) and a duty of care (to actively live up to their responsibility).

Shareholders may use the court system and sue the company if they feel that the company is being mismanaged. Knowing this helps to keep managers on their toes.

The law also protects the interests of other stakeholders, for example creditors and employees. Banks can demand compensation from board members and managers who have acted recklessly with their money. In some countries, employees have the right to elect members of the company's board.

Corporate governance would not be possible without some enforcement of property rights, and it certainly helps shareholders control managers. But it is not a perfect mechanism. Sometimes managers break the law. And shareholders may not be satisfied with a manager just because he abides by the law. Too many rules and too large penalties would lead to a loss of flexibility and risk aversion, which would make it difficult to do business.

Consider stock market regulation as a case.[2] Theoretically, a stock exchange is a firm that creates a market in shares (Mulherin et al., 1991). The market is attractive to buyers and sellers of shares because it economizes on their transaction costs, that is their search, information, bargaining, decision, policing and enforcement costs (Coase, 1992; Mulherin et al., 1991; Dahlman, 1979). An important instrument in this is a certain standardization of the shares traded (Telser, 1981) which reduces the need for a continuous detailed assessment of individual firms and transforms their stock into 'homogenous, fungible securities' (Pirrong, 1995). Standardization and other rules are provided by the law, by the exchanges themselves (Coase, 1992) through listing requirements and corporate governance codes (Cadbury Commission, 1992). This regulation applies to ownership and board structure, corporate governance practice, financial reporting, disclosure, capital structure, and firm size.

Governance rules and standards are valuable to investors and therefore also to issuers, because they reduce their cost of capital, but they come at a cost. There are direct costs, which include listing fees, fees for auditors and lawyers, liability and insurance costs, larger fees for non-executive and executive directors etc. In the USA the costs of compliance with the Sarbanes–Oxley act would fit into this category. Indirect costs would include costs of disclosure to competitors, loss of flexibility with regard to board structure, opportunity costs of top management time, box-checking and bureaucratic procedures. Most of these costs will be fixed, while the variable cost of trading shares will be negligible (Foucault and Parlour, 2004).

It is difficult to determine the optimal level of regulation with any degree of precision because regulation is so multifaceted. It is not a given, for example, that optimal regulation will maximize the number of listed companies or that it will minimize the number of delistings. However, it seems important to consider both costs and benefits. The widely used investor protection index originally proposed by La Porta et al. (1998) was justified to a large extent by a positive effect on the size of the stock market. This so-called 'anti-director rights' index summarized measures which were believed to strengthen the rights of minority investors vis-à-vis company boards.

The investor protection index constructed by La Porta et al. (1998) and updated by Pagano and Volpin (2005) is a sum of six dummy variables:

1 whether proxy by mail is allowed,
2 whether shares are/are not blocked before a shareholder meeting,
3 whether cumulative voting for directors is allowed,
4 whether oppressed minorities are protected,
5 whether the percentage of share capital required to call an extraordinary shareholder meeting is less than 10%, and
6 whether existing shareholders have pre-emptive rights at new equity offerings.

There are clearly both costs and benefits associated with these provisions. For example, the right to file lawsuits against boards involves cost, as does the right to call an annual meeting or a prohibition against dual class shares.

Theoretically, it can be argued that the optimal level of investor protection for listed companies is greater than zero since stock exchanges use regulation to lower the costs of exchange. It is equally plausible that there are limits to the optimal complexity of regulation (Kaplow, 1995; Ehrlich and Posner, 1974) and that more regulation will at some point have a negative effect.

As an example, La Porta et al. assert that investors are better protected when an investor can call an extraordinary general meeting if she has more than 10% of the stock. It is clear that an extraordinary meeting involves costs not just for the managers who have to defend their decisions, but also for the other shareholders who have to attend the meeting or live with the outcome if they stay away. But what would happen if this threshold was lowered to 5%; would investor protection

---

[2] This section builds on Thomsen and Vinten (2008).

be higher? If so, what about 1%? Or should any shareholder be able to call a shareholder meeting at any time? In most situations, the transaction costs for both the shareholder and for the company would probably become too high at some point; the other shareholders would consider delisting, or, at least, the company's market value would drop. In contrast, few would argue with the proposition that a qualified majority of the shareholders should be able to call an extraordinary meeting.

We therefore conjecture that there is a cost to stock market regulation, that more regulation is not necessarily better, and that regulation beyond a certain point will lead to fewer listed firms and lower firm value. We summarize these propositions in Figure 3.2.

3.5 Large owners

The vast majority (most likely 99%) of all companies are owned by one or two shareholders who also manage the company. It is not difficult to understand why. Owner-management aligns the interests of owners and managers. It is their own money so they have every incentive to manage it well. In other words, it is a solution to the moral hazard problem. Owner-management also addresses the adverse selection problem. Suppose that you inherit a firm, but you know that you are not a good manager. In this case you have an incentive to have someone else manage it; you might even see an incentive to sell it to somebody who can create more value than you can. It is your money and you have the incentives to manage it as well as you can. Both in theory and in practice it makes more sense to have a manager own the firm than somebody from the outside, because the manager has more information and is therefore in a better position to make decisions (Hart, 1995).

The vast majority of all firms are small, with no or only a few employees. Most of their owners are single individuals or family members so their corporate governance challenges are related to family business. There are also instances, however, when partners working together (for example lawyers, engineers, consultants) establish partnerships or joint stock corporations. Ownership in these companies is often intentionally equally distributed (e.g. 50:50), which creates special challenges related to deadlock and abuse of minority investors. Two partners, each with a 50% share, may disagree and their company may go completely limp as a result. In other cases, a minority investor

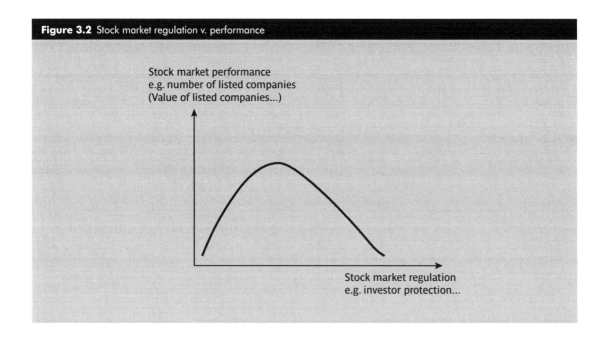

Figure 3.2 Stock market regulation v. performance

Stock market performance
e.g. number of listed companies
(Value of listed companies...)

Stock market regulation
e.g. investor protection...

with ⅓ of the shares may find that her shares have no value because the majority decide to pay no dividends and instead take out salaries to themselves. Since the shares are not listed she will typically be unable to sell her shares to others. In both cases the most effective solution is a shareholder agreement, which regulates governance and exit, and is signed when the company is founded, before the trouble starts. For an overview of shareholder agreements see Madelon and Thomsen (2009) and references therein. But it is well known that most partnerships do not have such clauses, because they are considered to be irrelevant at the beginning of the partnership which has to be founded on trust in any case (just like many people don't think about divorce the first time they marry). As a result, a lot of value is being destroyed across the world when unlisted companies break up. An effective solution would be to build in a generic shareholder agreement as default clauses in the standard corporate form which shareholders could then deviate from if they wanted (in the same way that newly weds do not normally have to think about divorce which is already built into law).[3] But this is still just an idea.

Even for listed companies, a blockholder can be a solution to a corporate governance problem because she has both the incentives and the power to influence what happens in the company. Large owners may therefore act as watchdogs on behalf of minority investors who can free ride on their efforts. Many blockholders even in large firms are individuals or families, but there is more variance here: governments, financial investors, other corporations and other entities may all be large owners.

Large owners are not a perfect solution. First, as a rule they will be more risk averse than other investors because they have invested so much in this particular company (i.e. they have placed all their eggs in one basket), and this will influence corporate strategy. Secondly, there is a risk that they may exploit the minority investors, particularly in countries with low investor protection. Tunnelling occurs when controlling owners take money out of the company, for example by organizing transactions on unfavourable terms with companies which they themselves own (this seems to have happened in the Italian Parmalat case). Large owners may also have idiosyncratic preferences which do not maximize shareholder value. For example, they may prefer that the company is managed by a family member or they may want to retain ownership in the family despite an attractive offer from the outside which the minority shareholders would prefer. Failed succession, e.g. from a clever father to a stupid son, is the Achilles heel of family-owned companies. Our discussion of family-owned companies will continue in Chapter 17.

The effects of large owners on corporate governance and performance depends critically on owner identity. A financial investor with a clear preference for shareholder value might be expected to exercise ownership in a way that is aligned with the interests of minority investors. In contrast, a government owner will usually have objectives which differ very much from shareholder value maximization. Families are probably somewhere in between. More on ownership structure will follow in Chapter 12.

So what is the relation between company performance and ownership concentration? Morck, Shleifer and Vishny (1988) were the first to examine the relationship between management ownership and market valuation of the firm, as measured by Tobin's Q. In a 1980 cross-section of 371 Fortune 500 firms, they found evidence of a significant non-monotonic relationship. They found that Tobin's Q first increases, then declines, and finally rises slightly as ownership by the board of directors rises. Their results suggested a positive relation between ownership and Q in the 0–5% board ownership range, a weak negative relation in the 5–25% range, and then perhaps a further positive relation beyond 25%. Their proposed interpretation was that the positive incentive effects dominate management ownership shares up to 5%, but that further ownership has negative effects because of entrenchment effects, which make it difficult for the other investors to replace the board. Beyond 25% the company is anyhow effectively dominated by the dominant owner who internalizes more and more of the costs of deviation from shareholder value as her ownership share increases and is therefore more aligned with shareholder value (Figure 3.3).

Others (e.g. McConnell and Servaes, 1990) have found bell-shaped curves which peak at much higher levels, and a bell-shaped curve has also been estimated for the share of the largest owner (see the ownership chapter for a survey).

---

[3] We are grateful to Professor Neville, University of Aarhus, for suggesting this idea.

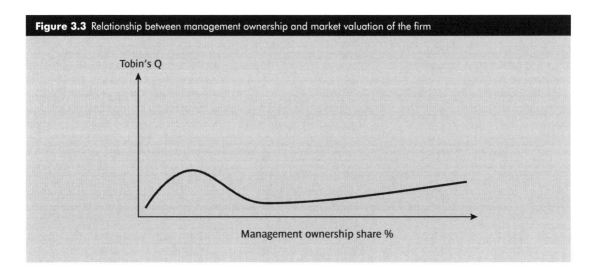

Figure 3.3 Relationship between management ownership and market valuation of the firm

3.6 Shareholder activism[4]

In the absence of a large owner, shareholders are much weaker, but it is not true that they have no power at all. They can turn up at annual meetings, they can criticize the management, and they can vote against it. Even if they lose a vote, the pressure can be unpleasant for the managers and it may damage their reputation. So managers have incentives to keep them happy.

Moreover, small shareholders may sell their shares: 'do the Wall Street walk'. This will tend to lower share prices and increase the costs of capital for the corporation. Corporate bondholders may sell out, too. This could make it more difficult for managers to compete, e.g. to grow the company, which provides an additional incentive to try to please shareholders. Shareholder pressure is obviously no less imperfect than all the other mechanisms. Small shareholders cannot be expected to be well informed, and there are 'free rider' problems between them: if one shareholder makes an effort he bears all the costs while all the other shareholders benefit as well.

The research on shareholder activism has studied the effects on firm value or shareholder returns, and has primarily studied pension funds and hedge funds rather than private individuals. Attempts by pension funds to reform corporate governance by making proposals at shareholder meetings are regarded by many researchers as unsuccessful in influencing firms and increasing their value (Gillan and Starks, 2000), although there is some evidence that voting against proposals by the board in targeted firms may have positive value effects (Del Guercio, Seery and Woidtke, 2008).

In contrast, so-called entrepreneurial shareholder activists like hedge funds and private equity firms are found to be quite successful in influencing companies (Gillan and Starks, 2007). Activist investment funds (Becht, Franks, Mayer and Rossi, 2009), hedge funds (Brav, Jiang, Partnoy and Thomas, 2008; Klein and Zur, 2009), corporate raiders (Holderness and Sheehan, 1985) and large blockholders (Barclay and Holderness, 1989, 1991) have all been found to have a positive effect on firm value. Becht et al. (2009) and Klein and Zur (2009) found that such entrepreneurial investors are very successful in accomplishing their objectives, for example in replacing board members, changing corporate strategy or opposing a merger.

Formally, shareholders' annual general meetings serve as an arena for face-to-face interaction between shareholders and management, where shareholders can hold management to account (Lawton and Rigby, 1992; Stratling, 2003). However, large shareholders including major institutional investors are known to favour private negotiations with management over public appearances

---

[4] This section draws on Poulsen, Strand and Thomsen (2010).

(Keasey and Short, 1999a). This tendency is reinforced by proxy voting in favour of the board (Stratling, 2003), and sidestepping the general meetings has undoubtedly contributed to a drop in meeting attendance (Nilsson and Hassel, 2003; Stratling, 2003). Annual general meetings are often seen only as rituals (Aggarwal, 2001; Hodges, Macniven, and Mellett, 2004; Schilling and Steensma, 2001) or 'annual headaches' at which management is questioned by social activists (Apostolides, 2007; Saxon, 1966). Nonetheless, even when ownership concentration is high, meetings may still contribute to accountability, since minority shareholders can criticize managers at the meetings with an element of surprise, which forces managers to be on their toes (Catasús and Johed, 2007; Gray, Owen and Maunders, 1988).

Following Pozen (1994), activism can be regarded as rational (in a financial sense) when shareholders balance the expected costs and benefits and take action only when the benefits exceed the costs. The costs of activism are determined by factors such as the opportunity cost of share ownership, analysis costs, management time, possible reprisals by the incumbent management, legal uncertainty (possible liability for insider trading, cornering the market, etc.), number of shareholders to be contacted, their identity and association with the firm and the level of engagement intended. The benefits of activism are determined by factors such as the probability of successful intervention, the shareholder's investment and expected holding period, the volatility of the stock and general economic uncertainty.

The expected rationality of activism goes beyond these apparent costs and benefits. First, it may be possible to exercise influence on management or the ruling coalition of shareholders through social pressure. Second, for professional investors, activism at an annual general meeting may serve a broader purpose, i.e. it may be part of a general campaign for or against certain management practices or a deterrent against unwanted behaviour in other companies which learn about events through the media (Nordén and Strand, 2009). While activity in one context may appear symbolic, it may be fully rational if understood in a broader setting. This also applies if a fund manager uses the public limelight to draw attention to a fund as an opportunity for investment. Finally, some activism may be privately optimal for a particular fund manager. Some may enjoy public visibility per se, while others may use it to prepare future careers in politics or public administration (Woidtke, 2002).

3.7 Takeovers

Hostile takeovers are a famous and dramatic governance mechanism. If company performance is bad, the stock price drops, and a raider can make a tender offer for its shares, acquire control, fire the management, restructure and sell his shares again at a significant gain.

However, empirically we observe few hostile takeovers. Thus, while they can make a contribution in some cases, they only rarely work in practice. One simple reason is that most companies around the world (including the USA) employ takeover defences specifically geared to prevent hostile takeovers. Another reason is that hostile takeovers may not create value for the acquirer, since significant costs are involved, whereas the gains to a very large extent go to the incumbent shareholders who almost always get a value premium.

To see why (following Grossmann and Hart, 1980; Becht et al., 2003), imagine a raider contemplating a bid for a firm, which he can restructure and thereby increase the value of the shares by $V = 1$ if he succeeds in getting more than 50% of the shares (votes). In contrast under the current management there will be no value increase, $V = 0$. He makes a conditional offer to the incumbent shareholders of a price premium of p per share. If there is competition among raiders, other raiders will have an incentive to overbid (raise p), until $p = 1$, in which case there is no incentive to raid. In jargon, the incumbent shareholders appropriate all the rents. This may happen even if there is no rent. The incumbent shareholders get p per share, if they sell. But if they hold and wait for the raider to restructure the firm, they get 1. So, they will only sell if $p \geq 1$! Hence, since the raider will have to pay a premium of $p = 1$ =>, he will have no incentive to raid, and there will be no takeover (and there will be no value increase, i.e. $V = 0$). Solutions to this problem could be reduced disclosure (so that a raider could secretly acquire control without paying a premium), 'squeeze out' rules (which force minority shareholders to sell to

a seller which controls more than e.g. 90% of the votes) or doing away with the mandatory bid rule which requires raiders to make a bid for all shares and pay the same price to all shareholders. However, these suggestions limit minority investor rights and may therefore be impossible to get passed.

There is empirical evidence that takeovers improve company performance and that barriers to hostile takeovers reduce it (Masulis et al., 2007). Gompers et al. (2003) and Bebchuk et al. (2009) find that takeover defences are negatively related to company performance. But as mentioned they are clearly no panacea. Empirically, far from all hostile takeovers are directed at companies with bad corporate governance and bad performance. M&A may even be a symptom of bad governance as when a company with plenty of free cash flow uses it to build empires by buying other companies.

3.8 Boards

Boards are a generic corporate governance mechanism. They are elected by shareholders with the explicit aim to address corporate governance issues. Since it would be costly for shareholders to meet and to monitor the company, they hire a group of professionals to do it for them. Boards meet regularly to examine company performance, to ratify major investment decisions, and if necessary, to replace management.

The basic theory of boards is agency theory. Boards deal with moral hazard by monitoring managers and motivating them through incentives (like stock options) and sanctions (like dismissal). They may also play a role in type 2 agency problems by safeguarding the interests of minority shareholders against dominant blockholders.

Fama and Jensen (1983) argue that boards will arise whenever there is separation of ownership and control. It is then necessary for shareholders to delegate monitoring. The solution is to elect a board consisting of a number of board members who can monitor each other as well as the managers. In contrast, Fama and Jensen argue that there is less of a role for boards when ownership is concentrated and owners can do their own monitoring. However, boards are known also to have functions other than the agency theoretic control role, for example they provide advice to managers and they help create networks to important stakeholders. These latter roles, advice and networking, may still be valuable even though ownership is concentrated. In addition, the boards of companies with multiple owners may function as a platform for resolving conflicts among the owners, particularly in small firms with a few large shareholders.

While there are no doubt many vigilant boards, and while corporate governance would no doubt be worse without them, boards are only a partial solution to the governance problem. For one thing, boards can be no better than the shareholders who elect them. If the shareholders are badly informed, or foolish, it is unlikely that they will elect the best board members, that they will monitor them well, and that they will replace bad board members. Secondly, board members have little knowledge about what goes on in the company compared with the CEO. Board members should not know too much, since they should not interfere with the day-to-day management of the company. Moreover, board culture appears to make it psychologically difficult for an outside board member to voice a critical opinion; see the following quote by the second richest man in the world, who has extensive board experience.

> *It's almost impossible, for example, in a boardroom populated by well-mannered people, to raise the question of whether the CEO should be replaced. It's equally awkward to question a proposed acquisition that has been endorsed by the CEO, particularly when his inside staff and outside advisors are present and unanimously support his decision. (They wouldn't be in the room if they didn't.) Finally, when the compensation committee – armed, as always, with support from a high-paid consultant – reports on a mega grant of options to the CEO, it would be like belching at the dinner table for a director to suggest that the committee reconsider …'[5]*

There is much more about boards in Chapters 8 and 9.

---

[5] Buffet (2003).

3.9 Incentive systems

By incentive systems we mean the incentives given to managers. Managerial pay (compensation) consists of fixed salary, bonuses, stock options, stock grants, and other benefits (i.e. health insurance, fringe benefits or pension scheme). Changes over the past decades imply that US managers in large listed companies are currently paid mostly according to performance (i.e. bonus or stock options schemes) while the greater part of management compensation in continental Europe is still fixed (i.e. a fixed amount per month).

Incentive systems can clearly give managers incentives to work in the interest of the shareholders; they can help address governance problems both of the moral hazard and the adverse selection variety. But incentive systems are not perfect solutions. Badly designed incentives are more part of the disease than the cure since they involve large transfers of money from the shareholders to the managers, which is exactly what many shareholders want to avoid in corporate governance. Moreover, programmes may lead to perverse incentives, for example earnings management, accounting fraud or excessive risk taking. Finally, because of risk aversion, performance-based pay should theoretically be higher than fixed pay, which is consistent with what we observe in practice.

There is more on executive pay in Chapter 10.

3.10 Creditors and capital structure

If companies need to borrow, creditors exercise tremendous influence on what they do. Banks may make demands on board composition, management and capital structure as a condition for lending. They may also insist on covenants which limit the strategic flexibility of companies (for example, new investments may need to be approved by creditors). In some cases a meeting with a major creditor may be more important than a board meeting for deciding the future of the company. Banks often influence who sits on boards of distressed firms, and in some countries like Germany the bankers themselves often sit on company boards even in well-performing firms. As an alternative to both equity and bank loans, companies may also issue corporate bonds to the market. Since bondholders have no voting rights, they have less influence on corporate governance, although bond prices may influence the company's cost of capital.

Empirically, credit (bank finance) is much more important than outside equity as a source of finance. Banks finance small corporations which cannot access the stock market and lend even in countries with underdeveloped equity markets. One reason may be that loan contracts are relatively simple (pay back or go bankrupt!) compared with equity which requires an elaborate system of governance (shareholder meetings, boards, annual reports and so on). However, there are also important agency costs of debt which banks incur and charge on to firms in the form of interest premiums. For example, managers may take excessive risks which will benefit the shareholders if they go well, while creditors lose if they don't. Many corporate finance textbooks therefore propose a graph as shown in Figure 3.4.

Here very high and very low levels of debt are believed to be associated with high average cost of capital as the threat of bankruptcy, financial distress and creditor–shareholder conflicts is weighted against agency problems of overcapitalization (e.g. excessive spending). In between the two there is a relatively long flat bottom where capital structure is less critical.

The classic paper on agency theory by Jensen and Meckling (1976) was an integrated theory of ownership and capital structure based on similar arguments. Subsequently Jensen (1986, 1989) championed the idea that debt finance could be an effective way to restrain managers from using up free cash flow. Hoshi et al. (1991) and many other studies (reviewed in Degryse, Ongena and Tümer-Alkan, 2008) find empirical support for this idea by observing that investment is less correlated with

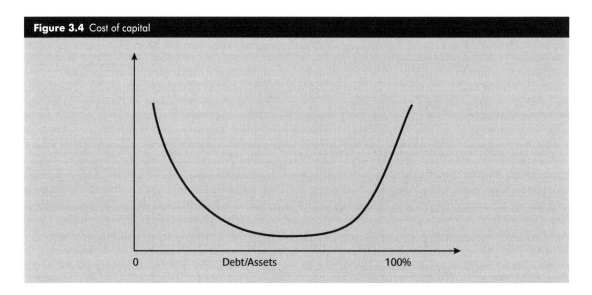

Figure 3.4 Cost of capital

cash flow in companies with strong bank relationships. Jensen argued that many large companies could benefit from higher leverage and that the demise of the public corporation was at hand. A wave of private equity investment during the next two decades did exactly that. Companies sought what they believed to be appropriate (typically higher) leverage. However, with the advent of the financial crisis of 2008, many companies again found themselves lacking equity finance when faced with a credit crunch.

Intermediates such as banks play a key role in debt markets (Degryse, Ongena and Tümer-Alkan, 2008). Instead of financing companies directly, savers put their money in the bank or another intermediary. Diamond (1984) provides a rationale by observing that the firms in pure credit markets may be capital-rationed and unable to finance all positive NPV projects. Banks take deposits (typically short term) and give short- or long-term loans to customers to suit their needs. In dealing with large company clients banks therefore come to play a role in corporate governance as the borderline between equity and debt becomes blurred. The saying goes that if you owe the bank a million you have a problem, but if you owe it a billion, the bank has a problem. Banks will hesitate to declare a big client bankrupt and will often interfere with the company in what is called relationship banking. They monitor company behaviour and regulate it by loan conditions (covenants), demanding to have certain people on the board etc. Debt can be regarded as conditional equity so in times of crises banks often effectively come to own companies. The influential role of banks in Germany and many other economies has led observers to talk of bank governance as distinct from market governance. There is more on banking in Chapter 13.

Altogether, the evidence indicates that banks play a valuable role in corporate governance, but there are also limitations to creditor monitoring. First of all, it only works when companies have significant debt. There are many kinds of companies which banks are reluctant to finance: for example, those companies with highly specialized and immaterial assets which cannot be used as collateral. In contrast, businesses with collateral value – property, land and inventory – are easier to debt finance. Secondly, creditors are naturally risk averse; unlike shareholders they do not gain when things go better than expected, but they lose when things go worse than expected and firms are unable to pay their debts. Since there is a trade-off between risk and return, lower risk will lead to lower returns, and lower overall performance. Finally, creditors may use their market power to extract rents from companies so that on average companies do not gain from more debt finance (Degryse, Ongena and Tümer-Alkan, 2008).

3.11 Auditors

Accounting and auditing are part of the corporate governance system (Watts and Zimmerman, 1978, 1986, 1990). Monitoring by shareholders and debt holders is much easier if an audit of the company's accounts can ensure that they present a 'true and fair view' of the company's performance and its financial situation. Auditing can reduce the information asymmetry which is at the core of the agency problem and thus help solve governance problems. Company managers have an incentive to use external auditors with a good reputation to audit their accounts because this will increase investor and business confidence in the company (and make it easier to attract finance or do business). The auditor has an incentive to provide accurate information because this will influence demand for her services.

Watts and Zimmerman show that auditing and accounting practices emerged in the British Ipswich guild as far back as 1200 and continued up to the British and US joint stock banks in the mid-19th century and the present day, when they have become law. Generally, positive account theory (Watts and Zimmerman, 1986) sees accounting and auditing practices as efficient (value enhancing) methods to reduce agency problems.

There is some evidence, however, that neither accounting nor auditing is always accurate and that managers opportunistically exploit accounting practices (Watts and Zimmerman, 1990). There is support for a bonus plan hypothesis, i.e. that managers influence earnings by accounting practices in order to maximize their bonuses. There is also support for the debt equity hypothesis which states that managers will seek to maximize accounting income when the debt/equity ratio is high. Finally, there is support for the political cost hypothesis, i.e. that large and more publicly visible firms will seek to understate their profitability in order to avoid political attention.

One way of looking at this is to say that auditors and accountants are also agents which gives rise to a new set of agency problems. Audit and accounting are not free, so there is a limit to the demand for auditing services. Moreover, more information does not always lead to greater transparency. The number of pages in annual reports has increased rapidly over the past decade, but it is not clear whether they have become more informative. In fact, for some users, they have become more confusing and less transparent. The move from historical cost accounting to market-based valuation may in some respects have made accounts more subjective and easier for managers to manipulate. And the auditing business has probably become more competitive. Auditors who are paid by companies have an incentive to accommodate the wishes of company managers for 'creative accounting'.

Altogether, like other governance mechanisms, accounting and auditing can help address agency problems, but they cannot solve them completely.

3.12 Analysts

Analysts employed by investors, stockbrokers, and rating agencies issue reports which help shareholders and creditors understand companies and evaluate company performance. This provides information which is useful for shareholders who have neither the capacity nor the time to do their own analysis and may help shareholders act more intelligently in corporate governance. A reasonably correct stock price is an important signal for shareholders and directs capital allocation in a market economy. But the value of analysis for corporate governance is limited when analysts have incentive problems of their own. For example, analysts have been criticized for issuing too many 'buy' recommendations in order to stimulate trading and commissions, which is how their employers make their money. Rating agencies in particular were criticized for having been far too optimistic up to the financial crisis, in part because they are paid by client companies who ask for a rating. Thus analysis may in principle contribute to better governance but is clearly no panacea.

Theoretically, analysts are up against strong fundamentals since the efficient markets hypothesis indicates that all relevant publicly available information is already incorporated in stock prices. But empirically many studies (Bjerring, Lakonishok and Vermaelen, 1983; Dimson and Marsh, 1984; Beneish, 1991; Womack, 1996; Barber et al., 2001; Jegadeesh et al., 2004) have found that analysts' recommendations do have a positive and significant impact on stock prices, either because they are good at their job or because the market believes in them. However, there is also evidence that stock market forecasts are too optimistic, e.g. too many buy relative to sell recommendations (Elton et al., 1986; Lin and McNichols, 1998). The most common explanation appears to be conflict of interests relative to clients. Analysts often depend on communication with corporate executives and analysts in particular may be pressured by their employers (stockbrokers, investment banks and rating agencies) to favour their customers. This is evident for sell-side analysts employed at stockbrokers or banks, but buy-side analysts at pension funds (and alike) may also have vested interests if they are employed by institutions which already own significant amounts of stock.

3.13 Competition

Competition in the market for products and services is a fundamental correction mechanism for any kind of inefficiency in a market-based system, and this also includes inefficiency in corporate governance. Bad management will ultimately lead to higher costs, loss of competitiveness, slower growth, decline or bankruptcy. But competition will tend to lower profit rates and shareholder returns. Thus, from a shareholder viewpoint, it is not a satisfactory solution even though it works well for society as a whole. Moreover, it may take a long time for competition to eliminate a large company, even if it is inefficient.

Competition can help address governance problems in several different ways (Nickell, 1996; Nickell et al., 1997). It can eliminate companies with persistently bad governance through price competition and eventual bankruptcy. It can also reduce slack and thereby limit managerial discretion and agency problems in those firms which are sufficiently flexible to adapt and cut costs. Moreover, shareholders can benchmark their company against competitors (Hart, 1983). This can make it more transparent whether bad performance is attributable to bad management or to more general conditions. It is also possible that product market competition makes profits more responsive to the actions of managers, so that owners have a greater incentive to monitor which will keep managerial effort and company performance high.

Nickell (1996) and Nickell et al. (1997) find evidence that productivity growth is higher in companies which are faced with competition. This is important from a social viewpoint since productivity generates economic growth. Shareholders will also benefit from high productivity and low costs, but profits will obviously be squeezed by price competition, so shareholders have an incentive to avoid competition. Chou et al. (2008) find that governance has no significant impact on stock market returns when product market competition is low.

Most economists would claim that the market ultimately gets it right. Grossly inefficient firms will adapt or go out of business. But it may take a long time, particularly if they are sitting on large amounts of cash or have strong market positions. In the meantime (and when the market fails to do the job) there is a role for other governance mechanisms.

3.14 Discussion

Altogether, if you think about it, there is an impressive array of corporate governance mechanisms. We can argue that they all work to some extent but have their strengths and weaknesses which make them more or less appropriate in a given situation. In other cases the same mechanism may create more problems than it solves. For example, personal ownership may be a blessing under an enlightened owner, but a curse under his idiot son. However none of the governance mechanisms, not even all of them together, can completely eliminate the governance problem.

In the real world these mechanisms are not independent. On the contrary, there are strong causal connections between them. For example, boards are elected by shareholders. Thus there must be a causal connection between ownership structure and board structure. In other words, governance mechanisms are parts of a system (Holmström and Milgrom, 1994). There may be both substitutability and complementarity between mechanisms so that some mechanisms tend to substitute for each other (i.e. if you have one, you do not need the other), while other mechanisms tend to coexist. These interdependencies are what make governance mechanisms form a system.

Moreover, some governance mechanisms are logically prior to others. For example, individual shareholders or board members will usually not be able to influence laws and regulation, which they have to take for granted. However, laws and regulation will influence ownership structure. In the same way, the shareholders elect the board and are therefore logically prior to board members who are again logically prior to the managers which they hire and fire. Chinese managers and boards, for example, are constrained by their majority shareholders (often government organizations) who are again constrained by the political system (communism). Finally, not all governance mechanisms are equally important. Most economists tend to emphasize product market competition (Allen and Gale, 1999), some financial economists emphasize takeovers, and there is widespread scepticism with regard to boards' morality.

We try to address some of these complexities in the next chapter on international corporate governance.

Minicase

Armand Hammer and Occidental Petroleum

In 1989, Occidental Petroleum announced that it would build and run a museum to house the art collection of its chairman and CEO, Armand Hammer, then aged 89. Armand Hammer was a legendary business tycoon and colourful personality: a stout Republican and world traveller, personal friends with Lenin and a friend of the Soviet Union during the Cold War. Rumour has it that he was named Arm-and-Hammer by his socialist father after the symbol of the American Socialist Party. Hammer had grown the company from only three employees to a major listed corporation. The company clearly benefited from his investments and international connections. The company announcement claimed that the museum would add to the company's goodwill. It later turned out that Hammer had used the company's money to buy some of the exhibits.

The announcement led to a furore among investors and some lawsuits. *Time Magazine* called most of the collection 'junk'. Oxy (Occidental Petroleum) was planning to spend $86 million on the museum, substantially more than is allowed in the US for charitable giving. Hammer also had other privileges, among them a (then) very attractive salary of $2 million guaranteed for 10 years. On the day Hammer died in 1990, Oxy's value increased by $500 million.

We do not have precise information about the ownership structure, but let's assume that Hammer had a large minority share of 11% and the rest was quite dispersed. We also don't have information on the capital structure but let's assume that it was conservatively managed with little debt and large cash reserves. The board consisted mainly of company insiders (Oxy executives, company lawyers and Hammer's friends). Rumour had it that Hammer had written resignation letters in his desk drawer. Half of the board members were over 72. Executive pay was mainly fixed – by Hammer. The courts declined to intervene because of the business judgement rule.

Source: This classic corporate governance case was first developed by Monks and Minow in *Corporate Governance* (Wiley-Blackwell, 2003). This minicase builds on their work. See also http://en.wikipedia.org/wiki/Armand_Hammer.

Discussion questions

1 Is there an agency problem here? If so what kind is it? Type I, II or III?
2 How do the standard governance mechanisms work:
   ■ The law?
   ■ Ownership pressure?
   ■ The board?
   ■ CEO incentives?
3 What other mechanisms could be at work?
4 What (if anything) could/should be done about it?

Summary (learning points)

■ There are many mechanisms which can address agency problems.
■ None of them works perfectly.
■ Social norms lead managers to behave decently even in the absence of incentives and sanctions.
■ Reputation concerns can also reduce agency problems.
■ The law punishes extreme agency problems like criminal behaviour.
■ Large owners have both the incentives and the power to induce managers to act in their interests.
■ The board is the formal, organizational solution to agency problems.
■ Incentives (pay for performance) can motivate managers to act in the interest of shareholders.
■ Capital structure (creditor monitoring) can also help control agency problems.
■ Information providers (auditors, analysts) reduce agency problems by providing information to shareholders and other stakeholders.
■ Ultimately competition helps reduce agency problems because inefficient firms with large agency problems will be outcompeted and disappear.

 ## References and further reading

Aggarwal, R. (2001) Value-Added Annual Shareholders Meetings: Reflections on People's Capitalism at Wal-Mart, *Journal of Retailing and Consumer Services*, 8 (6), 347–349.

Allen, F. and Gale, D. (1999) *Corporate Governance and Competition*, Vol. 28; Vol. 99 of working paper series, Financial Institutions Center, Wharton School, University of Pennsylvania.

Apostolides, N. (2007) Directors versus Shareholders: evaluating corporate governance in the UK using the AGM scorecard, *Corporate Governance: An International Review*, 15 (6), 1277–1287.

Arrow, K.J. (1962) Economic Welfare and the Allocation of Resources for Invention, in *The Rate and Direction of Inventive Activity: Economic and Social Factors*, National Bureau of Economic Research, 609–626.

Arrow, K.J. (1963) Uncertainty and the Welfare Economics of Medical Care, *American Economic Review*, 53 (5), 941–973. Reprinted in Arrow, K.J., *Collected Papers of Kenneth J. Arrow* (1985), Vol. 6, Applied Economics, Harvard University Press.

Arrow, K.J. (1969) *The Organization of Economic Activity: Issues to the Choice of Market versus Non-market Allocations*, Published in Arrow, K.J., *Collected Papers of Kenneth J. Arrow* (1983), Vol. 2, General Equilibrium, Harvard University Press.

Arrow, K.J. (1972) Gifts and Exchanges, *Philosophy & Public Affairs*, **1** (4), 343–362.

Arrow, K.J. (1973) Social Responsibility and Economic Efficiency, *Public Policy*, **21** (?), 303–318. Reprinted in Arrow, K.J., *Collected Papers of Kenneth J. Arrow* (1985), Vol. 6, Applied Economics, Harvard University Press.

Barber, B., Lehavy, R., McNichols, M. and Trueman, B. (2001) Can Investors Profit from the Prophets? Security Analyst Recommendations and Stock Returns, *Journal of Finance*, **56** (2), 531–563.

Barclay, M.J. and Holderness, C.G. (1989) Private benefits from control of public corporations, *Journal of Financial Economics*, **25** (2), 371–395.

Barclay, M.J. and Holderness, C.G. (1991) Negotiated Block Trades and Corporate Control, *Journal of Finance*, **46** (3), 861.

Bebchuk, L., Cohen, A. and Ferrell, A. (2009) What Matters in Corporate Governance?, *Review of Financial Studies*, **22** (2), 783–827.

Becht, M., Bolton, P. and Roell, A. (2003) Corporate Governance and Control, in *Handbook of the Economics of Finance: Corporate Finance*, Constantinides, M., Harris, M. and Stulz, R. (eds), Elsevier: Amsterdam.

Becht, M., Franks, J., Mayer, C. and Rossi, S. (2009) Returns to Shareholder Activism: Evidence from a Clinical Study of the Hermes UK Focus Fund, *Review of Financial Studies*, **23** (3), 3093–3129.

Beneish, M.D. (1991) Stock Price and the Dissemination of Analysts' Recommendation, *Journal of Business*, **64** (3), 393–416.

Bjerring, J.H., Lakonishok, J. and Vermaelen, T. (1983) Stock Prices and Financial Analysts' Recommendations, *Journal of Finance*, **38** (1), 187–204.

Brav, A., Jiang, W., Partnoy, F. and Thomas, R. (2008) Hedge Fund Activism, Corporate Governance, and Firm Performance, *Journal of Finance*, **63** (4), 1729–1775.

Buffett, W. (2003) Letter to Berkshire Hathaway Shareholders.

Cadbury Commission (1992) Code of best practice: Report of the committee on the financial aspects of corporate governance, Gee and Co: London.

Catasús, B. and Johed, G. (2007) Annual general meetings—rituals of closure or ideal speech situations? A dual analysis, *Scandinavian Journal of Management*, **23** (2), 168–190.

Chou, W., Ng, L. and Wang, Q. (2008) Product Market Competition and Corporate Governance, Georgia Institute of Technology, Working Paper.

Coase, R.H. (1992) Contracts and the Activities of Firms, *Journal of Law and Economics*, **34** (2), 451.

Constantinides, G.M., Harris, M. and Stulz, R.M. (eds) (2003) Control, in *Handbook of the Economics of Finance*, Elsevier, Edition 1, Vol. 1, Chapter 1, pp. 1–109. Updated in ECGI Working Paper Series in Finance (2005), European Corporate Governance Institute.

Dahlman, C.J. (1979) The problem with Externality, *Journal of Law and Economics*, **22** (1), 141.

Degryse, H., Ongena, S. and Tümer-Alkan, G. (2008) Corporate Governance: A Review of the Role of Banks, in *The Economics of Corporate Governance and Mergers*, Gugler, K. and Yurtoglu, B.B., Edward Elgar Publishing: Cheltenham.

Del Guercio, D., Seery, L. and Woidtke, T. (2008) Do Boards Pay Attention When Institutional Investor Activists "Just Vote No"?, *Journal of Financial Economics*, **90** (1), 84–103.

Diamond, D. (1984) Financial Intermediation and Delegated Monitoring, *Review of Economic Studies*, **51** (3), 393–414.

Dimson, E. and Marsh, P. (1984) An Analysis of Brokers' and Analysts' Unpublished Forecasts of UK Stock Returns, *Journal of Finance*, **39** (5), 1257–1292.

Dyck, A. and Zingales, L. (2002) The Corporate Governance Role of the Media, in *The Right to Tell: The Role of Mass Media in Development*, The World Bank: Washington.

Ehrlich, I. and Posner, R.A (1974) An Economic Analysis of Legal Rulemaking, *Journal of Legal Studies*, **3** (1), 257–286.

Elton, E.J., Gruber, M.J. and Grossman, S. (1986) Discrete Expectational Data and Portfolio Performance, *Journal of Finance*, **41** (3), 699–714.

Fama, E.F. (1980) Agency Problems and the Theory of the Firm, *Journal of Political Economy*, **88** (2), 288–307.

Fama, E.F. and Jensen, M.C. (1983) Separation of Ownership and Control, *Journal of Law and Economics*, **26** (2), 301.

Foucault, T., and Parlour, C.A. (2004) Competition for Listings, *RAND Journal of Economics*, **35** (2), 329–355.

Franklin, A. and Douglas, G. (1999) *Corporate Governance and Competition*, Wharton Financial Institutions Center, Working Paper 99–28, University of Pennsylvania.

Franks, J., Mayer, C. and Rossi, S. (2004) Ownership: Evolution and Regulation, *Review of Financial Studies*, **22** (10), 4009–4056.

Gillan, S.L. and Starks, L.T. (2000) Corporate Governance Proposals and Shareholder Activism: The Role of Institutional Investors, *Journal of Financial Economics*, **57** (2), 275–305.

Gillan, S. and Starks, L. (2007) The evolution of shareholder activism in the United States, *Journal of Applied Corporate Finance* **19** (1), 55–73.

Gompers, P., Ishii, J. and Metrick, A. (2003) Corporate Governance and Equity Prices, *Quarterly Journal of Economics*, **118** (1), 107–155.

Gray, R., Owen, D. and Maunders, K. (1988) Corporate Social Reporting: Emerging Trends in Accountability and the Social Contract, *Accounting, Auditing & Accountability Journal*, **1** (1), 6–20.

Grossmann, S.J. and Hart, O.D. (1980) Takeover bids, the free-rider problem, and the theory of the corporation, *Bell Journal of Economics*, **11** (1), 42.

Hart O. (1983) The Market Mechanism as an

Incentive Scheme, *Bell Journal of Economics*, **14** (2), 366–382.

Hart, O. (1995) *Firms, Contracts and Financial Structure*, Oxford University Press: New York.

Hodges, R., Macniven, L. and Mellett, H. (2004) Annual General Meetings of NHS Trusts: Devolving Power or Ritualising Accountability?, *Financial Accountability & Management*, **20** (4), 377–399.

Holderness, C.G. and Sheehan, D.P. (1985) Raiders or saviors? The evidence on six controversial investors, *Journal of Financial Economics*, **14** (4), 555.

Holmstrom, B. and Milgrom, P. (1994) The Firm as an Incentive System, *American Economic Review*, **84** (4), 972–991.

Hoshi, T., Kashyap, A. and Scharfstein, D. (1991) Corporate Structure, Liquidity, and Investment: Evidence from Japanese Industrial Groups, *Quarterly Journal of Economics*, **106** (1), 33–60.

Jegadeesh, N., Kim, J., Krische, S. and Lee, C. (2004) Analyzing the Analysts: When do Recommendations Add Value?, *Journal of Finance*, **59** (3), 1083–1124.

Jensen, M. (1986) Agency Costs of Free Cash Flow, Corporate Finance and Takeovers, *American Economic Review*, **76** (2), 323–329.

Jensen M. (1989) Eclipse of the Public Corporation, *Harvard Business Review*, **67** (5), 61–75.

Jensen, M. (1998) *Foundations of Organizational Strategy*, Harvard University Press: New York.

Jensen, M. and W. Meckling, W. (1976) Theory of the Firm: Managerial Behavior, Agency Costs and Ownership Structure, *Journal of Financial Economics*, **3** (4), 305–360.

Kaplow, L.(1995) A Model of the Optimal Complexity of Legal Rules, *Journal of Law, Economics & Organization*, **11** (1), 150–163.

Keasey, K. and Short, H. (1999) Managerial ownership and the performance of firms: Evidence from the UK, *Journal of Corporate Finance*, **5** (1), 79–101.

Keasey, K. and H. Short (1999a) *Institutional Shareholders and Corporate Governance in the United Kingdom*, The International Library of Critical Writings in Economics: Corporate Governance.

Klein, A. and Zur, E. (2009) Entrepreneurial Shareholder Activism: Hedge Funds and Other Private Investors, *Journal of Finance*, **64** (1), 187–229.

Kreps, D.M. (1990) Corporate Culture and Economic Theory, in *Perspectives on Positive Political Economy*, Alt, J.E. and Shepsle, K.A. (eds) Cambridge University Press: New York.

La Porta, R., Lopez-de-Silanes, F., Shleifer, A. and Vishny, R. (1998) Law and Finance, *Journal of Political Economy*, **106** (6), 1113–1155.

Lawton, P. and Rigby, E. (1992) *Meetings, Their Law, and Practice*, Pitman: London.

Lin, H.W. and McNichols, M.F (1998) Underwriting Relationships, Analysts' Earnings Forecasts and Investment Recommendations, *Journal of Accounting and Economics*, **25** (1), 101–127.

Madelon, C. and Thomsen, S. (2009) Contracting Around Ownership: Shareholder Agreements in France, in *The Modern Firm, Corporate Governance and Investment*, Bjuggren, P.O. and D.C. Mueller (eds), Edward Elgar Publishing: Cheltenham.

Masulis, R.W., Wang, C. and Xie, F. (2007) Corporate Governance and Acquirer Returns, *Journal of Finance*, **62** (4), 1851–1889.

McConnell, J. and Servaes, H. (1990) Additional Evidence on Equity Ownership and Corporate Value, *Journal of Financial Economics*, **27** (2), 595–612.

Monks, R. A. G. and Minow, N. (2003) *Corporate Governance*, T. J. International: Cornwall.

Morck, R., Shleifer, A. and Vishny, R.W. (1988) Management ownership and market valuation: An empirical analysis, *Journal of Financial Economics*, **20**, 293–315.

Mulherin, J.H., Netter, J.M. and Overdahl, J.A. (1991) Prices Are Property: The Organization of Financial Exchanges from a Transaction Cost Perspective, *Journal of Law and Economics*, **42** (2), 591.

Nickell, S.J. (1996) Competition and Corporate Performance, *Journal of Political Economy*, **104** (4), 724–746.

Nickell, S.J., Nicolitsas, D. and Dryden, N. (1997) What makes firms perform well?, *European Economic Review*, **41** (3–5), 783–796.

Nilsson, S. and Hassel, L.G. (2003) Corporate Governance: Attendance at the Annual General Meetings in Large Swedish Companies, *Vestnik*, **4**, 128–133.

Nordén, L. and T. Strand, T. (2009) Shareholder activism among portfolio managers: rational decisions or 15 minutes of fame?, *Journal of Management and Governance*, **15** (3), 375–391.

Pagano, M. and Volpin, P. (2005) The Political Economy of Corporate Governance, *American Economic Review*, **95** (4), 1005–1030.

Pirrong, S.C. (1995) The Efficient Scope of Private Transactions-Cost-Reducing Institutions: The Successes and Failures of Commodity Exchanges, *Journal of Legal Studies*, **24** (1), 229–255.

Poulsen, T., Strand, T. and Thomsen, S. (2010) Voting Power and Shareholder Activism: A Study of Swedish Shareholder Meetings, *Corporate Governance: An International Review*, **18** (4), 329–343.

Pozen, R.C. (1994) Institutional investors: The reluctant activists, *Harvard Business Review*, **72** (1), 140–149.

Saxon, G.O. (1966). Annual Headache: The Stockholders Meeting, *Harvard Business Review*, **44** (?), 132–137.

Schilling, M. and Steensma, H. (2001) The use of modular organizational forms: an industry-level analysis, *Academy of Management Journal*, **44** (6), 1149.

Stickel, S. (1992) Reputation and Performance Among Security Analysts, *Journal of Finance*, **47** (5), 1811–1836.

Stratling, R. (2003) General Meetings: A Dispensable Tool for Corporate Governance of Listed Companies? *Corporate Governance: An International Review*, **11** (1), 74–82.

Tadelis, S. (1999) What's in a Name? Reputation as a Tradeable Asset, *American Economic Review*, **89** (3), 548.

Telser, L.G. (1981) Why There Are Organized Futures Markets, *Journal of Law and Economics*, **24** (1), 1–22.

Thomsen, S. and Vinten, F.C. (2008) Delistings in Europe, in *Essays on Private Equity*, Frederik Christian Vinten, Copenhagen Business School Press: Frederiksberg.

Watts, R. L. and Zimmerman, J. L. (1978) Towards a positive theory of the determination of accounting standards, *The Accounting Review*, **53** (1), 112–134.

Watts, R. L. and Zimmerman, J. L. (1986) *Positive Accounting Theory*, New Jersey: Prentice-Hall.

Watts, R. L. and Zimmerman, J. L. (1990) Positive accounting theory: a ten-year perspective, *The Accounting Review*, **65** (1), 131–156.

Woidtke, T. (2002) Agents watching agents? Evidence from pension fund ownership and firm value, *Journal of Financial Economics*, **63** (2), 99–131.

Womack, K. L. (1996) Do brokerage analysts' recommendations have investment value?, *Journal of Finance*, **51** (1), 137–167.

Chapter 4

International Corporate Governance

Chapter contents

4.1   Introduction

There are many different corporate governance mechanisms used to varying degrees in different countries. For this reason, corporate governance researchers often talk of different corporate governance systems. For example, the United States and the United Kingdom have traditionally relied upon the stock market as an important source of company finance, whereas Germany has relied more upon bank finance, and in Japan the keiretsu (i.e. cross-ownership) system is prevalent. There are, as we will document, many important differences and varieties of corporate governance around the globe.

Before we start to analyse them, it is important to note that these differences correspond to broad typologies. The typologies have been constructed by scholars and practitioners to understand the heterogeneous corporate governance arrangements around the world. The broad-brush systems that we describe are, in some sense, fictional, but nevertheless helpful for understanding and classifying complex corporate governance arrangements. For example, not all US firms are listed. In fact, the vast majority of firms in any country are not listed. When we characterize 'systems' we tend to focus on the largest, most visible companies in a nation. But most companies in any nation are small and unlisted and in all nations these small and medium-sized companies account for the bulk of business activity. As far as we know, these small and medium-sized companies tend to be broadly similar in their corporate governance: closely held by founders or by families. Thus we may exaggerate the differences. For example, banks are not active participants in the governance of all German companies, but appear to concentrate on the largest firms.

There are also other substantial parts of corporate governance which are not normally visible in international comparisons; this is the role of not-for-profit firms, government organizations, cooperatives, associations, mutuals and subsidiaries of foreign firms. Some of these entities can be very large and collectively they dwarf the listed companies. We find these organizations in all countries – in the USA as well as in Europe. With the exception of government organizations, we know little about their importance and their relative efficiency. Indeed, the reason scholars now know so much about some of the largest public firms is because of enhanced corporate governance disclosure requirements that have been trending to more openness over the last twenty years or so.

Moreover, the corporate governance systems we describe here change over time. Over the past decade or so, German banks have been tending to reduce their shareholdings in German companies and are no longer the major blockholders they once were. So one might ask whether Germany can still be cited as a case of purely bank governance. France is another example; it used to be well known for government ownership of firms and nationalization. However, many of France's leading firms have now been privatized and in consequence do not look like standard state-controlled firms. This last empirical observation raises an important theoretical and practical question. Are corporate governance arrangements around the globe converging? Is there pressure towards a uniform and universal model of corporate governance? Is there a set of characteristics that seems to resolve the underlying agency problems of moral hazard that we described in previous chapters, or are heterogeneous governance arrangements likely to remain the norm? In short, a central hypothesis to be explored in the international corporate governance literature is whether or not corporate governance systems will tend to converge over time.

4.2   Theoretical context: a taxonomy

We define a country's corporate governance system as a set of governance mechanisms in use in a given country or context. The fact that they are used in combination indicates some degree of consistency and stability. By 'system' we mean a set of practices, mechanisms, institutions and rules that remain stable over sufficiently long periods of time.

It is possible to classify systems along several important dimensions (Aguilera and Jackson, 2010). These features define some of the most salient aspects of the institutional environment. Consider the following possible factors or taxonomies:

- Government vs. private ownership. This was the great distinction between the former communist economies of the USSR and its satellites and the market economies of the United States and open societies. Government ownership and control of economic activity is still extremely important in many companies across the world (e.g. China), and this influences the corporate governance arrangements in place in these economies.
- Market vs. bank-based systems. This is the disintermediation or intermediation of corporate finance arrangements. In some countries, such as Germany or Japan, financial transactions between large companies and banks tend to be based on stable relationships rather than anonymous trades. There is a close relationship between firms and the suppliers of finance. In other economies, such as the USA or the UK, corporate finance arrangements are more likely to be based on market-based contracting arrangements.
- Dispersed vs. concentrated ownership. Even many countries with well-developed stock markets are controlled or majority-owned by large blockholders such as families or even the state (e.g. Singapore). However, there are some very clear patterns of corporate ownership. In some countries, such as the USA and the UK, firms are owned by many shareholders, each of whom owns a small fraction of the company's shares. In other countries, such as China, there is often a single (or few) very large shareholders who own a large fraction of the firm's shares.
- Stakeholder- vs. shareholder-based systems. In some countries, the legal structure confers rights to stakeholders that are not apparent in other countries. For example, one important issue is whether or not labour is represented on the board of directors and is able to influence companies. This differs substantially across the world. In Germany, for example, there are employee representatives on the board of directors. This is unheard of in the major publicly traded firms of the United States.
- Legal system (common vs. civil law). The legal system is an important institutional feature that varies around the world. There are, broadly speaking, two types of system: common and civil law. Common law countries include the United Kingdom, the United States and countries that use case law as the mechanism to resolve legal disputes and protect shareholder rights. Many countries in the world tend to have various kinds of civil law (e.g. China) which are rule-based systems codified by governments and the state (e.g. France).

4.3 Substitution and complementarity

Corporate governance mechanisms are not independent. There are logical and causal ties between them. In terms of causal structure, macro factors like culture and politics logically precede company law which logically precedes ownership structure. Disentangling these causal relationships is often very difficult. There are quite specific laws which regulate how much a bank or an institutional investor can own, and these laws differ between nations. This is an important cause of the differences in global corporate governance arrangements (Roe, 1994a). For example, a political change will often lead to the creation of new laws, which in turn can influence corporate ownership structure. However, a change in corporate ownership structure will not directly change the law. Board structure is decided by the owners under the limits laid down by law, which are often quite specific. The board decides on management incentives and on a number of other issues, but it delegates significant responsibility to managers, who again delegate to their employees the implementation of their decisions. We have here a series of agency relationships.

Another type of dependency is the degree to which governance arrangements can be considered as complements or substitutes (Holmström and Milgrom, 1994). Suppose there are five distinct governance mechanisms that can be defined and agreed upon: reputation, law, large owners, boards and incentives. One can then ask the question: what are the interdependencies between them? Are they complementary, meaning that an incremental increase in one of the activities increases the (marginal) valuation of one of the others? Alternatively, are they substitutes, meaning that (marginal) increases in one activity reduce the (marginal) benefit to using one of the mechanisms? In shorthand, we can simple sign these as positive or negative: complementarity (+) or substitution (−). Complementary governance mechanisms will tend to support and reinforce each other, while substitutes will tend to replace each other, i.e. you will have one or the other. In Table 4.1 we sketch some *hypothetical* relationships concerning these interdependencies. We do not claim to do a complete diagnosis of all the interdependencies, but rather want to stress the idea of governance as an interconnected system. Indeed, it is a useful exercise to think why these mechanisms might be complements or substitutes.

For example, there seems to be some degree of substitutability between formal law and informal governance by reputation. Over time formal law has probably replaced custom law. If laws are well defined there is less of a need to rely on reputation to sanction corporate governance (see Poppo and Zenger, 2002 for a counter argument).

Moreover, law, e.g. investor protection via the legal system in place in a country, enables atomistic share markets and dispersed ownership (i.e. the market model) to function, while strong owners may be necessary to control firms in systems with weak investor protection, so there is substitutability between law and large owners (La Porta et al., 1998). It is also true, however, that it is difficult to have any kind of ownership in the absence of law, so there are also complementarities here.

The link between reputation and ownership is less obvious, since both firms with large owners and firms with diversified ownership are sensitive to their reputation. However, we propose a negative relationship. Large owners (e.g. founding families) appear to rely heavily on reputation, but this is more difficult and less necessary for small investors who can (individually) buy and sell without much of an effect on the firm. Large owners will usually have a longer time horizon since they retain their shares for a longer period of time, sometimes over many generations. This will make the mechanism of building a reputation more attractive. In contrast, firms with atomistic ownership are constantly for sale and may be merged or broken up.

Boards have their key rationale when there is separation of ownership and control with dispersed ownership, whereas large owners do not have to rely on the board to represent them vis-à-vis managers (Fama and Jensen, 1983). Large owners often participate directly in the management of the firm, and in this case it is superfluous for the board to monitor the managers on behalf of the owners. Thus, we propose a substitution effect between board and ownership control.

The relationship between boards and law or reputation is more uncertain. Boards are typically created by law, but we know that they arise spontaneously even in firms which are not required to have them (Bennedsen, 2002). It also seems possible to argue that boards need to do less when the governance problem is already addressed by either of the two other mechanisms.

Table 4.1 A hypothetical sketch of substitution (−) and complementarity (+) between governance mechanisms

	Reputation	Law	Large owners	Boards	Incentives
Reputation					
Law	−				
Large owners	+	−			
Boards	−	−	−		
Incentives	−	+	−	−	

Management incentives (performance pay) seem less necessary if there is already a strong ownership incentive. Theoretically, board monitoring to reduce information asymmetries will tend to reduce the need to incentivize. Moreover, by focusing on profit maximization in the short or medium term, management incentives may attenuate reputation building. Put differently, if managers are adequately motivated by reputation concerns, there is no reason to give them more incentives. The direct relationship between law and incentives is more uncertain, but we tentatively hypothesize a positive association because well-developed share markets with a strong legal infrastructure will need additional motivation of managers.

Much more can be said about these interdependencies. We propose the hypotheses in Table 4.2 as a way to illustrate the concept of interaction effects rather than a specific theory of such interactions.

4.4   Why systems?

The dominant streams of research have emphasized the role of formal institutions, for example the legal system and investor protection rules, as determinants of these differences (Shleifer and Vishny, 1997; La Porta et al., 1998, 1999, 2002). The legal systems perspective has led to a growing number of supportive empirical studies (Claessens et al., 2000; Denis and McConnell, 2003; Durnev and Kim, 2005; La Porta et al., 1999). The implication here seems to be that countries develop constitutions and basic institutions which have a deep and lasting impact on their corporate governance systems.

This emphasis on formal institutions is also characteristic of the so-called political theory of corporate governance (Roe 1991, 1994b), which emphasizes the regulation of financial institutions as a source of corporate governance differences. The pervasiveness of these differences within systems and the persistence of differences between systems is explained in terms of complementary institutions and rent seeking, which may effectively block changes in corporate governance (Coffee, 1999; North 1991; Roe, 1994b). The argument is that the organizations created in a specific system, e.g. banks or institutional investors, will tend to lobby politicians to protect their own interests including the system which supports them. However, the political theory indicates that corporate governance systems can change when the policies change.

Licht (2001) has proposed a cultural theory of corporate governance. If countries differ systematically in terms of risk aversion, time horizons, obedience to authority, and other cultural factors, this could influence their choice of corporate governance system. It is also possible that the legal origins are related to differences in ideology (e.g. liberalism vs. socialism).

4.5   International systems

Table 4.2 summarizes a large amount of information on corporate governance in six countries. For simplicity we count the three small Scandinavian countries (Norway, Sweden and Denmark) as one. The columns list countries. The rows list corporate governance mechanisms. We label them with tentative titles to identify their governance systems. In Table 4.3 we fill in numbers from various and more or less consistent sources. Since the sources are uneven, and since the data are not collected at different points in time, the numbers must in some cases be regarded as guesstimates.

We label the first two countries (the USA and the UK) market-based systems. This is at least partly because they have large stock markets both in terms of the **number of listed firms** and in terms of **stock market capitalization** relative to GDP (Table 4.2, bottom rows). Stock market capitalization here is the total value of all listed firms (stock price × number of shares) divided by the gross domestic product in the country. There were more than 5600 listed firms in the USA. But relative to the size of the population there were even more listed companies in Britain, more than 2400. The German economy is much larger than the UK economy, but the number of listed British firms was almost four times larger than

Table 4.2 Corporate governance systems – qualitative description

	USA	UK	Japan	France	Germany	Scandinavia
	Market governance	Investor governance	Network governance	Public governance	Stakeholder governance	Stakeholder governance
Legal system	Common	Common	Civil	Civil	Civil	Civil
Investor protection	High	High	Low	Medium	Medium	Medium
Ownership concentration	Low	Low	Medium	Medium	Medium	High
Typical owners	Institutions	Institutions	Cross ownership	Cross ownership	Families	Families
Board system	One tier	One tier	One tier	One tier	Two tiers	Two tiers
Managers on board	Yes	Yes	Many	Yes	No	No
Chair = CEO	Yes	No	No	Yes	No	No
Employees on board	No	No	No	No	Yes	Yes
Bank influence	Low	Low	High	High	High	Low
Performance pay	High	Medium	Low	Medium	Medium	Low

Sources: *The World Bank (2010), Djankov et al. (2008), Conyon et al. (2011).*

Table 4.3 Corporate governance systems – quantitative description

System label	USA Market governance	UK Investor governance	Japan Network governance	France Public governance	Germany Stakeholder governance	Scandinavia Stakeholder governance
Investor protection 1–5	3	5	4.5	3.5	3.5	3.5
Anti-self-dealing 0–1	0.65	0.95	0.50	0.38	0.28	0.39
Ownership concentration	19	21	10	47	69	25
Board levels	1	1	1	1	2	2
Managers on board %	25%	35%	90%	40%	0%	10%
Chair = CEO	80%	10%	10%	80%	0%	0%
Employees on board %	0%	0%	0%	0%	50%	30%
Bank credit % GDP	223	212	292	126	125	211
Performance pay	70%	50%	30%	40%	40%	30%
Listed firms 2008	5603	2415	3299	966	638	766
Market cap % GDP 2008	83	69	65	52	30	40

Sources: Guestimates based on various sources and years (latest figures), including *The World Bank Governance Indicators, Djankov et al. (2008), Conyon et al. (2011), Bebenroth and Danghao (2007), Coles (2008), Jeanjean, Thomas & Stolowy, Hervé (2009), Dahya, Dimitrov, and McConnell (2009).*

the German. In this way, we can distinguish between market-based governance systems (in the USA and the UK) and the control- or bank-based systems found in continental Europe and Japan (Bebchuk and Roe, 1999). However, the stock market is not all there is to it. Compared with Europe, the US and the UK rely much more on market mechanisms in terms of a relatively small government sector, a pro-market competition policy and flexible labour markets. In comparison many European countries have large welfare states, promote or at least accept large national monopolies and have highly unionized labour forces.

We label Germany and Scandinavia 'stakeholder systems' because of the role that employees, banks and other stakeholders play in these systems. For lack of a better word we label the French system 'public governance' because of a high level of government intervention. With regard to legal systems, the two market-based economies are common law systems, and this is perhaps no accident. Some researchers claim that legal systems have important implications for corporate governance (La Porta et al., 1998). In the common law system which is used in the English-speaking world, law is in principle made by the courts based on specific decisions which thus create precedence, and thereby influence future decisions. In short, law is made from the bottom up, and the courts are regarded as private institutions which side with other private institutions against the government in the protection of property rights. In contrast, in the civil law systems of Europe and Japan the law is in principle regarded as an instrument which the government uses to achieve its goals, and it is by nature much less protective of property rights. Law is made top down by politicians, civil servants and law professors. So the theory goes that common law systems are more likely to protect property rights, including the rights of minority investors, and that this is why the stock market is so well developed in common law countries.

In practice, the distinction between common and civil law countries is less clear. Why should lawmakers in continental Europe not be able to adopt the rules which they consider most conducive for stock market development (even to imitate common law countries if necessary)? Moreover, there are many examples of top-down legislation in the USA: Sarbanes–Oxley is a recent example.

However, there is empirical support for the hypothesis that company law in the USA and the UK tends to be more protective of shareholder rights than the law in other countries. One important and widely-used measure is the investor protection index constructed by La Porta et al. (1998) and updated by Pagano and Volpin (2005) – known as the LSSVPV index. The LSSVPV index is correlated with other kinds of minority investor protection: for example the Djankov et al. (2008) anti-self-dealing index. The anti-self-dealing index measures legal limitations to self-dealing by controlling owners. For example, self-dealing can include transactions with other entities (i.e. those owned by the controlling owner) at inflated or reduced prices which will benefit their own interests and which harm minority investors. These limitations can include mandatory disclosure, a mandatory approval by the minority investor, the ability to challenge such transactions in court, etc.

European (particularly North European) countries score higher on an alternative, broader governance measure: the World Bank governance index, which combines measures of political freedom (e.g. freedom of speech, association, voting), regulatory quality (e.g. costs of regulation, efficient enforcement, presence of generally accepted codes, company law) and quality of the legal system (e.g. quality of contract enforcement and court system). Every second year since 1996 the World Bank has published a set of six different country-level governance indicators for 209 countries (see Kaufmann et al., 2005, 2010). The six governance indicators are: 1) voice and accountability, 2) political instability and violence, 3) government effectiveness, 4) regulatory quality, 5) rule of law, and 6) control of corruption.

Market-based systems are characterized by low ownership concentration. Especially in the largest US companies the largest owner typically holds only a few percent of the stock, in the UK less than 5% (Barca and Becht, 2001), although the percentage tends to decrease with company size. The dispersion of ownership is obviously related to the size of the market. When more small shareholders invest, the size of the market increases and the average ownership share declines. Moreover, the increasing liquidity is attractive both for buyers and sellers of shares, and this leads to even more market participants (investors, companies). Ownership concentration is higher than this in Japan and much higher in the three European systems (France, Germany, and Scandinavia).

The typical shareholders both in the USA and the UK are institutional investors (i.e. pension funds, insurance companies, mutual funds, etc.). While many institutions are also large enough to take a high share of ownership in individual firms without undue risk to their portfolio, they are prevented from this by legal placement limits (which limit the share ownership of many investors to less than 5% of an individual company) as well as by an obligation to diversify risk (Roe, 1991). In the USA, there are also many individual 'mom and pop' investors, which further disperses the ownership of US companies. In comparison, the control-based systems are characterized by higher levels of ownership concentration by founding families, corporate investors (cross-holdings), banks, and governments (Barca and Becht, 2001).

As a result, it is difficult for US and UK managers to have an ongoing dialogue with their shareholders. Instead the price system is the communication mechanism. If the shareholders are not satisfied, they will sell and the stock price will fall. In contrast, in the European system a founder or a founding family will probably be able to express his/its opinion verbally (and probably in no uncertain terms). Management responsibility in the USA and the UK is diffuse (to the public), whereas it is direct and personal in Europe. In the USA and the UK, we find strong managers and weak owners, while the situation in Europe is the opposite (Roe, 1994b).

The dominant owners in Japan and France are other corporations. Japan has the so-called keiretsu system in which members of a company group (a keiretsu) hold shares in each other.

Mitsubishi heavy industry will own shares in Mitsubishi motors. They will both own shares in the Mitsubishi bank, which in turn holds shares in the other two. See Chapter 14 for more on the Japanese model. Although each shareholding is small, when they are summed up, they constitute an effective defence against takeovers.

With regard to **board systems,** the USA, the UK, and Japan have one-tier systems, while Germany and Scandinavia have two-tier systems.[1] The difference between one and two-tier systems is illustrated in Figure 4.1.

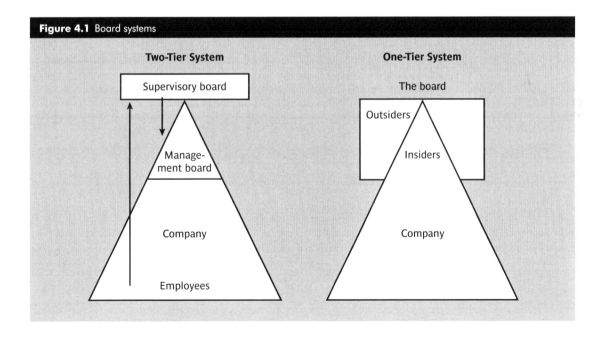

Figure 4.1 Board systems

[1] We define a two-tier system simply as a system in which the law requires companies to have two levels of management. This is the case in both Sweden and Norway, and so we define these countries as two-tier systems. Some people would disagree and claim that for example all decision power in Swedish companies is vested in the board which only delegates some of these functions to the management as a practical issue. We would maintain that Sweden is a two-tier system, although it is different from the German two-tier system. Japan (and China) also refer to a two-tier system with a 'board of statutory auditors' monitoring the management board, but since the auditors audit rather than hire and fire the managers or ratify strategies, we regard them as auditors rather than boards.

In two-tier systems (Germany, Scandinavia, Finland, Austria), shareholders elect supervisory board members, who are part-time non-executive directors, and occasionally also a minority of executive directors to a supervisory board which evaluates company performance, hires and fires the management (the executives), and must approve all major decisions. This is similar to one-tier systems, but unlike one-tier boards, supervisory boards cannot run the company on their own. They must appoint a management board.

In one-tier systems, shareholders elect the board, which then appoints the executives. Executives may or may not be board members, but typically some of them are. In Europe and the USA most of the board members are now non-executive directors (this holds in the USA and Europe, but not in Japan). Non-executive directors are typically part-time, and generally, in accordance with best-practice codes, a majority are independent also in the sense that they have no other material ties with the firm (e.g. the company lawyer, for example, is not an independent board member). Many non-executive directors have demanding jobs as executives, managers in other firms, lawyers or professors.

French companies have a choice between one- and two-tier boards, and the vast majority of them have chosen to stay with the traditional one-tier system. This is interesting, since it indicates that the one-tier board structure would win if the choice between one-tier and two-tiers was left to the market participants. It may be that the one-tier model is more effective or it may be that managers dislike the added control. However, it is also possible that many French companies hold on to the old board structure because of conservatism.

Turning to board composition, executives are prohibited from taking a seat on German supervisory boards, but in the USA, the UK and France companies have a fairly large percentage of managers on their board, although not a majority. In Scandinavia, the majority of the supervisory board members must (by law) be non-managers. In Denmark it is now regarded as best practice that managers do not sit on the supervisory board at all. Japan is famous for a very large percentage of insiders on boards. Historically, boards in Japan tended to be quite large (up to 30 or 40 members) which is perhaps too many for the board to make effective decisions. However, they have since shrunk down to an average size of 10. In the USA and France, the chief executive can also be chairman of the board (i.e. duality), but this is prohibited in two-tier systems. The French title is PDG: President + Director General. In the UK, the two positions – chairman and managing director – are now typically separated following corporate governance recommendations (Cadbury, 1992).

In Germany and Scandinavia **employees** of a company have a right to elect members of the supervisory board: typically ⅓ of the board members (Denmark, Norway, Sweden and Austria). But in some large German companies, up to 50% of the board will be employee representatives. Despite employee representation, the shareholder-elected board members have a majority of the votes (e.g. in Germany the vote of the chairman is decisive in the case of a split). Employee representation is not found on the shareholder-friendly US and UK boards, nor is it found in France. Interestingly, French unions have historically been unwilling to assume responsibility by employee representation. The differences are directly attributable to company law. In some countries, employee representation is mandatory by law and this is where you will find it. In other countries, employee representation is not mandatory, and the result is that most companies choose not to have it.

Banks have little influence in the (stock) market-based systems in the USA and the UK, but they continue to play a role in German corporate governance. Figure 4.2 illustrates the key difference between market-based and bank-based governance systems. In a market-based system, savers invest directly in shares and bonds of listed companies. In a bank-based system, they put their money in the bank which then lends it to the corporations or invests some of it directly in their shares. In the bank-based system, the bank acts as an intermediary and we therefore talk about intermediation. In the market-based system, or in a transition to a market-based system, we refer to 'disintermediation'. To be sure, even in market-based systems many people prefer to invest in a mutual fund rather than investing directly in stocks, but in this case, the role of the intermediary is much more limited. Banks used to be central actors in most corporate governance systems and may become important again in the future. Growing stock and bond markets shifted the balance towards disintermediation up to the financial crisis in 2008, but this process now seems unlikely to continue.

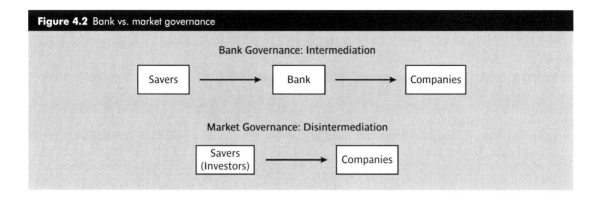

Figure 4.2 Bank vs. market governance

In Germany the importance of banks for corporate governance is magnified by a number of special characteristics. First, banks are allowed to make large investments in stock even to the point of controlling some of the largest German corporations. Secondly, bankers often act as custodians for German shareholders and they may be entitled to vote on their behalf at shareholder meetings. Thirdly, bankers often sit on the boards of non-financial companies. Legal and other considerations discourage bank managers from sitting on the boards of non-financial companies in the USA or the UK. So, despite a recent trend towards the reduction of their shareholdings in Germany, banks remain powerful actors in the German system. It is interesting, however, that German banks do not appear to provide more credit to the business sector than in the USA, which combines high levels of bank lending and a large number of listed companies. In other words, banks and markets may be complements rather than substitutes. More can be found on the German system in Chapter 13.

Japanese banks are powerful actors in the Japanese corporate governance system since they play a role as 'main banks' at the centre of many keiretsus. As in the USA, Japanese banks cannot hold controlling shares greater than 5% in non-financial companies. This is no accident since the Japanese regulation was written by the Americans during the occupation after the Second World War. However, one interpretation of the keiretsu system is that it is a way to circumvent these rules so that banks can retain control despite the rules.

Again, there are very concrete legal reasons why banks are less powerful in the USA and the UK. Commercial banks are prohibited from taking large positions in non-financial companies in the USA and also (albeit less formally) in the UK. Moreover, traditionally US banks have been kept small by a forced specialization among investment and commercial banks (due to the Glass–Steagall Act). For a long time in the USA banks were prevented from merging across state boundaries (due to the bank holding company act). Only recently, in 1999, some of these restrictions were lifted. Now, with post-crisis financial regulation, they may return.

The extent of **performance pay** for senior managers differs widely across systems although recently there appears to have been some convergence. Total pay levels for CEOs appear to be much higher in the USA and, to a lesser extent, in the UK than in continental Europe and Japan. Moreover, a much larger percentage (e.g. 70%) of US executive pay depends on performance (in the largest companies). Overall, this means that US and to some extent UK managers have much stronger performance incentives than do European or Japanese managers.

4.6 Country models

Instead of comparing corporate governance mechanisms, it is interesting to examine the individual countries to explain their historical and cultural characteristics (Pedersen and Thomsen, 1997). Charkman (1994) makes an interesting, if somewhat speculative, attempt.

Great Britain was the first nation to industrialize, and funds for large enterprises had to be attracted from a number of individual investors. The fortunes of the landed gentry and the merchant class were to a large extent channelled into manufacturing at arm's length via the City of London. Social prestige dictated that occupations in finance and economics enjoyed a higher status than engineering.

France has a historical tradition for government intervention and centralization which, according to some, can be traced back to Louis XIV (Charkman, 1994). Features of the French system like the almighty chairman-CEO (the PDG combined President and Director General) also fit a hypothesis of centralization. More recently, the large share of government ownership in France which is partly a consequence of nationalization after the Second World War and partly a result of the Mitterand government in the early 1980s is now undergoing large-scale privatization. The French tradition for government intervention is no doubt strengthened by strong personal ties in the elite that graduate from 'grand ecoles' and who occupy top jobs in business and government (Charkman 1994).

Another interesting feature of French ownership structure is the role played by holding companies which were originally established by industrial companies to overcome financing constraints (Levy-Leboyer 1980). This helps to explain the frequency of cross-holdings. After privatization there seems to have been a tendency for this system to reappear, as companies join in a hard core of cross-ownership to avoid being taken over by 'Anglo-Saxons'.

In Germany, banks played an active role in the industrialization process and financial institutions continued to exercise dominant minority control over many large companies (Feldenkirchen 1988), but have sold out in the past decades. Individual company profiles reveal that bank participation has often come about unintentionally as the result of financial distress (Charkman 1994). In addition, Social Democratic politics have clearly played a role in the emergence of employee representation both in Germany and in Scandinavia. Both countries are characterized by more friendly relations between capital and labour than in the market-based governance systems.

A high frequency of family and cooperative ownership in Scandinavia is partly attributable to the scarcity of large companies and partly to industry effects. Norway has many shipping companies (which tend to be family owned). Denmark has many food producing companies, which are still dominated by co-ops. Foundation ownership is often regarded as a response to high tax pressure.

4.7   Convergence[2]

Corporate governance systems are quite stable in the short run (e.g. from year to year), but they do sometimes change over longer periods of time (e.g. decades).

A decade ago, a consensus seemed to emerge among academics and executives alike that the Anglo-American corporate governance model had won and that European systems were converging to US/UK standards (e.g. Hansmann and Kraakman, 2000, 2002; Coffee 1999, 2002a, 2002c; Denis and McConnell, 2003). During the 1990s, examples were easy to find. Examples included the growing importance of stock markets in most economies, the increasing importance of institutional investors (Coffee, 1999; van den Berghe, 2002), the increasing number of hostile takeovers (*The Economist*, 2000) and suggestions to open the European markets further by a break-through rule (Bolkestein report, 2001), the spread of stock option-based managerial compensation (Murphy, 1999), or increases in leverage through share buy-backs and higher dividends (Warner, 1998).

However, contrary to general beliefs, it is possible to argue for a mutual convergence hypothesis (Thomsen, 2003). Not only has European corporate governance converged to US standards, US corporate governance has also effectively converged to European standards in several important respects since the 1980s. Comparative research in corporate governance has emphasized that Anglo-American corporate governance is characterized by low ownership concentration, one-tier

---

[2] This section draws heavily on 'The Convergence of Corporate Governance Systems to European and Anglo-American Standards', European Business Organization Law Review, 4 (1), 2003.

boards and shareholder value norms, whereas high levels of insider ownership, two-tier boards and stakeholder concerns are more characteristic features of continental Europe (Baums, 1994; Roe, 1994b; Prowse, 1995; Gugler, 2001; Vives, 2000; Barca and Becht, 2001). But during the 1990s ownership concentration in the USA/UK increased due to growing managerial ownership and institutional investment (Holderness et al., 1999; Meyer, 1998; Investor Relations Business, 2000). Moreover, management and control in the USA/UK have increasingly been separated by the appointment of non-executive directors (Monks and Minow, 2001), subcommittees composed of non-executives (Cadbury Code, NYSE code), and separation of the roles of CEO and board chair (e.g. the Cadbury and Higgs codes in the UK). Furthermore, the stakeholder approach attracted increasing attention in US management research and practice during the 1990s (Clarkson, 1995; Donaldson and Preston, 1995; Jones, 1995; Mitchell et al., 1997; Agle et al., 1999; Jones and Wicks, 1999; Jawahar and McLaughlin, 2001). Finally, financial deregulation has relaxed the separation of investment and commercial banking and has allowed banks to assume a more prominent role in the American economy (Financial Services Modernization Act, 1999; *The Economist*, 1999). That too is a step in a European direction.

The leading convergence theorists, Hansmann and Kraakman (2000), pointed to three mechanisms of governance convergence: logic (persuasive arguments for the superiority of one model), example (of competitive success of one model), and demonstrated competitive advantages. These forces work in the same direction when influential shareholders or company managers adopt international governance structures that are perceived to work better, for example, when European managers adopt US/UK governance principles because comparable companies in the US/UK have higher market value, lower capital costs, or other advantages. In global capital markets this may be the direct result of an attempt to attract capital from the same investors, or it may be a more indirect imitation of new management practices. Studies by van der Elst reported in van den Berghe (2002) document the significant internationalization of European equity markets which implies global competition to attract shareholder funds. Among listed companies international share ownership has increased considerably as a percentage of total ownership in most European countries over the period 1990 to 1998. In rough figures international ownership increased from 12% to 15% in Germany, from 14% to 35% in France, from 8% to 12% in Italy, from 16% to 36% in Spain, and from 12% to 24% in the UK. It also increased significantly by more than 30% in the Nordic countries (Thomsen, 2001), but only marginally in the USA from 7% to 7%+. Likewise, Coffee (2002a, 2002c) documents an increasing tendency for foreign firms to list on the New York Stock Exchange up to 2001 which was significant given the size and importance of the large companies in question (e.g. Daimler Benz) although the numbers (20–50 new firms a year during the 1990s) are probably too small to affect global changes in corporate governance in their own right.

Hansmann and Kraakman (2000) also mention harmonization and changes in corporate law as a weak force towards convergence. Convergence in regulation may come about if politicians imitate the laws and policies of other countries because they are persuaded by logical arguments and/or the desire to improve international competitiveness, economic growth, or employment. For example, a case in point is the proposed EU takeover directive (Bolkestein report, 2001; EU Commission, 2002) which aims to stimulate the market for hostile takeovers in Europe. Alternatively, governance structures may converge if corporate decision makers respond in the same way to similar challenges (e.g. the growing importance of institutional investors).

Clearly, these forces must be weighed against other powerful forces which block convergence or even promote divergence, for example the same factors that created corporate governance differences in the first place. Bebchuk (1999) and Bebchuk and Roe (1999) explain why ownership concentration will not automatically adjust to efficient levels, and particularly why a controlling shareholder structure with high ownership concentration (which we will call a control structure) does not automatically develop into a non-control structure (which we will call a market-based structure), even when the market-based structure maximizes the financial value of the firm.

One important reason is the existence of private benefits to controlling shareholders, which are not shared with minority investors (Bebchuk 1999; Bebchuk and Roe, 1999). When firms have already adopted a mixed ownership structure with some minority investors, prospective gains by selling more shares to the public must be shared by these investors, and this reduces the incentive to give up private control benefits (Bebchuk and Roe, 1999). Bebchuk (1999) therefore predicts that control-based governance systems will emerge when the private benefits of control are large. In market-based systems, managerial control benefits may give rise to persistence of market-based governance structures (dispersed ownership). Because of vested interests in maintaining the status quo, incumbent managers may resist the formation of controlling blocks (Bebchuk and Roe 1999) and fight hostile takeovers. Gains from the formation of large blocks of control will again be shared with the market, reducing the incentive to form such blocks in market-based systems (Shleifer and Vishny, 1986).

Other factors at the system level also create barriers to change of ownership structure (Bebchuk and Roe, 1999). Ceilings and other limitations on ownership by financial institutions, as in the USA, limit their ownership shares of individual firms (Roe, 1991). The existence of complementary institutions in a given system, e.g. a large and well-functioning stock market as in the USA/UK or an active bank sector as in Germany, may influence the ownership and capital structures of firms based in that system (Roe, 1994b). Legal systems may provide varying degrees of protection of minority investors (La Porta et al., 1998). Finally, the incumbent organizations/institutions will lobby for continuation of their own existence (North, 1991).

However, even though the formal governance structure is unchanged, there may be convergence in behaviour. Gilson (2001), and later La Porta et al. (2000), makes the important distinction between formal and functional convergence: companies within a particular institutional framework may change their behaviour in order to succeed or survive in international competition even though the formal structure is unchanged. Coffee (1999) argues that a number of forces pull and push towards convergence: the growth of European stock markets, disclosure harmonization, the growth of institutional investors, harmonization of international accounting standards and the need for global economies of scale. But these forces clash with path dependency, complementarity and other strong forces that block formal changes in the legal system. The outcome of this dilemma, Coffee argues, is that formal governance structures change very little, but that functional convergence in corporate governance takes place as European companies change behaviour to align with American standards.

Theoretically, functional convergence can be seen as a special case of Coasian contracting (Coase, 1960). If there are gains to trade or coordination, market participants have an incentive to contract around the prevailing formal structures of law and ownership to approach a first best allocation of resources. An obvious channel for this type of convergence is the internationalization of equity markets in which profit-seeking investors can strike mutually advantageous deals with companies in other governance systems and thus they may contract around formal barriers. This may, for example, have resulted in a functional reorientation of corporate governance in continental Europe.

More recently, papers by Markarian, Parbonetti and Previts (2007) or Martynova and Renneboog (2010) point to convergence in disclosure and legal system. Papers on the topic surveyed by Yoshikawa and Rasheed (2009) are more ambiguous, but very few find evidence of divergence. Large country differences remain in ownership structure, board systems and incentive pay. The speed of convergence is often found to be slow and to depend on the country context, but there is little doubt about the direction of change. For example some countries adopted corporate governance codes faster than others during past decades, but gradually they have all adopted such codes. It is highly plausible that some of the convergence was superficial and symbolic (and the underlying structure and behaviour remained relatively unchanged), but it is also possible to see convergence as a process in which symbolic adoption gradually becomes better rooted as laws, regulations and attitudes change.

In recent years convergence appears have been strengthened by macro trends. Figures 4.3 and 4.4 show the size of the stock market over time in terms of stock market capitalization to GDP and the number of listed companies. Market capitalization has dropped in all countries from levels of as high as 200% of GDP to below 100% today, first at the bursting of the dot.com bubble (2000–2003) and secondly during the financial crisis (2007–2008). During the same period the number of listed companies fell dramatically in the USA from a peak of 8850 companies in 1997 to 5603 in 2008, while it generally increased or remained roughly constant in Europe and Japan. In effect, US businesses have increasingly opted out of the market model, while Europe and Japan have opted in. The result is that the two continents are slowly converging.

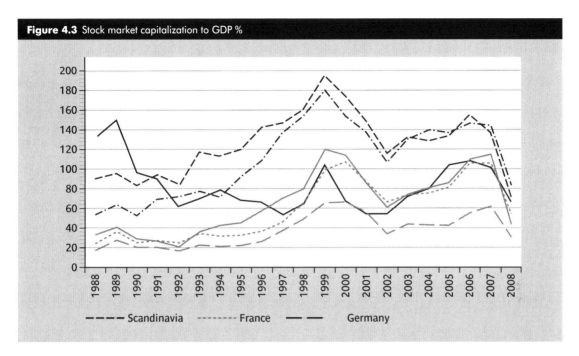

Figure 4.3 Stock market capitalization to GDP %

- − − − Scandinavia   ⋯⋯⋯ France   ▬ ▬ Germany

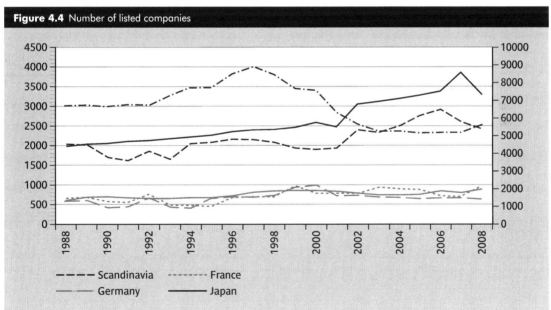

Figure 4.4 Number of listed companies

- − − − Scandinavia   ⋯⋯⋯ France
- ▬▬▬ Germany   ▬▬▬ Japan

4.8 Discussion

Corporate governance systems differ because countries use different mechanisms to control and direct companies. Some rely on more markets and price signals, others rely more on large owners such as families, business groups or governments. Some rely on economic incentives such as pay for

performance, others rely more on social sanctions. Some integrate stakeholders such as employees into the formal governance system; others keep them at arm's length distance to companies. Over time the different mechanisms are adjusted to fit into the bundles which identify as corporate governance systems.

These systemic differences shape the way governance is practised and the way companies do business. For better or worse companies in some countries have to listen more to their employees or their banks, while others need to spend time convincing the stock market that they are on the right track. Managers have much more autonomy in market-based systems, while owners are more influential where ownership is concentrated. They are more incentivized to maximize shareholder value in the market-based systems of the USA or the UK, but conform more to social norms in Japan.

The differences may be overstated, however. Small companies around the world tend to have similar (owner-managed) governance. Moreover, governance systems do change over time, and we can see elements of convergence over time. For example, companies around the world have adopted market-based governance mechanisms over the past three decades and now face much more regulation and government interference regardless of system. To some extent companies can now free themselves of their national origins and adopt individual governance models. It is often possible to contract around legal limitations if this is believed to create economic value.

Minicase

A match made in heaven – DaimlerChrysler 1998–2007

On 7 May 1998, Daimler Benz and Chrysler announced a merger – a match made in heaven, it was called. The merger was greeted with enthusiasm. Share prices rose, especially Chrysler's, and the combined value of the two companies increased. The merger was announced as a merger of equals with no need for job cuts since there was little overlap between Chrysler's operations in the USA and Daimler's in Europe. The equality was reflected in the management. There were two CEOs and parallel organizations. At one stroke DaimlerChrysler was the world's third largest car maker.

The governance of the two entities changed as a result of the merger. The ownership structure became more dispersed as Deutsche Bank's share in the combined entity fell and Chrysler's largest shareholder Kirk Gregorian sold out. The supervisory board became quite large with members from both companies. The German employees gracefully allowed United Auto Workers one of their board seats. Management pay for the German executives was adjusted upwards to the US level.

The market optimism did not last. Share prices started dropping on news that Chrysler's earnings had to be revised downwards, that former Chrysler executives were retiring, that DaimlerChrysler was dropped from the S&P 500 index (no longer being a US company), and that the company was having merger talks with Nissan (shares rose again when the talks were dropped). S&P deregistration alone drove share prices down by 15%. The US managers were replaced by Germans. But change was slow. Share prices took 10 years to recover to the 1998 level and then tumbled in the financial crisis of 2008. Growth slowed and the company eventually began to shrink. Return on net assets dropped to single figures. Credit ratings fell.

Finally, in 2007, Daimler gave up and sold Chrysler to Cerberus, a US private equity fund. Chrysler went bankrupt during the crisis and was taken over by the US government. But the world dream is not forgotten. Chrysler was recently sold to Fiat!

Source: Blasko, M., Netter, J. and Sinkey J. (2000). Value creation and the challenges of an international transaction. The Daimler Chrysler merger. *International Review of Financial Analysis*, **9** (1), 77–102.

Discussion questions

1 What are the key governance differences between US and German firms?
2 What problems could this create for the merged company?
3 What do you think about 'the merger of equals'?
4 Did governance become stronger or weaker after the merger?
5 Why do you think share prices fell during the talks with Nissan?
6 Was DaimlerChrysler doomed to failure?
7 Do you think Fiat-Chrysler will work?

Summary (learning points)

- Countries tend to have distinctive governance systems conditioned by history, politics and interdependencies among governance mechanisms.
- The UK and the USA broadly conform to the market model: they have large liquid stock markets, dispersed ownership, high investor protection, and widespread use of incentive pay and independent one-tier boards.
- Germany, in contrast, has a much smaller stock market, more concentrated ownership, two-tier boards with employee representation and influential banks. The system can be described as a stakeholder model.
- Japan is characterized by powerful banks, ownership ties between business firms, insider-dominated boards and limited use of performance pay. We describe it as a network system.
- France has medium ownership concentration, primarily one-tier boards with a powerful President Directeur General and a tradition for government intervention. We therefore characterize the French model as 'public governance'.
- Scandinavia has strong elements of the stakeholder model, which are taken even further by specific features such as strong welfare states, a gender quota (in Norway) and industrial foundations (in Denmark).
- Governance systems are not constant and we see some signs of convergence over time.

 ## References and further reading

Agle, B.R., Mitchell, R.K. and J.A. Sonnenfeld, J.A. (1999) Who Matters to CEOs? An Investigation of Stakeholder Attributes and Salience, Corporate Performance, and CEO Values, *Academy of Management Journal*, **42** (5), 507–525.

Aguilera, R. and Jackson, G. (2003) The Cross-National Diversity of Corporate Governance: Dimensions and Determinants, *Academy of Management Review*, **28** (3), 447–465.

Aguilera, R.V. and Jackson, G. (2010) Comparative and International Corporate Governance, *Annals of the Academy of Management*, **4**, 485–556.

Aguilera, R.V. and William, C.A. (2009) Law and Finance: Inaccurate, Incomplete, and Important, *Brigham Young University Law Review*, 6, 1413–1434.

Allan, F. and Gale, D. (1999) Corporate Governance and Competition, in *Corporate Governance: Theoretical and Empirical Perspectives* (2006), Vives, X. (ed.), Cambridge University Press: Cambridge.

Barca, F. and Becht, M. (2001) *The Control of Corporate Europe*, Oxford University Press: Oxford.

Barclay, M.J., and Holderness, C.G. (1989) Private Benefits from Control of Public Corporations, *Journal of Financial Economics*, **25** (2), 371–395.

Baums, T. (1994) The German Banking System and

its Impact on Corporate Finance and Governance, in *The Japanese Main Bank System*, Aoki, M. and Patrick, H. (eds) (1995), Oxford University Press: Oxford.

Baums, T., Buxbaum, T. and Hopt, K.J. (1994) *Institutional Investors and Corporate Governance*, Walter De Gruyter: Berlin.

Bebchuk, L. (1999) *A Rent Protection Theory of Corporate Ownership and Control*, NBER Working Paper, No. 7203, Cambridge, Massachusetts.

Bebchuk, L.A. and Roe, M. (1999) A Theory of Path Dependence in Corporate Ownership and Governance, *Stanford Law Review*, **52** (1), 127–170.

Becht, M. and Mayer, C. (2001) Introduction, in *The Control of Corporate Europe*, Barca, F. and Becht, M. (eds), Oxford University Press: Oxford.

Bennedsen, M. (2002) *Why Do Firms Have Boards?*, Working Paper, No. 03/2002, Copenhagen Business School: Frederiksberg.

van den Berghe, L. (2002) *Corporate Governance in a Globalising World: Convergence or Divergence? A European Perspective*, Kluwer Academic: Dordrecht.

Berle, A., and Means, C. (1932) *The Modern Corporation and Private Property*, Harcourt, Brace & World: New York.

Blair, M.M. (2002) *Post-Enron Reflections on Comparative Corporate Governance*, Georgetown University Law Center, Working Paper series in Business, Economics and Regulatory Law, No. 316663.

Blair, M.M. and Roe, M.J. (1999) *Employees and Corporate Governance*, The Brookings Institution: Washington DC.

Bolkestein report (2001) http://europa.eu.int/comm/ internal_market/en/company/companynews/ hlg01-2002.pdf

Bolton, P. and Von Thadden, E. (1998) Blocks, Liquidity, and Corporate Control, *Journal of Finance*, **53** (1), 1–25.

Braendle, U.C. and Noll, J. (2005) *The Societas Europaea – A Step Towards Convergence of Corporate Governance Systems?* (April 15, 2005), available at SSRN: http://ssrn.com/abstract=704881.

Burkart, M., Gromb, D. and Panunzi, F. (1997) Large Shareholders, Monitoring, and the Value of the Firm, *Quarterly Journal of Economics*, **112** (3), 693–728.

Burkart, M., Gromb, D. and Panunzi, F. (1998) Why Higher Takeover Premia Protect Minority Shareholders, *Journal of Political Economy*, **106** (1), 172–204.

Cadbury report, Sir Adrian Cadbury (1992) Report of the Committee on the Financial Aspects of Corporate Governance, Gee and Co.: London.

Calian, S.S. and Booth, T. (2000) Ethical Investing Grows in the United Kingdom, *Wall Street Journal*. New York, June 19.

Carlin, W. and Mayer, C. (2000) How do Financial Systems Affect Economic Performance?, in *Corporate Governance: Theoretical and Empirical Perspectives*, Vives, X. (ed), Cambridge University Press: Cambridge.

Charkman, J.P. (1994) *Keeping Good Company: A Study of Corporate Governance in Five Countries*, Oxford: Clarendon Press.

Chung, K.H. and Pruitt, S.W. (1994) A Simple Approximation of Tobin's q, *Financial Management*, **23** (3), 70–74.

Claessens, S., Djankov, S. and Lang, L.H.P. (2000) The Separation of Ownership and Control in East Asian Corporations, *Journal of Financial Economics*, **58** (1–2), 81–112.

Clarkson, M.B.E. (1995) A Stakeholder Framework for Analysing and Evaluating Corporate Social Performance, *Academy of Management Review*, **20** (1), 92–117.

Coase, R.H. (1960) The Problem of Social Cost, *Journal of Law and Economics*, **3** (Oct.), 1–44.

Coffee, J.C. (1999) The Future as History: The Prospects for Global Convergence in Corporate Governance and its Implications, *Northwestern University Law Review*, **93** (3), 641–708.

Coffee, J.C. (2002a) *Racing Towards the Top? The Impact of Cross-Listings and Stock Market Competition on International Corporate Governance*, Columbia Law School, Center for Law and Economic Studies, Working Paper No. 205.

Coffee, J.C. (2002b) *Understanding Enron: It's About the Gatekeepers, Stupid!*, Columbia Law School, Center for Law and Economic Studies, Working Paper No. 207.

Coffee, J.C. (2002c) Convergence and Its Critics: What are the Preconditions to the Separation of Ownership and Control?, in *Corporate Governance Regimes: Convergence and Diversity*, McCahery, J.A., Moerland, P., Raaijmakers, T. and Renneborg, L. (eds) Oxford University Press: New York.

Cohen, S. and Boyd, G. (2000) *Corporate Governance and Globalization*, Edward Elgar: Cheltenham.

Coles, N. D. L. (2008) Boards: Does one size fit all? *Journal of Financial Economics*, **87** (2), 329–356.

Commission of The European Communities (EU Commission, Brussels, 2002) Proposal for a Directive of the European Parliament and of the Council on Takeover Bids, Com (2002) 534 Final, 2002/0240(Cod).

Conyon, M.J., Peck, S.I. and Sadler, G.V (2011) New perspectives on the governance of executive compensation: an examination of the role and effect of compensation consultants, *Journal of Management and Governance*, **15** (1), 29–58.

Demirguc-Kunt, A. and Levine, R. (1999) *Bank-based and market-based financial systems: Cross-country comparisons*, World Bank Policy Working Paper No. 2143.

Demsetz, H. (1983) The Structure of Ownership and the Theory of the Firm, *Journal of Law and Economics*, **26** (2), 375–394.

Demsetz, H. and Lehn, K. (1985) The Structure of Corporate Ownership: Causes and Consequences, *Journal of Political Economy*, **93** (6), 1155–1177.

Denis, D.J., and Sarin, A. (1999) Ownership and Board Structures in Publicly Traded Corporations, *Journal of Financial Economics*, **52** (2), 187–223.

Denis, D.K. and McConnell, J.J. (2003) International Corporate Governance, *Journal of Financial and Quantitative Analysis,* **38** (1), 1–36.

Djankov, S., La Porta, R., Lopez de Silanes, F. and Shleifer, A. (2008). The law and economics of self-dealing, *Journal of Financial Economics,* **88** (3), 430–465.

Donaldson, T. and Preston, L.E. (1995) The Stakeholder Theory of the Corporation: Concepts, Evidence, and Implications, *Academy of Management Review,* **20** (1), 65–91.

Durnev, A. and Han Kim, E. (2005) To Steal or Not to Steal: Firm Attributes, Legal Environment, and Valuation, *Journal of Finance,* **60** (3), 1461–1493.

Dyck, A. and Zingales, L. (2004) Private Benefits of Control: An International Comparison, *Journal of Finance,* **59** (3), 537–600.

Dyck, A., Zingales, L. and Volchkova, N. (2008) The Corporate Governance Role of the Media: Evidence from Russia, *Journal of Finance,* **63** (3), 1093–1135.

Easterbrook, F.H. (1997) International Corporate Differences: Market or Law, *Journal of Applied Corporate Finance,* **9** (4), 23–29.

Fama, E.F. and Jensen, M.C. (1983) Agency Problems and Residual Claims, *Journal of Law and Economics,* **26** (2), 327–349.

Feldenkirchen, W. (1988) *The Concentration Process in the Entrepreneurial Economy Since the Late 19th Century,* Franz Steiner Verlag: Stuttgart.

Ferran, E. (1999) *Company Law and Corporate Finance,* Oxford University Press: Oxford.

Financial Services Modernization Act (1999), Act of the 106th United States Congress, Public Law 106-102.

Flynn, J. (1999) Use of Performance-Based Pay Spreads Across Continental Europe, Survey Says, *Wall Street Journal,* Nov. 17, New York.

Freeman, R.E. (1984) *Strategic Management: A Stakeholder Approach,* Cambridge University Press, New York.

Friedman, B.M. (1996) Economic Implications of Changing Share Ownership, *Journal of Portfolio Management,* **22** (3), 59–70.

Gerschenkron, A. (1962) *Economic Backwardness in Historical Perspective: A Book of Essays,* Belknap Press of Harvard University Press: Cambridge, MA.

Gilson, R.J. (2001) Globalising Corporate Governance: Convergence of Form or Function, *American Journal of Comparative Law,* **49** (2), 329–357.

Goergen, M., Martynova, M. and Renneboog, L.D.R. (2005) Corporate Governance Convergence: Evidence from Takeover Regulation Reforms in Europe, *Oxford Review of Economic Policy,* **21** (2), 243–268.

Granovetter, M. (2005) The Impact of Social Structure on Economic Outcomes, *Journal of Economic Perspectives,* **19** (1), 33–50.

Guest, P. M. (2008) The Determinants of Board Size and Composition Evidence from UK, *Journal of Corporate Finance,* **14** (1), 51–72.

Gugler, K. (2001) *Corporate Governance and Economic Performance,* Oxford University Press: Oxford.

Gugler, K., Mueller, D.C. and Yurtoglu, B.B. (2004) Corporate Governance and Globalization, *Oxford Review of Economic Policy,* **20** (1), 129–156.

Guillen, Mauro F. (2000) Corporate Governance and Globalization: Is There Convergence Across Countries?, *Advances in International Comparative Management,* **13**, 175–204.

Hamilton, J.D. (1994) *Time Series Analysis,* Princeton University Press, NJ.

Hansmann, H. and Kraakman, R. (2000) *The End of History For Corporate Law,* Yale School of Management Working Papers, Working Paper No. 136.

Hansmann, H. and Kraakman, R. (2001) The End of History for Corporate Law, *Georgetown Law Journal,* **89** (2), 439–468.

Hansmann, H. and Kraakman, R. (2002) Toward A Single Model of Corporate Law, in *Corporate Governance Regimes: Convergence and Diversity,* McCahery, J.A., Moerland, P., Raaijmakers, T. and Renneborg, L. (eds), Oxford University Press: Oxford.

Healy, P.M. and Palepu, K. (2002) *Governance and Intermediation Problems in capital markets: Evidence from the Fall of EnronHarvard,* NOM Research Paper O, 02–27, August.

Hellwig, M. (1998) On the Economics and Politics of Corporate Finance and Control, paper presented at the Conference on Corporate Governance of the Institut Català de Finances, Sitges, 23–24 October.

Himmelberg, C.P., Hubbard, R.G. and Palia, D. (1999) Understanding the Determinants of Managerial Ownership and the Link Between Ownership Structure and Performance, *Journal of Financial Economics,* **53** (3), 353–384.

Holderness, C.G. (2003) A Survey of Blockholders and Corporate Control, *Economic Policy Review,* **9** (1), available at http://ssrn.com/abstract=281952.

Holderness, C. and Sheehan, D. (1988) The Role of Majority Shareholders in Publicly Held Corporations: An exploratory analysis, *Journal of Financial Economics,* **20** (1–2), 317–346.

Holderness, C.G., Kroszner, R.S. and Sheehan, D.P (1999) Were the Good Old Days that Good? Changes in Managerial Ownership since the Great Depression, *Journal of Finance,* **54** (2), 435–469.

Holmstrom, B. and Milgrom, P. (1994) The Firm as an Incentive System, *American Economic Review,* **84** (4), 972–991.

Investor Relations Business (2000) Reversal of Fortune: Institutional Ownership is Declining, **5** (9).

Jawahar, I.M. and McLaughlin, G.L. (2001) Toward a Descriptive Stakeholder Theory: An Organizational Life Cycle Approach, *Academy of Management Review,* **26** (3), 397–414.

Jeanjean, T. and Stolowy, H. (2009) Determinants of board members' financial expertise – Emperical evidence from France, *The International Journal of Accounting,* **44** (4), 378–402.

Jensen, M.C. and Meckling, W.H. (1976) Theory of the Firm: Managerial Behaviour, Agency Costs, and

Ownership Structure, *Journal of Financial Economics*, **3** (4), 305–360.

Johnson, S. and Shleifer, A. (2001) *Coase and Competence in Development*, Harvard University, Working Paper.

Jones, T. and Wicks, A.C (1999) Convergent Stakeholder Theory, *Academy of Management Review,* **24** (2), 206–221.

Jones, T.M. (1995) Instrumental Stakeholder Theory: A Synthesis of Ethics and Economics, *Academy of Management Review*, **20** (2), 404–437.

Kaufmann, D. (2005) Back to Basics—10 Myths About Governance and Corruption, in *Finance and Development*, a quarterly magazine of the IMF, **42** (3).

Kaufmann, D., Kraay, A. and Mastruzzi, M. (2006) *Measuring Corruption: Myths and Realities,* The World Bank.

Kaufmann, D., Kraay, A. and Mastruzzi, M. (2010) *The Worldwide Governance Indicators: Methodology and Analytical Issues*, World Bank Policy Research Working Paper No. 5430.

Khanna, T., Kogan, J. and Palepu, K. (2006) Globalization and Corporate Governance Convergence? A Cross-Country Analysis, *Review of Economics and Statistics*, **88** (1), 69–90.

La Porta, R., Lopez-de-Silanes, F. and Shleifer, A. (2002) Government Ownership of Banks, *Journal of Finance*, **57** (1), 265–301.

La Porta, R., Lopez-de-Silanes, F., Shleifer, A. and Vishny, R. (1997) Legal Determinants of External Finance, *Journal of Finance*, **52** (3), 1131–1150.

La Porta, R., Lopez-de-Silanes, F., Shleifer, A. and Vishny, R.W.(1998) Law and finance, *Journal of Political Economy*, **106** (6), 1113–1155.

La Porta, R., Lopez-de-Silanes, F., Shleifer, A. and Vishny, R.W. (1999) Corporate ownership around the world, *Journal of Finance*, **54** (2), 471–517.

La Porta, R., Lopez-de-Silanes, F., Shleifer, A. and Vishny, R.W. (2000) Investor Protection and Corporate Valuation, *Journal of Financial Economics*, **58** (1–2), 3–27.

Levy-Leboyer, M. (1980) The large corporation in modern France, in *Managerial Hierarchies: Comparative Perspectives on the Rise of the Modern Industrial Enterprise,* Chandler Jr, A.D. and Daems, H. (eds), Harvard University Press: Cambridge, MA.

Licht, A.N. (2001) The Mother of all Path Dependencies: Toward a Cross Cultural Theory of Corporate Governance Systems, *Delaware Journal of Corporate Law*, **26** (1), 147–205.

Markarian, G., Parbonetti, A. and Previts, G.J. (2007) The Convergence of Disclosure and Governance Practices in the World's Largest Firms, *Corporate Governance: An International Review*, **15** (2), 294–310.

Martynova, M. and Renneboog, L.D.R. (2010) *A Corporate Governance Index: Convergence and Diversity of National Corporate Governance Regulations*, Discussion Paper 2010-012, Tilburg University, Tilburg Law and Economic Center.

McCahery, J.A., Moerland, P., Raaij, T. Makers and

Renneborg, L. (eds) (2002) *Corporate Governance Regimes: Convergence and Diversity*, Oxford University Press: Oxford.

Meyer, P. (1998) Board Stock Ownership: More, and more again, *Directors & Boards*, **22** (2), 55–61.

Mitchell, R.K., Agle, B.R. and Wood, D.J. (1997) Toward a Theory of Stakeholder Identification and Salience: Defining the Principle of Who and What Really Counts, *Academy of Management Review*, **22** (4), 853–886.

Monks, R.A.G and Minow, N. (2001) *Corporate Governance*, 2nd edition, Wiley-Blackwell: Chichester.

Monks, R.A.G. and Minow, N. (2008) *Corporate Governance*, 4th Edition, Wiley-Blackwell: Chichester.

Morck, R., Shleifer, A. and Vishny, R. (1988) Management Ownership and Firm Value: An Empirical Analysis, *Journal of Financial Economics*, **20** (1), 293–315.

Most, B.W. (2002) Socially Responsible Investing: An Imperfect World for Planners and Clients, *Journal of Financial Planning*, **15** (2), 48–55.

Murphy, K.J. (1999) Executive Compensation, in *Handbook of Labor Economics*, Ashenfelter, O. and Card, D. (eds) Vol. 3, Part 2, Elsevier: Amsterdam.

Myers, S.C. and Majluf, N.S. (1984) Corporate Financing and Investment Decisions When Firms Have Information That Investors Do Not Have, *Journal of Financial Economics*, **13** (2), 187–222.

New York Stock Exchange Corporate Accountability and Listing Standards Committee (2002), Report submitted to the NYSE's Board of Directors, June 6, 2002.

North, D.C. (1991) Institutions, *Journal of Economic Perspectives*, **5** (1), 97–112.

Oxelheim, L. (1998) Regulations, Institutions and Corporate Efforts – The Nordic Environment, in Oxelheim, L. et al. (eds), *Corporate Strategies to Internationalise the Cost of Capital*, Copenhagen Business School Press: Copenhagen.

Pagano, M. and Volpin, P. (2005) The Political Economy of Corporate Governance, *American Economic Review*, **95** (4), 1005–1030.

Pedersen, T. and Thomsen, S. (1997) European Patterns of Corporate Ownership, *Journal of International Business Studies*, **28** (4), 759–778.

Pedersen, T. and Thomsen, S. (1999) Economic and Systemic Explanations of Ownership Concentration among Europe's Largest Companies, *International Journal of the Economics of Business*, **6** (3), 367–381.

Poppo, L., and Zenger, T. (2002) Do Formal Contracts and Relational Governance Function as Substitutes or Complements? *Strategic Management Journal*, **23** (8), 707–726.

Prowse, S. (1995) Corporate Governance in an International Perspective: A Survey of Corporate Control Mechanism among Large Firms in the U.S., U.K., Japan and Germany, *Financial Markets, Institutions & Instruments*, **4** (1), 1–63.

Roe, M.J. (1991) A Political Theory of Corporate Finance, *Columbia Law Review*, **91** (1), 10–67.

Roe, M.J. (1994a) Some Differences in Corporate

Governance in Germany, Japan and America, in *Institutional Investors and Corporate Governance*, Baums,T., Boxhaul, T. and Hop, K.J. (eds) Walter De Gruyter & Co.: Berlin.

Roe, M.J. (1994b) *Strong Managers, Weak Owners: The Political Roots of American Corporate Finance*, Princeton University Press: Princeton, NJ.

Roe, M.J. (2001) The Shareholder Wealth Maximization Norm and Industrial Organization, *University of Pennsylvania Law Review*, **149** (6), 2063–2082.

Shleifer, A. and Vishny, R.W. (1986) Large Shareholders and Corporate Control, *Journal of Political Economy*, **94** (3), 461–488.

Shleifer, A. and Vishny, R.W. (1997) A Survey of Corporate Governance, *Journal of Finance*, **52** (2), 737–783.

Short, H. (1994) Ownership, Control, Financial Structure and the Performance of Firms, *Journal of Economic Surveys*, **8** (3), 203–249.

Tadelis, S. (1999) What's in a Name? Reputation as a Tradable Asset, *American Economic Review*, **89** (3), 548–563.

The Economist (1999) Finance and economics: The wall falls, **353** (8143), 79–81.

The Economist (2000) Europe's New Capitalism: Bidding for the Future, **354** (8157), 71–74.

Thomsen, S. (2001) Convergence Goes Both Ways: An Alternative Perspective on the Convergence of Corporate Governance Systems, in *The Internationalisation of Companies and Company Laws*, M. Neville and K.E. Sørensen (eds), DJØF, Copenhagen.

Thomsen, S. (2003) The convergence of corporate governance systems to European and Anglo-American standards, *European Business Organization Law Review*, **4** (1), 31–50.

Thomsen, S. and Pedersen, T. (1998) Industry and Ownership Structure, *International Review of Law and Economics*, **18** (4), 385–402.

Thomsen, S. and Pedersen, T. (2000) Ownership Structure and Economic Performance in the Largest European Companies, *Strategic Management Journal*, **21** (6), 689–705.

Thomsen, S. and Pedersen, T. (2003) Ownership Structure and Value of the Largest European Firms: The Importance of Owner Identity, *Journal of Management and Governance*, **7**(1), 27–55.

Vives, X. (2000) Corporate Governance: Does It Matter? in *Corporate Governance: Theoretical and Empirical Perspectives*, Vives, X. (ed.) Cambridge University Press: Cambridge, UK.

Vives, X. (2006) *Corporate Governance: Theoretical and Empirical Perspectives*, Cambridge University Press: Cambridge, UK.

Warner, J. (1998) Buyback Fever Hits Europe; Continental Companies are Snapping up their Shares, *Business Week*, **3577**, 46.

Watts R. and Zimmerman, J. (1978) Towards a Positive Theory of the Determination of Accounting Standards, *Accounting Review*, **53** (1), 112–134.

Watts, R. L. and Zimmerman, J. (1979) The demand for and supply of accounting theory: the market for excuses, *The Accounting Review*, **54** (2), 273–305.

Watts R. and Zimmerman, J. (1983) Agency Problems, Auditing, and the Theory of the Firm: Some Evidence, *Journal of Law and Economics*, **26** (3), 613–633.

Watts R. and Zimmerman, J. (1986) *Positive Accounting Theory*, Prentice Hall: Englewood Cliffs, NJ.

Watts R. and Zimmerman, J. (1990) Positive Accounting Theory: A Ten Year Perspective, *Accounting Review*, **65** (1), 131–156.

Womack, K., (1996) Do Brokerage Analysts' Recommendations have Investment Value?, *Journal of Finance*, **51** (1), 137–167.

The World Bank (2010). Corporate Governance Indicators. http://info.worldbank.org/governance/wgi/index.asp

Yoshikawa, T. and Rasheed, A.A. (2009) Convergence of Corporate Governance: Critical Review and Future Directions, *Corporate Governance: An International Review*, **17** (3), 388–404.

Zeckhouser, R., and Pound, J. (1990) Are Large Shareholders Effective Monitors? An Investigation of Share Ownership and Corporate Performance, in *Asymmetric Information, Corporate Finance and Investment*, G.R. Hubbard (ed), Chicago University Press.

PART **2**

Mechanisms

Part contents

Chapter 5

Informal Governance

Chapter contents

5.1 Introduction

Most corporate governance is focused on formal governance mechanisms like law, ownership or boards. But these mechanisms are only the tip of the iceberg as we try to illustrate in Figure 5.1. If everybody was trying to cheat all the time, it would be impossible or at least extremely costly to do business or have any kind of corporate governance. Countries without a basic level of social capital cannot have good governance despite formal institutions like boards, courts or company law. In this chapter we address the (90%) of behaviour which is regulated by informal governance: social norms, ethics, reputation, codes and other soft mechanisms.

We begin by discussing social norms: informal rules which regulate behaviour in a society or one of its many subgroups. These rules influence governance because the nature of the relevant agency problems differs from country to country as well as over time. Even if companies cannot influence social norms, they can be realistic and take them into consideration which should help reduce the costs. For example they can adapt their governance structures to a country context, or they may be able to select managers with attractive social norms.

Companies can also try to cultivate ethical codes which set them aside from other companies. In other words, business ethics can be part of corporate governance. We show how such codes can make sense both for society and individual firms, if they address issues which competition and regulation fail to cope with, and which the company is especially capable of handling.

We go on to examine reputation as a governance mechanism. Bad performance and lack of responsibility will spill over to a bad reputation that will make it more costly for the company to do business and therefore reduce profits in the long run. A bad reputation will also influence the social status of CEOs and other managers, and this is an added incentive to improve.

Finally we examine voluntary corporate governance codes which have become very important in recent decades. We show that most corporate governance codes are tailored to address the demands of institutional investors.

5.2 Social norms

Social norms are behavioural rules founded on a shared understanding about what actions are obligatory, permitted or forbidden (Ostrom, 2000). For example social norms may compel managers in some cultures to be honest, to work hard and to be loyal to their superiors. At the same time social

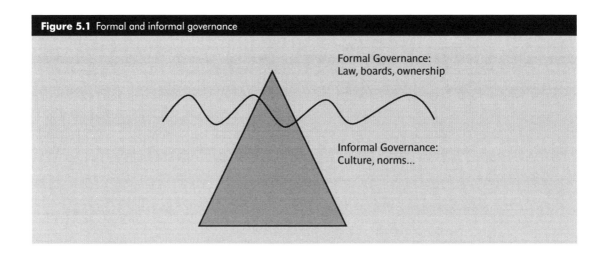

Figure 5.1 Formal and informal governance

norms may or may not allow them to bargain for the highest possible pay. Finally social norms may forbid them from taking or receiving bribes, or from working on Sundays.

We know from evolutionary psychology that human beings have an inherited propensity to learn social norms (Ostrom, 2000). Humans emerged originally as small bands of hunter-gathers whose survival depended on their ability to cooperate and resolve collective action problems in hunting and food provision, security and child-raising. So the ability to form social norms is in our genes. The basic norms and attitudes are probably formed by socialization in childhood and have to be taken for granted in corporate governance, but companies can also to some extent influence their employees and stakeholders through their policies. Conservative companies have been ridiculed for seeking to recruit employees with a good family background and to recruit them early so that they could be moulded. But this is precisely a way for companies to recognize the importance of social norms.

In principle all governance problems could be handled if people had only internalized the right social norms, which would require them to do just what is needed in a specific situation. This may be feasible in a traditional society of hunter-gathers where people are constantly facing the same problems. But there are also costs to governance by norms, particularly in a dynamic society. Technical change and economic growth require that behaviour is flexible and that people interact not just with their own small group but also in a large society where economic agents do not know each other and may disagree about what norms to apply. Finally, economic incentives remain important so that investments in monitoring and sanctioning (i.e. governance) are necessary for solutions that are sustainable in the long run.

Game theory (and particularly the prisoners' dilemma game described briefly in Chapter 3) provides a convenient theoretical framework for analysing these issues (Hardin, 1971) once it is recognized that governance systems must deal with individuals of different types, e.g. egotists vs. co-operators, which are likely to coexist in any given population. It is obviously an exaggeration to distinguish only between 'good guys' and 'bad guys' since people can behave quite differently in different roles, for example in their private and social life. Moreover people can change over time. But it is a start.

Applied to corporate governance, social norms like honesty, fairness and modesty go a long way towards addressing agency problems. Shareholders can trust 'decent' managers not to waste their money and to give them a return on their investment. 'My word is my bond.'

However, it is well known that social norms work better in small communities where the identities, histories and behaviour of the members are known by all. So all else being equal we will predict that governance by social norms will tend to break down in large stock markets where many issuers and shareholders interact. In such markets we need securities laws and other mechanisms, although social norms continue to play a role.

Another problem is the end game paradox. If the number of games is finite, the players lose their incentive to behave well and if it is known that cooperation will cease in the last game, they have no incentive to cooperate in the second to last game and so on until the entire game unravels. For example, if companies do not need to attract funds from the stock market late in their life cycle, they have no incentive to pay dividends, but if they have no incentive to pay dividends or please investors in other ways, investors may prefer not to invest, and the market breaks down. There are many examples of small communities and small stock exchanges where cooperation appears to have broken down and there is little new investment.

A third problem is the uncertainty which is at the heart of the agency problem. If financial results and stock prices drop because of some complex external event (such as perhaps the 2008 financial crisis), shareholders may lose faith in the market even if managers were in fact well behaved. Again, formal law may be necessary to re-establish investor confidence. It is interesting for example that a three-year slide in the US stock market was halted just after the draconian Sarbanes–Oxley law was passed in 2002.

So when will social norms work? The Nobel Laureate Elinor Ostrom's design principles for long-lived self-organized resource systems can function as an inspiration for when and how corporate governance can rely on social norms (Table 5.1).

Table 5.1 Design principles for self-organized resource systems

1. Clear boundary rules: who does and who does not belong to the organization/community
2. Fair resource allocation (or agents will leave)
3. Participants must be able to participate in influencing the rules – they cannot be dictated top-down
4. The rules must be enforced by (or accountable to) the participants who practise them
5. Sanctions must be graduated, i.e. mild at first then more severe (e.g. exclusion)
6. There must be a forum for rapid, low-cost resolution of conflict

One particularly important aspect of governance by norms is that it cannot take place top-down. For example managers can decree that a corporate culture has now changed to fit the most recent management fashion, but this will only influence behaviour to the extent that employees endorse the new values. Neither can they change the company's reputation by an advertising campaign. In contrast, Ostrom emphasizes government standardization, technology change and failure to transmit norms as some of the most important obstacles for governance by social norms.

In governance terms an ethical code is a governance mechanism which serves the same purpose as others: to coordinate economic activity. The market or price mechanism is another institution. So is (hierarchical) coordination by way of authority which takes place between bosses and their subordinates in most organizations.

Different mechanisms governing the supply of blood provide an illustration of social norms as an economic governance mechanism, what economists call an 'institution' (Titmuss, 1971; Arrow, 1972; Institute of Economic Affairs, 1973). A supply of blood can be obtained from voluntary donors (as often in the UK), it can be bought on the market (often in the USA), soldiers can be ordered to give blood, it can even be taken from prisoners (as is known to be the case in some military dictatorships). In principle, a blood firm could even be started in which an entrepreneur employed people with particularly excellent blood vessels (although this would probably be impractical for both medical and economic reasons).

Each of these institutions provides a mechanism which brings about a desired outcome: donors are presumably motivated by good feelings, social status, etc., sellers are paid according to the quantity supplied, employed blood-givers would be paid a fixed salary per month, soldiers and prisoners obey for fear of punishment.

Institutional economics predicts that non-market governance mechanisms will arise under conditions of market failure: '… when the market fails to achieve an optimal state, society will, to some extent at least, recognize the gap and non-market institutions will arise attempting to bridge it' (Arrow, 1963, p. 21). Market failure arguments can motivate government intervention in the markets, but also other types of non-market institutions:

> *Certainly, the government, at least in its economic activities, is usually implicitly or explicitly held to function as the agency which substitutes for the market's failure. I am arguing here that in some circumstances other social institutions will step into the optimality gap.*[1]

As an illustration of this principle, Arrow (1963) argued that a medical ethic among doctors is a way to overcome failures in the market for medical services due to information asymmetries between doctors and patients. Because patients generally lack information about the nature of their illness and effectiveness of alternative treatments, doctors could manipulate them in their own interest. A medical ethic among doctors enforced by powerful collective sanctions helps to

---

[1] Arrow, 1963, p. 22.

overcome this problem (Arrow, 1973, p. 139). Arguably, this medical ethic would not have been necessary had the prevailing social ethic been strong enough to prevent opportunistic behaviour from occurring among all citizens (doctors included). And to the extent that all doctors are motivated by a medical ethic it is not necessary for individual hospitals to introduce their own ethical codes.

The general implication is that there will be a rationale for ethical codes when alternative governance mechanisms (pure markets, hierarchies, government, social norms …) fail to achieve a social optimum. For example, an ethical business code encouraging all employees to give blood once a year would increase social welfare to the extent that an adequate blood supply is neither generated by market forces nor the political system or by voluntary action.

Can ethics fail? The answer is yes. A social norm can be unethical if it blocks economic and social progress. Obviously this does not mean that ethics in general is unethical (a viewpoint which was explicitly voiced by Nietzsche). For example, as emphasized by Schumpeter and Max Weber, capitalism itself is founded on a set of ethical principles (rationalism, hard work, saving). But it can be argued that social ethical standards will tend to be too conservative. For example, this seems to be a natural interpretation of the influential line of research in game theory that models ethics (cooperation) as the outcome of repeated games of the prisoners' dilemma type among selfish individuals (Hausman and McPherson, 1993; Binmore, 1994). If so, this will have detrimental direct effects on behaviour as well as spill-over effects on policies and markets.

In conclusion, failures in the prevailing social ethic combined with other governance failures create an important governance role for business ethics.

5.3   Business ethics as corporate governance

Assuming that problems of a general and recurrent nature are handled by government intervention or by the general social ethic, ethical codes should mainly be concerned with firm-specific issues which the firm is in a unique position to solve. This is consistent with the resource-based view of the firm which sees firm-specific resources and as the fundamental rationale for the existence of firms (Wernerfelt, 1984; Collis and Montgomery, 1997). A prime example of such assets is firm-specific information (core competencies etc.). Firm-specific resources can create economic profits and give the firm a certain freedom of action which is absent in perfectly competitive markets that presumably force firms to apply a common set of market-determined standards. For the same reason, firms which have access to proprietary information can afford to take ethical considerations into account.

One way to incorporate this into ethical management is for the individual firm to distinguish between general ethical codes to which it must adhere and firm-specific codes in areas on which it has superior information. The general codes should reflect the firm's perception of universal values in business (e.g. the work ethic, honesty and rationality, believed by Weber to be the ethical foundations of capitalism). In contrast, firm-specific codes may sometimes differ from the ethical views held by the rest of society. A biotechnology firm experimenting with technology and products which are uncharted territory for the general public carries a special responsibility both for safety and product standards and an obligation to overcome social resistance (including ethical criticism) from the establishment. In a change-resistant environment the social interest may be served by the nurture of ethical codes which differ from the prevailing social ethic.

In conclusion, there is a clear rationale for ethical codes in institutional economics. But are they privately optimal for the firm? Are they consistent with profit maximization? If ethical codes increase the welfare obtainable in the business, this creates a source of potential profits for the ethically constrained firm which is not available to the pure profit maximizers and which may outweigh the expected losses due to ethical constraints. In game theory terms, ethical codes are an example of commitment to a certain range of actions and the *value of tying one's hands* has been analysed extensively (for example by Schelling, 1960). Tirole (1988) uses the following example:

"*An oft-quoted example is that of two armies who wish to occupy an island situated between both countries and which is connected to each country by a bridge. Each army prefers to let its opponents have the island by fighting. Army 1, which is somewhat knowledgeable in game theory, occupies the island and burns the bridge behind it. Army 2, then, has no option other than to let Army 1 have the island, because it knows that Army 1 has no choice other than to fight back if Army 2 attacks. This is the paradox of commitment: Army 1 does better by reducing its set of choices.*"

In the same way, firms can benefit by reducing their set of choices. For example, a manufacturer of computers can commit itself to give after-sales service free of charge and to hold on to such a commitment even in the event that production of computers will prove unprofitable and will be shut down at a later date. It may be profitable *ex ante* to make this commitment binding because this will make customers more likely to buy the computer and reduce the probability that production will be unprofitable and thus have to be shut down. An ethical code can have the same function and may thereby increase both profits and social welfare, but to make the scheme work, it is necessary that the firm *burns its bridges* and commits to ethical behaviour even in the event that this should *ex post* prove to be suboptimal from the company's viewpoint.

Ethical behaviour may also be optimal from a selfish viewpoint in a sequence of repeated games (Schotter, 1981; Binmore, 1994) in which the stakeholders of a firm get to know each other over time, and where selfish behaviour may be optimal in the short run, but will be punished in subsequent games, and is therefore discouraged. As indicated in the previous discussion, this may be an argument for ethical standards in general more than for business ethics. But if the firm is perceived to be at the beginning of a repeated game, it may have an incentive to commit to a strong code of ethics. We discuss the role of reputation shortly.

A strong corporate culture or a mission which can motivate employees to make an effort beyond what is immediately selfish are among the important examples of the economic value of commitment (which may arise in prisoners' dilemma games and a number of other games, see Hausman and MacPherson, 1993). Studies by Chen, Sawyers and Williams (1997) and Nwachukwu and Vitell (1997) confirm that corporate cultures can support firm-specific ethical codes. In the theory of clans (Ouchi, 1980; Ouchi and Price, 1993; Alvesson and Lindkvist, 1993), common values are regarded as an optimal organizational form in unstable environments where there is uncertainty with regard to both means and objectives: for example, in product development where there is uncertainty both about the expected results and the best way to structure the work effort. If socially optimal ethical codes support strong corporate value systems, this may provide an additional argument for their consistency with profit maximization.

In spite of these economic incentives to adopt ethical business codes which are both privately and socially optimal it seems unreasonable to assume that economic forces will always lead to optimality. Access to unique resources may be considered to be a monopoly advantage which the unregulated, uncensored, profit-maximizing firm has an obvious incentive to exploit with as few constraints as possible. It can therefore be argued that the firm privileged by ownership of specific resources also carries a special responsibility to use those resources in an ethical way.

Even though it may be advantageous for the firm to a priori commit to certain values, there are also costs: for example the risk that the world may change so that these values are no longer ethically or commercially viable. The decision to commit to an ethical code can thus be understood as an irreversible investment decision under uncertainty in which the firm chooses to forsake certain future options, and the cost can therefore in principle be measured by real asset option theory (Dixit and Pindyck, 1994). Giving up flexibility by committing to ethical codes is equivalent to giving away put options, the opportunity costs of which are in principle given by their market value which will increase with uncertainty facing the business. For a profit-maximizing company to incur these costs, there must be offsetting benefits (i.e. a value as well as a cost of commitment).

A profit-maximizing firm may find it difficult to commit irreversibly to an ethical code. A standard objection to introducing non-profit objectives in company decision making is that the markets for corporate control will eliminate managers who do not pursue value-maximization strategies (e.g. Ehrhardt, 1995). Shleifer and Summers (1988) argue that the source of value gains from mergers and acquisitions is a breach of implicit contracts, mainly with employees. Suppose, for example, that a company commits itself to long-term employment policies to encourage its employees to invest in human capital dedicated to that particular firm. But what is to prevent takeovers and renegotiation of these implicit contracts in bad times? And if the firm cannot credibly commit itself, will the employees not recognize this and refuse to make the necessary investments in human capital *ex ante*? Dilemmas like this imply a close connection between businesses ethics and corporate governance. The value of ethical commitments which do not reflect the preferences of company owners is open to doubt. And, if ownership is to function as a basis for long-term ethical commitments, a certain degree of stability and accountability is necessary as well. It may not be impossible, for instance, to ensure loyalty to standard ethical codes among institutional investors, but the sustainability of this commitment is open to doubt if the same investors do not commit to a minimum holding period. In contrast to the Anglo-American corporate governance model, more long-term commitment may be found in Japanese or German models (e.g. Charkham, 1994) which tend to have a much higher degree of ownership concentration and longer holding periods.

There is no doubt, however, that it will be in the interest of the profit-maximizing firm to signal a commitment to ethical values if signalling costs are small and if this is perceived to have a positive financial effect (Harrington, 1989; Frank, 1989). An implication is that business managers will find it in their interest to mimic ethical behaviour to the extent that the public cannot distinguish between honesty and dishonesty. The plethora of ethical business codes with unclear empirical content (small signalling costs) provide circumstantial evidence of this.

5.4 Reputation and governance

A growing body of research (e.g. Franks, Mayer and Rossi, 2004; Coffee, 2001; Rajan and Zingales, 2002) has highlighted the role of trust and reputation as informal governance mechanisms. In this section we analyse the role of reputation and status in corporate governance based on previous research (Kreps, 1990; Bernheim, 1994; Weiss and Fershtman, 1998; Akerlof and Kranton, 2005).

Franks, Meyer and Rossi (2004) find that the British stock market historically flourished without formal investor protection, but very much based on trust in smaller, local stock exchanges. Coffee (2001) argues that trust can substitute formal law as a governance mechanism to protect minority investors in the Scandinavian countries, which are small tightly networked societies. Dyck and Zingales (2002) propose that media exposure may in itself be an important governance mechanism, partly because bad performance may damage the reputation of managers and board members.

This view can draw on a growing body of research on the economics of status and reputation, including Kreps (1990), Prendergast (2003), and Akerlof and Kranton (2005). For reviews see Weiss and Fershtman (1998) or Akerlof and Kranton (2005). The basic theme in this literature is that social rewards (like status) may be a valuable substitute for purely economic incentives because they can help address market failures (e.g. externalities).

Following Kreps (1990) companies can overcome prisoners' dilemma games with other market participants (buyers, sellers, employees and investors) by investing in reputation through consistently honest and fair behaviour. Under uncertainty this reputation can be a valuable asset because it influences consumers, employees and investors to do business with the firm. For example, employee and customer loyalty can translate into lower cost and higher profit. A good brand name makes it easier to attract customers, which saves marketing costs. Being regarded as a blue chip stock by investors can lower the costs of capital.

If managers and board members care about their reputation, and if their personal reputation is influenced by the company's reputation (Dyck and Zingales, 2002), the risk of losing a good reputation may serve as a governance mechanism which induces managers and board members to be efficient. Such mechanisms may be particularly strong in small societies with dense social networks such as the Scandinavian countries (Coffee, 2001). Johnson, Young and Welker (1993) found that the personal reputation of CEOs as rated by financial analysts was sensitive to both stock returns and changes in accounting profitability (489 firms, 896 CEOs, 1975–1987, 5528 firm years). The personal reputation of the CEO is also likely to influence her pay. Milbourn (2003) finds that proxies for CEO reputation (including favourable press coverage) positively influence pay for performance elasticity. Personal reputation may also influence the career prospects of CEOs and board members (Fama, 1980).

Aside from monetary benefits, individual managers and board members may care about their own and the company's reputation for intrinsic reasons. A growing literature has emphasized that individuals are concerned about their status and may identify with the companies that they work for (Akerlof and Kranton, 2005). Bernheim (1994) explicitly models the desire for social esteem as a driving force for individual behaviour.

In accordance with this literature we propose that reputation is a relatively simple alternative corporate governance mechanism. Companies that underperform damage their reputation and this spills over to the personal reputations of the top management team (management and supervisory boards). Bad personal reputation has a negative impact on their future careers (e.g. eligibility for new jobs or board positions), but more importantly it has a strong and direct negative effect on their personal utility. Like academic economists, who are believed to be motivated primarily by the recognition of their peers, experienced business people care strongly about their professional reputation. Following Akerlof and Kranton (2005) the top management team comes to identify with the company that they manage. In contrast to altruism, status-seeking is motivated not by feelings for other people, but by what other people feel about the status-seeker (Bernheim, 1994). This implies that status is a more powerful disciplining device for managers and board members of large, visible companies which attract more public attention. Greater transparency is also likely to make reputation and status concerns a more effective solution to agency problems.

5.5   Corporate governance codes[2]

Corporate governance codes are an example of soft law. They are sets of recommendations on good corporate governance, primarily concerning the structure, organization and decision processes of the board, but also to some extent dealing with executive pay, information disclosure and investor relations. The codes are most often written by committees composed of influential business people at the initiative of a government organization. Most codes are voluntary on a 'comply or explain' basis in the sense that companies may deviate from the recommendations but need to explain why they do so. They are not law, but they can be regarded as 'soft law', particularly since compliance rates tend to be high (e.g. Laing and Weir, 1999; Rayton and Cheng, 2004). Rayton and Cheng (2004) find that 98.9% of 402 large listed UK firms have an audit committee and that the same proportion have remuneration committees.

Codes of best practice are found in many other areas: for example, in the form of ethical, professional and technical guidelines (Héritier, 2002). Theoretically, they are a special kind of social institution (Arrow, 1969, 1973; Schotter, 1981; Thomsen, 2001) that can increase overall welfare if they contribute to the solution of market failures that are not adequately addressed by other means (e.g. law or private regulation) and if the costs of writing and enforcing the code do not exceed the benefits (Thomsen, 2001).

The question is: which market failure are corporate governance codes supposed to address? This is not an easy question to answer since the code writers are often not explicit about the nature of the problem and they certainly do not cloak their discussions in economic vocabulary. Moreover, the relationship between company law and corporate governance codes is often unclear. For instance, codes will occasionally make recommendations that are already included in the law.

---

[2] This section draws on Thomsen (2003).

Nevertheless, corporate governance codes appear to be concerned with the same themes, for example, transparency, the role of the board, investor protection, fraud avoidance, or how to provide a favourable investment climate to attract international capital. Using the analogy of consumer protection, it appears that the codes are regarded as a solution to asymmetric information problems between investors and companies, i.e. the principal–agent problem (Ross, 1973; Jensen and Meckling, 1976; MacNeil and Li, 2006). Firms, or their managers, clearly know much more than investors know about the firm and how it is run. It is well known that information problems of this kind can lead to an undersupply of capital and that these problems can, to some extent, be overcome by regulation and information provision. For example, government regulation may require that the cocoa content in products labelled 'chocolate' is no less than $x\%$ and that the cocoa content of a chocolate bar must be disclosed on the package. The problem here is that consumers know much less about the true quality of the product and, therefore, cannot make informed decisions. Moreover, producers have an incentive to cut costs and lower quality because this will not affect the price that they can charge to the ignorant consumers.

In the same way, adherence to a corporate governance code appears to be regarded as a guarantee that certain standards of good governance are met. Investors can then invest with greater confidence knowing that these standards are met. Instead of consumer protection, the codes provide investor protection (Cuervo, 2002; Aguilera and Cuervo-Cazurra, 2004).

There are several reasons why this kind of quality assurance would appeal to shareholders. Some, the 'widows and orphans' type, clearly do not have the intellectual ability or inclination to undertake it on their own. Others, like institutional investors, want to (and are obliged to) diversify their portfolio over a large number of shares and can save on information costs if they know that all companies meet the specified standards. It is well known that many institutional investors index their portfolio and do not invest much in information collection or bother to vote at shareholder meetings (Zeikel, 1978; Cuthbert and Dobbins, 1980; Rudd, 1986; Woolley and Bird, 2003; Clearfield, 2005). Some may want to invest in stocks in faraway countries about which they know little and would be assured by minimum standards (Aguilera and Cuervo-Cazurra, 2004).

One concern with this hypothesis is that the principal–agent problem is hardly new. It has existed at least as long as the joint stock company itself. The codes, however, are a fairly new occurrence within the past two decades or so. The main difference between now and then appears to be that the composition of shareholders has changed from individuals to institutions. Institutions hold larger blocks of shares than individuals and thus may have more of an effect on stock prices. Even more importantly, unlike individuals, they tend to hold a large total number of shares in many companies and so they are able to influence stock exchanges and policymakers. The corporate governance agenda is therefore to a large extent created and shaped by institutional shareholders. The massive build-up of capital in pension funds (Becht et al., 2003) clearly makes them attractive as a source of funding and creates incentives for companies, governments and exchanges to cater to their needs.

The hypothesis that corporate governance codes reflect rent seeking by institutional investors can explain a number of the 'code puzzles'.

1 *The mismatch with existing research*. Researchers have generally been concerned with the overall performance of firms, but corporate governance codes may have the more limited concern of representing the interests of institutional investors. Thus it is perhaps less surprising that empirical studies have not found any systematic effect of compliance on overall corporate performance (e.g. Laing and Weir, 1999).
2 *The specificity of the recommendations*, for example, in terms of minimum levels of independent board members defined in a particular way, is a puzzle given that the code writers do not know the specific circumstances of the companies they address. But from the viewpoint of institutional investors, who tend to hold shares in hundreds of companies, the specificity makes sense because it makes the codes easy to monitor.
3 *The focus on listed companies* is understandable given that this is where the bulk of the share investments by institutional investors takes place. The same investors are increasingly

involved in private equity, but they have not been pushing for transparency or independence in this area, where they tend to take much larger stakes and they tend to have more direct influence.

4 ***The advent of corporate governance codes in the 1990s*** is understandable given the increasing weight and continued massive increase in institutional savings in this period. It is also no surprise that the corporate governance agenda was first launched in the United States and the United Kingdom, where pension funds began to grow earlier than in most other countries around the world.

5 ***'One size fits all'*** is no longer a puzzle if one takes into consideration the demand side. While firms are very different, institutional investors around the world are relatively similar. They provide the same standard commodity to their customers using more or less the same financial techniques: in particular, portfolio diversification. The one big difference that does emerge from current research is between private and political pension funds (Woidtke, 2002). Private pension funds which also cater to corporate customers are generally much more discrete and pragmatic in advocating the corporate governance agenda. In contrast, political pension funds, like TIAA-CREF or CalPERS, with strong ties to unions or governments are generally much more outspoken.

6 ***The strong international similarities*** in corporate governance codes are a puzzle considering the large international differences in corporate governance. Why should the codes, relatively speaking, be so similar? Again, one important reason is that while countries are very different, institutional investors are relatively similar across the world. Another reason, of course, is competition for capital in an international market for shares in which UK and US institutions are still very large players.

7 ***The contents of the codes***, for example the focus on independence, is paradoxical given that so many other factors like competencies or personalities may be more important. But such factors are vague and difficult to monitor, and institutional investors have instead been demanding increases in board member independence and corporate transparency. For example, many codes around the world now demand that a majority of board members must be independent of both managers and the majority owners, with whom institutional investors compete for corporate control.

8 ***The focus on firms*** rather than, for example, investors, seems to be another example. With few exceptions, existing corporate governance codes focus on what companies and their boards can do to improve corporate governance, while the role of the investors is played down or ignored altogether. Only recently have stewardship codes for investors emerged. If codes are intended to cater to institutional investors, it is understandable that they mainly concern what companies can do for the investors rather than vice versa.

9 ***The choice of soft rather than hard law*** may be a matter of expediency from the viewpoint of investors as well as companies. Laws take time to change and policymakers may demand an overall social rationale for adopting them. This could mean that the powerful actors may prefer to exercise their influence directly.

While the codes tend to be similar across the world, they are not identical. National codes generally attempt to take into consideration country-specific characteristics like board structure (one- or two-tier), employee representation, takeover legislation, and so forth. In public choice terms, they may therefore be regarded as a negotiated compromise between existing stakeholders (e.g., incumbent owners, banks, labour unions, etc.) and the institutional investors. For example, it can be hypothesized that the contents of national corporate governance codes would reflect the relative bargaining power of the institutional investors in different countries.

It is noticeable that the growth of institutional investment since the 1990s coincided with the deregulation and internationalization of stock markets (e.g. Thomsen, 2003). Internationalization may have altered the nature of the bargaining game, since it may now be more difficult for incumbent stakeholders (owners, labour unions and national governments) to capture domestic institutions and/or to enter into implicit contracts with them. Moreover, given the size and turnover of US/UK

stock markets, it is understandable that US/UK standards should to some extent be exported to other countries (Thomsen, 2003).

Institutional investors have natural allies in their bargaining game with the incumbent stakeholders. For example, auditing firms are not generally opposed to transparency and disclosure, which generates new business for them. Consulting and search firms tend to promote professional non-executive directors, partly perhaps because some of them earn their living by recruiting. Stock exchanges, investment banks and stockbrokers compete internationally for business and governments also desire large national capital markets. In contrast, incumbent owners (e.g. founding families), employer organizations, employees, and to some extent banks may tend to be opposed to the interests of the institutional investors.

There has not been much previous research on the contents of corporate governance codes. However, Thomsen (2003) examines 52 national corporate governance codes gathered from a range of countries around the world. Subjecting these codes to a statistical analysis (principal components analysis) reveals a remarkable homogeneity. Ninety-five per cent of the variance is common and can therefore be attributed to a single factor or component. In other words, it is a good first assumption that codes are much alike (and do not display much country-specific variation). Table 5.2 examines 52 national corporate governance codes gathered from a range of countries around the world.[3] Most

Table 5.2 Summary statistics of 52 international corporate governance codes

Code provision/Code characteristic	Percentage of codes
Authorized by government/stock exchange	65.4
Applies only to listed firms	78.9
Mandatory 'comply or explain' recommendation	61.5
'One share – one vote' recommendation	21.2
Equal treatment of shareholders	73.1
Recommendation on pyramids	19.2
Recommendation on voting caps	21.2
Recommendation on shareholder agreements	13.5
Recommendation on the board of directors	98.1
Recommendation on monitoring role of the board	90.4
Recommendation on advisory role of the board	94.2
Recommendation on board size	15.4
Recommendation on independence of board members	94.2
Recommendation on independence of chairman	7.8
Total n = 52 codes	100

Source: The background data for this table was gathered by Morten Bennedsen, Copenhagen Business School (2004).

---

[3] Countries: the United Kingdom, the United States, Singapore, Greece, Portugal, Australia, Iceland, Thailand, Hong Kong, the Philippines, Malta, India, New Zealand, Mexico, Malaysia, China, Hungary, Canada, Pakistan, Cyprus, Spain, the Netherlands, Sweden, Belgium, Norway, France, Indonesia, Commonwealth countries, Russia, Romania, Italy, Lithuania, Macedonia, OECD, Kenya, Austria, Bangladesh, South Korea, Denmark, Germany, Poland, Slovenia, Peru, Turkey, Switzerland, Europe, Finland, Brazil, Latin America, Czech Republic, Slovakia, the world (ICGN).

of the codes are authorized by governmental organizations, for example, securities and exchange commissions, or by stock exchanges. While stock exchanges are generally organized as private institutions, they do to some extent produce a public good (and they are highly regulated). The rest of the codes are for the most part issued by professional associations. Some institutional investors, like CalPERS, publish their own corporate governance guidelines, but these are not included in the sample.

Generally the codes apply to listed firms only (78.9%), although 20% apply to all firms (listed or not). Admittedly, there are a few codes around the world that apply only to unlisted (e.g. small and medium-sized) companies, but the main focus is clearly on the listed ones.

More than 60% of the codes are adopted on a complete or partial 'comply or explain' basis, whereas the rest are merely recommendations.

As for the contents, almost all codes are concerned with boards (98%), board independence (94%), and the advisory (94%) or monitoring (90%) roles of the board. However, only very few (8%) go so far as to recommend independent board chairs.

In contrast to the many recommendations on board structure and practices, only a minority of the codes contain recommendations on ownership structure (dual class shares, pyramids, voting caps, or shareholder agreements). This is interesting since some outspoken investors like CalPERS explicitly advocate a 'one share–one vote' policy, which they associate with shareholder democracy. The one ownership issue that does gather general support is 'equal treatment of shareholders', which appears in 73% of the codes.

In summary, an analysis from the demand side (i.e. from the viewpoint of the institutional investors) can explain a number of characteristics of corporate governance codes, for example, the 'one size fits all' approach as well as the timing and diffusion of codes along with massive growth in institutional investment.

If corporate governance codes tend to reflect the preferences of institutional investors, this raises the question of their overall contribution to social welfare. There is nothing illegitimate *per se* about self-interest seeking. Given the increasing proportion of global savings, which is mediated by institutions, it is reasonable to be concerned with how this money can be put to good use.

It is not clear, however, that institutional investors are best suited to address all corporate governance problems. In fact, it can be argued that institutions are the source of rather than the solution to corporate governance problems because they are bound to prefer diversification of risk to monitoring and, thus, free ride on other market participants. There are indications that the costs of governance – including codes as well as other kinds of regulation – have become a serious problem for listed companies. Auditing and compliance costs have increased rapidly, and delistings have increased in both the United States and in Europe. An added concern is that increasing corporate governance bureaucracy at the top management level could have a detrimental effect on overall corporate performance and competitiveness.

5.6 Discussion

In this chapter we have examined four kinds of informal governance: social norms, business ethics, reputation and corporate governance codes. All these mechanisms can help reduce agency problems and thus contribute to corporate governance. It would be difficult to have any kind of corporate governance without them. However, they are also costly. Social norms can be too rigid. Business ethics can be just so much hot air. Reputation can be based on media populism rather than fact. Codes try to fit all companies to one size. As usual good corporate governance is all about matching governance mechanisms to the company and its situation.

Minicase

The Philips group

Philips is a large Dutch electronics company with 122,000 employees. It is a world leader in healthcare, lifestyle and lighting. Its shares are listed on Euronext and the New York Stock Exchange. The company is thus required to comply with the Dutch corporate governance rules, the US Sarbanes–Oxley Act and the New York Stock Exchange rules. The company is something of an icon in the Netherlands. Shaped by the Dutch business environment it has developed a strong interest in sustainability and social responsibility.

The executive management of Philips is entrusted to its management board of currently nine members chaired by the President/Chief Executive Officer. Executive board members and the CEO are elected by the shareholders on the recommendation of a supervisory board, which also ratifies all major decisions and supervises the company's operations and finances as well as its strategy and CSR issues.

In compliance with the Dutch corporate governance code, Philips has risk management and control systems in place, board committees, maximum term limits, disclosure of takeover defences, individual disclosure of executive pay, investor relations policies and so on. However, in some respects Philips is a management-controlled company. To protect the company from hostile takeover a foundation, Stichting Preferente Aandelen Philips, may call for the automatic issuance of as many preference shares as there are ordinary shares in the company outstanding at that time. The object of the Foundation is to represent the interests of the company and safeguard its autonomy and identity. The foundation board members are self-electing, but not members of the company board(s).

Philips' performance has been debated. The share price is, if anything, lower than it was 10 years ago. Average return on equity is around 3% over the 2008–2010 period. This could be seen as unsatisfactory but the same applies to many other mature European firms.

Sources:

Philips Corporate Governance Report

http://www.philips.com/shared/assets/Investor_relations/pdf/corporategovernance/CorporateGovernanceReport2010.pdf

Philips Financial Ethical code

http://www.philips.com/shared/assets/Investor_relations/pdf/businessprinciples/FinancialCodeofEthics_091112.pdf

Phillips Annual Report

http://www.phillips.com/newscenter

Dutch Corporate Governance Code

http://commissiecorporategovernance.nl/page/downloads/DEC_2008_UK_Code_DEF__uk_.pdf.

Discussion questions

1 How would you rate corporate governance at Philips as documented in its corporate governance report?
2 What role could ethical codes play in Philips' governance?
3 What do you think really drives governance at Philips?
4 How do you interpret the company's performance? As a sign of agency problems? Of adverse business conditions? Of stakeholder wealth maximization?

Summary (learning points)

- A large part of human activity is regulated informally rather than by formal governance arrangements.

- Social norms make people behave well (or less well) because they feel this is the right thing to do.

- Ethical business codes may in some cases lead to higher profits and benefit society, but it is not clear that companies use them in this way.

- Reputation also gives organizations and individuals an incentive to behave and thus contributes to the solution of agency problems.

- Corporate governance codes can also create value, but are strongly influenced by the interests of institutional investors.

References and further reading

Aguilera, R. and Cuervo-Cazurra, A. (2004) Codes of Good Governance Worldwide: What is the Trigger? *Organization Studies*, **25** (3), 415–443.

Aguilera, R. and Jackson, G. (2003) The cross-national diversity of corporate governance: Dimensions and determinants, *Academy of Management Review*, **28** (3), 447–465.

Akerlof, G.A. and Kranton, R.E (2005) Identity and the Economics of Organizations, *Journal of Economic Perspectives*, **19** (1), 9–32.

Alchian, A.A. (1950) Uncertainty, Evolution and Economic Theory, *Journal of Political Economy*, **58** (3), 211–221.

Alvesson, M. and Lindkvist, L. (1993) Transaction Costs, Clans and Corporate Culture, *Journal of Management Studies*, **30** (3), 427–452.

Anderson, E. (1990) The Ethical Limitations of The Market, *Economics and Philosophy*, **6** (2), 179–205.

Arrow, K.J. (1963) Uncertainty and the Welfare Economics of Medical Care, *American Economic Review*, **53** (5), 941–973, reprinted in *Collected Papers of Kenneth Arrow*.

Arrow, K.J. (1969) The Organization of Economic Activity, in Arrow K.J., *General Equilibrium, Collected Papers of Kenneth Arrow*, Vol. 2 (1983), Basil Blackwell.

Arrow, K.J. (1972) Gifts and Exchanges, *Philosophy and Public Affairs*, **1** (4), 343–362.

Arrow, K.J. (1973) Social Responsibility and Economic Efficiency, *Public Policy*, **21**, 303–318, Reprinted in *Collected Papers of Kenneth Arrow*, Vol. 6 (1985).

Arrow, K.J. (1974) *The Limits of Organization*, W.W. Norton & Co.

Arrow, K.J. (1997) Invaluable Goods, *Journal of Economic Literature*, **35** (2), 757–765.

Banfield, E.C. (1958) *The Moral Basis of a Backward Society*, The Free Press: Glencoe.

Baumol, W.J. (1991) *Perfect Markets and Easy Virtue, Business Ethics and the Invisible Hand,* Blackwell: Oxford.

Baums, T., Buxbaum, T. and Hopt, K.(1993) *Institutional Investors and Corporate Governance*, Walter De Gruyter: Berlin.

Becht, M., Bolton, P. and Roëll, A. (2003) Corporate Governance and Control, in *The Handbook of the Economics of Finance*, Constantinides, G., Harris, M. and Stulz, R. (eds) North-Holland: Amsterdam.

Berle, A.A. and Means, G.C. [1932] (1968) *The Modern Corporation and Private Property*, Harcourt, Brace & World: New York.

Bernheim, B.D. (1994) A Theory of Conformity, *Journal of Political Economy*, **102** (5), 841–877.

Binmore, K. (1994) *Game Theory and the Social Contract*, Vol. 1: Playing fair, MIT Press: Cambridge and London.

Buchanan, J.M. (1967) *The Demand and Supply of Public Goods*, Rand McNally: Chicago.

Buchanan, J.M. (1991) *The Economics and The Ethics of Constitutional Order*, University of Michigan Press: Ann Arbor.

Buchanan, J.M. and Tullock, G. (1999) *The Calculus of Consent: Logical Foundations of Constitutional Democracy*, Liberty Fund: Indianapolis, IN.

Cadbury Commission (1992) *Code of Best Practice: Report of the Committee on the Financial Aspects of Corporate Governance*, Gee and Co: London.

Charkham, J.P. (1994) *Keeping Good Company – A Study of Corporate Governance in Five Countries*, Clarendon Press: Oxford.

Chen, A.Y.S., Sawyers, R.B. and Williams, P.E. (1997) Reinforcing Ethical Decision Making Through

Corporate Culture, *Journal of Business Ethics*, **16** (8), 855–865.

Clearfield, A.M. (2005) With Friends Like These, Who Needs Enemies? The Structure of the Investment Industry and Its Reluctance to Exercise Governance Oversight, *Corporate Governance*, **13** (2), 114–121.

Code Group (2004) *Swedish Code of Corporate Governance*, Ministry of Finance: Stockholm.

Coffee Jr, J.C. (2001) The Rise of Dispersed Ownership: The Roles of Law and the State in the Separation of Ownership and Control, *Yale Law Journal*, **111** (1), 1–82.

Collis, D. and Montgomery, C. (1997) *Corporate Strategy. Resources and the Scope of the Firm*, Irwin: Chicago.

Copenhagen Stock Exchange Committee on Corporate Governance (2005) *Revised Recommendations for Corporate Governance in Denmark.*

Cuervo, A. (2002) Corporate Governance Mechanisms: A Plea for Less Code of Good Governance and More Market Control, *Corporate Governance*, **10** (2), 84–93.

Cuthbert, N. and Dobbins, R. (1980) Managerial Participation by Pension Funds and Other Financial Institutions, *Managerial Finance,* **6** (3), 43.

Daily, C.M., Dalton, D. and Canelli Jr, A. (2003) Corporate Governance: Decades of Dialogue and Data, *Academy of Management Review,* **28** (3), 371–383.

Danley, J.R. (1992) Redefined: Business Ethics and Political Economy, *Journal of Business Ethics,* **10** (12), 915–933.

Debreu, G. (1959) *The Theory of Value. An Axiomatic Analysis of Economic Equilibrium*, John Wiley: New York.

Dixit, A.K. and Pindyck, R.S (1994) *Investment under Uncertainty*, Princeton University Press.

Dyck, A. and Zingales, L. (2002) The corporate governance role of the media, in R. Islam (ed.), *The Right to Tell: the role of mass media in economic development*, World Bank: Washington, DC, 107–40.

Dyck, A. and Zingales, L. (2004) Private benefits of control: An international comparison, *Journal of Finance*, **59** (2), 537–600.

Ehrhardt, M. (1995) *The Search for Value*, Harvard Business School Press: Boston.

Elster, J. (1989) Social Norms and Economic Theory, *Journal of Economic Perspectives*, **3** (4), 99–117.

Etzioni, A. (1988) *The Moral Dimension*, Free Press: New York.

European Commission (2004) Commission Recommendation 2004/913/EC of 14 December 2004 fostering an appropriate regime for the remuneration of directors of listed companies, *Official Journal of the European Union*, L 385/55.

European Commission (2005) Commission Recommendation 2005/162/EC of 15 February 2005 on the role of non-executive or supervisory directors of listed companies and on the committees of the (supervisory) board, *Official Journal of the European Union,* L 52/51.

Evensky, J. (1993) Ethics and The Invisible Hand, *Journal of Economic Perspectives*, **7** (2), 197–205.

Fama, E.F. (1980) Agency problems and the theory of the firm, *Journal of Political Economy*, **88** (2), 299–307.

Fernández-Rodríguez, E., Gómez-Ansón, S. and Cuervo-García, Á. (2004) The Stock Market Reaction to the Introduction of Best Practice Codes by Spanish Firms, *Corporate Governance*, **12** (1), 29–46.

Foss, N.J. (1997) Ethics, Discovery and Strategy, *Journal of Business Ethics*, **16** (11), 1131–1142.

Frank, R.H. (1987) If Homo Economicus Could Choose His Own Utility Function, Would He Want One with a Conscience? *American Economic Review*, **77** (4), 593–604.

Frank, R.H. (1989) If Homo Economicus Could Choose His Own Utility Function, Would He Want One with a Conscience? Reply in *American Economic Review*, **79** (3), 594–596.

Franks, J., Mayer, C. and Rossi, S. (2004) *Spending Less Time with the Family – The Decline of Family Ownership in the United Kingdom*, National Bureau of Economic Research, University of Chicago Press.

Friedman, M. (1970) The Social Responsibility of Business Is to Increase Its Profits, The New York Times, September 13, 1970, quoted from Hoffman, W. and Frederick, R.E., *Business Ethics*, McGraw-Hill: New York (1995).

Ghemawat, P. (1991) *Commitment: The Dynamics of Strategy*, Free Press: New York.

Government Commission (2003) *German Corporate Governance Code (The Cromme Code).* http://www. corporate-governance-code.de/index-e.html

Grant, C. (1991) Friedman Fallacies, *Journal of Business Ethics*, **10** (12), 907–914.

Hamlin, A.P. (1986) *Ethics, Economics and the State*, Wheatsheaf Books: Brighton.

Hardin, R. (1971) Collective Action as an Agreeable n-Prisoners' Dilemma, *Behavioral Science*, **16** (5), 472–481.

Harrington, J.E. (1989) If Homo Economicus Could Choose His Own Utility Function, Would He Want One with a Conscience? Comment, *American Economic Review*, **79** (3), 588–593.

Hart, O. (1995) Corporate Governance: Some Theory and Implications, *The Economic Journal*, Vol. 105, pp. 678–89. Reprinted in *Corporate Governance*, K. Keasey, S. Thompson and M. Wright (eds) (1999), Edward Elgar Publishing: Cheltenham.

Hausman, D.M. and McPherson, M.S. (1993) Taking Ethics Seriously: Economics and Contemporary Moral Philosophy, *Journal of Economic Literature*, **31** (2), 671–731.

Héritier, A. (2002) New Modes of Governance in Europe: Policy Making without Legislating? *IHS Political Science Series*, **81**.

Hermalin, B.E., and Weisbach, M. (2005) Trends in Corporate Governance, *Journal of Finance,* **60** (5), 2351–2384.

Institute of Economic Affairs (1973) *The Economics of Charity. Essays on the Comparative Economics and Ethics of Giving and Selling, with Applications to Blood*, London.

Jensen, M.C. and Meckling, W. (1976) Theory of the firm: Managerial behavior, agency costs and ownership structure, *Journal of Financial Economics*, **3** (4), 305–360.

Johnson, W.B., Young, S.M and Welker, M. (1993) Managerial Reputation and the Informativeness of Accounting and Market Measures of Performance, *Contemporary Accounting Research*, **10** (1), 305–332.

Josephson, M. (1995) Teaching Ethical Decision Making and Principled Reasoning, Quoted from Hoffman, W. and Frederick, R.E. *Business Ethics*, McGraw-Hill: New York.

Keynes, J.M. (1936) *The General Theory of Employment, Interest, and Money*, Harcourt, Brace & World: New York.

Knight, F. (1921*) Risk, Uncertainty and Profit*, Houghton Mifflin: Boston.

Kreps, D. (1990) Corporate Culture and Economic Theory, in J. Alt and K. Shepsle, (eds) *Perspectives on Positive Political Economy*, Cambridge University Press.

Laing, D. and Weir, C.M. (1999) Governance structures, size and corporate performance in UK firms, *Management Decision, 37* (5), 457–464.

MacNeil, I. and Li, X. (2006) *'Comply or Explain': Market Discipline and Non-Compliance with the Combined Code, Corporate Governance: An International Review*, **14** (5), 468–496.

Milbourn, T.T. (2003) CEO reputation and stock-based compensation, *Journal of Financial Economics*, **68** (2), 233–262.

Mintzberg, H. (1979) *Structuring of Organizations*, Prentice-Hall: Englewood Cliffs.

Mitchell, W.G. and Simmons, R.T. (1994) *Beyond Politics. Markets, Welfare and the Failure of Bureaucracy*, Westview Press: Oxford.

Noe, T.H. and Rebello, M.J. (1994) The Dynamics of Business Ethics and Economic Activity, *American Economic Review*, **84** (3), 531–547.

North, D.C. (1990) *Institutions, Institutional Change and Economic Performance*, Cambridge University Press: Cambridge.

Nwachukwu, L.S. and Vitell Jr., S.J. (1997) The Influence of Corporate Culture on Managerial Ethical Judgments, *Journal of Business Ethics*, **16** (8), 757–776.

Olson, M. (1965) *The Logic of Collective Action*, Harvard University Press: Cambridge MA.

Ostrom, E. (2000) Collective Action and the Evolution of Social Norms, *Journal of Economic Perspectives*, **14** (3), 137–158.

Ouchi, W. (1980) Markets, Bureaucracies and Clans, *Administrative Science Quarterly*, **25** (1), 129–141.

Ouchi, W. and Price, R. (1993) Hierarchies, clans and theory Z: a new perspective on organization development, *Organizational Dynamics, 21* (4), 62–70.

Peltzman, S. (1976) Towards a More General Theory of Regulation, *Journal of Law and Economics*, **19** (2), 211–240.

Prendergast, C. (2003) The Limits of Bureaucratic Efficiency, *Journal of Political Economy*, **111** (5), 929–958.

Primaux, P. and Stieber, J. (1997) Managing Business Ethics and Opportunity Costs, *Journal of Business Ethics,* **16** (8) 835–842.

Radin, M.J. (1996) *Contested Commodities*, Cambridge University Press: Cambridge.

Rajan, R.G. and Zingales, L. (2002) *Banks and Markets: The Changing Character of European Finance*, CRSP Working Paper No. 546, January 2003.

Rayton, B. and S. Cheng, S. (2004) *Corporate Governance in the United Kingdom: Changes to the Regulatory Template and Company Practice from 1998–2002*, University of Bath Working Paper Series, No. 13.

Reilly, B.J. and Kyj, M.J. (1990) Economics and Ethics, *Journal of Business Ethics*, **9** (3), 691–698.

Ross, S.A. (1973) The Economic Theory of Agency: The Principal's Problem, *American Economic Review*, **63** (2), 134–139.

Rudd, A. (1986) Portfolio Management: Another Look at Passive Management, *Journal of Accounting, Auditing & Finance*, **1** (3), 242.

Schelling, T.C. (1960) *The Strategy of Conflict*, Harvard University Press: Cambridge MA.

Schelling, T.C. (1984) *Choice and Consequence*, Harvard University Press: Cambridge MA.

Schotter, A. (1981) *The Economic Theory of Social Institutions*, Cambridge University Press: Cambridge MA.

Schumpeter, J.A. (1934) *The Theory of Economic Development*, 2nd edition, Harvard University Press: New York.

Schumpeter, J.A. (1950) *Capitalism, Socialism and Democracy,* Harper & Row: New York.

Sen, A. (1993) Does Business Ethics Make Economic Sense, in *The Ethics of Business in a Global Economy*, P.M. Minus (ed), Kluwer Academic Publishers: Boston.

Shleifer, A. and Summers, L. (1988) Breach of Trust in Hostile Takeovers, in *Corporate Takeovers: Causes and Consequences*, A. J. Auerbach (ed), University of Chicago Press.

Shleifer, A. and Vishny, R.W. (1997) A survey of corporate governance, *Journal of Finance*, **52** (2), 737.

Singer, A.E. and Singer, M.S. (1997) Management-Science and Business-Ethics, *Journal of Business Ethics*, **16** (4), 385–395.

Smith, A. [1776] (1981), *An Inquiry into the Nature and Causes of the Wealth of Nations*, 1st edition, Liberty Classics: Indianapolis.

Stigler, G.J. (1971) The Theory of Economic Regulation, *Bell Journal of Economics and Management Science*, **2** (1), 3–21.

Sugden, R. (1989) Spontaneous Order, *Journal of Economic Perspectives*, **3** (4), 85–97.

Thomsen, S. (2001) Ethical Codes as Corporate Governance, *European Journal of Law and Economics*, **11** (2), 153–164.

Thomsen, S. (2003) The Convergence of Corporate Governance Systems to European and Anglo-American Standards, *European Business Organization Law Review*, **4** (1), 31–50.

Thomsen, S. (2004) Corporate values and corporate governance, *Journal of Corporate Governance*, **4** (4), 29–46.

Tirole, J. (1988) *The Theory of Industrial Organization*, MIT Press.

Titmuss, R. (1971) *The Gift Relationship. From Human Blood to Social Policy*, Random House: New York.

Weiss, Y. and Fershtman, C. (1998) Social status and economic performance: A survey, *European Economic Review*, **42** (3–5), 801–820.

Wernerfelt, B. (1984) A Resource-Based View of the Firm, *Strategic Management Journal*, **5** (2), 171–180.

Woidtke, T. (2002) Agents watching agents? Evidence from pension fund ownership and firm value, *Journal of Financial Economics*, **63** (2), 99–131.

Woolley, P. and Bird, R. (2003) Economic implications of passive investing, *Journal of Asset Management*, **3** (4), 303–312.

Zeikel, A. (1978) Pension Funds-Indexed Portfolios, *Journal of Accounting, Auditing & Finance*, **1** (2), 136.

Chapter 6

Corporate Social Responsibility

Chapter contents

6.1 Introduction

Corporate social responsibility (CSR) has become a central corporate governance issue in recent years. Definitions of CSR abound. We define Corporate Social Responsibility to be the way in which firms seek to voluntarily align the interests of owners and other stakeholders with the long-term best interests of society. These other stakeholders might include consumers, employees, suppliers, governments, the environment, and the wider social community. The stakeholders are constituencies in addition to other investors who have a financial claim to the enterprise such as equity and debt holders. The terms 'CSR' and 'stakeholder' are fluid and somewhat imprecise concepts. A legitimate stakeholder for one person may not be so for another person. For example, in some countries in continental Europe such as Germany there is a culture of allocating decision rights to employees as board members. This practice is hardly ever observed in the United States. Also, determining the best long-term outcomes for society is controversial and depends upon political systems and country culture. One challenge for the CSR community is to figure out who are the relevant stakeholders and what the societal interest is. Another challenge is to find the ideal balance between the competing objectives of multiple interest groups (for example, the firm's pursuit of profit might conflict with environmental objectives, or with employee welfare).

Debates about CSR have their proponents and detractors. The proponents argue that there is a strong business case to be made for CSR. Namely, firms receive tangible benefits by making strategic decisions that are more long-term oriented compared with focusing on immediate short-term profits. On the other hand, critics argue that CSR deflects CEOs from the fundamental economic role of the firm, which is to maximize the profits of the firm. Others argue that CSR is merely window dressing (or tokenism) and not a completely sincere attempt to align stakeholder interests with society (e.g. on matters related to the environment).

Our view treads the middle ground. We argue that CSR is critical to the success of firms and society, especially in contexts where it leads to greater value creation by organizations. CSR is an important strategy that firms can follow to meet the preferences of societies and the individuals in those societies. As such, we do not see any fundamental conflict of interest between creating value for firms and society on the one hand and stakeholders on the other hand. Indeed, as Michael Jensen (2001) has pointed out, the notions of 'Enlightened Value Maximization' and 'Enlightened Stakeholder Theory' are broadly equivalent in terms of leading to the best societal outcomes.

The concept of CSR is amorphous. It is a term used to express a number of different ideas. The European Commission's definition of CSR is: 'A concept whereby companies integrate social and environmental concerns in their business operations and in their interaction with their stakeholders on a voluntary basis.'[1] It implies that CSR is not merely philanthropy; it captures the idea that firms take actions that promote social interest beyond that which is required of them by law, and that dialogue with multiple stakeholders is crucial. But because the terminology is somewhat ill-defined, Tirole and Bénabou (2009) state: 'An analysis of CSR must therefore clarify its exact meaning, and in particular the presumed impact of CSR on the cost of capital. Some CSR advocates argue that there is a business case for good corporate behaviour, while others discuss it in terms of sacrificing some profit in the quest for the social good.' It is important to stress that there is no overall agreement on the definition of CSR; instead it is a broad argument that maximization of the interests of all communities in a society leads to the best overall outcome for that society. As we shall see below, some academics have challenged this notion.

Carroll (1999) documents that the CSR construct came into being from the 1950s through the 1960s. Its use proliferated during the 1970s. During the 1980s, more empirical research began to happen. New themes such as the relation between corporate social performance and stakeholder theory emerged. However, it is important for those who use it to clarify precisely what they mean

---

[1] http://ec.europa.eu/enterprise/policies/sustainable-business/corporate-social-responsibility/index_en.htm (accessed 10 October, 2010).

and in what context. We will return to these issues later on below. First consider the (controversial) approach to CSR proposed by Nobel Laureate Milton Friedman.

Stakeholders and shareholders

The standard objective function of the organization is the profit maximization hypothesis. By appealing to the fundamental theorems of welfare economics, it is possible to show that resource allocation in an economy is optimal and cannot be improved upon if firms and individuals maximize their own preferences. In the case of firms, preferences are profits and in the case of individuals it is 'utility'. For this theoretical result to hold in practice requires some heroic assumptions, including the absence of externalities. Externalities can be thought of as missing markets, whereby a transaction does not have a market price. An important negative externality is pollution. If externalities are present, then it opens the door for possible intervention.

Stakeholder theories of the firm challenge the standard economic model and the underlying presumption of naïve profit maximization. Donaldson and Preston (1995) articulate the advantages and benefits of the stakeholder theory of the firm. This theory has a much broader conceptualization of the firm in modern society. They argue that stakeholder theory is highly robust and has been persuasively justified in the scholarly management literature. Specifically, stakeholder theory has three features that make it very useful: its descriptive accuracy, its instrumental power, and finally its normative validity. Donaldson and Preston (1995) assert that these features are interrelated and mutually supportive. They argue that the normative conception of stakeholder theory, which describes how firms ought to be run, is fundamental. Importantly, as a descriptive model, they illustrate the connections between various constituencies including governments, investors, political groups, customers, communities, employees, trade associations, and suppliers.

Michael Jensen (2001) revisited the theory of the firm and specifically whether firms should optimize shareholder value or focus on stakeholder objectives. Ultimately, he comes down in favour of an enlightened value maximization theory that is logically similar to an enlightened stakeholder model whereby successful firms consider all constituencies as they try to create value in society.

Jensen (2001) offers some important critiques of stakeholder theories of the firm. He argues that firms should logically have a single-valued objective function. The reason for this is that it enables CEOs, managers and decision makers to know whether their actions are successful or not; it is a means to keep score. In addition, it provides decision makers with a tool to evaluate the trade-offs between alternative courses of action. He demonstrates that if there are multiple objectives within the firm then problems arise. Suppose, hypothetically, a manager has to decide between maximizing employee welfare and maximizing profits. How is this to be done? Profits can be increased by lowering wages, but employee welfare can be improved by increasing wages. What is the correct course of action? The problem is that there are multiple objectives, and Jensen argues that stakeholder models are deficient in that they do not adequately specify a mechanism to deal with these kinds of trade-offs between competing objectives that arise naturally in everyday business life. Enlightened stakeholder and value models, Jensen argues, specify the goal of the firm so that managers understand how the score is to be kept and whether the strategies they ultimately select are successful.

6.2   CSR: The Milton Friedman critique

Milton Friedman also expressed a very strong view about CSR: that business has no responsibilities beyond the pursuit of profits. The late Nobel Laureate opened his classic 1970 article by stating: 'When I hear businessmen speak eloquently about the "social responsibilities of business in a free-enterprise system", I am reminded of the wonderful line about the Frenchman who discovered at the age of 70 that he had been speaking prose all his life.' He leaves his readers in no doubt about his views on CSR: 'Businessmen who talk this way [about corporate social responsibilities] are unwitting puppets of the intellectual forces that have been undermining the basis of a free society these past decades.'

Milton Friedman makes the following arguments. CEOs, executives and managers are employees (i.e. agents) of those who employed them (the principal). As discussed in previous chapters, the principal–agent model is a reasonably uncontroversial characterization of the modern corporate world. As such the primary duty of the CEO, executive or manager is to the firm (at least contractually). Optimizing the owners' welfare, therefore, should be the main objective of the agent. If the idea of CSR is to have traction then it implies that the CEO or manager can take actions that can be in conflict with the owner's welfare. For example, a CEO may spend sums of money on reducing pollution in excess of what is required by law or is optimal for the firm because of the manager's personal desire to improve the environment. In this case the CEO has taken the decision to reallocate someone else's money to promote what the CEO believes to be in the 'social interest'. Because the CEO's spending decisions increase her own welfare based on her own perception of the social interest it has reduced the available funds to shareholders, as she is spending their money.

Friedman argues that instead of managers making this decision, shareholders themselves could make the decision about how to spend money on philanthropy, if indeed they wanted to. For Friedman the idea of CSR rests on a trade-off (or substitution effect) between the manager's actions and the owners' welfare. That is, increasing the manager's welfare reduces the welfare of the owners. Complementarities between the owners and the manager (or win–win situations) are ruled out. If there were complementarities then the agent (CEO) is really acting in the interests of the principals (shareholders). The CEO or manager is spending other people's money (namely shareholder funds) to pursue her own interests, and she is also trying to second-guess the shareholders' preferences. Friedman asserts that it is better to give the money back to the owners and let them make their own decisions. The legitimate role of the CEO/manager is to act as an agent on the behalf of shareholders for which she was employed. As Friedman remarks: 'The whole justification for permitting the corporate executive to be selected by the stockholders is that the executive is an agent serving the interests of his principal. This justification disappears when the corporate executive imposes taxes and spends the proceeds for "social" purposes. He becomes in effect a public employee, a civil servant, even though he remains in name an employee of a private enterprise.'

In summary, Milton Friedman provides an important market-based critique of some of the underpinnings of CSR and stakeholder theories of the firm. His famous 1970 paper makes the case against CSR by arguing that in free societies individuals, not unelected bureaucrats located in firms, should make decisions regarding their incomes. A simple example illustrates this. Suppose one invests $1000 in a firm and the firm actually needs to spend only $800 dollars to finance positive net present value projects and to achieve healthy capital appreciation or to pay dividends on your investment. The remaining $200 is surplus to the firm's requirements. What should the firm's CEO do? The CEO can return the money to you, or may spend the money on a social project deemed important by the CEO. If the company chooses to spend money on the CEO's pet project then this does not necessarily align owners' preferences or those of society. The investor may have different preferences on how the capital should be allocated to socially desirable projects.

6.3   Contemporary views on CSR

Views about CSR have been considerably refined over the years. The economist Jean Tirole (Tirole and Bénabou, 2009) identifies three different approaches to CSR. The first view is 'win–win' ('doing well by doing good'). The second is delegated philanthropy (the firm as a channel for the expression of citizen values). The third view is insider-initiated corporate philanthropy. Each of these is worth expanding upon. We summarize the main arguments associated with each.

The 'win–win' ('doing well by doing good') view is that engaging in good works (CSR) also leads to better profits for firms (increases the principal's welfare). It contrasts to the Friedman perspective. The important issue for the win–win view is to provide supporting evidence that CSR really does provide benefits to the firm. As Tirole states: 'for such a claim to be more than management consultants' promise of a "free lunch", it requires elaboration, as well as supporting evidence.' One way to motivate the win–win theory is to argue that markets are incomplete in some way or there are important externalities. Another motivation is that managers have psychological biases that cause them to miss profit-maximizing opportunities by focusing on short-term profits at the expense of long-term profit opportunities. One of the consequences of such externalities or psychological biases is that CEOs and managers often focus too much on short-term payoffs. In contrast, by committing to projects that come under the umbrella of 'corporate social responsibility', CSR strategies help managers focus on the long-term. This is because big ideas about society, community, and the environment are complex and help managers think beyond short-term financial considerations.

One can construct plausible examples of how markets might fail and so CSR would be useful. The CEO's career at the firm is finite. Indeed, one might think that CEO tenure is about five years. This provides potentially weak incentives for the CEO to care about the value of the firm beyond the expected career termination date. The CEO may care, therefore, only about boosting projects that yield returns now, rather than in the much more distant and unknowable future. Another example is CEO financial incentives. Stock option compensation might lead CEOs to fire workers in order to boost short-term profits and stock prices. This can be at the expense of the long-term future of the firm. This particular action clearly destroys the welfare of one important stakeholder group, namely the employees who were fired. However, the firm's short-term decision may have further unintended consequences. The firm may not be able to hire new motivated workers because they fear opportunistic action by management, so long-term profits and firm value suffer. It may also damage its reputation among consumers who may not buy the product. By getting managers to focus on the long term and to care in this case about employee welfare and not renege on implicit labour contracts, this business case for CSR leads to a clear win–win situation for the firm and for the stakeholders.

Tirole's delegated second notion is the philanthropy view (the firm as a channel for the expression of citizen values). This is the idea that stakeholders (investors, employees, customers) have a preference for the firm engaging in philanthropic actions on their behalf. Here it is important to ask why firms should do this rather than the stakeholders doing it for themselves, or indeed, why isn't the activity done through specialist not-for-profit organizations, churches, charities and the like. One reason is the presence of significant information asymmetries and transactions costs. One may construct an example to illustrate the point. Consider the firm Starbucks, the famous coffee retailer. Consumers alone may not know the intricacies of the trading and labour agreements between far-away coffee suppliers and retailers of coffee closer to home. Consumers may be concerned about fairtrade arrangements and ethical treatment of labour in coffee-supplying countries. It may be possible to set up a not-for-profit firm to specialize in the supply of fairtrade coffee, but transaction costs are lower if undertaken by the corporation itself. The consumers demand for CSR therefore economizes on transaction costs and is efficiently supplied by the firm at hand. Another example could be a not-for-profit firm that creates employment opportunities, or investment funds, in low income and low wealth communities who otherwise do not have access to scarce capital. Consumers and societies may find this desirable but do not have the relevant information to implement it. Therefore, the firm that initiates this is adding value.

Tirole's third view of CSR is termed 'insider-initiated corporate philanthropy'. This perspective suggests that CSR is motivated in part by the CEO's or executives' desire to allocate money based on their own preferences. Balancing the demands of other stakeholders such as investors, consumers or employees does not really motivate the expenditures. Instead CEOs may provide funds to political parties, charities and not-for-profit organizations for personal, and often well-intentioned, reasons. For example, the CEO or one of the board members may be connected to a not-for-profit organization and decide to donate money to this worthy cause. In this situation, and in contrast to the previous views of CSR, long-term profits might not be maximized because the CEO is making personal decisions rather than making a calculation based on the myriad interests of all stakeholders.

This last version is precisely the type of corporate philanthropy that concerned Milton Friedman so much in 1970. The argument is that managers (no matter how well intentioned) should not do philanthropy with other people's money. Instead, they should return free cash flow to investors who then make their own philanthropic decisions. Alternatively, managers may use their own wealth to make personal giving decisions. This type of philanthropy raises significant corporate governance concerns. First, if investors demand only high yields on investments and management engage in large-scale philanthropy then this indicates that managers may be entrenched. Second, if corporate mission and value statements accentuate wider stakeholder objectives then the firm may not be able to raise capital at low cost compared with shareholder value focused firms. Third, focusing on multiple constituencies may harm managerial accountability. A CEO brought to task for missing earnings targets may simply respond that he was balancing different stakeholder interests even if the missed target was due to insufficient effort on the part of the CEO. In short, too many objectives for the firm are, in fact, no objective at all.

In reality it might be difficult to discriminate between the different theories of CSR. What seems clear though is that under some contexts (Tirole's view #1 and #2) CSR may help boost long-term company performance. In other contexts (the Milton Friedman critique) CSR can be harmful to firm profitability. Perhaps one way forward is to look at the growing empirical evidence on CSR.

6.4 Some empirical examples

To get a better feel for the practice of CSR we will provide a few empirical examples. The first is a straightforward company example. The second shows how a leading social rating agency for investors evaluates CSR.

Many companies promote CSR. The reasons are myriad. It is good for business, their customers demand it, it improves corporate reputations, and it increases the financial performance of the firm. Or quite simply CSR firms might decide it is the right thing to do ethically.[2] Consider the case of Apple Inc.[3] Apple proudly asserts its commitment to progressive environmentalism. One of its current flagship products is the MacBook Pro. The company stresses the importance of how the product is engineered to reduce environmental impact. This includes an arsenic-free display glass, BFR-free, mercury-free LED-backlit display, PVC-free, highly recyclable aluminum and glass enclosure, reduced packaging volume, the product meets ENERGY STAR Version 5.0 requirements, and so on. More generally the company is highly committed to protecting the environment and reducing its carbon footprint. If one visits the company's website for investors, Apple's role in protecting the environment figures prominently (https://www.apple.com/investor/). There is a detailed discussion of the total footprint life-cycle from manufacturing to transportation to product use to recycling to facilities. As Apple states: 'We know that the most important thing we can do to reduce our impact on the environment is to improve our products. That's why we design them to use less material, ship with smaller packaging, be free of many toxic substances, and be as energy efficient and recyclable as possible. With every new product, we continue our progress toward minimizing our environmental impact.' How does this help Apple's financial position, because such commitment costs money? It happens in various ways: Apple can charge a product price premium, and consumers are willing to pay this. Customer willingness to pay arises because customers view the product as superior and many customers attach value to Apple's environmental stances. Apple can attract high quality employees because of its progressive policies. The commitment to environmentalism forces Apple to be even more innovative in terms of product design and engineering. The symbiotic relation between each of these elements results in a 'win–win' situation. Namely, environmental commitment is a positive-sum outcome: the firm wins and society / the environment wins.

Another way to look at the importance of CSR is to focus on rating agencies and how they evaluate firms' CSR. KLD Research & Analytics, Inc. (KLD) is a leading authority on social research

---

[2] In this chapter we do not get into the different approaches to making ethical decisions. For example, consequentialist ethics such as utilitarian theory evaluates morality based on outcomes. In contrast, deontology theory evaluates ethics based on specific acts rather than third-party outcomes. In either case, we just suppose that the firm/individual/society has decided on how to evaluate what is 'right'.

[3] Full disclosure: one of the authors is an Apple Mac user and supporter!

for institutional investors. To meet the needs of social investors, KLD provides research, benchmarks, compliance and consulting services analogous to those provided by financial research service firms. The data we report are an annual snapshot of the environmental, social and governance performance of companies in 2007. The data on their Domini Social Index (DS 400), which is a portfolio of ethically screened stocks, has been used in prior research. We simply report some aggregate statistics based on nearly 3000 US firms.

KLD provides CSR evaluations across a number of distinct groups. These include human rights, corporate governance, diversity, employment relations, military involvement, nuclear involvement, tobacco involvement, gambling involvement and firearms involvement. Within each of the groups KLD then identifies whether the company is strong in that area or whether there are concerns that should be signalled. Given that there are many indicators, we will report on only one: the environment.

KLD analyses a focal company (for example, Apple Inc or the Gap) and then evaluates its environmental performance (or other area of CSR). For each indicator variable KLD rates the focal firm by giving it a positive rating (strength) or a negative rating (concern) or no rating (neutral). Different indicator variables are provided separately for the environmental 'strengths' and 'concerns' categories. KLD has developed distinct indicators for rating the environmental strength of the focal firm. For example, 'Clean Energy' means 'the company has taken significant measures to reduce its impact on climate change and air pollution through use of renewable energy and clean fuels or through energy efficiency. The company has demonstrated a commitment to promoting climate-friendly policies and practices outside its own operations'. Other measures include 'Beneficial Products and Services' meaning 'the company derives substantial revenues from innovative remediation products, environmental services, or products that promote the efficient use of energy, or it has developed innovative products with environmental benefits'. Another is 'Pollution Prevention' meaning 'the company has notably strong pollution prevention programs including both emissions reductions and toxic-use reduction programs'. Yet another is 'Recycling' meaning 'the company either is a substantial user of recycled materials as raw materials in its manufacturing processes, or a major factor in the recycling industry'. KLD has similarly developed measures that identify environmental concerns at the focal company. These include 'Climate Change' which is equal to one if 'the company derives substantial revenues, directly or indirectly, from the sale of coal or oil and its derivative fuel products'. The second indicator is 'Ozone Depleting Chemicals' if 'the company is among the top manufacturers of ozone depleting chemicals such as HCFCs, methyl chloroform, methylene chloride, or bromines'. Another measure is 'Hazardous Waste' meaning 'the company has substantial liabilities for hazardous waste, or has recently paid significant fines or civil penalties for waste management violations'. 'Regulatory Problems' means 'the company has recently paid substantial fines or civil penalties for violations of air, water, or other environmental regulations, or it has a pattern of regulatory controversies under the Clean Air Act, Clean Water Act or other major environmental regulations'. Each of these measures, as is intuitive, document the strengths and weaknesses of CSR as rated by KLD.

In a similar way KLD identifies the social responsibility of firms in terms of employment practices. The categories here include Retirement Benefits (Concern), Health and Safety (Strength), Union Relations, Health and Safety (Concern), Workforce Reductions, Employment Relations Other Concerns, and Employment Relations – the Number of Concerns. They also consider Union Relations (Strength), Cash Profit Sharing, Employee Involvement, Retirement Benefits (Strength), Employment Relations Other Strength, and finally Employment Relations – Number of Strengths.

The mean statistics (and standard deviations) are provided in Table 6.1. In terms of the environment mostly the mean fraction of companies with concerns is quite low. For example, there are climate change concerns in about 4.8% of the 2937 firms. However, looking at the employment and management practices portion of the table we see a slightly different picture. There are retirement benefit concerns in 28.8% of the sample companies. The importance of KLD data, we think, is that it provides the basis of measuring accurately CSR issues that can then be tested in a model to see what the benefits to firms and other stakeholders are of adopting good practices.

Table 6.1 KLD assessment of environment and employment social responsibility

	# of observations	Average	Standard deviation
Environment			
Climate Change (from 1999)	2937	0.048	0.213
Hazardous Waste	2937	0.036	0.187
Regulatory Problems	2937	0.056	0.230
Ozone Depleting Chemicals	2937	0.001	0.026
Substantial Emissions	2937	0.045	0.208
Agriculture Chemicals	2937	0.006	0.078
Environment Other Concerns	2937	0.016	0.124
Environment – Number of Concerns	2937	0.208	0.630
Beneficial Products and Services	2937	0.019	0.136
Pollution Prevention	2937	0.011	0.104
Recycling	2937	0.014	0.117
Clean Energy	2937	0.034	0.182
Environment Other Strength	2937	0.003	0.052
Environment – Number of Strengths	2937	0.126	0.472
Employment			
Management Systems Strength	2937	0.045	0.208
Retirement Benefits Concern	2937	0.288	0.453
Health and Safety Strength	2937	0.048	0.213
Union Relations	2937	0.022	0.146
Health and Safety Concern	2937	0.122	0.327
Workforce Reductions	2937	0.034	0.181
Emp. Relations Other Concerns	2937	0.059	0.235
Emp. Relations – Number of Concerns	2937	0.524	0.710
Union Relations	2937	0.035	0.185
Cash Profit Sharing	2937	0.041	0.198
Employee Involvement	2937	0.056	0.230
Retirement Benefits Strength	2937	0.067	0.251
Emp. Relations Other Strength	2937	0.027	0.163
Emp. Relations – Number of Strengths	2937	0.275	0.600

Source: KLD (Wharton Research Data Services, WRDS).

6.5 Some empirical evidence

Many studies have examined the determinants and effects of CSR. The European Union's Competitiveness report in 2008 investigated the link between CSR and economic competitiveness. It provides a contemporary overview of how CSR can contribute to competitiveness.[4] The report assessed the impact of CSR along six distinct measures of firm-level competitiveness. The outcome measures considered were the firm's cost structure, human resource management, customer perspective, innovation, risk and reputation management, and financial performance. In addition the report investigates the relation between CSR and macro-level competitiveness and at the level of individual industrial sectors. What does the report conclude? It finds some but not universal evidence of a positive impact of CSR policies on firm competiveness. It states that 'the strength of that impact, and the extent to which it is relevant to all companies, varies. The business case for CSR is specific to different sectors, sizes and circumstances of companies' (EU, 2008, p. 118).

The EU report finds that the best evidence of a positive relation between CSR on competitiveness is in the domain of human resources, risk and reputation management, and innovation. In terms of human resources (attracting, retaining and motivating employees) the report concedes that for some companies the extra costs of CSR might still outweigh the benefits at least in the short run. The evidence for a positive effect of CSR on the stock market performance, though, is mixed. Stock prices are an important indicator of the economic performance of firms since they reflect the discounted present value of the firm's operational activities. So, investigating the effect, say, of a firm investing in environmental CSR on stock prices is important. Here the EU report concludes that: 'Research indicates conclusively that there is a positive but small correlation between CSR and financial performance. The nature of the causal link is not clear, however.' Despite this there is increasing attention to CSR policies in the valuation of assets and firms, so CSR may become increasingly important for investors.

Other academic reviews of CSR yield similar findings. Margolis, Elfenbein and Walsh (2007) conducted a meta-analysis of the relationship between CSR and the financial performance of firms. They investigated 167 separate studies appearing in leading journals from 1972 to 2007. Different types of CSR are studies including charitable contributions (e.g. donations to foundations), corporate policies (e.g. apartheid in South Africa), environmental policies (e.g. policies, toxic release data etc.), corporate misdeeds (e.g. arrests, fines etc.), and transparency (e.g. the public provision of data). In addition they analysed self-reported measures of social performance, observers' perceptions of CSR, third party audits (e.g. KLD), and the use of screened mutual funds (e.g. the Domini 400).

Overall, this wide-ranging review finds only small (but nevertheless positive) effects of CSR on financial performance. They find that the association between CSR and financial performance is strongest for the analysis of the specific dimensions of charitable contributions, revealed misdeeds, and environmental performance and when CSR is assessed more broadly through observer perceptions and self-reported social performance. On the other hand, they find only a weak association for specific dimensions of corporate policies and transparency and when [corporate social performance] is assessed more broadly through third-party audits and mutual fund screens. The link between corporate financial performance and CSR is an important topic for continued research. This is because if such a link can be demonstrated robustly then it will be easier for firms to convince investors and owners of the merits of CSR policies.

Other research also shows that CSR leads to different actions by managers and firms. Chatterji and Toffel (2010) investigated US firm reactions to ratings by professional external rating agencies. They find that firms that initially received poor ratings subsequently improved their environmental performance more than other firms. In addition, they find that such differences were more salient and pronounced in regulated industries and by firms with more low-cost opportunities to exploit. This suggests that receiving poor ratings has the effect of modifying corporate social behaviour.

---

[4] http://ec.europa.eu/enterprise/policies/sustainable-business/corporate-social-responsibility/competitiveness/index_en.htm (accessed on 20 October, 2010).

Lev et al. (2010) studied the relation between charitable giving and future sales growth in a sample of US firms between 1989 and 2000. They find evidence that charitable contributions increase firms' revenue growth. They find that giving is associated with subsequent sales growth after controlling for other important determinants of sales growth. However, they find that the results are contingent upon types of sector, such as consumer sectors, retailers and financial services. Lev et al. (2010, p. 198) remark that: 'Doing good is apparently good for you under certain circumstances. We go beyond documenting an association between contributions and subsequent growth by identifying customer satisfaction as the mechanism underlying this relation.'

6.6 Discussion

CSR has emerged as a significant area of corporate governance over the last three decades. Key issues include the definition of CSR: what is it and how is it to be made operational. We are agnostic and offer the following definition. CSR is the way in which firms seek to voluntarily align the interests of owners and other stakeholders with the long-term best interests of society. The key issues then become who are the stakeholders, how is social welfare defined and how do we balance competing interests? These are challenging but worthwhile and important tasks.

CSR is an important issue for firms. Many firms stress the importance of CSR to their overall business strategy. We have discussed the competing views of CSR. Milton Friedman was highly critical of CSR policies, believing that CEOs had no right to engage in philanthropy with investors' funds. Contemporary views are more sanguine. Tirole stressed the importance of win–win strategies, where both society and firms are better off by promoting CSR policies. One way to think about this is to say that contemporary views of CSR represent a positive-sum outcome. The Friedman view is a negative or zero-sum outcome at best.

The empirical evidence on CSR is mixed. Studies find that CSR policies improve a company's product reputation, and are successful in attracting talented employees to the firm and motivating them. However, CSR comes at a cost to the firm, and it is less clear that the costs of CSR are strictly less than the benefits at least in the short term. The findings on the relation between CSR and financial performance, then, have been less strong. The consensus view seems to be that there are small positive effects of CSR on performance, but teasing at the causal effect has proved tricky. Even if firms do not always secure better financial returns, one might argue that there is an ethical reason for promoting CSR because it fits with societies' preferences. A good example is the case of South Africa during the apartheid regime. Citizens in many countries simply demanded that firms not do business with the then oppressive South African regime, even if this meant company profits would suffer. Overall, the study of CSR has implications for corporate governance, business ethics and the delicate balance between firms and governments.

Minicase

Walmart

Many major companies provide reports and comprehensive audits in relation to their commitment to corporate social responsibilities. These focus on how the company contributes to the welfare of customers, the environment and society.

Consider the case of Walmart. Walmart provides an annual Global Sustainability Report. It gives an annual progress update. It makes commitments in the area of Energy (its goal is to be supplied by 100% renewable energy), Waste (its goal is to create zero waste) and Products (its goal is to sell products that sustain people and the environment). In the social arena Walmart makes significant contributions in the areas of responsible sourcing, improving supply chain management, in terms of its internal purchasing practices, its customers, and it supports communities and helps the career advancement of its associates.

In 2010, Walmart helped support communities in a multitude of ways. 'Walmart and its domestic and international foundations donate hundreds of millions of dollars to create opportunities for people to live better in the communities our business touches around the world. By helping these communities and the people who live there, we are keeping our promise to be a good neighbor. We award grants to organizations whose programs address needs that vary from hunger to educational access. In total around the globe, Walmart, its Foundations, its customers and associates supported communities with more than $624 million in charitable contributions during FYE10.'[5]

There are many examples of giving by Walmart. In 2009, the Walmart Foundation awarded the US Conference of Mayors (USCM) and Business and Professional Women's Foundation (BPW) grants totalling $5.4 million to support the creation of green jobs in the US In 2010, Walmart provided more than $1.5 million in financial support in response to the earthquake in Haiti, including in-kind contributions such as donations of pre-packaged food kits, blankets and face masks.

Walmart has received many awards for its contributions to a broad range of CSR activities. These include the 2009 Waste Reduction Awards Program Winner – California Integrated Waste Management Board. It was ranked #3 out of 35 other retailers in the Q3 2009 Covalence Ethical Reputation Ranking and it won the 2009 Green Choice Award – *Natural Health* magazine.

Source: http://walmartstores.com/sites/sustainabilityreport/2010/social_supporting_communities.aspx

Discussion questions

1 Do you think that Walmart is a socially responsible company? Can you think of arguments for and against?

2 Do you think that CSR in Walmart is maximizing profits? If so, how? And is it then 'real' CSR or just shareholder value maximization?

3 How could CSR at Walmart evolve in the future? Can you give examples of how this would or would not be consistent with shareholder value?

4 Which of Tirole's three theories is most applicable to Walmart?

Summary (learning points)

- Corporate social responsibility (CSR) is the way in which firms seek to voluntarily align the interests of owners and other stakeholders with the long-term best interests of society.

- Milton Friedman argues that shareholders themselves could make the decisions about how to spend money on philanthropy if they wanted to: firms should return money to investors who make their own decisions. For Friedman this is not the job of firms.

- The economist Jean Tirole argues the case for CSR based on three steps. The first is 'win–win' ('doing well by doing good'). Second, delegated philanthropy (the firm as a channel for the expression of citizen values). Third, insider-initiated corporate philanthropy. Each provides a rationale for corporations to engage in CSR.

- Areas where firms engage in CSR are the environment (e.g. reducing carbon footprint), communities (e.g. fostering community development), workplace practices (e.g. work–life balance), macroeconomic policy engagement (e.g. giving to individuals or by opposing oppressive regimes).

References and further reading

Allen, F., Carletti, E. and Marquez, R. (2009), *Stakeholder Capitalism, Corporate Governance and Firm Value*, discussion paper, electronic copy available at http://ssrn.com/abstract=9681411.

Carroll, A.B. (1999) Corporate Social Responsibility: Evolution of a Definitional Construct, *Business & Society*, **38** (3), 268–295.

Chatterji, A.K. and Toffel, M.W. (2010) How firms respond to being rated, *Strategic Management Journal*, **31** (9), 917–945.

Donaldson, T. and Preston, L. (1995) The Stakeholder Theory of the Corporation: Concepts, Evidence, and Implications, *Academy of Management Review*, **20** (1), 65–91.

EU (2008) *European Competitiveness report*, http://ec.europa.eu/enterprise/policies/sustainable-business/corporate-social-responsibility/competitiveness/index_en.htm

Friedman, M. (1970), Social Responsibility of Business, *The New York Times*, September 13.

Jensen, M. (2001), Value Maximization, Stakeholder Theory and the Corporate Objective Function, *Journal of Applied Corporate Finance* **14** (3), 8–21.

Lev, B., Petrovits, C. and Radhakrishnan, S. (2010) Is doing good good for you? How corporate charitable contributions enhance revenue growth, *Strategic Management Journal*, **31** (2), 182–200.

Margolis, J.D., Elfenbein, H.A. and Walsh, J. P. (2007) *Does it pay to be good? A meta-analysis and redirection of research on the relationship between corporate social and financial performance*, Working Paper, Ross School of Business, University of Michigan.

Tirole, J. (2001), Corporate Governance, *Econometrica*, **69** (1), 1–35.

Tirole, J. and Bénabou, R. (2009) Individual and Corporate Social Responsibility, *Economica*, **77** (305), 1–19.

Chapter 7

Corporate Ownership

Chapter contents

7.1   Introduction

In this chapter we examine ownership of companies as a governance mechanism. We start by reviewing ownership as a set of rights and obligations which can vary from firm to firm. We then go on to describe the importance of ownership structure and owner identity. We also describe two very different ownership types: cooperatives and private equity. More on specific ownership structures (investors, families, business groups etc.) will be found in subsequent chapters.

7.2   What is ownership?

Since Roman times it has been recognized that ownership is a set of rights (and obligations) concerning assets such as (Whinston and Segal, 2010):

- user rights (*usus*): right to use an asset;
- profit rights (*usus fructus*): if you own a piece of land you also own the fruits of the land;
- disposal rights (*abusus*): including rights to sell or even physically destroy the asset;
- control rights: the rights to determine who is going to use the asset.

In addition, ownership confers responsibility. For example, if you are a farmer you are responsible for not letting your livestock trample over another person's land. If you own a handgun, you are responsible for storing it in such a way that your neighbour's children cannot easily find it.

These rights may be endlessly combined and recombined. Doing so can be an important source of value creation.

Consider some of the combinations. If you rent an apartment you may have the right to use a washing machine (user rights), but you would not have the right to sell laundry services (profit rights); to determine whether, when and how the other tenants can use the washer (control rights); nor to sell the machine; nor, for that matter, would you have the right to sell your user rights. But suppose you go on a vacation and the machine stands idle during the summer. Would it not be economically beneficial to be able to lease your rights to somebody else during that period of time? In a larger setting, reconfigurations like this can create a lot of value for everyone.

Or consider your body. You can use it, you can profit by using your muscles and brain, you can control it, but you cannot sell it, since slavery is forbidden. Yet some people die of hunger. Would everyone be better off if they were allowed to sell themselves as slaves? What about body parts? Should you be allowed to sell your liver?

For a less controversial application, much new deregulation is based on the premise that you can distinguish between the infrastructure (the railway, the telephone lines, the airport, etc.) and the services they provide. Property rights to the infrastructure do not necessarily mean that the infrastructure service cannot be provided by many different firms.

7.3   Ownership of the firm

In a typical limited liability joint stock company, owners (shareholders) do not have the rights to use corporate assets. They can dissolve the company if they wish, but they cannot just grab corporate assets for their private use. However they do have the right to profit, a right to control (vote), and a right to sell their shares. In a limited liability company, owners are usually free of responsibility for how the company is managed and they do not pledge for the debt which the managers incur beyond the share capital which they have invested. This means that they do not have to constantly keep track of what happens in the firm. This is a major convenience making it much more attractive to buy shares, which is perhaps the foundation for modern capitalism. In legal jargon there is a veil between the company and its shareholders. However, if it can be shown that a company is used as an instrument with an unlawful purpose (e.g. drug trafficking) courts are sometimes (very reluctantly) willing to 'lift the veil' of the corporation and hold the owners responsible for its actions.

Not all companies share the ownership characteristics of publicly limited firms. Companies may for example issue different types, or classes, of shares: some with and some without voting rights (to the extent this is allowed by law). In this case, owners of the non-voting shares will have no voting rights, but they will have the same rights as other shareholders to buy and sell shares and to receive dividends. In the literature on dual class shares, profits rights are sometimes called cash flow rights.

Owners may also have profit and control rights without transfer rights. This is true in cooperatives in which you are a member; you can vote, you can receive dividends, but you cannot sell your membership to another person. In addition, voting in cooperatives is typically one vote per person rather than one vote per share. Moreover, in cooperatives, farmers often have the right and the obligation to do certain kinds of business with the coop. For example, members may be obligated to sell all their milk to the cooperative dairy; the dairy, in turn, is obliged to accept it. This certainty of supply is a key competitive advantage for agricultural cooperatives.

Shareholder agreements may limit the rights of family members and others to sell their shares and they may oblige them to vote together on certain issues. In general, corporate ownership is simply one large shareholder contract so that shareholder agreements can restructure ownership completely, within the confines of the law.

Hedge funds may buy shares in a company and hedge their risk (e.g. by an options deal). They can then vote their shares without any economic responsibility (i.e. they are insured against losses or gains). They can even go short in a stock, buy voting rights, and influence the firm to activities which will reduce the stock price. This is a decoupling of voting rights from profit and transfer rights.

7.4 Ownership structure[1]

In publicly listed companies, there are two key elements of ownership structure: ownership concentration and owner identities. Or in other words: who are the owners and how much of the firm does each of them own? Whereas ownership concentration measures the power of shareholders to influence managers, the identity of the owners has implications for their objectives and the way they exercise their power. This is reflected in company strategy with regard to profit goals, dividends, capital structure and growth rates (cf. the work of Henry Hansmann, 1988; 1996).

Ownership concentration can be measured as a first-cut approximation by the share of the largest owner of total stock. According to agency theory, the choice of a privately optimal ownership structure involves a trade-off between risk and incentive efficiency (Jensen and Meckling, 1976; Fama and Jensen, 1983; Demsetz, 1983; Shleifer and Vishny, 1997). Ceteris paribus, larger owners will have a stronger incentive to monitor managers and they will have more power to enforce their interests. This should increase the inclination of managers to maximize shareholder value. But generally the owner's portfolio risk will also increase the larger the ownership share becomes. To the extent that companies differ in terms of firm-specific risk, the privately optimal ownership share of the largest owner will therefore vary. Furthermore, the nature and complexity of activities carried out by individual firms may also vary, which will influence the marginal effect of monitoring (e.g. Demsetz and Lehn, 1985, Zeckhauser and Pound, 1990). Finally, the relationship between ownership concentration and economic performance need not be uniform (Fama and Jensen, 1983; Morck et al., 1988; Shleifer and Vishny, 1997). Fama and Jensen (1983) suggest that managerial ownership above

---

[1] This section and the next borrow from Thomsen and Pedersen (2000): Ownership Structure and Economic Performance in the Largest European Companies, *Strategic Management Journal*.

a certain level will allow managers to become entrenched and expropriate the wealth of minority shareholders.

This leads to the idea of a bell-shaped relationship between ownership concentration (share of the largest owner) and economic performance, which we can measure by firm value, accounting rates of profitability, shareholder value creation, or other variables (Figure 7.1).

Up to a certain point, all shareholders benefit from greater ownership concentration because a large owner has the power and incentives to maximize firm performance or to see to it that the management maximizes performance. The larger the share of the largest owner, the greater her incentive will be and the more certain she can be of her ability to influence the managers.

Beyond a certain point, however, the entrenchment effect kicks in. The largest owner nears complete control and, in effect, manages the company. But she is very difficult to get rid of and she may start to enjoy private benefits of control, e.g. fringe benefits and all sorts of other things which reduce the value of the firm. Moreover, her risk aversion becomes more and more serious because of an increasingly unbalanced portfolio.

Once the point of full control (entrenchment) is reached, the curve may turn upwards again. From this point on a higher ownership share means that the majority owner now has less and less of an incentive to deviate from value maximization (i.e. she will be paying for it out of her own pocket).

7.5   Ownership and performance

The implication of Figure 7.1 would be that owners of firms with low ownership concentration could benefit from buying more shares, while the owners of firms with high ownership would benefit from selling out (this would increase the value of their shares). So why do they not do so? Demsetz argued theoretically that the ownership structure of the firm is 'an endogenous outcome of competitive selection in which various cost advantages and disadvantages are balanced to arrive at an equilibrium

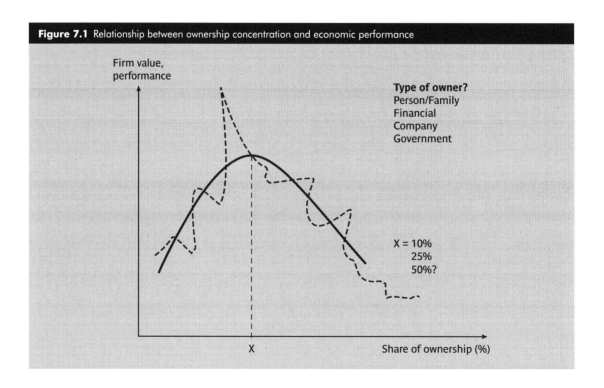

Figure 7.1 Relationship between ownership concentration and economic performance

organization of the firm' (Demsetz, 1983, p. 1164). So again, if owners could increase their profits by rearranging their portfolios, why do they not do so?

One answer to this question could be that the estimated performance effects of ownership concentration are statistical artefacts. In support of this view, Loderer and Martin (1997) and Cho (1998) found the performance effect to be insignificant in a simultaneous estimation of causes and effects of ownership concentration.

Another answer may be free-rider problems among small investors (Shleifer and Vishny, 1986): if one shareholder attempts to acquire a large ownership stake the gains will (largely) be captured by the other shareholders who sell their shares at a premium price reflecting the anticipated increase in the value of the firm. But while free riding among small shareholders provides an argument for a positive effect on company economy performance, the strength and significance of this effect is an empirical question.

A third answer may be that the tacit agency-theoretical assumption of value-maximizing shareholders is incorrect. In other words, owners may have their own reasons for not reshuffling their portfolios to capture the gains from arbitrage. The *identity* of owners may be important with implications for corporate strategy and performance. We develop this idea in the following section.

7.6 Owner identity[2]

The standard assumption in agency theory is that owners want the company to maximize economic profits or, in modern terms, shareholder value. Although this assumption may be sufficient for many purposes, it is strictly speaking only an approximation of the more general idea that owners (like managers) may be expected to maximize their utility which may depend on other factors. One simple reason is that many owners (institutional investors, banks, other companies and governments) act as intermediate agents for final owners. Furthermore, even theoretically, profit maximization is only well-defined when markets are complete (e.g. when all risk is diversifiable). When markets are incomplete, even profit-maximizing owners may disagree about corporate strategy because of different preferences regarding risk and the time profile of expected cash flows.

Following Hansmann (1988, 1996) and Thomsen and Pedersen (1998), we can use the relative costs and benefits of ownership for each owner category as a benchmark for assessing its dominant objectives. To model the firm as a nexus of contracts with a number of different stakeholders such as (in this case) institutional investors, banks, business partners, managers or the government, there are transaction costs associated with each of these contracts. Ownership can in principle be assigned to any one of these stakeholders who will then incur the costs of ownership, but is relieved of the costs of market contracting. The (opportunity) costs of assigning the ownership rights to another stakeholder consist of the sum of added ownership costs plus added costs of market contracting. All else equal, the optimal ownership type, j, minimizes transaction costs which consist of ownership costs (CO) and costs of market contracting (CC) (i.e. it solves the optimization problem):

$$\text{Min } (CO_j + \Sigma_{i \neq j} CC_i) \text{ by } j,$$

where i is an index of the firm's stakeholders. Furthermore, regardless of the optimality of the present owners, the economic behaviour of individual ownership types is likely to be influenced by their ownership costs and benefits.

An example

Table 7.1 gives a numerical application of Hansmann's formula. Imagine that there are four 'patrons' (you can also call them stakeholders or just 'possible owners'): investors, suppliers, managers and government. And imagine that the cost of contracting and ownership are given by the numbers in the table.

2 This section draws on Thomsen and Pedersen (2000).

Table 7.1 Applying Hansmann's formula – a numerical example

Patron	Costs of ownership	Costs of contracting	Total cost
Investors	1	8	19
Suppliers	2	7	21
Managers	3	6	23
Government	4	5	25

From the investor viewpoint, the cost of acquiring ownership would be the sum of the direct ownership costs plus the costs of market contracting with other participants, that is total transaction costs of

$$1 + 7 + 6 + 5 = 19$$

For suppliers, the total transaction costs would be:

$$2 + 8 + 6 + 5 = 21$$

If you go through the last two rows, you will see that estimated transaction costs are still higher. It follows that investors, whose transaction costs of ownership are the lowest in this case, should take ownership (provided that the benefits of ownership exceed the cost).

In Hansmann's framework, the costs of market contracting include the conventional losses attributed to market power distortions (double marginalization, Tirole, 1992, pp. 170–171), ex post transaction costs associated with asset specificity (of the type emphasized by Williamson, 1985), and information costs (Arrow, 1975). Transaction costs of this kind incurred by one particular stakeholder or group of stakeholders can be avoided to some extent if these stakeholders become owners and thereby internalize their transactions with the firm. The costs of ownership include monitoring and risk-bearing costs (as emphasized by Jensen and Meckling, 1976), but also costs of collective decision making (Hansmann, 1988), which may be large if the owners are a large and heterogeneous group.

For example, companies run by an owner-manager avoid the transaction costs by hiring the services of professional managers (i.e. the incentive and information problems studied in standard agency theory), but have to incur market transaction costs in financing (i.e. to use debt rather than equity capital) since the firm cannot at the same time internalize its transactions with managers and outside investors. In contrast, investor-owned companies can obtain equity finance from the stock markets, but have to contract out for the services of professional managers. Hybrid solutions (e.g. when shareholders share ownership with managers) are clearly possible, but they may give rise to conflicts of interest between the two owner categories, in which case the objectives of the dominant category seem more likely to prevail (although the exact relationship between ownership concentration and owner 'power' is complex, Cubbin and Leech, 1983).

Furthermore, the objectives imposed on the company by any given dominant ownership category are likely to reflect the ownership costs and benefits of that category. In the case of owner-managed companies ('proprietorships'), financial problems due to capital rationing, short time horizons, and risk aversion are particularly likely to influence the company (Fama and Jensen, 1985). For example, compared with investor-owned companies, owner-managed companies seem less likely to undertake ambitious investment programmes to exploit economies of scale and are more likely to pursue niche strategies related to flexibility or differentiation. For the same reason Chandler (1977, 1990) regarded separation of ownership and control as an essential part of the enduring logic of industrial success in exploiting scale economies.

Below we comment briefly on the characteristics of some standard ownership structures for listed companies which are analysed in greater detail in subsequent chapters. We then go on to treat some other ownership structures in greater detail: cooperatives and private equity firms.

Investor ownership has advantages in terms of easy access to capital, low risk aversion and a relatively long time horizon. Furthermore, institutional investors are characterized by portfolio investments and arm's length relationships with firms. In comparison with other owner categories, they are relatively specialized as owners, their performance is often measured in terms of financial success, and their objectives can therefore be described as shareholder value and liquidity. However their usually low ownership shares impair their ability to influence management. Nevertheless, empirical studies have found a positive effect of investor ownership on company performance (e.g. Pedersen and Thomsen, 2000). There is more on institutional investor ownership in Chapter 12.

Family ownership is often associated with a double role for the family as owners and managers of the firm. In economic terms, families make firm-specific investments in human capital which makes them reluctant to give up control (Maug, 1996). This, and the fact that founding family owners of larger corporations are likely to be relatively wealthy, may create a long-term commitment to the survival of the company. However, since a disproportionate share of their wealth is invested in the company, and since families often do not want to risk losing control by attracting equity from the stock markets, family-owned companies may be relatively risk averse, and they are more likely to be capital-rationed than other companies. Furthermore, families may derive private benefits from running the company at the expense of minority shareholders (expropriation) (Fama and Jensen, 1983; La Porta et al., 1998). In support of the expropriation hypothesis, Johnson et al. (1985) find that the stock market reacts favourably to the unexpected death of CEOs with large ownership stakes. Generally empirical studies have found that first-generation family firms (founder-owned companies) outperform other ownership structure, but after succession to the next generations performance drops to average levels and perhaps below that. You can find more on family ownership in Chapter 17.

Bank ownership is illegal in the USA and generally avoided in the UK, but it plays an important role in the so-called German model (Charkham, 1994) in which banks function as universal providers of financial services (Hausbanks) to industrial companies. Since bank-owned companies have (at least partly) internalized their banking relationships, they may have privileged access to capital, information, and other services which the banks have to offer. In support, Cable (1985) finds a positive performance effect of bank ownership among West German firms, and Hoshi et al. (1990a, 1990b, 1991) and Ramirez (1995) indicate that members of bank-based business groups are less likely to be credit-rationed. However, it is also possible that banks use their power over firms to extract higher interest rates. More on bank ownership in Chapter 13.

Corporate ownership ties are an integral feature of the Japanese keiretsu, the French cross-holding structures, and Swedish business groups (Kester, 1992; Charkham, 1994). Vertical ties between companies at different stages of the value chain appear to play an important role in those groups which are not bank-based. In this case, the company has internalized its transactions with the providers of a critical input which makes sense under conditions of high asset specificity and transaction frequency (Williamson, 1985). As demonstrated by Caves (1996), the multinational company's choice of foreign direct investment over exports reflects similar reasoning. In particular corporate ownership ties may facilitate knowledge transfers. Nevertheless, as recognized by Kester (1992) the advantages of business group membership come at a cost: for example loss of flexibility and risk of deficient mutual monitoring. Hundley and Jacobson's finding (1998) that keiretsu members do worse in terms of export performance than non-members indicates that the costs may sometimes exceed the benefits. There is more on corporate ownership in keiretsus in Chapter 14.

Government ownership internalizes the relationship between government and company which may or may not make overall sense, but which functions as an institutional alternative to regulation. With regard to economic performance, the literature (e.g. Shepherd, 1989; Laffont and Tirole, 1993; Hart et al., 1996) suggests that governments are likely to pay special attention to political goals such as low output prices, employment, or external effects relative to profitability. In fact, non-profit maximizing behaviour is a key rationale for government ownership in welfare economics (e.g. Arrow, 1969), since it is expected to correct market failures by acting differently from private firms (e.g. Shepherd,

1989). Ceteris paribus, government-owned enterprises are therefore expected to be low performers in terms of conventional performance measures. On the other hand, governments are usually relatively wealthy, which implies a relative advantage for government-owned companies in terms of credit, liquidity, or costs of capital. Moreover, governments are often more likely to tolerate state-owned monopolies which can make it easier for government firms to make money. We examine the costs and benefits of government ownership more closely in Chapter 15.

Non-profit firms are quite frequent among hospitals, universities, research institutions, museums and schools. Non-profit enterprises such as universities, monasteries or church institutions are far older than joint stock corporations. The non-profit status does not mean they cannot make profits, but rather that they do not distribute the profits to outside owners. So-called commercial non-profits which buy and sell goods or services will obviously make a profit if revenues exceed costs. But instead of paying them out as dividends they accumulate or reinvest profits or alternatively use them to expand their activities. According to a review by Malani, Philipson and David (2003) there are three main theories in the literature on commercial non-profits: 1) the altruism model, 2) the worker cooperative model, and 3) the non-contractible quality model. In the altruism model non-profits are motivated by a charitable purpose which differs from profit maximization (e.g. the Red Cross). In the worker cooperative model doctors at a hospital or professors at a university effectively own their organizations and choose the non-profit enterprise as a convenient organizational form. Profits are distributed to doctors or other workers as salaries. In the quality uncertainty model it is regarded as a disadvantage for certain types of firms to have owners who may prefer to pay out dividends rather than service their customers properly. This may be the case in charitable foundations or other institutions which receive most of their revenues from donors who are reluctant to see their donations paid out as dividends to shareholders (Fama and Jensen, 1983). They therefore prefer to give to non-profit entities. Industrial foundations are foundations which own normal business companies. Thus ownership structure is quite common in Northern Europe. We will look at it more closely in Chapter 16.

7.7   Cooperatives[3]

Cooperatives are member-based associations which own business firms. For example, milk farmers may get together and establish a dairy or customers in a village may join forces to establish their own grocery store or electricity plant. They may also want to establish their own bank or insurance company as a financial mutual. Cooperatives dominate many industries in food and agriculture and have substantial market shares in others such as financial services and utilities (water, electricity, and housing).

Classical efficiency rationales for cooperatives have focused on the cooperative form as a way to overcome the monopsony problems that occur when a group of farmers face a single buyer (e.g. an intermediary producer such as a dairy or slaughterhouse). Under these circumstances, optimal behaviour by the intermediary producer can be shown to lead to double marginalization, a market distortion compared with perfect competition. The monopsonist/monopolist intermediary is predicted to both reduce its demand for the primary product to lower input prices and to reduce its supply to the end market to obtain higher prices for the final product (e.g. Tirole, 1992). Under these circumstances the farmers can overcome the monopoly distortion and can increase their joint profits by establishing their own dairy, slaughterhouse and electricity plant in cooperative form. However, there are various other ways to overcome such monopoly problems. Tirole (1992) discusses the range of vertical restraints as possible solutions, and additional explanations are required for when the cooperative will be the most preferred (cost-efficient) alternative. Why would it be necessary to form an association to have vertical integration?

---

[3] This section draws on Thomsen and Pedersen (1998): Industry and Ownership Structure, *International Review of Law and Economics*. For a useful survey of agricultural cooperatives see Cook, Chaddad and Iliopoulos (2004).

One argument could be that decentralized ownership of farming is most efficient for incentive reasons. Due to moral hazard problems owner-managed farms could be a first best solution to the allocation of ownership (Hart, 1988). Since this would make it inefficient for the manufacturer to own the farms, the alternative would be to have the farmers own the dairy. Forming an association for this might then be seen as a suitable response.

Another approach based on Hansmann (1988) is to stress the transaction costs advantages of internalizing transactions with suppliers or customers. For example, cooperative slaughterhouses can achieve greater capacity utilization and lower costs because farmers are contractually bound to sell their pigs to the slaughterhouse. Moreover, farmers can be sure that they can sell their pigs, i.e. they have the right as well as the obligation to sell their products to the cooperative. This reduces uncertainty, marketing and production costs at the farm level. Slaughterhouses and farmers can also more readily share information and cooperate on quality standards etc. because they are part of the same entity. However, internalizing supplier or customer relations means that capital and management services have to be produced on market terms with added transaction costs.

Hansmann (1988) argues that the costs of collective decision making are typically high in cooperatives, but that the commonality of interests and extensive information sharing that is characteristic of rural/farm communities reduce these problems. This provides an explanation for why the cooperative form is widely used for farm-related activities (dairies, slaughterhouses, and retailers based in the countryside) but is comparatively rare in other parts of the economy. In sum, a high frequency of cooperatives is expected in farm-related activities or activities based in the countryside. Because of problems in attracting outside equity the frequency of cooperative ownership should be negatively related to the amount of firm-specific capital necessary to operate in an industry, and, in particular, cooperatives should be rare in industries characterized by large firms and high sunk costs.

Value maximization in cooperatives is different from shareholder value maximization in listed firms. In a cooperative, farmers are paid a provisional price per kilo of input (meat or milk) corresponding ideally to marginal costs. Then, at the end of the year, if the cooperative makes a profit it is distributed pro rata per unit input rather than per share (or unit of equity capital) as in joint stock companies. In other words, cooperatives seek to maximize profits per unit of input while joint stock companies seek (at least in principle) to maximize profits per unit of capital (return on equity). The two principles can easily create disagreements in joint ventures between cooperatives and outside investors, as when cooperative members want high input prices to maximize farm profits and outside investors want low input prices to maximize shareholder value.

Corporate governance in cooperatives also differs from governance in listed companies. Members vote personally (one person – one vote) rather than per unit of capital (one share – one vote) or unit of input (one pig – one vote). This means that they come to resemble political organizations to some extent although the members have a clear economic interest in the process. Alternatively cooperatives can be compared to listed companies with extremely diversified ownership in which free-rider problems are an ever-present risk. Partly in response to inefficiencies in the political process like time inconsistency, agenda sensitivity or minority abuse, the democratic election process is invariably indirect with many checks and balances. For example members do not decide directly on most issues (direct democracy), but use indirect democracy to elect representatives, for example having members first elect a board of representatives which then elects the company board.

Another characteristic of cooperative ownership is that members cannot sell their shares (or membership rights), the value of which stays in the company when they leave (e.g. retire). This implies conflicts of interest between older and newer members (Hansmann, 1996). Older members are rationally opposed to long-term investments financed by lower dividends, which younger members may rationally favour. As the saying goes, you come in naked and you leave naked, that is you do not have to pay to get in but neither do you get paid for leaving. The absence of a secondary market for ownership rights means that cooperatives do not have a stock price which reflects the overall value of the company. It also means that the members care much more about dividends and that it may be difficult to establish a strong equity base in the company. As a result cooperatives tend to be more leveraged than listed companies, which may make it more difficult for them to invest in research and development and other long-term projects. This tendency is reinforced in farm cooperatives when the farmers are relatively poor because of tough competition and low profit margins, and when they have a lot of debt in their farm business.

Strategically, farm cooperatives tend to be low cost volume maximizers rather than technology leaders, advertisers or product differentiators. This is partly because of their obligation to buy all the produce of their members, partly because quality differences among producers will tend to lead to conflicts of interests, and partly because of the leveraged capital structure. Farm products which are relatively stable, standardized commodities appear to fit the bill quite well.

Cooperative boards are often elected in constituencies representing different groups of members (e.g. a certain geographical area). In other words, boards are not necessarily a team who work together for a common goal but guard their own special interests. It may be necessary, for example, to close down a slaughterhouse, but in what region should it be? Perhaps for the same reason cooperative boards also tend to be very large and to be composed of members (e.g. farmers) rather than professional non-executive directors. This may tend to skew the balance of power towards the professional managers. On the other hand, farmers in farm cooperatives are quite knowledgeable about farming and not too patient with their money. Another risk may be that the board members tend to focus more on issues like production which they understand well and less on marketing, product development or international expansion.

International production raises special problems in cooperatives whose members have to decide whether to allow suppliers in other countries to become members. This may create cultural problems, particularly in countries where cooperative companies are uncommon. An alternative may be to establish wholly owned foreign subsidiaries, which will then have to be financed exclusively by home country members with relatively high opportunity costs of capital. In this case internationalization is likely to be slower than in competing listed companies, and this may be a competitive disadvantage for cooperatives. Finally, they may attract capital in the host country by partial listing which will then give rise to the predictable conflicts of interest described above. Faced with these and similar challenges many former cooperatives have decided to transform themselves into share companies or to sell out to other companies with a different ownership structure.

Financial mutuals have many of the same characteristics and challenges as farm cooperatives (McKillop, 2005). They are in principle just cooperatives whose members are customers of banks, insurance companies, building societies, credit providers etc. However, there are also some crucial differences. In some cases the members are prohibited by law from dissolving the company and seizing the assets, in which case their ownership rights are severely curtailed. It may be more correct to talk of them as member-governed rather than as member-owned companies. Secondly the nature of the services they provide means that member loyalty may be more fleeting than in agricultural commodities. Many members of a financial mutual may not regard themselves as owners or even members in any meaningful sense since they become members by choosing the cheapest product. Thirdly, the standardized nature of the product provided means that competition is a powerful governance mechanism. If the firm cannot provide competitive products at competitive prices, its members can vote with their feet and take their business to a competitor. For example, unlike shareholders, depositors in a (listed or cooperative) bank can take out their deposits and place them with another bank. In the same way, the bond market may constrain the financing of an inefficient mortgage institution.

It is relatively easy to point to potential inefficiencies in cooperatives and all other ownership structures. Therefore the important point is how inefficient they are relative to, for example, the agency problems in listed companies. Over time agricultural cooperatives have gained market share in food products. This indicates some competitive advantages. In past decades financial mutuals lost market share due to de-mutualization, but appear to have weathered the financial crisis much better than other financial firms, partly because they are more conservative. Altogether the evidence indicates that there is a role to play for cooperatives as for other ownership structures.

7.8   Private equity[4]

Private equity (PE) is a relatively new kind of ownership structure, which emerged during the 1980s in the US when private equity funds became famous for hostile takeovers. It gradually spread to the rest of the world in the next few decades, partly as a result of the internationalization of US PE firms like Blackstone and KKR, partly by the emergence of new PE firms in Europe and elsewhere.

Unlike venture capital firms which specialize in early stage financing of high-technology firms in biotech and IT, private equity funds specialize in buying mature firms, restructuring them and selling them again after some years (on average around five years). Therefore they are often called buy-out funds. However, to the confusion of the general public, the academic literature often refers to private equity as an overall term encompassing both venture capital and buyout funds. Some even refer to venture capital firms as the generic term for both venture capital and private equity. It is true that there are similarities in the organization of the two types of funds (partnership organization, incentive schemes), but their focus is different. Venture capital starts or develops new firms. Private equity restructures mature firms. It is equally important to distinguish private equity funds from other funds such as sovereign wealth funds or pension funds (sovereign wealth funds are government-owned investment funds typically set up to reinvest earnings from oil or other raw materials).

Private equity firms are typically organized as partnerships managed by a general partner (the private equity firm) and financed by limited partners (investors), who invest in a fund managed by the firm (Ribstein, 2009). One reason why they are organized this way is that the structure is tax-transparent so that the investors do not have to pay taxes twice on capital gains. The private equity firm itself typically consists of a limited number of partners and employees, perhaps a dozen or so. When the fund is raised investors commit a sizeable amount of money to the fund, which the private equity firm (the general partner) can 'call' when it has identified a company to invest in or a follow-up investment in one of the existing portfolio companies. Typically the investors have no say in how the money is invested. They have to come up with it when it is called by the general partner. The fund typically has a fixed duration, e.g. 10 years, after which it is dissolved. General partners who perform well will obviously find it much easier to raise new funds while bad performers will find it impossible. Reputation and track record is therefore a key governance mechanism for private equity funds. The limited time span also helps foster what the private equity funds call 'a sense of urgency'. Recently, however, some large firms have changed their business model and become listed entities themselves.

Private equity funds use high-powered performance incentives (Prowse, 1998; Zong, 2005). The fund managers (general partners) charge an administration fee of perhaps 2% of assets under management. However, when their performance exceeds a benchmark of typically 8% return a year the general partner is paid a 'carry' (fee) of perhaps 20% of the excess profits. It has been much discussed whether this fee should be taxed with capital gains or income tax, but in any case the private equity firm does not invest the equivalent 20% of the capital in the fund. However it is quite customary that managers in the private equity firm also co-invest in the fund. Moreover, they typically also ask the managers and board members of the acquired firms to co-invest with them. This implies a strong economic interest in creating shareholder value in the acquired firms.

Private equity funds are known to rely heavily on leverage, i.e. borrowed money (Kaplan, 2007; Wright, Gilligan and Amess, 2009), so much in fact that they are sometimes known as leveraged buy-out funds. At least before the financial crisis they would typically leverage their investment three or four times, so that they put in for example 1 billion of their own equity and borrow 2 billion to finance an acquisition of 3 billion. If the value of the acquired firm then doubles over a 5-year period (a not unusual situation in the past) and it is sold for 6 billion, the fund has made $4 - 1 = 3$ billion and the private equity firm has added $0.2 * (4 - 1 * 1,08^5) = 506$ million to its expected fee (Table 7.2).

---

[4]   For useful readings on private equity see Acharya, Kehoe and Reyner (2009); Wright, Amess, Weir and Girma (2009) or Zong (2005) on governance practices; Wright, Gilligan and Amess (2009) on profitability and economic effects; Wright Bacon and Amess (2009) on the impact on human resource policies; and Wood and Wright (2009) for a general survey.

Table 7.2 Structure of a leveraged buyout

	Purchase	Sale
Equity	1	4
Debt	2	2
Total firm value	3	6

In this case they typically do not get the 2% annual administration fee. Carry is usually not calculated deal by deal but fund by fund, however, so it may be that other firms in the portfolio turn out to be less lucrative. However, when asset prices are rising private equity firms tend to make a lot of money because of the leverage.

The same leverage effect could of course also be achieved on the stock market, i.e. borrow 2 billion against an investment of 1 billion and invest 3 billion in a stock market index. If share prices double, you would have a return of 300% on your investment (excluding debt costs and dividends). So naturally, we would expect higher returns in a leveraged portfolio, when asset prices increase, but most investors prefer to avoid this kind of leverage because of the obvious risk: what if prices fall? A price drop of ⅓ from 3 to 2 is enough to wipe out their equity. It is important to notice the asymmetry in compensation here: if the market goes up, the private equity firm gets a carry of 20%. If it goes down they do not lose, but get the administration fee of 2% a year. So successful private equity managers have made enormous amounts of money in the past, much more than they could ever have earned as CEOs in listed firms. However, the fact is that investors like pension funds have been willing to invest an increasing amount of their money on these terms. Why?

Private equity firms do more than leverage, of course. First of all, unlike other investors such as families (who own because they inherited) or pension funds (who hold a stock market index +/–), private equity funds only invest if they think they can make money, i.e. if they have an investment hypothesis of how to take the company from A to B and make money in the process. They often use one of two generic strategies: acceleration or reversal. Acceleration is when they invest in a profitable company and want to accelerate its growth, for example by M&A. In this case they typically work with the incumbent management and try to support their ideas, perhaps modify them a little to maximize shareholder value. Reversal is when they want to undo an existing strategy, for example break up a company which has expanded by conglomerate diversification, i.e. adding more business areas. In that case private equity firms will often want to replace the incumbent managers, perhaps by a hostile takeover. They will want to break up the company by focusing on core business and selling off business units in other areas. Most likely they may also want to slash overheads, cut down on the workforce, renegotiate contracts with suppliers and so on. In many cases they use combinations of the two generic strategies, but it will typically be possible to classify the overall strategy in one box or the other. Since the equity funds do not have the inside knowledge or industry experience, they will typically either focus on some relatively clear and robust strategies or alternatively rely on insiders and experts to come up with more original ideas.

Once they have taken over there is evidence that private equity firms manage their portfolio firms differently from other owners. First and foremost they act as owners, not passive investors (Wright, Gilligan and Amess, 2009). The approach is hands on rather than arm's length distance. They engage in active ownership through frequent talks with managers in the portfolio companies (in and outside board meetings), they have their partners or employees sit on portfolio company boards, they participate actively in key decisions relating to M&A, capital structure etc. in which they have special expertise, and sometimes they lead special development projects on supply chain management, IT or other important company issues. They are known to be quicker at replacing underperforming executives or board members. The balance of power between shareholders and managers is therefore different (and much more favourable to owners) than in companies with dispersed ownership.

The financial performance of private equity is a much debated issue. The private equity industry itself often claims to achieve spectacular returns much above those in listed companies. And individual PE firms routinely claim to beat the market year after year. After all, this is part of their fund raising. However, given uncertainty and measurement error the empirical evidence is more consistent with normal returns when adjusting for leverage, risk and fees (Wright, Gilligan and Amess, 2009). Nevertheless, unlike for other investment fund managers the academic literature has found evidence of persistence in returns so that the best private equity funds, who achieve abnormal returns, will tend to do so year after year. Many pension funds and other investors therefore attempt to invest only in the best funds with a good track record (and are therefore able to charge higher fees).

In conclusion, private equity funds are important to corporate governance, because they account for an increasing share of the global economy, and because they have distinct governance characteristics. In recent years firms with other ownership structures, including investor and family-owned companies, have tried to learn from the best private equity firms – leveraging their capital structure, focusing on board competencies, restructuring and repackaging business units, incentivizing the management team and so on.

7.9 Best owner

In conclusion, we conjecture that each of the ownership categories has different objectives with implications for corporate strategy and performance. The analysis indicates that institutional investors are more focused on conventional performance measures like shareholder value while the other ownership types typically have other business relationships with the firm (e.g. the bank that is both owner and creditor). Accordingly, these owners try to optimize across the entire range of relationships with the firm, so that their objective vis-à-vis the company becomes a composite of ownership and the other stakeholder interests.

While corporate ownership used to be taken for granted, it is increasingly becoming part of business strategy and value creation. Private equity funds believe that they can create value by new ownership and so do the many other acquirers. New financial instruments like hedging or advanced combinations of debt and equity can decouple ownership rights from cash flow rights and make it easier to finance new ownership structures.

A third increasingly important part of the ownership calculation is outsourcing, which is addressed by the make-or-buy decision: should we have an IT department or outsource it to IBM (or CSC)? Should we run our own call centre or outsource it to India?

The 'best owner' of a company, or an asset, is the owner which can create most value with it, which involves weighing costs and benefits of ownership. In an open auction, this 'best owner' will win because she will be paying the highest price for the company. It is interesting therefore to inquire what makes one owner better than another. While a complete theory remains to be developed, it is possible to identify some important determinants (Dobbs, Huyett and Koller, 2010).

At the core this is a matching problem where a range of potential owners with given characteristics are matched with firms which also have different characteristics.

- **Capital** is the traditional reason for going public. If some owners have capital and others do not, the firm may be more valuable for the capital-rich owners who can invest more in it.
- **Risk aversion**. The more risk averse the potential owner is, the less likely it is that she will take ownership.
- **Information**. All else equal, the individuals who run a company are the best owners since they have more and better information than anybody else.
- **Competence**. Some potential owners have acquired an expertise in running businesses which others do not have. Owner competence may be industry- and country-specific. The 'stupid son' does not automatically inherit the competence of the 'clever father'.
- **Strategic fit**. Sometimes a business unit does not fit into the overall strategy of a corporation which would like to concentrate its effort elsewhere. It may, therefore, be put up for sale.

- **Business relations**. Other companies are more likely to acquire a company with which they have on-going business relations, particularly if they involve mutual dependency (asset specificity).
- **Preferences**. Individuals have different preferences, and preferences may change over time. Some may be interested in acquiring ownership and some in divesting it.
- **Government regulation**. Some companies or individuals are occasionally not allowed to acquire certain companies, for example because of anti-trust legislation or national security. There may also be legal ceilings on the amount of stock that investors can own in an individual firm.

7.10 Active ownership

Ownership does not automatically influence company behaviour. It needs to be exercised, and can be exercised more or less intelligently. Passive owners, like some institutional investors or founding families, do not interfere with their firms and therefore implicitly delegate responsibility to managers or other owners. Some investors do not bother to show up or vote at the annual shareholder meetings. The result may be a power vacuum in which managers completely dominate corporate decision making.

Other owners are much more active. Owner-managers take an active part in running the business. Even if they don't, they may play a role as non-executive board members or as active watchdogs at shareholder meetings.

Institutional investors may also be more or less active as we will see in the Chapter 12. Some like CalPERS or TIAA-CREF have made a name for themselves by targeting, naming and shaming badly behaving companies. Others are quieter about it and have a dialogue with managers where they can suggest improvements. Yet others just sell if they are not satisfied. And many don't do anything at all, but simply hold on to their stock.

So-called engagement funds have tried to profit from stockholder negligence by pressuring managers to make value-enhancing decisions. For example hedge funds (organized as private equity funds, but with a much shorter time horizon) buy a non-trivial amount of stock and use their shareholdings to pressure managers to increase shareholder value. If they are successful they stand to gain from the ensuing share price increase.

It is not true however that active ownership is always better, not even from a shareholder perspective. The optimal level of activism will depend on owner competence, for example. Children of a successful company founder may be better off by being passive and delegating more decisions to managers and other professionals. Shareholder wealth and risk preferences may also be important. In many cases it is optimal for owners to keep some distance from the firm.

Private equity funds and venture capitalists can be more or less active in the portfolio companies that they control. They can sit on the company board, communicate directly with company managers, and take charge of key decisions like M&A or special development projects in the companies (thus sidestepping company managers). Alternatively, they can keep their distance and let the companies be run by professional board members and managers. Private equity funds typically have more than one portfolio company which diversifies their portfolio and this creates a distinction (distance) between firm and fund risk profiles.

Likewise, politicians may decide to intervene in a government organization like the navy or a state-owned enterprise and be active participants in the organization. Alternatively, they may decide to fix the organization's objectives and leave the rest to professionals. They may decide to run a state-owned enterprise from the ministry or let it establish independent headquarters outside, which would also add to governance distance.

The value of distance probably emerges from a specialization of management and control functions. If controllers become too involved in management, they lose their objectivity because they effectively have to monitor their own decisions. Moreover they forego the advantages of delegation. Both factors will reduce organizational efficiency. Thus, as organizations grow and the complexity of their tasks increases, we would expect to observe increasing distance between companies and their owners.

On the other hand it may well be that very distant controllers lose touch with the organization they are supposed to monitor and that the optimal distance between controllers and managers will therefore be less than infinite (i.e. less than complete separation of the two functions). Thus boards, for example, are not only charged with hiring and firing managers, but also have a role in strategic decision making. Or large owners may decide to put some of their own people on the boards of companies they control. Even the purview of ordinary shareholders is not limited to electing the board; they must also approve or reject major decisions which change the nature of the company. Thus we hypothesize the familiar bell-shaped relationship between distance and economic performance such that performance first increases with distance but starts to decline as we approach full separation.

7.11 Discussion

Ownership matters. It may not matter much whether a large listed firm is owned by this or that set of institutional investors, but it matters whether the company is owned by investors, a family or some other big blockholder. For large blockholders the identity of the owners is important because owners have different competencies and resources. Distinct ownership structures such as cooperatives or private equity firms have their own governance styles and special governance problems which need to be addressed. It is impossible to find a single universally superior governance model, but for individual companies it may be possible to find a 'best owner'.

Owners can be more or less active. Some operate hands on, others maintain arm's length distance. The level of activity will also depend on firm-specific factors.

Minicase

Privatizing a telecommunications firm[5]

A government in a small country is considering whether to privatize a telecommunications firm which was formerly a state monopoly. The firm has a high, but falling market share, particularly in the diminishing fixed line segment, and a substantial free cash flow. It is investing in other European telecommunications firms, mobile telephony, broadband and internet services like on-line music. The telecommunications market is being liberalized and competition is increasing, but the market is large and growing.

Several privatization options are being discussed. The company could be listed and the government could gradually sell its shares. The company might then continue with dispersed ownership primarily by institutional investors. Critics claim that the share price might fluctuate wildly if the company becomes an object of speculation by large foreign hedge funds. It might also be snapped up by a foreign competitor, several of which are expanding internationally. In this case it would become a foreign subsidiary. Or a consortium of private equity funds might buy it. The government could counter this by a takeover defence like retaining a golden share which gives it the right to veto takeovers. Some suggest that the company should be sold to a large domestic owner, but this is against international competition rules.

The government could also stick to the status quo and retain its shares. Alternatively, it could privatize only a part of the company and keep a majority share. This could be combined with the adoption of standard governance principles like a professional board and stock option compensation for the executives.

---

[5] This case is fictional, but inspired by real world events. Telecommunication firms around the world have been or are being privatized. They are sometimes sold to the public, sometimes to other firms, sometimes they are bought by private equity funds.

Discussion questions

1 Could there be an agency problem in this company? What kind?
2 Would the country and the company be served by privatization?
3 Is there some truth in what the critics say about market short-termism and hedge funds?
4 Would the company's long-term progress be served by dispersed ownership?
5 What would be the costs and benefits of foreign ownership?
6 What might a private equity firm do to the company?
7 How about a domestic blockholder taking a large share? Would that work?
8 What would you advise the government to do?

Summary (learning points)

■ Ownership is a set of rights to use, control, profit from and transfer assets.

■ Shareholders usually have rights to control (vote), profit (dividend) and transfer (sell) shares.

■ Ownership matters most when ownership is concentrated.

■ Ownership identity matters because different owners (individuals, institutions, companies, governments, non-profits) have different goals, competences and resources.

■ Each ownership structure has its costs and benefits which makes it appropriate for certain firms.

■ A higher ownership share can lead to positive incentive effects and negative entrenchment effects.

■ Private equity funds specialize in buying, owning and selling firms. They typically target mature firms with a high cash flow.

■ Cooperatives are associations which may own business firms. They are particularly common in farm-related businesses.

References and further reading

Acharya, V.V., Kehoe, C. and Reyner, M. (2009) Private Equity vs. PLC Boards in the U.K.: A Comparison of Practices and Effectiveness, *Journal of Applied Corporate Finance*, **21** (1), 45–56.

Alchian, A.A. and Demsetz, H. (1972) Production, Information Costs, and Economic Organization, *American Economic Review*, **62** (5), 777–795.

Amihud, Y. and Lev, B. (1981) Risk reduction as a managerial motive for conglomerate mergers, *Bell Journal of Economics*, **12** (2), 605–617.

Arrow, K.J. (1969) The organization of economic activity: issues pertinent to the choice of market versus nonmarket allocation, in *The Analysis and Evaluation of Public Expenditure: The PPB System*, Vol. 1, U.S. Joint Economic Committee, 91st Congress, 1st Session, US Print Office: Washington DC.

Arrow, K.J. (1975) Vertical Integration and Communication, *Bell Journal of Economics*, **6** (1), 173–183.

Bergh, D.D. (1995) Size and relatedness of units sold, *Strategic Management Journal*, **16** (3), 221–240.

Bergström, C. and Rydqvist, K. (1990) The Determinants of Corporate Ownership. An Empirical Study on Swedish Data, *Journal of Banking and Finance*, **14** (2), 237–253.

Berle, A. and Means, C. (1932) *The Modern Corporation and Private Property*, Macmillan: New York.

Bethel, J.E. and Liebeskind, J. (1993) The effects of ownership structure on corporate restructuring, *Strategic Management Journal*, **14** (Summer Special Issue), 15–31.

Blaine, M. (1994) Comparing the Profitability of Firms in Germany, Japan and the United States, *Management International Review*, **34** (2), 125–148.

Bogetoft, P. (2005) An information economic rationale for cooperatives, *European Review of Agricultural Economics*, **32** (2), 191–217.

Cable, J. (1985) Capital Market Information and Industrial Performance: The Role of West German Banks, *Economic Journal*, **95** (377), 118–132.

Caves, R. (1996) *Multinational Enterprise and Economic Analysis*, Cambridge University Press: Cambridge, UK.

Chandler, A.D. (1977) *The visible hand: The managerial revolution in American Business*, Bellknap Press: Cambridge, MA.

Chandler, A.D. (1990) *Scale and Scope*, Harvard University Press: Cambridge MA.

Charkham, J.P. (1994) *Keeping Good Company – A Study of Corporate Governance in Five Countries*, Clarendon Press: Oxford.

Cho, M. (1998) Ownership Structure, Investment, and The Corporate Value: An Empirical Analysis, *Journal of Financial Economics*, **47** (1), 103–121.

Cook, M., Chaddad, F. and Iliopoulos, C. (2004) Advances in Cooperative Theory since 1990: A Review of Agricultural Economics Literature, in *Restructuring Agricultural Cooperatives*, Hendrikse, G.W.J. (ed), pp. 65–90.

Cubbin, J. and Leech, D. (1983) The Effect of Shareholding Dispersion on the Degree of Control in British Companies: Theory and Measurement, *Economic Journal*, **93** (370), 351–369.

Cumming, D., Siegel, D.S. and Wright, M. (2007) Private equity, leveraged buyouts and governance, *Journal of Corporate Finance*, **13** (4), 439–460.

De Jong, H. (1995) European Capitalism: Between Freedom and Social Justice, *Review of Industrial Organization*, **10** (4), 399–419.

Demsetz. H. (1983) The Structure of Ownership and The Theory of the Firm, *Journal of Law and Economics*, **26** (2), 375–394.

Demsetz, H. and Lehn, K. (1985) The structure of corporate ownership: Causes and consequences, *Journal of Political Economy*, **93** (6), 1155–1177.

Dennis, D.D., Denis, D.K. and Sarin, A. (1997) Agency problems, equity ownership and corporate diversification, *Journal of Finance*, **52** (1), 135–160.

Dobbs, R., Huyett, B. and Koller, T. (2010) Are you still the best owner of your assets?, *McKinsey Quarterly*, **1** 107–111.

Fama, E. (1980) Agency Problems and the Theory of the Firm, *Journal of Political Economy*, **88** (2), 288–307.

Fama, E.F. and Jensen, M.C. (1983) Agency Problems and Residual Claims, *Journal of Law and Economics*, **26** (2), 327–349.

Fama, E.F. and Jensen, M.C. (1985) Organizational Forms and Investment Decisions, *Journal of Financial Economics*, **14** (1), 101–119.

Gedajlovich, E. and Shapiro, D. (1998) Management and Ownership Effects: Evidence from 5 Countries, Strategic Management Journal, **19** (6), 533–555.

Gerson, J. and Barr, G. (1996) The Structure of Corporate Control and Ownership in a Regulatory Environment Unbiased toward One-Share-One-Vote, *Corporate Governance*, **4** (2), 78–93.

Gibbs, P.A. (1993) Determinants of corporate restructuring: The relative importance of corporate governance, takeover threat, and free cash flow, *Strategic Management Journal*, **14** (S1), 51–68.

Hansmann, H. (1988) Ownership of the Firm, Journal of Law, Economics and Organization, **4** (2), 267–305.

Hansmann, H. (1996) *The Ownership of Enterprise*, The Belknap Press of Harvard University Press: Cambridge, MA.

Hart, O. (1983) The Market Mechanism as an Incentive Scheme, *Bell Journal of Economics*, **14** (2), 366–382.

Hart, O. (1988) Incomplete Contracts and the Theory of the Firm, *Journal of Law, Economics and Organization*, **4** (1), 119–139.

Hart, O., Shleifer, A. and Vishny, R.W. (1996) *The Proper Scope of Government*, Theory and an Application to Prisons, National Bureau of Economic Research, Working Paper 5744, September.

Hill, C.W.L. and Snell, S.A. (1989) Effects of ownership and control on corporate productivity, *Academy of Management Journal*, **32** (1), 25–46.

Holderness, C. and Sheehan, D. (1988) The Role of Majority Shareholders in Publicly Held Corporations, *Journal of Financial Economics*, **20** (1), 317–346.

Hoshi, T., Kashyap, A. and Sharfstein, D. (1990a) Banking, Monitoring and Investment. Evidence from the Changing Structure of Japanese Corporate Banking Relationships, in *Asymmetric Information, Corporate Finance and Investment*, G.R. Hubbard (ed), University of Chicago Press: Chicago.

Hoshi, T., Kashyap, A. and Sharfstein, D. (1990b) The Role of Banks in Reducing the Costs of Financial Distress in Japan, *Journal of Financial Economics*, **27** (1), 67–88.

Hoshi, T., Kashyap, A. and Sharfstein, D. (1991) Corporate Structure, Liquidity and Investment. Evidence from Japanese Industrial Groups, *Quarterly Journal of Economics*, **106** (1), 35–60.

Hoskisson, R.E., Johnson, J.R.A and Moesel, D.D. (1994) Corporate divestiture intensity in restructuring firms, Effects of governance, strategy and performance, *Academy of Management Journal*, **37** (5), 1207–1238.

Hundley, G. and Jacobson, C.K. (1998) The effects of the Keiretsu on the export performance of Japanese companies: Help or hindrance?, *Strategic Management Journal*, **19** (10), 927–937.

Jensen, M. (1986) Agency Costs of Free Cash Flow, Corporate Finance and Takeovers, *American Economic Review*, **76** (2), 323–329.

Jensen, M. (1989) Eclipse of the Public Corporation, *Harvard Business Review*, **67** (5), 61–75.

Jensen, M. (1993) The Modern Industrial Revolution,

Exit and the Failure of Internal Control Systems, *Journal of Finance*, **48** (3), 481–531.

Jensen, M.C. (2010) Active Investors, LBOs, and the Privatization of Bankruptcy, *Journal of Applied Corporate Finance*, **22** (1), 77–85.

Jensen, M.C. and Meckling, W.H. (1976) Theory of the Firm: Managerial Behavior, Agency Costs, and Ownership Structure, *Journal of Financial Economics*, **3** (4), 305–360.

Johnson, W.B., Macgee, R.P., Nagarajan, N.J. and Newman, H.A. (1985) An Analysis of the Stock Price Reaction to Sudden Executive Deaths. Implications for the Managerial Labour Market, *Journal of Accounting and Economics*, **7** (1), 151–174.

Kaplan, S. (2007) *Private Equity: Past, Present, and Future*, Presentation, The Economics of Private Equity, SIFR Conference, August 30–31, 2007.

Kaplan, S. and Schoar, A. (2005) Private Equity Performance: Returns Persistence and Capital, *Journal of Finance*, **60** (4), 1791–1823.

Kelsey, D. and Milne, F. (2010) Takeovers and cooperatives: governance and stability in non-corporate firms, *Journal of Economics*, **99** (3), 193–209.

Kester, C.W. (1992) Industrial Groups as Systems of Contractual Governance, *Oxford Review of Economic Policy*, **8** (3), 24–44.

La Porta, R., Lopez-de-Silanes, F., Shleifer, A. and Vishny, R.W. (1998) Law and Finance, *Journal of Political Economy*, **106** (6), 1113–1155.

Laffont, J.J. and Tirole, J. (1993) *Theory of Procurement and Regulation*, MIT Press: Cambridge, MA.

Lane, P.J., Cannella Jr., A.A., and Lubatkin, M.H. (1998) Agency problems as antecedents to unrelated mergers and diversification: Amihud and Lev reconsidered, *Strategic Management Journal*, **19** (6), 555–578.

Le, T. and Buck, T. (2011) State ownership and listed firm performance: a universally negative governance relationship?, *Journal of Management & Governance*, **15** (2), 227–248.

Leech, D. and Leahy, J. (1991) Ownership Structure, Control Type Classifications and the Performance of Large British Companies, *Economic Journal*, **101**, (409), 1418–1437.

Levin, S.M. and Levin, S.L. (1982) Ownership and Control of Large Industrial Firms: Some New Evidence, *Review of Business and Economic Research*, **14**, 37–49.

Li, M. and Simerly, R. (1998) The moderating effect of environmental dynamism on the ownership and performance relationship, *Strategic Management Journal*, **19** (2), 169–179.

Lloyd, W.P., Hand, J.H and Modani, N.K. (1987) The Effect of the Degree of Ownership Control on Firm Diversification, Market Value and Merger Activity, *Journal of Business Research*, **15** (4), 303–312.

Loderer, C. and Martin, K. (1997) Executive stock ownership and performance, *Journal of Financial Economics*, **45** (2), 223–255.

Malani, A., Philipson, T. and David, G. (2003) Theories of Firm Behavior in the Nonprofit Sector. A Synthesis and Empirical Evaluation, in Glaeser, E.L. (ed), *The Governance of Not-for-profit Organizations*, University of Chicago Press.

Maug, E. (1996) Corporate control and the market for managerial labour: On the decision to go public, *European Economic Review*, **40** (3), 1049–1057.

Mazzolini, R. (1990) The International Strategy of State-owned Firms: An Organizational Process and Politics Perspective, *Strategic Management Journal*, **1** (2), 101–118.

McConnell J.J. and Servaes, H. (1990) Additional evidence on equity ownership and corporate value, *Journal of Financial Economics*, **27** (2), 595–612.

McKillop, D.G. (2005) Financial Cooperatives: Structure, Conduct and Performance, *Annals of Public & Cooperative Economics*, **76** (3), 301–305.

Morck, R., Shleifer, A. and Vishny, R. (1988) Management Ownership and Market Valuation: An Empirical Analysis, *Journal of Financial Economics*, **20** (1), 293–315.

Nickel, S., Nicolitsas, D. and Dryden, N. (1997) What makes firms perform well?, *European Economic Review*, **41** (30), 783–796.

Nobes, C. and Parker, R. (1998) *Comparative International Accounting*, Prentice Hall: London.

Oswald, S.L. and Jahera Jr., J.S. (1991) The influence of ownership on performance: An empirical study, *Strategic Management Journal*, **12** (4), 321–326.

Pedersen, T. and Thomsen, S. (1997) European Patterns of Corporate Ownership, *Journal of International Business Studies*, **28** (4), 759–778.

Pedersen, T. and Thomsen, S. (1999) Economic and Systemic Explanations of Ownership Concentration among Europe's Largest Companies, *International Journal of the Economics of Business*, **6** (3), 367–381.

Prowse, S.D. (1998) *The Economics of the Private Equity Market*, Federal Reserve Bank of Dallas.

Ramirez, C.D. (1995) Did J.P. Morgan's Men Add Liquidity? – Corporate Investment, Cash Flow, and Financial Structure at the Turn of the Twentieth Century, *Journal of Finance*, **50** (2), 661–678.

Ribstein, L.E. (2009) Partnership Governance of Large Firms, *University of Chicago Law Review*, **76** (1), 289–309.

Sexty, R.W. (1980) Autonomy Strategies of Government Owned Business Corporations in Canada, *Strategic Management Journal*, **1** (4), 371–384.

Shepherd, W.G. (1989) Public Enterprise: Criteria and Cases, in *The Structure of European Industry*, H.W. de Jong (ed), Kluwer Academic: Dordrecht.

Shinong, W., Nianhang, X. and Qingbo, Y. (2009) State Control, Legal Investor Protection, and Ownership Concentration: Evidence from China, *Corporate Governance: An International Review*, **17** (2), 176–192.

Shleifer, A. and Vishny, R.W. (1986) Large Shareholders and Corporate Control, *Journal of Political Economy*, **95** (3), 461–488.

Shleifer, A. and Vishny, R.W. (1997) A Survey of

Corporate Governance, *Journal of Finance*, **52**, (2), 737–783.

Short, H. (1994) Ownership, Control, Financial Structure and the Performance of Firms, *Journal of Economic Surveys*, **8** (3), 203–249.

Thomsen, S. and Pedersen, T. (1998) Industry and Ownership Structure, *International Review of Law and Economics*, **18** (4), 385–402.

Thomsen, S. and Pedersen, T. (2000) Ownership Structure and Economic Performance in the largest European Companies, *Strategic Management Journal*, **21** (6), 689–705.

Tirole, J. (1992) *The Theory of Industrial Organization*, MIT Press: Cambridge MA.

Wei, S. and Chen, L. (2009) Firm Profitability, State Ownership, and Top Management Turnover at the Listed Firms in China: A Behavioral Perspective, *Corporate Governance: An International Review*, **17** (4), 443–456.

Whinston, M.D. and Segal, I.R. (2010) *Property Rights*, Stanford Law and Economics Olin Working Paper No. 394, forthcoming in *Handbook of Organizational Economics*.

Williamson, O. (1985) *The Economic Institutions of Capitalism*, Free Press: New York.

Wood, G. and Wright, M. (2009) Private equity: A review and synthesis, *International Journal of Management Reviews*, **11** (4), 361–380.

Worldscope-Disclosure (annually). Compact D – CD-ROM. Disclosure Inc., Bethesda, MD.

Wright, M., Amess, K., Weir, C. and Girma, S.

(2009) Private Equity and Corporate Governance: Retrospect and Prospect, *Corporate Governance: An International Review*, **17** (3), 353–375.

Wright, M., Bacon, N. and Amess, K. (2009) The Impact of Private Equity and Buyouts on Employment, Remuneration and other HRM Practices, *Journal of Industrial Relations*, **51** (4), 501–515.

Wright, M., Gilligan, J. and Amess, K. (2009) The economic impact of private equity: what we know and what we would like to know, *Venture Capital*, **11** (1), 1–21.

Wright, M., Renneboog, L., Simons, T. and Scholes, L. (2006) Leveraged Buyouts in the U.K. and Continental Europe: Retrospect and Prospect, *Journal of Applied Corporate Finance*, **18** (3), 38–55.

Wright, R.E. (2010) Partnership Governance of Large Firms, *McKinsey Quarterly*, **4**, 23–25.

Wruck, K.H. (2008) Private Equity, Corporate Governance, and the Reinvention of the Market for Corporate Control, *Journal of Applied Corporate Finance*, **20** (3), 8–21.

Zeckhouser, R. and Pound, J. (1990) Are Large Shareholders Effective Monitors? – An Investigation of Share Ownership and Corporate Performance, in *Asymmetric Information, Corporate Finance and Investment*, G.R. Hubbard (ed) University of Chicago Press: Chicago.

Zong, L. (2005) Governance Lessons from the Private Equity Industry, *Journal of Private Equity*, **9** (1), 63–66.

Chapter 8

Board Theories and Board Structure

Chapter contents

8.1   Introduction

Boards of directors are central to corporate governance. To some 'the board of directors' and the concept of 'corporate governance' are almost synonymous. It is easy to see why, given the visibility of the board in controlling the organization. In the policy arena the board of directors has for a long time been seen as paramount. The original Cadbury committee that investigated the financial aspects of corporate governance in the UK placed considerable emphasis on the board of directors. It said: 'Corporate governance is the system by which companies are directed and controlled. Boards of directors are responsible for the governance of their companies. The shareholders' role in governance is to appoint the directors and the auditors and to satisfy themselves that an appropriate governance structure is in place.' From this it is clear that the board is a central corporate governance institution.

In this chapter we will identify the main roles of the board of directors in the operation of corporate governance. We outline the main theories and discuss the empirical evidence relating to board structure. Our discussion of the board of directors is broad. We encompass both economic and management theories of the board. To this end our discussion provides an overview of the main contributions of each, rather than an in-depth literature review of the board of directors in each functional discipline. The discussion will try to cut across systemic differences between one- and two-tier boards, which are covered in Chapter 3 and in the country chapters (11 to 17). This chapter looks at board structure. In Chapter 9 we examine board behaviour further.

8.2   The board of directors

Formally, the board of directors is an intermediary between the firm's shareholders and its top management team. The board of directors is elected by shareholders and is the final arbiter of all major decisions made by the firm. The board has decision-making rights over the firm's assets, ceded to it (on a limited basis) by the owners of the firm. This includes evaluating company performance, hiring and firing the company CEO and top managers, ensuring an ideal business strategy, and deciding on a number of issues in which managers have a special interest such as auditing, compensation or nomination of new board members.

The board of directors is invariably a group of individuals made up of a limited number of members. Ten members would be considered typical for a medium to large company, but this can easily vary. In some cases boards can be as large as 30 to 40 members, but this is rare (de Andres, Azofra and Lopez, 2005; Conyon and Peck, 1998; Adams et al., 2010). On the other hand, corporation law typically specifies a minimum number of directors for an organization (two or three). Companies that have smaller boards will have a different group dynamic compared with companies with large boards. This means that small-group psychology and board dynamics are relevant to the study of boards.

Many but not all firms have boards even when it is not mandatory (Bennedsen, 2002). This indicates that boards are endogenous to firms and that they play a valuable, but not indispensable, role in corporate governance. If they did not exist they would have to be invented. Organizations have boards of directors not only because the law compels them to but because boards provide useful functions. This indicates that boards are endogenous to firms and that they play a valuable role in corporate governance. The issue of endogenous boards has become a central theme in the economics of boards of directors. Scholars in this tradition stress that board structure is not fixed or exogenously given. Instead, there are complex reasons for the observed patterns of board structures.

A hallmark feature of the unitary board of directors is that it is made up of inside and outside directors. The inside directors are also called executive directors, and the outside directors are called non-executive directors. Most outside board members are now part-time, non-executive directors who do not work for the company except when they show up for board meetings and special occasions like the annual shareholder meeting (Adams et al., 2010). This was not always so and is still not the case in Japan, where most board members are still executives. Corporate governance by non-executive directors has emerged from the corporate governance debate, particularly best-practice codes. However, in most systems except Germany it is customary for the CEO and perhaps a few other managers to sit on the board.

Another central feature of the board of directors is the question of whether the Chief Executive Officer (CEO) is also the chairman of the board. When the CEO is also the chairman this is often referred to as 'CEO duality'. In the United States the CEO is often the chairman of the board. The CEO is also the chairman of the board in some other countries too, such as France. However, in other countries such as the United Kingdom the CEO is rarely the chairman of the board. Indeed, in about 80% of cases the roles are separated. Why the CEO and chair roles are combined in the USA but not in the UK is especially interesting since these countries share similar governance structures (e.g. common law, shareholder-centric, single board governance models). Partly, the difference is due to culture, and also due to other institutions. For example, the governance code in the UK emphasizes separating the posts of CEO and chair in order to provide an effective separation of powers.

Another important question is whether the outside directors are independent. Theoretically, as we discuss below, this is required since the outside directors act as a check on any potential self-interested behaviour by the insiders. If the outsiders were not independent then their effectiveness would be blunted. Board members (directors) are said to be independent if they have no ties to the firm and therefore no special interests apart from their responsibility as board members (we provide an extended definition below). Executives are by definition dependent, but non-executive directors are not independent either if they have economic ties to the firm or its managers. For example, the company lawyer or relatives of the CEO are clearly not independent even though they are not members of the management team. Many non-executive directors have demanding jobs as managers in other firms, are lawyers, or even professors. Some specialize in board work and have many other board positions. They are often known as professional or (better) full-time board members (since most board members will be professional in some sense).

Boards tend to meet between six and eight times per year, and occasionally will meet more often but rarely more than twelve times a year (Vafeas, 1999). There is little scientific evidence as to the duration of board meetings, but a normal meeting is believed to average somewhere from 3–4 hours up to a whole day in large corporations. Company directors interviewed by consulting companies indicate that they spend some 180–200 hours a year (i.e. 4–5 working weeks) on board-related tasks (PricewaterhouseCoopers, 2005; USC/Mercer Delta, 2005). For example, the US-based National Association of Corporate Directors estimates that board members spent on average 204.5 hours on a board position in 2010. Survey studies agree that the time spent on board work has increased over the past few years.

Although it is not unusual for major shareholders to be represented on the board, most board members are not major shareholders. Outside the US most non-executive directors appear to be paid a fixed fee rather than variable pay. The UK governance code and other codes advise against stock options for non-executives. However stock options are a common means of payment for US directors (73% of firms), and their wealth has been calculated to increase by US$285,000 for a one-standard-deviation increase in market capitalization (Adams et al., 2010).

Boards of directors make the most important decisions in the firm about the firm's strategy, major acquisitions, disposals, and so on. They also make decisions on hiring, firing and compensating the CEO. Board members make collective (i.e. non-hierarchical) decisions. Unless otherwise decided in the bylaws, voting is democratic (one member – one vote). Decisions are officially made by the board as a whole. In most cases decisions are unanimous. From an agency theory perspective, group work like this could create free-rider problems since individual directors can free ride on the activities of others. This is an example where it is important to understand the nuances of small-group decision making in order to understand the overall effectiveness of the board of directors.

To carry out their many important tasks, boards of directors have developed an efficient committee structure. These committees are assigned central tasks and then report back to the main board.

Most listed firms currently have committees for auditing, compensation, and corporate governance (which is sometimes called the nominations committee). In large listed US firms, board committees meet separately in 3–4 meetings per year (Adams, 2005). These committees are mandatory in many jurisdictions, but some companies also have committees for strategy, CSR, acquisitions or other important issues. Committees are typically formed as a subgroup of three or more board members and the key committees are composed exclusively or at least mainly of independent non-executive directors, since they deal with issues in which the executives may have a private interest. Auditing committees, for example, deal with financial reports, control systems, and choice of auditor. Intuitively, the rationale seems to be to ensure that information provided to the board is reliable and not biased by the executives in their own favour. Remuneration (compensation) committees set the pay of the executives, in which they also have a vested interest. Finally, the nomination committee is concerned with selecting board members and managers, so independence is intended to ensure that managers do not bias board composition in their own favour.

8.3 Board structure in the USA

Boards of directors have been becoming smaller over the last few decades in the United States. However, there is no evidence that they are continuing to decrease in size. Equilar (2011), a professional services firm that specializes in corporate governance and executive compensation analysis, estimates that most boards contain between eight and ten directors. In 2010, the majority of companies in the S&P 1500 had between eight and ten members. Figure 8.1 (from Equilar) shows the distribution in firm size and recent trends.

It is also the case that board size increases with company size. For example, small cap companies have boards of about eight members, whereas mid-cap firms have boards of about nine members, and large boards contain about eleven directors.

Equilar reports that there have been some interesting governance changes in the leadership structure of US boards. Since 2010, US firms have been required under new SEC disclosure requirements to add a discussion of their leadership structure to the board's proxy statement. Specifically, boards are now required to make a statement as to whether they combine or separate the posts of CEO and board chair. There is also a discussion of why the firm believes its decision is most appropriate for the company. Figure 8.2 (from Equilar) shows that 51.3% of S&P 1500 companies combine the posts of CEO and chair, and 13.2% have an executive chairman. The study finds that about 33% of boards have a non-executive chair. There are important size effects. Large-cap companies are more likely to combine the posts of CEO and chair compared with smaller companies.

An important development is the rise of the lead director at US firms. Corporate governance advocates have suggested that companies which combine the roles of CEO and chair should nominate an independent director to serve as the lead or presiding director. Equilar research shows that among the S&P 1500 companies, more than half (nearly 60%) have adopted a lead director to serve as the leader of the board. More importantly, the lead director is much more likely to be observed when the company has combined the roles of CEO and board chair. Equilar research shows that 82.2% of companies that combine the roles of CEO and board chair have a lead director. This finding confirms that firms are more likely use alternative governance solutions (the lead director) when agency problems are potentially more severe (combining the posts of CEO and chair).

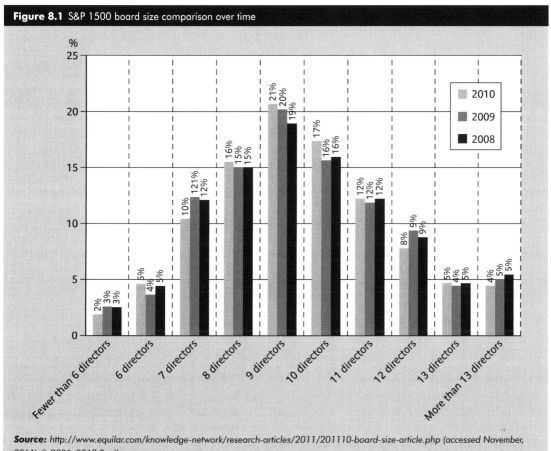

Figure 8.1 S&P 1500 board size comparison over time

Source: http://www.equilar.com/knowledge-network/research-articles/2011/201110-board-size-article.php (accessed November, 2011) © 2001–2012 Equilar.

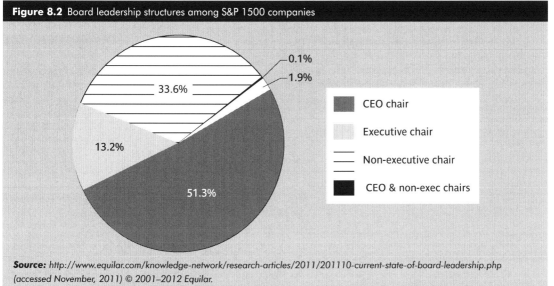

Figure 8.2 Board leadership structures among S&P 1500 companies

Source: http://www.equilar.com/knowledge-network/research-articles/2011/201110-current-state-of-board-leadership.php (accessed November, 2011) © 2001–2012 Equilar.

8.4   The theory of boards

Economic theories of the board often appeal to principal–agent theory as well as incomplete contracting. According to **agency theory** (Fama and Jensen, 1983) boards will arise as a control mechanism when there is separation of ownership and control. In other words, agency problems are the raison d'être for boards. When there is separation of ownership and control there are important asymmetries of information. The owners of the firm (shareholders) do not run the firm directly but instead assign this task to a CEO and top management team. However, the shareholders do not know for certain whether the CEO is acting in their best interests or if he is behaving opportunistically and pursuing his own interests. In the language of agency theory there is a moral hazard problem as the efforts of the CEO are not fully revealed. The shareholders could design contracts (performance-based rewards, for example) to solve this problem. However, such contracts are necessarily incomplete. It is extremely difficult to design a contract that specifies every single contingency that will ever happen and assign a reward to it. It is even more difficult to write such a set of contracts that can be enforced by a neutral third party (e.g. a court). This is where boards of directors are important. They are an institution that can make decisions that have not been specified in advance in some set of contracts. They are the vehicle by which unforeseen real-world decisions can be resolved. In this deep sense boards are endogenous institutions that deal with the twin issues of incomplete market contracts and cost of asymmetric information between shareholders and the CEO.

Information asymmetries, costs of collective decision making, and free-riding problems all imply excessively high transaction costs for direct shareholder democracy. It is unrealistic to get all shareholders together very often. And even if it were, most shareholders might not know what to say. Compared with shareholder meetings, boards can give more continuous and flexible feedback to the management which will often be in the company's best interest. One implication of this is that boards primarily have a role to play in companies with dispersed ownership.

Agency theory provides an argument for why monitoring is done by a group rather than a single individual: mutual monitoring lowers the likelihood that the board will collude with the management. The board members watch each other as well as the management team. This is called horizontal monitoring: a situation where an efficient equilibrium monitoring of the team is successfully implemented between team members rather than in a hierarchical top-down fashion.

Fama and Jensen (1983) argued that boards (i.e. non-executives) and managers will specialize in different stages of corporate decision making. They outlined a reasonable set of steps in any decision-making process. A decision process will involve several distinct phases: first, there is the initiation of decision proposals; second, there is the ratification stage, where approval or rejection of the suggested decisions is made; third, there is the implementation of the proposal. Finally, in step four, there is the monitoring phase, whereby the initiated, ratified and implemented decisions are finally evaluated. At this evaluation stage the appropriate rewards, or penalties, are decided. Fama and Jensen argue that an effective and efficient division of labour is where the CEO takes charge of initiation and implementation (steps 1 and 3), while outside directors on the board carry out the ratification and monitoring (steps 2 and 4). A visual sketch is given in Figure 8.3.

In other words, managers come up with decision proposals (new strategies, M&A and the like) and the board ratifies (or rejects) these proposals. Management thereafter implements the decision, and the board monitors whether this is satisfactory. One can see this process as akin to an effective separation of powers. The CEO and managers are insiders and are responsible for the initiation and implementation of core strategies. The outside directors on the board are responsible for ratification and monitoring of those decisions by the CEO. By separating these functional tasks there is an effective separation of powers on the unitary board that provides the appropriate checks and balances. There is no need in this scheme for a dual board system as is the case in Germany for example. There, the supervisory board deals with the ratification/monitoring role and the management board with the initiation/implementation of decisions.

While boards have the formal power to reject all proposals, they very rarely do so. Berle and Means (1932) argue that executives are effectively in control of the board because of their control of

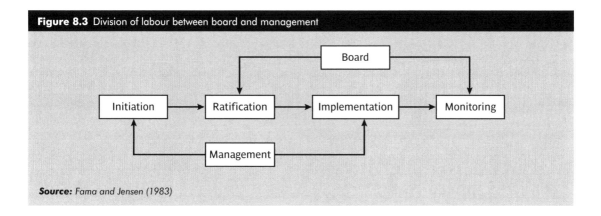

Figure 8.3 Division of labour between board and management

Source: Fama and Jensen (1983)

proxy committees. Mace (1971) and Lorsch and MacIver (1989) emphasize the power of the CEO over the board and downplay the importance of board control. Warther (1998), summarizing the earlier literature, argues that critical board members who voted against the management tend to leave or be ejected. Hermalin and Weisbach (1998) show how successful CEOs can accumulate power over time by influencing the composition of the board. Boone et al. (2007) find empirical support for their ideas. A formal argument for board inactivity or 'rubber-stamping' of CEO proposals can be found in the distinction between formal and real authority (Aghion and Tirole, 1997; Weber, 1968). Although boards have formal authority to overrule executives, non-executive directors have insufficient information to decide whether this is the right thing to do. Even if they retain formal control, Aghion and Tirole show that boards will rationally rubber-stamp management decision proposals as long as they have no independent sources of information and if they can assume that the decision proposal is no worse than the benchmark of doing nothing (in other words, assuming that managers and board members have a shared interest in selecting projects that at least cover the opportunity costs of capital). In this case, the agent has the real authority. Boards may recognize this and delegate formal authority to managers who will then want to contribute more information to the board because their interests are safeguarded. In both cases, greater board involvement, understood as overruling of more management decisions or rejection of more project proposals, will harm organizational performance.

8.5 Alternatives to agency theory

To the classic board functions ('the control role') management scholars would add 'service' and networking roles (Johnson et al., 1996). Service involves giving advice and input to strategy discussions. For example, a lawyer on the board may advise on legal issues (Daily et al., 2003). Networking (the so-called resource dependence role) consists of establishing and maintaining contacts to important constituencies, including investors, banks, customers and others (e.g. Pfeffer and Salancik, 1978; Stearns and Mizruchi, 1993). We can summarize these different roles as the three Cs:

- **The Control role** (i.e. the monitoring function stressed by agency theory);
- **The Consulting role** (i.e. the service function stressed by stewardship and resource dependence theory);
- **The Contact role** (i.e. the networking function stressed by resource dependence theory).

The three roles are not mutually exclusive, but are nevertheless distinct. Imagine for example that you manage to persuade Bill Gates to sit on the board of your newly started firm. As an experienced business manager he would probably be very good at spotting slack and other deviations from shareholder value and so could help with the control function. But if you were the single owner-manager, control might not be much of an issue since you would have every incentive to be efficient in your use of scarce resources. However, with his extensive business experience he might help you with business advice (consulting), which would be very valuable even though control was not necessary. Then again, it might be that he was so busy that he could never attend board meetings and did not even have time to read your financial statements. Nevertheless, just having his name on the letterhead might open a lot of doors, make it easier for you to negotiate with your bank, and contact potential customers, even though he did not carry out his control or consulting roles. And of course, an occasional lead to a large US customer might come in very handy. In other words, he would be very valuable in the contact role.

8.6 The service role

Non-executive board members can be seen as members of the management team to which they provide valuable inputs and thus contribute to value creation. This is the role emphasized in **stewardship theory** (Donaldson, 1990; Donaldson and Davis, 1991, 1994), which regards most managers as intrinsically motivated to do a good job. According to stewardship theory the elaborate controls of corporate governance are therefore at best unnecessary and at worst harmful to company performance. It may for example be preferable to have the CEO act as chairman of the board to avoid unnecessary conflicts. The service role is emphasized in theories of '**friendly boards**', which cooperate with rather than control the CEO (Adams and Ferreira, 2007). Likewise Pearce and Zahra (1991) argue that the empowerment of boards does not need to come at the cost of managerial autonomy, but can be seen as a win–win situation.

Westphal (1999) proposes 'the collaborative board model', in which dependence and social ties promote exchange of knowledge with executives and thus help boost board performance by reducing information asymmetries. The argument is that a certain level of trust is necessary to facilitate this since managers need to confess to uncertainty and/or to reveal problems in the organization – information which can potentially be used against them on the board. Trust is facilitated by social ties. Management and board members form friendship ties which oblige them to come to each other's defence and to care for each other's welfare. Greater openness in turn is likely to induce other board members to be more open as well and to create greater collaboration on the board. Thus a virtuous circle is created. In addition, Westphal argues that better information will make boards more efficient in monitoring so that even the control function improves in collaborative boards. While board control with the CEO may be momentarily reduced by collaboration it may be enhanced in the long run because of better information (consistent with Aghion and Tirole, 1997). McNulty, Roberts and Stiles (2005) therefore argue against any perceived trade-off between service and control roles. A more meaningful distinction, they argue, is between a more or less active role for non-executive directors.

A collaborative style may thus enable boards to participate in decision management as well as decision control. In particular the board can be active in developing as well as ratifying strategies and thus potentially add more value to the company (Huse, 2007). Pugliese et al. (2009) survey literature on the board's involvement in strategy. They find it to be a contested issue, but observe that boards do in fact tend to become more involved in business strategy over time. Therefore, as argued by Westphal (1999), overemphasis on independence and control in corporate governance codes and regulation may actually reduce board task performance.

Opening the black box in order to examine the small group interaction of company boards opens the door to board behaviour and board processes (Forbes and Milliken, 1999). Factors like the 'cohesiveness' of the board, its effort norms or cognitive conflict may influence its function, i.e. board task performance. Effective board task performance partially consists in avoiding or breaking psychological deadlocks. Westphal argues that non-executive directors display 'pluralistic ignorance' (i.e. underestimate that other board members may also be critical of the CEO) (Westphal and Bednar, 2005). However, greater openness by some members makes it more likely that others will also reveal their concerns which should facilitate more efficient decisions.

Deadlocks may occasionally be deliberate and opportunistically created by the CEO which reintroduces conflicts between executive and non-executive directors. The CEO may try to appease critical non-executives by ingratiation (Westphal, 1998), or troublesome directors may be subjected to 'social distancing' through personal networks (Westphal and Khanna, 2003). Board failures like these may lead to 'groupthink', i.e. inability to respond rationally to new information.

Successful board leadership also requires attention to putting the right team together. Belbin (1993) distinguished between different team roles such as coordinators, implementers, monitors and idea-generators ('plants'). He shows that team performance depends on an appropriate mix of role, and this is also likely to apply to company boards.

8.7 The contact role

The contact role of boards is emphasized in the **resource dependence theory** of the firm (Pfeffer and Salancik, 1978; Hillman, Withers and Collins, 2009), according to which companies seek to manage external dependence by forming ownership ties and board connections. For example, more externally dependent organizations may have larger boards and a higher number of outside directors.

The theory suggests that directors can contribute resources such as advice, access to outside information, preferential access to external resources, and legitimacy. This may benefit companies in regulated industries or communist countries like China, where political connections are supremely important. It may be a good idea for example to have a chairman who is a senior member of the communist party. Stakeholder directors may benefit the company's social responsibility. Directors from the financial community may facilitate access to particular kinds of finance like venture capital or bank loans (Stearns and Mizruchi, 1993). Resource access may be particularly important in small firms, whereas monitoring (the control role) may be correspondingly less important because they have less slack.

Board ties have been studied in social network theory (e.g. Grannovetter, 1985), which stresses the social context (embeddedness) of social phenomena like corporate governance rather than attributes of individual persons or firms. Network theory clearly emphasizes the contact role of boards. One example is politically connected directors (Adams et al., 2010). Agrawal and Knoeber (2001) find that firms which are dependent on political decisions tend to hire directors with a political background, for example those which sell to the government. They also find that electric utilities prepared for deregulation by hiring political directors. As a tangible expression of the value of such connections, Goldman et al. (2009) find abnormal stock returns when political directors are appointed and that firm value may increase if your side wins in an election, but may fall if the other side wins. Another example is bankers, who may facilitate firm access to financial markets (Güner, Malmendier and Tate, 2008), although they are understandably reluctant to sit on the boards of firms with funding deficits (i.e. firms which are most in need of their network).

Another type of resource provision is human and social capital, which may benefit both control, service and network functions. For example ex-politicians might be better at assessing whether firm management was effective at lobbying, give better advice on politically sensitive issues and create connections to current politicians and bureaucrats. Human capital may be measured by education and experience, whereas social capital may be measured by connections.

8.8 The challenge of institutional theory

Institutional theory (Meyer and Rowan, 1977; Powell and Dimaggio, 1991; Scott, 2001) emphasizes that organizational practices such as corporate governance may spread as a result of social pressures (imitation, ideology and coercion) as well as economic efficiency. Moreover, corporate governance may facilitate such social pressures. Social network research has found that board ties (an individual sitting on the boards of two companies) may be a source of information diffusion. Practices such as multidivisional organization, investor relations and diversification have been shown to spread more easily between firms if they have a board member in common (Shropshire, 2010). This is fully consistent with resource dependence theory and social network theory. Unfortunately, questionable practices (such as golden parachutes, poison pills, stock options backdating and financial misrepresentation) are known to spread in the same virus-like way (Shropshire, 2010).

Fashion waves in corporate governance are an indication that all is not decided by economic rationality. The spread of practices such as shareholder value, poison pills, stock options, corporate social responsibility, corporate governance codes etc. shows that firms tend to imitate each other rather than find individual solutions to their own problems. Corporate governance codes adopt a one-size-fits-all approach although academic research often points to the importance of contingencies and firm-specific solutions.

This raises important questions for corporate governance. To what extent can we rely on existing governance practices to be efficient, and to what extent are they results of social 'myths' with little empirical justification? One way to decide is to use empirical evidence on the covariance of the various practices with company performance. To the extent that boards choose optimal solutions we should expect to see firm differences and little systematic covariance between governance practices and company performance. However, if governance practices are adopted solely to imitate others, this introduces an exogenous variation in governance practices which can be used to identify the effect of these practices on company performance.

8.9 Empirical evidence

In this section we consider some of the empirical evidence on board structure. There are important themes. First, board structure (such as the independence of the board, or board size, or combining the CEO and chair positions) can have an effect on observable organizational performance. For example, these board variables might affect stock market or operational measures such as stock returns or return on assets. There are many studies that have documented the correlations between such variables and in effect they are evaluating the consequences of board structure. Second, there are other studies that evaluate the determinants or antecedents of board structures. These types of studies assert that board structures are neither fixed nor are exogenous but instead are determined by a host of factors that influence the firm's operating environment. Taken together, these studies show that boards are endogenous. That is not only do boards affect factors such as organizational performance but there are also other factors that affect the type of boards that are observed in practice.

The endogenous nature of boards is a fundamental issue for empirical studies of boards. For example, one might argue that boards with more independent directors on them lead to better performance. However, it is also the case that better performing companies, run by high-quality CEOs and managers, are more likely to populate their boards with more outside independent directors. Disentangling endogeneity to arrive at the true causal effect of board structure on firm performance is a major research challenge (Adams, Hermalin and Weisbach, 2010).

8.10 Board structure and company performance

In this section we discuss how board structure has affected organizational performance. As discussed above, boards tend to have certain structures. Typically, such structures are slowly changing: characteristics of boards such as board size, level of board independence (e.g. percentage of independent directors), duality (coincidence or not of chair and CEO), board diversity, as well as organizational traits such as adoption and composition of board committees. Our goal is to summarize how these board features affect (if at all) the performance of organizations. This is a central corporate governance question. Policymakers and academics have spent a lot of time arguing that particular structures might have certain advantages over other types of structures. For example, it is frequently asserted that boards containing more outsiders are 'better' because they provide more oversight of potentially errant CEOs. Another hypothesis holds that smaller boards are more effective than larger boards because they do not suffer from free-rider problems. If these and other similar hypotheses were true then ultimately we would expect it to show up in superior patterns of organizational performance. A recent comprehensive review of boards has been provided by Adams, Hermalin and Weisbach (2010).

There have been hundreds of academic studies relating board structure to measures of company performance. However, the consensus of scientific evidence is that the empirical findings relating board independence to firm performance are at best mixed. Studies have found few general results demonstrating the universal positive benefits of board structures on firm performance. Johnson et al. (1996) summarize an extensive literature review as follows:

> ‖ *To our knowledge, there has been no documented evidence of the existence of a unicorn. With tongue slightly in cheek, there can be two general rationales for our failure to 'discover' this legendary species. First, this animal simply does not exist. Second, we have not searched in the right place, at the right time, with the right equipment … In many ways an aggregation and summary of the boards of directors/financial performance/other outcomes literature has this same character. Maybe such relationships simply do not exist in nature. Or, if they do exist, their magnitude is such that they are not of practical importance. Alternatively, given the heterogeneity of typical independent variables, it may be unrealistic to reasonably compare and summarize this body of work.*[1] ‖

Other scholars have investigated further the relation between firm performance and independence of the board of directors. The results are mixed. Dalton, Daily, Ellstrand and Johnson (1998) provide a meta-analysis of several studies and conclude that it is difficult to isolate any systematic effect of board independence (159 samples, $n = 40{,}160$) or duality (69 samples, $n = 12{,}915$) on company performance. Several studies, including Bhagat and Black (2002), Agrawal and Knoeber (1996) and Klein (1998), find a negative correlation between board independence and organizational performance. Other studies have found no (or little) relationship between board structure and firm performance. These include Hermalin and Weisbach (1991), Adams et al. (2010), and Mehran (1995). These results are salient because corporate governance scholars argue that board independence facilitates better monitoring of the CEO and the management team and should therefore show up in superior economic performance.

There are several methodological issues which complicate empirical studies of board structure and performance. The most important is that we have strong reasons to believe that board structure and board behaviour depend upon ownership and capital structure, law and other governance mechanisms as well as on company performance. Boone et al. (2007), Raheja (2005), Baker and Gompers (2003), Denis and Sarin (1999), and Hermalin and Weisbach (1998) find that board structure is influenced by ownership structure, board size, company performance, and other economic variables. To estimate the effects of board structure, we need to take this interdependence into consideration, which means estimating simultaneous equation systems with many dependent equations. Very few studies have done this. An exception is Bhagat and Bolton (2008), who estimate ownership, governance, performance and capital structure in four simultaneous equations. They find that board structure (measured by the fraction of independent directors) has no significant effect on firm value and has a negative effect on accounting returns. However, it is difficult to find instrument variables which influence either performance or governance without influencing the others, so causality is a problem even in large simultaneous equation models. The issue of endogeneity of board structure has been considered most recently by Wintoki, Linck and Netter (2011). They used dynamic panel data (GMM) estimators to address the endogeneity problems relating to the effect of board

---

[1] Johnson et al. (1996) p. 433.

structure on firm performance, as well as the main determinants of board structure. Using a panel of about 6,000 firms from 1991 to 2003 they find no causal relation between board structure and the firm's current performance. This, and similar studies, attests to the importance of controlling for the endogenous selection of boards (Adams et al., 2010).

All this indicates that boards are part of a complex system of governance mechanisms. In many cases, board structure and board behaviour will be determined by other corporate governance mechanisms in combination with firm-specific variables. For example, large owners often want to be represented on the board. Moreover, even if they are not present on the board, the expectations of large owners can condition board decisions to a very large extent. A board may, for example, feel compelled by anticipated shareholder reactions to fire the CEO after three years of bad performance. Or banks may make demands on board composition as a condition for extending credit to an insolvent firm, and the board may feel compelled to fire the CEO because of manifest or anticipated pressure from creditors. The point is that board structure and behaviour are endogenous, and when this is taken into account, the part of company behaviour and performance which is attributable to the board as such is diminished.

8.11   Board independence

Independence is by far the most discussed aspect of board structure. There is a clear agency logic behind it. Agents cannot monitor themselves, nor can other agents with a vested interest be expected to do a good job.

Are the board members independent of the management team so that they reject its proposals when called for and if necessary replace it? Coming from a situation where the majority of the board members were executives of the firm, the first push was to increase the number of non-executive directors, since executives could hardly be expected to turn down their own proposals or fire themselves. However, it was soon realized that even non-executive board members might have ties to management which prevent them from acting independently. This could be family ties (i.e. relatives of the CEO), economic ties (i.e. a lawyer with the firm as a client) or an employee (who could be fired by the chief executive). Considering an ever-increasing number of possible conflicts of interest has led to an expanding definition of 'dependence' and an ever-narrower definition of independence.

According to the UK governance code a director is dependent if she:

- has been an employee of the company or group within the last five years;
- has, or has had within the last three years, a material business relationship with the company either directly, or as a partner, shareholder, director or senior employee of a body that has such a relationship with the company;
- has received or receives additional remuneration from the company apart from a director's fee;
- participates in the company's share option or a performance-related pay scheme, or is a member of the company's pension scheme;
- has close family ties with any of the company's advisers, directors or senior employees;
- holds cross-directorships or has significant links with other directors through involvement in other companies or bodies;
- represents a significant shareholder;
- has served on the board for more than nine years from the date of their first election.

There is a clear agency logic to many of these definitions. An employee might for example be afraid to turn down a proposal from his boss for fear of repercussions. So may a person with a material business relationship with the company (e.g. the lawyer, consultant, banker or supplier). A large supplier might not be afraid, but could on the other hand have a vested interest in the purchase or finance decisions. In the same way it makes sense that somebody with family ties to executives or persons with a business relationship to the company must be regarded as dependent. Cross-directorships or other significant links might also make directors more reluctant to go up against the management.

Other provisions could be justified by group psychology. It is not clear from an agency perspective why a board member with long tenure (> 9 years) is more dependent on the management team than one with a short tenure (say 2 years). On the contrary it seems likely that a director with long tenure has a better understanding of the firm, which could make her a better monitor. The argument appears to be that long-tenured directors come to identify with the management because of socialization, which could be justified by reference to group psychology.

From an agency theory viewpoint it is also surprising that large shareholders or their representatives are regarded as dependent even if they are not part of the management team. Large owners have strong profit incentive in harmony with the interests of minority shareholders, and for this reason large owners are not regarded as dependent by the NYSE code, for example. A more convincing argument could be that large owners might have different interests from minority shareholders (type 2 agency problems).

Even if a director is independent according to the above criteria, she may not be independent in other respects. According to the UK and other governance codes it is up to the board to decide whether a board member can be considered independent. The board might take other information into account than that mentioned in the dependence criteria, for example a known close friendship with the chief executive. It seems necessary in this connection to distinguish between formal dependence (as expressed in the code) and substantial independence (as in the ability to stand up to the CEO). For example, personal friends of the CEO, retired directors who are dependent on the board fee or consultants with a potential client relationship to the firm may be independent in name, but not in substance. In practice however, boards very rarely take such extended dependence criteria into account.

It is possible to find examples of directors who are formally dependent but substantially independent. For example, on the board of a family firm (perhaps listed) the brother of the CEO may be formally dependent, but in a much better position to challenge his brother's decision than the formally independent outside board members who can be fired at a whim. The same of course goes for the long-tenured board member or the dominant owner mentioned above.

As mentioned, there is no consensus in the literature on the effect of board independence. Dahya and McConnell (2007) find a positive effect of adding more independent directors in the UK, and Dahya et al. (2002) find that CEOs are more easily replaced as a result of this. But other studies find negative or insignificant effects (e.g. Duchin et al., 2010).

A more promising approach may be to examine under what circumstances board independence has the expected positive effect. Duchin, Matsusaka and Ozbas (2010) find this to be the case when the activities of the firm are relatively transparent and there is limited information asymmetry. Likewise, Gani and Jermias (2006) find that independent directors add value for companies that pursue cost leadership strategies, but not for companies that pursue innovation strategies.

There are a number of studies of special situations, e.g. the role of the board in replacing CEOs, shareholder defences, executive compensation and M&A, and here there is more evidence that board independence matters (Johnson et al., 1996; Hermalin and Weisbach, 2003). However, the implications for overall company performance are often unclear. It may be that independent boards are more likely to replace CEOs when performance is bad, but it is unclear whether this is the right decision. Second, even when performance is measured (as in event studies) it is unclear whether a positive effect on the performance effects of certain types of decisions (like adopting a poison pill) will hold for other types of decisions as well. In fact, it seems likely that greater independence and more monitoring can have adverse effects on information sharing (Adams and Ferreira, 2007). Empirical observations often run counter to expectations. In a meta-study of 38 studies with 69 samples ($N = 30,650$), Deutsch (2005) concludes that greater board independence is associated with higher executive pay, more unrelated diversification and more takeover defences, all contrary to expectations in a standard agency model (although more complex stories can make sense of some of it; Hermalin, 2005).

8.12   Board size

Agency theorists have argued that firm and board performance is negatively correlated to firm performance. Jensen (1993), Lipton and Lorsch (1992) and Yermack (1996) have each argued that large boards can be less effective than small boards. Larger boards are more prone to free-rider problems which reduce the board's capacity to monitor effectively. The basic idea is that when boards get to be too big, agency problems increase and the board becomes more symbolic and less a part of the management decision-making process. The group dynamics of running a large board are often challenging. Jensen (1993) argued that when boards get beyond seven or eight people they are less likely to function effectively. In addition, they become easier for the CEO to control.

Several studies have examined the hypothesized negative correlation between board size and firm performance. In an early study, Yermack (1996) examined the relation between Tobin's Q (the market value of the firm to its replacement cost) and board size in a sample of large US corporations, controlling for other variables that are likely to affect Tobin's Q. He found a significant negative relation. Eisenberg et al. (1998) also found a negative association between firm performance and board size in a sample of small and midsize Finnish firms. The pattern of results is found elsewhere in Europe too. Conyon and Peck (1998) examined the effects of board size on measures of corporate performance across a number of European economies. They too found a negative relationship between firm performance and board size. They used fixed effects techniques on panel data between 1992 and 1995 for the UK, France, Netherlands, Denmark and Italy. When firm performance was measured as the return on equity, they identified a significant negative association between board size and firm performance. However, when firm performance was measured as the market to book value (approximating Tobin's Q) the negative effect could only be established for the UK and the Netherlands.

However, the empirical evidence relating to board size is now more ambiguous and therefore inconclusive. In their early survey of the economic literature, Hermalin and Weisbach (2003) conclude that 'board composition is not related to corporate performance, while board size is negatively related to corporate performance'. However, other studies have produced conflicting evidence. Research by Dalton, Daily, Johnson and Ellstrand (1999), using evidence from a meta-analysis of 131 samples and 20,620 observations, find the opposite: '... the results for our overall meta-analysis of the board size–financial performance association strongly suggest a nonzero, positive relationship ... these relationships are consistent for market-based and accounting based firm performance measures' (Dalton et al. 1998). So perhaps there is really no consensus on board size effects on performance after all. Moreover, new evidence by Coles et al. (2008) indicates that board size may actually increase firm value in diversified and leveraged firms. In a subsequent review Adams, Hermalin and Weisbach (2010) no longer regard a negative board size effect as a stylized fact. There are many reasons for this. One, of course, is that the results from studies find mixed evidence and this alone means it is difficult to draw robust conclusions. Another reason is that the causal interpretation is inaccurate because board size is endogenous. Rather than board size affecting firm performance it is plausible that firm size is driven by many considerations including organizational performance itself.

8.13   Board diversity

The issue of board diversity has become an increasingly important topic for corporate governance scholars. The US Securities and Exchange Commission (SEC) now requires companies to provide enhanced disclosure on how they consider diversity in the director nomination process. In addition, the global debate about women board directors has intensified. In parts of Europe, quotas specifying the percentage of women on boards have been introduced.

The standard business case for diverse boards is that it increases the quality of board decision-making, and ultimately business performance. This provides a powerful basis for addressing the diversity composition of the board. Boards that are diverse in ethnicity, gender, experience, education and background possess a considerable range of different knowledge and skills. Directors on diverse boards have greater insights into markets, customers, employees and business opportunities. This leads to a better understanding of business conditions, and in turn to better company performance.

Another benefit is that diverse boards can reduce 'groupthink', a situation where directors too easily reach consensus because of their shared similarities. Groupthink leads to poorer quality decisions because sound alternatives are too often dismissed. Diverse viewpoints, in contrast, tend to encourage healthy debate in the boardroom, different types of conversations, different perspectives, and challenges to each other's viewpoints. In short, diversity can improve the quality of boardroom debate and decision making.

In addition, there are moral and social justifications for diverse boards. The current diversity of boards does not reflect the diversity in the wider population, their companies' client base, or often their workforces. In addition, the board's diversity does not capitalize fully on the available talent pool in the labour force. Increasing board diversity is desirable, and consistent with promoting equality as a public policy goal.

Diversity is not without its challenges. Research shows that groups that are too dissimilar can lead to lower levels of cohesiveness and teamwork. Sharp dissimilarities in team membership can lead to an inability to agree on mutual goals, increased conflict, and reduced information sharing. If this situation arises in the boardroom then it can unfavourably affect the quality of board performance, and decision making. Companies must, therefore, balance the benefits of greater diversity against the potential challenges.

Although it is sometimes claimed that there is a business case for board diversity, the empirical evidence does not support it. In a study of large US firms, Adams and Ferreira (2009) find insignificant or negative effects of US gender diversity on company performance (ROA and Q). Ahern and Dittmar (2010) find that the Norwegian gender quota (which mandates at least 40% women) has a significant negative effect on company performance. Bohren and Odegaard (2006) find a negative performance effect of gender before the quota. Masulis, Wang and Xie (2010) examine the impact of international directors in S&P 1500 companies and find a negative effect of international board membership on firm value and accounting profitability and negative stock market reactions to announced appointments of international directors. Thus, if anything, the available and emerging empirical literature finds negative performance effects of diversity. This is clearly an area where further research is warranted.

8.14   Employee representation

As we have seen previously several European countries, for example Germany, Austria, Denmark, Norway, Sweden, Slovenia, have mandatory employee representation on company boards (Jackson, 2005; Thomsen, Rose and Kronborg, 2010). There have also been voluntary experiments with so-called Employee Representation Plans in the USA, Australia and other countries (Patmore, 2007). Historically, the US movement appears to have been started by J.D. Rockefeller Junior as part of a union avoidance strategy (Patmore, 2007). It involved a dialogue between managers and employees and even (in rare cases) voluntary board representation. At their peak such programmes covered about as many employees as labour unions. However, their importance has waned since the 1930s.

Some academics, such as Roberts and van den Steen (2001), have argued that employee representation is necessary to ensure employee investment in firm-specific skills, particularly in firms where human capital is important, such as law firms, accounting firms and consulting firms. In the absence of co-determination, they argue, employees will use other more costly ways to seek influence, such as strikes. Limited employee influence, they further argue, is only sustainable in highly flexible labour markets such as the USA and the UK. In contrast, Jensen and Meckling (1979) argue that firms with high levels of employee determination run the risk of becoming labour-managed firms or at least being pushed in that direction. In their view labour-managed firms will become less competitive

because of less access to outside equity and governance problems of circular governance (employees controlling the managers who control the employees).

Evidence on the effect of employee representation is emerging. Gorton and Schmid (2004) examine the performance effects of equal (50%) employee representation on the boards of the largest 250 German nonfinancial companies in 1989–1999. They find that firm value is on average 31% lower with 50% employee representation than with ⅓ participation. As might be expected employee representatives in equal representation appear to use their power to secure employment so that labour costs are around 50% higher. Guedri and Hollandts (2008) examine employee ownership and employee board representation in 250 French companies in 2000–2005. They find no significant effect of employee board representation, but a curvilinear effect of employee ownership. However, in a sample of 786 listed German firms active in 2003, Fauver and Fuerst (2006) find no overall significant effect, but rather that a moderate employee representation of 33–50% of the board is actually good for company performance, while performance decreases when employees are in the majority. They propose and find empirical support for the idea that employee representation will be particularly valuable for firms operating in industries that require coordination and special skills or knowledge.

8.15 Other studies of board structure

In Table 8.1 we provide an overview of influential studies of other elements of board structure and their impact on company performance.

Duality, i.e. the CEO also being chairman of the board, does not make much sense from an agency perspective because it enables the agent extensive control of his own monitoring. Even in the USA the percentage of companies with duality dropped from 71% in 2005 to 60% in 2010 (*Financial Times* 14 March 2011). However, in a stewardship or collaborative board perspective this concentration of power may facilitate the speed and efficiency of decision making. Moreover, as emphasized by Adams et al. (2010) there may be reverse causality: well-performing CEOs may find it easier to gain the trust

Table 8.1 Some empirical studies of board structure and company performance

	Effect	Representative studies
Duality (chair = CEO)	0	Brickley et al. (1997) Dalton et al. (1998) Adams et al. (2005)
Board interlocks (CEOs sit on each other's boards)	–	Fahlenbrach et al. (2008) Larcker et al. (2005)
Busy directors (with many board positions)	–	Fich and Shivdasani (2006)
Staggered boards (election periods for board members)	–	Bebchuk et al. (2002) Bebchuk and Cohen (2005) Guo et al. (2008)
Director experience	+	McDonald et al. (2008) Tian et al. (2011)
Financial expertise on bank boards	–	Minton et al. (2011) Ferreira et al. (2010)
Board committees	+/–	Conyon and Peck (1998) Reeb and Upadhyay (2010)

of the non-executive board members and to capture the position as chairman. Some studies have found that it is more difficult to replace the CEO when they are also chairman of the board, but this is not necessarily bad for performance in general.

In the same way as an enlightened monarchy may be best of all political governance systems, duality may be efficient with a good CEO, but a disaster with a bad one. Seen in this way it is not surprising that empirical studies have not found systematic negative (or positive) effects of duality.

Board interlocks (i.e. two CEOs sitting on each other's boards) would theoretically dampen the board's supervision of the CEO, and empirical studies have in fact found a negative effect on company performance.

Busy directors, i.e. directors with many other board positions, may or may not harm firm performance. Busy directors are more likely to be capable individuals, and in some cases they may add valuable information because they sit on many company boards. But they also have less time to spend on individual board positions and so may be less diligent in monitoring. Fich and Shivdasani (2006) find that the negative effects predominate for outside directors, who have more than three board positions.

Staggered boards, i.e. fixed election terms for directors of 2 or more years, are widely regarded as a takeover defence, since even a majority shareholder will only gradually be able to replace board members if boards are staggered. According to agency theory, this should reduce firm performance and firm value, and this is what empirical studies have in fact found. Staggered boards are often regarded as takeover defences since they may prevent a hostile bidder from taking control for a couple of years.

After the financial crisis, some research found that board independence was positively rather than negatively correlated with financial distress among banks such as requiring support from the troubled assets relief fund (Adams 2009, Ferreira et al. 2010). In contrast it was clear that many bank boards were insufficiently informed and/or insufficiently aware of the risks banks were taking. This raised the issue of whether a lack of banking experience and or financial literacy on the boards of banks and other financial institutions contributed to the financial crisis. However, papers by Minton et al. (2011) and Ferreira et al. (2010) indicate that this was not the case. Minton et al. argue that boards with greater financial expertise rationally took greater risks knowing that they would be bailed out by the taxpayers.

Board committees can be regarded as a way to professionalize board works which allows greater attention to specific functional areas. Reeb and Upadhyay (2010) find that committees add to firm value in larger boards with a greater ratio of independent directors, but lower firm value in smaller insider dominated boards. In a small board of say three members, committees do not make much sense.

8.16　Discussion

Boards clearly play an important role in corporate governance. You can imagine firms without boards, and some firms do in fact exist and thrive without boards (Bennedsen, 2002). But in a world without boards they would probably be reinvented because they are an efficient way to handle agency problems, get advice and connect the company to important constituencies. Agency problems include both type 1 problems between owners and managers, type 2 problems between owners and type 3 problems between owners and stakeholders. For example, minority owners may insist on a board seat to ensure that their economic interests are respected, and creditors may demand a seat on the board as a condition for providing bridging finance to a distressed company.

In addition to the control role, boards can be useful as in-house consultants providing advice to the management and as ambassadors proving contact to shareholders, customers, regulators, banks and other important constituencies. They can help with strategy, risk management, headhunting, pay negotiations, auditing, legal issues etc. However, with limited time and knowledge there are also limits to how much non-executive directors should be expected to do.

Minicase

The collapse of Lehman Brothers

With assets of $639 billion the bankruptcy of Lehman Brothers filed on 15 September 2008 was the biggest in history. Lehman was later criticized for aggressive and excessive risk taking and overexposure to subprime bonds. With the benefit of hindsight, the bank went down because of overexposure to bad mortgage loans. This raises a rather obvious question: where was the board in all this? Why didn't it intervene?

Here are the board members as of 2008:

- Richard S. Fuld, Jr. Chairman and CEO since 1994, joined Lehman Brothers in 1969
- Michael L. Ainslie. Former President, Sotheby's Holdings
- John F. Akers (age 74). Retired Chairman, IBM
- Roger S. Berlind, (age 75). Theatrical producer
- Thomas H. Cruikshank (age 77). Retired CEO of Halliburton Company
- Marsha Johnson Evans. Rear Admiral, United States Navy (Retired)
- Sir Christopher Gent. Non-Executive Chairman of GlaxoSmithKline plc
- Jerry A. Grundhofer. Retired CEO, US Bancorp, entered 2008
- Roland A. Hernandez. Retired Chairman and CEO, Telemundo Group
- Henry Kaufman (age 81). Retired, Salomon Brs, Chairman of the Finance and Risk Committee
- John D. Macomber (age 80). Former CEO, Celanese Corporation, a director of Lehman Brothers Holdings Inc. since 1994.

CEO Richard (Dick) Fuld had a substantial equity investment (estimated at 1.4% of the firm or more than half a billion dollars' worth before the stock dropped during the crisis). Fuld is reported to have made hundreds of millions of dollars during his tenure as CEO of Lehman Brothers.

Sources: Compiled from a number of sources including: *Richard Fuld punched in face in Lehman Brothers gym* by Jon Swaine, The Telegraph, 7 October 2008, and *How Much Did CEO Dick Fuld Really Make?* by James Sterngold, Bloomberg Businessweek, 29 April 2010.

Discussion questions

1 Can Lehman's collapse be attributed to agency problems? If so, what kind?
2 Did Lehman's board have the capacity to stop the bank's excessive risk taking?
3 Was the board sufficiently independent?
4 Was its size appropriate?
5 With the benefit of hindsight, what changes in board structure would you propose?

Summary (learning points)

- Boards are small groups who hold the decision-making authority in companies (and most other organizations).
- According to agency theory, boards exist to solve the agency problems which dispersed owners have in dealing with company managers. They are monitors elected by the shareholders.

- In management theory, boards are said to have other functions in addition to control such as advising managers and networking.
- To exercise effective control boards must be independent of the managers they are supposed to supervise.
- They must also be sufficiently small to allow effective decision making.
- There is little evidence that board structure has any systematic effect on company performance.

References and further reading

Adams, R.B. (2005) What do Boards do? Evidence from Board Committee and Director Compensation Data, (March 13, 2003), EFA 2005 Moscow Meetings Paper, available at SSRN: http://ssrn.com/abstract=397401.

Adams, R. (2009) Governance and the financial crisis, in Thomsen S., Rose C. and Risager O. (eds), *Understanding the Financial Crisis: Investment, Risk and Governance*, SimCorp StrategyLab.

Adams, R.B. and Ferreira, D. (2007) A Theory of Friendly Boards, *Journal of Finance*, **62** (1), 217–250.

Adams, R. and Ferreira, D. (2009) Women in the boardroom and their impact on governance and performance, *Journal of Financial Economics*, **94** (2), 291–309.

Adams, R.B., Almeida, H. and Ferreira, D. (2005) Powerful CEOs and Their Impact on Corporate Performance, *Review of Financial Studies*, **18** (4), 1403–1432.

Adams, R.B., Hermalin, B.E and Weisbach, M.S. (2010) The Role of Boards of Directors in Corporate Governance: A Conceptual Framework and Survey, Journal of Economic Literature, *American Economic Association*, **48** (1), 58–107.

Aghion, P. and Tirole, J. (1995) Some implications of growth for organizational form and ownership structure, *European Economic Review*, **39** (3/4), 440–455.

Aghion, P. and Tirole, J. (1997) Formal and real authority in organizations, *Journal of Political Economy*, **105** (1), 1–29.

Agrawal, A. and Knoeber, C. R. (1996) Firm Performance and Mechanisms to Control Agency Problems between Managers and Shareholders, *Journal of Financial and Quantitative Analysis*, **31**(3), 377–397.

Agrawal, A. and Knoeber, C. R. (2001) Do Some Outside Directors Play a Political Role?, *Journal of Law and Economics*, **44** (1), 179–198.

Ahern, K.A. and Dittmar, A. (2010) *The Changing of the Boards: The Value Effect of a Massive Exogenous Shock*, Unpublished working paper.

Almazan, A. and Suarez. J. (2003) Entrenchment and severance pay in optimal governance structures, *Journal of Finance*, **58** (2), 519–547.

Anderson, R.C. and Reeb, D.M. (2003) Founding-Family Ownership and Firm Performance: Evidence from the S&P 500, *Journal of Finance*, **58** (3), 1301–1328.

Andres, de P., Azofra, V. and Lopez, F. (2005) Corporate Boards in OECD Countries: size, composition, functioning and effectiveness, *Corporate Governance: An International Review*, **13** (2), 197–210.

Baker, M. and Gompers, P. (2003) The Determinants of Board Structure at the Initial Public Offering, *Journal of Law & Economics*, **46** (2), 569–598.

Bear, S., Rahman, N. and Post, C. (2010) The Impact of Board Diversity and Gender Composition on Corporate Social Responsibility and Firm Reputation, *Journal of Business Ethics*, **97** (2), 207–221.

Bebchuk, L.A. and Cohen, A. (2005) The Costs of Entrenched Boards, *Journal of Financial Economics*, **78** (2), 409–433.

Bebchuk, L.A., Coates, J.C. and Subramanian. G. (2002) The Powerful Antitakeover Force of Staggered Boards: Theory, Evidence, and Policy, *Stanford Law Review*, **54** (5), 887–950.

Belbin, M. (1993) *Team Roles at Work*, Butterworth-Heinemann: Oxford.

Bennedsen, M. (2002) *Why Do Firms Have Boards?*, Available at SSRN: http://ssrn.com/abstract=303680 or doi:10. 2139/ssrn. 303680.

Bennedsen, M., Perez-Gonzalez, F. and Wolfenzon, D. (2006) *Do CEOs Matter?*, NYU Working Paper No. FIN-06-032. Available at SSRN: http://ssrn.com/abstract=1293659.

Berle, A.A. and Means, G.C. (1932) *The Modern Corporation and Private Property*, Harcourt, Brace and World.

Bhagat, S. and Black, B. (2002) The Non-Correlation between Board Independence and Long Term Firm Performance, *Journal of Corporation Law*, **27** (2), 231–273.

Bhagat, S. and Bolton, B. (2008) Corporate

governance and firm performance, *Journal of Corporate Finance*, **14** (3), 257–273.

Bøhren, Ø. and Ødegaard, B. (2006) Governance and performance revisited, in Ali, P.U. and Gregoriou, G. (eds) *International Corporate Governance after Sarbanes-Oxley*, Wiley.

Bohren, Ø. and Strom, R.Ø. (2006) *Aligned, informed, and decisive: Characteristics of value-creating boards* BI, Norwegian School of Management Working Paper.

Bohren, Ø. and Strom, R. (2010) Governance and Politics: Regulating Independence and Diversity in the Board Room, *Journal of Business Finance & Accounting*, **37** (9/10), 1281–1308.

Boone, A.L., Field, L.C., Karpoff, J.M. and Raheja, C.G. (2007) The Determinants of Corporate Board Size and Composition: An Empirical Analysis, *Journal of Financial Economics*, **85** (1), 66–101.

Brick, I., Palmon, O. and Wald, J. (2006) CEO compensation, director compensation, and firm performance: Evidence of cronyism?, *Journal of Corporate Finance*, **12** (3), 403–423.

Brickley, J., Coles, J. and Jarrell, G. (1997) Leadership Structure: Separating the CEO and the Chairman of the Board, *Journal of Corporate Finance*, **3** (3), 189–220.

Buffet, W. (2003) *Letter to Shareholders, Berkshire Hathaway Inc.*

Cadbury Report, Sir Adrian Cadbury (1992) Report of the Committee on the Financial Aspects of Corporate Governance, Gee and Co.: London.

Carlsson, R.H. (2007) Swedish Corporate Governance and Value Creation: owners still in the driver's seat, *Corporate Governance: An International Review*, **15** (6), 1038–1055.

Chan, K.C. and Li, J. (2008) Audit Committee and Firm Value: Evidence on Outside Top Executives as Expert-Independent Directors, *Corporate Governance: An International Review*, **16** (1), 16–31.

Coles, J.L., Daniel, N.D and Naveen, L. (2008) Boards: Does One Size Fit All?, *Journal of Financial Economics*, **87** (2), 329–356.

Conyon, M.J. and Peck, S.I. (1998) Board Control, Remuneration Committees, and Top Management Compensation, *Academy of Management Journal*, **41** (2), 146–157.

Corley, K. (2005) Examining the Non-Executive Director's Role from a Non-Agency Theory Perspective: Implications Arising from the Higgs Report, *British Journal of Management*, **16** (S1), S1–S4.

Dahya, J. and McConnell, J.J. (2007) Board Composition, Corporate Performance, and the Cadbury Committee Recommendation, *Journal of Financial and Quantitative Analysis*, **42** (3), 535–564.

Dahya, J., McConnell, J.J. and Travlos, N.G. (2002) The Cadbury Committee, Corporate Performance, and Top Management Turnover, *Journal of Finance*, **57** (1), 461–483.

Daily, C., Dalton, D. and Rajagopalay, N. (2003) Governance through ownership: centuries of practice, decades of research, *Academy of Management Journal*, **46** (2), 151–158.

Dalton, D.R., Daily, S.M., Ellstrand, A.E. and Johnson, J.J. (1998) Meta-Analytic Reviews of Board Compensation, Leadership Structure and Financial Performance, *Strategic Management Journal*, **19** (3), 269–290.

De Andres, P., Azofra, V. and Lopez, F. (2005) Corporate Boards in OECD Countries: size, composition, functioning and effectiveness, *Corporate Governance: An International Review*, **13** (2), 197–210.

Denis, D.J. and Denis, D.K. (1995) Performance Changes Following Top Management Dismissals, *Journal of Finance*, **50** (4), 1029–1057.

Denis, D. and Sarin, A. (1999) Ownership and board structures in publicly traded corporations, *Journal of Financial Economics*, **52** (2), 187–223.

Deutsch, Y. (2005) The Impact of Board Composition on Firms' Critical Decisions: A Meta-Analytic Review, *Journal of Management*, **31** (3), 424–444.

Donaldson, L. (1990) The Ethereal Hand: Organizational Economics and Management Theory, *Academy of Management Review*, **15** (3), 369–381.

Donaldson, L. and Davis, J.H. (1991) Stewardship Theory or Agency Theory: CEO Governance and Shareholder Returns, *Australian Journal of Management*, **16** (1), 49–64.

Donaldson, L. and Davis, J.H. (1994) Boards and Company Performance – Research Challenges the Conventional Wisdom, *Corporate Governance: An International Review*, **2** (3), 151–160.

Duchin, R., Matsusaka, J.G. and Ozbas, O. (2010) When are outside directors effective?, *Journal of Financial Economics*, **96** (2), 195–214.

Dulewicz, V. and Herbert, P. (2004) Does the Composition and Practice of Boards of Directors Bear Any Relationship to the Performance of their Companies? *Corporate Governance: An International Review*, **12** (3), 263–280.

Eisenberg, T., Sundgren, S. and Wells, M.T. (1998) Larger board size and decreasing firm value in small firms, *Journal of Financial Economics*, **48** (1), 35–54.

Fahlenbrach, R., Low, A. and Stulz, R.M. (2008) Why Do Firms Appoint CEOs as Outside Directors?, *Journal of Financial Economics*, **97** (1), 12–32.

Fama, F.F. and Jensen, M.C. (1983) Separation of Ownership and Control, *Journal of Law and Economics*, **26** (2), 301.

Fauver, L. and Fuerst, M. E. (2006) Does good corporate governance include employee representation? Evidence from German corporate boards, *Journal of Financial Economics*, **82** (3), 673–710.

Ferreira, D., Kirchmaier, T. and Metzger, D. (2010) *Boards of Banks*, ECGI – Finance Working Paper No. 289/2010.

Fich, E.M. and Shivdasani, A. (2006) Are Busy Boards Effective Monitors? *Journal of Finance*, **61** (2), 689–724.

Financial Times (2011) *A very British split at the top*, By Geoffrey Owen, March 14 .

Finegold, D., Benson, G.S and Hecht, D. (2007)

Corporate Boards and Company Performance: review of research in light of recent reforms, *Corporate Governance: An International Review*, **15** (5), 865–878.

Forbes, D.P. and Milliken, F.J. (1999) Cognition and corporate governance: understanding boards of directors as strategic decision-making groups, *Academy of Management Review*, **24** (3) 489–505.

Gani, L. and Jermias, J. (2006) Investigating the effect of board independence on performance across different strategies, *International Journal of Accounting*, **41** (3), 295–314.

Goldman, E., Rocholl, J. and So, J. (2009) Do Politically Connected Boards Affect Firm Value?, *Review of Financial Studies*, **22** (6), 2331–2360.

Gorton, G. and Schmid, F.A. (2004) Capital, Labor, and the Firm: A Study of German Codetermination, *Journal of the European Economic Association*, **2** (5), 863–905.

Granovetter, M. (1985) Economic action and social structure: The problem of embeddedness, *American Journal of Sociology*, **91** (3), 481–510.

Greene, E.F. and Falk, B.B. (1979) The Audit Committee — A Measured Contribution to Corporate Governance? A Realistic Appraisal of its Objectives and Functions, *Business Lawyer*, **34** (3), 1229.

Guedri, Z. and Hollandts, X. (2008) Beyond Dichotomy: The Curvilinear Impact of Employee Ownership on Firm Performance, *Corporate Governance: An International Review*, **16** (5), 460–474.

Güner, A., Malmendier, U. and Tate, G. (2008) Financial Expertise of Directors, *Journal of Financial Economics*, **88** (2), 323–354.

Guo, R.-J., Kruse, T.A. and Nohel, T. (2008) Undoing the Powerful Anti-takeover Force of Staggered Boards, *Journal of Corporate Finance*, **14** (3), 274–288.

Hermalin, B.E. (2005) Trends in Corporate Governance, *Journal of Finance*, **60** (5), 2351–2384.

Hermalin, B. and Weisbach, M. (1991) The effects of board composition and direct incentives on firm performance, *Financial Management*, **20** (4).

Hermalin, B. and Weisbach, M. (1998) Endogenously Chosen Boards of Directors and Their Monitoring of the CEO, *American Economic Review*, **88** (1), 96–118.

Hermalin, B.E. and Weisbach, M.S. (2003) Boards of directors as an endogenously determined institution: a survey of the economic literature, *Economic Policy Review, Federal Reserve Bank of New York*, issue Apr, 7–26.

Hillman, A. and Dalziel, V. (2003) Boards of Directors and Firm Performance: Integrating Agency and Resource Dependence Perspectives, *Academy of Management Review*, **28** (3), 383–396.

Hillman, A., Withers, M. and Collins, B. (2009) Resource Dependence Theory: A Review, *Journal of Management*, **35** (6), 1404–1427.

Huse, M. (2007) *Boards, Governance and Value Creation: The Human Side of Corporate Governance*, Cambridge University Press: Cambridge

Huson, M.R., Malatesta, P. and Parrino, R. (2004) Managerial Succession and Firm Performance, *Journal of Financial Economics*, **74** (2), 237–275.

Jackson, G. (2005) Employee Representation in the Board Compared: A Fuzzy Sets Analysis of Corporate Governance, Unionism and Political Institutions, *Industrielle Beziehungen*, **2005** (3), 252–279.

Jensen, M.C. (1993) The modern industrial revolution, exit, and the failure of internal control systems, *Journal of Finance*, **48** (3), 831–80.

Jensen, M.C. and Meckling, W.H (1979) Rights and Production Functions: An Application to Labor-Managed Firms and Codetermination, *Journal of Business*, **52** (4), 469–506.

Johnson, J.L., Daily, C.M. and Ellstrand, A.E. (1996) Boards of directors: a review and research agenda, *Journal of Management*, **22** (3), 409–438.

Kaplan, S.N. and Minton, B.A. (2006) *Has the CEO Turnover Changed? Increasingly Performance Sensitive Boards and Increasingly Uneasy CEOs*, National Bureau of Economic Research Working Paper 12465.

Klein, A. (1998), Firm Performance and Board Committee Structure, *Journal of Law & Economics*, **41** (1), 275–303.

Kor, Y.Y. and Misangyi, V.F. (2008) Outside directors' industry-specific experience and firms' liability of newness, *Strategic Management Journal*, **29** (12), 1345–1355.

Krivogorsky, V. (2006) Ownership, board structure, and performance in continental Europe, *International Journal of Accounting*, **41** (2), 176–197.

Larcker, D.F., Richardson, S.A., Seary, A. and Tuna I. (2005) *Director Networks, Executive Compensation, and Organizational Performance*. Unpublished.

Linck, J.S., Netter, J.M. and Yang, T. (2009) The Effects and Unintended Consequences of the Sarbanes–Oxley Act on the Supply and Demand for Directors, *Review of Financial Studies*, **22** (8), 3287–3328.

Lipton, M. and Lorsch, J.W. (1992) A modest proposal for improved corporate governance, *The Business Lawyer*, **48** (1).

Lohse, D. (2006) Tackling Corporate Governance, Interview with Prof. David Larcker, *Stanford Business Magazine*, August.

Lorsch, J. and MacIver, E. (1989) *Pawns or Potentates*, Harvard Business School Press: Boston, MA.

Lynall, M., Golden, B. and Hillman, A. (2003) Board Composition From Adolescence To Maturity: A Multitheoretic View, *Academy of Management Review*, **28** (3), 416–431.

Mace, M.L. (1971) Directors: Myth and Reality, in *Theories of Corporate Governance*, T.Clarke (ed), Routledge: New York.

Masulis, R.W., Wang, C. and Xie, F. (2010) *Globalizing the Boardroom – The Effects of Foreign Directors on Corporate Governance and Firm Performance*, ECGI-Finance Working Paper No. 242.

McDonald, M.L., Westphal, J.D. and Graebner, M.E. (2008) What do they know? The effects of outside director acquisition experience on firm acquisition performance, *Strategic Management Journal*, **29** (11), 1155–1177.

McNulty, T. and Pettigrew, A. (1999) Strategists on the Board, *Organization Studies*, **20** (1), 47–74.

McNulty, T., Roberts, J. and Stiles, P. (2005). Undertaking Governance Reform and Research: Further Reflections on the Higgs Review, *British Journal of Management*, **16** (s1), S99–S107.

Mehran, H. (1995) Executive Compensation Structure, Ownership, and Firm Performance, *Journal of Financial Economics*, **38** (2), 163–184.

Meyer, J.W. and Rowan, B. (1977) Institutionalized organizations: Formal structure as myth and ceremony, *American Journal of Sociology*, **83** (2), 340–363.

Minton, B.A., Taillard, J. and Williamson, R.G. (2011) *Do Independence and Financial Expertise of the Board Matter for Risk Taking and Performance?* (June 20). Fisher College of Business Working Paper No. 2010-03-014. Available at SSRN: http://ssrn.com/abstract=1661855

Oliver, R.W. (2000) The Board's Role: Driver's Seat or Rubber Stamp?, *Journal of Business Strategy*, **21** (4), 7–9.

Patmore, G. (2007) Employee representation plans at the Minnequa steelworks, Pueblo, Colorado, 1915–1942, *Business History*, **49** (6), 844–867.

Pearce, J. and Zahra, S. (1991) The relative power of CEOs and boards of directors: Associations with corporate performance, *Strategic Management Journal*, **12** (2), 135–153.

Petrovic, J. (2008) Unlocking the role of a board director: a review of the literature, *Management Decision*, **46** (9), 1373–1392.

Pfeffer, J. and Salancik, D.R. (1978) *The external control of organizations: A resource-dependence perspective*, Harper & Row: New York.

Powell, W.W. and Dimaggio, P.J. (1991) *The new institutionalism in organizational analysis*, University of Chicago Press: Chicago.

PricewaterhouseCoopers (2005) What Directors Think, *Corporate Board Member Magazine*, published by Board Member Inc.

Pugliese, A., Bezemer, P., Zattoni, A., Huse, M., Van den Bosch, F.J. and Volberda, H.W. (2009) Boards of Directors' Contribution to Strategy: A Literature Review and Research Agenda, *Corporate Governance: An International Review*, **17** (3), 292–306.

Raheja, C. (2005) Determinants of Board Size and Composition: A Theory of Corporate Boards, *Journal of Financial & Quantitative Analysis*, **40** (2), 283–306.

Ravina, E. and Sapienza, P. (2010) What Do Independent Directors Know? Evidence from Their Trading, *The Review of Financial Studies*, **23** (3), 962–1003.

Reeb, D. and Upadhyay, A. (2010) Subordinate board structures, *Journal of Corporate Finance*, **16** (4), 469–486.

Roberts, J. and Van den Steen, E. (2001) Human Capital and Corporate Governance, in *Corporate Governance: Essays in Honor of Horst Albach*, Albach, H. and Schwalbach, J. (eds), Springer Verlag: Berlin.

Roberts, J., McNulty, T. and Stiles, P. (2005) Beyond Agency Conceptions of the Work of the Non-Executive Director: Creating Accountability in the Boardroom, *British Journal of Management*, **16** (s1), 5–26.

Scott, W.R. (2001) *Institutions and Organizations*, Sage: Thousand Oaks, CA.

Shropshire, C. (2010) The Role of the Interlocking Director And Board Receptivity in The Diffusion of Practices, *Academy of Management Review*, **35** (2), 246–264.

Simon, H. (1986) The Failures of Armchair Economics, *Challenge*, Nov–Dec, 18–25.

Stearns, L.B. and Mizruchi, M.S. (1993) Board composition and corporate financing: The impact of financial institution representation on borrowing, *Academy of Management Journal*, **36** (3), 603–618.

Terjesen, S., Sealy, R. and Singh, V. (2009) Women Directors on Corporate Boards: A Review and Research Agenda, *Corporate Governance: An International Review*, **17** (3), 320–337.

Thomsen, S., Rose, C. and Kronborg, D. (2010) *Minimizing employee representation on Nordic boards*, Unpublished working paper.

Tian, J., Haleblian, J. and Rajagopalan, N. (2011) The effects of board human and social capital on investor reactions to new CEO selection, *Strategic Management Journal*, **32** (7), 731–747.

USC/Mercer Delta (2005) Corporate Board Survey Results (March 2004).

Vafeas, N. (1999) Board meeting frequency and firm performance, *Journal of Financial Economics*, **53** (1), 113–142.

Warther, V.A. (1998) Board effectiveness and board dissent: A model of the board's relationship to management and shareholders, *Journal of Corporate Finance*, **4** (1), 53–70.

Weber, Max (1968) *Economy and Society*, Bedminster Press: New York.

Westphal, J. (1998) Board Games: How CEOs Adapt to Increases in Structural Board Independence from Management, *Administrative Science Quarterly*, **43** (3), 511–538.

Westphal, J.D. (1999) Collaboration in the Board Room: Behavioral and Performance Consequences of CEO-Board Ties, *Academy of Management Journal*, **42** (1), 7–24.

Westphal, J. and Bednar, M. (2005) Pluralistic Ignorance in Corporate Boards and Firms' Strategic Persistence in Response to Low Firm Performance, *Administrative Science Quarterly*, **50** (2), 262–298.

Westphal, J. and Khanna, P. (2003) Keeping Directors in Line: Social Distancing as a Control Mechanism in the Corporate Elite, *Administrative Science Quarterly*, **48** (3), 361–398.

Wintoki, M. Babajide, L., James S. and Netter, J.M. (2011) Endogeneity and the Dynamics of Internal Corporate Governance (August 4), *Journal of Financial Economics*, Forthcoming. Available at SSRN: http://ssrn.com/abstract=970986.

Yermack, D. (1996) Higher market valuation of companies with a small board of directors, *Journal of Financial Economics*, **40** (2), 185–211.

Chapter 9

Board Behaviour

Chapter contents

9.1 Introduction

In this chapter we consider how board behaviour can enhance or reduce organizational and board performance. One important constraint on board behaviour are the duties and obligations that directors must carry out according to the legal structures that are in place in their respective countries. What is more difficult to understand fully are the underlying dynamics of how directors interact with each other in groups. While it is possible to define, and even to some extent measure, board structure, there is an aura of mystique about how behaviour in the boardroom is conducted in practice. For academic scholars, understanding board processes creates practical dilemmas. We cannot actually observe what goes on at board meetings, and because of confidentiality it is difficult to get board members to talk about it. In the theory of boards, it is customary to refer to board behaviour as a 'black box'. This metaphor is borrowed from the theory of the firm and resonates well with the mystique and is enhanced by knowing that the board is the main decision-maker in firms. In this chapter we try to open the black box and peer inside. We examine the legal duties of directors and what is expected of them according to best-practice codes and the few studies of what actually goes on. Because of the procedural formality of board meetings it turns out that the black box metaphor is somewhat ill-founded; we may actually know more about what goes on in boardrooms than one might initially suspect.

9.2 Directors' duties

An important and binding constraint on director behaviour is company law. Company law is different in each country, but across the world it defines and regulates what board directors must do and in addition the law places constraints on what they must not do. The exact legal philosophy and wording differs from corporate governance system to system, and country to country, but essentially they contain the same elements. The law typically prescribes that organizations must have a board of directors and that the board must contain a certain number of directors. The law also outlines the parameters that provide the boundaries to director behaviour..

Consider US law as a reference point and the duties of the company director. As we have discussed elsewhere in this book, the USA is a shareholder-centric common law system. American case law operates a 'business judgement rule' which provides directors with considerable protection from the effects of their actions. The business judgement rule says that the court will not review the business decisions of directors who performed their duties in good faith, with care and loyalty. The business judgement rule is a presumption in favour of the board of directors, meaning that they are effectively absolved from liability for decisions that result in harm or adverse consequences for the organization. The directors' duties are:

- The fiduciary duty to act in the best interest of the shareholders (within the limits set by law). This underlines that boards are fiduciaries (agents) acting on behalf of shareholders.
- The duty of loyalty to the company is the duty of directors to keep the company's best interest in mind and not act for personal gain.
- The duty of fair dealing can be regarded as a special case of the duty of loyalty. A director is not allowed to personally take advantage of a business opportunity in the company's business area unless the transaction is first offered to the company and turned down. Directors must therefore disclose any personal interest in a transaction (for example at a board meeting). If there is a vote on the issue, it must be decided by a majority of the non-interested directors.
- The duty of care is the duty to exercise the duty of loyalty with the care that could be expected of a reasonable 'prudent' person. This includes for example the duty to meet regularly to assess company performance and to read and react on information provided to the board. It includes

the duty to ask for additional information, but it usually does not obligate the director to second guess information provided by company management or other board members. Trust is allowed.

In summary, the business judgement rule provides boards of directors with a safe harbour regarding their decisions. The business judgement rule affords the boards of directors considerable protections. Specifically it says the directors of a corporation 'are clothed with that presumption, which the law accords to them, of being actuated in their conduct by a bona fide regard for the interests of the corporation whose affairs the stockholders have committed to their charge'. In short, directors are assumed to be acting in the best interests of the firm. In order to challenge the decision of the board of directors, a complainant or plaintiff must provide the burden of showing that the directors themselves breached one of the triads of their fiduciary duty. Namely, they did not act in good faith, loyalty, or undertake due care. If a complainant cannot show this then the plaintiff is not entitled to remedies under the law. In short, the courts do not want to hold directors liable for decisions made in good faith with a reasonable level of care. They will trust their judgement. But if it can be demonstrated that the board did not exercise sufficient care it is up to the board members to prove that their decisions were in fact fair to all shareholders.

In the United Kingdom, the UK Companies Act of 2006 governs directors' duties. The Companies Act has been reformed many times and the 2006 Act is the most recent. The UK system of corporate governance is based on common law, as in the United States. However, the most recent Companies Act (2006) has shifted the emphasis of directors' duties away from a purely shareholder-centric model to one of protecting stakeholder interests too. The duties of directors are outlined in Sections 171 to 177 of the new Companies Act (2006). To enumerate these: §171 says that directors must act within their powers provided in the company's articles of association; §172 requires directors to promote the success of the company; §173 requires independent judgement; §174 requires them to exercise reasonable care, skill and diligence; §175 requires them to avoid conflicts of interest; §176 requires directors not to accept benefits from third parties; and §177 requires director to declare any interest in a proposed transaction with the company.

Section 172 was perhaps the most controversial aspect of the new changes since it required directors to promote the long-term 'success' of the company for the benefit of the company's members (shareholders) and its other stakeholders, including employees, customers and creditors. The directors must serve all shareholders, not just the majority. Section 172 does require the board of directors to act in a way that benefits the shareholders as a whole, but there is an additional set of factors that they must take into account when making their decisions. These include the interest of employees, relationships with suppliers, customers and others, the impact on the community and the environment, and the need to maintain a reputation for high standards of business conduct and to act fairly between the different members.

9.3   Country codes of conduct

Another key insight into board behaviour is what boards are expected to do according to codes of best practice. A list of country codes is maintained by the European Corporate Governance Institute (ECGI). For each country a corporate governance code is provided, and this gives directions on the types of behaviours and duties that boards are expected to follow (see http://www.ecgi.org/codes/all_codes.php).

Consider the context of the UK. The UK Corporate Governance Code, which was formerly the Combined Code, establishes the standards of good practice in relation to board leadership and effectiveness, remuneration, accountability and relations with shareholders. The most recent Code was published in May 2010. It applies to financial June 2010.

The purpose of the Code 'is to facilitate effective, entrepreneurial and prudent management that can deliver the long-term success of the company'. The Code sets out principles and provisions that govern director behaviour. The principals contained in the Code are central and every director must understand them. The following are a few examples.

Section A deals with leadership of the company. Principle A1 deals with the role of the board. It says: 'Every company should be headed by an effective board which is collectively responsible for the long-term success of the company.' Principle A2 asserts that 'There should be a clear division of responsibilities at the head of the company between the running of the board and the executive responsibility for the running of the company's business. No one individual should have unfettered powers of decision.' In addition, A3 requires that: 'The chairman is responsible for leadership of the board and ensuring its effectiveness on all aspects of its role.' A4 makes requirements of the non-executive directors: 'As part of their role as members of a unitary board, non-executive directors should constructively challenge and help develop proposals on strategy.'

Section B of the new UK Governance Code deals explicitly with board effectiveness and requires the following board behaviour. Principle B1: 'The board and its committees should have the appropriate balance of skills, experience, independence and knowledge of the company to enable them to discharge their respective duties and responsibilities effectively.' Appointments to the board are governed by Principle B2: 'There should be a formal, rigorous and transparent procedure for the appointment of new directors to the board.' Principle B3 requires diligence from the directors: 'All directors should be able to allocate sufficient time to the company to discharge their responsibilities effectively.' B4 requires regular training of the directors: 'All directors should receive induction on joining the board and should regularly update and refresh their skills and knowledge.'

Section C of the Code deals with accountability. This acts as an important constraint on director behaviour. In terms of the financial position of the company, Principle C1 states: 'The board should present a balanced and understandable assessment of the company's position and prospects.' In terms of risk management and control, C2 states: 'The board is responsible for determining the nature and extent of the significant risks it is willing to take in achieving its strategic objectives. The board should maintain sound risk management and internal control systems.'

Section E of the new Code requires directors to engage proactively with the firm's owners. Principle E1 states: 'There should be a dialogue with shareholders based on the mutual understanding of objectives. The board as a whole has responsibility for ensuring that a satisfactory dialogue with shareholders takes place.' Principle E2 requires effective use of the annual general meeting: 'The board should use the AGM to communicate with investors and to encourage their participation.'

It is clear that the principles and provisions contained in the Code of Conduct place duties and obligations on directors. The UK Code of Conduct, though, is based on the concept of 'comply or explain'. It is not legally binding, but if directors and companies do not follow the principles and provisions it contains they are required to explain why not. However, as one might expect, the code conveys much weight and there is a strong social norm to follow its recommendations.

The 'to do list' contained in the Code is perhaps somewhat daunting. Board members should (at least in part) be entrepreneurs, accountants, controllers, strategists, human resource specialists, pay consultants, risk managers, investor relations officers and corporate governance evaluators. One wonders whether this is realistic for large complex companies with less than two months of work. At the very least it must require a very special kind of individual. Certainly, in smaller, perhaps unlisted companies it is unrealistic to expect directors to accomplish all of this. Nevertheless the UK code does provide an ideal yardstick for what boards ought to do.

In addition to these obligations there are numerous special tasks for the chairman and the senior independent director. The senior independent director, also (in the US) called a 'lead director', is expected to be a sounding board for the chairman and a spokesperson for the other non-executives.

The tasks of chairs and lead directors (UK governance code) are:

- The chair and the senior independent director should hold meetings with the non-executive directors without the executives present. In the USA these meetings are for some strange reason called executive sessions.
- Led by the senior independent director, the non-executive directors should meet without the

chairman present at least annually to appraise the chairman's performance, and on such other occasions as are deemed appropriate.

- The chairman should ensure that the directors continually update their skills and the knowledge and familiarity with the company required to fulfil their role both on the board and on board committees. The company should provide the necessary resources.
- The chairman should ensure that the views of shareholders are communicated to the board as a whole.
- The chairman should discuss governance and strategy with major shareholders.
- The senior independent director should attend sufficient meetings with a range of major shareholders.

The tasks of board committees (UK governance code) are:

- The nomination committee should lead the process for board appointments and make recommendations to the board.
- For the appointment of a chairman, the nomination committee should prepare a job specification.
- The remuneration committee should have delegated responsibility for setting remuneration for all executive directors and the chairman, including pension rights and any compensation payments.
- The (remuneration) committee should also recommend and monitor the level and structure of remuneration for senior management. The definition of 'senior management' should normally include the first layer of management below the board level.
- The board should establish an audit committee to review the company's internal financial controls and to review and monitor the external auditor's independence and objectivity
- And the effectiveness of the audit process, taking into consideration relevant professional and regulatory requirements;
- Develop and implement policy on the engagement of the external auditor to supply non-audit services;
- Review arrangements by which staff of the company may, in confidence, raise concerns about possible improprieties in matters of financial reporting or other matters;
- Monitor and review the effectiveness of the internal audit activities;
- Have primary responsibility for making a recommendation on the appointment, reappointment and removal of the external auditors.

9.4 What do boards do?

Because researchers are normally barred from attending board meetings we have relatively few studies of what happens in board meetings. But based on minutes and casual observation we can infer that board meetings tend to follow a common agenda structure, which is occasionally even written into the rules of procedure or the bylaws (Colley et al., 2003):

1 Quorum/approval of agenda
2 Approval/signature of minutes
3 Messages (non-decision/consent items)
4 Committee reports
5 Current financial status
6 Proposals
7 Briefings
8 Any other business.

The current financial status will invariably include a report by the management on the financial situation, how the company performs relative to the budget and explanations for the deviations. Critics have argued that a lot of time is therefore spent discussing the past rather than the future.

Traditionally, it was held that boards did not do very much (Adams et al., 2010). Based on a large number of interviews with non-executive directors, Lorsch and MacIver (1989) concluded that non-executive directors were pawns more than potentates vis-à-vis the management, partly because they did not have sufficient time and were forced to rely on the chairman/CEO for most of their information. They also documented that most US non-executive directors felt an ambiguous and partly conflicting set of responsibilities to all stakeholders rather than just to shareholders. They argued that more empowered directors would benefit company performance. Partly as a result of the corporate governance debate, this may actually have happened, so that boards now are more empowered and important. For example, in current surveys most board members feel that they have a role in setting strategy (Adams et al., 2010).

After interviewing 108 non-executive directors, McNulty and Pettigrew (1999) conclude that 'the initiation and generation of strategy are much more likely to be led by executive directors. It is the executive board members, acting outside the boardroom, who tend to generate the content of strategy'. However, they argue that some boards shape strategic decisions through consultation with the executives (often outside board meetings), while 'only a minority of boards shape the context, content, and conduct of strategy'. Boards ratify most proposals by the executives (90–95%), but Pettigrew and McNulty maintain that non-executives shape strategy by an on-going dialogue with the management in and outside board meetings.

Adams (2005) approaches the study of board behaviour indirectly. She examines the time and compensation of committee work as a proxy for director effort. Using this proxy, she concludes that company boards devote more time to monitoring (audit, compensation, and nomination committees) than to strategy or network roles, but that many do have strategy and stakeholder committees which account for respectively 4% and 1% of total director compensation. However, she also infers that most board work takes place outside the committees.

Huse and Zattoni (2008) relate case studies of board work in three small Norwegian firms to the corporate life cycle. In a start-up firm they find that the board was mainly involved in enhancing the firm's legitimacy. In a growth firm they find that the advisory role of the board was primary, while control was most important in a firm hit by a crisis.

Based on seven case studies, Nicholson and Kiel (2007) found that boards play very different roles (control, service or contact) depending on the firm in question and the challenges it faces.

Tuggle, Sirmon, Reutzel and Bierman (2010) examine minutes of board meetings using content analysis to infer time spent on monitoring and find that boards monitor more if performance decreases and monitor less if it increases. Duality (CEO = chair) reduces the level of monitoring. Zhang, Baden-Fuller and Pool (2011) examine boards of high-tech venture capital firms and find that boards play roles which are more consistent with cooperation (Westphal, 1998) than with the pure control role emphasized in agency theory.

Altogether, the available evidence indicates that boards do in fact have a number of functions including control, advice and networking.

9.5 Theorizing about board behaviour

The most important aspect of board behaviour is arguably the division of labour between management and the outside independent directors of the board. Which decisions are made by the management, and which have to be taken to the independent board members?

First certain key decisions, the core board activities, cannot be outsourced or shared with the CEO because of conflicts of interest. These include the basic functions like tracking company performance, hiring/firing the CEO, nomination, auditing and remuneration decisions. The CEO should not control himself, set his own pay, control his controllers, or measure his own or the company's performance. For these activities, if there were no board, you would have to invent it.

Beyond this, boards should intuitively deal with overall principles while day-to-day management of the business is left to the executives (Figure 9.1).

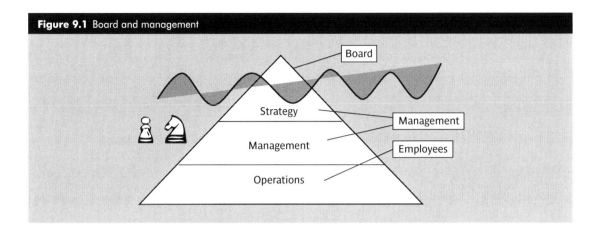

Figure 9.1 Board and management

It would be tempting to say that boards deal with strategy, while managers deal with tactics and operations, but the non-executive directors are usually in no position to decide the strategy without consulting the CEO. Fama and Jensen (1983) argue that management proposes the strategy and the board ratifies it (or rejects it in rare cases). An alternative may be that management proposes the strategy, while the board modifies and then ratifies. Another formulation may be that the board 'vets' the strategy.

This means that strategy is a grey area between the board and the management. What decisions are sufficiently strategic to be taken to the board? A formal expression of this limit will often be found in the rules of procedure which limit the size of transactions which the CEO can undertake without board approval. One guiding principle can be whether an activity is business as usual, in which case it need not be presented to the board, or whether it represents something new, which the board should then approve. Another guiding principle is size; if transactions are very large, they are of course unusual for that very reason.

The division of labour between board and management can obviously vary between firms and over time. Boards may be expected to be more active in crisis situations, when the company and the CEO are performing badly and in the interim period between CEOs until the new CEO is firmly in charge. In some cases when the CEO dies or suddenly quits, board members may feel obliged to take on additional responsibility.

With regard to differences between firms, small firms are more likely to call on advice from the board and to seek its assistance in forming business relationships. Boards may also be more active in companies that depend more on a few large, but relatively generic decisions (e.g. property companies) compared with more opaque and continuous businesses which rely more on managerial judgement.

Board involvement

A related question is how much the board should become involved. If we measure board involvement by number of board meetings or hours worked, we would theoretically postulate a bell-shaped effect on company performance for an increasing number of hours (Figure 9.2).

The marginal productivity of board work is probably quite high initially. It makes a big difference whether there is some control of management or none at all. But as the graph indicates, the marginal productivity of board effort is likely to decline and at some point become negative. For example, non-executive board members have an information disadvantage compared with managers and will therefore make worse decisions if they delegate less. Moreover, there is a trade-off between management and control. The more effort boards put in, the more they will become involved in management and the less objective they can be in controlling the self-same management (Adams and Ferreira, 2007).

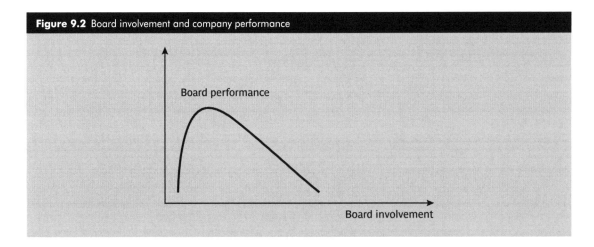

Figure 9.2 Board involvement and company performance

For example, company performance may increase as the board puts in more effort and the number of board meetings is doubled from 1 to 2 to 4 meetings a year and maybe also (but less steeply) from 4 to 8 meetings. But company performance will increase very little and probably even decline if the number of annual board meetings is doubled from 8 to 16 meetings a year. And certainly a redoubling from 16 to 32 board meetings a year would be ridiculous. Redoubling again to 64 board meetings a year would definitely change its work to infringe much more on management. For example, board members are likely to get more involved in management and operations, which they do not know well enough, and the CEO must devote an increasing share of his time tending the board rather than minding his business. Good boards will therefore try to find a golden mean where they don't overdo it.

CEO/board relationships

The relationship between the board and the CEO is clearly one of the most important elements of corporate governance. If the CEO is unwilling to share information, the board will often have too little information to monitor performance accurately. On the other hand, strong and capable CEOs may have a professional interest in boards which can appreciate what they are doing. This may be a matter of getting the board to buy in or be motivated by a desire to be praised for good performance.

Pearce and Zahra (1991) illustrate some of the possible outcomes of this tension. They examine the relative power of the CEO and the board. Arguing that both the CEO and the board can be more or less powerful they construct a 2 × 2 matrix to illustrate the different power constellations (Table 9.1).

- Caretaker boards are dysfunctional with low board power and low CEO power. The board is 'a legal necessity' void of decision-making power and leadership.
- Statutory boards 'reflect the prototypical image of ineffective boards', i.e. the rule of the imperial CEO. The board rubber-stamps the decisions of the CEO, who has power while the non-executive directors do not.
- Proactive boards are active, vigilant and empowered by shareholder activism and director liability. They influence strategy and control executive search and selection as well as committee work. To some extent their power derives from gaining ground in a zero-sum game with the CEO.
- Participative boards are boards in which both parties are empowered. According to Pearce and Zahra their working style is characterized by 'discussion, debate and disagreement' resolved ultimately by formal mechanisms such as voting. Proactive boards will spend considerable time trying to negotiate a consensus.

Table 9.1 Relative CEO and board power

		Board power	
		Low	High
CEO power	High	Statutory boards	Participative boards
	Low	Caretaker boards	Proactive boards

Based on a survey of 139 Fortune 500 boards, Pearce and Zahra find that empowered and particularly participative boards have the best overall performance.

Power relations are likely to change over time, reflecting the experience and track record of the CEO and the board (Hermalin and Weisbach, 1998). Successful CEOs may see their power grow as the board becomes more reluctant to fire them. They may be able to influence the composition of the board, nominating members who are friendly to them. They become more experienced and less likely to make mistakes. They also get to know the board better and get better at handling it. Their power will probably continue to grow until they approach retirement age, at which point their power will decrease rapidly, particularly after retirement has been announced.

The power of chairs and ordinary board members will probably increase over time with their experience until it drops off just before retirement. However, we expect a less steep power curve for the board than for CEOs given that they are part-time and that company success is attributed more to the CEO than to the board.

Over long periods of time other factors will change as well. The competitive advantage of most firms will be eroded over time by the forces of competition. This will leave both the board and the CEO in a more vulnerable position, but particularly the CEO, who is generally held more accountable for company performance. Random events like macroeconomic crises are also more likely to occur at least once over longer periods of time. The risk is that the CEO will be held accountable for at least some of the ensuing drop in company performance. However, ownership structures of individual firms may become less concentrated as controlling owners sell out. This will then increase both CEO and board power.

CEO and board turnover will also influence power relations. Newly hired CEOs will probably be more cautious and more loyal to the board that hired them. In the same way new board members will be more reluctant to take drastic steps until they have a better grasp of the situation.

9.6 Discussion

The black box metaphor has generated an aura of mystique about what goes on in board meetings. Since confidentiality concerns have prevented researchers from participating, we cannot say precisely what is going on. However, boards are more regulated than any other part of the company, so we know quite a lot about what they must and must not do, and what they are expected to do. Moreover, the agenda format regulates how boards deliberate and make their decisions.

As in any other organizational unit, decisions need not actually be made at the meeting. Many items will be clarified informally outside the boardroom, for example in informal bilateral meetings between the chair and the CEO, between board members or between board members and shareholders.

As for what boards do, we know that they spend time on control, advice and contact tasks. The priority given to these tasks will vary from firm to firm and over time. In younger, smaller, unlisted firms advice and contacts are generally more important, whereas control is more important in large listed companies. However, since boards carry the overall responsibility for the success of the company any pertinent question (risk management, search and selection, macroeconomics) can be brought up at a board meeting.

However, one should also be realistic. With a yearly workload of perhaps a month per member, there is a limit to what non-executive board members can effectively handle. Many of the board's responsibilities will therefore be discharged by delegation to the CEO, staff members, or outside consultants like auditors and pay consultants.

Minicase

The new venture[1]

I

Because of your skills in governance and finance you have just been elected to be a board member in a publicly listed company. The company is a mature producer of food additives with organic growth of 2–3% a year, but it is quite profitable (return on equity 23% over the last 5 years) and well consolidated (equity/assets of 60%). But the share price is low and has been flat for many years.

Management proposes a new biotech business project. The project is small, but could be important as a development project. It involves producing smaller quantities of a number of additives (emulsifiers) using genetically modified organisms. It has a projected payback time of less than 2 years. The other board members are ordinary businessmen with little or no knowledge of biotech. They seem hesitant. You notice that the share prices of biotechnology companies are much higher than those of food producers.

What do you say?

II

After two years the project turns out to be much more costly than expected (customers are reluctant to buy). As a result the budget has been exceeded by 100%. The new venture is still small compared with the rest of the company, but annual profits are affected. The long-term prospects are still promising, the managers say (they present a new, revised investment case). The innovative approach has generated favourable international publicity. An experienced biotech manager has been hired to head the new venture. They ask for an extension.

What do you say?

III

After 4 years the project has exceeded budget by 500% and now reduced total earnings by 50%. A senior board member says that he believes the project should be closed. But the chairman and the CEO are hesitant. 'We would lose all,' the chairman says.

What do you say?

---

[1] This fictionalized case is based on an actual business situation.

Discussion questions

1 With the benefit of hindsight, would you say that the board was acting correctly?
2 What warning signals do you see now?
3 What should be the optimal go/no go rule for new ventures in the company?
4 How about your own role on the board, would you have acted differently?

Summary (learning points)

- Boards are obligated by law to act in the best interest of the shareholder and the company, to exert a reasonable amount of effort and not let their private interests get in the way.

- According to best-practice codes they are expected to review company performance, approve strategy and major decisions, hire and fire the chief executive and oversee a number of other tasks such as risk management, social responsibility, shareholder contacts, financial control etc.

- Board meetings tend to follow a fairly similar agenda.

- Boards play many different roles (monitoring, advising, networking) depending on the challenges facing the company.

- The balance of power between boards and executives varies from company to company.

- We propose a bell-shaped relationship between board involvement and company performance. Board involvement adds value up to a point after which it may become excessive and do more harm than good.

References and further reading

Adams, R.B. (2005) *What do Boards do?* Evidence from Board Committee and Director Compensation Data (March 13, 2003), EFA 2005 Moscow Meetings Paper.

Adams, R.B. and Ferreira, D. (2007) A Theory of Friendly Boards, *Journal of Finance*, 62 (1), 217–250.

Adams, R.B., Hermalin, B.E. and Weisbach, M.S. (2010) The Role of Boards of Directors in Corporate Governance: A Conceptual Framework and Survey, *Journal of Economic Literature*, American Economic Association, 48 (1), 58–107.

Bauguess, S. and Stegemoller, M. (2008) Protective governance choices and the value of acquisition activity, *Journal of Corporate Finance*, 14 (5), 550–566.

Colley, J.L., Doyle, J.L., Stettinius, W. and Logan, G. (2003) *Corporate Governance*, McGraw-Hill.

Faleye, O., Hoitash, R. and Hoitash, U. (2011) The costs of intense board monitoring, *Journal of Financial Economics*, 101 (1), 160–181.

Fama, F.F. and Jensen, M.C. (1983) Separation of Ownership and Control, *Journal of Law and Economics*, 26 (2), 301–325.

German Company law – http://www.bundesrecht. juris.de/aktg/

Gillette, A.B., Noe, T.H. and Rebello, M.J. (2003) Corporate Board Composition, Protocols, and Voting Behavior: Experimental Evidence, *Journal of Finance*, 58 (5), 1997–2032.

Hambrick, D.C., Werder, A.V. and Zajac, E.J. (2008) New Directions in Corporate Governance Research, *Organization Science*, 19 (3), 381–385.

Hermalin, B. and Weisbach, M. (1998) Endogenously Chosen Boards of Directors and Their Monitoring

of the CEO, *American Economic Review*, 88 (1), 96–118.

Huse, M. and Zattoni, A. (2008) Trust, Firm Life Cycle, and Actual Board Behavior: Evidence from One of the Lads in the Board of Three Small Firms, *International Studies of Management & Organization*, 38 (3), 71–97.

Huse, M., Hoskisson, R., Zattoni, A. and Viganò, R. (2011) New perspectives on board research: changing the research agenda, *Journal of Management & Governance*, 15 (1), 5–28.

Huse, M., Nielsen, S. and Hagen, I. (2009) Women and Employee-Elected Board Members, and Their Contributions to Board Control Tasks, *Journal of Business Ethics*, 89 (4), 581–597.

Kroll, M., Walters, B.A. and Wright, P. (2008) Board vigilance, director experience, and corporate outcomes, *Strategic Management Journal*, 29 (4), 363–382.

Letendre, L. (2004) The dynamics of the boardroom, *Academy of Management Executive*, 18 (1), 101–104.

Lorsch, J. and MacIver, E. (1989) *Pawns or Potentates*, Harvard Business School Press: Boston, MA.

McDonald, M.L. and Westphal, J.D. (2010) A little help here? Board control, CEO identification with the corporate elite, and strategic help provided to CEOs at other firms, *Academy of Management Journal*, 53 (2), 343–370.

McNulty, T. and Pettigrew, A. (1999) Strategists on the Board, *Organization Studies*, 20 (1), 47–74.

McNulty, T., Pettigrew, A., Jobome, G. and Morris, C. (2011) The role, power and influence of company chairs, *Journal of Management & Governance*, 15 (1), 91–121.

McNulty, T., Roberts, J. and Stiles, P. (2005) Undertaking Governance Reform and Research: Further Reflections on the Higgs Review, *British Journal of Management*, **16** (S1), S99–S107.

Nicholson, G.J. and Kiel, G.C. (2007) Can Directors Impact Performance? A case-based test of three theories of corporate governance, *Corporate Governance: An International Review*, **15** (4), 585–608.

Paul, D.L. (2007) Board Composition and Corrective Action: Evidence from Corporate Responses to Bad Acquisition Bids, *Journal of Financial & Quantitative Analysis*, **42** (3), 759–783.

Pearce II, J.A. and Zahra, S.A. (1991) The relative power of CEOs and boards of directors: associations with corporate performance, *Strategic Management Journal*, **12** (2), 135–153.

Stern, I. and Westphal, J.D. (2010) Stealthy Footsteps to the Boardroom: Executives' Backgrounds, Sophisticated Interpersonal Influence Behavior, and Board Appointments, *Administrative Science Quarterly*, **55** (2), 278–319.

The UK corporate governance code – Financial Reporting Council, http://www.frc.org.uk/corporate/ukcgcode.cfm

Tuggle, C.S., Sirmon, D.G., Reutzel, C.R. and Bierman, L. (2010) Commanding board of director attention: investigating how organizational performance and CEO duality affect board members' attention to monitoring, *Strategic Management Journal*, **31** (9), 946–968.

US (Delaware company law) http://delcode.delaware.gov/title8/c001/sc04/index.shtml

van Ees, H., van der Laan, G. and Postma, T.M. (2008) Effective board behavior in The Netherlands, *European Management Journal*, **26** (2), 84–93.

van Ees, H., Gabrielsson, J. and Huse, M. (2009) Toward a Behavioral Theory of Boards and Corporate Governance, *Corporate Governance: An International Review*, **17** (3), 307–319.

Westphal, J. (1998) Board Games: How CEOs Adapt to Increases in Structural Board Independence from Management, *Administrative Science Quarterly*, **43** (3), 511–538.

Westphal, J.D. and Fredrickson, J.W. (2001) Who directs strategic change? Director experience, the selection of new CEOs, and change in corporate strategy, *Strategic Management Journal*, **22** (12), 1113–1137.

Westphal, J.D. and. Zajac, E.J. (1995) Who Shall Govern? CEO/Board Power, Demographic Similarity, and New Director Selection, *Administrative Science Quarterly*, **40** (1), 60–83.

Zhang, J.J., Baden-Fuller, C. and Pool, J.K. (2011) Resolving the Tensions between Monitoring, Resourcing and Strategizing: Structures and Processes in High Technology Venture Boards, *Long Range Planning*, **44** (2), 95–117.

Chapter 10

Executive Compensation

Chapter contents

10.1   Introduction

Executive compensation is a central feature of the corporate governance system. It is also very controversial. Politicians, the public, taxpayers, the media, as well as some academics have been highly critical of executive pay practices. The financial crisis of 2008 led to even greater scrutinizing of executive pay, especially the large salaries received by CEOs of banks and financial institutions. Authorities in the USA and around the world are in the process of enacting new laws to improve upon executive pay arrangements and associated corporate governance arrangements. The goal of this chapter is to provide a descriptive analysis of executive compensation and incentives, and to provide some explanations for those outcomes.

At least three factors are driving the unprecedented recent interest in CEO pay. First, as the financial crisis deepened many bank employees received lavish bonuses at the same time as their firms lobbied for massive government bailouts. For example, at American International Group (AIG) $218 million was paid in bonuses to employees of its financial services division. The public was outraged. Second, many CEOs do receive very large amounts of money, and the dollar amounts can attract significant attention. The median CEO in the S&P 500 earned about $8 million dollars in 2008. Annual growth rates in CEO pay can often exceed 10%. Executive pay critics also contend that CEO compensation is not sufficiently tied to the performance of their firms. Third, increasingly US CEOs are doing better when their incomes are compared with that of the typical American household. In 1993, average total pay of CEOs was approximately 100 times greater than median household income and by 2006 it was more than 200 times greater (Kaplan, 2008). Because of these kinds of factors, interest in executive compensation has spiked.

There are two competing perspectives on executive compensation. The first is 'optimal contracting' theory. According to this perspective, markets ultimately determine executive compensation. CEO pay arrangements, whilst not always perfect, reflect the costs and benefits of arm's-length bargaining between boards and CEOs. Executive pay contracts provide efficient incentives for dealing with agency costs (Core and Guay, 2010; Holmström, 1979). The second perspective is the 'managerial power' theory. It states that executive pay arrangements are not the outcome of arm's-length contracting. CEO pay arrangements are fundamentally flawed and managerial excess is widespread. This view sees executive compensation as part of the corporate governance problem, rather than the solution (e.g. Bebchuk and Fried, 2004). This chapter describes executive compensation and incentives, investigating whether outcomes are consistent with economic theory.

10.2   Executive compensation

The economic objective of executive compensation is to align the interests of the CEO and the firm's owners (Murphy, 1999). HR professionals frequently talk about the need to attract, retain and motivate talented individuals. In theory, shareholders do not set pay directly. They do so indirectly by electing a board of directors to act on their behalf. In practice, therefore, the firm's board of directors sets pay acting faithfully on behalf of the company shareholders. If the board fails in its fiduciary duties of care and loyalty to the principal, then this can lead to poorly designed compensation contracts (Bebchuk and Fried, 2004).

Optimal contracting view

The economics of executive compensation is generally motivated by principal–agent considerations (Holmström, 1979). A risk-neutral owner and rational self-interested utility maximizing CEO is assumed. There is an asymmetry of information between the owner of the firm (the 'principal') and the CEO (the 'agent') who makes decisions on behalf the owner. This gives rise to a moral hazard problem, namely that the actions or care taken by the CEO are not perfectly observable, at zero or low cost, to the owner. The CEO can opportunistically pursue his own interest at the expense of shareholders because he is better informed about his own actions.

As a practical matter, moral hazard can come in many forms. First, the CEO can enjoy the quiet life by picking easy-to-manage tasks. A risk-averse CEO may avoid undertaking risky projects with positive net present values, especially if the *ex post* outcomes of such projects turn out to be poor and lead to termination. Second, the CEO may engage in self-interested empire building. One mechanism to achieve this is via mergers and acquisitions. Third, the CEO may make excessive or unwarranted use of company perks that may not be beneficial for shareholders. This may include use of corporate aircraft, financial services, or club memberships. In the extreme, moral hazard also includes intentional misappropriation of shareholder funds, including fraud and theft. Corporate accounting scandals such as Enron, or the Ponzi scheme perpetrated by former investment banker Bernard Madoff are examples.

To solve the moral hazard problem, the firm's owners design a contract that makes management rewards contingent upon firm performance. Economists say that the contract should be incentive compatible: the CEO chooses the correct (i.e. optimal) action (i.e. focus on firm performance) because it is in his best interests to do so (i.e. leads to greater personal wealth). Agency theory provides the underlying logic for 'pay-for-performance' plans in organizations (Murphy, 1999).

Economic models predict that executive pay contracts include stock options, accounting earnings, and individual performance metrics that provide a signal of the executive's effort. This is the 'informativeness' principle. Any variable that yields information about CEO effort may be legitimately used in the compensation contract. Two immediate points are worth noting about this optimal contracting approach. First, agency theory predicts that second-best contracts reduce opportunistic behaviour on the part of executives. The use of compensation that is at risk for the CEO, such as stock options, motivates individual effort. Second, agency costs are not completely eliminated. Instead, the firm evaluates the incremental benefits and costs of designing, implementing and verifying the contract. In this sense the contract is optimal but not perfect (in the economist's sense of it being first best).

Managerial power view

A popular alternative view of executive compensation is that CEOs set pay in their own rather than shareholder interests. It has been termed the managerial power view (or sometimes 'skimming' hypothesis) and contrasts with optimal contracting theory (Bebchuk and Fried, 2004). It argues that bargaining between corporate boards and CEOs is not determined by arm's-length bargaining and that executive pay is excessive. The resulting pay contracts are not in shareholders' interests. How are CEOs able to get this extra pay? After all, most individuals in organizations (you and me) cannot simply demand a premium over the market rate and expect to receive it.

One version of the theory is that CEOs exercise power and influence over their boards, and use this to lobby for high pay levels. The 'excess pay' constitutes an economic rent, an amount greater than required for the CEO to provide labour services to the firm. Corporate boards are viewed as relatively weak compared with the CEO. What constitutes a weak board? The extant literature typically argues that a board is poorly constituted if it is too large, and therefore it is difficult for directors to oppose the CEO, or if the CEO has appointed the outside directors, who are beholden to the CEO for their jobs. In addition, directors may serve on too many other boards, making them too busy to be effective monitors; or if the CEO is also chair of the board, conflicts of interest may arise. The board may be too friendly with the CEO, coming from the same social or friendship groups, and therefore pay insufficient attention to their fiduciary duties to shareholders. When boardroom governance is poor, managerial power theories predict that excess pay will result.

There are limits on how high CEO pay can be. Too much compensation can severely damage an executive's reputation or cause embarrassment. Bebchuk and Fried (2004) term this 'outrage costs'. Outrage matters because it can impose on CEOs both market penalties (such as devaluation of a manager's reputation) and social costs. They argue that market constraints and the social costs

coming from excessively favourable pay arrangements are not sufficient in preventing significant and widespread deviations from optimal contracting. Overall, the insight offered by the managerial power view is that CEO pay is not the solution to the corporate governance problem, but instead is actually part of the problem.

10.3 The design of executive compensation

Changes in US compensation disclosure requirements in 1992 led to significantly enhanced information about salaries, options and bonuses reported in proxy statements. Disclosure was enhanced in other countries too. In the UK, the Cadbury report in 1992 ushered in a new era of corporate governance. This led to a series of other governance reports. Specifically, the Greenbury report increased pay disclosure from 1995 onwards. However, in continental Europe and parts of Asia, disclosure of executive compensation is less complete. Executive compensation typically contains four broad elements: an annual salary, an annual bonus, equity compensation in the form of stock options and restricted stock, and other benefits in the forms of retirement pay and perks (Murphy, 1999). The sum of these individual elements is an estimate of total annual executive compensation.

CEO salaries are positively correlated with firm size, and the statistical association is significant and economically large. Research suggests that an increase in firm size of 50% can increase CEO pay by approximately 20%. The elasticity of executive pay to firm size is estimated at about 0.4 (Murphy, 1999) and is often interpreted as the economic returns to managerial talent, as larger firms require better managers to run them. Table 10.1 shows that CEO salaries are about $1 million in large S&P 500 firms. Salaries are lower in smaller mid-cap and small-cap firms. Average pay is greater than

Table 10.1 CEO pay

Study	Year	Average pay ($000s)	Median pay ($000s)	Comments
Conyon, Core and Guay (2011)[1]	1997	$3,522	$975	1,327 firms
	2003	$4,651	$1,121	1,511 firms
Core and Guay (2010)[2]	1997	–	$3,800	S&P 500 firms
	2008	–	$7,600	S&P 500 firms
Kaplan (2008)[3]	2000	$16,000	$7,000	S&P 500 firms
	2006	$8,000	$8,000	S&P 500 firms
Larcker and Tayan (2011)[4]	2008/09	–	$11,357	Top 100 US firms
		–	$1,588	Largest 4000 US firms
Conference Board (2009)	2008	$4,331.65	$2,462.98	Large US firms
Bizjak, Lemmon and Nguyen[5]	2006/07	–	$3,880	Large US firms

Notes: Superscript: 1. Table 1 of the study; 2. Table 1 of the study; 3. Based in Figure 1 of the study, these figures are approximate; 4. Derived from Larcker and Tayan (2011) 'Seven Myths of Corporate Governance'. Exhibit 2. Total annual CEO pay is the sum of salary, bonuses, options and other flow period pay; CEO pay is the sum of salary, bonus, other annual compensation, the total value of restricted stock granted, the total value of stock options granted (based on the Black–Scholes method), and long-term incentive payouts, and all other pay. It is variable TDC1 in the Execucomp database. Non-S&P 500 firms are selected; 5. Bizjak et al. (2011) Table 1.

median, illustrating that CEO pay data is positively skewed: there are a few very well paid CEOs who drag the average upwards. Note that the average salary as a percentage of total pay is smaller for larger firms, suggesting that larger firms have more pay at risk.

CEOs also receive annual incentives – a bonus that is generally paid in cash. The performance measure triggering the bonus is usually an internal company accounting variable, such as budgeted earnings. External or market-based performance measures such as stock returns or share price returns relative to the market are rarely used in driving bonus pay – internal accounting measures are predominant (Murphy, 1999). The expected payment (i.e. the typical payoff schedule) for CEO bonuses is non-linear. This means that the executive may be able to strategically alter the performance measure in order to receive better pay outcomes. For example, the executive may shift reported firm revenues across periods. Alternatively, the executive may lobby for softer, easier performance targets. The typical CEO bonus plan, found in many companies, can easily lead to unintended but nevertheless predictable CEO behaviour.

Stock options

A major element of executive compensation is stock options, and other forms of equity compensation such as restricted stock (Murphy, 2009). A stock option is a contract that gives the holder the right to purchase the underlying stock at some predetermined price in the future. If the stock goes up, the option holder gains. There is no obligation to buy, so if the stock price goes down in the future the option simply lapses. The use of stock options as a central form of executive compensation expanded greatly in the 1990s. Research shows that perhaps up to 50% of a CEO's total pay came in the form of options by the late 1990s. Stock options became increasingly common in parts of Europe too, especially the UK (Conyon and Murphy, 2000).

Stock options are a potentially effective way to align the interests of managers with firms, and solve agency problems. Stock options are the right but not the obligation to purchase a share in the firm at some pre-specified price at some date in the future. The pre-specified price is known as the exercise or strike price. The period of time that the executive has to exercise the option is called the maturity term. In the case of options given to executives this is between seven and ten years. When the option is initially awarded, the executive cannot exercise it for a period of time, generally around three years. This is called the vesting period, at the end of which ownership transfers to the executive and he may exercise the option until the expiry of the option at maturity. The window of opportunity for the executive to make gains from the option is therefore between about three and ten years. Although a US executive has to wait three years before the option vests, a UK executive frequently has a performance vesting criteria attached to the option too. UK CEOs have to attain a performance level as well. The performance measure is usually earnings per share or total shareholder returns target.

A central question is how to value the stock option. The end-of-contract value is not known with certainty at the time the option is granted. The problem for the board of directors, and the remuneration committee, is to figure out how much the option given to an executive is worth. It is customary to value stock options as the economic cost to the firm of granting an option to the executive. This is the opportunity cost to the firm that is forgone by not selling the call option in the open market. The basic idea is to ask what value the firm could have got for issuing options in the market rather than allocating them to the executive. The expected value (i.e. present value) can be obtained by using an augmented version of the Black and Scholes (1973) option pricing formula. The Black–Scholes equation for a European call option on a share that pays dividends is:

$$\text{Option value} = c = Se^{-qt}N(d_1) - Xe^{-rt}N(d_2)$$

$$\text{where } d_1 = (\ln(S/X) + (r - q + \sigma^2/2)t) / \sigma\sqrt{t}, \text{ and } d_2 = d_1 - \sigma\sqrt{t}.$$

The term c is known as the call value of the option. With information on six basic input variables it is possible to assign a present value estimate to the call option. The input variables are: S is the stock price, X the exercise price, t the maturity term, r the risk-free interest rate, q the dividend yield, and

σ the volatility of returns. $N(.)$ is the cumulative probability distribution function for a standardized normal variable. Using this formula, the excepted value of the option can be calculated.

To use the formula, we first define a 'standard' option. Suppose that the stock price S is $100 and that the option is granted at the money so the exercise price is also $100 (i.e. $X = \$100$). The stock volatility is set at 30%, the annual risk-free interest rate is 2.0%, the option maturity term is set at 7 years, and the stock's dividend yield is 2.0%. In this case, the Black–Scholes value of the option, given by the formula above, is calculated as $26.82. It is important to note that the option has economic value, even though in this case the so-called intrinsic value of the option is zero. The *intrinsic value* of the option is the stock price minus the exercise price $(S - X)$, and when an option is granted at-the-money this value is zero. This does not mean that the option has zero value. Positive economic value comes from the so-called *time value* of the option. This reflects the fact that the option has time before it needs to be exercised (in this example 7 years) and there is a probability that the options will end up in the money. As the contract nears maturity, the time value of the option diminishes and most of the value of that time is given by the (hopefully) positive intrinsic value.

A myth about executive pay and stock options is that they do not reward performance or have downside risk. This is not the case. Options as a form of executive compensation are linked to firm performance. If an executive owned a common share (as opposed to a stock option) the pay-for-performance link is simple. A unit increase in the stock price increases the value of the share by one unit. There is an automatic one-to-one linear relation between the asset value and the underlying share price. For stock options we want to know the answer to the same question: how does the value of the option vary with the underlying price of the asset, namely the share price? Unlike an ordinary share, the value-to-asset price relation is not one-to-one and is in fact non-linear. The Black–Scholes model shows that holding all other variables constant, the value of the option displays a convex relation to the share price.

A simple example illustrates the convexity in the option contract. Using the standard option (defined above) suppose now that the stock price increases by 10% (i.e. by $10), and the values assigned to the other input variables are held constant. Using the Black–Scholes formula the value of the stock option increases from $26.82 to $32.70. However, the percentage increase in the expected value of the option is 21.92%. The key point is that the percentage increase in the share price has resulted in a *more than proportionate* increase in the value of the stock option. Another way of saying this is that the elasticity of the call value with respect to the underlying price of the asset (the stock price) is greater than one. If we were describing a common stock, and not a stock option, the $10 increase in the share price would have increased the value of share by exactly $10 too (the elasticity of the stock value to the share price is one). However, the convexity of the stock option payoff schedule leads to a greater than proportionate effect on the value of the option for a given increase in the share price, other things equal. In this sense, share options, rather than ordinary shares, provide greater incentives for executives to raise share prices.

The Black–Scholes pricing equation also shows that the option value is positively correlated with the stock price. The convexity of the option contract, and hence the high-powered incentives the contract creates, can be seen by the 'hedge-ratio'. The change in the call value of the option with respect to the underlying price of the asset is given as $dc/dS = \delta = e\text{-}qTN(d_1)$, where the delta term varies between zero and one $(0 < \delta < 1)$. This is the *option delta* or *hedge ratio*. For the standard option defined above and granted at the money, the option delta is approximately 0.569, meaning that a dollar change in the stock price increases the value of the option by about 56.9 cents. Fundamentally, then, option pay is connected to firm performance.

The option delta is not fixed. If the stock price increases to $110 (other things held constant) the option delta also increases. Now it is approximately 0.607, meaning now that at the new price a dollar change in the stock price will increase the value of the option at the margin by about 60 cents.[1] Geometrically, it is possible to show that the line tangent to the option payoff curve, evaluated at each new stock price, becomes steeper as the underlying asset price increases. The behavioural consequence is that an option recipient has greater (financial) incentives to increase the stock price; this is precisely because the option payoff schedule is convex.

---

[1] Really, we are talking about instantaneous rates of change here.

Stock options then are an important way to link pay to performance and focus the CEO's attention on creating increased value. It is important to stress some of the implicit assumptions underlying the Black–Scholes model (at least from an executive pay perspective). A complete derivation of the option pricing equations may be found in Hull (2009). First, in the context of the executive labour market, many assumptions underlying the Black–Scholes model are unlikely to hold in practice. In particular, the assumption of risk-neutrality of the option recipient is likely to be violated, or hold only by luck. This means that the CEO will likely place a different value on the option compared with the expected value of the option arising from the Black–Scholes equation. A standard way to think about this is that executives are typically risk (and effort) averse, undiversified, and prevented from trading the options or hedging their risk by selling short the company stock. Since these are binding constraints, executives will (in general) place a lower value on the stock option compared with the Black–Scholes value. How much lower is difficult to assess. There is little research on this issue, and there is clearly a fertile area for further studies. Ultimately, it will depend on assumptions about the form of the CEO's utility (or payoff) function, the degree of CEO risk-averseness and the CEO's wealth inside and outside the firm.

Second, the differences in the option valuations between the firm and the option recipient have important implications for the use of stock options as a compensation instrument. For the CEO to accept the contract in an open market, the firm must pay a premium to motivate the CEO to accept the risky option versus risk-free cash compensation. In consequence, firms will want to make sure that the resulting increase in executive and firm performance from using options covers this risk premium. In this sense, stock options are an expensive way to reward executives compared with simply providing risk-free cash to the executive. However, the use of options is beneficial if they induce sufficient extra effort or performance by the executive to cover the incremental costs. There is evidence that differences in risk preferences can account for differences in compensation practices across countries. Conyon, Core and Guay (2011) study US CEOs and compare these with CEOs in Europe. They find that median US CEO pay in 2003, defined as the sum of salary, bonus, grant date value of restricted stock and options, and benefits and other compensation, is about 40% greater than for UK CEOs. However, US CEOs hold more risky pay in the form of equity, and are therefore likely to demand a risk premium. After controlling for risk (and here they have to make a number of assumptions) they show that the US risk-adjusted pay is about the same as that of UK CEOs. Using a different methodology, Fernandes, Ferreira, Matos and Murphy (2009) arrive at a similar conclusion. They find that the US CEO pay premium falls significantly if one controls for the riskiness of the pay package held by US CEOs.

Stock options and asset price variability

One concern with stock options is that they may promote excessive risk-taking on the part of the CEO. Actually, providing risk-taking incentives might have been one of the original intentions of such instruments in an earlier era when CEOs took too few risks. This was precisely the point made by Jensen and Murphy (1990) when they claimed that CEOs were paid like bureaucrats in the pre-1990s era. CEO compensation depended on salaries, stability of operating incomes and not on the stock value of the firm.

The stock option pricing model discussed above can be used to show two things. First, the value of the stock option is positively correlated to firm risk, measured by the volatility of the stock price. Second, the percentage increase in the value of the option is less than the percentage increase in the value of the volatility term.[2]

---

[2] Using the values for the standard option defined earlier we can evaluate how changes in the firm's stock volatility alter the value of the option. Initially, we suppose that $S = \$100$, $X = \$100$, stock volatility = 30%, the risk-free rate = 2%, the maturity term = 7 years, and the dividend yield = 2%. As before, the value of the option is about $26.8. We now increase the stock volatility by 50% (from 30% to 45%), holding the values of the other variables constant. The value of the option increases from about to $26 to approximately $39, an increase of about 45%. In mathematical finance, this is referred to as the option 'vega'. Vega is the derivative of the option value with respect to the volatility of the underlying asset.

How might this affect managerial behaviour? First, the positive correlation between option value and price volatility means that the manager has an incentive to increase this volatility (i.e. he may engage in risky behaviour). This creates a potential tension between investors and managers, if investors prefer less variance in asset prices. Second, the effect of a change in price volatility on the option value is less than the effect of a change in the level of the stock price on option value. Although managerial behaviour is tilted towards increasing the volatility of the option (other things held constant), the incentive is less than the motivation effect arising from a change in the stock price alone. Third, it is reasonable to suppose that underlying asset prices and therefore the volatility of the firm's stock price is endogenous from the perspective of the CEO. His actions affect both the level and distribution of asset prices. In consequence, there are regions of the stock price and risk mapping that the CEO might exploit that might not be in the interests of the investor. For example, the CEO may try and increase the level of the stock price only modestly (perhaps to thwart potential hostile takeover attempts) but enhance the value of the option by taking actions that increase the volatility of the firm's stock prices.

The key takeaway is that if asset prices and volatilities are endogenous, then CEOs may drive wealth by increasing both variables. In the latter case, it is not clear that investors will like the greater price risk.

The shift to restricted stock

Stock options were very important in the 1990s. By 2001, options accounted for about 50% of pay. Since then the use of stock options has declined somewhat. Now it is estimated that options are about 30% of pay for US CEOs. Why is this? It is not because fixed pay has increased as a percentage (this has remained fairly constant at about 20% of total pay). What has changed is the use of restricted stocks by firms to compensate their CEOs.

Restricted stocks are shares that are restricted in the sense that they have a time-vesting element. That is, the CEO does not own the shares until a particular amount of time has elapsed. There are no performance hurdles to clear though. This practice differs from countries such as the UK where options and (performance) shares become owned based on the achievement of performance targets, such as earnings per share growth or the stock price relative to the market.

Restricted stock became important in the USA because of changes in accounting rules. FAS123 in 1995 suggested but did not mandate companies to expense stock options using the Black–Scholes (or similar) method. Few companies did. This is because the alternative was to expense options based on their intrinsic value (the stock price minus the exercise price). For options granted at the money this was zero! In consequence, firms had few incentives to use the economically preferred expected value method. However, in 2005 accounting standards changed and FAS123R now required companies to expense options using a fair market value method such as Black–Scholes. This effectively levelled the playing field between options and restricted stock, because previously restricted stock did not receive this favourable accounting treatment. So, from around 2005 it looks as if there was a rebalancing of the way the firms delivered equity pay to the CEOs. Options became less favoured and restricted stock more so. And this coincided with the changes in accounting regulations, so it seems natural to think that this might have been an important reason for this change.

10.4 Empirical evidence

Next we turn to empirical evidence on executive pay. Some of this evidence is summarized in Table 10.1. The Conference Board conducts an annual review of US executive compensation. They define total compensation as the sum of annualized salary, bonus, non-equity incentive compensation,[3]

---

[3] Defined as short-term and long-term cash awards based on pre-established, performance-based criteria in situations where outcome is substantially uncertain at time of award.

the reported grant date present value of options, the value of stock awards,[4] the change in pension value[5] and earnings on non-qualified deferred compensation, and all other compensation.[6] The 2009 Conference Board report provides compensation details for executives in 2,108 publicly traded firms in the United States in 2008.

The Conference Board (2009) data show that median CEO compensation was $2,462,982 in 2008. Average total CEO pay was $4,331,655. This reveals an important point. The executive pay distribution is positively skewed. This is because CEO pay is bounded below at zero, and there are far fewer executives who make large sums of money at the top of the pay distribution. One or two CEOs earning large (outlier) sums have the effect of dragging the average upwards. In consequence, average pay is higher than the median. At the 10th percentile CEO pay was $699,698 and at the 90th percentile it was $9,507,437.

CEO cash compensation and total compensation (which includes the grants of options, stock etc.) varies positively with firm revenues. The Conference Board (2009) data show that for firms in the middle of the distribution of firm revenues,[7] median CEO cash compensation is $948,147. Median total compensation is $2,118,466. CEOs at the largest firms make the most compensation. This finding is consistent with a vast amount of academic literature on executive compensation

Core and Guay (2010) provide time-series evidence from 1993 to 2008 on executive compensation in the United States. They show that median CEO pay in the S&P 500 firms increased from approximately $2 million in 1993 to about $7.7 million in 2008, and the annual rate of growth in pay was approximately 9.4%. The S&P 500 firms are large firms, so it is expected that compensation is higher for the CEOs of these firms. Total annual pay is calculated as the sum of salary, bonus, the value of stock and option grants and other pay in the year. Their evidence also shows that the growth in CEO pay (9.4%) is positively correlated with growth in firm market values over the period 1993 to 2008 (10.1%) and that CEO pay as a fraction of firm market value has remained approximately constant over time. This is consistent with economic models that predict that the growth in CEO pay reflects the growth in the complexity of the organizations and the difficulties of managing those assets (Gabaix and Landier, 2008). It contradicts the managerial power view since there appears to be a legitimate reason for changes in pay (i.e. increased rewards for managing increases in organizational complexity).

The level of pay is only part of the story. The overall mix of pay is also very important. That is, how much of total pay is delivered in cash salary? How much is delivered in stock options? How much is delivered in annual incentives? CEOs of companies that deliver compensation all in the form of salaries have fewer incentives to focus on improving the stock price of the company and long-term shareholder wealth. CEOs receiving only salaries could enjoy the quiet life. The Conference Board data provide answers to these questions.

The Conference Board also investigates executive compensation mix by firm revenues, based on splitting the data into ten equal-sized bins (deciles). Consider the companies in the middle category, with firm revenues between about $599 million and $912 million. For this group of firms, the Conference Board finds that the CEO's salary is approximately 33.8% of total compensation. The bonus represents about 5.3% of total pay. Incentive pay (short-term and long-term cash awards based on pre-established, performance-based criteria) is 13.36% of total pay. Stock options are about 15.92% of total pay. Stock is about 25.99% of total pay. Pensions make up 2.57% of total pay. Finally, other compensation makes up about 3.48% of total pay. The important point is that about two-thirds of pay is 'at risk', in the sense that payouts from the contract are not guaranteed. They are uncertain. The guaranteed portion of CEO pay is the salary, and for this group of firms and CEOs it is about

---

[4] Options are the grant date present value of options (from the 'Grant of plan-based awards table' of the proxy statement). The value of stock awards are the values as reported in Summary Compensation Table 'Stock awards' column.

[5] Actuarially determined change in value of defined benefit pensions and non-qualified deferred compensation earnings, including supplemental plans. Reported in Summary Compensation Table 'Change in pension value and non-qualified deferred compensation earnings' column.

[6] All other compensation is the incremental cost of perquisites ($10,000 or more), tax gross-ups, company contributions to qualified and non-qualified defined contribution plans, preferential stock purchase, relocation, etc. Reported in Summary Compensation Table 'All other compensation' column.

[7] Namely, the median decile calculated on the basis of firm revenues.

one-third of the CEO's total pay package. Another feature of the executive compensation data is that CEOs of larger firms have more pay at risk. Consider the CEOs of the largest firms in the survey, with revenues exceeding $9,636.62 million dollars. In these firms the CEO's salary is about 13.5% of total pay. The rest, namely about 85%, is pay that is 'at risk', since it is performance contingent and therefore not guaranteed.

Is executive pay linked to performance?

Critics of CEO pay frequently contend that CEO pay is not sufficiently linked to firm performance, implying the interests of executives and shareholders are not well aligned. Jensen and Murphy (1990) showed that US CEOs were paid like bureaucrats. The problem, they argued, was that executives received most of their compensation in the form of salaries and cash pay, and hardly any in the form of corporate equity such as stock options and restricted stock. The implication was that executives had few financial incentives to focus on wealth creation, and instead could enjoy the quiet life, or even built leviathan empires since salaries were paid to the size (not performance) of the firm.

Since the publication of Jensen and Murphy's seminal article the executive compensation landscape has changed radically. As documented in many studies, the level of executive compensation has increased significantly. However, so too has the structure of compensation. Specifically, contemporary executive compensation contracts contain a significant amount of equity compensation in the form of options and restricted stock. The shift away from base salaries to the use of equity pay, especially the accumulation of equity pay by executives, is a major source of executive incentives.

Pay for performance is the idea that changes in compensation should be the result of changes in measures of performance. Above we showed that stock options and ordinary equity (common shares) are automatically directly related to firm performance. As the stock price increases so too does the value of the CEO's holdings of options and shares. In this sense pay is linked to firm performance. This relation can be called the direct 'pay-for-performance' link. One can also calculate an indirect relation between pay and performance. Salaries are not automatically and mechanically linked to the firm's stock price in the same way that options or shares are. However, it is possible to carry out a regression analysis and examine whether there is a statistical association between pay and performance in the data. Indeed, when this exercise is carried out there is usually a positive relation, but the correlation of pay to performance is often much weaker than the pay-for-performance link arising from the use of stock and options.

The relation between pay and performance is a fundamental issue in the executive compensation literature. From an economic perspective the link is informative about the severity of the agency problem. The stronger is pay-for-performance, the less severe are agency concerns. But in a more general sense, pay-for-performance tells us the compensation received by the CEO is justified by improvements in firm performance. In this sense, the CEO 'deserves' the compensation increase. It is a true 'reward'. Some critics have argued that there is a fundamental disconnect between pay and performance. Empirically, this is not the case on average. It is, of course, possible (and regrettable) to find instances of unreasonable CEO pay packages. However, on average there is a positive correlation between executive pay and performance.

It is important to distinguish between 'CEO pay' and 'CEO incentives'. The latter relates to the wealth that the CEO has in his or her company. CEO pay is the amount of remuneration received in a given period of time in exchange for labour services. This includes salaries, bonuses received, the value of option grants and other share-based compensation granted during the reporting period and so on. In contrast, CEO incentives are the incremental change in total CEO wealth brought about by an incremental change in performance. This, more accurately, is pay-for-performance. CEO wealth is made up not only of the grants of options this year, but also includes the value of all of the equity-based compensation held by the CEO in the firm, usually accumulated over time (Murphy, 1999; Core and Guay, 2010).[8]

---

[8] One measure of incentives is the dollar change in the value of the CEO wealth from a 1% change in the stock price. Incentives are the dollar change in executive portfolio wealth arising from a 1% increase in shareholder wealth. An

Several academics have documented a positive correlation between CEO wealth and firm performance, each using slightly different methodologies, but all showing the same overall picture: US CEOs' compensation is tied to the performance of their firms. In the early 1990s it was shown that the primary driver of pay for performance was not cash compensation, but equity ownership. Consider recent evidence by Professor David Larcker (Larcker and Tayan, 2011), based on US data in 2008 and 2009. Using data on a very large sample of US public firms, he shows that the median value of a CEO's equity stake in his or her firm is about $4.6 million. Equity includes the estimated fair value of stock directly held by the CEO as well as equity grants, such as stock options and restricted stock the CEO owns in the firm. The median value of the firms in the sample is about $332 million. Larcker shows that a 1% increase in the company's stock price is associated with an increase in the value of CEO wealth of about $54,000. Moreover, if the CEO doubles the stock price (i.e. a 100% increase in stock) the CEO's expected gain is about $5.2 million. Given that median total annual compensation is about $1.6 million during the same time period, the pay-for-performance incentives are significant. Doubling the stock price is worth about two and half times annual compensation for the CEO. The empirical evidence is consistent with the hypothesis that compensation packages are designed to create value for long-term shareholder wealth. We do not think, as critics contend, that compensation packages are designed to destroy shareholder wealth or lead to excess risk-taking.

Jensen and Murphy's (1990) original research showed that CEO wealth increased only $3.25 for every $1,000 change in shareholder wealth, suggesting that CEOs had only weak incentives to promote shareholder value. An important reason for the lack of incentives in the original Jensen–Murphy data was the relative low level of equity ownership by CEOs. Hall and Liebman (1998) extended the analysis by Jensen and Murphy, asking whether CEOs really were paid like bureaucrats. Their hand-collected data showed that since about the mid-1980s stock options had become a critical feature of CEO pay. The hypothesis that CEO pay was not linked to performance was overturned. Importantly, they showed a strong positive correlation between CEO compensation and firm performance, arising almost entirely from changes in the value of CEO holdings of stock and stock options. In addition, they demonstrated that both the level of CEO compensation and the sensitivity of compensation to firm performance increased dramatically since 1980, largely because of increases in stock option grants.

Core and Guay (2010) demonstrate how CEO pay and incentives changed from 1993 to 2008. They find that in year 2000 the median CEO had incentives of $50.2 million. If the stock price fell by 20% then the CEO's incentives would fall by $10.4 million (i.e. minus 20% times $50.2). This figure is much greater than the median CEO's total compensation for year 2000, which in their data was $6.3 million. The same effect was observed for different years. The important point is that CEO wealth incentives are much greater than CEO annual pay each year.

Core and Guay (2010) find strong evidence that CEO pay is correlated to performance. For the years 1993 to 2008 the S&P 500 firms are sorted into deciles based on the stock return performance of the firms. They find that stock returns in the lowest decile are negative –44.7% and returns in the top decile are positive 68.8%. As many critics contend, changes in annual CEO pay are only weakly related to stock market performance. In the lowest ranked decile, despite stock returns of –44.7%, CEO pay falls by only –13.7%. In the top decile, despite returns of +68.8%, annual CEO pay increases by +19.7%. However, this misses the central point that wealth and equity incentives drive the pay-for-performance relation. In the bottom decile (firms with negative stock returns of –44.7%) CEOs see losses of $32 million on their beginning-of-year wealth incentives. In the top decile (firms with positive stock returns of +68.8%) CEOs enjoy gains of $31.4 million on their beginning-of-year wealth incentives. Core and Guay conclude that stock price changes can cause large changes in the CEO's portfolio and wealth even though changes in annual compensation might be fairly small.

alternative measure found in the literature and used by Jensen and Murphy (1990) measures CEO incentives as the dollar change in CEO wealth from a $1000 dollar change in firm wealth. This measure varies between $0 (no incentives) to $1000 (the CEO receives all the increase in generated firm wealth). This measure views incentives as being driven by fractional ownership of the firm. Both measures have appeared in the economics, finance and accounting literature.

Many studies find that pay is strongly linked to performance, and that magnitude of this is driven by the CEO's holding of equity in the firm. These data illustrate how and why.

The picture from the United States is that CEO pay has grown significantly since the 1980s. What is more the compositions seems to have shifted away from guaranteed compensation in the form of cash salaries, towards pay-at-risk in the form of stock options and equity. It is noteworthy that the period since the 1980s (namely the last thirty years or so) is unusual in the larger sweep of corporate history. Frydman and Saks (2010) analysed long-run trends in US executive compensation using a hand-collected panel data set from 1936 to 2005. They collected information for all available years for the largest 50 companies in 1940, 1960 and 1990, a period covering most of the 20th century. A number of striking conclusions emerge. First, Frydman and Saks (2010) find the median value of real executive compensation was actually remarkably flat from around the late 1940s until the mid-1970s. This suggests the correlation between executive pay and firm growth was actually pretty weak at this time. Second, the authors show that very large increases in CEO pay, sometimes in excess of 10% per annum, have occurred since the mid-1970s, but especially since the 1980s. Prior to this, modest growth in executive pay of 1% per annum was the norm. A key takeaway from this analysis, then, is that the growth in executive pay is, in the wider historical context, a comparatively recent phenomenon.

International executive compensation

Collecting and comparing global executive compensation is a difficult task, complicated by many factors. First, a single easy-to-use electronic data source is not readily available. Most data sets that do exist are single-country data sets (e.g. S&P's ExecuComp data in the United States). Second, the disclosure of executive compensation information varies significantly around the world, in both quality and amount of material produced. Third, differences in tax rates, government transfers, macro-economic and cultural factors make international comparisons particularly problematic. However, international executive pay research is worthwhile since a richer set of theories (e.g. arbitrage theories, competitive labour market theories) can be evaluated. We expect that over time more data and, in consequence, more international research will be undertaken.

There are a few nascent international studies at present. Several questions are asked. First, is the level of pay converging? At the root of this hypothesis is the law of one price, or no arbitrage condition. In competitive factor markets (i.e. no transaction costs, tax distortions etc.) identical factors cannot trade at different prices. As executive labour markets become more global, one hypothesis is that CEO pay levels converge to their competitive level. In practice, authors have examined the US and compared it with other countries and asked whether the Americanization of pay has led to non-US firms 'catching up'. A second question concerns the mix of pay. That is the amount of total pay in the form of stock options, restricted stock and other forms of pay at risk. Again, the issue is whether non-US firms are increasingly adopting US practices and using more stock options, equity pay etc.

What do we know so far? Conyon and Murphy (2000) studied a cross-section of US firms and British firms, using data from 1997. They demonstrated that US CEO pay was significantly higher than executive pay in the UK. After controlling for economic and governance drivers of executive pay, CEOs in the United States still enjoyed a significant pay premium. Although the US pay premium was lower when controlling for firm size, and other economic and governance variables, the magnitude remained statistically significant. They concluded that factors other than agency costs, such as political economy of pay and cultural factors might be responsible for the observed international differences in CEO pay, especially the relatively high CEO pay observed in the USA.

A number of studies have shown that US CEO pay is significantly higher than executive pay in other countries. Fernandes, Ferreira, Matos, and Murphy (2010) document the level and structure of CEO compensation in 14 countries around the world in 2006. Their comprehensive study is important as it uses firm-level financial data (i.e. not survey estimates) that is broadly comparable across countries. The basic pay findings from their study are reported in Table 10.2. It shows that in 2006 median US CEO compensation was about $3.3 million compared with $1.6 million in non-US countries. This is a fundamental finding; the raw data show that US CEOs receive a pay-premium

Table 10.2 CEO pay in 2006 by country

	2006 CEO pay ($million) Mean	2006 CEO pay ($million) Median	Salary	Other	Bonus	Stock and options
Australia	$2.4	$1.7	46%	10%	26%	18%
Belgium	1.6	0.9	58%	5%	27%	10%
Canada	3.1	2.2	33%	10%	26%	32%
France	2.4	0.9	61%	2%	22%	15%
Germany	3.6	2.4	39%	10%	41%	10%
Ireland	2.4	1.7	44%	8%	25%	22%
Italy	5.2	2.7	56%	4%	29%	12%
Netherlands	2.4	1.4	44%	12%	23%	22%
Norway	1.7	1.0	56%	3%	25%	15%
S. Africa	1.7	1.3	43%	7%	36%	14%
Sweden	1.7	1.1	62%	18%	19%	2%
Switzerland	6.1	2.3	50%	4%	21%	25%
UK	2.9	1.7	42%	9%	19%	30%
Non-US	$2.8	$1.6	46%	8%	24%	22%
US	$5.5	$3.3	28%	6%	27%	39%

Source: Fernandes et al. (2010). Based on their Table 1, making up 1,648 US firms and 1,251 non-US firms. Year of data is 2006. Data is from S&P's ExecuComp database (US) and BoardEx (non-US). CEO pay is defined as the sum of salaries, bonuses (including all non-equity incentives), benefits, and grant date values for stock options, restricted stock, and performance shares.

compared with non-US counterparts. Outside of the United States, other 'high' paying countries include Canada, Ireland, Germany, Italy, Switzerland and the UK, each with median pay greater than $1.5 million. Countries who pay their CEOs less than $1.5 million include Belgium, France, the Netherlands, and Norway. In addition, the raw data show that US CEOs have more 'pay-at-risk' compared with non-US CEOs. The fraction of total pay made up of salary is an estimate of the certain income to be received by the CEO. The remainder (such as bonuses and options) is 'at-risk' in the sense that it is contingent on performance outcomes. US CEOs have 28% of pay comprised of salary, implying 72% is 'at risk'. In stark contrast, non-US CEOs (on average) have 46% of their total pay comprised of salary, implying that 54% of their pay is at risk. The data are consistent with the hypothesis that US CEOs bear more compensation risk than non-US CEOs.

Why is the level of pay in the US higher than in non-US countries? Conyon, Core and Guay (2011) argue it can be explained by risk factors. They computed risk-adjusted US CEO pay and compared it with UK and continental European CEOs. This is important first because it helps explain international differences in the level of CEO pay. In addition, it also helps answer the question as to whether CEOs are overpaid or not. They hypothesized that it is important to control for the necessary risk premium inherent in holding risky forms of equity pay. Controlling for firm and industry characteristics, they find that US CEOs have higher pay (as might be expected). In addition, they

find that US CEOs also bear much higher stock and option incentives than UK CEOs. An important finding is that using reasonable estimates of risk premiums, they find that risk-adjusted US CEO pay does not appear to be large compared with that of UK CEOs. That is, controlling for risk premiums, US and UK pay are very similar on a risk-adjusted basis. They also examine differences in pay and equity incentives between a sample of non-UK European CEOs and a matched sample of US CEOs. They find that risk-adjusting pay may explain about half of the apparent higher pay for US CEOs. So, there is a residual gap that still needs to be explained (and this may be attributable to tax, or cultural differences). However, even comparing the US with continental European countries, risk-premium associated with compensation incentives is important.

Fernandes et al. (2010) investigated CEO pay across 14 countries using 2006 data. They confirm that US executives are paid significantly more than their foreign counterparts. In addition, such CEOs receive a much larger share of their compensation in the form of stock options and restricted shares. Importantly, they show that the US pay premium is much reduced after controlling for firm, ownership, and board characteristics. After controlling for the risk of equity-based pay, it is statistically insignificant. The results accord with Conyon, Core and Guay (2011). Fernandes et al. (2010) illustrate that there is not a significant US pay premium (or significant differences in use of equity-based compensation) when US firms are compared with 'internationalized' non-US firms exposed to international capital and product markets, or to 'Americanized' non-US firms exposed to US capital and managerial labour markets. The authors also provide evidence of CEO pay convergence, using data from 2003 to 2008. US and non-US pay practices have largely converged over this time period. They suggest this may reflect international convergence in the accounting treatment of stock options. Finally, the authors consider the political economy of executive pay. They argue that cross-country differences in the use of equity-based pay might reflect idiosyncratic events and government intervention that either encouraged or discouraged the use of equity incentives. This is especially so for US CEOs who receive a larger amount of stock options and restricted stock in their pay packet.

10.5 The governance of executive pay

The institutions of pay setting are important if pay practices are to be designed effectively to align managerial and owner interests. In practice shareholders are too numerous and too diverse to set pay. Instead the board of directors sets pay on behalf of shareholders. Do boards set executive pay appropriately? We briefly consider some salient issues in the light of changes in regulations in the US and the UK.

Too much CEO power?

Critics of executive compensation claim that CEO pay is too high, too generous and frequently inefficient (Bebchuk and Fried, 2004). Managerial power theorists argue that CEO power leads to levels of pay above the arm's-length negotiated optimal contracting level. Corporate boards are relatively weak, and acquiesce to CEO demands. CEO pay does not increase indefinitely because of 'outrage' costs. However, according to the critics, CEO power and influence is sufficiently widespread that deviation from market forces and optimal contracting are common. There are many potential tests of the managerial power hypothesis, and a challenge for research is to design tests that rule out the competing efficiency (optimal contracting) explanation. Much of the existing literature seeking to test the effects of board power uses measures of 'power' that are at best only proxies for 'power'; this makes testing particularly tricky.

One important research hypothesis is that weak boards lead to high CEO pay (Bebchuk and Weisbach, 2010). The corporate governance literature typically designates a board as poorly constituted if it is too large, and therefore it is difficult for directors to oppose the CEO, or if the CEO has appointed the outside directors, who are obligated to the CEO for their jobs. In addition, boards may be termed as weak when directors serve on too many other boards, making them too busy to be effective monitors; or if the CEO is also chair of the board, since conflicts of interest arise. Alternatively, the board may be too friendly with the CEO, coming from the same social or friendship groups, and therefore pay insufficient attention to their fiduciary duties to shareholders (Westphal 1998). The available empirical evidence supports the claim that agency costs are greater when boards are poorly constituted. The evidence shows that in a cross-section poorly designed board structures are associated with greater excess pay (Core et al., 1999). Using more subtle measures of power such as CEO duality (where the CEO also holds the position of board chair) and the number of directors appointed to the board after the CEO's appointment as determinants of this power dynamic, the empirical evidence is somewhat mixed. Westphal and Zajac (1994) suggest this latter measure is positively related to CEO pay. Duality appeared to be an important predictor in some studies (Main et al., 1995) though others found no such effects (Boyd, 1994). Deutsch (2005) provides a meta-analysis of some 38 studies related to the issue of outsider (rather than strictly independent) status and finds no robust relationship.

One important piece of evidence is the relation between executive pay and independent directors over time. Boards of directors have become more independent over time, at the same time that executive pay has increased. Another way of stating this is that executive pay has increased as boards of directors have become stronger and more independent. The time-series data, at first glance, is at odds with the managerial power view of CEO pay. It predicts that as governance quality goes up CEO pay should go down. However, the converse is true in the United States, and other countries too (such as the UK).

Compensation committees

A key feature of the executive pay setting process is the compensation committee. It makes the process of pay setting much more transparent, and hopefully more independent by removing the CEO from deliberations about compensation. Ineffective pay committees give the CEO an opportunity to promote his interests at the expense of shareholder welfare. Previous studies have found little evidence that compensation committees are ineffective. Conyon and Peck (1998) investigate the relation between board control, the compensation committee and executive pay, using panel data on the 100 largest UK firms between 1991 and 1994. The quality of governance increases over time. In 1991, 78% of firms have a compensation committee, increasing to 99% in 1994. The proportion of independent directors on the committee increases from 87% in 1991 to 91% in 1994. The study shows that CEO pay is greater in firms with compensation committees or those with a greater fraction of outsiders on the committee. However, they find the link between pay and performance is greater in firms with a greater proportion of outside directors on the compensation committee.

In another study, Daily et al. (1998) investigate 200 Fortune 500 companies in 1992. They find no relationship between CEO pay and the proportion of affiliated directors on the compensation committee. Other studies from the US and the UK have also failed to find that compensation committees result in excess CEO pay or poorly designed compensation contracts (Anderson and Bizjak, 2003; Conyon and He, 2004; Gregory-Smith, 2009; Bender, 2003). Other studies drawing on more behavioural theories of how boards operate have, however, isolated some interesting results; O'Reilly et al. (1988) showed that CEO pay was positively associated with the pay levels of both compensation committee members and other outside directors. They suggest that social comparisons become an important mechanism in the pay-setting behaviour, a theme that may become particularly important is social comparisons based on friendship ties (Westphal, 1998).

Compensation consultants

Compensation consultants are firms who advise the board of directors about executive pay practices. Critics argue that pay consultants lead to excessive CEO pay and poorly designed contracts (Waxman, 2007; Bebchuk and Fried, 2004). While boards are not mandated to use any external advisers when considering pay in their organization, in the United Kingdom, the key public policy review of CEO compensation, the 1995 Greenbury Committee, recommended, 'the [compensation] committees should … have access to professional advice inside and outside the company' (Greenbury Report 1995, Recommendation A7). It is argued here that the primary function of the consultant is to provide expert advice on the design and structure of CEO pay. The process of consultant advice may have implications for the design of CEO pay, in particular when the consultants make extensive use of surveys and social comparisons. Bebchuk and Fried (2004) argue that consultants are not sufficiently independent and suffer from conflicts of interest because they sell other services to their clients and are thus wary of provoking the CEO for fear of jeopardizing this other business. If true, the CEO pay contract is not best from the shareholder's perspective. On the other hand, the optimal contracting view argues that compensation consultants are experts who provide valuable information and data to busy boards of directors. Their presence ameliorates opportunistic behaviour by CEOs and leads to well-structured optimal compensation contracts. Do pay consultants promote the best interests of the firm's owners or do they simply enrich entrenched CEOs?

The available empirical evidence shows that consultants have a relatively limited effect on CEO pay and incentives. It was perhaps thought that consultants would explain a large amount of the variation in CEO pay, and this does not seem to be the case. Consultants do not appear to be the primary driver of the recent growth in executive pay. Nor does the available evidence suggest that contracts are especially badly designed by consultants. Murphy and Sandino (2010) find evidence in both the US and Canada that CEO pay is greater in companies where the consultant provides other services. In addition, they find that pay is higher in Canadian firms when the fees paid to consultants for other services are large relative to the fees for executive-compensation services. This evidence suggests that greater agency costs lead to higher compensation. However, they unexpectedly find that CEO pay is higher in US firms where the consultant works for the independent board rather than for management.

In another study, Cadman, Carter and Hillegeist (2010) investigate compensation consultants' potential cross-selling incentives using 755 firms from the S&P 1500 for 2006. Conditional upon the firm retaining a consultant, the authors Cadman et al. (2010, p. 263) are 'unable to find widespread evidence of higher levels of pay or lower pay-performance sensitivities for clients of consultants with potentially greater conflicts of interest'. They conclude there is little evidence that potential conflicts of interest between the firm and its consultant are a primary driver of excessive CEO pay. Conyon, Peck and Sadler (2009) also perform a comparative study of the relation between CEO pay and consultants using British and American data for 2006. They find that CEO pay is generally greater in firms that use compensation consultants, which is consistent with the managerial power theory of executive pay. They also show that the amount of equity used in the CEO compensation package, such as stock options, is greater in firms that use consultants. This is consistent with alignment of manager and shareholder interests, and the optimal contracting theory of pay. Finally, there is little evidence that using consultants with potential conflicts of interest, such as supplying other business to client firms, leads to greater CEO pay or the adverse design of pay contracts. The evidence is consistent with Cadman, Carter and Hillegeist (2010). In a related study, Conyon, Peck and Sadler (2011) suggest that some significant behavioural process may work in the operation of consultants; the market for such consultants is quite concentrated and often boards can be interlocked both through the use of consultants and board members. Such high contact interlocks can provide a significant basis for recommending pay arrangements based on social comparisons, and they find that CEO pay is indeed related to such shared director–consultant use.

Say on pay

In an effort to reform executive pay arrangements, several countries, including the USA and the UK, have given shareholders the right to vote on executive compensation. These voting arrangements are known colloquially as 'say on pay'. In the UK, shareholders vote on the board's compensation report annually. They do not vote on the specifics, such as the level of pay, the amount of options etc. Instead, they vote on the report in its entirety. Typically, shareholder voting on executive pay is not binding on the board's management. So, if shareholders vote against the CEO's compensation package, the board of directors is not obliged to amend pay arrangements. However, common sense suggests that if shareholders are terribly unhappy about pay then the board will in all likelihood react and accommodate their position in some way. Of course, voting on pay is only one way that shareholders can force a dialogue with the firm's management and owners may voice opinion in other ways. Arrangements for voting on CEO pay in the United States were ushered in with the passage of the Dodd–Frank Act in 2010. The consequences of this Act for shareholder voting and CEO pay are yet to be fully evaluated.

Existing academic research yields mixed findings on 'say on pay'. Conyon and Sadler (2010) investigate the relation between shareholder voting and CEO pay using UK data between 2002 and 2007. They find that less than 10% of shareholders abstain or vote against the mandated Directors' Remuneration Report (DRR) resolution. In addition, this figure had been falling over time. This suggests that (despite media claims) shareholders are not as dissatisfied with pay arrangements as to vote against them. Second, Conyon and Sadler find that investors are more likely to vote against executive pay resolutions compared with non-pay resolutions. Pay resolutions are more unpopular than other kinds of resolutions. Third, they find that shareholders are more likely to vote against general executive pay resolutions, such as stock options, long-term incentive plans and bonus resolutions compared with non-pay resolutions. In addition, the evidence shows that firms with higher CEO pay attract greater voting dissent. Fifth, there is little evidence that CEO pay is lower in firms that previously experienced high levels of shareholder dissent. In addition, there is little evidence that the mix of CEO pay, measured as the amount of CEO equity pay, is higher in such firms. Overall, Conyon and Sadler find only limited evidence that, on average, 'say on pay' materially alters the subsequent level and design of CEO compensation. However, their data stops immediately prior to the financial crisis. It would be interesting to know what happened after 2007 with the advent of the financial crisis to see if anything has changed.

Ferri and Maber (2011) also study voting effects on CEO pay. They find little effect on the level and trends in CEO pay. However, they find that firms respond to high voting dissent by removing controversial compensation provisions, such as long notice periods and retesting provisions for option grants. In addition, they find a significant increase in the sensitivity of CEO pay to poor performance, particularly among firms that experience high dissent at the first vote. The USA has just introduced such shareholder voting on pay; the evidence from the UK suggests (at present) that the observed effects in the USA might well be quite modest.

Bank CEO pay

Since the 2008 crisis, bank CEO pay has become an important issue. A salient question is whether incentives at banks were 'perverse' and encouraged excess risk-taking. Emerging studies on the relation between bank executive compensation and the financial crisis have produced mixed findings. Having said this, there is some emerging consensus. In general it has proved difficult to document a causal link between the structure of compensation in banks and the crisis.

Fahlenbrach and Stulz (2011) conclude that compensation arrangements at US banks were fundamentally flawed. They find that CEOs with incentives that are better aligned to shareholders actually performed worse in the crisis. They argue that CEOs took decisions they expected to be optimal for shareholders before the crisis, but ultimately these turned out to perform badly. In addition, one might think that if CEOs had advance knowledge that their decisions would not optimize shareholder value then they would have taken actions to insulate their own personal wealth from adverse price movements. However, Fahlenbrach and Stulz find no evidence of unusual share selling or other hedging activity by bank executives in advance of the crisis. They also show CEOs' aggregate stock and option holdings are more than eight times the value of annual compensation. The amount of CEO wealth at risk prior to the financial crisis makes it improbable that a rational CEO knew of an impending financial crash, or knowingly engaged in excessively risky behaviour. Therefore, while there appears to be a correlation between compensation structures and performance during the crisis, it seems that the companies who did the worst in the crisis are those that had the better executive incentives pre-crisis.

There is another set of research that shows that compensation practices encouraged excessive risk-taking. Bebchuk and Spamann (2010) assert that the capital structure at financial institutions led to increased risk-taking by bank CEOs before the financial crisis. They use several arguments suggesting that leverage structure led CEOs to focus on increasing stock prices. In addition, Cai et al. (2010) also assert that CEO pay structures are designed with shareholders' perspective in mind. However, this does not necessarily benefit debt holders such as banks, bondholders, and depositors. The idea is that with more debt and leverage in banking, there is a bias toward excessive risk-taking. This is reminiscent of the Jensen and Meckling (1976) agency cost of debt problem. At present there is insufficient empirical evidence that compensation structures lead to such actions in practice. In addition, the current hypothesis that 'bank incentives caused the crisis' does not explain why this happened in the years 2007 and 2008 as opposed to earlier times. Bank CEO incentives have been relatively constant over time.

The emerging new studies on banks show interesting findings, and there are bound to be many more in the future as scholars investigate the causes of the recession. The challenge, of course, is to show that in time-series data there is a *causal* relation between compensation contracts and (well-defined) excessive risk-taking, ex post. As more data become available, we expect future articles to address empirically the precise relation between pay incentives at banks and risk-taking behaviour. However, other factors will also be studied such as the quality of loans made by the banks, securitization of assets, off-balance sheet accounting, loose monetary policy and contagion effects. All of these are important when trying to understand the causes of the financial crisis.

Recent developments in elements of compensation plan design

Since the Dodd–Frank Act was passed in 2010, many publicly traded US companies appear to have been changing their executive compensation packages to further align CEO compensation with stockholder interests. The academic evidence is perhaps too new to assess at the moment, but various professional firms are documenting some interesting changes in CEO pay arrangements.

Equilar (2011a)[9] find that several aspects of pay are changing. First, they find that the prevalence of Fortune 100 companies with publicly disclosed executive stock ownership policies increased from 87.4% to 88.4% from 2009 to 2010. In addition, they find that the prevalence of holding requirements at Fortune 100 companies increased from 2009 to 2010, rising from 47.4% to 50.5%. Their report finds that ownership guidelines are based on targets as a multiple of base salary. These make up 80.8% of all ownership guidelines. Thus, ownership retention is becoming increasingly important.

One might ask what type of equity counts towards ownership targets. Equilar (2011a) find that stock options are least likely to be counted towards meeting executive ownership guidelines. For those companies with guidelines, they found that 10.3% allow options to be applied toward ownership targets, while 38.5% of firms explicitly exclude stock options from ownership goals. In contrast, restricted stock is more likely to be counted towards the guidelines, at over 40%. The report finds that in 2010 the median value of target stock ownership levels for CEOs was about $7.0 million.

Another issue is hedging arrangements. There is a concern that CEOs and executives may try to unwind the risk imposed upon them by boards hedging in some way. However, Equilar (2011a) finds that companies have hedging policies, specifically restricting such activities. They find that the disclosure of such hedging restrictions significantly increased from 46.3% in 2009 to 71.6% in 2010.

The Dodd–Frank Act (2010) also included important provisions for companies to recover erroneously awarded compensation. Specifically, section 954 of the Dodd–Frank Act requires the SEC to adopt new rules in this area. Companies must implement a 'clawback' policy to recoup incentive compensation for specific triggers, for example for financial restatements. Failure will risk penalties. Equilar (2011b) showed that clawback policies 'have become increasingly complex, broader in scope, and much more likely to impact all compensation vehicles'. They find that remarkable change over a short period of time. From 2006 to 2011, clawback policies increased from 17.6% to 84.2% at

---

[9] We would like to thank Equilar for providing us with the reports used in this chapter.

Fortune 100 firms (as disclosed in the proxy statements). The triggers for clawbacks included financial restatements (89% of firms) or ethical misconduct (79% of firms).

Equilar (2011c) shed light on the perquisites and benefits in compensation packages. Generally, Equilar find that the value of 'other' compensation has fallen over 30% from 2008 to 2010. They find that contentious benefits also fall. 'The median value of perquisites related to the personal use of corporate aircraft by Fortune 100 chief executives fell by 20.0 percent, from $115,588 in 2009 to $92,421 in 2010. The prevalence of aircraft perquisites also decreased ...' In addition, they find that the value of tax gross-ups (which shield executives from tax payments) fell 48.4% from $26,936 in 2009 to $13,911 in 2010. Importantly, the prevalence of such tax gross-ups decreased from 50.0% in 2009 to 25.3% in 2010.

What these various Equilar reports show is that executive compensation continues to change and is in flux. There is a strong likelihood that CEO pay will continue to change in the future, perhaps due to public pressure and changes in legislation.

10.6 Discussion

Executive compensation is a very controversial subject in corporate governance. High levels of pay received by CEOs frequently attract the attention of the media. There is a popular concern that CEOs are able to set their own level of pay, and this is not in the interests of either shareholders or society. In an attempt to improve upon executive compensation arrangements, especially since the 2008 financial crisis, new legislation has been enacted (e.g. Dodd–Frank Act 2010).

From an economics perspective, executive compensation is supposed to be the solution to widespread agency problems. The design of optimal contracts can motivate individual effort without the need for excessive monitoring by boards of directors. However, managerial power theorists argue that CEO pay is part of the problem, not part of the solution. They argue that pay outcomes are not the consequence of arm's-length bargaining.

Managerial power theorists claim that CEOs exert power over their boards and are able to achieve higher pay than is necessary. An important academic research theme is attempting to distinguish between these hypotheses. Executive compensation has increased over time, especially since the mid-1980s. The reasons for this are not fully understood. Proponents from the optimal contracting and managerial power schools each assert that the empirical evidence best supports their case. The economic case for managerial power outcomes seems to us to have considerable sway. Undoubtedly, the executive compensation debate will continue. The financial crisis has added to this impetus as well as regulatory changes in the form of 'say on pay', clawbacks and proxy access ushered in with Dodd–Frank.

Minicase

Corporate governance and executive compensation at Apple Inc.

Apple Inc. designs, manufactures and markets personal computers, mobile communication devices and portable digital music and video players, and sells a variety of related software, services, peripherals and networking solutions.

Apple's Board of Directors oversees the Chief Executive Officer and other senior management in the competent and ethical operation of Apple on a day-to-day basis and assures that the long-term interests of shareholders are being served. To satisfy the Board's duties, directors are expected to take a proactive, focused approach to their positions, and set standards to ensure that Apple is committed to business success through the maintenance of high standards of responsibility and ethics."

In each of the years 2008 to 2010, Steve P. Jobs, the former Chief Executive Officer of Apple, received an annual salary of $1 (i.e. one single dollar). He received no bonus, no stock awards, no option awards or other form of annual compensation. Tim Cook, the Chief Operating Officer, in 2010 received a salary of $800,016, a bonus of $5,000,000, stock awards of $52,334,250, non-equity incentive plan compensation of $900,000, and other compensation of $58,306, yielding a 2010 total of $59,092,572.

On December 17, 2010, Steve Jobs beneficially owned 5,546,451 shares of common stock. If Apple's shares are worth about $380 then Jobs' wealth in the firm is about $2 billion dollars. Tim Cook owned 13,659 shares of common stock. At that date there were about 921,043,522 common shares in Apple.

On August 24, 2011, Steve Jobs announced his resignation from his role as Apple's CEO. Speculation was that this was due to ill health, as Jobs was suffering from a string of health problems. In his letter of resignation, Jobs strongly recommended that the Apple executive succession plan be followed and Tim Cook be named as his successor.

It was with great regret and sadness that we heard of Steve Jobs' death on October 5, 2011. His humanity and leadership were inspirational. He left the world a far better place, making a real difference to millions of people worldwide.

Source: http://investor.apple.com/governance.cfm

Discussion questions

1 What do you think of Apple's board of directors?
2 What do you think of the design of Steve Jobs' compensation package?
3 What do you think of Apple's CEO succession plan?
4 What do you think of the company's incentive programme?
5 How would you rate the overall corporate governance arrangements at Apple?

Summary (learning points)

■ Executive compensation is controversial. Optimal contract theorists think that compensation plans are designed in the best interests of shareholders. Managerial power theorists think that CEOs can too easily set their own pay.

■ Executive compensation has been increasing significantly in recent years, not only in the United States but in other countries too.

■ Executive pay is made up of cash pay including a fixed salary and cash annual incentives (bonuses). In addition, executives receive non-cash pay such as stock options, restricted stock, etc.

■ US CEOs receive a relatively large fraction in the form of pay-at-risk, such as annual incentives and stock options. In contrast, continental European countries are more likely to pay executives with fixed salaries. The global trend is towards more pay-at-risk.

 # References and further reading

Andersen, R.C. and Bizjak, J.M. (2003) An empirical examination of the role of the CEO and the compensation committee in structuring executive pay, *Journal of Banking & Finance*, **27** (7), 1323–1348.

Bebchuk, L.A. and Fried, J.M. (2004) *Pay Without Performance: The Unfulfilled Promise of Executive Remuneration*, Harvard University Press: Cambridge, MA.

Bebchuk, L.A. and Fried, J.M. (2006). Pay without Performance: Overview of the Issues, *Academy of Management Perspectives* **20** (1), 18–24.

Bebchuk, L.A. and Spamann, H. (2010) Regulating Bankers' Pay, *Georgetown Law Journal*, **98** (2), 247–287.

Bebchuk, L.A. and Weisbach, M.S. (2010) The State of Corporate Governance Research, *Review of Financial Studies*, **23** (3), 939–961.

Bender, R. (2003) How executive directors' remuneration is determined in two FTSE utilities, *Corporate Governance: An International Review*, **11** (3), 206–217. Available at SSRN: http://ssrn.com/abstract=465517.

Bertrand, M. (2009) CEOs, *Annual Review of Economics*, **1** (1), 121–150.

Bizjak, J., Lemmon, M. and T. Nguyen, T. (2011) Are all CEOs above average? An empirical analysis of compensation peer groups and pay design, *Journal of Financial Economics*, **100** (3), 538–555.

Black, F. and Scholes, M. (1973) The Pricing of Options and Corporate Liabilities, *Journal of Political Economy*, **81** (3), 637–654.

Bolton, P. and M. Dewatripont, M. (2005) *Contract Theory*, MIT Press.

Boyd, B.K. (1994) Board Control and CEO Compensation, *Strategic Management Journal*, **15** (5), 335–344.

Cadman, B., Carter, M.E. and Hillegeist, S. (2010) The incentives of compensation consultants and CEO pay, *Journal of Accounting and Economics*, **49** (3), 263–280.

Cai, J., Cherny, K. and Milbourn, T. (2010) Compensation and Risk Incentives in Banking and Finance, Federal Reserve Bank of Cleveland.

Conference Board, The (2009) *The 2009 Top Executive Compensation Report* (Report Authors Kevin Hallock and Judit Torok).

Conyon, M. and He, L. (2004) Compensation committees and CEO compensation incentives in US entrepreneurial firms, *Journal of Management Accounting Research*, **16** (1), 35–56.

Conyon, M.J. and Murphy, K.J. (2000). The Prince and the Pauper? CEO pay in the US and UK, *Economic Journal*, **110** (467), F640–671.

Conyon, M. and Peck, S.I. (1998) Board Control, Remuneration Committees, and Top Management Compensation, *Academy of Management Journal*, **41** (2), 146–157.

Conyon, M. and Peck, S.I. (2011) *Executive Compensation, Pay for Performance and the Institutions of Pay Setting.*

Conyon, M. and Sadler, G. (2010) Shareholder Voting and Directors' Remuneration Report Legislation: Say on Pay in the UK, *Corporate Governance: An International Review*, **18** (4), 296–312.

Conyon, M.J., Core, J.E. and Guay, W.R. (2011) Are US CEOs Paid More than UK CEOs? Inferences from Risk-Adjusted Pay, *Review of Financial Studies*, **24** (2), 402–38.

Conyon, M.J., Peck, S.I. and Sadler, G.V. (2011) New perspectives on the governance of executive compensation: an examination of the role and effect of compensation consultants, *Journal of Management and Governance*, **15** (1), 29–58.

Conyon, M.J., Sadler, G.V. and Peck, S.I. (2009) Compensation Consultants and Executive Pay: Evidence from the United States and the United Kingdom, *Academy of Management Perspectives*, **23** (1), 43–55.

Core, J.E. and Guay, W.R. (2010) Is CEO pay too high and are incentives too low? A wealth-based contracting framework, *Academy of Management Perspectives*, **24** (1), 5–19.

Core, J.E., Holthausen, R.W. and Larcker, D.F. (1999) Corporate governance, chief executive officer compensation, and firm performance, *Journal of Financial Economics*, **51** (3), 371–406.

Daily, C.M., Johnson, D.F., Ellstrand, A.E. and Dalton, V. (1998) Compensation committee composition as a determinant of CEO compensation, *Academy of Management Journal*, **41** (2), 209–220.

Deutsch, Y. (2005) The Impact of Board Composition on Firms' Critical Decisions: A Meta-Analytic Review, *Journal of Management*, **31** (3), 424–444.

Equilar (2011a) Executive Stock Ownership Guidelines Report: *An Analysis of Ownership Guidelines at Fortune 100 Companies*, www.equilar.com

Equilar (2011b) Clawback Policy Report: *Compensation Recovery Policies at Fortune 100 Companies*, www.equilar.com

Equilar (2011c) CEO Benefits and Perquisites Report: *An Analysis of Key Benefits and Perquisites at Fortune 100 Companies*, www.equilar.com

Fahlenbrach, R. and Stulz, R.M. (2011) Bank CEO Incentives and the Credit Crisis, *Journal of Financial Economics*, **99** (1), 11–26.

Fernandes, N.G., Ferreira, M.A., Matos, P.P. and Murphy, K.J. (2011) *Are US CEOs Paid More? New International Evidence* (October 12, 2011). EFA 2009 Bergen Meetings Paper; AFA 2011 Denver Meetings Paper; ECGI – Finance Working Paper No. 255/2009. Available at SSRN: http://ssrn.com/abstract=1341639

Ferri, F. and Maber, D.A. (2011) *Say on Pay Votes and CEO Compensation: Evidence from the UK* (March

11, 2011). Available at SSRN: http://ssrn.com/abstract=1420394

Frydman, C. and Saks, R.E. (2010) Executive Compensation: A New View from a Long-Term Perspective, 1936–2005, *Review of Financial Studies*, **23** (5), 2099–2138.

Gabaix, X. and Landier, A. (2008) Why has CEO Pay Increased so Much? *Quarterly Journal of Economics*, **123** (1), 49–100.

Gregory-Smith, I. (2009) Chief Executive Pay and Non-Executive Director Independence in the UK: Optimal Contracting vs. Rent Extraction, Nottingham University Business School Research Paper No. 2009–02. Available at SSRN: http://ssrn.com/abstract=1345926.

Hall, B. and Liebman, J. (1998). Are CEOs really paid like bureaucrats? *Quarterly Journal of Economics*, **113** (3), 653–691.

Holmström, B. (1979). Moral hazard and observability, *Bell Journal of Economics*, **10** (1), 74–91.

Holmström, B. and Milgrom, P. (1987) Aggregation and Linearity in the Provision of Intertemporal Incentives, *Econometrica*, **55** (2), 303–328.

Jensen, M. and Meckling, W. (1976) Theory of the Firm: Managerial Behavior, Agency Costs, and Ownership Structure, *Journal of Financial Economics*, **3** (4), 305–360.

Jensen, M.C, and Murphy, K.J. (1990) Performance pay and top-management incentives, *Journal of Political Economy*, **98** (2), 225–264.

Kaplan, S.N. (2008) Are U.S CEOs underpaid?, *The Academy of Management Perspectives*, **22** (2), 5–20.

Laffont, J-J., and Martimort, D. (2002) *The Theory of Incentives: The Principal-Agent Model*, Princeton: Princeton University Press.

Larcker, D.F. and Tayan, B. (2011) Seven Myths of Executive Compensation, Stanford Graduate School of Business, Closer Look Series: *Topics Issues and Controversies in Corporate Governance*, CGRP-16 (06/01/11).

Main, B.G.M., O'Reilly, C. and Wade, J. (1995) The CEO, The Board of Directors and Executive Compensation: Economic and Psychological Perspectives, *Industrial and Corporate Change*, **4** (2), 293–332.

Milgrom, P. and Roberts, J. (1992) *Economics, Organizations and Management*, Prentice Hall.

Murphy, Kevin J. (1999). Executive Compensation, in Ashenfelter, O. and Card, D. (eds.), *Handbook of Labor Economics*, Volume 3, 2485–2563, North Holland, Elsevier: Amsterdam.

Murphy, K.J. (2009) *Compensation Structure and Systemic Risk*, Marshall School of Business Working Paper No. FBE 34-09.

Murphy, K.J. and Sandino, T. (2010) Executive pay and "independent" compensation consultants, *Journal of Accounting and Economics*, **49** (3), 247–262.

O'Reilly, C.A., Main, B.G and Crystal, G.S. (1988) CEO salaries as tournaments and social comparisons: A tale of two theories, *Administrative Science Quarterly*, **33** (2), 257–274.

Tirole, J. (2006) *The Theory of Corporate Finance*, Princeton University Press.

Waxman, H. (2007) *Executive Pay: Conflicts of Interest Among Compensation Consultants*, United States House of Representatives Committee on Oversight and Government Reform, December.

Westphal, J. (1998) Board Games: How CEOs Adapt to Increases in Structural Board Independence from Management, *Administrative Science Quarterly*, **43** (3), 511–538.

Westphal, J.D. and Zajac, E.J. (1994) Substance and Symbolism in CEOs' Long-Term Incentive Plans, *Administrative Science Quarterly*, **39** (3), 367–390.

PART 3

International Systems

Part contents

Chapter 11

Corporate Governance in the United States and the United Kingdom

Chapter contents

11.1 Introduction

This chapter provides an overview of corporate governance arrangements in the United States and the United Kingdom. The design of optimal corporate governance remains a central issue in these countries. Lawmakers and regulators are ever watchful, and the framework of corporate governance is constantly evolving. Periodically, corporate scandals have erupted and acted as catalysts for change. In the United States the 2002 Sarbanes–Oxley Act followed from the Enron scandal in 2001, and the 2010 Dodd–Frank Act stemmed from the 2008 financial crisis. In the United Kingdom, the 1992 Cadbury Corporate Governance code followed from the Bank of Credit and Commerce International (BCCI) scandal of 1991. The 1995 Greenbury report originated from alleged executive compensation abuses, especially in the newly privatized utilities. In each case, lax corporate governance arrangements were presumed partly responsible. In the extreme, senior executives exploited weaknesses in the existing systems of corporate checks and balances to further their own interests.

The need for effective corporate governance arrangements arises from the separation of firm ownership from corporate control. Because shareholders do not directly run the firm, management might take actions that benefit themselves at the expense of shareholders. This is the agency problem associated with corporate governance: managers may take self-interested actions that impose significant costs on shareholders. The problem for shareholders and society is to design a system of governance so that managers do not opportunistically expropriate shareholders wealth. The goal of the system is to minimize (but not necessarily eliminate) these agency costs. The solution includes institutional features such as a board of directors to safeguard shareholder interests, skilled directors who are independent from management, an audit committee to check the finances of the firm, and external auditors who provide expert opinion on the veracity of financial statements. The optimal governance system reduces agency costs. It does so up to the point justified by the expenditures on these monitoring and compliance mechanisms.

Corporate governance arrangements in the United States and United Kingdom are market-oriented and shareholder-centric. The United States is the canonical model. The term 'market-based model' is used as shorthand for a system that embodies particular governance characteristics. The core elements of this model include a large capital market relative to gross domestic product, security and protection of property rights, and a relatively low role for the state in the affairs of business. The owners of publicly traded firms are many and diffuse. Each owns a relatively low stake in the firm. There is a single unitary board of directors, led by the Chief Executive Officer (CEO). The board also contains independent non-executive directors. Executive compensation arrangements promote equity ownership and financial instruments such as stock options. The primary goal of the corporation is to maximize shareholder value. The interests of shareholders are dominant, and tend to be protected in company law and securities market regulations.

US and UK corporate governance arrangements contrast to the stakeholder-centred model that is more common throughout continental Europe. An example is Germany. The stakeholder approach emphasizes the legitimacy of multiple constituencies such as employees, unions, customers and suppliers. German corporate governance provisions stand in marked contrast to the USA and the UK. There is a two-tier board structure consisting of a management board and a separate supervisory board. The supervisory board contains employee and trade union representatives, which is unheard of in American companies. In addition, German boards often contain bank representatives with links to debt financiers.

11.2 Corporate governance in the United States

Publicly traded listed firms make up a significant part of economic activity in the United States, and market-based economies. In 2007, the market capitalization of US listed companies, as a percentage of gross domestic product (GDP), was about 142%. This compared with about 85% for the Euro Area

as a whole (World Bank, 2011). In Germany the market value of listed firms' shares to GDP was about 60%. In addition, US investors are offered a high degree of protection. The World Bank strength of legal rights index, which measures the degree to which collateral and bankruptcy laws protect the rights of borrowers and lenders, was 8.0 in 2007 (it ranges from 0 to 10, with higher scores indicating better laws). The index value for the Euro Area was 6.2 in 2007. Strong property rights, and the protection of investor rights, are the bedrock of sound US corporate governance.

The goal of publicly traded US firms is to optimize shareholder value. The New York Stock Exchange enshrines this in its corporate governance principles (NYSE, 2010). Why might this be? Economists can show, under fairly strict conditions, that profit-maximizing firms (and consumers maximizing their own preferences) lead to optimal (i.e. best) outcomes. The first fundamental theorem of welfare economics shows that firms and individuals operating in a competitive market lead to a Pareto optimal equilibrium. Pareto efficiency (a standard economic welfare criteria) occurs when it is not possible to reallocate resources to improve the welfare of one person without making at least one person worse off. The second fundamental theorem states that every efficient allocation can be supported by some set of market prices. In short, individuals and firms pursuing their own private interests lead to optimal economic outcomes. However, the necessary conditions for equating private efficiency with economy-wide efficiency are frequently violated in the real world. Often there are externalities (transactions that are not priced in the market), imperfect market information, monopolies, or missing markets. In such cases the general equilibrium ideal is not obtained. An example is environmental pollution. Pollution is a negative externality. Because it is not priced in a private exchange, the firm produces 'too much' pollution compared with what is socially optimal. Such externalities can be dealt with in various ways, including government taxation and/or regulation, or alternatively by creating a market for the externality.

Another reason to give more weight to shareholder interests is their 'residual claimant' status. Shareholders are only entitled to the difference between what the firm has produced and the payments it is contracted to make. That is, they get the 'residual' from the economic activities of the firm. They are the last in a long line of claimants to the firm's income stream. In contrast, debt financiers have contracts specifying fixed interest payments, and a pecking order of payments if the firm is bankrupt and its assets wound up. Employees receive compensation contracts specifying payments in return for labour supply. General suppliers of raw materials to the firm (and consumers of the firm's output) exchange goods and services at agreed market prices. Shareholders, as residual claimants, are therefore more vulnerable compared with these other stakeholders. Maximizing shareholder interests may maximize the size of the pie to be distributed among all claimants.

The board of directors

In the United States, the board of directors is the primary mechanism for exercising control at publicly traded firms in principle. The board ensures that the management acts in the best interests of shareholders. There is a single board of directors. The unitary board structure in the USA contrasts to the dual board structures that exists in Germany or France where a mixture of single and dual board structures prevail. The CEO is the most senior executive and is almost always a member of the board. The size of the board of directors increases with the size of the firm. This reflects the increased complexity of running large firms. Start-ups, early-stage firms and initial public offerings have smaller boards than large long-established firms. The typical size of the board of directors at a large US company is about ten members.

CEOs at publicly traded firms are professional managers. Typically, they are not the original founders of the firm. Nor do they own a significant share stake in the firm (CEO share stakes above 5% are rare). Instead the CEO tends to be a professional manager hired by the board of directors to run the firm in the interests of shareholders. For example, Jeff Immelt is the CEO of US conglomerate General Electric. He was selected by GE's board of directors in 2000 to replace Jack Welch. Previously, Jeff Immelt was the CEO and president of GE's Medical Systems division, now known as GE Healthcare. Companies such as Google and eBay also quickly hired professional CEOs in the early years of becoming publicly traded firms. Google recruited Eric Schmidt to become CEO;

he was previously CEO of Novell. Google's founders, Sergey Brin and Larry Page, remained active participants on the board of directors. EBay hired Meg Whitman in 1998 as CEO. EBay's founder, Pierre Omidyar, remained a board member.

The role of the board of directors, according to economist Michael Jensen, is to hire, fire and compensate the CEO. The board is the shareholders' first line of defence against self-dealing by management. The list of appropriate board functions is a matter for debate. The following are especially important. First, the board of directors identifies and selects the chief executive officer. Second, the main board recruits and retains candidates for the board of directors. Third, the board of directors evaluates the performance of the CEO, in relation to company strategy, operations, and financing. This includes designing the best compensation and incentive package to motivate the CEO. Fourth, the board of directors makes sure that the company is in compliance with all applicable laws and regulations affecting the firm.

The board of directors is made up of executive and non-executive directors. Non-executive directors, in particular, are charged with the responsibility of protecting shareholder interests. In this respect, non-executive directors are required to be 'independent', reflecting their impartiality from the company's senior executive team and their ability to proffer objective advice. Independent directors are normally drawn from senior positions at non-affiliated companies, not-for-profit organizations or universities. For example, the board at General Electric contains a banker and university president (see Minicase 1). The executive directors are responsible for decision making, such as proposing and implementing strategy or financing decisions. The non-executive directors are responsible for decision control, such as ratifying and evaluating the outcome of strategic or major financial decisions. The distinction between executive and non-executive board members supports the system of checks and balances on the main board.

To carry out its various functions the board of directors establishes relevant committees. Especially important are the audit committee, the compensation committee and the governance (or nomination committee). The main board may set up other salient committees as required. The executive directors are not members of the compensation or audit committee for example. If they were, then they might be able to engage in inappropriate self-serving behaviour (such as setting their own pay). These committees are made up wholly of non-executive (and independent) directors.

Non-executive directors form the overwhelming majority of the board in publicly traded US firms. Typically, the only executive directors on the main board are the CEO and the Chief Financial Officer. They are referred to as insiders, as they are full-time employees of the firm whose interests are tied to the firm. The remaining board members are non-executive directors, or outsiders. The proportion of non-executive directors (outsiders) is about 80% on a standard ten-person board. The outside directors are not full-time employees of the company, but instead are drawn from an array of business and other occupations to provide experience and oversight for the board. Their services are supplied on a part-time basis. A key issue is the independence of the non-executive directors. Independence is ultimately a subjective metric. Indeed, there are many consulting firms who provide assessments of 'independence'. The New York Stock Exchange listing rules require boards to have at least two-thirds of the board's directors to be independent. Independence requires that the non-executive's objectivity not be compromised. This is usually measured by material business transactions with the firm, whether the non-executive director is a former full-time employee, whether the non-executive is a family member or has other relationships with the company or its officers.

US firms generally combine the posts of CEO and chairperson, namely, the same person performs both jobs. Frequently, this is referred to as CEO–chair 'duality'. This practice might cause a conflict of interest, since the CEO is simultaneously the most senior executive and the most senior shareholder guardian in the firm. Can the CEO really dispassionately evaluate the performance of the CEO when he is, in fact, the CEO? In many countries the norm is for different people to be CEO and chairperson, as is the case in the UK. Set against this concern is a counter-argument. Combining the posts leads to clear and decisive leadership of the organization. To ameliorate concerns about potential conflicts of interest, many US companies have identified a presiding or 'lead' director to assume a leadership role in board affairs. This person is a senior director with considerable experience and gravitas, a person who ensures that there is sufficient transparency, accountability, checks and balances at the apex of

the corporation. Minicase 1 shows that this is the solution adopted by General Electric. The newly enacted Dodd–Frank Act requires firms to discuss whether the posts of CEO and chair are combined or not.

Corporate ownership

Corporate ownership of US publicly traded firms has two main characteristics. First, there are many small shareholders. Second, each shareholder typically owns only a tiny fraction of the firm's common outstanding shares. This is the traditional understanding, and the implications are profound. They were first espoused by Berle and Means in their classic text *The Modern Corporation and Private Property* in 1932. Berle and Means hypothesized that the pattern of legal ownership in the USA gave rise to an effective separation of ownership and control. The shareholders (who are the firm's legal owners) elect the board of directors who then manage the firm's assets on behalf of the owners. However, because each shareholder owns a very small fraction of the firm's shares she has weak incentives to monitor management. Any shareholder so inclined would bear the full costs of actively monitoring management, but would only realize benefits proportional to her equity holdings. If monitoring incentives are weak for any one shareholder, they are weak for all since everyone has only a small fraction of the firm's outstanding shares. The result is that no one has strong incentives to monitor management, and effective control of the firm is ceded to management insiders. There is a collective action problem. Moral hazards might run rampant as executives pursue their own, rather than shareholders' interests. Mark Roes succinctly characterized this as a problem of 'weak owners and strong managers'. The fundamental problem is that small, isolated individual investors do not have sufficient power or coordination abilities to effectively control an errant management.

Because there are many shareholders and each shareholder has a small percentage ownership, ownership is not concentrated. It is rare for an individual shareholder to own more than 5% of a US firm's outstanding common shares. This is especially true in larger public firms. Ownership patterns in the USA contrast to continental European firms where shareholders own large blocks of shares, and so ownership is more concentrated. Owners of European firms may be families, other companies, or even the state. In the USA, firms report shareholdings above a threshold of 5%, under the Securities and Exchange Commission rules. The identity and number of shares owned is revealed in the definitive proxy statements. In addition, firms report the beneficial share ownership of the board of directors, no matter what that percentage is. For example, Minicase 1 shows that General Electric has one external shareholder with greater than 5% holdings: BlackRock Inc.[1] BlackRock is a global investment management firm. There are more than 10 billion common shares outstanding in GE. Directors, including the CEO, typically own a very small fraction of the firm's shares. Ownership, then, is diffuse with many shareholders. It is not difficult to see that individual shareholders might find it difficult to exercise effective control.

Who owns corporate shares? Historically, individuals and households were the main holders of equity shares, rather than institutions such as pension funds. The Conference Board provides data showing significant growth in institutional share ownership in the USA over a long period of time. In 1950 institutions accounted for approximately 6.1% if total outstanding equity. In 1970 this figure had increased to 19.4%, and by 1980 to 20.4%. During the 1990s and early 2000s the Conference Board estimates that institutions accounted for about 50% of total outstanding equity. The latest Conference Board study illustrates that institutional ownership appears to have plateaued at about this level. In 2009 institutional holdings were about 51% of total equity (The Conference Board, 2010). Aggarwal et al. (2011) confirm these findings. In the USA they show that institutional holdings in a firm's stock as a percentage of its market capitalization was 40.3% in 2003, rising to approximately 57.8% in 2007. The average yearly change in institutional ownership during the data period was about 4.4%. The evidence is consistent with a marked shift away from individual shareholding towards institutional holdings in the United States. In contrast, institutional holdings are less prominent in some continental stakeholder-oriented European countries, although some

---

[1] Calculated as (573,904,247 / 10,672,871,990) × 100 = 5.4%

change has been recorded since 2000. Aggarwal et al. (2011) report that in Germany the percentage of firm stock held by institutions was 16.5% in 2003, increasing to 27.7% in 2007. The level of institutional holdings is lower compared with the United States, but the growth rate is positive.

The changing structure of corporate ownership might have far-reaching implications for the control of US firms. Many shareholders with small share-stakes find it difficult to take collective action, or resolve latent agency problems associated with management. This problem is the essence of the 'strong-manager and weak-owner' hypothesis. However, as ownership becomes more concentrated it becomes easier for owners to act in a concerted fashion. The American Bar Association (2009) remarks: 'To the extent that shareholdings are concentrated among a smaller group of shareholders, the collective action element of the classic accountability problem can be overcome by institutional investors.' The concentration of ownership and the rise of active investors suggests that owners have a more important say in the direct governance of firms.

Executive compensation practices

The market-model uses executive compensation contracts as a means to resolving agency problems. The significant issues here are the level and structure of US executive compensation. US executives receive high levels of pay, especially at large firms. CEO pay in the USA appears to be greater than in most European countries. Executive pay appears to have increased significantly since the 1980s. This seems to have occurred at the same time that measures of income inequality started to increase significantly. The precise reasons for the increase in executive pay are unknown, and the subject of academic research. Some authors suggest management exerts power and influence over the board and is able to extract greater than necessary pay. Alternatively, the level and structure of CEO pay may be driven by the operation of the executive labour market. This could include the globalization of product and labour markets, or increased demand for general managerial skills.

The market-model stresses the use of equity compensation to motivate executives. Since the 1980s stock options have become a significant part of the typical CEO's compensation contract. Estimates suggest that by year 2000 about 50% of a typical S&P 500 firm's CEO pay was made up of stock options. From an agency perspective this provides significant incentives to promote shareholder value, as the value of the option increases as the price of the underlying asset increases. An interesting corollary here is that the use of options (and other forms of equity pay, such as restricted stock) puts significant compensation risk on CEOs. Standard economic theory predicts that individuals need to be compensated for increasing risk. In consequence, the increase in the level of pay might, in part, be a reflection of the need to compensate CEOs for increasing the riskiness of compensation contracts.

The takeover market

The takeover market, or market for corporate control, imposes significant constraints on CEOs and managers in the market model. Firms that do not optimize shareholder value face the distinct possibility that their firm will be taken over by a raider. The bidding company then has the option to replace the target firm's management with its own slate. The threat of takeover, other things equal, ensures managers take decisions in the interests of owners. Takeovers are more common in the USA than other countries.

One impediment to effective governance is the use of takeover deterrents by the firm. These are widespread and often controversial among shareholders. Management defends their use on the basis that they enable the firm to focus on the long-run rather than have to be excessively concerned with quarterly earnings and short-term stock prices. Takeover defences significantly impede the possibility of a corporate takeover. Generally, they work by imposing significant costs on the raider, but not the incumbent shareholders. Anti-takeover measures generally work by making it costly for a bidder to acquire a target. A shareholder rights plan, colloquially known as a 'poison pill', is a popular US defence against a takeover, especially in the early 1980s. They do not require shareholder approval to be implemented by the board (e.g. for companies incorporated in Delaware). In the UK, shareholder approval is required. The target company issues rights to existing shareholders to acquire a significant number of shares if anyone acquires more than a set amount of the company's stock (say, 15%). The bidder firm does not have these rights, so effectively diluting the percentage of the target owned by the bidder, making it very expensive to acquire control of the target. Other ways of imposing costs on a bidder firm by the target are 'golden parachutes'. These are costs the acquiring firm will have to pay the CEO and other senior managers in the event of a change of control. The effect of these is to blunt the effectiveness of the market for corporate control as a disciplining mechanism.

Securities regulation and corporate governance

The US Securities and Exchange Commission (the SEC) regulates publicly traded firms.[2] The SEC was created in 1934. It enforces the main securities legislation in the United States. These include the Securities Act of 1933, the Trust Indenture Act of 1939, the Investment Company Act of 1940, Investment Advisers Act of 1940, the Sarbanes–Oxley Act of 2002, and other salient acts. Most recently the SEC is responsible for implementing regulatory initiatives ushered in by the Dodd–Frank Wall Street Reform and Consumer Protection Act (2010). The Dodd–Frank Act was enacted as a direct consequence of the 2008 financial crisis. In the decade since 2000 there have been two significant pieces of legislation affecting the governance of firms. One is the Sarbanes–Oxley Act (2002), and the other is the Dodd–Frank Act (2010).

Sarbanes–Oxley Act, 2002

President Bush signed Sarbanes–Oxley (SOX) into law in 2002. It followed the high-profile corporate scandal at Enron. Enron was an innovative energy company that used aggressive accounting techniques that inflated the company's financial position. Enron collapsed in 2001 amid accounting irregularities. The firm's auditor was Arthur Andersen. It was complicit by misrepresenting the company's financials, and shredded important documents during regulatory investigations. Arthur Andersen collapsed because of its unprofessional activities. Other notable scandals around this time were WorldCom and Tyco. There was a public appetite to regulate excesses at public firms. The Sarbanes–Oxley Act introduced major changes to the regulation of financial practice at publicly traded firms and corporate governance standards.

The Sarbanes–Oxley Act is made up of eleven separate titles, each containing its own set of sections. They are intended to help investors and society by improving compliance, accountability and good governance. The Act is wide ranging, and applies to public and not private companies. Sarbanes–Oxley imposes compliance costs on firms. Ultimately, the success of the Act depends on whether its benefits (e.g. better accountability, increased transparency, motivated management) outweigh the costs (e.g. arising from compliance, introduction of information systems, hiring new personnel). The academic evidence in this area is still being amassed, and the current findings are mixed. Some academics are critical of the mandatory nature of the provisions contained in SOX (Romano, 2005).

The Sarbanes–Oxley Act is a significant piece of legislation and covers a myriad of governance issues. *Title I establishes the Public Company Account Oversight Board (PCAOB)*. It provides independent oversight of audit companies, and enforces mandates associated with SOX. *Title II addresses Auditor Independence*. Specifically, it mitigates conflicts of interest by prohibiting auditors from providing non-audit related services to clients. *Title III deals with Corporate Responsibility*. It addresses issues from public company audit committees, corporate responsibility for financial reports, penalties for officers and directors, to rules of responsibility for attorneys. Section 302 requires that the Chief Executive Officer (CEO) and Chief Financial Officer (CFO), as the firm's principal officers, certify the integrity and veracity of the financial reports.

Title IV addresses Enhanced Financial Disclosures, and contains nine sections. Specifically, Section 401 requires a financial statement to be accurate and presented in a way that does not contain

---

[2] The SEC's website provides much corporate governance information. http://www.sec.gov/

incorrect statements. Financial statements must also include all material off-balance sheet liabilities, obligations or transactions. Section 404 requires the issuing firm to establish internal controls for assuring the accuracy of financial reports and disclosures. It mandates both audits and reports on those controls. The auditing firm must attest to the effectiveness of internal controls. Section 409 requires timely reporting of material changes in the financial or operational condition of the company.

Title V deals with Analyst Conflict of Interests. It makes provisions to mitigate securities analyst conflict of interests, and requires disclosure of knowable conflicts. *Title VI relates to Commission Resources and Authority.* It contains four sections on issues including the authorization of appropriations, and appearance practice before the commission. *Title VII deals with Studies and Reports.* It requires the Comptroller General and the SEC to perform various studies and report their findings. These are to include the effects of consolidation of public accounting firms, and the role of credit rating agencies in the operation of securities markets.

Title VIII relates to Corporate and Criminal Fraud Accountability. It outlines specific criminal penalties for manipulation, destruction or alteration of financial records. It also affords certain protections for whistle-blowers who report evidence of corporate malfeasance. *Title IX deals with White-Collar Crime Penalty Enhancements.* It makes provision to increase criminal penalties associated with white-collar crimes and conspiracies. It advocates stronger sentencing guidelines. Failure to certify corporate financial reports becomes a criminal offence. *Title X relates to Corporate Tax Returns* and requires the CEO to sign the company's tax returns. *Title XI deals with Corporate Fraud Accountability.* It makes corporate fraud and records tampering criminal offences. It gives specific penalties for violations.

Sarbanes–Oxley is a significant piece of legislation, with many key provisions. We highlight one area in particular. SOX Section 404 addressed the Assessment of Internal Control and was perhaps the most contentious part of the legislation. Section 404 was costly for firms to implement, because documenting and keeping appropriate records requires significant resources and effort. The costs include millions of dollars and many hours of increased labour time. Academic research has shown suggestive evidence that Sarbanes–Oxley is associated with increased private costs to firms (Zhang, 2007).

The Dodd–Frank Act, 2010

The second major piece of governance legislation since 2000 was the Dodd–Frank Wall Street Reform and Consumer Protection Act (Pub.L. 111-203, H.R. 4173).[3] President Obama signed the 'Dodd–Frank Act' into law on 21 July 2010. The Act is a direct response to the 2008 financial crisis, and the public outrage at the activities of some Wall Street firms. It is the most fundamental piece of financial regulation in the United States since the Great Depression. Dodd–Frank objectives are 'to promote the financial stability of the United States by improving accountability and transparency in the financial system, to end "too big to fail", to protect the American taxpayer by ending bailouts, to protect consumers from abusive financial services practices, and for other purposes'. The Act is extraordinarily long, covering 848 pages. It leaves most of the 'fine details' to be promulgated by several government bodies. These agencies include the SEC, the Federal Reserve System, the Department of Treasury, the Commodity Futures Trading Commission, the Financial Stability Oversight Council, the Federal Deposit Insurance Corporation, the Federal Trade Commission, the Government Accounting Office, and the Office of the Comptroller of the Currency. DavisPolk (2010) estimate that Dodd–Frank requires regulators to create 243 new rules, conduct 67 studies, and issue 22 periodic reports. Dodd–Frank focuses on three main areas of corporate governance at financial institutions and public companies (DavisPolk, 2010). Firstly, Dodd–Frank requires certain financial and non-financial companies to establish a risk committee. Secondly, it requires firms to provide

---

[3] See the information contained at http://www.llsdc.org/Dodd-Frank-Act-Leg-Hist/ (accessed June 2011).

additional disclosure regarding organizational structure. Lastly, Dodd–Frank gives the SEC authority to promulgate proxy access.

While ostensibly focused on regulating firms in the financial services industry, the Act also imposes corporate governance reforms on all large publicly traded US firms. These are contained in Title IX, Subtitles E and G. Section 951 imposes so-called 'say on pay'. Shareholders will be asked to approve the company's executive compensation practices in a non-binding vote occurring at least every three years. In addition, companies are required to disclose, and shareholders are asked to approve, golden parachute payments in connection with mergers, tender offers, or going-private transactions. Section 954 deals with clawbacks. Companies must implement and report policies for recouping payments to executives based on financial statements that are subsequently restated. The rule applies to any current or former executive officer (an expansion of Sarbanes–Oxley, where only the CEO and CFO were subject to clawbacks).

In terms of governance and compensation issues, Sections 953, 955 and 972 deal with enhanced disclosures. Companies must report the ratio of CEO compensation to the median pay for all other company employees. Companies must analyse and report the relation between realized compensation and the firm's financial performance, including stock-price performance. In addition, companies must disclose their policies regarding hedging by employees to protect against reductions in company stock prices. Finally, the Dodd–Frank Act requires companies to disclose their policies and practices on why the company chooses either to separate the chairman and CEO positions, or combine both roles. Section 952 deals with compensation committee independence. Following Sarbanes–Oxley (2002) requirements for audit committees, publicly traded companies are required to have compensation committees comprised solely of outside independent directors (where 'independence' takes into account any financial ties the outside directors might have with the firm). Section 971 deals with proxy access by stockholders. Additionally, companies must assess the independence of compensation consultants, attorneys, accountants and other advisers to the compensation committees. Certain shareholders are permitted to nominate their own director candidates in the company's annual proxy statements.

As noted above, Dodd–Franks is far reaching. The expected future benefits include financial stability, a better environment to conduct business, and the eradication of 'too big to fail'. However there are significant costs to implementation. Not least are the complexities of implementation, which may hamper the competitive position of US firms, various government agencies are given access to significant resources to set up departments and conduct research associated with the Act. The *Wall Street Journal* reports that costs could run to about $2.9 billion over five years.[4] Furthermore, a significant number of federal government personnel have been tasked to Dodd–Frank duties, and more staff recruitment directly related to Dodd–Frank regulation is being considered.

Ethical standards and corruption

The USA holds firms to very high ethical standards. This is achieved through the various acts discussed earlier. In addition, the Foreign Corrupt Practices Act (FCPA) is a federal law enacted in 1977. It prohibits companies from paying bribes to foreign government officials and political figures for the purpose of obtaining business. Persons subject to FCPA are issuers (US or foreign), any citizen, national or resident of the USA. The Act covers firms and persons. The Foreign Corrupt Practices Act has two key provisions. Firstly, there is an anti-bribery provision. It is unlawful to make a payment to a foreign official for the purpose of obtaining or retaining business for or with, or directing business to, any person. The law is enforced by the Department of Justice. Secondly, the FCPA also requires companies whose securities are listed in the United States to meet its accounting provisions. Notable cases of firms and individuals subject to FCPA include BAE Systems, Baker Hughes, Daimler AG, KBR, Lucent Technologies, Monsanto, Siemens, and Avon Products.

---

[4] http://blogs.wsj.com/economics/2011/03/28/gao-implementing-dodd-frank-could-cost-2-9-billion/ (accessed June 2011).

11.3 Corporate governance in the United Kingdom

As in the United States, UK listed firms make up a significant part of economic activity. In 2007 the market capitalization of UK listed companies, as a percentage of gross domestic product (GDP), was about 138%. This compared with about 85% for the Euro Area as a whole (World Bank, 2011). The World Bank strength of legal rights index, measuring laws to protect the rights of borrowers and lenders, was 9.0 in 2007 (in the range 0 to 10). The index value for the Euro Area was 6.2 in 2007. As in the USA, strong property rights and the protection of investor rights are important elements of corporate governance.

The goal of the firm is somewhat broader than shareholder value maximization. UK directors face a complex set of responsibilities to all stakeholders, not just to shareholders. One might think of this as a move to accommodate broad stakeholder interests. The UK 2006 Companies Act, Section §172 focuses on the duties of the board of directors. Specifically, it argues that there is a 'duty to promote the success of the company'. The areas discussed include:

> *A director of a company must act in the way he considers, in good faith, would be most likely to promote the success of the company for the benefit of its members as a whole, and in doing so have regard (amongst other matters) to (a) the likely consequences of any decision in the long term, (b) the interests of the company's employees, (c) the need to foster the company's business relationships with suppliers, customers and others, (d) the impact of the company's operations on the community and the environment, (e) the desirability of the company maintaining a reputation for high standards of business conduct, and (f) the need to act fairly as between members of the company.*

It is clear from this that in discharging their duties, directors are formally instructed to consider a wider set of stakeholders than just shareholders. This approach to corporate law appears to be an important deviation from the pure shareholder model. Whatever benefits there may be in adopting such a broad stakeholder view, a multi-valued (and possibly partly conflicting) objective function beyond profit or value maximization does not make it easier for company directors to make decisions or for shareholders to hold them accountable.

The takeover market

As in the USA, the UK has an active takeover market compared with the bank-based continental European model. This acts as an important constraint on managerial opportunism. Managers who do not enhance the value of the enterprise face being taken over and, presumably, losing their jobs. UK M&A activity is buoyant. The UK Office for National Statistics (ONS) reports there were 587 mergers and acquisitions in the UK by UK companies in year 2000, 769 in 2005 and 296 in 2010.[5]

The UK Panel on Takeovers and Mergers implements policy on takeovers. It oversees the UK's Companies Act dues, including rules in the European Directive on Takeover Bids (2004/25/EC) for public companies. The Companies Act 2006 (section 979) gives a takeover bidder who has acquired 90% of a company's shares the right to compulsorily purchase stock from the remaining shareholders. Section 983 of the Act allows minority shareholders to insist that their stakes are bought out. In addition, the City Code on Takeovers and Mergers, known as 'City Code' or 'Takeover Code', sets out takeover rules and is found in the Blue Book. Since 2006 the UK Code is now statutory in order to comply with the European Directive on Takeovers.[6]

The Code requires that all shareholders be treated equally. It regulates the information that companies are able to release publicly in relation to the bid. It sets timetables for elements of the takeover bid. The rules state (but are not limited to) that a shareholder must make an offer when its

---

5 See information at http://www.statistics.gov.uk/StatBase/Product.asp?vlnk=72&Pos=1&ColRank=1&Rank=240 (accessed June 2011).

6 See the information contained at http://www.thetakeoverpanel.org.uk/ (accessed June 2011).

shareholding reaches 30% of the target. In addition, a bidder must make an announcement if rumour affects a company's share price. Also, the level of the offer must not be less than any price paid by the bidder in the three months before the announcement of a firm intention to make an offer.

The board of directors

The UK model of corporate governance shares many features of the US model. They are similar enough to be grouped under the concept of the market model or Anglo-Saxon model. However, this does not mean they are identical. At the level of the firm, the board of directors is the main decision-making body. The board, like in the USA, is a single-tier or unitary board. Board size increases with firm size, so the largest firms on the London Stock Exchange have bigger boards. The typical board size is approximately ten members. The board also has three main committees: an audit committee, a remuneration committee, and a governance (or nominating) committee. The remuneration committee is the UK nomenclature for a compensation committee. These carry out broadly the same functions as they do in the United States.

There are important differences in the design of UK boards when compared with those in the United States. In the UK, most publicly traded firms separate the posts of CEO and chairperson. Two different people occupy these roles. Estimates suggest that in excess of 80% of UK listed firms separate the posts. Second, executive directors are more prevalent on UK boards. Estimates suggest that approximately 50% of the board is made up of executive directors, and the remainder non-executive directors. However, executive directors do not serve on audit committees and rarely on remuneration committees. Implicitly, comparing two boards of equal size in the USA and the UK there are more independent outside directors on US boards.

Minicase 2[7] gives an example of the main board arrangements at J. Sainsbury plc in the United Kingdom. Sainsbury's is one of the largest chains of supermarkets in the UK. It is listed on the London Stock Exchange and is a constituent of the FTSE 100 Index. Sainsbury's was founded in 1869. It grew rapidly through various innovations and became a significant entity during the 1980s. Other leading supermarkets vying for market share are Tesco and Asda (which currently are in positions one and two in terms of market share). Minicase 2 shows the board of directors contains 12 members, of which three are women. The balance between executive and non-executive directors is more balanced than would be typically observed in the USA. There are eight non-executive directors, and four executive directors. In addition to the CEO, Justin King, the executive members include the Chief Financial Officer, Group Commercial Officer and the Group Development Director. Sainsbury, like most UK public firms, separates the role of CEO and chairman: Justin King is the CEO and David Tyler is the chairman. Consistent with the UK's corporate governance code, Sainsbury has a remuneration, an audit and a nomination committee, the members of which are all non-executive. In addition, Sainsbury has a corporate governance responsibility committee.

Sainsbury is a family firm, and the family still retains a significant fraction of the firm's shares. Significant shareholdings above 3% of the firm's shares include: Judith Portrait (a trustee of various settlements, including charitable trusts) 4.09%, Legal and General Group plc 3.99%, Lord Sainsbury of Turville 4.99%. However, the firm's major shareholder is Qatar Holdings LLC with a 25.99% share stake. This is a sovereign wealth fund and investment vehicle of the Qatari royal family. Ownership in Sainsbury is therefore concentrated.

Corporate governance arrangements

UK corporate governance arrangements follow the doctrine of 'comply or explain'. This means that instead of establishing mandatory laws in the field of corporate governance, government regulators establish a 'code of conduct'. Publicly traded firms may choose to comply with it, or not. This principle began with the Cadbury Code in 1992, and has been endorsed ever since. If firms choose not to comply with aspects of the governance code they must explain publicly the reasons for non-compliance. The UK Corporate Governance Code employs this doctrine. It sets out minimum requirements for the

---

[7] 2011 Annual Report and Accounts available at: http://www.j-sainsbury.co.uk/ (accessed June 2011).

design of boards in terms of the proportion of non-executive directors, separating the posts of CEO and chairperson, audit committees, and compensation committees. Firms can choose to comply or explain their position in relation to the prevailing standard. The underlying logic of the 'comply or explain' principle is that it allows companies to decide on how best to organize governance in their own unique circumstances. It may be thought of as a partial market solution to find the optimal governance arrangement. The 'comply or explain' principle eschews the notion that there is one form of corporate governance that is appropriate for all firms (i.e. that one size fits all). Indeed, the market can impose penalties on firms. If the firm chooses not to comply and investors dislike this then the firm's stock price will be discounted. In effect, the market disciplines firms rather than strict legal rules.

The regulatory rules pertaining to UK listed companies are outlined in the most recent UK Corporate Governance Code of 2010. The Financial Reporting Council implemented the code; it is part of the Financial Services Authority's Listing Rules. As noted above, the Governance Code adopts a principles-based approach, providing general guidelines to 'best practice' for UK listed firms. It contrasts with a rules-based approach that precisely defines what companies must do.

The current Governance Code is the latest statement of a set of 'best practice' principles that started with the Cadbury committee in 1992. The Cadbury committee focused on the financial aspects of corporate governance in the wake of various scandals including the banking and financial frauds perpetrated at Bank of Credit and Commerce International (BCCI) and the pension funds deception perpetrated by Robert Maxwell. The Cadbury report recommended strengthening the audit committee functions and internal risk management to make such financial risks less likely and to protect investors. In consequence, all UK boards have an audit committee made up only of non-executive directors. Cadbury also recommended that the CEO and chairman of companies should be separate; also that boards should have at least three non-executive directors. In short, Cadbury tried to put in place a system of checks and balances to restrain self-interested activities by too-powerful executives.

The Cadbury report became the bedrock of corporate governance reforms. Indeed, many of the corporate governance codes that sprang up around the world since have been heavily influenced by the insights of the Cadbury committee. In the UK, several committees of enquiry, probing various aspects of corporate governance, followed Cadbury. The 1995 Greenbury committee, chaired by the former chairman of Marks and Spencer Sir Richard Greenbury, focused on executive pay. Set against public concerns over high levels of pay, including those at recently privatized firms, it recommended that firms establish remuneration committees made up entirely of non-executive directors. Importantly, executive pay should be linked to long-term measures of performance. The report was critical of the role of share options and discussed the importance of alternative long-term incentive plans. In 1998 the Hampel report drew together the emerging themes and produced a Combined Code, reflecting then current best practices. It argued for more involvement by institutional investors. In particular, they should consider voting their shares; compulsory voting was ruled out. Hampel also resulted in more disclosure about executive pay, including executive pension arrangements.

The Higgs review in 2003 investigated the role and effectiveness of non-executive directors, as well as the audit and remuneration committees, to improve the existing Combined Code. The review discussed the role of non-executive directors, their induction to the board, their remuneration and independence. It recommended that a senior independent director be identified who can be available to shareholders. The report endorsed the 'comply or explain' principle, rather than rigid rules. At around the same time (i.e. 2005) the Smith report considered the independence of auditors, given the US accounting scandals surrounding Enron and auditors Arthur Andersen. It is now incorporated into the UK governance code.

How do corporate governance arrangements in the UK compare with those in the USA? Firstly, there are strong similarities to broad corporate governance in the two economies, not least the commitment to open markets, and the protection of investor rights. Secondly, UK company law is slightly less bureaucratic and cumbersome. The UK has not adopted Sarbanes–Oxley style rules and therefore enforcement is less rigid. As a result, foreign companies currently might find it more attractive to have shares listed in London than in New York. This is not to say that the UK has not had its share of bureaucracy. But the regulation has been less stringent and has been of a different kind. As noted, beginning with Cadbury (1992), the UK has relied more on self-regulation (i.e. corporate governance codes). This has probably led to lower costs of regulatory governance.

Thirdly, UK ownership seems slightly less dispersed than in the USA, at least partly because the percentage of private shareholders is smaller. Moreover, the distribution of shares among large investors is more even (Barca and Becht, 2002). On average, the largest owner of a British company holds 5% and the share of the second largest owner is not much lower. Moreover, because of informal networks within the business elite (i.e. the 'old boys' clubs'), investors find it easier to act in concert. This means that the 5–10 largest owners (which are normally institutional investors) have a direct influence on company managers. The UK system may therefore be described as 'pension fund governance'. In consequence, owners are somewhat stronger, and managers are somewhat less powerful than in the USA. Finally, again partly as a result of less powerful managers, executive pay is much lower for similar sized companies and the use of takeover defences is more limited. Since Cadbury (1992), there have not been any major financial scandals in the UK on the scale of Enron, Tyco, or WorldCom.

Ethical standards and corruption

The UK introduced a Bribery Act in 2010, which covers the criminal law relating to bribery. It is claimed that the Act has wide jurisdiction, and permits the prosecution of an individual or company with links to the United Kingdom, regardless of where the crime occurred. The crime of bribery is described in Section 1 of the Act as occurring when a person offers, gives or promises to give a 'financial or other advantage' to another individual in exchange for 'improperly' performing a 'relevant function or activity'. Bribery of foreign public officials is a distinct crime under the Act (Section 6). In this case an individual will be guilty if they promise, offer or give a financial or other advantage to a foreign public official, where such an advantage is not legitimately due. If a person is successfully prosecuted, individuals are subject to fines, imprisonment and disqualification from holding directorships. The newness of the Act means that it is yet to be evaluated properly. One concern is that it may make illegal certain acts that may be socially unacceptable market practice in one part of the globe but acceptable in other regions. This may have an impact on the competitiveness of British industry.

11.4 Discussion

Corporate governance arrangements in the United States and the United Kingdom are shareholder-centric and responsive to market forces. The core features are: a large capital market relative to gross domestic product, security and protection of property rights, and a relatively low role for the state in the affairs of business. The owners of publicly traded firms are many and diffuse. Each owns a relatively low stake in the firm. There is a single unitary board of directors, led by a Chief Executive Officer (CEO). The board also contains independent non-executive directors. Executive compensation arrangements promote equity ownership and financial instruments such as stock options. The primary goal of the corporation is to maximize shareholder value. The interests of shareholders are dominant, and tend to be protected in company law and securities market regulations.

Minicase 1

The Board of Directors at General Electric in 2009

- W. Geoffrey Beattie, 49, President and Chief Executive Officer, The Woodbridge Company Limited, Toronto, Canada. Director since 2009.
- James I. Cash, Jr., 62, Emeritus James E. Robison Professor of Business Administration, Harvard Graduate School of Business, Boston, Massachusetts. Director since 1997.
- Sir William M. Castell, 62, Former Vice Chairman, General Electric Company, Fairfield, Connecticut. Director since 2004.
- Ann M. Fudge, 58, Former Chairman of the Board and Chief Executive Officer, Young & Rubicam Brands, global marketing communications network, New York. Director since 1999.

- Susan Hockfield, 58, President of the Massachusetts Institute of Technology, Cambridge, Massachusetts. Director since 2006.
- Jeffrey R. Immelt, 54, Chairman of the Board and Chief Executive Officer, General Electric Company, Fairfield, Connecticut. Director since 2000.
- Andrea Jung, 51, Chairman of the Board and Chief Executive Officer, Avon Products, Inc., beauty products, New York. Director since 1998.
- Alan G. (A.G.) Lafley, 62, Chairman of the Board and former Chief Executive Officer, Procter & Gamble Company, personal and household products, Cincinnati, Ohio. Director since 2002.
- Robert W. Lane, 60, Chairman of the Board and former Chief Executive Officer, Deere & Company, agricultural, construction and forestry equipment, Moline, Illinois. Director since 2005.
- Ralph S. Larsen, 71, Former Chairman of the Board and Chief Executive Officer, Johnson & Johnson, pharmaceutical, medical and consumer products, New Brunswick, New Jersey. Director since 2002.
- Rochelle B. Lazarus, 62, Chairman of the Board and former Chief Executive Officer, Ogilvy & Mather Worldwide, global marketing communications company, New York. Director since 2000.
- James J. Mulva, 63, Chairman of the Board and Chief Executive Officer, ConocoPhillips, international, integrated energy company, Houston, Texas. Director since 2008.
- Sam Nunn, 71, Co-Chairman and Chief Executive Officer, Nuclear Threat Initiative, Washington, D.C. Director since 1997.
- Roger S. Penske, 73, Chairman of the Board, Penske Corporation and Penske Truck Leasing Corporation, Chairman of the Board and Chief Executive Officer, Penske Automotive Group, Inc., diversified transportation company, Detroit, Michigan. Director since 1994.
- Robert J. Swieringa, 67, Professor of Accounting and former Anne and Elmer Lindseth Dean, S.C. Johnson Graduate School of Management, Cornell University, Ithaca, New York. Director since 2002.
- Douglas A. Warner III, 63, Former Chairman of the Board, J.P. Morgan Chase & Co., The Chase Manhattan Bank, and Morgan Guaranty Trust Company, investment banking, New York. Director since 1992.

GE's leadership structure is described as: 'Our CEO also serves as the Chairman of the Board and we have an independent presiding director with broad authority and responsibility. The presiding director, Ralph S. Larsen, the former chairman of the board and chief executive officer of Johnson & Johnson, has the following responsibilities: (1) to lead meetings of the non-management directors, which are scheduled at least three times a year, and to call additional meetings of the non-management directors as he deems appropriate, (2) to advise the Nominating and Corporate Governance Committee on the selection of committee chairs, (3) to advise on and determine with the concurrence of the Chairman the agenda for Board meetings, (4) to determine, with the Chairman, the nature and extent of information that should be provided to the Board in advance of Board meetings, (5) to work with the Chairman to propose an annual schedule of major discussion items for the Board's approval, (6) to provide leadership to the Board if circumstances arise in which the role of the Chairman may be, or may be perceived to be, in conflict, and otherwise act as Chairman of Board meetings when the Chairman is not in attendance, and (7) to perform such other functions as the Board may direct.'

Audit committee: 'The members of the Audit Committee are directors Warner, who chairs the committee, Beattie, Cash, Lane, Mulva and Swieringa. The Board has determined that Messrs. Beattie, Lane, Mulva, Swieringa and Warner are "audit committee financial experts," as defined under SEC rules.'

Management Development and Compensation Committee: 'The members of the MDCC are directors Larsen, who chairs the committee, Cash, Jung, Lane, Nunn and Warner.'

Nominating and Corporate Governance Committee: 'The members of the Nominating and Corporate Governance Committee are directors Lazarus, who chairs the committee, Hockfield, Jung, Lafley, Larsen and Warner.'

Information on stock ownership

Table 11.1 includes all GE stock-based holdings, as of December 31, 2009, of our directors and the named executives, our directors and executive officers as a group, and all those known by us to be beneficial owners of more than 5% of our common stock.

Table 11.1   Common stock and total stock-based holdings

Name	Stock[1]	Total[2]	Name	Stock[1]	Total[2]
W. Geoffrey Beattie[3]	20,458	30,717	Ralph S. Larsen[3]	165,316	251,893
BlackRock, Inc.[4]	573,904,247	573,904,247	Rochelle B. Lazarus[3]	71,601	162,665
James I. Cash, Jr.	76,480	134,808	James J. Mulva[3]	4,105	32,222
William M. Castell	280,273	306,731	Michael A. Neal	2,434,935	5,570,174
Ann M. Fudge	59,713	136,497	Sam Nunn	150,000	270,202
Susan Hockfield	0	22,752	Roger S. Penske	150,000	290,781
Jeffrey R. Immelt[3]	4,558,529	5,998,343	John G. Rice[3]	2,577,797	5,597,102
Andrea Jung[3]	61,519	126,831	Keith S. Sherin[3]	2,279,994	5,169,914
John Krenicki[3]	1,035,807	3,453,612	Robert J. Swieringa	3,754	78,123
Alan G. Lafley[3]	49,150	128,655	Douglas A. Warner III[3]	212,879	275,408
Robert W. Lane	14,500	72,387			
Common stock holdings of all directors and executive officers as a group (25) were 16,543,486.[5]					

[1] The company indicates: 'This column lists beneficial ownership of voting securities as calculated under SEC rules, including restricted stock held by certain of the named executives over which they have sole voting power but no investment power.' We also note that there are 10,672,871,990 voting shares in GE.

Sources:
http://www.sec.gov/Archives/edgar/data/40545/000119312510048722/ddef14a.htm
GE's corporate governance principles can be found at: www.ge.com/company/governance
http://www.sec.gov/Archives/edgar/data/40545/000119312510048722/ddef14a.htm.

The Board of Directors at Sainsbury plc

1. David Tyler, Chairman Appointed to the Board on 1 October 2009. David became Chairman on 1 November 2009. He is Non-Executive Chairman of Logica plc and a Non-Executive Director of Experian plc and Burberry Group plc, where he also chairs the Remuneration Committee. He was previously Finance Director of GUS plc (1997–2006) and has held senior financial and general management roles with Christie's International plc (1989–96), County NatWest Limited (1986–89) and Unilever PLC (1974–86). He was also Chairman of 3i Quoted Private Equity plc (2007–09) and a Non-Executive Director of Reckitt Benckiser Group plc over the same period.

2. Justin King, Chief Executive Appointed to the Board on 29 March 2004. Justin is also Chairman of the Operating Board. He has been a Non-Executive Director of Staples, Inc. since September 2007 and was appointed to the board of the London Organizing Committee of the Olympic Games and Paralympic Games in January 2009. He is a member of the CBI President's Committee, is a patron of Skillsmart Retail, the national sector skills council for retail, and is a Visiting Fellow of Oxford University's Centre for Corporate Reputation. Justin was formerly Director of Food at Marks and Spencer Group plc and prior to this held a number of senior positions at ASDA/WalMart and Häagen Dazs UK. He spent much of his early career with Mars Confectionery and Pepsi International.

3. John Rogers, Chief Financial Officer Appointed to the Board on 19 July 2010. John is also a member of the Board of Sainsbury's Bank plc. John joined Sainsbury's in March 2005 as Director of Corporate Finance and then became Director of Group Finance from March 2007 to June 2008. In June 2008 John was appointed to the Operating Board as Property Director. Prior to Sainsbury's, John was Group Finance Director for Hanover Acceptances, a diversified corporation with wholly owned subsidiaries in the food manufacturing, real estate and agri-business sectors.

4. Mike Coupe, Group Commercial Director Appointed Group Commercial Director on 19 July 2010, and is responsible for trading, marketing, IT and online. Mike has been a member of the Operating Board since October 2004 and an Executive Director since 1 August 2007. He joined Sainsbury's from Big Food Group where he was a Board Director of Big Food Group plc and Managing Director of Iceland Food Stores. He previously worked for both ASDA and Tesco, where he served in a variety of senior management roles. He is also a member of the supervisory board of GSI UK.

5. Darren Shapland, Group Development Director Appointed Group Development Director on 19 July 2010 and responsible for Convenience, Property, Sainsbury's Bank, Strategy and New Business Development. Before taking on this role, Darren was Chief Financial Officer from 1 August 2005. He is also Chairman of Sainsbury's Bank plc. Darren was appointed a Non-Executive Director of Ladbrokes plc in November 2009. He was formerly Group Finance Director of Carpetright plc (2002–05) and Finance Director of Superdrug Stores plc (2000–02). Between 1988 and 2000, Darren held a number of financial and operational management roles at Arcadia plc including Joint Managing Director, Arcadia Home Shopping; Finance Director of Arcadia brands; Finance Director, Top Shop/Top Man (Burton Group); and Director of Supply Chain Programme (Burton Group).

6. Val Gooding, Non-Executive Director Appointed to the Board on 11 January 2007. Val was formerly Chief Executive of BUPA (1998–2008), which she joined from British Airways. She is a Non-Executive Director of Standard Chartered Bank plc, the Lawn Tennis Association, the BBC and the Home Office. She is a Trustee of the British Museum and the Rose Theatre. She was formerly a Non-Executive Director of Compass Group plc and BAA plc.

7. Gary Hughes, Non-Executive Director Appointed to the Board on 1 January 2005. Gary is Chief Financial Officer of the Gala Coral Group, a Director of the Scottish Exhibition Centre

Limited and an advisor to Ibis Capital plc. Formerly he was Chief Executive of CMP Information Limited – a division of United Business Media plc (2006–08), Group Finance Director of Emap plc (2000–05), Group Finance Director of SMG plc (1996–2000), and Deputy Finance Director of Forte plc (1994–96). Prior to this Gary held a number of senior management positions with Guinness plc in the UK and in North America.

8. Bob Stack, Non-Executive Director Appointed to the Board on 1 January 2005. Bob was a Director of Cadbury plc until December 2008, having joined Cadbury Beverages in the USA in 1990, and was first appointed to the Board of Cadbury Schweppes plc in May 1996 as Group Human Resources Director. In March 2000 he was appointed Chief Human Resources Officer and took on responsibility for communication and external affairs in addition to HR. Bob is Trustee and Non-Executive Director of Earthwatch International and also a Non-Executive Director and Chairman of the Remuneration Committee of IMI plc.

9. John McAdam, Non-Executive Director Appointed to the Board on 1 September 2005. John is the Senior Independent Director. He is Chairman of Rentokil Initial plc and United Utilities plc. He is also a Non-Executive Director of Rolls-Royce Group plc and Sara Lee Corporation. John joined Unilever plc as a management trainee in 1974 and went on to hold a number of senior positions in Birds Eye Walls, Quest and Unichema, before the sale of the Specialty Chemical Businesses to ICI in 1997. He was Chief Executive of ICI plc, until its sale to Akzo Nobel, and was formerly a Non-Executive Director of Severn Trent plc (2000–05).

10. Anna Ford, Non-Executive Director Appointed to the Board on 2 May 2006. Anna retired from the BBC in 2006, after 32 years in News and Current Affairs. She is a Non- Executive Director of N Brown Group plc and has been a Trustee of the Royal Botanical Gardens in Kew, London; a Fellow of the Royal Geographical Society; a Trustee of Forum for the Future; Chancellor of Manchester University; and an Honorary Bencher of Middle Temple.

11. Mary Harris, Non-Executive Director Appointed to the Board on 1 August 2007. Mary is a member of the supervisory boards of TNT NV and Unibail-Rodamco S.E. She previously spent much of her career with McKinsey & Company, most recently as a partner, and her previous work experience included working for PepsiCo in Greece and the UK as a sales and marketing executive.

12. Matt Brittin, Non-Executive Director Appointed to the Board on 27 January 2011. Matt is Managing Director of Google in the UK & Ireland. Before joining Google at the start of 2007, Matt spent much of his career in media and marketing, with particular interests in strategy, commercial development and sales performance. This included Commercial and Digital leadership roles in UK media. He is also a Director of charities The Climate Group and The Media Trust.

13. Lord Sainsbury of Preston Candover KG, Life President Reproduced by kind permission of Sainsbury's Supermarkets Ltd.

Discussion questions

1 What are the primary ownership and control mechanisms in the United States and the United Kingdom?

2 How are the governance arrangements in the UK and USA similar? And where are they different?

3 Evaluate the importance of stock options and other forms of executive pay arrangements in the USA and the UK.

4 What are the most significant changes in corporate governance in the USA and the UK since 1990?

5 How effective are boards in the UK at delivering shareholder and stakeholder value?

Summary (learning points)

■ Corporate governance in the USA and the UK is based on the Anglo-Saxon system of governance.

■ It is based on the rule of law and the protection of property rights.

■ Firms and individuals are governed by Acts and securities regulations. In the UK the Cadbury Committee set the standard for governance arrangements that followed (e.g. Greenbury, Higgs). In the USA, the Securities Act 1933, Sarbanes–Oxley and currently Dodd–Frank are the primary governance instruments.

■ The board of directors in the USA and the UK are unitary in structure consisting of executive directors and independent outside directors.

■ The ownership of firms is typically based on many small investors each owning only a small fraction of the firm. This gives rise to the classic divorce between the ownership of firms and their control.

■ Executive compensation arrangement place emphasis on stock options and other forms of long-term pay in order to align the interests of owners and managers.

■ The goal of the firms is more shareholder centred in the USA compared with the UK. The Companies Act gives other stakeholders more sway in the UK, relative to the USA.

 References and further reading

Aggarwal, R., Erel, I., Ferreira, M. and Matos, P. (2011) Does governance travel around the world? Evidence from institutional investors, *Journal of Financial Economics*, **100** (1), 154–181.

American Bar Association (2009) *Report of the Task Force of the ABA Section of Business Law Corporate Governance Committee on Delineation of Governance Roles and Responsibilities*, http://apps.americanbar.org/buslaw/committees/CL260000pub/materials/20090801/delineation-final.pdf.

Barca, F. and Becht M. (eds) (2002) *The Control of Corporate Europe*, OUP: New York.

Conference Board, The (2010) *The 2010 Institutional Investment Report: Trends in Asset Allocation and Portfolio Composition*, http://www.conference-board.org.

DavisPolk (2010) Summary of the Dodd–Frank Wall Street Reform and Consumer Protection Act, Enacted into Law on July 21, 2010.

Ho, V.H. (2010) 'Enlightened Shareholder Value': Corporate Governance Beyond the Shareholder-Stakeholder Divide, *Journal of Corporation Law*, **36** (1), 59–112.

Larcker, D. (2008) *Models of Corporate Governance: Who's the Fairest of them All?* Rock Center for Corporate Governance, CG-11.

New York Stock Exchange (2010). *Report of the New York Stock Exchange Commission on Corporate Governance*, 23 September.

Romano, R. (2005) The Sarbanes–Oxley Act and the Making of Quack Corporate Governance, *Yale Law Journal*, **114** (7), 1521–1611.

World Bank (2011) *Market Capitalization of Listed Companies as a Percentage of GDP*, http://data.worldbank.org/indicator/CM.MKT.LCAP.GD.ZS/countries?display=default (retrieved: 30 May 2011).

Zhang I.X. (2007) Economic consequences of the Sarbanes–Oxley Act of 2002, *Journal of Accounting and Economics*, **44** (1–2), 74–115.

Chapter **12**

Corporate Ownership: Institutional investors and activist shareholders

Chapter contents

12.1   Introduction

This chapter describes the nature of corporate ownership in the US and the UK and some of the consequences of the observed patterns of ownership. Specifically, the chapter focuses on the role of institutional and activist shareholders. The pattern of corporate ownership in the United States and the United Kingdom is characterized by the presence of numerous shareholders, each of whom has a relatively small share stake in the firm. However, this does not mean that shareholders are necessarily powerless. There are important mechanisms through which they can exercise power and influence. First, if shareholders are unhappy with the way in which the firm is being run they can sell their shares. From the shareholders' perspective this represents an 'exit' from the firm (the Wall Street Walk: shareholders are voting with their feet). This can be costly for shareholders (especially if their selling decisions have a price effect in the asset market). Second, shareholders can exercise 'voice'. They can try to influence the board of directors directly regarding major issues facing the firm. The board has a fiduciary duty to make decisions on behalf of the firm's owners, so it is sensible for the board to heed these requests. If shareholders are unhappy with the board's decisions they can seek to replace the board of directors via proxy measures and voting resolutions. This could include having the directors of the board, and even the CEO, replaced. There is a balance to be struck, then, between the relative costs and benefits of exercising 'voice', and the costs and 'benefits "exit"' by selling shares. The activist – institutional distinction has been identified before (Larcker and Tayan, 2011).

In this chapter we discuss broadly the role of shareholders as investors and owners. We then discuss the nature of institutional ownership in Anglo-Saxon economies such as the US and the UK. Finally we discuss the role of activist investors.

12.2   Corporate ownership: shareholders

The firm's shareholders are individuals or institutions that legally own one or more shares of stock in a public or private corporation. Shareholders of US and UK companies typically own the firm's shares, but typically do not participate in the day to day running of the firm itself. Shareholders are granted rights and privileges associated with the class of stock that they own. The different classes of stock can include common (or ordinary shares) and preferred shares. The rights shareholders enjoy can include the following: the right to sell the shares; the right to vote on the individual directors nominated by the main board; the right to nominate their own directors; the right to propose shareholder resolutions; the right to dividend payments if declared by the board; the right to purchase new shares issued by the company, and the right to residual assets if the company is liquidated. Different classes of shares might have different voting rights associated with them.

The standard economic view of the firm is that the board of directors maximizes shareholder wealth. From this perspective the purpose of corporate governance is to align the interests of owners (shareholders) with management. For example, this can be achieved via the use of compensation contracts, the use of audit committees, and the promotion of independent directors on the main board. According to this view, the primary goal of governance is to create shareholder value. However, several commentators consider shareholders to be only one subset among many different stakeholders. Other stakeholders may include anyone who has a direct or indirect interest in the business. This includes the company's employees, the firm's suppliers and customers, the community, etc. This is because these actors, too, can create long-term value for the firm. However, there is an additional issue. Shareholders themselves are not a homogenous group. One shareholder can differ radically from another in terms of their preferences. The presence of heterogeneous shareholders has implications for the effective control of the firm (Larcker and Tayan, 2011).

There are important differences between shareholders. First, shareholders can differ in their objectives and preferences. Second, shareholders can differ in their scale and size of holding. This heterogeneity between shareholders, as we show below, accentuates a 'free rider' and coordination problem, which in turn can lead to a lack of effective control of the firm. Solving this is one goal of effective corporate governance arrangements. Third, shareholders can differ in their type. Some shareholders are individuals, others are banks or relationship investors, others might be financial institutions such insurance companies (Larcker and Tayan, 2011).

Shareholders can have different objectives. For example, there might be differences in core objectives, overall investment time horizon and degree of activism. Institutional investors pool their income and invest in securities. They include banks, insurance companies, retirement or pension funds, hedge funds, investment advisors and mutual funds. The objectives of these different entities might differ in their objectives and the duration of their long position in their investment. A pension fund might have an objective to pursue long-term growth of the stock at reasonably low risk in order to provide retirement income to employees who invest in retirement savings. A hedge fund, on the other hand, might want to invest only for the short-term in a high-risk or distressed securities, with the hope of an associated high short-term return. Another class of investors might want to engage only in socially responsible investment strategies. This investment space has been increasing recently. Socially responsible investors avoid investments in assets that violate pre-determined principles, such as investments that cause environmental damage, or unacceptable breaches of human rights, or exploit employees. In addition, such investors might avoid investments in particular industries such as tobacco, nuclear, or defence. In short, different shareholders can have different objectives from each other (Larcker and Tayan, 2011).

In addition, shareholders might express different preferences regarding their investment time horizon. Some shareholders might be more long-term oriented and others short-term focused. There is a significant debate centred on whether the Anglo-Saxon model encourages short-termism and a quest for short term returns. Hedge funds, for example, might be deliberately short-term oriented Indeed, one benefit claimed for stakeholder models such as those in Germany and continental Europe is that management can focus on long-term goals, and are not needlessly diverted to give excessive attention to short-term results.

Investor preferences might vary depending on whether they are active or passive. An example of a passive investor is one that invests in assets such as an index fund. These funds are configured to mimic the returns on some pre-specified index such as the S&P500. These investors simply collect their returns, for a given risk class, and are usually less concerned with corporate governance or management issues. Other investors are more active. Activist investors take the view that being engaged with management, by improving corporate governance arrangements, leads to better long-term performance of firms. Although activist investors bear costs of their activism (for example financial costs and the opportunity costs of their time) the belief is that the benefits from these activities are even greater.

The second major difference between investors is in the scale or size of investment holding. An individual shareholder may have only a few shares in a company. Independent of his or her preferences, then, the individual's ability to influence management is likely to be minimal. The small investor does not have to be an individual. Another example might be a small faith-based investment company, which similarly might find it difficult to impact key management decisions. In contrast, other investors hold very large equity positions in a firm. Their power and influence increases with the size of their holding. A prime example here is Black Rock Inc. Black is one of the world's most prominent investment firms, and headquartered in New York. It has been estimated total assets of $178 billion and has current market value of $36 billion. It operates throughout the US, Europe and Asia. However, it could be a family or other controlling interest.

There are two consequences associated with heterogeneity in shareholder preferences and size. First, size might lead to an underinvestment in monitoring of management. To see this suppose that investor A owns α percent of the firm (e.g. α might be 2%) and another investor B owns β percent of the firm (e.g. β might be 4% but can also be 1%). Suppose that shareholder A monitors management at a private cost of γ dollars. These costs include the financial as well as the opportunity costs of the investor's time. The (positive) change in firm value is ΔV, but shareholder A only receives benefits proportional to their ownership, that is $\alpha \Delta V$. Recall that the investor has borne all the costs (γ dollars)

of monitoring. As long as the change in value of the firm is greater than the cost (i.e. that $\alpha\Delta V > \gamma$) then monitoring is (at first glance) privately beneficial. The smaller the the investor's shareownership (i.e. lower α) the less likely is private monitoring. In the limit, as the fraction of total ownership gets very small (α tends to zero) monitoring of management becomes non-existent (Conyon and Lecch, 1994). The role of shareholder power has been considered by Cubbin and Leech (1983).

In addition, shareholder A has borne all the costs of monitoring and secured benefits proportional to his ownership. In addition, shareholder B has secured benefits $\beta\Delta V$ and has paid none of the costs. B, in this case, free rides on A. It might have been better for shareholder A to act like investor B. That is A should not have not have engaged in monitoring and hoped that some other investor (e.g. B) does engage in costly monitoring and improves the performance of the firm (because $(\alpha\Delta V - \gamma) < \alpha\Delta V$). The rational strategy, therefore, might be to hope that other investors monitor management and then free ride on their efforts. But if this is optimal for one investor, it is optimal for all and in the end there is not enough monitoring (Conyon and Leech, 1994; Cubbin and Leech, 1983). One solution for this is to promote larger ownership stakes (i.e. α and β relatively big) so that each investor has sufficient skin in the game to make monitoring pay off. Alternatively, investors A and B could coordinate their activities to achieve this (because α plus β is better than α or β alone). However, this leads to a second problem: one of coordination. Suppose A and B do not have identical preferences. Investor A could be a hedge fund and investor B could be pension fund. With different preferences the shareholders might not be able to agree on the optimal strategy to pursue. Another problem is that of coordination technology. There may be rules prohibiting coordination between shareholders, or binding technologically constraints meaning they cannot effectively coordinate. Acting in concert might therefore be quite difficult.

In summary, when discussing shareholders there is a tendency to think of there being only one 'type' of shareholder. Shareholders might actually come in different types, with different preferences, and in different sizes (Larcker and Tayan, 2011). These differences have consequences for the ability of shareholders to act in concert, or alone.

12.3　Institutional ownership

Since Berle and Means (1932) the common understanding of corporate ownership is that there are numerous shareholders each with a relatively small percentage holding. Historically, individuals and households were the main holder of equity shares, rather than institutions such as pension funds. However, the empirical evidence demonstrates that institutions have become very important. Investors with a significant share stake in the firm are termed blockholders (Larcker and Tayan, 2011). Blockholders are usually institutions rather than individuals. There is a distinction between blockholders who are external to the firm, rather than internal to the firm such as an officer or director such as the CEO.

What does the pattern of US ownership look like? Data from the Conference Board shows significant growth in institutional share ownership in the US over a long period of time (The Conference Board, 2010). In 1950 institutions accounted for approximately 6.1% of total outstanding equity. In 1970 this figure had increased to 19.4%, by 1980 to 20.4%. During the 1990s and early 2000s the Conference Board estimates that institutions accounted for about 50% of total outstanding equity. The latest Conference Board study illustrates that institutional ownership appears to have plateaued at about this level. In 2009 institutional holdings were about 51% of total equity (The Conference Board, 2010). Aggarwal et al (2011) confirm these findings. In the US they show that institutional holdings in a firm's stock as a percentage of its market capitalization was 40.3% in 2003, rising to approximately 57.8% in 2007. The average yearly change in institutional ownership during the data period was about 4.4%. The evidence is consistent with a marked shift away from individual shareholding towards institutional holdings in the United States.

The importance of institutional blockholders is also confirmed in other data sets. Larcker and Tayan (2011) use data from the Thomson Reuters Institutional (13f) Holdings data set (s34). Firms in the United States publicly ownership positions. They show that 90% of publicly listed firms have an institutional shareholder with at least a 1% share stake in the firm. 79% of firms have at least a 3% share stake and 68% have at least a 5 percent position.[1]

In terms of exercising control over the firm, block shareholders can have considerable influence. Influence can be approximated by the degree of ownership concentration in the public firm or the likelihood of winning contested vote (Cubbin and Lecech, 1983). Share ownership of the largest few blockholders can be relative large. can be significant If so, then coordination between blockholders is feasible then effective control of the firm might well be possible. Such share ownership positions might influence context elections for directors, or the outcome of a takeover battle, or even lead to board representation (Larcker and Tayan, 2011).

Table 12.1 shows the largest shareowners for Apple Inc at the end of 2009, based on the Thomson Reuters data. The largest blockholder is Fidelity management Research, with over 45 million shares. This represents approximately 4.99% of the company's outstanding shares. The next largest owner is State Street Corporation and the next Vanguard Group. The combined ownership share of the five largest blockholders is about 16.87% of total shares outstanding.

The dominant form of corporate ownership in the United States, then, is institutional investment. Institutional investors (or for convenience 'institutions') are organizations which invest large amounts of money on behalf of others in order to provide financial services to them. They include pension funds, insurance companies, mutual funds and other investment companies. Sometimes banks are also regarded as institutional investors, but later we single out banks as a distinct group because they have a special role to play in corporate governance (see chapter 13 on bank governance). We will also not include hedge funds, venture capital or private equity funds, because they are less bound to diversify risk. Neither will we include private foundations and endowments, companies or governments because these entities invest on their own behalf rather than to provide financial services (pension, insurance) to the public. These entities have governance issues of their own.

Institutional investors are dominant corporate owners, especially in market based economies such as the US or UK. This does not mean that they are the only important ownership form in those economies. For example, family businesses continue to play a very important role in the US economy, even in the very largest listed companies (Anderson and Reeb, 2004). Institutional investors are also important in economies like Germany and Japan. Institutional investors are ubiquitous, and they are driving the corporate governance agenda almost everywhere. In many countries around the world their influence is counterbalanced by other large blockholders like families, governments or bank/based business groups. Institutional investors are very important in the US or UK. In a typical listed firm, particularly in a large one, the largest owner will be an institutional investor such as Fidelity or Prudential holding 3–5% of the stock (more in the UK, less in the US). This small share is no accident since institutions investing other people's money are bound both legally and morally to invest cautiously and to diversify risk.

Institutional investors act as intermediaries for individuals who save for retirement (usually greater than 65 years of age), to insure against accidents or simply to get a return on their investment. The question is: why do they need an intermediary (Black, 1992a)? Why not invest directly in stocks and bonds. Some tentative answers are that institutional investors can do this more effectively than individuals because they possess financial competencies, because they can pool risks and because they can save transaction costs. In addition many pension schemes are mandatory or quasi/mandatory as part of government or union schemes that force individuals to invest collectively. Moreover, tax policies routinely subsidize collective saving schemes.

The rationale for financial competence is surprisingly not as strong as might be expected. It is known that few institutional investors, if any at all, can outperform the simple index strategy of holding the market portfolio. Moreover it does not take many securities in a portfolio to come very close to market returns. In addition, changes in technology have lowered the cost of day trading, and

---

[1] Using this data set for the year 2009 (December quarter reporting period) we also calculated that approximately 80% of firms had at least one blockholder with a 1% stake. In addition, approximately 60% of firms had at least one blockholder with a 5% stake.

Table 12.1 Apple Inc. Ownership: Largest institutions, 2009

Institution	Shares	Ownership %
Fidelity Management & Research	45173344	4.99
State Str Corporation	31980670	3.53
Vanguard Group, Inc.	31216671	3.45
T. Rowe Price Associates, INC.	24545605	2.71
Janus Capital Management LLC	19804140	2.19
Amvescap PLC London	17008269	1.88
AXA Financial, INC.	15242132	1.68
Capital World Investors	13428200	1.48
Northern Trust Corp	12498780	1.38
Wellington Management Co, LLP	12465540	1.38
Mellon Bank NA	11724791	1.30
Capital Research Gbl Investors	11015000	1.22
MSDW & Company	9785440	1.08
Jennison Associates LLC	9085761	1.00
Marsico Capital MGMT, LLC	8708293	0.96
College Retire Equities	8673979	0.96
J.P Morgan Chase & Co.	8565104	0.95
Bank of America Corporation	6423860	0.71
Goldman Sachs & Company	6334312	0.70
Riversource Investments, LLC	6155792	0.68
UBS GBL Asset MGMT (Americas) IN	5768985	0.64

Source: *Thomson Reuters Institutional Holdings (13f). December 2009.*

there is a rising level of education among many in regards to finance. This means that individuals can trade securities easily and inexpensively. Moreover institutions are not free, they typically charge 1–2% of assets under management. Nevertheless the combination of professionalism, economies of scale and government nudging has been strong enough to channel an ever increasing share of total savings into institutions during the past many decades. It is no doubt an added benefit that collective savings schemes such as institutional investment act under an implicit government guarantee. If you lose your individual savings, you have a problem, but if your pension fund loses your savings, the government has a problem! Another example of the consequences of too big to fail!

Given that institutional investors exist the most important question is how they influence corporate governance. Since the inception of corporate governance with the Cadbury and Hampel reports in the UK, it has been fashionable to assign to them a special role as guardians of shareholder interests (Tricker, 1998, Baums and Hopt, 1992). One reason is that they are large investors. However, they typically hold only minority positions which are somewhat larger than those of private investors, but insufficient to give them direct control (i.e. in excess of 50%). In the US and UK the rise of institutions may have meant an increase in ownership concentration (as noted earlier) but probably the reverse in Europe and the rest of the world, where they take over from families, business groups, governments and other very large shareholders.

A better reason to expect institutions to influence corporate governance is their overall size and general interests in the stock market which enables them to compare companies and if necessary sanction bad behaviour by excluding them from their portfolio. Moreover, their combined size of their shareholdings in individual firms is often sufficient to give them collective control when ownership is dispersed. This presupposes that the institutions can overcome the important free rider problems that potentially exist between them, which is not always evident. In addition, it is also possible that competition between investors can play a positive role by keeping the exploitation of the private benefits of control in check. Black (1992a) argues that institutional investors as well as watching managers can also monitor each other. Finally, institutional investors might value pure shareholder value creation more than other large shareholders like families, governments or business groups, which often have other reasons to own shares (Thomsen and Pedersen, 2000).

Empirical studies

Many studies have examined the determinants and consequences of institutional investors (Larcker and Tayan, 2011). Franks, Mayer and Rossi (2009) investigated the evolution of ownership and regulation in the United Kingdom from 1900 to 2000. The study is significant because it is a long-run analysis of the evolution of the ownership of firms. A standard hypothesis in the finance literature is that that dispersed ownership is facilitated by investor protection. This idea is often marshalled as evidence as to why civil law countries such as those in Germany have large concentrated share stakes instead of liquid diversified ownership patterns. Investor protection provided under common law systems reduces risks and promotes widely held share ownership. However, Franks et al (2008) find that common law did not promote investor protection in the UK, and investor protection was actually quite weak until the 1920s and was strong only since the 1950s. However, ownership had become dispersed at this time in spite of weak investor protection. They argue that ownership dispersion was promoted instead on the basis of informal mechanisms of trust rather than formal mechanisms of regulation. Stockholders might not have had recourse in the courts for disputes, but they did have influence in their communities where the firms were located. In this earlier stage of capitalist development, trust relations were sufficient to promote ownership dispersion.

Studies have investigated the relation between ownership structure and company performance. Evidence is mixed on the effects that institutions have, and it continues to be an important area of research. Gompers and Metrick (2001) investigated institutional investors' demand for stock characteristics and the consequent effect on the firms' stock prices and returns. Empirically, they found that large institutional investors nearly doubled their share of the stock market from 1980 to 1996. This attests to the earlier evidence on the contemporary importance of institutional investors. The authors found that the increase in demand for the stock of large companies was a substitute for the stock of small companies: 'The compositional shift can, by itself, account for a nearly 50 percent increase in the price of large-company stock relative to small-company stock and can explain part of the disappearance of the historical small-company stock premium.' Gompers and Metrick (2011, p. 229)

McConnell and Servaes (1990) investigated the relation between Tobin's Q (the market value of a firm to its replacement costs) and the structure of equity ownership for a sample of 1,173 firms for 1976 and 1,093 firms for 1986. Importantly they found a significant positive association between Tobin's Q and the fraction of shares owned by institutional investors. This is consistent with the view that firm value is a function of the structure of the firm's equity ownership. In addition, they found a concave relation between measured Q and the fraction of common stock owned by corporate insiders.

Bushee (1998) focused on the relation between institutional investors and research and development investment spending as a measure of firm performance. The economic, finance, and accounting literature has debated whether institutional investors promote short-termism by cutting R&D to boost earnings. Bushee (1998, p305) found that: "that managers are less likely to cut R&D

to reverse an earnings decline when institutional ownership is high, implying that institutions are sophisticated investors who typically serve a monitoring role in reducing pressures for myopic behaviour'. Although the author documents some caveats, in general he finds that institutional investors impede myopic managerial behaviour. In another study Bushee, Carter and Gerakos (2009) study the association between institutional investors and corporate governance mechanisms. Overall, they find little evidence of an association between total institutional ownership and governance mechanisms. However, they do find that: 'that firms with a high level of ownership by institutions sensitive to shareholder rights exhibit significant future improvements in shareholder rights, consistent with shareholder activism.'

Otherstudies including Steiner (1996), Han & Suuk (1998), Thomsen and Pedersen (2000) and Woidtke (2001) have found a positive impact of (private) institutional investor ownership on firm value. (Pedersen and Thomsen, 2003). However Woidte (2001) makes the important distinction between private and political institutions (e.g. government pension funds) and shows that the political institutions tend to underperform. Rose (2005) found the same for Danish political pension funds although it is unclear whether institutional investors cause lower market values or whether they (prudently) prefer to invest in cheap companies. However, window-dressing, selling off shares that have sharply declined in value at year-end (Lakonishok et al., 1991), implies an artificial positive association between institutional investment and firm value. Early research by Black (1992b) surveyed evidence on whether large outside shareholders undertake valuable monitoring. His survey concluded that the direct evidence on institutional oversight was limited and that, in fact, institutions at that time did little monitoring (Black, 1992b p. 897).

The pattern and type of ownership can affect other dimensions of corporate decision making. Studies have shown that the pattern of ownership can affect CEO pay. In a classic study, Hartzell, and Starks (2003) find that companies with higher levels of institutional ownership have lower levels of CEO compensation but in contrast tend to use more performance-based compensation contracts. The results confirm a monitoring role for institutional shareholders in mitigating agency costs. Shin and Seo (2011) also show that CEO pay is determined institutional investor type. They argue that institutional investors' incentives and capabilities to monitor CEO pay are determined by the fiduciary responsibilities, conflicts of interest, and information asymmetry that institutional investors face. Using US data from 1998 to 2002 they find that CEO pay and incentives are affected public pension fund ownership more negatively (and oppositely) than mutual fund ownership.

A complicating factor is that institutions may sometime exert their influence by selling, and this may in fact lead to changes in company behaviour. For example Parrone et al. find that institutional investment tends to drop prior to CEO dismissals. Although this may have the desired effect, it will not be in the best interest of those institutions which do not experience the value increase supposedly following governance change. In fact, investors with a passive buy and hold strategy may be better off because the investor free-rides on the exit decisions of the other investors.

Risk and portfolio allocation

Institutions treasure liquidity and arms lengths relationships to the companies that they invest in. This is mostly because diversification allows them to eliminate or at least reduce firm specific risk by putting their eggs in many baskets. However, risk diversification can be achieved with a relatively limited number of stocks (Elton and Gruber, 1977). If risk is measured by the standard deviation of portfolio return, something close to full diversification is achieved with about 20–30 stocks as illustrated in Figure 12.1.

Most institutions hold many more stocks than this, which is a problem for corporate governance since the portfolio such managers very quickly lose track of what is going on within the individual firms. This prevents them from acting effectively as active owners. Managers may delegate responsibility to lower level employees or outsource it to specialized portfolio managers. But delegation creates a new set of agency problems. Specialized managers tend to be optimistic with regard to the segment that they cover. And outsourcing is not cheap. It often costs 1–2% of assets under management.

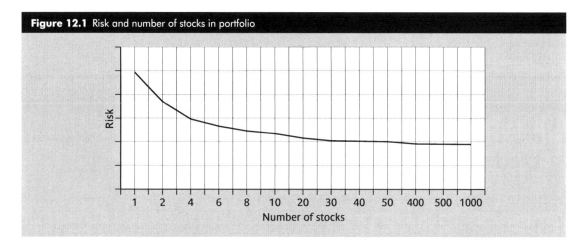

Figure 12.1 Risk and number of stocks in portfolio

Many institutions index their portfolio. Based on an overall decision of how much to invest in a given stock market, they use the market weights as a guide for how much to invest in a given company. If a share accounts for 1% of the total value (market capitalization) of the stock market, they invest 1% of their funds in it. They may be underweighted (hold less than the market weight) or overweighted (hold more than the market weight) in a given company, but they will typically not stray much from the market portfolio. In some cases the institution will set limits for how much portfolio managers can deviate from the market portfolio (how large the 'tracking error' can be) in order to prevent them from taking excessive risks.

Indexing is a solution to many of the issues raised here. It is a simple way to decide how to invest. Simple means cheap: you do not need a large staff to implement it. It also means objective in the sense that many internal and external disagreements can be avoided by simply mimicking the market. It is a risk management tool that can be used to keep the idiosyncrasies (optimism or pessimism) of fund managers in check. It is theoretically well founded in modern finance, where many studies have shown that it is difficult and perhaps impossible to beat the market, If market prices follow a random walk it is absurd for portfolio managers to have opinions about which companies to invest in.

However, indexing also creates problems, particularly for corporate governance. Since it tends to lead to very diversified portfolios, it is impossible for institutions to exercise active ownership in all the companies that they invest in. It is difficult enough to understand what is going on in one company, so who can keep track of 100? Even if it was possible, it would probably not be economically rational to do so because of free rider problems: other investors (who hold the vast majority of the shares) get most of the benefit, but do not share in the costs. As a result there is an undersupply of company information in the investment community. This contributes to asymmetric information and agency problems.

Another problem is that indexing may be a suboptimal investment strategy in the medium and long term. While stock markets are sufficiently chaotic to very nearly follow a random walk in the short term they may be subject to mean reversion in the medium and long term. Thus, stock prices that are very high relative to earnings might tend to fall in the long term. Conversely cheap stocks will tend to appreciate which forms the rationale for value investment (buy low, sell high). A curious consequence of indexing is that a stock that increases excessively also becomes more significant in terms of market weight and therefore institutions are obligated to buy more of them, which may fuel further price increases. Thus there is a real chance that indexing can actually contribute to stock market bubbles.

Even apart from portfolio concerns there are sound reasons why institutions would like to diversify. Liquidity is one. Small shareholdings in large firms can be easily divested without depressing the stock price. This is one reason why many institutions prefer to invest in large blue chip companies (Del Guercio, 1996, Gillan and Starks, 2003 pp. 8–9). In contrast large shareholdings in small firms can be very difficult and costly to get rid of. Very often the institutions will have to accept a large discount on the current stock price if they want to sell, and potential buyers may have to make the same offer to all other shareholders as well because of the so-called mandatory bid rule.

Another reason is insider trading. Large owners will often obtain company information which makes it illegal for them to trade their shares, and therefore they lose their flexibility. Even if they have no inside information they may be suspected of having it with the implied legal risks. Finally, small shares do not attract attention. In case of a scandal in the company, investors will not be held accountable.

12.4 Investor activism

For a large part of recent corporate history, institutional investors have been relatively passive (Black 1992b). Increasingly, investors are becoming more active. Their level of engagement may range from the very limited to just short of managing the company. For example, the types of things that investors may actively engage in include: reading the annual report; analyzing publicly available information; attending shareholder meetings, voting; asking questions at shareholder meeting; speaking at shareholder meeting; informal meeting with managers; voicing critical opinions; rallying other shareholders; campaigning against the management when the shareholders disagree with management; nominating their own slate of directors; buying or selling blocks of shares; and orchestrating ownership change; and taking seats on the main board of directors.

Shareholder activists might have many objectives, but ultimately they try and use 'voice' rather than 'exit' as a mechanism to change major corporate policies. Examples of such activism include pension funds that manage assets on behalf of current and future older workers; institutional investors who are committed to promoting social policies (e.g. the environment); hedge funds who seek higher risk and returns; and individuals who try to lobby firms in relation to their own concerns.

How can an activist shareholder influence corporate decisions? One mechanism is for the shareholder to table resolutions for voting at the company's Annual General Meeting (AGM). A shareholder proposal is a recommendation or requirement that the company and/or its board of directors take action that the shareholder intends to present at a meeting of the company's shareholders. In the US shareholder proposals are governed by Rule 14a–8. Only registered security holders can make proposals. In addition, to be eligible to submit a proposal the shareholder must have continuously held at least $2000 market value of shares or 1% of the company's securities for at least one year by the date of the proposal. Proposals are limited to five hundred words. The company can exclude the shareholder proposal for several reasons. If the proposal violates state or federal law it can be excluded. For example, if the proposal was implemented it would lead the company to violate a state, federal or foreign law to which it is subject. The company can exclude the proposal if it is based on special interest or a personal grievance. For example, proposals that seek to benefit one shareholder at the expense of another body of shareholders can be excluded from consideration.

In the UK the board generally tables all resolutions at an AGM although shareholders can table their own resolutions but this requires a minimum 5% share ownership or the co-ordination of 100 shareholders. Section 338 of the Companies Act 2006 governs the process (see Subsection 3) and as such, shareholder requisitioned resolutions are rare. The outcome of any shareholder resolution can be formalized in several ways. For many years, non-contentious resolutions have been passed on a simple 'show of hands' basis, where each member (or proxy thereof) present at the AGM has one vote regardless of the size of their shareholding. An Ordinary resolution requires a simple majority (i.e. greater than 50%) of hands voting for the resolution to be passed; a Special resolution requires 75% in favor to be passed. Other than asking questions of directors from the floor, this show of hands vote provides the most tangible way for the shareholders who have attended the AGM to provide a collective expression of their concerns and opinions. However, there is no guarantee such a vote will take place and indeed this largely symbolic mechanism has in recent years begun to disappear, and instead firms have a vote on all resolutions. Typically shareholders can register their proxy vote

in advance, either by post, or by email (if held in a nominee account) and increasing numbers of companies now provide the provision for shareholders to vote via a website.

What type of proposals do shareholders pursue? Gillan and Starks (2007) show that shareholder proposals traditionally focus on issues that dilute shareholder rights and/or power, or issues that lead to an entrenched management. For example, shareholder proposals include repealing classified or staggered boards. Staggered boards exist when only a set fraction of the board (normally a third) is electable each year. Removing an entire board would therefore require a sustained (three-year) campaign. Other shareholder proposals include eliminating poison pills. Poison pills (or shareholder rights plans) make it more difficult for another firm to acquire the target company. In consequence, this insulates management from market pressures. More recently, boards of directors and executive compensation issues have become more pronounced. In particular, shareholder proposals have focused on promoting an independent director to be the chair of the board of directors, or alternatively separating the posts of CEO and chairperson. In addition, alleged excessive compensation has emerged as a touch stone issue. The form that the 'excess' takes is variable. It can be too generous payments in the event that the CEO leaves the firm (so-called 'golden parachutes'), to insufficient long-term incentives and to much guaranteed pay, to simply too high pay relative to comparable peer CEOs. Because of the concern over CEO pay, several countries have now directly sponsored 'say on pay' legislation that gives shareholders rights to vote specifically on executive pay matters. In the UK, this change came about in 2002 with the Directors Remuneration Report legislation. This gave shareholders a vote on the whole compensation report (not the specifics of pay). However, the outcome of the vote is non-binding on management, but a 'no-vote' would be fairly damaging to the company and hard to ignore. In the US the Dodd-Frank Act (2010) ushered in an era of 'say on pay'. Shareholders can vote on pay, but as in the UK the outcome of the vote is non-binding on management.

How successful have shareholders been in voting? ISS (Institutional Shareholder Services) 2010 post-season provides detailed data on voting at issuing firms.[2] In terms of newly enacted executive compensation voting they found that three companies-Motorola, Occidental Petroleum, and KeyCorp-failed to receive majority approval from investors during management-sponsored advisory votes on executive compensation. However, these appeared to be outliers. The average support for corporate pay practices was 89.6 percent, which was up from 87.4 percent in 2009. On key issues related to the board of directors there was about 58% average support for majority voting in director elections, 59% average support for the repeal of classified boards and 73% average support for the repeal of supermajority voting. Other measures were less successful. For example, there was only 28% average support for having an independent chair. In terms of compensation matters, there was also less support. There was about 45% average support for an advisory vote on executive pay and about 23.5% average support for a retention period for executive stock options. Despite these outcomes voting can be effective. It is not so much whether the vote is won or lost, but even a lost vote can be a signal for change.

Empirical studies

In general, does shareholder activism lead to better performance of firms? This is an on-going research question. The empirical evidence is mixed. There is an important empirical evidence to suggest that that activism by institutional shareholders is not positively correlated to organizational performance (Black (1998); Gillan and Starks (1998); and Karpoff (2001)). A study by Smith (1996) examined the determinants and consequences of shareholder activism for 51 firms targeted by CalPERS. The author found that firm level of institutional holdings predicted the probability of being targeted by CalPERS, and that about three-quarters of the proposals made by CalPERS were adopted. Firm value increased for firms that adopted CalPERS recommendations and decreased for firms that did not. However, although CalPERS affected firm behavior the author found no statistically significant change in operating performance. There are several reasons why institutional activism does not lead to better

---

[2] http://www.issgovernance.com/docs/2010USPostSeasonReport (accessed June 2011).

firm performance. Activist investors might lack the necessary skills or information. They might not monitor sufficient because of free-riding problems discussed earlier. There may be impediments to effective coordination among investors, or different objectives between investors creating conflict between them. There are other reasons why these earlier studies do not find robust positive associations between activism and performance. For example, the activism decision itself might be endogenous. Not only does activism theoretically predict performance, but firm performance would drive the degree of activist engagement. Disentangling such effects is difficult. In addition, there might be anticipation effects. The threat of activism can alter managerial behavior without actual activism occurring. Firm performance might increase via this indirect mechanism which is difficult to observe empirically.

Recently, however, Becht, Franks, Mayer and Rossi (2010) studied the private engagements by an activist fund using data on about 30 UK companies. The data are from Hermes, the fund manager owned by the British Telecom Pension Scheme, on engagements with management in companies targeted by its UK Focus Fund. A unique aspect of the research is that shareholder activism can be studied through predominantly *private* interventions that would be unobservable in studies that rely purely on public information. The set of governance objectives that the activist shareholder pursued ranged from initiating board changes to financial policies standards to improving shareholder relations. In terms of board changes thesactivist objectives included changing the CEO, chairman, non-executive directors and adding independent elements to the board. The authors found that the fund's objectives are often met. In addition, the Hermes activist fund substantially outperformed other benchmarks. Overall, the study provides empirical evidence that activism improves firm performance.

Other evidence on shareholder monitoring comes from hedge fund studies. Brav et al (2008) study hedge fund activism and firm performance using United States data from 2001 to 2006. They find that hedge monitor by engaging with firms on strategic, operational, and financial isssues. In two thirs of cases they are successful in their objectives. The authors study finds a 7% abnormal return at the time of hedge fund announcement. They find evidence that firm performance increases along a number of dimensions. They show that target firms increase operating performance and payouts. In addition, they find that the CEO turnover rate is higher. Overall, the data show important benefits from shareholder activism. Klein and Zur (2009) also examined hedge fund activism. Specifically, they examined recent confrontational activism campaigns by hedge funds and other private investors. They find positive performance effects and that hedge funds are able to achieve their objectives. Specifically, they find a positive market reaction for the target firm around the initial Schedule 13D filing date, as well as over the following year. Some of the hedge funds objectives include changing board composition, the target firms should pursue alternative strategies, and an issue related to a merger. They find activists frequently gain board representation through real or threatened proxy solicitations. As in Brave et al (2008) this study shows the benefits from shareholder monitoring.

Determinants of the activism decision

How do investors decide whether or not to be activists? Like many other issues in corporate governance, the decision to be a shareholder activist or not is endogenous and driven by a number of considerations. Theoretically (following the analysis in Poulsen, Strand and Thomsen 2010), investors will decide how active to be depending on the costs and benefits of activism (Pozen 1994). Poulsen-Strand-Thomsen conjectured that investors either give up and sell their shares or increase their level of engagement if previous attempts have failed. Activism is a 'voice' activity, and the costs and benefits will be weighed against exit (doing the 'Wall Street Walk' by selling the shares) or loyalty (continuing as a passive shareholder) (Hirschman, 1971). The easiest (and least costly) approach will typically be a dialogue with the incumbent management, which may be persuaded to take into consideration the views of the shareholder in informal meetings (Gillan and Starks, 2000). If this approach does not work, the institution may give up (exit or loyalty) or become more active at increasing costs by informally contracting other shareholders. This will involve more meetings and some risk of reprisals by management or being accused of cornering the market. Subsequently

– having failed to reach a settlement informally behind the scene – they may again give up or engage in overt activism, i.e. making proposals or voicing dissent at the annual meeting or perhaps even campaign against the incumbent management in the media at still higher costs.

Ryan and Schenider (2002) propose that some funds are more likely to be active, particularly those which are large, have a long time horizon, are partly politically motivated, do not (like banks or insurance companies) have a client relationship with potential targets, are not subject to legal restraints and outsource to portfolio managers. In an empirical study Rubach and Sebora (2009) find that size and time horizon and in/house rather than outsourced fund management.

We conjecture that the decision to become active and the level of activism will depend on the perceived costs and benefits of activism compared to alternative strategies (exit, loyalty). The expected costs include opportunity costs of share ownership, analysis costs, management time, possible reprisals by the incumbent management, legal uncertainty (possible liability for insider trading, cornering the market etc.), number of shareholders to be contracted, their identity and association with the company, the level of engagement intended etc. Fixed costs include information costs of monitoring and evaluating strategic policies, costs incurred in the supervision of management to enforce accountability to shareholders, and different costs of shareholder relations (e.g. communication and dissemination of information about the firm among members of the coalition). Variable costs include costs of shareholder relations. They depend on the participating institutions' ability to collude and are likely to depend on sociological as well as organizational factors.

The expected benefits will depend on the probability of successful intervention, the institution's investment and expected holding period, the volatility of the stock and general economic uncertainty. Activism may be wasted if the company does not change course, even though voicing opinions may have both long and short run effects. The institution will benefit the more she has invested and the longer she expects to keep her stock. Even if activism is successful in changing the direction of the company general stock price fluctuations and macroeconomic shocks may lead to economic losses.

In firms with dispersed ownership, firms where minority institutions wish to challenge a larger shareholder or firms where several larger shareholders compete for power, activism also becomes a matter of collecting support and forming coalitions. If a controlling coalition of shareholders cannot be formed without the largest shareholder then activism in the above sense is useless without the consent of this shareholder. To a large extent, the futility of shareholder activism is therefore determined by the ownership structure in place at the time of the shareholder meeting.

Who governs the institutions? Implicitly, the benefit of investors monitoring firms is premised on the notion of zero agency costs at the institutions themselves. Given the increasing importance of institutional investors, it is worth asking how they themselves are governed. The answer is: usually not very well (Stewart and Yermo, 2009). Many are government, quasi-government or union-based organizations that are very difficult to hold accountable for performance. It may be very costly

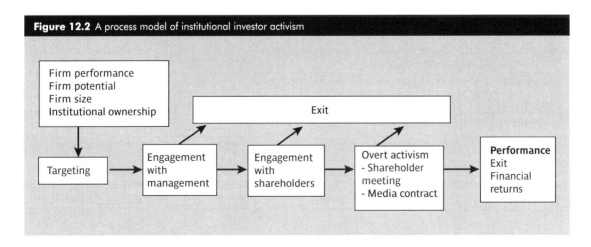

Figure 12.2 A process model of institutional investor activism

or impossible for pension fund members to move which gives many of them a monopoly status. The boards may not be particularly competent (Stewart and Yermo, 2009) and are often chosen for political reasons. It may therefore not be particularly surprising that the political pension funds have been found to underperform (Woidtke, 2002). The same funds have been found to be most activist and many of them leader in the corporate governance debate.

12.5   Discussion

This chapter has provided more detail on corporate ownership structures. Specifically, we have focused on institutional investors, and on activist investors. Institutions are blockholders such as pension funds. They may be simply tracking funds. Activist investors, in contrast, take positions on issues and try and change these issues by influencing company management.

We have discussed the broad patterns in the data and also the empirical evidence.

Minicase

CalPERS

As an organization, California Public Employees' Retirement System (CalPERS) provides retirement and health benefits to more than 1.6 million public employees, retirees, and their families and more than 3,000 employers. CalPERS maintains a 'focus list' of what it considers to be underperforming companies in corporate America. It then uses this list as starting point to understand how shareholder activism can add value by changing corporate governance practices.

CalPERS takes the view that corporate governance leads to better investment performance. In consequence, they actively seek changes in governance practices to enhance value. They use numerous strategies, some of which are aimed at specifically turning around poorly performing companies. CalPERS used to maintain a list of poorly structured firms. However, in November 2010, CalPERS adopted a new strategy. The new approach is to engage through private contacts and proxy actions rather than by posting a public 'name-and-shame'. CalPERS claim that: 'Key findings of a new 10-year Wilshire Consulting study of CalPERS corporate engagements within the Focus List program, includes public and private contacts, demonstrated outperformance against the sector and benchmark in both three and five year time periods by over 15% and 9%, respectively.' (CalPERS, Corporate Governance, 2010, page 3).

In addition, CalPERS is addressing issues of diversity in the boardroom. As is well know the percentage of women in boardroom leadership roles in the United States is lamentably low. CalPERS is developing ways to identify talent for nomination to corporate boards. This initiative is called: the Diverse Director Data-Source (3D). The goal is to challenge 'group think' that plagues boardrooms, and to bring 'fresh perspectives, skills and experience which boards need to ensure effective risk management and sustained value creation.' These kinds of activist approaches, CalPERS hopes, will lead to increased value added.

Source; Facts at A Glance: Corporate Governance. http://www.calpers.ca.gov/index.jsp?bc=/about/press/news/invest-corp/home.xml

Discussion questions

1 What is the goal of a pension fund like CalPERS? What should it be?
2 Do you think that its active corporate governance policy can make a difference? What are the arguments for and against?
3 Would it be better to sell the shares of badly governed firms?
4 What corporate governance mechanisms does CalPERS use?

References and further reading

Aggarwal, R., Erel, I., Ferreira, M. and Matos, P. (2011) Does governance travel around the world? Evidence from institutional investors, *Journal of Financial Economics*, **100** (1), 154–181.

Baums, T., Buxbaum T. and Hopt, K. J. (Eds) (1994) *Institutional investors and corporate governance*, De Gruyter: Berlin.

Bebchuk, L.A. and Fried, J.M. (2003) Executive Compensation as an Agency Problem, *Journal of Economic Perspectives*, **17** (3), 71–92

Becht, M., Franks, J., Mayer, C. and Rossi, S. (2010) Returns to Shareholder Activism: Evidence from a Clinical Study of the Hermes UK Focus Fund, *Review of Financial Studies* **23** (3), 3093–3129

Black, B.S. (1998) Shareholder Activism and Corporate Governance in the U.S. in Newman, P. (ed.) *The New Palgrave Dictionary of Economics and the Law*. Palgrave Macmillan: London and Basingstoke.

Black, B.S. (1992a) Agents Watching Agents: The Promise of Institutional Investor Voice, *UCLA Law Review* **39** (4), 811–893.

Black, B.S. (1992b) The Value of Institutional Investor Monitoring: The Empirical Evidence *UCLA Law Review* **39** (4), 895–939.

Brav, A., Jiang, W., Partnov, F. and Thomas, R. (2008) Hedge Fund Activism, Corporate Governance, and Firm Performance, *The Journal of Finance*, **63**: 1729–1775.

Bushee, B.J. (1998) The influence of institutional investors in myopic R&D investment behavior, *Accounting Review*, **73** (3), 305–333.

Bushee, B.J., Carter, M.E. and Gerakos, J.J. (2009) Institutional Investor Preferences for Corporate Governance Mechanisms Available at SSRN: http://ssrn.com/abstract=1070168

Conyon, M.J. and Leech, D. (1994) Top Pay, Company Performance and Corporate Governance, *Oxford Bulletin of Economics and Statistics*, **56** (3), 229–47.

Cubbin, J. and Leech, D. (1983) The effect of shareholding dispersion on the degree of control in British companies: theory and measurement. *Economic Journal*, **93** : 351–369.

Davis, E. (2002) Institutional investors, corporate governance and the performance of the corporate sector, *Economic Systems*, **26** (3), 203–229.

Davis Polk (2010) Summary of the Dodd-Frank Wall Street Reform and Consumer Protection Act, Enacted into Law on July 21, 2010

Del Guercio, D. (1996) The Distorting Effect of the Prudent-Man Laws on Institutional Equity Investments, *Journal of Financial Economics*, **40** (1), 31–62.

Elton, E. J. and Gruber, M. J. (1977) Risk Reduction and Portfolio Size: An Analytic Solution, *Journal of Business* 50 : 415–37

Franks, J., Mayer, C. and Rossi, S. (2009) Ownership: Evolution and Regulation, Review of Financial Studies 22 (10), 4009–4056

Gillan, S. L., and Starks, L. T. (1998) A Survey of Shareholder Activism: Motivation and Empirical Evidence, *Contemporary Finance Digest* 2 (3), 10–34.

Gillan, S., & Starks, L. (2000) Corporate governance proposals and shareholder activism: the role of institutional investors, *Journal of Financial Economics*, **57** (2), 275–305.

Gillan, S., & Starks, L. (2003) Corporate Governance, Corporate Ownership, and the Role of Institutional Investors: A Global Perspective, *Journal of Applied Finance*, **13**(2), 4–22.

Gompers, P.A., and Metrick, A. (2001) Institutional Investors And Equity Prices, *Quarterly Journal Of Economics* 116 (1), 229–259.

Han, K.C. and Suk, D.Y. (1998) The effect of ownership structure on firm performance: Additional evidence, *Review of Financial Economics*, 7(2), 143–155.

Hartzell, J. C. and Starks, L.T. (2003) Institutional Investors and Executive Compensation, *The Journal of Finance*, **58**: 2351–2374. doi: 10.1046/j.1540-6261.2003.00608.x

Ho, V.H. (2010) Enlightened Shareholder Value: Corporate Governance Beyond the Shareholder-Stakeholder Divide, *Journal of Corporation Law*, **36** (1), 59–112.

Holmström, B.R. and Kaplan, S.N. (2003) The State of U.S. Corporate Governance: What's Right and What's Wrong? ECGI – Finance Working Paper No. 23/2003. Available at SSRN:http://ssrn.com/abstract=441100.

Karpoff, J.M. (2001) The Impact of Shareholder Activism on Target Companies: A Survey of

Empirical Findings, Working paper, University of Washington.

Klein, A. and Zur, E. (2009) Entrepreneurial Shareholder Activism: Hedge Funds and Other Private Investors, *The Journal of Finance*, 64 (1), 187–229. doi: 10.1111/j.1540-6261.2008.01432.x

Larcker, D. (2008) *Models of Corporate Governance: Who's the Fairest of them All?* Rock Center for Corporate Governance, CG–11.

Larcker, D. and Tayan, B. (2011) *Corporate Governance Matters: A Closer Look at Organizational Choices and the Consequences*, Pearson Education

Mallin, C. (2002) Editorial: Institutional Investors and the Growth of Global Influence, *Corporate Governance: An International Review*, 10 (2), 67.

McConnell, J.J. and Servaes, H. (1990) Additional evidence on equity ownership and corporate value, *Journal of Financial Economics*, 27 (2), 595–612, ISSN 0304-405X, 10.1016/0304-405X(90)90069-C.

New York Stock Exchange (2010) *Report of the New York Stock Exchange Commission on Corporate Governance*, 23 September 10.

Parrino, R., Sias, R.W. and Starks, L.T. (2003) Voting With Their Feet: Institutional Investors and CEO Turnover, *Journal of Financial Economics* 68 (1), 3–46.

Pedersen, T. and Thomsen, S. (2003) Ownership structure and value of the largest European firms: the importance of owner identity, *Journal of Management and Governance*, 7, 27–55.

Rappaport, A. (1981) Selecting strategies that create shareholder value. *Harvard Business Review*, May-June: 139–149

Rappaport, A. (1986) *Creating shareholder value: the new standard for business performance*, Free Press: New York.

Romano, R. (2005) The Sarbanes-Oxley Act and the Making of Quack Corporate Governance, *The Yale Law Journal*, 114 (7), 1521–1611

Rose, C. (2007) Can institutional investors fix the corporate governance problem? Some Danish evidence, *Journal of Management & Governance*, 11(4), 405–428.

Rubach, M. and Sebora, T. (2009) Determinants of Institutional Investor Activism: A Test of the Ryan-Schneider Model, *Journal of Managerial Issues*, 21(2), 245–261.

Ryan, L. and Schneider, M. (2002) The Antecedents of Institutional Investor Activism, Academy of Management Review, 27: 554–573.

Skog, R. (2005) A Remarkable Decade: The Awakening of Swedish Institutional Investors. *European Business Law Review*, 16(5), 1017–1031.

Shin, J.Y. and Seo, J. (2011) Less Pay and More Sensitivity? Institutional Investor Heterogeneity and CEO Pay, *Journal of Management*, 37 (6), 1719–1746.

Smith, M.P (1996) Shareholder Activism by Institutional Investors: Evidence from CalPERS, *Journal Of Finance*, 51 (1), 227–252.

Steiner, T.L. (1996) A re-examination of the relationships between ownership structure, firm diversification, and Tobin's q, *Quarterly Journal of Business and Economics*, 35(4), 39–48.

Stewart, F., & Yermo, J. (2009) Pension Fund Governance: Challenges and Potential Solutions. *OECD Journal: Financial Market Trends*, 2008(2), 223–264.

Thomsen, S. & Pedersen, T. (2000) Ownership structure and economic performance in the largest European companies, *Strategic Management Journal*, 21(6), 689–705.

Tricker, R. (1998) Editorial. The Role of the Institutional Investor in Corporate Governance, *Corporate Governance. An International Review*, 6(4), 213–216.

Woidtke, T. (2002) Agents watching agents?: evidence from pension fund ownership and firm value, *Journal of Financial Economics*, 63(1), 99–131.

World Bank (2011) Market Capitalization of Listed Companies as a Percentage of GDP, http://data.worldbank.org/indicator/CM.MKT.LCAP.GD.ZS/countries?display=default (Accessed: 30 May 2011).

Zhang Ivy Xiying (2007) Economic consequences of the Sarbanes–Oxley Act of 2002, *Journal of Accounting and Economics*, 44 (1–2), 74–115.

Chapter 13

Germany and Bank Governance[1]

Chapter contents

[1] Comments by Steffen Brenner, Jana Oehmichen, Steffen Rapp and Michael Wolff are gratefully acknowledged.

13.1   Introduction

In most countries around the world banks provide the bulk of business firm financing. This implies a governance model which is different from that of equity finance. Bankers rather than markets get to choose what projects should be financed. Rather than with anonymous market participants firms must deal with bankers in an ongoing banking relationship. The familiar agency problems of adverse selection and moral hazard do not disappear, but banks handle them differently. In this chapter we begin with a discussion of bank governance. In the standard Anglo-Saxon model that we have discussed in this book, external control over managers is exerted by the threat of takeover and replacement if they engage in non-present value maximization. Outsider independent directors, as members of unitary boards, exercise their judgement in favour of the shareholders. Examples of this type of system are the USA and the UK. In contrast, other systems are organized such that substantial portions of equity in each company are under the control of blockholders and banks. There are long-term commitments to the firm and lending strategies. Strong bank and firm relationships are more common. Hostile takeovers are less prevalent or nearly impossible. The main example of such an economy is Germany. In consequence, the second half this chapter considers corporate governance arrangements in Germany. German corporate governance was traditionally regarded as a prime example of a bank-based model. However, we find the role of banks in the German economy to be more elusive than commonly assumed. Importantly, as we will discuss, there are other characteristics like two-tier boards representation which point more to a social democratic stakeholder model which the Germans themselves call the social market economy. Other features of the German corporate governance model also stand out. The German firm has few constraints imposed on managers by the market for corporate control in the form of hostile takeovers. Large shareholders are very prevalent as are cross-holdings between firms and, of course, significant bank or creditor monitoring. The two-tier 'management-supervisory' board is a hallmark of the German system: legal structures establishing co-determination between shareholders and employees are at the heart of the system. In addition, CEO compensation patterns appear different in Germany compared to, say, the USA and the UK. Above all, it appears that the German corporate governance system reflects the deeper antecedents of the German culture, the social democratic tradition, and Germany's long-standing legal system.

13.2   Bank governance in theory

From a corporate governance perspective banks exist because they provide a solution to moral hazard and adverse selection problems in finance (Stiglitz and Weiss, 1981; Diamond, 1984). In open markets these agency problems would be much more difficult to address because of free rider problems among investors, and this would not only be wasteful, but also lead to systematic underinvestment (Myers and Majluf, 1984). In the absence of agency problems companies could easily issue debt or other marketable securities to the public and cover all of their financing needs in this way. But in practice, because of agency costs, this would not be feasible or at least would be much more expensive than using a bank to channel savings into loans.

Adverse selection problems relate to credit quality: it is difficult for lenders to distinguish between good and bad loans. Charging a high interest rate to compensate for potential losses may tend to drive away good borrowers and so lead to self-selection of bad ones. Moral hazard problems relate primarily to borrower behaviour. Borrowers may for example take risks, which will benefit them if things go well, while the bank loses if things go wrong. Both problems are attributable to information asymmetries (hidden knowledge, hidden action). These information problems can to some extent be overcome by screening (evaluating borrowers by information collection), careful contracting and monitoring of borrower behaviour. However, if lenders are highly diversified, as portfolio concerns would dictate, each individual lender has little incentive to engage in these activities because she has so little at stake and the other lenders would reap most of the potential benefits. The result would be a market failure which can be remedied by an organizational solution: banks. Instead of lending directly to companies or other borrowers, savers can put their money in a bank which can finance the entire loan and therefore has much stronger incentives to monitor. As specialized institutions with loan histories and many clients banks will develop competencies which can enable them to do this much better than the average saver.

Some companies which are large enough and have sufficiently good reputations may obtain their financing directly from savers through company bonds and stock. They can afford to invest in marketing their own securities and cooperate with underwriters to assure potential investors that they have a sufficiently good business case and sufficiently good corporate governance to control agency problems. However, for most businesses, in particular small and medium-sized enterprises, it will be cheaper to rely on bank loans.

Basic loan contracts are simple and easy to enforce. As long as the borrower meets her debt payments, there is little or no reason for intervention by the lender. If the borrower does not pay back as agreed, the bank seizes her assets. Bank loans to companies can therefore be viewed as contingent equity: loan capital converted to equity in the event of default. This is easier and less costly to administer than the elaborate governance system set up to organize equity finance. Jensen (1986) argued that leverage is an optimal governance mechanism for companies with high free cash flow – a point which private equity companies around the world have taken to heart.

Altogether, it is no accident that banks provide much more finance to companies than stock markets. But there are obviously costs as well as benefits with bank finance. First, banks charge for their services and sometimes they can use a strong bargaining position to charge high fees and loan margins and thereby extract rents from their clients (Rajan, 1992). Secondly, loan contracts work much better if the assets have a resale value which can be used as collateral. This applies to buildings and some standard commodities, but investments in research and development or specialized machinery have little or no collateral value and banks will routinely refuse to finance them. In fact banks may have little incentive to declare bankruptcy if they do not gain by doing so (as will often be the case when they have lent to companies with specialized assets). Companies acting rationally will realize this and therefore have an incentive to default strategically to renegotiate their debt and reduce their debt burden. Rational banks will realize that this may happen and will be even more reluctant to lend to companies with little or no collateral.

The situation may be different if there are many creditors each of which can force liquidation. This will make it more difficult to negotiate a settlement (which creditor should take a 'haircut' of what size?) and increases the chances of bankruptcy. The likelihood that a bankruptcy will be called may provide a deterrent against strategic liquidation. This then paradoxically may make it easier to obtain market credit in the first place (Dewatripont and Maskin, 1995).

13.3 Governance role of banks

Banks can exercise optimal corporate governance in several different ways: as lenders, advisers, owners, trustees or board members. In some cases, they play these roles simultaneously in the same firm, which gives them tremendous influence. In other cases, they concentrate on lending, which still makes their role less visible in well-functioning firms, while they tend to become more active in cases of financial distress.

1 By deciding to give or withhold credit to firms they influence which projects go ahead. They have an obvious interest in avoiding bad loans and risky empire building, which runs parallel to shareholder interests. However, because of the standard loan contracts (according to which banks lose when things go bad, but do not gain much when things go well) banks will typically be more conservative and risk averse than shareholders. The empirical evidence is ambiguous (Degryse and Ongena, 2008), which indicates that there are in fact both cost and benefits to bank

finance. However a close, long-term bank relationship probably tends to improve shareholder value and profitability (Degryse and Ongena, 2008). For example, share prices tend to rise when new loans are announced and to fall when the company's bank goes bankrupt.

2 Covenants. By imposing covenants (loan conditions) on firms banks are often much more directly involved in company affairs. Covenants specify what firms are allowed to do and what price they have to pay for their loans conditional on their ability to fulfil loan conditions. A critical decision is loan maturity with a choice between long-term loans and short-term loans, which are rolled over and are therefore subject to renegotiation. Short-term loans may give banks more power, but firms will often be reluctant to finance long-term investment in this way. Long-term loans, in contrast, require more monitoring by the banks to safeguard their interests.

3 Banks may own shares in companies, often in companies with which they do a lot of business. Ownership often comes about as a result of debt being converted into equity when clients are unable to repay. However, countries differ in how much they allow banks to own of individual firms. In the USA, UK and many other countries across the world a 5% limit is imposed, but not so in Germany. While banks in the USA used to be prevented from owning significant amounts of stock in non-financial companies, more relaxed regulation following the financial services modernization act of 1999 enabled investment banks to exercise some control indirectly through special investment vehicles. Several studies have found a positive effect of bank ownership on firm value (Gorton and Schmid, 2000; Edwards and Nibler, 2000), while Morck, Nakamura and Shivdasani (2000) find ambiguous evidence in Japan which they interpret as evidence of rent extraction when banks hold relatively small blocks of shares.

4 Banks as trustees. Banks may represent other shareholders as custodians of their shares or as managers of investment companies (see below on Germany). In this case they have control rights while others have cash flow rights and carry the risk (Santos and Rumble, 2006). In principle this could create scope for private benefits (e.g. that banks let their interests as lenders sway their ownership interest), but mechanisms like reputation or regulation may limit such behaviour.

5 Banks may place their people on company boards. Bankers on a board can provide expertise to the company and also facilitate trust which may make it easier for them to obtain credit. However, they may also influence company policies to promote bank interests, e.g. towards risk aversion. As board members they are accountable to the company and its shareholders, but a double role as bank employees and board members can create conflicts of interests. The empirical evidence indicates that banks tend to sit on the boards of large and stable firms with high collateral (Degryse and Ongena, 2008), i.e. precisely those firms who would find it easy to get credit anyway. Dittmann et al. (2010) even find that bankers on the board cause a decline in firm value.

13.4 Relationship banking[2]

The relationship between a company and its bank is perhaps the single most important of all business relationships after ownership relations. The relationship creates obvious links between the two parties via the credit relationship which may more or less completely determine the activities of individual firms and which has, in some cases, led to the bankruptcy of even large banks. In addition to capital transfer, bank relationships involve information transfers to assess the financial risks involved in the company's activities. Generally, they are multi-functional involving many kinds of financial services such as short-term credit, long-term loans, new equity issues, payment systems, portfolio management, as well as various kinds of advice (Holland, 1994). Banks have enthusiastically endorsed relationship building, and relationship banking has been a catchword among bankers since the beginning of the 1980s.

---

[2] This section draws heavily on Steen Thomsen (1999) The Duration of Business Relationships: Banking Relationships of Danish Manufacturers 1900–1995. Unpublished working paper.

A higher level of information, trust and resource commitment may enable banks to better assess the risks involved in a company's business and thus to extend more credit, give better advice, etc. Hodgman (1963) found in a series of interviews that 'bankers preferred to lend to applicants who were most likely to maintain a long term deposit relationship with them' (Holland, 1994). Likewise, companies may be willing to take on more debt if they have developed close banking relationships over time. In addition, Holland (1994) emphasizes that close relations are regarded as implicit insurance for both banks and companies. Companies expect the bank to help them in hard times, and in turn, banks expect companies to give them a relatively certain share of their regular bank business. Social bonds (Håkansson and Snehota, 1995) also appear in relationship banking. Thus, Donaldson (1969) found that finance officers 'placed considerable emphasis on the importance of cultivating a close relationship with the lending officer – a relationship usually regarded as a highly personal one involving mutual trust and continuous communication' (Holland, 1994, p. 369).

In accordance with practice, the economics literature views bank relationships as a way to overcome credit rationing and adverse selection under asymmetric information (Stiglitz and Weiss, 1981; Diamond, 1984). Information asymmetries between lenders and borrowers may cause lenders to limit the supply of capital which may have unfortunate effects if profitable investments cannot be funded and especially so in times of financial distress (Stiglitz and Weiss, 1981). Long-term relationships may provide banks with better information on the nature of the company and its business which may reduce these problems. In comparison with anonymous bond markets, banks are in a better position to monitor the borrowers (Fama, 1985). Furthermore, the prospect of future business is an added incentive for banks to provide bridging finance for a client in trouble. This implies a significant survival value of a close bank relationship from the viewpoint of the company. Empirical studies indicate that credit increases with the durability of the firm's bank relationship (Degreyse and Ongena, 2008).

From the viewpoint of the bank, reduced information asymmetries may in some cases overcome credit rationing and may generate extra business or, in other cases, may help to avoid bad loans. Furthermore, bank loans may also spill over into other kinds of bank business including cash management, short-term credits, transactions, and investment banking (see Figure 13.1 for an illustration of a universal bank). A loyal customer base implies a secure source of revenue. And a better understanding of the clients is in itself an important asset which may support new product development, marketing, etc.

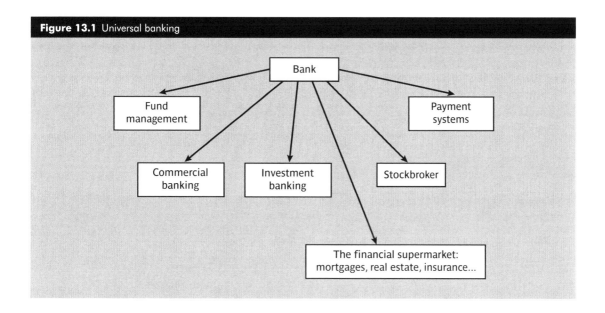

Figure 13.1 Universal banking

This would seem to imply that bank relationships are particularly valuable (and durable) when companies are credit rationed, e.g. when they have insufficient equity or internal funds to finance their investments.

Bank monitoring and financial control may reduce managerial discretion and agency costs. For example, banks have an obvious interest in persuading companies to avoid managerial inefficiency and unprofitable projects which endanger their ability to repay loans. Close relations with other companies may also provide a valuable source of advice on recruitment, acquisition targets, restructuring, etc.

In contrast to this rosy picture, some research has stressed that there is a dark side to banking relationships (Rajan, 1992). Greenbaum et al. (1989) argue theoretically that the interest rate charged by banks on loans to a company will increase in the duration of the relationship which predicts that companies will eventually switch banks as competitors give them a better offer. Sharpe (1990) argues that relationship banks gain access to an information monopoly which they can exploit to the firm's disadvantage unless checked by reputation.

13.5   An overview of corporate governance arrangements in Germany

Corporate governance arrangements in Germany are very distinct from those in the Anglo-Saxon market model that characterize the United States and the United Kingdom. One of the more salient features of the German system is the relationship between organizations and corporate financing. Unlike in the United States and the United Kingdom, bank-based finance is especially important in Germany – as we discuss below. In the USA and UK the equity markets are large and liquid. In Germany much more emphasis is placed on the role of the bank in credit financing, and firms often develop very close relationships with their banks.

However, bank financing is only one feature of the German corporate governance model. The German system of governance is different from that of many other countries in terms of ownership structure, the market for corporate control, the role and structure of the board of directors, the structure of executive compensation contracts, the role of employees and other stakeholders, and the general development of the corporate legal and governance framework. Goergen, Manjon and Renneboog (2005) characterize the German system in the following way: 'the German system is characterised by the existence of a market for partial corporate control, large shareholders, cross-holdings and bank/ creditor monitoring, a two-tier (management-supervisory board) with co-determination between shareholders and employees on the supervisory board, a non-negligible sensitivity of managerial compensation to performance, competitive product markets, and corporate governance regulations largely based on EU directives but with deep roots in the German legal doctrine' (page 285).

In the remainder of this chapter we provide an overview of corporate governance arrangements in Germany. Goergen, Manjon and Renneboog (2008) provide a recent comprehensive survey of historical and contemporary corporate governance developments.

13.6   The role of banks in Germany

Traditionally, Germany is regarded as the prime example of a bank-based corporate governance system, where the majority of external finance to companies is provided by banks rather than stock markets or corporate bonds. Goergen et al. (2008) argue that one of the most important features of the German corporate governance system is the relationship between the firm and the bank. The bank fulfils a similar role to that of large shareholders in the Anglo-Saxon model by monitoring the firm. The banks typically have large credit stakes in the firm so have an incentive to monitor management. The lending relationship between the bank and the firm gives the bank considerable power. The bank is typically represented on the firm's supervisory board. In this role the bank has access to significant amounts of corporate information. Goergen et al. (2008) argue that the reason why banks are so powerful in German is because the banks owning shares in the firm were also the firm's main bank providing long-term loans to the company. This main bank is known as the Hausbank.

The firm–bank relationship is not easy to characterise as this. Recent empirical evidence suggests that banks in Germany might not be especially different in lending proportions from those in other countries. As can be seen in Figure 13.2, German banks now provide less credit to their economy than their counterparts in the market-based models. In fact, judging from these figures Japan is the bank-based system par excellence.

The picture is the same if we consider credit to the private sector only. There are also other signs that the governance role of German banks is waning. Banks have been selling their shares in large German companies, for example. Nevertheless, banks still influence German corporate governance. Banks remain powerful as custodians for minority shareholders and by representation on company boards.

However, traditionally banks have played a central role in German economic development. Companies have turned to their 'house banks' for credit, investment bank services, asset management, transactions, and all other financial services. Germany's tradition for universal banks – which combine all of these services in one bank – allowed banks to grow large and thereby better able to manage large accounts with undue financial risk. The tradition was – and is – therefore to finance companies by long-term bank debt rather than by issuing equity to the stock market. Moreover, many company pension funds are not separately funded, but remain part of corporate liabilities and do not, therefore, add to the size and liquidity of the financial markets.

German banks are allowed to possess controlling stakes in non-financial firms and historically they have done so to a considerable extent. Thus, bank capitalism has led to more ownership control of large German firms than we find in large US firms. Since the major banks concentrate their shares in large companies, the combined share of the three largest banks could historically add up to effective control (since the merger between Dresdner and Commerzbank the two largest banks are now Commerzbank and Deutsche Bank).

In addition to direct ownership, German banks act as custodians for ordinary shareholders and may represent them at shareholder meetings. This further increases their power. German banks also control the votes of mutual funds, whose shares they can vote if necessary. Moreover, bankers often sit on the supervisory boards of non-financial companies. Altogether, German banks historically dominated corporate governance in Germany through ownership, ownership representation, board membership, and lending relationships. However, the German model appears to be changing. In global competition with other banks and stimulated by new tax laws (which no longer tax appreciation on long-term shareholdings when the banks sell them), German banks have sold off shares and reduced

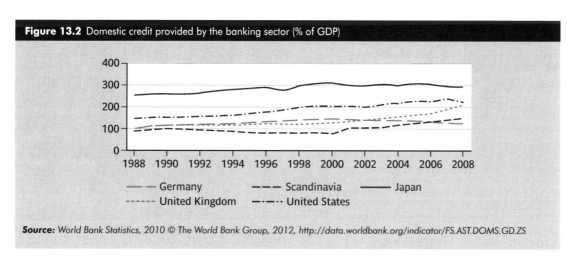

Figure 13.2 Domestic credit provided by the banking sector (% of GDP)

Legend: Germany, Scandinavia, Japan, United Kingdom, United States

Source: World Bank Statistics, 2010 © The World Bank Group, 2012, http://data.worldbank.org/indicator/FS.AST.DOMS.GD.ZS

loans to large German companies in recent years. Their ownership stake has been reduced from 4.7% in 1997 to 0.6% in 2006, and their share of supervisory board members fell from 7.6% to 4.3% over the same period (Rapp et al., 2009). Voting caps and dual class shares which made takeovers more difficult have been abolished by law (2003), although it is still possible to issue non-voting preference shares. Moreover securitisation – selling loans to investors – may have weakened the loan monitoring role of banks. As a result, German corporate governance has converged towards the market model, although it still retains many distinctive features.

Hackethal et al. (2005) argue that the demise of the banks may lead to a power vaccum in corporate governance, since Germany lacks many disciplining mechanisms of the market model (such as takeovers, leverage or intense labour mobility). The result could be a 'managerialist' regime in which professional managers rule relatively unchecked.

13.7　The German legal system

The German **legal system** is civil law which according to La Porta et al. (1998) is associated with less protection of minority investors. However, La Porta et al. (1998 and subsequent research) note that the quality of enforcement in Germany is high so that effective investor protection is quite high. Compared with the USA and the UK a high priority is given to stakeholders. Company managers are obliged to act in the best interest of the company when faced with a takeover threat (Goergen et al., 2008). Corporate restructuring can be challenged and delayed for many years by minority shareholders.

13.8　The market for corporate control

The standard economic argument for hostile takeovers is that it improves economic efficiency. Managers and CEOs cannot run their firms inefficiently otherwise they are likely to be acquired. CEOs that enjoy the quiet life, or take excess perks, or make bad strategic decisions, are subject to a higher probability of takeover by a hostile raider. The acquirer will reallocate resources more efficiently, and make an economic profit. The CEO of the target firm is likely to be replaced after the takeover. The market for corporate control therefore disciplines CEOs ensuring they run their companies in the most profitable long-term way. Industrial and financial economists have debated this hypothesis for decades. The proposition is controversial and there is mixed evidence on the efficacy of the takeover mechanism in countries such as the USA and the UK. However, the underlying logic is clear – the possibility of a hostile takeover, at least in principle, acts as a binding constraint for managers promoting efficient behaviour.

A salient feature of German corporate governance is the near absence of hostile takeovers and merger and acquisition behaviour. Goergen et al. (2008) present the remarkable fact that since World War II there have only been three hostile takeovers in Germany: Feldmuhle Nobel in 1988–89, Hoesch in 1990–91, and Continental in 1991–92. In contrast, the UK had about 40 hostile mergers per year between 1984 and 1989. Goergen et al. (2008, p. 186) remark that: 'Hence, one can conclude there is no active market for corporate control in Germany.' The authors go on to analyse a slightly separate issue in which there is a market for partial control stakes in firms. They assert that this market is, indeed, often hostile and fairly active.

Mergers are still rare in Germany by international standards, and controversial given Germany's codetermination laws and commitments to a stakeholder model. The German firm Mannesmann AG was acquired by the British company Vodafone Group Plc in 2000. The deal was highly controversial as Germany had never previously seen such a large domestic firm acquired by a foreign entity. Ultimately, the hostile bid was backed by the management of Mannesmann and Vodafone. Non-hostile mergers do happen in Germany. In 1998 Daimler-Benz AG merged with the US car manufacturer Chrysler Corp. as a merger of equals. The deal was structured via an exchange of shares. As with other cases in Germany, the merger became highly contentious. Investors filed lawsuits arguing that the deal was not in fact a 'merger of equals' as claimed by the senior management who put the deal together. The combination really amounted to a Daimler-Benz takeover of Chrysler.

Changes in the German takeover code (1995 and revised in 1998), as well as the Takeover Act (2002), make it easier to facilitate a corporate change of control. For example, the takeover code, although voluntary, calls for a mandatory takeover bid as soon as one party has gained control of 50% of the votes of the firm. See Goegen et al. (2008, p. 189).

13.9 German ownership structure

Ownership structure in Germany has traditionally been concentrated so that most companies would have a large shareholder controlling more than 25% of the votes (Becht and Boehmer, 2001, 2003), and the controlling blockholder would rarely be challenged by other powerful blockholders.

As mentioned earlier, blockholder power has been attenuated by the withdrawal of the banks leaving as some see it a power vacuum. Certainly there are now many more companies with dispersed ownership. However, a large fraction of shares is held by non-financial companies, for example in pyramids where companies in a group hold stock in other members of that group. Strong ownership (and board) networks have given rise to the notion of a Germany Inc. (Deutschland AG) as a label for the business establishment. These firms tend to be more difficult to acquire, but it is not clear that their productivity suffers from it. For example, they have been found to have higher productivity than companies with dispersed ownership (Goergen et al., 2008).

A few important firms such as Volkswagen are wholly or partially government owned, but this is an exception. After German unification East Germany was characterized by mass privatization and little remains of the former planned economy.

With concentrated ownership and the strong emphasis on stakeholders it is understandable that takeover activity is very limited (Goergen et al., 2008). Apparently, block trades used to play a role, but this has become more difficult after the adoption of the mandatory bid rule (which obliges buyers to make the same bid to all shareholders when they acquire a block of shares).

13.10 German board structure

Germany has a mandatory two-tier board system. All companies must have a supervisory board (Aufsichtsrat) and a management board (Vorstand), whose roles very much resemble those of non-executive and executive directors in the UK. Overlap between the two boards is prohibited. The supervisory board is charged with many of the same functions as boards in the USA and UK:

- to review the performance of the company and take steps to avoid bankruptcy,
- to monitor the performance of managers and to replace them if necessary,
- to ratify major decisions (e.g. M&A).

Since the two tier system is mandatory for all German companies, it is difficult to isolate its economic effects from other German characteristics by statistical studies. Gillette, Noe and Rebello (2008) have compared one- and two-tier boards in an experimental setting. They find that two-tier boards tend to be more conservative than one-tier boards (i.e. that is two-tier boards tend to reject more projects). This is easy to justify theoretically following Sah and Stiglitz (1985, 1986). The two-tier board is a hierarchy, where the supervisory board is superior to the management board. The one-tier board is a polyarchy where all members have the same vote. Essentially the decision procedure in a two-tier board has two steps to it. First the management board considers a proposal. If it rejects it, the project

Table 13.1 Acceptance or rejection of a decision proposal in a two-tier board

	Supervisory board rejects	Supervisory board accepts
Management board rejects	Rejection	Rejection
Management board accepts	Rejection	Acceptance

The two-tier structure therefore works as a double sorting mechanism. In a one-tier board, in contrast, there is only one decision and so, all else equal, less of a chance that the proposal will fail.

is trashed and never heard of again. If they approve it, it faces another exam in the supervisory board, at which stage it may again be rejected or accepted. This gives rise to the following decision matrix.

Whether these theoretical considerations hold in practice is uncertain. The preamble to the German corporate governance code argues that '... the dual-board system ... and the single-board system are converging because of the intensive interaction of the Management Board and the Supervisory Board in the dual-board system'. Members of the management board will invariably be present at supervisory board meetings and will do most of the talking as they present their proposals. So it may be difficult to distinguish between one- and two-tier board meetings from observing the actual board interaction.

The management board (Vorstand) is a collective decision-making body appointed by the supervisory board. It is headed by a CEO (Sprecher), but in principle differences of opinion are settled by majority voting.

13.11 Employee representation

Employees have a right to elect up to half of the board members in larger corporations (those with more than 2000 German employees), but the shareholders maintain a voting majority since the vote of the chairman is decisive in case of a deadlock. In medium-sized companies (with fewer than 2000 but more than 500 employees), they are represented by one-third of the board, while companies with fewer than 500 employees do not need to have employee representation.[3] Paradoxically, this applies to German employees only. Non-German employees are not provided with a systematic voice under this system.

Academic studies of German codetermination (as the system is called) have indicated that firms with 50% employee representation have lower value than firms with 33% representation (Gorton and Schmid, 2004), while labour costs tend to be correspondingly 50% higher. Fauver and Fuerst (2006) find that a moderate employee representation of 33–50% of the board improves company performance compared with zero employee representation. However, because codetermination is determined by company size it is difficult for these studies to filter away related differences between large and medium-sized companies. Nor is it clear that the effects of codetermination should necessarily be measured at the company level. It may be that codetermination fosters a less adversarial and more cooperative relationship between capital and labour resulting in for example fewer work days lost because of strikes. It is also possible that the strong German tradition of craft-based education is related to greater cooperation between capitalists and workers. While the UK shareholder value system secures investor protection, the German stakeholder system seems designed to protect employees.

The system has been severely criticized within Germany itself. After joining the international European market many German companies have decided to incorporate in the UK, where they can escape mandatory codetermination. In 2006 1 in 7 of all new German limited liability companies did so (Frey et al., 2010).

---

[3] For references to studies on the effect of employee representation see Chapter 8.

In addition to employee representation at the board level, many decisions concerning labour issues must be discussed in work councils before they can be put into practice.

As mentioned, bankers may also sit on German company boards which further strengthens stakeholder viewpoints. Bankers and employees will typically agree on risk aversion because both stand to lose if things go badly, but do not gain if things go well for the company.

As mentioned, a tight director network has (along with bank and ownership ties) given rise to the phrase 'Deutschland AG', which sees German business as controlled by a relatively small business elite. Böhler, Rapp and Wolff (2010) find that strong network ties have a negative influence on company performance and argue that well-connected directors may feel more committed to their network than to the firms, which they are intended to supervise. Foreign ownership tends to reduce board ties, while domestic institutional investment tends to promote them. Oehmichen, Rapp and Wolff (2010) further find that tight board networks are negatively associated with female board participation, which is quite low on average (4%). However, Rapp, Schwetzler and Sperling (2009) find that ownership ties in German business decline over time and conclude that 'Germany AG' may be disappearing.

13.12   Executive compensation

One of the main goals of executive compensation contracts is to align the interests of CEOs with owners. In doing so, it is common for CEOs in the USA and the UK to receive payments that are contingent upon the performance of their firms. Short-term incentives are provided through bonuses that are tied to operational targets. Long-term incentives are provided to CEOs via the use of equity compensation such as stock options and restricted stock.

Under rules in effect until 2005, public companies in Germany were required to report only the aggregate cash compensation paid to all management directors; details on individual compensation or on stock options were not required. In 2000, following the Ackermann-Mannesman merger scandal, German legislators began working on new pay disclosure rules that would reveal individual pay packages. However, the landmark German disclosure legislation was not passed until 2005, requiring details on option grants but not option holdings; it also included a loophole to benefit secretive family-owned or closely held corporations: the company would not have to disclose pay details if 75% of the shares voted against such disclosure (Conyon et al., 2011).

German law prohibited the use of stock options for executives prior to 1998. One exception to this rule was if stock options were based on convertible bonds (the 'Wandelschuldverschreibung'). In the mid-1990s, two of Germany's largest companies – Daimler-Benz and Deutsche Bank – announced plans to offer convertible-bond-based options to their executives. The plans were attacked in both the media and the courts by shareholder groups, worker councils, politicians and executives in other firms (Sanders and Tuschke, 2007).

In April 1998, the 'Corporate Sector Supervision and Transparency Act' (KonTraG) effectively made 'naked' stock options (i.e. those not connected with convertible bonds) legal in Germany. Unlike options in France and the United Kingdom (or in the United States in the 1950s–1960s), options in Germany were taxed as ordinary income and not as capital gains. Nonetheless, several companies proposed to offer option plans: while less than 10% of DAX 100 firms used options prior to 1998, 50% of DAX 100 firms had adopted stock options by 2000 (Conyon et al., 2011).

German CEOs receive modest amounts of compensation and equity incentives, especially when compared to CEOs in the USA. The number of studies on German executive compensation is comparatively few, in part because disclosure of the elements of CEO and executive pay has been incomplete until quite recently. Early studies by Conyon and Schwalbach (1999, 2000a,b) showed that German executive compensation was low by European standards. However, they found that CEO pay was positively related to firm performance, suggesting partial alignment between managers and shareholder interests. In addition, the studies showed that firm size was a significant driver of CEO pay – the magnitude of the CEO pay and firm size elasticity was on a par with other executive pay studies. Goergen et al. (2008) used survey data from consultants Towers Perrin for the period 2001 to 2002 and showed that German CEO pay was about a quarter that of a US CEO and about similar to that of the typical UK CEO. Most of the CEOs' pay came in the form of base salary compensation, a point we return to below. Recently studies have showed that the use of incentive pay is gaining ground in Germany, although it is less widely and less extravagantly used than in the UK and USA (Andreas, Rapp and Wolff, 2010). Conyon et al. (2011) using data from 2008 found that the level of German pay was about half that of the USA and slightly higher than in the UK. Salaries accounted for about 39% of total pay, annual bonuses about 42%, equity pay (including stock options) about 9% of pay and other pay the remaining 11%. The lack of equity pay was salient: it compared to a European average of 19% and 46% observed in the USA. It seems that Germany CEOs receive comparable levels of total pay to their European counterparts, but much less of this is delivered in the form of stock options or restricted stock arrangements.

13.13 Corporate governance regulations

As noted above, German corporate governance operates a civil law, as opposed to common law, system. Common law systems provide a comparative in protecting shareholder interests and property rights. In addition, common law systems facilitate economic growth and the development of stock markets by encouraging initial public offerings. An implication of the benefits of common law systems favours the development of laws and regulatory codes that promote the development of financial markets.

Goergen et al. (2008) argue that recent changes in company law in Germany have favoured the growth in financial markets. This is perhaps not surprising given the globalization of companies since the late 1990s. In general, financial reforms in Germany have resulted in greater transparency and also in an environment more conducive to hostile takeovers. There have been several laws that impact directly on the external environment within which firms operate. These include the Securities Trading Act (1994), the Restructuring Act (1995), the Antitrust Act (1998), the Third Act on the promotion of financial markets (1998), the Corporate Control and Transparency Act (1998), the Takeover Code (1995, 1998) and the Takeover Act (2002), Capital Gains tax (2002) and the Fourth Financial Market Promotion Act (2002). These are discussed in detail in Goergen et al. (2008). However, the essence of these reforms is to promote transparency and good governance in an ever increasing global market.

In 2000 a Government-sponsored panel began drafting a corporate governance code to influence the behaviour of firms and boards. At its core was the notion of transparency and disclosure. Like the UK Cadbury Code the recommendations focused on the principle of 'comply or explain': follow the code's recommendation, or explain why there are deviations from it. The German Corporate Governance Code is split into the following major sections: Shareholders and the General Meeting, Cooperation between Management Board and Supervisory Board, Management Board, Supervisory Board, Transparency, Reporting and Audit of the Annual Financial Statements.

The German Corporate Governance Code presents essential statutory regulations for the management and supervision (governance) of German listed companies and contains internationally and nationally recognized standards for good and responsible governance. The Code aims at making the German Corporate Governance system transparent and understandable. Its purpose is to promote the trust of international and national investors, customers, employees and the general public in the management and supervision of listed German stock corporations.

13.14 Why is Germany different?

One might ask why the German corporate governance system is different. Charkham (1994) has suggested a cultural explanation: German corporate governance reflects deeply held views of how companies should be run and of the relationship between business and society. Private ownership is not a goal in itself, but is subordinate to the public interest. Ownership involves obligations as well as rights. The purpose of a company is to provide goods and services for the population, not to make money. These views, though difficult to verify, seem consistent with a strong industrial tradition in German business. Unlike in the UK, considerable social prestige is traditionally attached to engineering and physics, but not to economics and finance. Bright people, it is said, become engineers, philosophers or lawyers, not economists.

According to the cultural view, the industrial tradition – valuing the company as such (das Unternehmen an sich) – promotes long-term thinking, stakeholder interest and survival of the corporation as the overall goal. It is translated into long terms of office for executives who continue after retirement as supervisory board chairs. Conservative accounting seems to fit the picture.

Another related view turns to politics. There is a strong social democratic tradition in Germany, and German Christian conservatism has traditionally been more social and less liberal than the Conservatives and Republicans in the UK and the USA. Social democracy emphasized codetermination which led to employee representation. It may also be that Social Democrats found it easier to regulate banks and therefore preferred the bank-based model.

13.15 Discussion

Germany is clearly a rich society despite recent unification between East and West. GDP per capita is the same as in the UK, but a third lower than in the USA.

The bank-based German governance model may not have contributed adequately to the profitability and competitiveness of German corporations in the boom years up to the financial crisis. The banks themselves seem on the way to replacing it with a more market-oriented style of governance.

The board system, particularly employee representation, has been met with significant criticism in the business community. It seems to have led to larger supervisory boards in the 1970s when it was introduced, but average size has now dropped to nine in investor-owned firms and five in family firms (Achleitner, Kaserer, Kauf, Günther, Ampenberger, 2009). Schroeder and Shrader (1998) find that supervisory boards go through the motions, i.e. limit decisions to what is legally required. Gorton and Smid (2000, 2004) argue that firms with employee representation have lower performance and lower risk which is what you would theoretically expect: all else equal, employees have an interest in protecting their jobs and so they would want to influence their companies to risk less. If there is a trade off between risk and return, the greater risk aversion should lead to lower returns (see Figure 13.3).

The same logic can be applied to other parts of the German corporate governance system. Banks are naturally risk averse because they lose by downside risk, but they do not gain by upside risk. Banks would, therefore, naturally induce companies to take less risk, which would then lead to less risk taking and lower returns. As powerful actors in German corporate governance, banks and employees share a common interest in not inducing risk-taking pay-by-performance pay for executives.

At the macro level, all this might be expected to show up in less entrepreneurship and lower economic growth than would otherwise have been the case. If so, the lower risk taking will only be in the short-term interest of employees and banks, because both stand to benefit more than anything

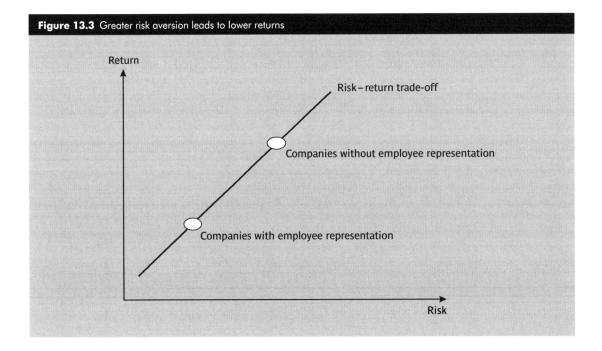

Figure 13.3 Greater risk aversion leads to lower returns

else from higher economic growth. This may be one reason why both bankers and unions now seem more susceptible to economic reform.

However, there are also advantages to limiting risk taking. The 2007–2009 financial crisis was widely attributed to excessive risk taking in banks and other financial institutions, particularly in the USA and the UK. The more cautious Germany emerged less scathed by the crisis with strong economic growth. Thus the battle of the systems – the competition between corporate governance systems, bank based versus market based – remains undecided (Levine, 2002; Beck and Levine, 2004).

Minicase

Daimler Benz

Based in Germany, Daimler AG is one of the world's largest premium car producers and the world's biggest manufacturer of commercial vehicles (trucks, vans, buses).

Deutsche Bank used to own one-third of Daimler, but today its ownership structure is dispersed with sovereign wealth funds from Kuwait and Abu Dhabi as the biggest single shareholders.

In accordance with German codetermination law, the Supervisory Board of Daimler AG consists of 20 members, of whom 10 are elected by the shareholders and 10 are representatives of the employees:

(As reported by the company, employee representatives are marked*)

- Dr. rer. pol. Manfred Bischoff, Chairman, Former Member of the Board of Management of the company
- Erich Klemm,* Deputy Chairman, Chairman of the General Works Council, Daimler Group and Daimler AG

- Dr. Paul Achleitner, Member of the Board of Management of Allianz SE
- Sari Baldauf, Former Executive, Nokia Corporation
- Dr. Clemens Börsig, Chairman of Deutsche Bank AG
- Prof. Dr. Heinrich Flegel,* Director Research Materials, Daimler AG
- Dr. rer.nat. Jürgen Hambrecht, Former Executive, BASF
- Petraea Heynike, Former Executive Vice President of Nestlé SA
- Jörg Hofmann,* District Manager of German Metalworkers' Union
- Dr. Thomas Klebe,* General Council of German Metalworkers' Union
- Gerard Kleisterlee, Former CEO of Royal Philips Electronics NV
- Jürgen Langer,* Works Council of the Frankfurt/Offenbach Dealership
- Ansgar Osseforth,* Manager Mercedes-Benz Research and Development
- Valter Sanches,* Secretary, Confederação Nacional dos Metalúrgicos
- Stefan Schwaab,* General Works Council, Daimler AG;
- Jörg Spies,* Chairman of the Works Council, Headquarters, Daimler AG
- Lloyd G. Trotter, Former Vice Chairman, General Electric,
- Dr. h. c. Bernhard Walter, Former Executive, Dresdner Bank AG
- Uwe Werner,* Chairman of the Works Council, Bremen Plant, Daimler
- Lynton R. Wilson, Chancellor, McMaster University, first elected, 1998

The Board of Management has the following composition:

- Dr. Dieter Zetsche (chair)
- Dr. Wolfgang Bernhard, Manufacturing and Procurement Mercedes-Benz Cars and Mercedes-Benz Vans
- Dr. Christine Hohmann-Dennhardt, Integrity and Legal Affairs
- Wilfried Porth, Human Resources & Labour Relations Director
- Andreas Renschler, Daimler Trucks
- Bodo Uebber, Finance & Controlling
- Prof. Dr. Thomas Weber, Group R&D

The present compensation system for managers has one fixed component and two variable, performance-related components: a fixed base salary, variable compensation in the form of an annual bonus and share-based compensation in the form of a four-year plan. In 2010 Dieter Zetsche received €8.6 million, €1.5 million of which was in the form of a fixed base salary and €4.8 million was in the form of a bonus. Members of the Supervisory Board receive a fixed fee in addition to expenses at the end of the financial year. This fee amounts to €100,000 for each member, but three times this amount for the Chairman.

Daimler's share price has been flat over the past 20 years. Its return on net assets 2005–2010 was 8%, but revenues have not grown. This might not seem impressive. However, it is well-known that the automobile sector is a difficult and mature market in which to compete. It is noteworthy that US rivals GM and Chrysler went bankrupt over the same period.

Source: Daimler Benz: http://www.daimler.com/; Board of Management remuneration in 2010, www.daimler.com, © 2011 Daimler AG

Discussion questions

1 What do you think of Daimler's board? Is it appropriate for a company of this kind?
2 How do you think the board structure influences Daimler's performance?
3 Do you think that Daimler is up for sale to the highest bidder?
4 What do you think of the company's incentive programme?
5 How would you rate the governance structure overall?

Summary (learning points)

■ Bank governance involves loan capital (rather than equity) by a single intermediary (a bank rather than a market) in a long-term banking relationship where a house bank handles all or most of the firm's banking business. The relationship can be cemented by ownership and board ties.

■ The close bank relationship can help overcome information asymmetries and agency problems (and thus improve the supply of capital).

■ In a long-term bank relationship the main bank is generally expected to provide crisis insurance in times of distress.

■ Germany was formerly characterized by bank governance, but banks have become less influential over time. German banks have for example reduced their shareholdings in German firms.

■ Germany has a two-tier board model with a clear separation between the management board and the supervisory board.

■ Germany also has mandatory employee representation on supervisory boards (up to 50% in large firms).

 ## References and further reading

Achleitner, A-K., Kaserer, C., Kauf, T., Günther, N. and Ampenberger, M. (2009) Listed Family Firms in Germany (in German) (October 19). Available at SSRN: http://ssrn.com/abstract=1490698

Andreas, J., Rapp, M.S. and Wolff, M. (2010) *Determinants of Director Compensation in Two-Tier Systems: Evidence from German Panel Data* (September 28). CEFS Working Paper 06-2010. Available at SSRN: http://ssrn.com/abstract=1486325.

Becht, M. and Boehmer, E. (2001). Ownership and voting power in Germany, in F. Barca and M. Becht (eds), *The Control of Corporate Europe*, Oxford University Press: Oxford.

Becht, M. and Boehmer, E. (2003) Voting control in German corporations, *International Review of Law and Economics*, 23 (1), 1–29.

Beck, T. and Levine, R. (2004) Stock Markets, Banks, and Growth: Panel Evidence, *Journal of Banking and Finance*, 28 (3), 423–442.

Black, B., Cheffins, B. and Klausner, M. (2005) Liability Risk for Outside Directors: a Cross-Border Analysis, *European Financial Management*, 11 (2), 153–171.

Böhler, D., Rapp, M. and Wolff, M. (2010) *Director Networks, Firm Performance, and Shareholder Base.* Unpublished working paper.

Charkman, J.P. (1994) *Keeping Good Company: A Study of Corporate Governance in Five Countries*, Clarendon Press: Oxford.

Chizema, A. (2008) Institutions and Voluntary Compliance: The Disclosure of Individual Executive Pay in Germany, *Corporate Governance: An International Review*, **16** (4), 359–374.

Conynon, M.J. and Schwalbach, J. (2000a) Executive Compensation: Evidence from the UK and Germany, *Long Range Planning* **33** (4) 504–526

Conyon, M.J. and Schwalbach, J. (2000b) European Differences in Executive Pay and Corporate Governance, *Zeitschrift für Betriebswirtschaft* ? (), 97–114.

Cromme, G. (2005) Corporate Governance in Germany and the German Corporate Governance Code, *Corporate Governance: An International Review*, **13** (3), 362–367.

Degryse, H.A. and S. Ongena (2008) Competition and regulation in the banking sector: A review of the empirical evidence on the sources of bank rents, in *Handbook of Financial Intermediation and Banking*, A. Thakor and A. Boot (eds), Elsevier.

Dewatripont, M. and Maskin, E. (1995) Credit and Efficiency in Centralized and Decentralized Economies, *Review of Economic Studies*, **62** (Oct), 541–555.

Diamond, D.W. (1984) Financial intermediation and delegated monitoring, *Review of Economic Studies* **51** (July), 393–414.

Dittmann, I., Maug, E. and Schneider, C. (2010) Bankers on the boards of German firms: What they do, what they are worth, and why they are (still) there, *Review of Finance*, **14** (1), 35–71.

Donaldson, G. (1969) *Strategy for Financial Mobility*, Harvard Graduate School of Business Administration.

Edwards, J. and Nibler, M. (2000) Corporate Governance in Germany: The Role of Banks and Ownership Concentration, *Economic Policy*, **15** (31), 237–267.

Edwards, J., Eggert, W. and Weichenrieder, A. (2009) Corporate governance and pay for performance: evidence from Germany, *Economics of Governance*, **10** (1), 1–26.

Elston, J.A. and Goldberg, L.G. (2003) Executive compensation and agency costs in Germany, *Journal of Banking and Finance*, **27** (7), 1391–1410.

Fama, E. (1985) What's different about banks?, *Journal of Monetary Economics*, **15** (1), 29–39.

Fauver, L. and Fuerst, M.E. (2006) Does good corporate governance include employee representation? Evidence from German corporate boards, *Journal of Financial Economics*, **82** (3), 673–710.

Frey, B.S., Osterloh, M. and Zeitoun, H. (2010) Voluntary Co-determination Produces Sustainable Competitive Advantage, in Sacconi, L. (ed.), *Corporate Social Responsibility and Corporate Governance: The Contribution of Economic Theory and Related Disciplines*, Palgrave MacMillan: London.

Gillette, A.A., Noe, T.H. and Rebello, M.J. (2008) Board Structures Around the World: an Experimental Investigation, *Review of Finance*, **12** (1), 93–140.

Goergen, M., Brewster, C. and Wood, G. (2009) Corporate Governance and Training. *Journal of Industrial Relations*, **51** (4), 459–487.

Goergen, M., Manjon, M.C. and Renneboog, L. (2008) Recent developments in German corporate governance, *International Review of Law & Economics*, **28** (3), 175–193.

Gorton, G. and Schmid, F.A. (2000) Universal Banking and the Performance of German Firms, *Journal of Financial Economics* **58** (1–2), 29– 80.

Gorton, G. and Schmid, F.A. (2004) Capital, Labor, and the firm: A Study of German Codetermination, *Journal of the European Economic Association*, **2** (5), 863–905.

Greenbaum, S., Kanatas, G. and Venezia, I. (1989) Loan pricing under the bank–client relationship. *Journal of Banking and Finance*, **13** (2), 221–235.

Hackethal, A., Schmidt, R.H. and Tyrell, M. (2005) Banks and German Corporate Governance: On the Way to a Capital Market-Based System? *Corporate Governance: An International Review*, **13** (3), 397–407. Available at SSRN: http://ssrn.com/abstract=725888.

Håkansson, H. and Snehota, I. (1995) *Developing Relationships in Business Networks*, Routledge: New York.

Hodgman, D. (1963) *Commercial Bank Loan and Investment Policy*. University of Illinois Press: Champaign, IL.

Holland, J. (1994) Bank lending relationships and the complex nature of bank-corporate relations. *Journal of Business Finance and Accounting*, **21** (3), 367–393.

Houston, J. and James, C. (1996) Bank information monopolies and the mix of private and public debt claims, *Journal of Finance*, **60** (5), 1863–1889.

Jensen, M. (1986) Agency costs of free cash flow, corporate finance and takeovers, *American Economic Review*, **76** (2), 323–329.

Köhler, M. (2010) *Corporate Governance and Current Regulation in the German Banking Sector: An Overview and Assessment*, ZEW – Centre for European Economic Research Discussion Paper No. 10-002. Available at SSRN: http://ssrn.com/abstract=1551270.

La Porta, R., Lopez-de-Silanes, F., Shleifer, A. and Vishny, R. (1998) Law and finance, *Journal of Political Economy*, **106** (6), 1113–1155.

Levine, R. (2002) Bank-based or market-based financial systems: Which is better? *Journal of Financial Intermediation*, **11** (4), 398–428.

Morck, R., Nakamura, M. and Shivdasani, A. (2000) Banks, Ownership Structure, and Firm Value in Japan, *Journal of Business*, **73** (4), 539–567

Moriarty, R., Kimball, R. and Gay, J. (1983) The Management of Corporate Banking Relationships, *Sloan Management Review*, Spring, 3–15.

Myers, S.C., and Majluf, N. (1984), Corporate financing and investment decisions when firms have information that investors do not have, *Journal of Financial Economics*, **13** (2), 187–221.

Oehmichen, J., Rapp, M. and Wolff, M. (2010) Der Einfluss der Aufsichtsratszusammensetzung auf die Präsenz von Frauen in Aufsichtsräten, in: *Zeitschrift für betriebswirtschaftliche Forschung* (zfbf), **62** (4), 504–533.

Rajan, R. (1992) Insiders and Outsiders: The Choice between Relationship and Arm's-Length Debt, *Journal of Finance*, **47** (4), 1367–1400.

Rapp, M., Schmidt, M., Schellong, D. and Wolff, M. (2010) Considering the Shareholder Perspective: Value-based Management Systems and Stock Market Performance, *Review of Managerial Science* 5 (2–3), 171–194.

Rapp, M. Schwetzler, B. and Sperling, M. (2009) *The Disappearing Deutschland AG – An Analysis of Block Trade in German Large Caps*, paper presented at the EURAM 2009 Annual Meeting.

Sah, R.K. and Stiglitz, J. (1985) Human Fallibility and Economic Organization, *American Economic Review*, **75** (2), 292–297.

Sah, R.K. and Stiglitz, J. (1986) The Architecture of Economic Systems: Hierarchies and Polyarchies, *American Economic Review*, **76** (4), 716–727.

Santos, J. and Rumble, A.S. (2006) The American Keiretsu and Universal Banks: Investing, Voting and Sitting on Nonfinancials' Corporate Boards, *Journal of Financial Economics*, **80** (2) 419–454.

Schroeder, U. and Schrader, A. (1998) The changing role of banks and corporate governance in Germany: Evolution towards the market? in: Black, S.W. and Moersch, M. (eds), *Competition and Convergence in Financial Markets*, Elsevier, 17–34.

Sharpe, S.A. (1990) Asymmetric information, bank lending and implicit contracts: A stylised model of customer relationships, *Journal of Finance*, **65** (4), 1069–1087.

Stiglitz, J.E. and Weiss, A. (1981) Credit rationing in markets with imperfect information, *American Economic Review*, **71** (3), 393–410.

Chapter 14

Japanese Corporate Governance[1]

Chapter contents

[1] I (Steen) am deeply grateful to the Research Institute of Capital Formation RICE at the Development Bank of Japan (DBJ) for awarding me the Shimomura Fellowship, which allowed me to write this paper as a DBJ guest. The financial, organizational and intellectual support of RICE has been invaluable. I am particularly grateful to Masaharu Hanazaki-san for helpful discussions and to Soko Nishizawa-san for research assistance.

14.1   Introduction

Twenty years ago Japan was widely admired for its corporate governance. Now after two decades of economic stagnation and stock market decline, Japanese governance is widely criticized for contributing to the financial crisis. The Nikkei index at less than 2,000 at year end 2010 was only 25% of the peak level (Figure 14.1). GDP per capita at $35,000 has barely grown during the same period.[2] And yet at the same time Japan is successfully producing and exporting the world's best cars, cameras, electronics and thousands of high-tech products.

In this chapter we review Japanese corporate governance. Is there a distinct Japanese corporate governance model? To what extent did it contribute to Japan's growth miracle? To what extent is it responsible for the current crisis? We begin with a review of the literature about the Japanese model and then go on to discuss its relationship to the boom and bust periods.

14.2   Is there a Japanese model?

Japanese corporate governance is said to have a number of special characteristics which separate Japan both from continental Europe and from the USA or the UK (Charkham, 1995; Lonien, 2007; Alexander, 2008).

Keiretsu (company groups) are the characteristic ownership mode for large listed firms (Prowse, 1992). At first glance, ownership is very dispersed and comparable to that in the USA or the UK, but closer scrutiny reveals that companies in a company group tend to hold shares in each other so it is usually impossible for an outsider to take over a Japanese company against the wishes of its management. Some keiretsu are formed among former subsidiaries in Japanese zaibatsu (family-owned business groups) which were broken up during the US occupation after the Second World

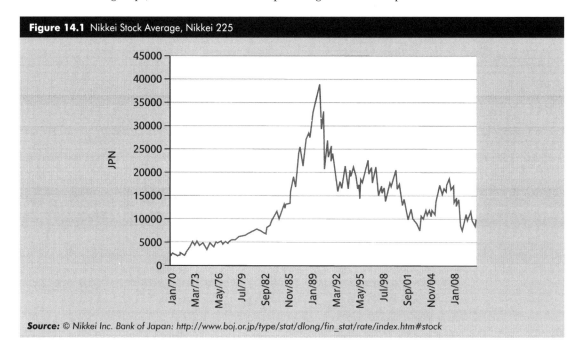

Figure 14.1 Nikkei Stock Average, Nikkei 225

Source: © Nikkei Inc. Bank of Japan: http://www.boj.or.jp/type/stat/dlong/fin_stat/rate/index.htm#stock

---

[2] Source: Statistical Handbook of Japan 2010, by Statistics Bureau, Japan, Chapter 3, pp. 23–24.

©War. These 'horizontal keiretsu' are often formed around 'main banks'. Others, vertical keiretsu, are formed along the supply chain so that a firm and its suppliers are united by ownership.

The keiretsu as an ideal type of Japanese ownership is not intended to overlook the existence of other ownership structures in Japan. Family ownership has recently been rediscovered as an important and well-performing part of Japanese business (Saito, 2008). Nor are business groups unique to Japan (Morck, 2005). The claim is rather that this particular kind of business group, often without a dominant owner, is the most distinctive characteristic of Japanese business.

While it is undisputed that many companies share the same name and hold ownership shares in each other, there is the more difficult question of what these company groups mean. To what extent are the companies acting independently, and to what extent do they form a coherent group? After all, the fact that the presidents of member companies meet once a month is not in itself an indicator of much coordination. The degree of group cohesion may have changed over time and is currently believed to be very weak in some of the bank-based groups in particular. Moreover, cross-shareholdings have been reduced in recent decades (Ahmadjian and Okumura, 2010).

Even in the absence of ownership ties, **industrial networks** between a firm and its suppliers are said to be highly stable and to be regarded as part of an on-going relationship rather than as a set of spot market transactions (Nakamura, 1992; Dyer and Ouchi, 1993; Dyer, 1994). However, while stable relationships appear to characterize the auto industry, they are not necessarily found in other industries (Hirakubo, Kublin and Topol, 2000).

Bank finance rather than equity finance was undisputedly the predominant mode of capital provision in Japan.[3] There are similarities to the traditional German bank-based model, but in Japan US-style 5% ownership ceilings were imposed during the occupation, and (although the ceilings were later raised to 10% in the revision to the Anti-Trust Act in 1953, just after restoration of Japanese sovereignty in May 1952) this has prevented Japanese banks from taking a dominant role in corporate ownership (Buck and Tull, 2000). However, because of financial deregulation, bank debt accounts for a much smaller proportion of firm liabilities, and bank shareholdings have also been reduced (Ahmadjian and Okumura, 2010).

The question is again: what does it mean? Some studies have found stronger monitoring and positive value effects of main bank ties. For example, Kang and Shivdasani (1995) find that managers are more likely to be fired for bad performance in firms with a main bank and outside succession is also more likely. After non-routine management replacement, company performance tends to improve. Kang and Shivdasani (1997) found that M&A is better appreciated by the stock market if the company has a main bank tie. This is also consistent with efficient monitoring. Others (Hoshi, Kashyap and Scharfstein, 1990) have found that bank ties help firms overcome financial distress. But satisfaction with the bank system has dried up in recent years. Rather than celebrating bank assistance, Hoshi (2006) talks of the disadvantages of keeping failing firms alive ('the economics of the living dead'). It is also possible that banks take advantage of their client relationships to charge higher interest and that they influence firms to become more risk averse (Weinstein and Yafeh, 1998). Another disadvantage of bank-based governance is that client firms with reciprocal ownership in their main bank are unlikely to be active owners and discipline bank managers, for example to prevent them from excessive lending in a property boom (Dinc, 2006). The net of these costs and benefits may well be negative. Hoshi and Kashyap (2001, pp. 200–201) review a number of empirical studies indicating that keiretsu firms have lower average profitability than stand-alone firms. This may reflect the fact that groups provide mutual insurance so that strong firms subsidize weak firms in the group.

The **Japanese board system** is essentially one-tier although with elements of a two-tier system with a statutory board of auditors. However, the board of auditors is mainly concerned with auditing and does not ratify strategic decisions, hire or fire managers or carry out other tasks associated with board work. A company law reform in 2002 introduced the option of an American-style board system with independent directors and committees for auditing, compensation and nomination (Aoki,

---

[3] In fact measured by domestic credit by the banking sector relative to GDP, Japan (163%) is a much more bank-oriented economy than Germany (107%) but so is the UK (211%)! (Source: The World Bank, 2010, http://data.worldbank.org/indicator/FS.AST.DOMS.GD.ZS).

2006). So far relatively few companies (< 100) appear to have chosen this model. However, there are currently proposals circulating which would mandate at least one truly independent director.

Boards tend to be large, historically sometimes as large as 30–40 members, but have been shrinking for years. They also tend to be composed primarily of company executives. Bebenroth and Donghao (2007) find an average board size of 10 and 7% outside directors (almost all of them in companies with the new board system). Consequently, board control of managers is virtually absent, while management control of boards is ubiquitous. While it is generally believed that lower board size has a positive effect on company performance, this was not found in Japan (Bebenroth and Donghao, 2007, Uchida 2011). Uchida (2011) shows that Japanese companies which reduce the size of their boards increase the number of officers proportionally so that the size of the total management team is unchanged.

In contrast, Kaplan and Minton (1994) found evidence that poor performance leads to (a higher probability of) appointment of outside directors, former bank or other corporate directors, and subsequent replacement of incumbent executives. They conclude that corporate shareholders play an important monitoring and disciplinary role in Japan. So boards can in fact make a difference. However, the appointment of a bank director is a rare event and it only has a positive effect on firm value where banks have an ownership interest, i.e. when bank and firm belong to the same business group (Morck and Nakamura, 1999).

Incentive pay appears to be less used and is less tied to shareholder value than in the USA (Kato and Kubo, 2006; Kubo and Saito, 2008). Kaplan (1994) found the same performance sensitivity as in the USA, but lower sensitivity to share price performance, which is understandable given that stock options were not allowed until 1996 (Ahmadjian, 2000). However, Kubo and Saito (2008) show that the performance sensitivity for CEO dismissals dropped after 1990. Neither do observed changes in incentive pay appear be associated with changes in company performance (Kubo, 2005). There may even be a negative effect (Sakawa and Watanabe, 2008). Average pay levels for managers tend to be lower than in the USA. Moreover, career progress seems to be determined by seniority more than performance. However, company-wide bonus systems for all employees appear to provide a collective incentive (Kato and Kubo, 2006).

Employee relations are characterized by long-term, often lifetime, employment with the same company (Charkham, 1995; Jackson, 2005). Japanese managers (salary men) and other employees tend to work in the same company throughout their careers. A system of enterprise unions, rather than trade unions, means that employees in the same company tend to be members of the same enterprise union.[4] They are therefore less likely to bargain for high wages when the company is in bad shape. The flip side of this company loyalty appears to be rather inflexible labour markets. It is very difficult to get a new job if you are fired. Recent papers conclude that the life-time employment model is alive and well for permanent employees (Shimizutani and Yokoyama, 2009; Suzuki, 2010). In fact Shimizutani and Yokoyama (2009) find that employment duration increased for permanent employees. Hassan and Hoshino (2009) document that companies have been willing to sacrifice profitability to maintain this goal. However, a new kind of non-regular (temporary) worker with less employment security has emerged, and the core of permanent employees is shrinking. Ono (2010) estimates that it is down to 20% of the labour force.

Government intervention has traditionally played some role in Japanese society, not least through so-called 'administrative guidance – gyōsei-shidō' (Schaede, 1994). For example, bank credit was apparently politically directed at certain sectors of the economy after WWII, and large parts of Japanese businesses are protected from international competition by tariffs and other trade barriers. However, it is not at all clear that government regulation is necessarily beneficial and over time many areas of the economy have been deregulated.

The role of the government is strengthened by appointment of former bureaucrats to bank boards (amakudari). It is conceivable that this practice can help increase the social responsibility of banks and other firms (Schaede, 1994), but it is also possible that it weakens financial supervision consistent with Stigler's hypothesis of capture of regulatory agencies (Stigler, 1971). Cosy ties between regulators

---

4   Interestingly, enterprise unions are not part of a traditional Japanese model. They were adopted during the 1950s to counter labour unrest.

and firms were criticized after the Fukushima nuclear disaster following the Tohoku earthquake and tsunami. Historically, banks without amakudari were found to have higher solvency (equity/assets) and fewer non-performing loans, although also slightly lower profitability (Hanazaki and Horiuchi, 2001; Horiuchi and Shimizu, 2001).

Company law in the civil law tradition was imported from Germany (Charkham, 1995). Although Japan scores highly on formal measures of investor protection (Djankov et al., 2007), the level of shareholder influence is very limited. Japanese companies are famous for holding their annual meetings on the same day (shuchubi) which effectively prevents small shareholders from attending most of them (Charkham, 1995; Ahmadjian and Okumura, 2010). Moreover, the meetings are said to be deliberately kept very short, for example 30 minutes. This is apparently to avoid embarrassing questions from so-called sokaiya, professional troublemakers with links to organized crime, who take bribes for keeping silent (Ahmadjian and Okumura, 2010). However the effect is to almost entirely sideline shareholder meetings.

Japanese culture is a popular explanation for differences in corporate governance. In *The Chrysanthemum and the Sword*, Ruth Benedict (1946) argued that the Japanese 'shame' culture is more social than the individualistic 'guilt' cultures of the West and that social motives like 'honour', 'obligation', or 'duty' play a much stronger role. Correspondingly, Charkham (1995) argued that Japanese corporate governance is shaped by mutual obligations between the company and its employees, a strong corporate family feeling, and decisions based on consensus and social responsibility. However, cultural stereotypes seem inconsistent with the dramatic changes in corporate governance during the past century (see below), while Japanese culture has presumably remained unchanged. Apparently, corporate governance is not only determined by culture, although culture may clearly be one of the important background variables.

Related to culture, **corporate objectives** as expressed by company managers seem to emphasize production, market share, stakeholder relations and company survival much more than shareholder value (Witt and Redding, 2009a). Hoshi and Kashyap (2001, p. 205) find high survival rates among listed firms in Japan compared with those in the USA, which they attributed to the keiretsu structure. Fewer bankruptcies may also reflect conservatism and lower risk taking, which is what we would expect in firms strongly influenced by banks, which are adverse to downside risk. Moreover, we would also expect to see an emphasis on growth given that Japanese managers are relatively autonomous and subjected to very little corporate governance. Neither shareholders, boards nor incentives appear to exert any strong influence on them or to induce them to create value, at least not shareholder value. Given this managerialist orientation of Japanese corporate governance it is not surprising that managers emphasize other goals over shareholder value, for example market share (Lonien, 2007) or stability of employment (Redding and Witt, 2008). It is of course possible that they are (or were) disciplined by other mechanisms (Schaede, 1994). After all, Kang, Shivdasani and Yamada (2000) found that the Japanese stock market generally reacts positively to M&A announcements which could indicate that acquiring firms were better governed and created more value than firms elsewhere.

All in all there appear to be several distinct characteristics of Japanese corporate governance. In the next two sections we consider two common denominators for these characteristics: bank governance and relational governance.

14.3 Bank governance

One way to summarize the Japanese system is 'bank governance' involving bank rather than equity financing of large corporations, close ties between (main) banks and their corporate clients, and cementing of these ties through cross-ownership (Aoki and Patrick, 1994; Hoshi and Kashyap, 2001). In this model, bankers rather than shareholders monitor companies and intervene if necessary.

Aoki (1988) has called the traditional Japanese model **'contingent governance'**, the logic of which seems to go something like this. Under normal circumstances, as long as the firm does not make a deficit which it cannot cover, management is left to its own devices. But in times of crisis, the main bank steps in and leads a rescue operation which takes charge of the subsequent restructuring.

Bank relationships thus reduce credit constraints in bankruptcy and financial distress. They provide an important source of insurance in an economy with a very small government sector and without a social safety net, e.g. without much employment insurance. In addition, inflexible labour markets make it difficult to find a new job. The closed markets for corporate control function appear particularly important under these circumstances.

This description of Japanese governance seems very similar to the traditional German bank-based system. But there are some variations. First and foremost, banks do not get to exert direct influence to the same extent. They do not own large blocks of shares and typically they do not place their own people on company boards. In this sense the Japanese company seems more autonomous than the German ideal type. Nor do Japanese employees get generous unemployment insurance or the right to elect directors to the company board. Instead they get greater job security.

The model is consistent in the sense that strong owners or takeovers are not necessary if banks do the monitoring. For the same reason independent boards are less necessary. Neither will bankers favour risk-taking by stock options compensation. In contrast a greater volume (production) will imply more bank business. It is in the interest of banks to avoid job losses which can increase their credit risk.

Even the role of the government in this model can be seen as an expression of contingent governance. Normally the government does not interfere (and in fact the Japanese government sector is very small) but in times of crisis it will step in to salvage failing banks.

14.4   Relational governance theory

An alternative but complementary view is that Japanese companies, and Japanese society, are ruled by relational governance (Kester, 1992; Gilson and Roe, 1993). Relational governance involves on-going relationships between market participants and other members of society. Instead of coordinating economic activity purely via the price mechanism, relational governance involves additional formal or informal contractual obligations. For example, instead of just buying and selling, an on-going relationship between buyer and seller may facilitate trust and mutually binding long-term contracts, or they may partially internalize the transaction by buying stock in each other. Social mechanisms like reputation and culture may reinforce or replace formal contracts.

Oliver Williamson (1975, 1985, 2005) has persuasively argued that such contractual governance can be (transaction) cost effective when the relationship is:

- on-going and long-term (i.e. characterized by a high frequency of transactions), and
- characterized by intermediate dependency (asset specificity).

For example, long-term contracts and ownership integration can insure the parties to the transaction against opportunistic behaviour and thereby increase their incentive to make transaction-specific investments.

Complete integration will involve a merger between the firms involved in a transaction, which implies a loss of local autonomy and incentives in the individual firms. An alternative, hybrid mode of organization is relational governance where firms form associations by partial ownership, interlocking boards, long-term contracts and social relationships. Such partial integration may promote trust and cooperation between the firms involved.[5]

Relational governance may be extended to a wider group of stakeholders like employees or consumers whose loyalty is a valuable asset for the firm. For example, a company which treats its employees well and does not fire them unless it is absolutely necessary, will build up loyalty in the workforce which makes employees less likely to change jobs. Among consumers, a track record of providing superior value at low prices will build brand loyalty.

---

[5] An alternative theory of keiretsu is that they are a mechanism to reduce competition and block entry, but this appears to be contrary to the empirical evidence (Weinstein and Yafeh, 1995).

By stabilizing economic relationships, relational governance can reduce risk, for example employment risk, and if market participants are risk averse this will be a competitive advantage.

14.5 The keiretsu system: an example

Keiretsu are groups of companies loosely connected by cross-ownership and sometimes also by a joint name (logo) and a common management philosophy. The shareholdings by group members, and sometimes also by business partners outside the group, are extremely stable and constitute an effective defence against hostile takeover. There are fewer ties between company groups.

It is unclear to what extent group members actually exercise their ownership. In some cases, executives from other group companies sit on the board, and some loose coordination apparently takes place at monthly 'Presidents' meetings'.

There are said to be two types of keiretsu: horizontal and vertical.

Horizontal keiretsu, like Mitsubishi, consist of companies in different industries. Traditionally there was only one company per industry and this meant there were no competitors. But more recently, there are examples of competition between group members. The result is a spider's web of small ownership shares (Figure 14.2). There is often a 'main bank' at the centre of such keiretsu which handles the banking business of the associated companies.

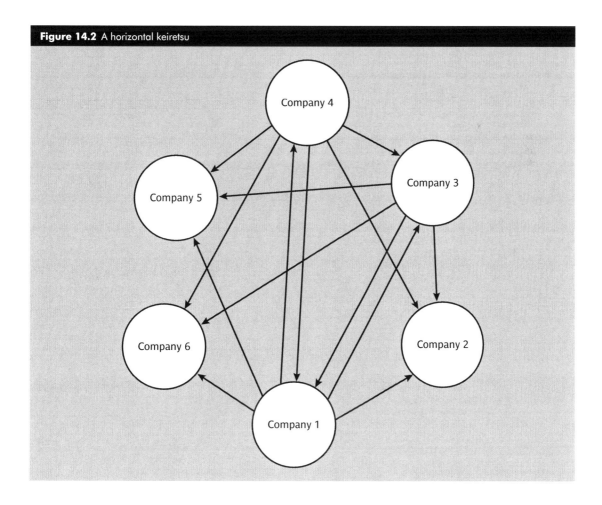

Figure 14.2 A horizontal keiretsu

An example of a horizontal keiretsu is the Mitsubishi group, which consists (among others) of the companies mentioned in Table 14.1. There are a number of different companies from many different industries.

The Mitsubishi zaibatsu was broken up in 1945 and today the members are increasingly regarded as independent companies. However, Mitsubishi Corporation, the core of the Mitsubishi Group, Japan's largest general trading house (sogo shosha), still provides services across the entire value chain for its business group members and other clients (see Table 14.2).

Vertical keiretsu, like the Toyota group, consist of firms in the same value chain from raw material to production to distribution. There is typically one leading firm that controls the chain which contributes to coordination of activities along the supply chain (Figure 14.3).

Table 14.1   The Mitsubishi Group

Asahi Glass Co., Ltd.
Mitsubishi Gas Chemical Company, Inc.
Mitsubishi Shindoh Co., Ltd.
The Bank of Tokyo-Mitsubishi UFJ, Ltd.
Mitsubishi Heavy Industries, Ltd.
Mitsubishi Steel Mfg. Co., Ltd.
Kirin Holdings Company, Ltd.
Mitsubishi Kakoki Kaisha, Ltd.
Mitsubishi UFJ Securities Co., Ltd.
Meiji Yasuda Life Insurance Co.
Mitsubishi Logistics Corp.
Mitsubishi UFJ Trust and Banking Corp.
Mitsubishi Aluminium Co., Ltd.
Mitsubishi Materials Corp.
Nikon Corp.
Mitsubishi Cable Industries, Ltd.
Mitsubishi Motors Corp.
Nippon Oil Corp.
Mitsubishi Chemical Corp.
Mitsubishi Paper Mills Ltd.
Nippon Yusen Kabushiki Kaisha
Mitsubishi Corporation
Mitsubishi Plastics, Inc.
Mitsubishi Construction Co., Ltd.
Mitsubishi Electric Corp.
Mitsubishi Rayon Co., Ltd.
Tokio Marine & Nichido Fire Insurance Co., Ltd.
Mitsubishi Estate Co., Ltd.
Mitsubishi Research Institute, Inc.

Source: Mitsubishi Group, www.mitsubishi.com

Table 14.2   Trade services offered by Mitsubishi Corporation

Sales agency: sales and exports for manufacturers

Marketing

Purchasing

Logistics (transport and storage)

Finance

Processing and producing goods

Investment: e.g. building plants and establishment of subsidiaries and affiliated companies

Business intelligence: gathering, analysing and supplying information on international affairs, legal matters and market trends

Business consulting

Technology search: R&D and technology transfers

Joint projects: cooperating with business partners, M&A, joint ventures, network formation

Source: Mitsubishi Group, www.mitsubishi.com

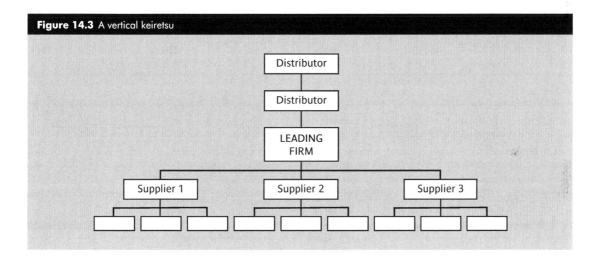

Figure 14.3 A vertical keiretsu

Many Japanese management innovations, e.g. just-in-time, the redevelopment of quality management, the kanban system, seem to spring from this type of coordination. This is consistent with 'Williamsonian' advantages of relational contracting.

14.6   The governance vacuum

In summary, there is no doubt that Japan has a unique governance model. It is more questionable whether the model addresses the agency problems which corporate governance is supposed to address. Does it effectively prevent managers from overinvesting? Does it guide investment towards effective allocation of capital? Does it replace managers when necessary?

Even in the traditional post-war model it was clear that managers acted relatively unrestrained by formal mechanisms such as active owners, independent boards or pay for performance. The main bank mainly became active when firms failed so there was little governance of successful firms.

Moreover, management autarchy appears to have been strengthened in recent decades as main banks and company groups became weaker. The weakened old mechanisms have not been replaced by new ones like independent boards or corporate takeovers. Some observers therefore talk of a vacuum in Japanese governance (Hanazaki and Horiuchi, 2001, 2003, 2004; Ahmadjian and Okumura, 2010).

It is clear that social norms to some extent have kept managerial opportunism in check. There have been relatively few scandals related to fraud, self-dealing and excessive pay. Moreover, international competition seems to have forced exporting firms to become effective. However, cultural norms have tended to preserve the status quo, e.g. zombie firms, rather than pressure managers to efficient use of capital and labour. And large areas of the Japanese economy are sheltered from competition. Thus, in the Japanese case weak governance may lead to low productivity growth rather than opportunism, i.e. to sins of omission rather than sins of commission.

Caballero, Hoshi and Kashyap (2008) study the social effects of zombie firms. By keeping unproductive firms alive, they argue, productivity growth is kept lower than it otherwise would be, but profit rates are also kept down, preventing profitable new entry and further investment.

14.7 Corporate governance and the crisis

In retrospect, Japanese governance arguably contributed both to the growth miracle and the subsequent crisis. A standard real economy story (à la Hayashi and Prescott, 2002, but different from theirs) goes something like this.

The post-war growth miracle took place in a period when productivity and labour costs had not yet reached the production possibility frontier. In addition the global economic climate up to 1974 was unusually favourable. The growth potential was enormous, and Japanese firms succeeded in exploiting it very well. Japanese governance effectively engineered firms into growth machines with few checks and stops. Autonomous managers not controlled by profit-seeking owners, independent boards or pay for performance are known to seek growth. Banks provided a source of inexpensive finance. The standard agency problems which corporate governance is expected to address were relatively small. Overinvestment and empire building are not really problematic if the growth potential is sufficiently large, and if managerial profligacy is kept reasonably in check by regulation, social norms and competition. Lifetime employment made sense since there was work enough for everyone.

As may be seen in Figure 14.4, the beginning of the economic crisis corresponds almost exactly to complete catch-up, when Japanese GDP per capita reached Western level. The subsequent distance between the two graphs can be seen as an indicator of unexploited growth potential in the Japanese economy.

During 1970–1990 the favourable conditions changed. Japan reached and in many sectors surpassed the productivity frontier, and the global economic climate worsened due to energy price shocks, protectionism and stagflation. But the miracle had created expectations of continuing growth in living standards, property prices etc. Moreover, Japanese corporate governance was in no way adapted to the new situation. The economy finally hit the wall with the bursting of the 1990 bubble. Post-crisis Japan is still in Aoki's words in a state of institutional flux, meaning 'an unfinished period of institutional change' (Aoki, 2006).

The new circumstances are such that the growth potential is smaller and of a different nature, related to productivity growth rather than factor growth. This means that overinvestment and excess labour is much more of an issue. Value creation by efficient use of resources, rather than increased employment of capital and labour, is the important challenge. Growth in this scenario is more likely to come from high-tech start-ups which require venture capital rather than bank finance. Even in established sectors like services, productivity growth is more likely to come from small and medium sized companies, which are less insulated from market mechanisms. This is likely to lead to creative destruction of existing firms, which will need to downsize and restructure. In the large companies efficient investment must involve attention to opportunity costs of capital rather than just breaking even. This will require governance structures which can impel managers to become more effective, including active ownership,

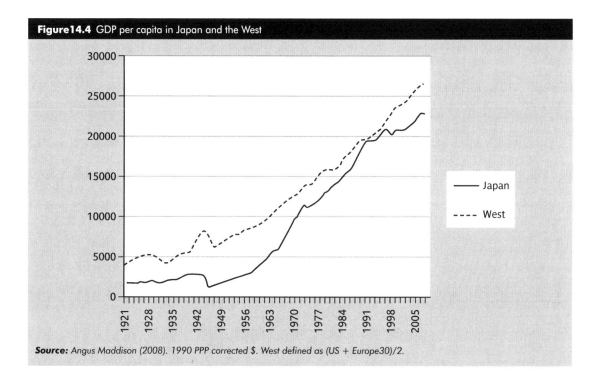

Figure14.4 GDP per capita in Japan and the West

Source: Angus Maddison (2008). 1990 PPP corrected $. West defined as (US + Europe30)/2.

independent boards and economic incentives. Balancing this need for change with attention to social harmony and political stability is likely to be the challenge of the next decades.

Superimposed on this real economy story is the **banking crisis**. Japanese banks lent excessively in the boom years up to 1990 and have been burdened with bad debts ever since. While there may be many other causes of the banking crisis, the question here is whether corporate governance had anything to do with it.

One view, associated with Aoki (1994) and Hellmann et al. (2000), is that the crisis was caused by deregulation of the financial sector, which loosened the bonds between firms and banks and lowered the incentives of banks to monitor firms. As firms were no longer governed, they overspent, and this created the crisis.

A somewhat different version, associated with Hoshi and Kashyap (2004), is that lopsided deregulation made it possible for large firms to fund themselves in the capital market, while household investment remained regulated and continued to be channelled into bank deposits. Banks therefore expanded their loans to construction and real estate, which fuelled the housing bubble and the subsequent burst. Because banks are afraid to recognize their losses, they continue to refinance failing zombie firms (Hoshi 2006), which has dramatic negative effects on productivity growth.

A third view, associated with Hanazaki and Horiuchi (2001, 2003, 2004), is that the crisis was caused by failure of bank governance. Unchecked managerial expense preference can explain why banks have grown so large, why they were allowed to lend excessively during the boom years, why high staff costs and low levels of bank profitability are tolerated, and why bank managers continue to refinance failing firms. Managerial autonomy is arguably less of a problem in industrial firms faced with international competition, which is absent in the banking sector. On the contrary, moral hazard has been stimulated through an implicit government safety net. Financial regulation on, for example, capital adequacy also appears to have been loosened.

Interestingly, all three views appear to involve corporate governance failure. As we have seen previously, safeguarding employment and supporting firms in financial distress are a characteristic of traditional Japanese governance. While these traits were consistent with high growth in the post-bubble era, they appear to have become a serious liability during the past two decades.

14.8 Discussion

To conclude, we return to the three key questions raised at the beginning of the chapter and try to provide clear, though tentative answers.

1 Is there a distinct Japanese governance model?

The answer is yes. Japanese corporate governance is not a clone of any existing governance system. There are similarities to the traditional German system of bank governance, but the company groups, long-term employment and absence of board controls are distinct Japanese characteristics. Neither does Japan share in the German codetermination system. There is no one-to-one correspondence between this system and Japanese culture, however. Governance is not destiny.

2 Was Japanese governance responsible for the growth miracle?

The answer is no. The fundamental driver of the growth miracle was probably a productivity catch-up such as we are seeing in emerging markets today. Japanese governance no doubt facilitated the growth miracle by providing plentiful finance to banks and by providing a stable and reasonably responsible institutional regime. But the growth would have happened anyway as it is happening in completely different institutional settings today, like China (communism and government ownership) or India (democracy and family business).

3 Is Japanese governance responsible for the crisis?

The answer here is yes, partly. Unlike the growth miracle or the global financial crisis of 2008 the prolonged Japanese crisis of 1990–2010 is a distinct Japanese phenomenon. Other Asian countries escaped relatively quickly from the Asian debt crisis of 1997, but Japan has been stuck for two decades. The surprise is not that the growth miracle ended, but rather that the Japanese economy has been unable to resume growth at the pace of other developed economies (e.g. 2% a year) despite record-low interest rates, a well-educated and dedicated workforce and a stable institutional environment. To progress in the global knowledge economy, a different capital market is probably needed with more emphasis on efficient allocation of capital, equity finance, small businesses growth and creative destruction. This requires a new kind of governance with a stronger role for owners, independent boards and profit incentives. It almost certainly also requires institutional reforms in other areas such as the labour market, competition policy and social security.

The good news is that the present situation is sufficiently unsatisfactory to be creating a growing discrepancy between Japan's economic potential and the status quo. The rewards to institutional change will therefore be growing over time. The probability that this opportunity will be seized is therefore growing over time.

Minicase

Mitsui Group

Mitsui Group is one of the largest corporate conglomerates (keiretsu) in the world. Companies in the Mitsui family include Mitsui & Co., Chuo Mitsui Trust Holdings, Japan Steel Works, Mitsui Chemicals, Mitsui Construction Co., Mitsui Engineering and Shipbuilding, Mitsui Fudosan, Mitsui-gold, Mitsui Mining & Smelting, Mitsui Oil Exploration Co. (MOECO), Mitsui OSK Lines Ltd., Mitsui Petrochemical Industries Ltd, Mitsui-Soko, Mitsui Sumitomo Insurance Group, Oji Paper Company, Pacific Coast Recycling, Sumitomo Mitsui Banking Corporation, Taiheiyo Cement, Toray Industries, Tri-net Logistics Management. Sony and Tokyo Broadcasting System are said to have close ties to the group. Many others, e.g. Toshiba, Toyota Motors, and Suntory, have become independent.

Mitsui & Co. is active in sales, logistics and financing and infrastructure projects. Its ownership is dispersed with the Master Trust Bank of Japan, Ltd. (9.04%), Japan Trustee Services Bank, Ltd. (6.80%) and Sumitomo Mitsui Banking Corporation (2.10%) as the largest shareholders.

The board consists of:

- Masami Iijima, Chief Executive Officer
- Joji Okada, Chief Financial Officer
- Takao Omae, Vice President
- Masayoshi Komai, Vice President
- Fuminobu Kawashima, Senior Executive Managing Officer
- Kiyoshi Masuko, Deputy Chief Operating Officer of EMEA Business Unit Masayuki Kinoshita, Executive Managing Officer
- Daisuke Saiga, Executive Managing Officer, Representative Director, Junichi Matsumoto
- Shoei Utsuda, Mitsui & Co. Ltd.
- Toshiro Mutoh, Mitsui & Co. Ltd.
- Satoru Miura, Mitsui & Co. Ltd.
- Motonori Murakami, Mitsui & Co. Ltd.
- Hideharu Kadowaki,. Mitsui Chemicals Inc.
- Seiichi Tanaka, Mitsui & Co. Ltd.
- Nobuko Matsubara, Daiwa Securities Group Inc.
- Naoto Nakamura, Asahi Group Holdings Ltd.
- Ikujiro Nonaka, Seven & I Holdings Co., Ltd.
- Hiroshi Hirabayashi, Toshiba Corp.
- Hiroyasu Watanabe, Nomura Co.
- Kunihiro Matsuo, Asahi Glass Co.

The company's revenue has decreased during the crisis, but its return on equity has remained over 10% on average for the last 5 years.

Sources: compiled from Reuters, Wikipedia, Google Finance; Mitsui & Co, for the corporate governance statement: http://www.mitsui.com/jp/en/company/governance/outlook/__icsFiles/afieldfile/2011/02/14/Outlook_CG_.pdf

Discussion questions

1 Does the Mitsui group make sense from a shareholder value perspective?
2 Do you think Mitsui & Co. could be targeted in a hostile takeover?
3 What do you think about its board?

Summary (learning points)

- The Japanese model is characterized by cross-ownership ties within business groups (keiretsu), insider-dominated boards, low and relatively fixed executive pay and limited protection of minority investors.

- This means that Japanese managers are unconstrained by most formal governance mechanisms. However, social norms may exert an important influence.
- Soft characteristics attributed to the Japanese model include loyalty (life-time employment), community and consensus.
- Increasing foreign investment and weakening of some business groups have led to some modernization of Japanese governance, but the process is slow.
- The model was highly successful in the growth period 1950–1990, but is believed to be partly responsible for two 'lost decades' 1990–2010.

References and further reading

Ahmadjian, C. (2000) Chapter 9. Changing Japanese Corporate Governance, *Japanese Economy*, **28** (6), 59–84.

Ahmadjian, C. (2008) Japan's Evolving Corporate Governance System, *Japan Spotlight*, **27** (3), 10–13.

Ahmadjian, C. and Okumura, A. (2010). Corporate Governance in Japan. Edward Elgar Handbook on International Corporate Governance. Forthcoming.

Alexander, A. (2008) The Japan Story, *International Economy*, **22** (3), 73–76.

Aoki, M. (1988), *Information, incentives and bargaining in the Japanese economy*, Cambridge University Press: Cambridge.

Aoki, M. (1994). Monitoring characteristics of the main bank system: An analytical and developmental view, in: Aoki, M., Hugh, P. (eds.), *The Japanese Main Bank System: Its Relevancy for Developing and Transforming Economies*, Oxford University Press: New York, 109–141.

Aoki, M. (2006) *Whither Japan's Corporate Governance*, Rock Center for Corporate Governance Working Paper No. 29. Available at SSRN: http://ssrn.com/abstract=918624.

Aoki, M. and Patrick, H. (eds) (1994) *The Japanese Main Bank System*, Clarendon Press: Oxford.

Aoki, M., Patrick, H. and Sheard, P. (1994) The Japanese Main Bank System: An Introductory Overview, in M. Aoki and H. Patrick (eds.), *The Japanese Main Bank System: Its Relevance for Developing and Transforming Economies*, Oxford University Press: Oxford, 3–5.

Basu, S., Hwang, L., Mitsudome, T. and Weintrop, J. (2007) Corporate governance, top executive compensation and firm performance in Japan, *Pacific-Basin Finance Journal*, **15** (1), 56–79.

Bebenroth, R.B. and Donghao, L. (2007) Performance Impact at the Board Level: Corporate Governance in Japan, *Asian Business & Management*, **6** (3), 303–326.

Benedict, R. (1946) *The Chrysanthemum and the Sword, Patterns of Japanese Culture*, Houghton, Mifflin Company: Boston.

Buck, T. and Tull, M. (2000) Anglo-American Contributions to Japanese and German Corporate Governance after World War Two, *Business History*, **42** (2), 119–140.

Caballero, R., Hoshi, T. and Kashyap, A. (2008) Zombie Lending and Depressed Restructuring in Japan, *American Economic Review*, **98** (5), 1943–1977.

Charkham, J. (1995) *Keeping Good Company: A Study of Corporate Governance in Five Countries*, Oxford University Press: Oxford.

Constand, R., and Pace, R. (1998) Another look at corporate ownership in Japan, *Global Finance Journal*, **9** (1), 127–147.

Dinc, S. (2006) Monitoring the Monitors: The Corporate Governance in Japanese Banks and Their Real Estate Lending in the 1980s, *Journal of Business*, (November), **79** (6), 3057–3081.

Djankov, S., McLiesh, C. and Shleifer, A. (2007) Private credit in 129 countries, *Journal of Financial Economics*, **84** (2), 299–329.

Djankov, S., La Porta, R., Lopez-de-Silanes, F. and Shleifer, A. (2008) The law and economics of self-dealing, *Journal of Financial Economics*, **88** (3), 430–465.

Dyer, J.H. (1994) Dedicated assets: Japan's manufacturing edge, *Harvard Business Review*, **72** (6),174–178.

Dyer, J.H. and Ouchi, W.G. (1993) Japanese-style partnerships: Giving companies a competitive edge, *Sloan Management Review* **35** (1), 51–64.

Flath, D. (2000) *The Japanese Economy*, Oxford University Press: Oxford.

Gedajlovic, E. and Shapiro, D. (2002) Ownership Structure and Firm Profitability in Japan, *Academy of Management Journal*, **45** (3), 565–575.

Gilson, R.J. and. Roe, M.J. (1993) Understanding the Japanese Keiretsu: Overlaps between Corporate Governance and Industrial Organization, *Yale Law Journal*, **102** (4), 871–906.

Hanazaki, M. and Horiuchi, A. (2001) A Vacuum of Governance in Japanese Bank Management, in

Banking, Capital Markets and Corporate Governance, Osano, H. and Tachibanaki, T. (eds.), Palgrave.

Hanazaki, M, and Horiuchi, A. (2003) A review of Japan's bank crisis from the governance perspective, *Pacific-Basin Finance Journal*, **11** (3), 305.

Hanazaki, M. and Horiuchi, A. (2004) Can the Financial Restraint Theory Explain the Postwar Experience of Japan's Financial System? in *Designing Financial Systems in East Asia and Japan*, (Joseph P.H. Fan, Masaharu Hanazaki and Juro Teranishi, eds.), RoutledgeCurzon, pp. 19–46.

Hassan, H. and Hoshino, Y. (2009) Long-Term Employment Contracts In Japanese Companies and the Corporate Profitability in the Post Economic Bubble Era, *Journal of Financial Management & Analysis*, **22** (2), 26–48.

Hayashi, F. and Prescott, E. (2002) The 1990s in Japan: A Lost Decade, *Review of Economic Dynamics*, **5** (1), 206.

Hellmann, T., Murdock, K. and Stiglitz, J. (2000) Liberalization, Moral Hazard in Banking, and Prudential Regulation: Are Capital Requirements Enough? *American Economic Review*, **90** (1), 147–165.

Hiraki, T., Inoue, H., Ito, A., Kuroki, F. and Masuda, H. (2003) Corporate governance and firm value in Japan: Evidence from 1985 to 1998, *Pacific-Basin Finance Journal*, **11** (3), 239.

Hirakubo, N., Kublin, M. and Topol, M. (2000) The Myth of Japanese Buyer–Supplier Relationships. *American Journal of Business*, **15** (2), 85–92.

Hirota, S., Kubo, K., Miyajima, H., Paul, H. and Young Won, P. (2010). Corporate mission, corporate policies and business outcomes: evidence from Japan, *Management Decision*, **48** (7), 1134–1153.

Horiuchi, A. and Shimizu, K. (2001) Did amakudari undermine the effectiveness of regulator monitoring in Japan?, *Journal of Banking & Finance*, **25** (3), 573–596.

Hoshi, T. (2006) Economics of the Living Dead, *Japanese Economic Review*, **57** (1), 30–49.

Hoshi, T. and Kashyap, A.K. (2001) *Corporate Financing and Governance in Japan: The Road to the Future*, MIT Press: Cambridge, MA.

Hoshi, T., and Kashyap, A. (2010) Will the U.S. bank recapitalization succeed? Eight lessons from Japan, *Journal of Financial Economics*, **97** (3), 398–417.

Hoshi, T., Kashyap, A. and Scharfstein, D. (1990) The role of banks in reducing the costs of financial distress in Japan, *Journal of Financial Economics*, **27** (1), 67–88.

Jackson, G. (2005) Stakeholders under Pressure: corporate governance and labour management in Germany and Japan, *Corporate Governance: An International Review*, **13** (3), 419–428.

Jacoby, S. (2007) Principles and Agents: CalPERS and corporate governance in Japan, *Corporate Governance: An International Review*, **15** (1), 5–15.

Jameson, M., Sullivan, M. and Constand, R. (2000) Ownership Structure and Performance of Japanese Firms: Horizontal Keiretsu, Vertical Keiretsu, and Independents, *Review of Pacific Basin Financial Markets & Policies*, **3** (4), 535.

Kang, J. and Shivdasani, A. (1995) Firm performance, corporate governance, and top executive turnover in Japan, *Journal of Financial Economics*, **38** (1), 29–58.

Kang, J. and Shivdasani, A. (1997) Corporate restructuring during performance declines in Japan, *Journal of Financial Economics*, **46** (1), 29–65.

Kang, J. and Shivdasani, A. (1996) Does the Japanese governance system enhance shareholder wealth? Evidence from the stock-price effects of top management turnover, *Review of Financial Studies*, **9** (4), 1061–1095.

Kang, J., Shivdasani, A. and Yamada, T. (2000) The Effect of Bank Relations on Investment Decisions: An Investigation of Japanese Takeover Bids, *Journal of Finance*, **55** (5), 2197–2218.

Kaplan, S. (1994) Top executive rewards and firm performance: A comparison of Japan and the United States, *Journal of Political Economy*, **102** (3), 510.

Kaplan, S. and Minton, B. (1994) Appointments of outsiders to Japanese boards: Determinants and implications for managers, *Journal of Financial Economics*, **36** (2), 225–258.

Kato, T. and Kubo, K. (2006) CEO compensation and firm performance in Japan: Evidence from new panel data on individual CEO pay, *Journal of the Japanese & International Economies*, **20** (1), 1–19.

Kester, W. (1992) Industrial Groups as Contractual Governance Systems, *Oxford Review of Economic Policy*, **8** (3), 24–44.

Kubo, K. (2005) Executive Compensation Policy and Company Performance in Japan, *Corporate Governance: An International Review*, **13** (3), 429–436.

Kubo, K. and Saito, T. (2008) The Relationship Between Financial Incentives for Company Presidents and Firm Performance in Japan, *Japanese Economic Review*, **59** (4), 401–418.

Lonien, C. (2007) Chapter 1. The Old Japanese Keiretsu Model. *Japanese Economy*, **34** (3), 5–36.

Maddison, A. (2008) Statistics on world population, GDP and per capita GDP, 1–2008 AD. http://www.ggdc.net/maddison/oriindex.htm.

Morck R.K. (ed.) (2005) *A History of Corporate Governance around the World: Family Business Groups to Professional Managers*, University of Chicago Press.

Morck, R. and Nakamura, M. (1999) Banks and Corporate Control in Japan, *Journal of Finance*, **54** (1), 319–339.

Morck, R. and Nakamura, M. (2005) Frog in a Well Knows Nothing of the Ocean: A History of Corporate Ownership in Japan, pp. 367–459, in Morck, R. (ed.) *A History of Corporate Governance around the World: Family Business Groups to Professional Managers*, University of Chicago Press.

Nakamura, H. (1992) *Beyond the Keiretsu* (in Japanese). NTT Publishing: Tokyo.

Noda, T. and Ichihashi, M. (2010) Governance Structures and Management Efficiency in Japanese Companies, *Japanese Economy*, **37** (2), 58–82.

Ono, H. (2010) Lifetime employment in Japan: Concepts and measurements, *Journal of the Japanese & International Economies*, **24** (1), 1–27.

Prowse, S. (1992) The Structure of Corporate Ownership in Japan, *Journal of Finance*, **47** (3), 1121–1140.

Redding, G. and Witt, M. (2008) The role of executive rationale in the comparison of capitalisms: some preliminary findings, INSEAD Working Paper No. 2004/15/ABCM/EARC7.

Saito, T. (2008). Family firms and firm performance: Evidence from Japan, *Journal of the Japanese & International Economies*, **22** (4), 620–646.

Sakawa, H. and Watanabe, N. (2008) Relationship between Managerial Compensation and Business Performance in Japan: New Evidence Using Micro Data, *Asian Economic Journal*, **22** (4), 431–455.

Schaede, U. (1994) Understanding Corporate Governance in Japan: Do Classical Concepts Apply?, *Industrial & Corporate Change*, **3** (2), 285–323.

Shimizu, T. and Tajima, K. (2010) Improving reputations, *International Financial Law Review*, 51–54. http://www.iflr.com/Article/2394961/Improving-reputations.html

Shimizutani, S. and Yokoyama, I. (2009) Has Japan's Long-Term Employment Practice Survived? Developments Since the 1990s, *Industrial & Labor Relations Review*, **62** (3), 313–326.

Statistics Bureau, Japan (2010) *Statistical Handbook of Japan 2010*.

Stigler, G. (1971) The theory of economic regulation, *Bell Journal of Economics and Management Science*, **2** (1), 3–21.

Sueyoshi, T., Goto, M. and Omi, Y. (2010) Corporate governance and firm performance: Evidence from Japanese manufacturing industries after the lost decade, *European Journal of Operational Research*, **203** (3), 724–736.

Suzuki, H. (2010) Employment Relations in Japan: Recent Changes under Global Competition and Recession, *Journal of Industrial Relations*, **52** (3), 387–401.

Uchida, K. (2011) Does Corporate Board Downsizing Increase Shareholder Value? Evidence from Japan, *International Review of Economics & Finance*, **20** (4), 562–573.

Weinstein, D. and Yafeh, Y. (1995) Japan's Corporate Groups: Collusive or Competitive? An Empirical Investigation of Keiretsu Behavior, *Journal of Industrial Economics*, **43** (4), 359.

Weinstein, D. and Yafeh, Y. (1998) On the Costs of a Bank-Centered Financial System: Evidence from the Changing Main Bank Relations in Japan, *Journal of Finance*, **53** (2), 635–672.

Williamson, O. (1975) *Markets and Hierarchies*, Free Press: New York.

Williamson, O. (1985) *The Economic Institutions of Capitalism*, Free Press: New York.

Williamson, O. (1996) *The Mechanisms of Governance*, Oxford University Press: Oxford.

Williamson, O. (2005) The Economics of Governance, *American Economic Review*, **95**, (2), 1–18.

Witt, M. and Redding, G. (2009) The Spirits of Capitalism: German, Japanese, and US Senior Executive Perceptions of Why Firms Exist. *INSEAD Working Papers Collection*, 2009 61, 1–58.

Witt, M. and Redding, G. (2009a) Culture, meaning and institutions: executive rationale in Germany and Japan, *Journal of International Business Studies*, **40** (5), 859–885.

Yabei, H. and Izumida, S. (2008). Ownership Concentration and Corporate Performance: A Causal Analysis with Japanese Panel Data, *Corporate Governance: An International Review*, **16** (4), 342–358.

Yoshikawa, T. and Phan, P. (2005) The Effects of Ownership and Capital Structure on Board Composition and Strategic Diversification in Japanese Corporations, *Corporate Governance: An International Review*, **13** (2), 303–312.

Yoshikawa, T. and Rasheed, A. (2010) Family Control and Ownership Monitoring in Family-Controlled Firms in Japan, *Journal of Management Studies*, **47** (2), 274–295.

Yoshikawa, T., Lai Si, T. and McGuire, J. (2007) Corporate Governance Reform as Institutional Innovation: The Case of Japan, *Organization Science*, **18** (6), 973–988.

Chapter 15

Corporate Governance in China[1]

Chapter contents

---

[1] This chapter draws heavily on research carried out by Lerong He and Martin Conyon. We thank Lerong for discussions and comments. See Conyon and He (2011a, b, c).

15.1   Introduction

China is the world's second largest economy. Its growth rate since the 1980s has been highly significant, exceeding 10% per annum. Even since the global macro-economic downturn beginning in 2008, China economy has proved to be robust. Also, since the 1980s China's corporate governance arrangements have shifted dramatically, as capital market reforms have deepened. In this chapter we discuss the evolution of corporate governance in China, paying attention to the ownership of firms, the board of directors and the changing structure of executive incentives.

China is the most populous state in the world, with in excess of 1.3 billion people. China is a single-party state dominated by the Communist Party of China (CPC) and is made up of over twenty-two provinces, five autonomous regions, four directly administered municipalities (Beijing, Tianjin, Shanghai, and Chongqing). There are two autonomous special administrative regions: Hong Kong and Macau. In 1978 Deng Xiao-Ping opened the Chinese economy to the rest of the world. Since then China's overall trade as a percentage of GDP has risen steeply from about 8% in 1977 to about 35% in 1999. In the last 35 years China's economic growth, reform and transition have skyrocketed.

As we show in more detail below, corporate governance arrangements in China deviate significantly from those found in Anglo-Saxon countries such as the United States. Perhaps the most important difference is that the Chinese State continues to play a major role in the ownership and control of enterprises. China remains a socialist economy, despite its economic reforms. Indeed, it seems interesting to us that economic convergence to market-style models in China appears to have outpaced political convergence to the Western democratic model.

China's economic evolution has important implications for entrepreneurship, innovation and the performance of firms. In this chapter we describe the main features of corporate governance in China. Our main focus is on the distinctive patterns of firm ownership, the board of directors and the incentives arising from executive compensation. We illustrate that since the early 2000s China has embarked upon a series of corporate governance reforms. The purpose of these was to further develop its capital markets and promote investor confidence in China. The overall picture of Chinese corporate governance is one of flux: China's firms are adapting to the modern global economy.

15.2   Institutional context

China's macro economy

Since the late 1970s China's economy has transformed from what was effectively a socialist centrally planned system to a more market-oriented one. These reforms can be considered as gradual rather than radical. They include increased autonomy for state-owned enterprises (SOEs), the opening up of the economy to foreign trade and investment, the development of domestic stock markets, and the rapid growth of the private sector. These have led to significant efficiency gains. A key year in the modern restructuring of China is 1978. Since then China's GDP has increased more than ten-fold. In 2010 China was the second-largest economy in the world after the USA. China's estimated 2010 GDP, at purchasing power parity, was about $9.8 trillion. In the same year, China's economy (GDP) grew at about 10% (Conyon and He, 2011c; Song et al., 2011).[2]

China's emergence as a global economic power since 1978 has been nothing short of staggering. In a recent study, Hsieh and Ossa (2011) estimate China's productivity growth, using industry level data, and quantify what the counterfactual case of what would have happened to real incomes throughout the world if nothing but China's productivity had changed. They find that average real

---

[2] Source: https://www.cia.gov/library/publications/the-world-factbook/geos/ch.html (retrieved 4 February 2011).

income in the rest of the world increased by a cumulative 0.48% from 1992 to 2007 due to China's productivity growth. The authors calculate that 2.2% of the cumulative worldwide gains from China's productivity growth accrued to the rest of the world.

Song et al. (2011) stress the importance of China's very unique growth path. There has been significant growth and sustained capital accumulation. The rate of return on investment is significantly above 20%, which is higher than most industrialized countries. In addition, China has experienced a significant increase in foreign reserves. The surplus has increased from US$21 billion in 1992 (5% of its annual GDP) to US$2,130 billion in June 2009 (46% of its GDP) (Song et al. 2011). China's foreign reserves increased further to about US$3,201 billion in September 2011.[3] China's foreign reserves are the most salient in the world and represent a significant fraction of global reserves.

One issue here is that China's exchange rate is being kept artificially low by the Chinese authorities. As of 2011, this continues to be a concern for China's trading partners and the international community. Rodrik (2010) discusses China's place in the world economy. The critics of Chinese economic policy assert that the Chinese currency, the renminbi, is seriously undervalued and accounts for China's global trade surplus. One potential solution is that China replaces its foreign demand for its goods with domestic markets. This will ensure future economic growth. Dealing with trade imbalances, burgeoning foreign reserves and the design of monetary policy at the same time as preserving domestic productivity, worker wages and employment, will be a significant challenge for China in the coming years.

It is difficult to divorce economic from political governance in China. The context in which firms operate should be seen in the broader context of the governance of society. The World Bank routinely produces information on governance arrangements for all countries around the world. Specifically, it gives information on voice and accountability, political stability and absence of violence, government effectiveness, regulatory quality, the rule of law and finally the control of corruption.

Figure 15.1 shows the ranking for China and compares it with the United States. The United States is chosen simply because it is often held up as the exemplar capitalist Anglo-Saxon corporate governance model. The figure shows that the United States is ranked in the highest percentiles for all indicators. The 'x-axis' measures the performance ranking from the zero-percentile to the top one-hundredth percentile across nation states. Of the two bars within each category, the top refers to the most recent year of data (which is 2007) and the bottom to the earlier time period (which is 1996). China performs poorly across many of the measures, especially voice and accountability. Unfortunately, China is in the lowest rankings (below median) for most measures, with the exception of government effectiveness.

Capital market innovations

The radical changes in China's macroeconomy have been accompanied by radical changes in its general infrastructure and capital markets. Modern capital market innovations occurred in 1990 with the opening of the Shanghai and Shenzhen Stock Exchanges. The Chinese Securities Regulation Commission (CSRC) regulates China's capital market. China's Securities Law was passed in December 1998 and became effective in July 1999. The law gave the CSRC wide-ranging powers to develop securities legislation. The law gives the CSRC the 'authority to implement a centralized and unified regulation of the nationwide securities market in order to ensure their lawful operation'. The CSRC oversees China's nationwide centralized securities supervisory system, with the power to regulate and supervise securities issuers, as well as to investigate, and impose penalties for, 'illegal activities related to securities and futures'. The CSRC is empowered to issue Opinions or Guideline Opinions, non-legally binding guidance for publicly traded corporations. Its functions are similar to the Securities and Exchange Commission in the United States.

Allen and Shen (2011) argue that China's securities market development is different from London or New York. Those markets evolved over many centuries, arising because of patterns of demand and supply of financial intermediation. In contrast, markets in China emerged in the 1980s following the

---

[3] Source: http://www.pbc.gov.cn/publish/html/2011s09.htm (retrieved 15 November 2011).

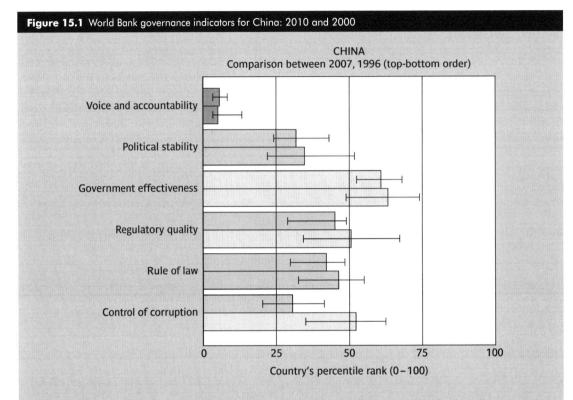

Figure 15.1 World Bank governance indicators for China: 2010 and 2000

Source: *Kaufmann D., A. Kraay, and M. Mastruzzi 2008: Governance Matters VII: Governance Indicators, 1996–2007. World Bank Policy Research Working Paper No. 4654.*

Note: *The governance indicators presented here aggregate the views on the quality of governance provided by a large number of enterprise, citizen and expert survey respondents in industrial and developing countries. These data are gathered from a number of survey institutes, think tanks, non-governmental organizations, and international organizations. The aggregate indicators do not reflect the official views of the World Bank, its Executive Directors, or the countries they represent. The WGI are not used by the World Bank Group to allocate resources or for any other official purpose.*

start of economic liberalization and were associated with tightly controlled exchanges established in the early 1990s in Shanghai and Shenzhen. Allen and Shen (2011) argue: 'These new markets have been designed to, and are largely limited to, serve state purposes. That is to assist in the financing of the state sector of the economy. Rather than evolving in a bottom-up pattern, they are controlled, top-down securities markets.' This raises questions about the efficacy of governance in China's capital markets.

The beginnings of China's capital market were actually quite modest, with few listed firms and low market capitalization. Markets began trading in 1990, and the estimated market value of publicly traded shares on 31 December 2009 was about $5 trillion. The value of China's stock market ranks third behind the United States and Japan. In this sense, China has developed a giant market. China's equity markets have grown significantly over time. In 1992 there were only 53 firms listed on the stock exchanges, but by the year 2000 there were 1088. The number of firms listed on the domestic exchanges has steadily increased and in 2009 there were a total of 1718 firms.[4] At the same time proceeds from Initial Public Offerings (IPOs) have also increased, illustrating the importance of capital market developments to the

---

[4] Source: Chinese Securities Regulatory Commission Annual Report, 2009. http://www.csrc.gov.cn/pub/csrc_en/about/annual/201011/P020101105493830315968.pdf.

Chinese economy.[5] Finally, the significance of capital market reforms is reflected in the fact that the combined market capitalization of the Shanghai and Shenzhen stock market accounted for 73% of China's GDP in 2009. This compares with about 45% in 2001 and 18% in 2005. As China moved from the 20th to the 21st century it has assumed a significant role in the global economy.

As stock markets have evolved in China, more attention has been given to the patterns in asset prices. Compared with developed capital markets, stock prices set in emerging markets may contain incomplete or inaccurate information. Morck et al. (2000) and Morck and Yeung (2002) point to the relative lack of information conveyed by stock prices in China and other emerging markets. They argue that stock markets in developing economies tend to rise and fall together, and this positive synchronization is 'functionally inefficient' (Morck and Yeung, 2002). For example, 70–80% of stocks in China have been found to move in the same direction in the same week versus only 58% in the USA (Morck and Yeung, 2002). Since stock prices tend to move together, investors may not be performing the information gathering and processing that is necessary to fine tune firm-specific stock prices, thus hindering capital allocation. As a result, a firm's stock market performance may not fully reflect the CEO's performance but instead be an indicator of the overall market movement.

Patterns of corporate governance in China

The context of corporate governance in China is radically different from Western economies. The governance of China's firms seems to borrow from both the Anglo-Saxon model and the continental European model. For example, China has recently introduced stock options to motivate executives, a move that seems akin to the American model. The use of stock options, though, is very new and there is little hard evidence on their use or impact at the moment. In the area of the board of directors, China is different from the US western model. China's public firms have a two-tier board system, which seems similar to the model exemplified by German governance. Using data from the papers by Conyon and He (2011a, b, c) it is possible to give a flavour of the main features of corporate governance arrangements in China. Specifically, we focus on three areas: a) the ownership of firms, b) the board of directors, and c) executive compensation contracts.

Ownership of publicly traded firms

China is a socialist economy, and the State continues to play a dominant role in directing economic activity. In this regard, the political system in China seems at variance with the economic reforms that are going on, as these are significantly oriented towards the market. One of the most important manifestations of State influence is in the ownership and control of public firms. First, the ultimate ownership of the firm is often in the hands of the State, i.e. the Chinese government. This facilitates significant State influence in the activities of the firm, especially in choosing the directors of the firm who will manage the assets. Second, the ownership of publicly traded firms is highly concentrated, especially compared with Western firms. There is often one single large shareholder. This shareholder may or may not be the State. It is not unusual for the single largest shareholder to own at least 40% of the firm. Compared with Western firms, especially those in the United States and the United Kingdom, this figure is indeed large. We now look more closely at the institutions of governance in China.

China has a very distinct pattern of firm ownership and control. Two central features stand out. First, the Chinese State is often a major shareholder in many publicly traded firms. Second, the ownership of company shares is highly concentrated. A few shareholders own a disproportionately large fraction of the firm's equity. Both of these facts stand in sharp contrast to patterns of ownership found in Anglo-Saxon economies. Anglo-Saxon models are often premised on the individual private ownership of firms, and ownership patterns are diffuse with no single shareholder holding a dominant position.

---

[5] An example of the significance of IPOs in China is Agricultural Bank of China (ABC). On 13 August 2010, it completed the world's largest initial public offering. It raised a total of US$22.1 billion. The offering beat the one set by Industrial and Commercial Bank of China in 2006 of US$21.9 billion.
Source: 'AgBank IPO officially the world's biggest', *Financial Times*, 13 August 2010.

15.3 Costs and benefits of ownership structures in China

The pattern of Chinese ownership has important consequences for the performance of firms. Several benefits and costs associated with the ownership structure in China can be enumerated. On the benefit side of the equation, State-concentrated ownership can have a number of effects. First, concentrated ownership helps resolve free-rider and monitoring problems that owners usually face. Owners with small share stakes have weak incentives to monitor. This is because monitoring management is costly to shareholders, and the returns from that monitoring are small because their ownership stake is low. In contrast, an owner with a large share ownership percentage has incentives to make sure that the firm is run in a value-maximizing way. This is because the owner receives a larger share of any increase in value resulting from engaging in costly monitoring of errant managers.

There are important costs to concentrated State ownership. A dominant owner may expropriate minority shareholders via tunnelling or other rent-seeking activities, i.e. the State can extract rents of other minority owners leading to lower market valuations. If an owner enjoys private benefits of control then the owner may pursue objectives that do not optimize the share price and therefore hurt the other minority shareholders. In the case of China these may include political objectives.

State ownership has important consequences for the dynamics of an economic system. State-owned firms in China might recruit different 'types' of managers than privately controlled firms. For a given level of ownership concentration the managers in a state firm might be more bureaucratic, and less innovative than managers in a privately controlled firm. One of the fundamental advantages of private ownership is the dynamic vitality it injects into an economic system. Of course, this is in part a matter of culture and intent. It is possible for some states, at least over the short period, to infuse dynamism and innovation into managers. But, over the long period the returns to that entrepreneurship are in the ownership it provides to those engaged in the economic activity. Overall, the pattern of ownership in China is a double-edged sword. It has significant potential costs in the form of entrenchment and blunting the incentives to innovation over the long-term. In the short run, the benefits of command and control may resolve free-rider problems as the State directs economic activity to meet its own goals.

We now describe in more detail the ownership of Chinese firms. There are three major classes of share ownership. First, the Chinese State owns shares, held through government agencies. Second, legal entities can own shares, held through State-controlled legal persons, or privately controlled legal persons. Finally, individuals, institutions and private businesses can own shares privately. When a state-owned enterprise (SOE) is listed, only a small proportion of equity is sold to private investors in the IPO process. The state and parent SOEs still retain sufficient shares in the form of state shares or legal person shares to retain voting control, which typically accounts for two-thirds of total shares outstanding. State shares and legal entity shares are (generally) non-tradable. There are circumstances when they can be exchanged, but the process of doing so is quite complex. Reforms began in 2005 to make all shares tradable. In addition, a Chinese company may also issue three types of tradable shares. Tradable 'A' shares are listed on the two domestic exchanges (Shanghai and Shenzhen) to domestic investors and denominated in renminbi (RMB). 'B' shares are issued to foreign investors traded in either US dollars or Hong Kong dollars. Finally, a Chinese firm may also trade on the Hong Kong Stock Exchange and issue so-called 'H' shares.

To show how ownership and control has evolved over time we use data on publicly traded firms. The data cover the period from 2001 to 2005, and include most firms that are listed on the two domestic main exchanges in each year. The pattern of ownership is shown in Table 15.1 (panel A) using the data supplied in Conyon and He (2011a). A number of empirical facts emerge. First, the data show that in most firms there is a single dominant shareholder whose large ownership stake presumably facilitates considerable power in the running of the firm. Second, the State was the ultimate owner in about 82% of firms in 2001 and only 71% in 2005. The corollary is that private ownership and control has more than doubled over this short time period. About 27% of firms were privately controlled in 2005 compared with 11% in 2001. The State's ownership control of firms has diminished, as market reforms deepened. Third, the ownership of publicly traded firms is

Table 15.1 Chinese ownership and control

Panel A: Ownership and control

Year	State ownership	Private ownership	Other ownership	Largest share stake	Second largest share stake	Third largest share stake
2001	0.82	0.11	0.07	0.44	0.08	0.03
2002	0.78	0.16	0.06	0.44	0.09	0.03
2003	0.74	0.22	0.04	0.43	0.09	0.04
2004	0.70	0.26	0.04	0.42	0.10	0.04
2005	0.71	0.27	0.02	0.41	0.10	0.04
Total	0.74	0.21	0.05	0.43	0.09	0.04

Panel B: Executive compensation and the board of directors

Year	Executive pay (RMB 000s)	CEO ownership (RMB 000s)	Board size	Independent directors (%)	Combined CEO and Chair	Compensation committee
2001	104.97	767.30	9.40	5.97	0.12	0.08
2002	127.56	1375.27	9.92	23.65	0.11	0.31
2003	162.88	1979.39	9.89	32.36	0.11	0.42
2004	195.75	3285.02	9.80	33.82	0.11	0.46
2005	153.51	3150.18	9.66	34.34	0.11	0.51
Total	151.48	2187.57	9.74	26.88	0.11	0.37

Panel A: 'State ownership' = 1 if the Chinese State is the ultimate firm owner. 'Private ownership' = 1 if the ultimate owner is a private institution; 'Other ownership' is the residual ownership category. 'Largest share stake': the percentage ownership of largest shareholder. Second and third largest share stakes are similarly defined.

Panel B: 'Executive pay': (RMB 000s); 'CEO ownership' (RMB 000s): value of CEO shareholdings is the number of shares held by the CEO multiplied by the firm's stock price (units = millions). 'Independent directors': the fraction of the board comprised of independent directors; 'Board size': Board size is measured as the number of individuals on the main board. 'Combined CEO and Chair': leadership structure of the firm is a dummy variable set equal to one if the posts of CEO and chairman are combined, and zero otherwise; 'Compensation committee': a dummy variable equal to one if the firm has a compensation committee and zero otherwise.
Source: derived from Conyon and He (2011a).

highly concentrated in China. As can be seen, the largest shareholder owns about 43% of the firm's shares, the next largest about 9% and the third largest about 4%. The difference in ownership stake between the first and second owner is important. The situation contrasts markedly with Anglo-Saxon economies.

As noted earlier, one benefit of concentrated ownership is that investors with large share stakes have incentives to engage in costly monitoring and avoid free riding. However, there are significant costs associated with ownership concentration. Large shareholders may expropriate

minority shareholders, or promote their own objectives over those of other shareholders. This may occur via tunnelling or other rent extraction strategies. The problem of expropriation by controlling shareholders is viewed as extremely severe in Chinese stock markets because information disclosure is more embryonic and in general the system corporate control mechanisms are more weak. One recent study showed that pay-for-performance incentives were weaker in firms where the major shareholder could expropriate funds via tunnelling activities. Another concern is that when the State is the firm's ultimate owner the CEO is more likely to be a bureaucrat or care more about political actions than about creating firm value. In consequence, State-controlled firms might pursue political or multiple objectives, such as employment growth, rather than profit maximization.

15.4 The board of directors

China operates a quasi two-tier board system consisting of a main board of directors and a supervisory board. However, the supervisory board in this case is an auditor and not a decision maker. It can make recommendations to the shareholders, but not hire or fire managers, veto investments, or the like. Traditionally, the State has huge influence on the appointment of board and supervisory board members. An enduring concern in the literature is that State-appointed bureaucrats are ineffective in monitoring management (Fan, Wong and Zhang, 2007; Hu et al., 2010). In response to shareholder pressure, and deepening market reforms, China's listed firms have increasingly adopted Anglo-Saxon style internal corporate governance structures (Allen, Qian and Qian, 2005; Jingu, 2007; Chen, Liu and Li, 2010). This includes adopting key committees such as audit, compensation and governance committees. The importance of the audit committee, of course, is that it signals the probity and veracity of the firm's financial and capital structure (assuming its members are sufficiently qualified and independent).

Another important example of this is the Code of Corporate Governance issued by the China Securities Regulatory Commission. This code required listed firms to add independent directors to the main board of directors and separate the posts of CEO and chairperson. The expectation is that one-third of the board should comprise independent directors. The corporate governance code defines director independence as: 'The independent director shall be independent from the listed company that employs them and the company's major shareholders.' According to this definition, a non-executive director may not necessarily be independent. A non-executive director does not hold a position in the listed firm but may hold a position in the parent company or major shareholder of the firm. If the reforms are effective we would expect to observe better decision-making by boards of directors in relation to key strategic variables. For example, we would expect to observe compensation contracts that better align owner and manager interests and motivate executives. We would expect to see boards of directors having an increased willingness to fire the CEO for poor performance. And, indeed, there is empirical evidence of these, and other, beneficial effects of more independent directors.

To see the basic structure of boards of directors in China, we again focus on the publicly traded firms from 2001 to 2005. Table 15.1 (panel B) contains information on boardroom structure. The noteworthy feature of the data is the increased adoption of Western-style boardroom governance practices. The percentage of independent members on the board has increased from about 6% in 2001 to about 34% in 2005. The significant increase in independent directors on the board is due to the regulation issued by the Chinese Securities Regulation Commission in 2001 that mandated at least one-third of board members be independent directors. Immediately, the presence of 'independent' directors increased. The size of the main board of directors is about ten members and has remained relatively constant over time. There are other noteworthy features. About 11% of firms combine the posts of CEO and chairperson over the sample period. Finally, the proportion of firms that have adopted a compensation committee for setting executive pay has increased from about 8% in 2001 to approximately 50% in 2005. The data show significant change and flux in the internal control and governance of Chinese firms during the early 2000s.

15.5 Executive compensation

Previous chapters in this book explained how executive compensation contracts motivate CEOs and align the interests of owners and managers. Historically, Chinese executives receive only cash salaries, bonuses and stipends. Equity compensation in the form of stock options has historically been very rare, and has been permissible only since 2006. In addition, Chinese executives often receive various perks from their companies, but the extent and value of these have been difficult to ascertain. These, then, are the main facts regarding Chinese executive pay. In the language of Jensen and Murphy (1990), the CEOs of China's public companies are paid like 'bureaucrats' in the sense that compensation contracts do not emphasize equity pay such as stock options or performance shares. Instead, most of the CEO's pay comes in the form of a fixed salary that does not necessarily vary with the stock performance of the firm.

In addition, Chinese executives might own shares in their own firms. They might have purchased these in open market transaction, or been given them. At the moment it is thought that CEOs own at least some shares in about 50% of the publicly traded firms. As we'll see below, the value of such share ownership is generally higher than the value of the CEO's annual cash compensation in those cases where it is possible to get sufficient information.

The disclosure of executive pay information is far weaker in China than in countries such as the USA. Investors and other end users of executive compensation data receive far less information than is available in countries such as the United States or the United Kingdom. However, the situation is improving with the passage of time and the deepening market reforms. The Chinese Securities Regulation Committee (CSRC) regulates the disclosure of executive compensation information in publicly traded firms. Early regulation (pre-2001) did not require public firms to disclose information about executive pay in their annual reports, although some firms did so but on a voluntary basis. From 2001 onwards the CSRC required publicly traded firms to report the aggregated sum of total compensation for the three highest-paid executives. Firms also had to report the total pay received by the board in total. The mix of salary, bonuses and other remuneration was not divulged, and so it is difficult to get a precise picture of the actual pay contract. From 2001 to 2006, disclosure of pay information for each individual was not required.

From 2006 onwards, publicly traded firms were required to report each individual board member and top management's total compensation separately as the sum of salary, bonuses, stipends, and other benefits. Importantly, the CSRC provided a framework to introduce equity incentives at this time. In order to promote better incentives within public companies, the CSRC promulgated the Trial Measures for the Administration of Equity Incentive Schemes of Listed Companies on 1 January 2006. Further to these measures companies could propose the adoption of equity incentive plans, including restricted stock and stock option plans. The total number of shares available for such incentive plans could not exceed 10% of the total shares outstanding. In addition, independent directors were excluded from participating in such incentive plans. The independent directors gave their opinion on the fairness of such equity plans. Once the board of directors adopted the plan, and providing the CSRC did not object, the firm was able to convene a shareholder meeting to review, and then adopt, the equity plan. The empirical evidence suggests that equity incentives were not commonplace in the early to mid-2000s. Overall, the direction of recent regulatory history suggests more information disclosure about executive pay and a move towards some forms of equity-based compensation. It is too early to evaluate how prevalent equity compensation will become in mainland China or what the effects of stock option pay will be on corporate performance.

Table 15.1 (panel B) uses data from Conyon and He (2011a) and shows some basic facts about the evolution of Chinese executive compensation. Over the period from 2001 to 2005 the average value of cash compensation was about 151,000 RMB (the Chinese unit of currency). The increased economic openness of the Chinese economy has been associated with a corresponding increase in the level of executive compensation. As noted earlier, it is not possible at this time to know how much of executive compensation is in the form of incentive bonuses and how much is in the form of salary. It is also difficult to value accurately non-disclosed perks such as schooling, medical, social welfare

provisions, pensions etc. The magnitude of such perk arrangements can range from approximately 15% to 30% of an executive's salary.

In addition, Table 15.1 (panel B) provides basic information on the average value of CEO shareholdings. This is the value of the shares that the CEO owns in his own company. As can be seen it is approximately 2,177,000 RMB. If one compares this with cash compensation, then the value of shares is approximately 14 times the value of annual pay. The significance of this is that share ownership can act as an important device to align owner and manager interests. Because the value of CEO share ownership varies directly with asset prices, it gives the CEO an incentive to create firm value. As such, the incentives to promote value creation might come at the expense of the ownership of firm stock rather than annual executive compensation. Capital market regulations are, of course, different in China and it is difficult to know about the buy and sell decisions of the CEO's own stock, or what trading constraints are imposed on the CEO.

This subsection has highlighted the following basic facts about Chinese executive pay. First, systematic information disclosure about executive pay only really began around 2000. This is much later than many other countries. Second, the level of pay in China is growing, but is low by international standards. Third, since 2006 more information about stock options and equity pay have been provided relative to earlier periods. It seems that executive payment systems in China are being configured to align the interests of owners and managers. Over the next few years a clearer picture of CEO pay arrangements should emerge.

15.6   Corporate governance in China: recent academic studies

There are now several academic studies investigating the effects of corporate governance in China. In this section we provide a flavour of some of these. We focus on the relation of governance and performance, corporate governance and management turnover, and corporate governance and executive compensation.

The effects of concentrated ownership are particularly salient in the context of China. One issue is the potential conflicts of interest that exist between controlling shareholders and minority shareholders. Wang and Xiou (2011) investigate this issue in the context of executive compensation contracts. They show that controlling shareholders' tunnelling (i.e. by diverting the firm's resources) leads to a reduction in the estimated pay-for-performance sensitivity of executive compensation. The results indicate that although incentive payment methods are increasingly used in Chinese listed companies, there are some issues. Specifically, controlling shareholders (the ones who achieve private benefits from control) have fewer incentives to strengthen the relationship between executive pay and firm performance.

Cheung et al. (2009) investigated the quality and consequences of corporate governance practices in the Fortune 100 largest listed Chinese firms in 2004. Based on the revised OECD Principles of Corporate Governance they develop a corporate governance index (CGI) to measure the aggregate quality of corporate governance and disclosure practices of the 100 largest listed Chinese firms. Their index is assembled from a set of about 90 questions probing the transparency, disclosure and rights of shareholders. The authors find that the quality of Chinese firms' governance has indeed improved. They find differences in corporate governance quality when comparing the top performing with the bottom performing firms: higher performance for better governance. In addition, the authors find that overseas-listed Chinese companies tend to have better governance, and increased information disclosure and transparency compared with non-overseas-listed Chinese companies. Importantly, the relation between firm performance and corporate governance is not particularly robust. The relation between the quality of corporate governance practices and the market valuation of firms is not statistically significant in their regression models. The results suggest that even though there may have been improvements in corporate governance, the benefits of this 'good corporate governance' have not been completely reflected in the market valuation of Chinese companies.

However, it is always important to bear in mind with such 'firm performance and corporate governance' that the underlying econometric requirements to identify causal relationships are often difficult to isolate. For example, ideally one would like the changes in governance to be exogenous and then study the consequent effects on performance, and compare this with a control group. In reality, it is often difficult to isolate truly exogenous changes, and as such the 'endogeneity problem' may be a concern.

As noted above, an enduring issue is the role played by bureaucrats in China's enterprises. Fan, Wong and Zhang (2007) investigate politically connected CEOs and their effects in China. They find that about one-quarter of the CEOs in a sample of 790 privatized firms are former or current government bureaucrats. Firms with politically connected CEOs have worse performance than those without politically connected CEOs. They find that the negative effect of the CEO's political ties also is evident on the first-day stock return. In addition, the study finds that firms led by politically connected CEOs are more likely to appoint other bureaucrats to the board of directors rather than directors with relevant professional backgrounds.

Yuan Lu and Jun Yao (2006) investigated the effects of state ownership and group control mechanisms on the interaction between diversification and performance of companies in China. They find that state ownership has enhanced the performance of group affiliated companies when they adopted higher degrees of diversification. In addition, the authors find that cash flow rights have a positive effect on the performance of companies only in companies with high diversification. In general, they find that group control rights have a negative impact on the performance. Ownership control mechanisms, derived mainly from pyramid ownership structures in China, 'enable the dominant owners to expropriate the value from minority shareholders or tunnel corporate resources for their own interest'.

Other studies have investigated how governance structures interact with accounting quality. Firth, Fung and Rui (2007a, b) investigate how ownership, two-tier board structure, and audits change the informativeness of China's firms. They measure informativeness by the earnings–returns relation, discretionary accruals, and audit opinion. They show that 'ownership concentration, the presence of foreign shareholders, the percentage of tradable shares, the type of dominant shareholder, the supervisory board, and independent directors affect the earnings response coefficients and discretionary accruals'. In addition, the type of shareholder, the size of the supervisory board, and the percentage of independent directors also has an effect on whether or not there is a modified audit opinion. The results clearly demonstrate that governance affects the information available to investors.

Studies have also examined the relation between CEO turnover, firm performance and corporate governance. Specifically, researchers ask questions such as: Are managers in China fired for poor performance? Do firms with more independent boards fire poorly performing managers more frequently? If the company's fortune declines (measured either by stock returns or some accounting measure of performance), does the CEO of the company face an increased likelihood of losing his job? The broad answer to these questions is 'yes'. A number of studies have shown that poor performance in China's firms leads to greater than expected CEO turnover. This provides evidence that the proposed corporate governance reforms are effective.

As an example, Kato and Long (2006b) examined Chinese CEO turnover in a pooled cross-section of data on about 600 firms from 1998 to 2002. They find a negative correlation between CEO turnover and firm performance, measured either as shareholder returns or return on assets. This suggests that managers are not completely insulated from their bad decisions, and are replaced for poor performance. The study also shows that corporate governance arrangements are important. Specifically, ownership concentration, the private control of firms and board governance all influence CEO turnover. They find that the link between CEO turnover and firm performance is stronger in firms with a majority shareholder and weaker for listed firms controlled by the state. This suggests that ownership concentration helps firm decision-making. However, firms with weak stock returns are more insulated from firing if the ultimate owner is the State rather than if privately controlled. The authors also find that the CEO turnover–performance sensitivity is more negative in firms with a greater fraction of outside directors. In addition, firms appear to subsequently experience greater performance improvement after the replacement of their CEOs when the firms are privately controlled or have a controlling shareholder. The negative correlation between CEO turnover and firm performance has been found in other studies too. Firth, Fung and Rui (2006a) also investigate CEO turnover in a sample of firms between 1998 and 2002. They find that CEO turnover is negatively correlated with a firm's profitability but not with stock returns. The authors report a moderating effect for majority share ownership but not for the presence of independent directors. Conyon and He (2011a) investigated the relation between CEO turnover and firm performance in China's publicly traded firms. They investigated how informative stock prices are as predictors of CEO replacement. They find that Chinese firms rely more on accounting performance than on stock market performance when determining CEO turnover. Firms with noisier performance measures and firms with larger growth opportunities rely less on both accounting and stock market performance in CEO replacement decisions. State-controlled firms were more likely to use accounting performance to determine CEO turnover.

Overall, the emerging evidence suggests that management turnover for poor performance is being influenced by changes in the internal governance of firms. Time will tell whether the changes in governance will have permanent long-lasting effects on the quality of board decision-making.

Executive compensation can solve the underlying agency problem by aligning the interests of owners and managers. The underlying presumption is that firms want to maximize shareholder value; this may not be the case in China, where the State still has a significant influence. If firms do want to optimize profits, then the provision of pay-for-performance is important. In Western firms, stock options and other forms of equity pay (restricted stock, long-term incentive plans etc.) are used to align the CEO and firm interests.

The number of studies on executive pay in China is increasing with the availability of data and enhanced pay disclosure rules. Kato and Long (2006a, b) investigate a sample of 937 publicly traded firms in China from 1998 to 2002. They document several important findings. First, executive cash compensation is positively related to firm performance. The authors perform a regression of the change in the logarithm of compensation on the change in the logarithm of shareholder wealth: the elasticity approach to retrieving the pay-for-performance sensitivity. Implicitly this approach filters out firm fixed effects in the corresponding underlying levels model. Second, they find evidence that the pay-for-performance link is weaker in firms with a high concentration of government ownership. They link the percentage of company shares owned by the government with shareholder return measures, and find that the sign is negative and significant. The implication is that the pay-for-performance relation is weaker in State-controlled firms. Because the data period ranges from 1998 to 2002 it does not study the effect of independent directors on the board on the pay-for-performance link. Other studies too find that pay is positively related to firm performance. Firth, Fung and Rui (2007a) examine a sample of 549 listed firms in China between 1998 and 2000. They find that cash compensation is related to firm performance and that ownership and governance factors are determinants of cash pay.

Recently, Conyon and He (2011a) investigate a larger set of 1342 firms from 2001 to 2005. They investigate the pay-for-performance relation controlling for management quality via the use of firm fixed-effects, the role of ownership structure, and the effect of independent directors on the main board. They find that executive total pay and incentives are positively correlated with the firm's stock market and accounting performance. They show that the pay-for-performance relation is robust to firm fixed effects. Second, they show that the pay-for-performance relation tends to be weaker in firms that are State controlled. This suggests that privately controlled firms provide better motivation to increase firm performance. Third, there is some evidence that the pay-for-performance relation is stronger in firms that have a greater fraction of independent outside directors on the main board. In addition, they compare executive compensation in China with that in the United States and find that American executives earn about 17 times more than their Chinese counterparts. The difference is significantly reduced after controlling for the economic determinants of executive pay. They show that the same variables determine pay in each country, particularly firm size and performance.

Overall, the emerging evidence suggests that executive pay is related to firm performance in China. This might be surprising to some, but executives are rewarded for good performance. Corporate governance also affects the determination of pay. The link between pay and performance might be less strong in State-controlled firms, and stronger in firms with more independent directors. As market reforms deepen, and options and equity pay become more widespread, we expect this relation to strengthen.

15.7 Discussion

China is the second largest economy in the world. Since 1978 the country's economic growth has skyrocketed. In tandem, China's capital markets have grown significantly in terms of the number of listed firms and also market value. Since the early 2000s the China Securities Regulation Commission has enacted various reforms aimed at strengthening corporate governance arrangements. The objective of these appears to be to generate investor confidence in a country that has well-known weaknesses in the wider political and economic sphere. These recent corporate governance innovations have increased transparency and, to an extent, strengthened owners' rights. As we demonstrated in this chapter, ownership of firms is still very concentrated in China, and this can lead to expropriation of minatory shareholders. This agency problem is a concern for minority investors. The problem might be more acute when the State is the ultimate owner of the firm, or where the State has objectives that are different from value maximization. In terms of internal corporate governance, China's listed firms are adding independent directors to the board and are improving incentive arrangements. What is clear is that there has been significant reform in a short timespan. We think that the governance system is still in flux. We hope that the reforms continue, and especially that high-quality practices are implemented to protect all investors' capital.

Minicase

China Mobile Limited

China Mobile Limited is a Chinese state-owned telecommunication company that provides mobile voice and multimedia through its mobile telecom network, the largest of its kind in the world. Also the most valuable mobile telecommunications company in the world, it is listed on the NYSE and Hong Kong exchanges. As of March 2011, China Mobile is the largest mobile phone company in the world, with over 600 million subscribers. Revenues in 2010 were about $73 billion. The company employed about 150,000 people.

'Ownership: China Mobile likely enjoys substantial benefits from China's government, but also experiences frequent government intervention in its business affairs. Government control is maintained through a presumably government-owned holding company, China Mobile Communications Corporation (CMCC), that owns 100% ownership of China Mobile (HK) Group Limited, which in turn holds over 70% ownership of China Mobile – the remainder being controlled by public investors. Established in 2000, CMCC is China Mobile Ltd's current parent company.'[6]

The board of directors consists of nine executive directors and four independent and non-executive directors. The executive directors are: Mr. WANG Jianzhou (Executive Director, Chairman & Chief Executive Officer), Mr. LI Yue (Executive Director & Vice President), Mr. LU Xiangdong (Executive Director & Vice President), Mr. XUE Taohai (Executive Director, Vice President & Chief Financial Officer), Madam HUANG Wenlin (Executive Director & Vice President), Mr. SHA Yuejia (Executive Director & Vice President), Mr. LIU Aili (Executive Director & Vice President), Madam XIN Fanfei (Executive Director & Vice President), and Mr. XU Long (Executive Director of the Company & President of Guangdong Mobile). The independent non-executive directors are Dr. LO Ka Shui, Mr. Frank WONG Kwong Shing, Dr. Moses CHENG Mo Chi, and the single non-executive director is Mr. Nicholas Jonathan READ.

Mr. Wang Jianzhou is aged 61, he is an executive director, chairman and Chief Executive Officer of the company, and joined the board of directors of the company in November 2004. Mr.

---

[6] Source: Compiled from a number of sources including www.chinamobileltd.com and http://en.wikipedia.org/wiki/China_Mobile

Wang is in charge of the overall management of the company. He is also the President of China Mobile Communications Corporation (the ultimate controlling shareholder of the company). The board has three principal committees: an audit committee, a remuneration committee and a nomination committee.

The annual report shows that in 2008 the CEO received HK$180,000 in fees, HK$1,172,000 in salary and allowances, HK$660,000 in performance-related bonuses, HK$285,000 in retirement benefits, a fair value estimate of options amounting to HK$849,000, yielding a 2008 total of HK$3,146,000. This is approximately half a million US dollars (1 Hong Kong dollar = 0.1283 US dollars).

Source: *2009 annual report and accounts. Available at: http://www.chinamobileltd.com/ir.php?menu=3*

Discussion questions

1 How would you evaluate the ownership structure of China Mobile?
2 How does the level and structure of CEO pay at China Mobile compare with pay at Western companies?
3 What are the costs and benefits of China's State-owned system?
4 What do you make of the board and committee arrangements at China Mobile?

Summary (learning points)

- China is a socialist economy, and the State continues to play a dominant role in directing economic activity.

- The single largest shareholder (often the Chinese State) has a controlling interest in excess of 40%.

- Executive compensation is low by international standards. However, estimating the value of government transfers (pensions, education, housing etc.) at purchasing power parity rates is difficult.

- Historically, equity pay such as stock options, have not been used in mainland China as a way of motivating executives. There are recent changes suggesting that options might be used as a compensation tool in the future.

- Corporate governance is evolving rapidly in China, as capital market reforms seek to reassure investors of the quality of investing in China.

- The Chinese Corporate Governance Code in 2002 ushered in an era of board reforms including a role for independent directors, and board committees (such as compensation, audit and nomination committees).

 ## References and further reading

Allen, W.T. and Shen, H. (2011) *Assessing China's Top-Down Securities Markets*, NBER Working Paper No. 16713.

Allen, F., Qian, J. and Qian, M. (2005) Law, finance, and economic growth in China, *Journal of Financial Economics*, **77** (1), 57–116.

Chen, J.J., Liu, X. and Li, W. (2010) The Effect of Insider Control and Global Benchmarks on Chinese Executive Compensation, *Corporate Governance: An International Review*, **18** (2), 107–123.

Cheung, Y., Leung, P.J., Piman, L. and Tong, L. (2009) Does corporate governance matter in

China? *China Economic Review*, **19** (3), September 2008, 460–479.

Chinese Security Law (1999) Rule number 16 of Chinese Security Law of 1999.

Conyon, M.J. and He, L. (2010) *Executive Compensation in China*, Working paper, the Wharton School.

Conyon, M.J. and He, L. (2011a) Executive Compensation and Corporate Governance in China, *Journal of Corporate Finance*, **17** (4), 1158–1175, 10.1016/j.jcorpfin.2011.04.006.

Conyon, M.J. and He, L. (2011b; forthcoming) CEO Turnover in China: the role of market-based and accounting performance measures, *European Journal of Finance*.

Conyon, M.J. and He, L. (2011c) Executive compensation and pay for performance in China, in *Handbook of Executive Compensation*, Thomas, R. and Hill, J. (eds) Edward Elgar: Cheltenham.

Coughlan, A.T. and Schmidt, R.M. (1985) Executive Compensation, Management Turnover and Firm Performance: An Empirical Investigation, *Journal of Accounting & Economics*, **7** (1–3), 43–66.

CSRC (1998) *Guidelines on contents and formats of information disclosure of annual report for listed companies—1998 version*. People's Republic of China: China Securities Regulatory Commission.

CSRC (2000) *Guidelines on contents and formats of information disclosure of annual report for listed companies—2000 version*. People's Republic of China: China Securities Regulatory Commission.

CSRC (2001) *Guidelines for introducing independent directors to the board of directors of listed companies*, People's Republic of China: China Securities Regulatory Commission.

CSRC (2002a) *Code of corporate governance for listed companies in China*, People's Republic of China: China Securities Regulatory Commission.

CSRC (2002b) *Guidelines on contents and formats of information disclosure of annual report for listed companies—2002 version*, People's Republic of China: China Securities Regulatory Commission.

CSRC (2005a) *Guidelines on contents and formats of information disclosure of annual report for listed companies—2005 version*. People's Republic of China: China Securities Regulatory Commission.

CSRC (2005b) *Regulation for the Stock Options Grants in Public Firms*.

DeFond, M.L., Wong, T.J. and Li, S.H. (1999) The impact of improved auditor independence on audit market concentration in China, *Journal of Accounting & Economics*, **28** (3), 269–305.

Ding, Y.H. and Zhang, J. (2007) Private vs state ownership and earnings management, *Corporate Governance: an International Review*, **15** (2), 223–238.

Fan, J.P.H., Wong, T.J. and Zhang, T.Y. (2007) Politically connected CEOs, corporate governance, and Post-IPO performance of China's newly partially privatized firms, *Journal of Financial Economics* **84** (2), 330–357.

Fan, J.P., Huang, J., Oberholzer-Gee, F. and Zhao, M. (2009) *Bureaucrats as Managers – Evidence from China*. Working paper, Harvard Business School.

Firth, M., Fung, P.M.Y. and Rui, O.M. (2006a) Corporate performance and CEO compensation in China, *Journal of Corporate Finance*, **12**, 693–714.

Firth, M., Fung, P.M.Y. and Rui, O.M. (2006b) Firm Performance, Governance Structure, and Top Management Turnover in a Transitional Economy, *Journal of Management Studies*, **43** (6), 1289–1330.

Firth, M., Fung, P.M.Y. and Rui, O.M. (2007a) How ownership and corporate governance influence chief executive pay in China's listed firms, *Journal of Business Research*, **60** (7), 776–785.

Firth, M., Fung, P.M.Y. and Rui, O.M. (2007b) Ownership, two-tier board structure, and the informativeness of earnings – Evidence from China, *Journal of Accounting and Public Policy*, **26** (4), 463–496, ISSN 0278-4254, DOI: 10.1016/j.jaccpubpol. 2007. 05. 004.

Hsieh, C-T. and Ossa, R. (2011) *A Global View of Productivity Growth in China*, NBER Working Paper No. 16778.

Hu, H.W., Tam, O.K. and Tan, M.G-S. (2010) Internal governance mechanisms and firm performance in China, *Asia Pacific Journal of Management*, **27** (4), 727–749.

Jensen, M. and Murphy, K.J. (1990) Performance pay and top-management incentives, *Journal of Political Economy*, **98** (2), 225–64.

Jingu, T. (2007) Corporate Governance for Listed Companies in China – Recent Moves to Improve the Quality of Listed Companies, *Nomura Capital Market Review*, **10** (2). Available at http://ssrn.com/paper=1016912.

Kato, T.K. and Long, C.X. (2006a) CEO turnover, firm performance, and enterprise reform in China: Evidence from micro data, *Journal of Comparative Economics*, **34** (4), 796–817.

Kato, T.K. and Long, C.X. (2006b) Executive turnover and firm performance in China, *American Economic Review*, **96** (2), 363–367.

Lu, Y. and Yao, J. (2006) Impact of state ownership and control mechanisms on the performance of group affiliated companies in China, *Asia Pacific Journal of Management*, **23** (4), 485–503, DOI: 10.1007/s10490-006-9017-0.

Morck, R. and Yeung, B. (2002) The puzzle of the harmonious stock prices, *World Economy*, **3** (3), 1–15.

Morck, R., Yeung, B. and Yu, W. (2000) The information content of stock markets: Why do emerging markets have synchronous stock price movements? *Journal of Financial Economics*, **58** (1–2), 215–260.

Qian, Y. (1995) Reforming corporate governance and finance in China, in Aoki, M. and Kim, H.-K. (eds) *Corporate Governance in Transitional Economies, The World Bank*, 215–252.

Rodrik, D. (2010) Making Room for China in the World Economy, *American Economic Review*, **100** (2), 89–93.

Song, Z., Storesletten, K. and Zilibotti, F. (2011)

Growing Like China, *American Economic Review*, **101** (1), 196–233.

Wang, K. and Xiao X. (2011) Controlling shareholders' tunneling and executive compensation: Evidence from China, *Journal of Accounting and Public Policy*, **30** (1), 89–100.

Xi, C. (2006), In search of effective monitoring board model: Board reforms and the political economy of Corporate Law in China, *Connecticut Journal of International Law*, **22** (1), 1–46.

Xu, L. (2004) *Types of large shareholders, corporate governance, and firm performance : evidence from China's listed companies*, Ph.D., School of Accounting and Finance, Hong Kong Polytechnic University.

Chapter 16

Stakeholder Governance in Scandinavia

Chapter contents

16.1   Introduction

In this chapter we examine the stakeholder view of corporate governance using as a case the Scandinavian countries (Denmark, Norway, Sweden), which may (to some extent at least) be said to practise this model. The stakeholder view is that companies should be run in the interest of all stakeholders, not just shareholders. We begin by examining what stakeholder value maximization might be and how it can be implemented by government regulation, ownership structures, board representation and informal mechanisms like reputation or culture. Next we describe corporate governance in the Nordic countries, i.e. Scandinavia and Finland. Despite several structural differences we can discern elements of a Scandinavian governance model: welfare states, concentrated ownership, strong labour unions, employees on the board, modest executive pay. The Nordic countries are world champions in 'social governance'. We go on to highlight two examples of how stakeholder concerns can influence ownership and board structure. First we examine a particular kind of ownership, majority ownership by charitable foundations, which is found in the Nordic countries, primarily in Denmark. We then examine how government regulation mandates diversity on company boards through the Norwegian gender quota which stipulates that at least 40% of board members of any listed company must be women. Finally, we provide a tentative assessment of costs and benefits of the Scandinavian model.

16.2   The stakeholder model[1]

In neoclassical economic theory firms are assumed to maximize profits. In the stakeholder model firms ideally maximize value creation for all stakeholders, that is the sum of values created by contracting with the firm relative to the best alternative use of resources (Kay, 1995; Holmström, 1999). This would include the sum of (positive or negative) value added to each stakeholder group. For owners, value added would be economic profits net of the cost of capital (Copeland et al., 1994) plus other benefits of control. For employees, it could be the sum of wage and utility differences relative to the best alternative job. For consumers, it could be the consumer surplus created (sum of utility net of price created to all consumers). For suppliers and creditors, it could be the risk-adjusted net profits on the firm's account. For governments and other citizens, value creation could imply the sum of tax revenues and the net value of positive and negative externalities created by the firm relative to the relevant alternative firm.

Company behaviour can be modelled as a balance struck between these alternative concerns, or (more formally) as maximizing the expected value of a corporate objective function defined on the range of potential performance measures. What matters is whether and how much potential goal variables influence the behaviour of the company. The company 'as such' is a legal fiction. It has no objectives of its own. But individual stakeholders may (or may not) maximize their respective utility functions, and the corporate objective function is an aggregate of their goals.

Conceptually, it is important to distinguish between goals that are valued for their own sake and goals that are valued as instruments or proxies for more basic, underlying goals (Holmström, 1979). However, neither in practice nor in theory is it possible a priori to classify goal variables as either means or ends. It may be standard practice to regard shareholder value creation as the overall goal and to regard variables like market share, cost efficiency, employee satisfaction and product safety as means to that end, but some managers may regard product safety and employee satisfaction as goals in their own right, and some may regard shareholder value creation as nothing but a necessary condition (or perhaps a necessary evil) to implement their business visions. They may pay lip service

---

[1] This section draws on Thomsen (2004, 2005b).

to goals like shareholder value and justify their views by arguing that product safety and employee satisfaction are means to that end. The semantics is less important than actual behaviour.

In a simple (linear) case, the corporate objective function is a weighted average, which attaches fixed weights $\alpha = (\alpha_1, ..., \alpha_i, ..., \alpha_n)$ between zero and one ($0 \le \alpha_i \le 1$) to the range of potential goals $p = (p_1, ..., p_i, ..., p_n)$. Intuitively, the weights should sum to one since there must be a trade-off between alternative objectives – if you put more emphasis on one objective, you will de facto place less emphasis on others. Some weights will be zero, reflecting the 'pragmatic reality that managers simply cannot attend to all actual or potential claims' (Mitchell et al., 1997). Company behaviour should then maximize the expected value of the objective function V:

$$\text{MAX } E(V(p)) = E(\alpha p).$$

In the standard common agency model (Bernheim and Whinston, 1986) weighted average corporate objective functions emerge if the principals have quasi-linear utility functions. But although this simple case is illustrative, it is probably not sufficiently general (see e.g. Dixit et al., 1997, p. 753). In practice, because of measurement problems and other transaction costs, total value maximization may be impossible (Hart, 1995; Holmström, 1999). This gives rise to a generalized corporate governance problem (Zingales, 2001), the type 3 agency problem between managers and stakeholders, which may be (imperfectly) addressed by alternative market and non-market mechanisms.

Markets

First, regular market transactions, contracting and private arbitration imply some degree of internalization. This may be the case when companies offer attractive wages and employment contracts to safeguard investments in firm-specific assets (Akerlof and Yellen, 1986) or if the law awards compensation to a certain group of stakeholders for a negative externality imposed on them (Coase, 1960).

Government regulation

Government regulation, for example investor protection or environmental legislation, may force firms to pay attention to certain stakeholder concerns. In theory, rational managers will recognize actual and potential challenges of this kind and de facto incorporate them into the corporate value function. However, in some cases, these mechanisms will be insufficient because of high transaction costs.

Ownership

One solution to contracting problems between a firm and a stakeholder or a group of stakeholders is to internalize the stakeholder–firm relationship through ownership (Hart, 1995; Williamson, 1996; Hansmann, 1996). Standard examples of this include vertical integration between up- and downstream firms (Williamson, 1975), supplier and customer cooperatives (Hansmann, 1996), government ownership (e.g. Shepherd, 1989; Laffont and Tirole, 1993; Hart, Shleifer and Vishny, 1997), employee ownership and partnerships (Hansmann, 1996). However, ownership integration cannot solve all market failures. Economic selection mechanisms may take a long time (Hill and Jones, 1992), and in some cases ownership structures may be perpetuated by government regulation or inertia (Roe, 1991, 1994; Hansmann, 1996). Moreover, because of the costs of ownership, not all critical stakeholders will possess ownership rights and this creates a need for alternative schemes (Tirole, 2001), such as explicit or implicit contracts, reputation, ethical codes and other kinds of (more or less credible) commitment. In other words there is a rationale for values that are related to those critical stakeholders. As emphasized by Hill and Jones (1992), managers effectively come to act as agents for all critical stakeholders (owners and non-owners alike) whose relationship with the firm is not efficiently coordinated by spot market contracting. In many cases incorporating their interests in the corporate objective function will be both privately and socially optimal although it is unlikely that a social optimum will be reached in this way alone (Arrow, 1973).

The board

A second mechanism shaping corporate objectives is board composition, or more generally the composition of the top management team. In companies that separate ownership and control, the responsibility for defining and changing corporate values is often effectively left to the management. Relationships with critical stakeholders may be internalized by having them represented on the board as non-executive members (Jones and Goldberg, 1982; Evan and Freeman, 1983; Luoma and Goodstein, 1999). Board members may effectively represent different ownership groups (for example founding families, large blockholders or institutional investors as well as owner-managers). In some countries (like Scandinavia, Germany or Austria), employees or governments are entitled to board representation. But owners may also voluntarily choose to appoint members with links to stakeholder groups (e.g. the financial community or research institutions) that are believed to be important to firm growth or survival.

This view of boards corresponds to the resource dependency function, one of the three generic board roles identified by Johnson et al. (1996). Luoma and Goodstein (1999) find that 14% of the board members in their sample of American companies can be categorized as stakeholder representatives, which may perhaps be enough to give voice to some stakeholder interests, but not enough to dominate corporate decision making.

Informal governance

A third way for companies to internalize stakeholder concerns is to increase their creditability and trustworthiness through implicit contracts based on reputation (Fombrun and Shanley, 1990; Kay, 1995) and corporate culture (Kreps, 1990) or socialization (Scott and Lane, 2000). Reputation may be built by consistent behaviour over a long period of time and facilitated by communication (Fombrun, 1996). Following Kreps (1990), a reputation for honesty is a valuable asset which will be lost if the company is not truthful, which implies an economic incentive to honesty. Commitments to employee satisfaction, customer value and creditor protection may also be valuable, self-sustainable assets. Arrow (1973), Sen (1993) and others have argued that ethical codes may improve economic efficiency when other social institutions fail to achieve optimal results, in particular the classic market failures when the firm has access to unique information (Arrow, 1973). Arrow (1969) proposes that non-market institutions may in fact arise in response to market failures.

Intuitively, the emphasis placed on different stakeholder values should reflect their relative bargaining power (Bernheim and Whinston, 1986; Mitchell et al., 1997; Scott and Lane, 2000), which should again reflect their impact on the overall value creation in the firm. For example, in labour-intensive industries where human capital is important relative to machinery and equipment, more emphasis might be placed on employee satisfaction. Socialization is another way in which stakeholder concerns may conceivably be internalized, not only in corporate values, but also even in the minds and identity of the managers. Scott and Lane (2000) argue that managers' identities are affected by representing the organization in its relationships with stakeholders so that they come to act consistently with the presented self-image (p. 47). Stewardship theory (Davis et al., 1997) holds that managers will identify with organizational values and prefer cooperative behaviour, which could facilitate implicit contracting with external stakeholders.

16.3   Nordic corporate governance[2]

The Nordic countries – Scandinavia (Denmark, Norway and Sweden) and Finland – are small, affluent welfare states. Their populations are respectively 5.5 million (Denmark), 4.8 million (Norway) and 9.2 million (Sweden). In 2008, the GDP per capita of Denmark was $63,000, $95,000 in Norway,

---

[2] This section draws on previous work, including Sinani et al. (2008).

$53,000 in Sweden and $51,000 in Finland (Norway's extraordinary richness being attributable mainly to oil). This is higher than in the US ($47,000) and much higher than in the EU ($32,000 in 2009), although the comparison is sensitive to correction for purchasing power and significant currency fluctuations during the recent financial crisis. The Nordic countries are all welfare states with a high level of government expenditure and the world's highest marginal tax rates (Gwartney and Lawson, 2006).

Nevertheless, the Nordic countries are economically dynamic with productivity growth rates of 1.2% (Sweden), 2% (Finland) and 0.8% (Denmark) against 1.2% in the US.[3] Three of the four largest EU knowledge economies are said to be Nordic (Norway is not a member). Economic growth has been above average in the Euro Area (see Table 16.1) and comparable to that in the USA over the past decade, particularly if one takes into consideration higher labour force growth in the USA.

The four countries are culturally similar (historically with a Protestant religion and alternating social democratic governments during the last 50 years) and the Scandinavian countries are quite homogeneous in terms of ethnic composition, language, religious beliefs and values etc. Income and wealth inequalities have deliberately been kept low with high tax rates and extensive welfare programmes. They have a history of social democratic governments and high government expenditure, which are reflected in the world's highest marginal tax rates (Gwartney and Lawson, 2006). The social-democratic influence shows up in employee representation on boards, for example. It also shows up in Norway's many government-owned companies, although the social democrats have historically been reluctant to intervene directly in the business sector and remain so in Denmark and Sweden, while most government-owned enterprises have been privatized in Finland. Social democratic values are reinforced by government-funded schools and universities, hospitals and social services. Company law, with a few exceptions, has been very similar and part of a conscious effort to foster Nordic harmonization. The greater Nordic region of Iceland, Estonia, Latvia and Lithuania and Northern Germany shares many institutional and cultural affinities with the Nordic countries, but the focus here will be on Scandinavia and Finland.

Obviously, the Nordic countries also differ in many ways. For example, for geographical reasons, mining, forestry and heavy industry have been strong in Sweden and Finland, while shipping and recently energy (particularly oil) have dominated the Norwegian economy. Denmark has traditionally been an agricultural country with many small and medium-sized enterprises in manufacturing. Both similarities and differences have left their mark on Nordic corporate governance.

Table 16.1 GDP growth per year

	Average 1996–2009
Denmark	1.4
Finland	2.8
Norway	2.5
Sweden	2.2
Nordic countries	2.3
United States	2.6
Euro Area	1.7

Source: OECD Economic Outlook database

---

[3] Source: OECD.

Table 16.2 highlights some corporate governance characteristics of the Nordic countries. To some extent this simplified expression is based on guesstimates and not all academics would agree with everything. Nevertheless, the table serves as a useful reference point for presenting the Nordic model.

Ownership

Compared with the USA and the UK, the Nordic countries are characterized by more concentrated ownership structures. The largest owner will typically have effective control of the company compared with the USA or the UK where the largest owner will typically own less than 5%. In Sweden and Denmark blockholder ownership is reinforced by dual-class shares such that one share class (typically held by the founders) carries more votes than the other (typically held by the public). Dual-class shares are also commonly used in family-owned Norwegian shipping companies.

Owner identities vary between the countries, but distinct ownership types are industrial foundations in Denmark (e.g. the Carlsberg Foundation), government ownership in Norway (e.g. Statoil) and business groups in Sweden (e.g. the Handelsbanken and Wallenberg spheres). Finland has evolved from substantial government ownership to more open stock markets with substantial foreign ownership. A majority of the mobile phone producer Nokia, for example, is now owned by international investors. The importance of the stock market in Scandinavia has historically been small compared with the Anglo-American market-based economies, while banks have been large and influential, as in Germany. However, during the past two decades the Swedish stock market has grown impressively and is now close to USA/UK figures relative to GDP.

All three countries have a significant degree of family ownership among listed companies (as most other countries across the world including the USA) and, in all of them, foreign ownership

Table 16.2 Stylized governance characteristics of the Nordic countries

	Denmark	Norway	Sweden	Finland
Ownership concentration	High	Medium	Medium	Low
Typical owners	Families Foundations Coops	Government Foreign	Business groups	Institutions Foreign
Board system	Two tiers	Two tiers	Two tiers	One tier
Managers on board	(–)	+	+	+
Employee representation	30%	30%	25%	0%
Bank influence	–	–	+	+
Average CEO pay $m	0.8	0.5	1.5	0.5
% performance based	20%	40%	50%	20%
Legal system	Civil	Civil	Civil	Civil
Listed firms 2008	216	209	341	126
Market cap/GDP %	38	27	52	56

In preparing the subjective assessments of this table, I was grateful for advice from and discussions with Professor Tom Berglund, Professor Trond Randoy and Professor Ken Bechmann. Any remaining errors are the author's own responsibility.

has increased significantly since the 1990s. In addition to having some of the world's largest farm cooperatives, Denmark is special as about two-thirds of listed firms are controlled by a majority shareholder (Eriksson et al., 2001; Krüger Andersen, 2004; Lausten, 2002; Rose and Mejer, 2003). In Norway traditional industries like shipping are still controlled mainly by families, but resource-intensive businesses like oil and power as well as banks are to a large extent owned by the state (La Porta et al., 1998, 2002b; Oxelheim, 1998; Randøy and Nielsen, 2002). Sweden has a tradition of large business groups and large industrial firms, as socialist governments, labour unions and industrialists together favoured large firms in the economy. Half of the stock market has long been controlled by the two business spheres of Handelsbanken and Wallenberg. Although foreign and institutional ownership has increased recently, they have to a large extent kept their dominance of the stock market (Agnblad et al., 2001; Collin, 1998; Högfeldt, 2004).

Scandinavian countries have a long tradition of strong owners. They achieve this control by dual-class shares, pyramids, and cross-shareholdings. Denmark has many dual-class shares, Norway uses pyramids (a few) and dual shares (a few), and Sweden uses all three to a much larger extent than the other two and indeed the rest of the world (La Porta et al., 1998). Majority ownership is also more common in Denmark and Norway. Despite this, there is little evidence of owners expropriating personal gains from minority shareholders (Dyck and Zingales, 2004; Nenova, 2003).

Boards

Company law in the three Scandinavian countries prescribes that there must be one or more responsible managers (a 'direktion' of one or more members in Denmark, an 'administrerende direktør' in Norway and a 'verkställande direktör' in Sweden). In addition joint stock companies (aktieselskaber) must have a board ('bestyrelsen' in Danish, 'styret' in Norwegian and 'styrelsen' in Swedish). In other words they can be regarded as two-tier board systems, although with a different division of labour between the two boards than in Germany. For example, unlike in Germany there is no absolute separation of members between the two boards in the Nordic countries. Boards in Scandinavia have some management responsibilities (but must not take part in daily management) and some legal scholars therefore categorize them as one-tier or hybrid systems. Moreover, managers can sit on their own supervisory boards, and this is quite common in Norway and Sweden (but not in Denmark). According to Henrekson and Jakobsson (2011), Swedish CEOs sit on the boards in roughly half of the listed companies. Finnish companies can choose between one- and two-tier systems, but most choose US style one-tier models. The same option is open to Danish companies after a company law reform was adopted in 2010, but so far few companies (if any) appear to have moved to the one-tier model or to a German style two-tier model.

The three Scandinavian countries all have employee representation on their supervisory boards, typically with around one-third of the directors being elected by the employees, although the exact representation rules vary slightly. This is a clear indication of a more stakeholder-oriented approach than is found in the USA or the UK, although less so than in Germany where many companies have 50% employee representation. Norway has experimented with further mandatory board representation by requiring equal gender representation (i.e. minimum 40% of each gender) in listed companies as of 2008. Social democrats in Sweden and Denmark have similar quotas on their agenda.

Scandinavian executive pay is typically more moderate than in the USA or Continental Europe, particularly after taxation. In rough figures, average total CEO pay is an estimated $1 million a year for listed companies which is substantially lower than in the USA, the UK or Germany (see Chapter 10). Moreover, performance incentives also appear to be lower in the Nordic model with estimates of variable to total pay ranging from 20% to 40% against 70% in the US, 50% in the UK and 40% in Germany. The low pay level and low fraction of variable pay may be partly attributable to monitoring by controlling shareholders, small-firm effects (many listed firms are small) or social pressures in egalitarian societies with social democratic traditions. It must be noted however that there is some uncertainty concerning the figures, particularly bonus levels, as well as the valuation of stock options.

Moreover, not all companies (particularly not all small and medium-sized companies) disclose CEO pay. This means that the reported figures are guesstimates based on available information rather than exact figures.

Finally, with regard to the legal system the Scandinavian countries have civil rather than common law, although they are occasionally assigned a special category of their own ('Scandinavian Civil Law') within the civil law tradition.

Altogether, it seems possible despite country differences to discern a Nordic corporate governance model, particularly among the three Scandinavian countries. Ownership is generally more concentrated than in the market-based systems. The board structure is semi-two-tier. Employee representatives sit on supervisory boards, but only in a minority up to one-third compared with 50:50 in some German firms. Executive compensation is more modest and less incentivized than in other high-income countries. Nevertheless the Nordic countries are by no means uniform in their approach to governance. For example, Finland appears to have opted for a more market-based approach to governance with one-tier boards and dispersed ownership. Even within Scandinavia the gigantic Swedish business groups differ substantially from Norwegian government ownership which again differs greatly from Danish industrial foundations.

16.4 Social governance

There is probably more to corporate governance than the structural factors outlined above. Institutional infrastructure such as efficient and accountable regulation, transparency and political stability are also part of the picture. In this section we go on to examine some of these softer factors using the World Bank Governance Indicators (cf. Table 16.3). For more than a decade the World Bank has rated countries on six governance variables defined as follows.

Voice and accountability is intended to measure 'the extent to which citizens in a country are able to participate in selecting their government, as well as freedom of expression, freedom of association, and a free media'.

Political stability and absence of violence/terrorism is intended to measure 'the perceptions of the likelihood that the government will be destabilized or overthrown by unconstitutional or violent means, including domestic violence and terrorism'.

Government effectiveness is intended to measure 'the quality of public services, the quality of the civil service and the degree of its independence from political pressures, the quality of policy formulation and implementation, and the credibility of the government's commitment to such policies'.

Regulatory quality is intended to measure 'the ability of the government to formulate and implement sound policies and regulations that permit and promote private sector development'.

Rule of law is intended to measure 'the extent to which agents have confidence in and abide by the rules of society, in particular the quality of contract enforcement, the police, and the courts, as well as the likelihood of crime and violence'.

Control of corruption is intended to measure 'the extent to which public power is exercised for private gain, including petty and grand forms of corruption, as well as "capture" of the state by elites and private interests'.

For each of these variables countries are ranked on a scale from 1 (low) to 100 (high). Without going into the obvious measurement problems of this approach, we compare the scores of the Nordic countries with the USA and the rest of Europe.

Table 16.3 The Nordic countries in the World Bank Governance Indicators (rank score 1–100 from low to high)

Voice and accountability	1996	1998	2000	2002	2003	2004	2005	2006	2007	2008
Denmark	96	96	97	99	100	100	100	100	97	98
Finland	95	96	100	100	99	100	100	100	98	97
Norway	99	97	96	98	97	98	98	97	100	100
Sweden	95	98	99	99	98	99	96	95	98	100
Nordic countries	96	97	98	99	98	99	98	98	98	99
United States	91	91	90	92	91	90	90	86	84	86
EU	84	87	86	86	88	89	88	87	88	87
Political stability – no violence	**1996**	**1998**	**2000**	**2002**	**2003**	**2004**	**2005**	**2006**	**2007**	**2008**
Denmark	92	93	94	94	90	85	82	76	82	82
Finland	98	97	99	100	100	100	100	99	99	97
Norway	99	97	97	98	96	95	92	90	94	97
Sweden	100	98	97	96	98	94	90	90	93	88
Nordic countries	97	96	97	97	96	93	91	89	92	91
United States	85	82	88	58	57	53	50	61	58	68
EU	77	79	80	82	77	73	73	73	74	75
Government effectiveness	**1996**	**1998**	**2000**	**2002**	**2003**	**2004**	**2005**	**2006**	**2007**	**2008**
Denmark	97	95	97	99	99	100	99	100	100	100
Finland	96	95	97	100	100	98	100	99	97	98
Norway	99	98	95	96	96	98	97	98	99	98
Sweden	97	99	98	96	98	97	97	97	98	99
Nordic countries	97	97	97	98	98	98	98	98	98	98
United States	98	91	93	93	93	93	92	91	91	93
EU	86	87	86	87	87	86	86	85	84	84
Regulatory quality	**1996**	**1998**	**2000**	**2002**	**2003**	**2004**	**2005**	**2006**	**2007**	**2008**
Denmark	93	97	96	97	99	98	98	99	100	99
Finland	91	98	99	99	100	100	99	97	96	94
Norway	89	93	83	87	90	93	92	90	90	89

Sweden	90	88	91	96	97	96	93	93	95	96
Nordic countries	91	94	92	95	96	96	95	95	95	94
United States	95	96	95	93	92	92	93	94	91	93
EU	85	86	87	88	88	87	87	87	87	88
Rule of law	**1996**	**1998**	**2000**	**2002**	**2003**	**2004**	**2005**	**2006**	**2007**	**2008**
Denmark	98	98	97	98	99	98	100	99	100	100
Finland	99	99	99	99	98	98	99	99	97	98
Norway	100	100	98	98	99	100	98	100	99	100
Sweden	97	96	97	97	97	97	96	98	98	98
Nordic countries	98	98	98	98	98	98	98	99	99	99
United States	93	93	93	92	93	92	92	92	92	92
EU	85	85	84	84	84	84	82	82	83	84
Control of corruption	**1996**	**1998**	**2000**	**2002**	**2003**	**2004**	**2005**	**2006**	**2007**	**2008**
Denmark	100	98	97	98	98	99	99	99	99	99
Finland	100	100	100	100	100	100	100	100	100	100
Norway	99	97	96	96	96	95	96	97	95	95
Sweden	98	100	99	98	98	98	97	98	98	98
Nordic countries	99	99	98	98	98	98	98	98	98	98
United States	92	93	93	93	93	93	92	89	92	92
EU	81	84	85	84	85	84	83	82	82	82

Source: *The World Bank, http://info.worldbank.org/governance/wgi/index.asp*

As will be seen, the Nordic countries score consistently higher than the USA and the rest of Europe on all indicators. In fact, as a group they score higher than all other countries on the planet. Consider for example voice and accountability, a democracy and transparency indicator, on which the Nordic countries score 99 out of 100 in 2008, while the USA scores 86 and the EU 87 respectively. Over time the position of the Nordic countries appears to be quite stable while there appears to be a gentle downward slide in the USA in recent years. Democracy matters, for example because it enables voters to hold politicians to account for inefficient regulation and self-dealing.

The Nordic countries score much higher than the USA and EU on political stability, more than 20 rank points over the USA (although somewhat lower than in the 1990s). Political stability is known to increase institutional stability and investor protection. On government effectiveness, rule of law and control of corruption the Nordic countries score 98 out of 100! Again this is much higher than the USA and the EU as a whole. Regulatory quality is the only indicator on which the USA comes close (only one point behind) the Nordic countries while the rest of the EU is five points lower.

It is surprising that the Nordic advantage is so robust over time and across the six different measures. With regard to social governance, more than corporate governance, they appear to be

world champions. While the determinants of social capital necessary to produce such results may seem to be somewhat outside the scope of corporate governance research, it clearly influences corporate governance in many ways. For example less cronyism doubtless makes it easier to enforce governance regulation impartially and effectively. The risk of fraud and other kinds of agency is almost certainly lower, and the extensive mistrust of managers implicit in agency theory and many US governance practices may be less appropriate in a Nordic context. This does not mean that all managers always behave or that corporate governance is irrelevant in a Nordic context but it is interesting and important to note that these very strong background institutions are likely to seriously influence the nature of corporate governance.

16.5 Industrial foundations[4]

In Northern Europe it is not uncommon for foundations to own and operate world-class companies such as Bertelsmann, Heineken, Robert Bosch, Carlsberg or IKEA. In Denmark, particularly, foundations own and operate a quarter of the 100 largest Danish corporations and control close to half the value of the major Danish stock index (KFX). Similar structures were not uncommon in the USA up to the 1969 laws, which effectively prevent US foundations from owning more than 20% of business companies (Fleishman, 2001).

While much debated among legal scholars, foundation ownership is something of an enigma to economic theory (Thomsen, 1996). Since the 1970s a large body of literature has emerged which emphasizes that risk diversification and incentives play a key role in efficient ownership of business companies (e.g. Jensen and Meckling, 1976; Putterman, 1993; Hart, 1995; Hansmann, 1996; Williamson, 1996; Shleifer and Vishny, 1997). A possible exception is non-profit organizations, which are clearly not monitored by owners, but rather by donors or users (Hansmann, 1980; Fama and Jensen, 1983a). But a non-profit organization is generally believed to be competitive only in certain industries (hospitals, universities, charities and the like) and not (in the absence of tax subsidies) to be a viable business model for commercial enterprises (Fama and Jensen, 1983b). The theoretical implication is that non-profit entities should be a rare phenomenon outside of these special industries, and in other industries their performance (in terms of profitability, growth, cost efficiency or other measures) would be expected to be below average. Non-profit enterprises lack a personal profit motive to monitor managers, and their ability to attract equity from outside investors is also limited. Altogether, agency theory would predict that foundation-owned companies would perform badly compared with investor-owned companies on criteria like profitability, growth and shareholder value.

But this is inconsistent with empirical studies, which have found the economic performance of foundation-owned companies to be no worse or even slightly better than that of companies with more common ownership structures, measured on accounting profitability, growth, stock market value or stock returns (Herrmann and Franke, 2002; Thomsen, 1996, 1999; Thomsen and Rose, 2004). Further research appears to enlarge rather than solve the puzzle (Thomsen, 1999). Taxation may to some extent explain the creation of foundations, but does not affect the relative performance of foundation-owned companies. The foundation-owned companies are more international than other companies and spread across a range of sectors so monopoly explanations do not work. Creditor monitoring as a substitute control mechanism is generally less important for foundation-owned companies which have significantly lower debt/equity ratios. Accounting biases are not a good explanation since foundation-owned companies tend to have the same Q-values and market rates of return as other companies even adjusting for the conventional risk measures.

Formally, an industrial foundation is an organization created to administer a large ownership stake in a particular company, very often donated to the foundation by the company's founder. The

---

[4] This section borrows liberally from a previous working paper (Thomsen, 2005a).

foundation itself is a non-profit entity. It has no owners. Its board of directors is often self-elective, constrained only by the law and its charter which frequently stipulates that the foundation should serve some broadly defined social purpose, e.g. to act in the company's 'best interest' and use excess revenue for charitable purposes. Often, but not always, the founder's family continues to play a role in the management of the company. The institutional set-up resembles what would have been the case if the Ford Foundation had maintained majority control of Ford Motor Company.

As an example consider William Demant, a listed Danish company, one of the world's largest producers of hearing aids. The company is majority-owned by the Oticon Foundation (Figure 16.1). One approach to foundation ownership is the theory of commercial non-profits. Another approach is to regard industrial foundations as an extension of family ownership.

Non-profit theory

According to the review by Malani, Philipson and David (2003), there are three main theories in the literature on commercial non-profits: 1) the altruism model, 2) the worker cooperative model, and 3) the non-contractible quality model.

The altruism model (Newhouse, 1970) assumes that non-profits differ from for-profits by having preferences with regard to the quantity and quality of output (e.g. running a hospital is a goal in itself). It seems straightforward to generalize this logic to concerns for employment security, labour standards, use of child labour among suppliers etc. These concerns may be motivated by pure altruism or by professional norms shaped by 'elite workers' (e.g. doctors), which implies the possibility of integrating the altruism model with the worker's cooperative model.

It seems difficult to rule out that altruism, or a desire to advertise a family name and make it famous into posterity (Glaeser, 2002), is a possible motive for establishing an industrial foundation by a large donation. Casual inspection of foundation charters indicates that they often make special provisions about high ethical standards in the conduct of business, concern for employees and their families or for product quality. For example Carlsberg is in this way committed to brewing beer of the highest quality. So a preference for high product quality could be a prediction of the altruism model (Malani, Philipson and David, 2003). While product quality is generally difficult to observe, it seems possible that foundation ownership may also be associated with a size preference, since foundation charters tend to regard running the company as a goal in itself. This prediction is supported by studies which find that US non-profits tend to be bigger than their for-profit competitors (Malani, Philipson and David, 2003).

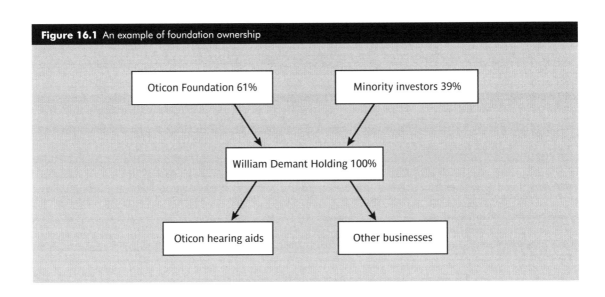

Figure 16.1 An example of foundation ownership

An alternative is to model non-profits as worker cooperatives (Pauly and Redisch, 1973). Glaeser (2002) models US non-profits as employee cooperatives that are captured by elite employees (doctors, university professors or priests, which in industrial foundations probably would be the top managers). However, the self-interest seeking of the managerial elite is tempered by competition and he therefore argues that competition is a key driver of economic efficiency in not-for-profit firms. A high degree of internationalization of the Danish foundation-owned companies is consistent with competition as a main determinant of their relatively good performance. But does competition mean that ownership is irrelevant? This would then imply that there is considerably more latitude for variations in the ownership and governance of business firms than is normally implied by the corporate governance literature.

At face value, the worker cooperative model would seem to imply high salaries per worker and lower levels of employment relative to output. However, if the capturing agents are top managers rather than elite employees, the model seems consistent with a size preference. Glaeser (2002) describes how there can be conflicts of interests between donors and professional managers in US non-profits, and how over time the professional managers tend to become more powerful as organizations grow, gain control of their own resources and so become less dependent on the donors. Similar trends and conflicts can be observed in industrial foundations between founding families and professional managers. Thus over long time periods the founding families probably tend to lose their control of the foundations and their boards.

The third body of theory is based on quality uncertainty (Hansmann, 1980; Glaeser and Shleifer, 2001). Hansmann (1980) explains the survival of non-profit institutions by a contract-failure argument: when the buyer is uncertain about the quality of a service provided to him, a market failure occurs since the producer has the capacity to reduce quality of the good in ways that cannot be detected by the buyer. To facilitate contracting under these circumstances, the supplier may organize as a non-profit enterprise, which is free of any profit-incentive to cheat on customers. Non-profit enterprise can therefore be seen as a binding commitment not to maximize profits opportunistically at the expense of buyers, and in principle the argument can be generalized to include safeguarding all economic relationships in which a company has decisive information advantages. It seems possible to generalize the argument to other economic relationships characterized by high asset specificity and/or hold up risks, e.g. relations with suppliers, bank relationships, inter-firm alliances, employee relations etc. All else equal a non-profit firm could be less likely to renege on implicit contracts with employees, banks or other firms because they value the extra profits less.

Glaeser and Shleifer (2001) develop this perspective formally in an incomplete contracts framework. Here, the problem is not asymmetric information per se, but rather that quality or certain aspects of it are unverifiable and cannot be contracted on. They conclude that there is scope for non-profit enterprise in sectors of the economy where there are opportunities for severe ex post expropriation of consumers, employees and donors.

In their model a firm has the opportunity to reduce cost at the expense of non-verifiable product quality to the buyer. The owner/managers of a for-profit firm will do this as long as the marginal cost reduction exceeds the marginal expense/effort involved (i.e. until marginal effort costs equals marginal cost reduction and profit increase). But on the assumption that the manager of a not-for-profit firm will value a marginal increase in profits by less than the owner-manager of a for-profit firm, she will have less of an incentive to reduce costs and lower quality. Therefore not-for-profit firms will invest less in cost reduction that reduces non-verifiable product quality and hurts the buyer. Buyers will recognize this and prefer to deal with the not-for-profit firm. Over time a more consistent pattern of honouring implicit contracts with customers and other stakeholders would of course be expected to result in a better reputation.

While unobserved and unverifiable aspects of quality are present to some degree in all economic relationships, their importance is likely to vary by nature of the product, the institutional environment and other characteristics. It may be that certain industries are characterized by greater information asymmetries but it may also be that a non-profit structure can support business strategies that rely on product quality differentiation even in relatively transparent industries. Obviously, these

possible benefits of non-profit ownership related to limiting the profit motive have to be weighed against the disadvantages of not being able to attract outside equity and lower cost efficiency because of less intense monitoring (Fama and Jensen, 1983b).

Foundation ownership can also be regarded as an extension of family ownership. Foundation-owned companies are often managed by the founding families, who continue to take a strong personal interest in the firm. Several recent studies (e.g. Anderson and Reeb, 2003; Amit and Villalonga, 2006) have emphasized the relatively strong performance of family-owned firms and it is possible that foundation-owned firms can benefit from this type of long-term commitment. Thomsen (1999) finds that half of the foundation-owned companies in Denmark retain a tie to the founding family and that the companies which do so also do better in terms of profitability. Founding-family ties are not a sufficient explanation of the relatively good performance of foundation-owned companies since even the slightly worse performing foundation-owned companies without ties to the founding family do not underperform compared with investor-owned companies. But it seems likely that foundation-owned companies retain more of the company's administrative heritage, since this is the explicit formal goal of the foundation structure.

16.6   Board diversity

In most countries across the world, company boards are composed of demographically similar individuals: men aged between 50 and 60, national citizens with an education in business, economics, law or engineering, with the same ethnic origin, similar backgrounds as managers in similar companies, from the same residential areas. Many of their companies have grown to become global businesses with a great diversity of product markets, workforce, customer base and stakeholders.

However, over the past decade corporate boards in the Nordic countries have become more diverse as a consequence of legal changes, globalization and social trends. A mandatory gender quota in Norway has generated a large-scale natural experiment. A similar quota was announced, but later cancelled in Sweden up to 2005. The Scandinavian countries also have mandatory employee representation. Boards have also become more diverse because of an increasing level of international board membership.

The most dramatic case is the Norwegian gender quota, according to which the fraction of women (and men) on company boards must be at least 40% (the quota was announced but not fully effective in 2005). The exact implementation is given in Table 16.4.

So if shareholders decide to elect six board members at the annual general meeting (AGM) of a publicly listed Norwegian company, three of them must be women. If they only decide to elect three, only one has to be a woman and so on. Strangely, the quota does not apply to employee representatives. Sweden had announced a similar quota which was, however, withdrawn after a change of government in 2005. Denmark has so far not adopted quotas, although the proposal has been put forward by the opposition Social Democrats, and the Danish best practice corporate governance code contains a mild endorsement of diversity.

With regard to international board membership, diversity has been increased by removal of regulation. Thus Danish company law (§ 50.2) contained the following provision: 'Members of the management board and at least half of the members of the board of directors shall be resident in this country, save where the Minister of Trade and Industry grants an exemption from this requirement'. A similar restriction was found in Norway (Norwegian company law § 6.11). This was later held to be in breach of the principles of the internal market and so removed for EU citizens.

In addition, mandatory employee representation imposes additional diversity on Nordic boards. As previously noted, above a certain size threshold (e.g. 35 employees), employees in Denmark, Norway and Sweden have a right to elect members to company supervisory boards.

Table 16.4   The Norwegian gender quota

Board members elected by shareholders	Minimum number of females	Minimum % women
3	1	33.3
4	2	50
5	2	40
6	3	50
7	3	43
8	3	38
9	4	44
10	4	40
11	4	40
12	5	40

Diversity theory

Theoretically, an important benefit of a diverse board could be access to a greater pool of qualified board members (Adams and Ferreira, 2009). It would be strange if the best board members of a multinational corporation all happened to have the same nationality, background, education, age and other demographic characteristics. On the contrary, such demographic concentration can be regarded as evidence of discrimination (Becker, 1971). Removing this source of inefficiency might in itself increase board and company performance. Becker (1971) models discrimination as an effect of preferences (prejudices) of leading managers, but predicts that companies will have to sacrifice some profitability and that this will only be sustainable in monopolistic situations. A second argument for diversity is greater independence. Boards which are independent of managers and other special interest groups may be more effective in monitoring managers on behalf of shareholders (Rosenstein and Wyatt, 1990; Cotter, Shivdasani and Zenner, 1997). Third, it may be that diverse boards are more creative and suffer less from groupthink.

There may also be costs to diversity. Studies in social psychology (e.g. Zander, 1979) have found that group loyalty depends on the similarity of group members. Athey, Avery and Zemsky (2000) argue that mentoring is more likely to occur between similar individuals. In management studies, Kanter (1977) proposed that trust is facilitated by similarity in top management teams. She emphasized that this kind of trust may be more necessary when environmental uncertainty is high (Adams and Ferreira, 2002). Pelled (1996) argues that demographic diversity may cause affective conflicts which reduce organizational performance. Greater diversity could also make boards less efficient and resolute, in monitoring as well as in decision-making. Thus the grandfather of agency theory, Michael Jensen (1993), argues that 'suggestions to model the board after a democratic political model in which various constituencies are represented are likely to make the process even weaker'. Finally, there is a risk that diversity imposed for reasons other than improving company performance (e.g. political correctness or equality) may force companies to employ sub-standard, less talented and less experienced board members.

So far most empirical studies have found a negative association between Nordic board diversity and company economic performance (Ahern and Dittmar, 2010; Bøhren and Ødegaard, 2006). For a discussion of costs and benefits see Chapter 8.

16.7   Discussion

While it is difficult to classify Scandinavia unambiguously on a scale between market and bank, it is clear that the standard US corporate governance model of 'strong managers and weak owners' and its related problems do not fit. On the contrary, Scandinavia has weak managers who are pressured by strong owners, independent boards, and strong labour unions. Thus, classical agency (type I) problems are much less serious than in the UK. One indicator of management weakness is that CEO pay has not increased to the same extent as in the USA.

Moreover, the strong owners in Scandinavia appear to be relatively decent, perhaps because of socialization and perhaps because social democratic politicians have historically been 'breathing down their necks'. For example, the value spread between voting and non-voting shares, an indicator of expropriation risk, is quite low.

Finally, stakeholder issues do not seem to be more serious in Scandinavia than in other countries. In fact, because of employee representation and strong labour unions, employees seem stronger in Scandinavia than anywhere else in the world, with the possible exception of Germany.

So, it is possible to argue that Scandinavia is a 'sweet spot' with few corporate governance problems. But it is also possible to argue that Scandinavia has too few governance problems and pays a price for its strong owners and strong unions. The price is opportunity cost. Small US states which are comparable to Scandinavia now have much higher per capita GDP. Adjusting for purchasing power, US GDP is only slightly higher, but small homogeneous countries should be able to do much better than that. One of the reasons for American dynamism is a strong capital market which will inevitably involve ownership dispersion and agency problems. It also involves dramatic restructuring, takeovers, and other issues which seem unpalatable to the cosy Scandinavian consensus. The point is that the gains of dynamic capital market, or more generally of a dynamic market economy, may be worth it.

The Nordic model has worked reasonably well, however, and it seems possible that it can be improved to work even better, for example by active ownership, improved investor protection, pension fund capitalism and responsible labour unions.

Minicase

Statoil

Statoil, the Norwegian oil firm, is the largest company in Scandinavia by market capitalization. It has production in 13 countries and retail sales (e.g. gas stations) in 8.

The company is ⅔ owned by the Norwegian government and its shares are listed in Oslo and New York.

By law, four members of the 10 supervisory board members are women. Three are non-Norwegians, three are employee representatives, three have previous experience in the energy industry, and two are former politicians.

In 2010, the CEO was paid roughly €1.5 million of which roughly half was fixed. The chairman of the board got roughly €87,000.

Table 16.5 gives the 2011 performance of Statoil and several similar oil companies.

Sources: http://en.wikipedia.org/wiki/Statoil
http://www.statoil.com/en/About/CorporateGovernance/GoverningBodies/Board/Pages/default.aspx
Enriching a Few at the Expense of Many by Gretchen Morgenson, The New York Times, 9 April 2011.

Table 16.5 Company performance 2011 (latest annual figures)

Company name	P/E ratio	Price-to-book	Mkt cap	Return on avg assets
Statoil ASA	5.98	1.86	73.05	6.24
Exxon Mobil Corporation	9.46	2.49	350.12	11.72
TOTAL S.A.	6.33	1.24	105.14	7.96
Royal Dutch Shell plc	7.09	1.35	198.84	6.66
Eni S.p.A.	7.81	0.96	68.36	5.92
Chevron Corporation	8.37	1.86	192.11	10.95
BP plc	5.97	1.30	119.30	–1.31
Suncor Energy Inc. (USA)	13.81	1.35	47.78	5.54
Marathon Oil Corporation	7.25	0.77	18.07	5.29

Source: Google Finance.

Discussion questions

1 How would you assess Statoil's ownership structure. Is it optimal for the company? For Norway?
2 How would you assess the board structure? Is it good for the company?
3 Is executive pay appropriate for the company?
4 How is Statoil's governance affected by its Scandinavian origin?
5 How would you rate Statoil's governance overall?

Summary (learning points)

■ The Nordic (Scandinavian) model may be said to consist of strong owners, two-tier boards, ⅓ employee representation, low and fixed executive pay.
■ Moreover the Nordic countries are bound together by strong social governance.
■ However, there are also pronounced differences ranging from dispersed investor ownership in Finland, to business groups in Sweden, state ownership in Norway and industrial foundations in Denmark.
■ A mandatory 40% gender quota has been implemented in Norway and is being debated in the other countries as well.

References and further reading

Adams, R. and Ferreira, D. (2002) *Diversity and Incentives in Teams: Evidence from Corporate Boards*, working paper, Federal Reserve Bank of New York and Getulio Vargas Foundation.

Adams, R. and Ferreira, D. (2009) Women in the boardroom and their impact on governance and performance, *Journal of Financial Economics*, **94** (2), 291–309.

Agnblad, J., Berglöf, E., Högfeldt, P. and Svancar, H. (2001) Ownership and control in Sweden – strong owners, weak minorities and social control, in Barca, F. and Becht, M. (eds), *The control of corporate Europe*, Oxford University Press: Oxford.

Ahern, K.R. and Dittmar, A.K. (2010) *The Changing of the Boards: the Value Effect of a Massive Exogenous Shock.* Available at SSRN: http://ssrn.com/abstract=1364470.

Akerlof, G.A. and Yellen, J. (1986) *Efficiency Wage Models of the Labor Market*, Cambridge University Press: Cambridge, MA.

Amit, R. and Villalonga, B. (2006) How do family ownership, control and management affect firm value?, Journal of Financial Economics, **80** (2), 385–417.

Anderson, R.C. and Reeb, D. (2003). Founding-family ownership and firm performance: evidence from the S&P 500, *Journal of Finance*, **58** (3), 1301–1328.

Arrow, K.J. (1969) The Organization of Economic Activity, in Arrow K.J., *General Equilibrium*. Reprinted in *Collected Papers of Kenneth Arrow, Vol. 2* (1983), Basil Blackwell.

Arrow, K.J. (1973) Social responsibility and economic efficiency, *Public Policy*, **21**, 303–318. Reprinted in *Collected Papers of Kenneth Arrow, Vol. 6, Applied Economics*, Belknap Press: Cambridge, MA (1985).

Athey, S., Avery, C. and Zemsky, P. (2000) Mentoring and Diversity, *American Economic Review*, **90** (4),765–787.

Barca, F. and Becht, M. (2001) *The Control of Corporate Europe*, Oxford University Press: Oxford.

Baums, T. (1994) The German Banking System and its Impact on Corporate Finance and Governance, in Aoki, M. and Patrick, H. (eds.) *The Japanese Main Bank System*, Oxford University Press: Oxford.

Becker, G.S. (1971) *The Economics of Discrimination* (2nd edn), University of Chicago Press: Chicago and London.

Bernheim, D.B. and Whinston, M.D. (1986) Common agency, *Econometrica*, **54** (4), 923–942.

Bøhren, Ø. and Ødegaard, B.A. (2001) Patterns of corporate ownership: Insights from a unique data set, *Nordic Journal of Political Economy*, **27**, 55–86.

Bøhren, Ø. and Ødegaard, B.A. (2006) Governance and performance revisited, in P.U. Ali and G. Gregoriou (eds) *International Corporate Governance after Sarbanes-Oxley*, Wiley.

Booth, J.R. and Deli, D.N. (1996). Factors affecting the Number of Outside Directorships held by CEOs, *Journal of Financial Economics*, **40** (1), 81–104.

Coase, R.H. (1960) The problem of social cost, *Journal of Law and Economics*, **3** (Oct), 1–44.

Coffee, J.C. (1999) The Future as History: The Prospects for Global Convergence in Corporate Governance and its Implications, *Northwestern University Law Review*, **93**, 641–708.

Coffee, J.C. (2001) *Do Norms Matter? A Cross-Country Examination of the Private Benefits of Control*, Columbia Law and Economics Working Paper No. 183.

Collin, S.-O. (1998) Why are these islands of conscious power found in the ocean of ownership? Institutional and governance hypotheses explaining the existence of business groups in Sweden, *Journal of Management Studies*, **35** (6), 719–746.

Copeland, T., Koller, T. and Murrin, J. (1994) *Valuation ± Measuring and Managing the Value of Companies*, John Wiley: New York.

Cotter, J., Shivdasani, A. and Zenner, M. (1997) Do Independent Directors Enhance Target Shareholder Wealth during Tender Offers?, *Journal of Financial Economics*, **43** (2), 195–218.

Davis, J.A., Schorman, D.F. and Donaldson, L. (1997) Towards a stewardship theory of management, *Academy of Management Review*, **22** (1), 20–47.

Demirguc-Kunt, A., and R. Levine. (1999) *Bank-based and market-based financial systems: Cross-country comparisons*, World Bank Policy Working Paper No. 2143.

Demsetz, H. and Lehn, K. (1985) The structure of corporate ownership: Causes and consequences. *Journal of Political Economy*, **93** (6), 1155–1177.

Demsetz, H. and Villalonga, B. (2001) Ownership structure and corporate performance, *Journal of Corporate Finance*, **7** (3), 209–233.

Denis, D.K. and McConnell, J.J. (2003) International Corporate Governance, *Journal of Financial and Quantitative Analysis*, **38** (1), 1–36.

Dixit, A., Grossman, G. and Elhanan, E. (1997) Common agency and coordination general theory and application to government policy making, *Journal of Political Economy*, **105** (4), 752–769.

Durnev, A. and Han Kim, E. (2002) *To Steal or Not to Steal: Firm Attributes, Legal Environment, and Valuation, Working Paper*, University of Michigan Business School.

Dyck, A. and Zingales, L. (2002) The Corporate Governance Role of the Media, in R. Islam, *The Right To Tell: The Role of Mass Media in Economic Development*, World Bank: Washington, D.C., pp. 107–140.

Dyck, A. and Zingales, L. (2004) Private benefits of control: An international comparison, *Journal of Finance*, **59** (2), 537–600.

Eriksson, T., Strøjer Madsen, E., Dilling-Hansen, M. and Smith, V. (2001) Determinants of CEO and board turnover, *Empirica*, **28** (3), 243–257.

Evan, W. and Freeman, R.E. (1983) A stakeholder theory of the modern corporation: Kantian capitalism, in Beauchamp, T. and Bowie, N. (eds), *Ethical Theory and Business*, pp. 75–93, Prentice Hall: Englewood Cliffs, NJ.

Fama, E.F. (1980) Agency Problems and the Theory of the Firm, *Journal of Political Economy*, **88** (2), 288–307.

Fama, E.F. and Jensen, M.C. (1983a) Separation of Ownership and Control, *Journal of Law and Economics*, **26** (2), 301–325.

Fama, E.F. and Jensen, M.C. (1983b) Agency Problems and Residual Claims, *Journal of Law and Economics*, **26** (2), 327–349.

Fama, E.F. and Jensen, M.C. (1985) Organizational Forms and Investment Decisions, *Journal of Financial Economics*, **14** (1), 101–119.

Fleishman, J. (2001) Public Policy and Philanthropic Purpose – Foundation Ownership and Control of Corporations in Germany and the United States, in Schlüter, A., Then, V. and Walkenhorst, P. (Bertelsmann Foundation) (eds.) *Foundations in Europe: Society, Management and Law*, London: Directory for Social Change, pp. 372–408.

Fombrun, C.J. (1996) *Reputation: Realizing Value from the Corporate Image*, Harvard Business School Press: Boston, MA.

Fombrun, C.J. and Shanley, M. (1990) What's in a name? Reputation building and corporate strategy, *Academy of Management Journal*, **33** (2), 233–258.

Franks, J., Mayer, C. and Rossi, S. (2004) *Ownership: Evolution and Regulation*, European Corporate Governance Institute Working Paper 09/2003 (revised 12/2004).

Franks, J., Mayer, C. and Rossi, S. (2005). Spending Less Time with the Family: The Decline of Family Ownership in the United Kingdom in R.K. Morck (ed.) *A History of Corporate Governance around the World: Family Business Groups to Professional Managers*, University of Chicago Press, 581–607.

Glaeser, E.L. (2002) The Governance of Not-for-Profit Firms. Harvard Institute of Economic Research Paper No. 1954. Cambridge MA. Published in *The Governance of Not-for-Profit Firms*, E.L. Glaeser (ed). University of Chicago Press, 2003.

Glaeser, E.L. and Shleifer, A. (2001) Not-For-Profit Entrepreneurs, *Journal of Public Economics, 81* (1), 99–115.

Granovetter, M. (2005) The Impact of Social Structure on Economic Outcomes, *Journal of Economic Perspectives*, **19** (1), 33–50.

Gugler, K. (2001) *Corporate Governance and Economic Performance*, Oxford University Press: Oxford.

Gwartney, J.D. and Lawson, R.A. (2006) The impact of tax policy on economic growth, income distribution, and allocation of taxes, *Social Philosophy and Policy*, **23** (2), 28–52.

Hallock, K.F. (1997) Reciprocally Interlocking Board of Directors and Executive Compensation, *Journal of Financial and Quantitative Analysis*, **32** (3), 331–344.

Hansmann, H. (1980) The Role of Non-profit Enterprise, *Yale Law Review*, **89** (5), 835–901.

Hansmann, H. (1987) Economic Theories of Non Profit Organization, in Powell, W.W. (ed.) *The Non-profit sector – A Research Handbook*, Yale University Press.

Hansmann, H. (1988) Ownership of the Firm, *Journal of Law, Economics and Organization*, **4** (2), 267–304.

Hansmann, H. (1996) *The Ownership of Enterprise*, The Belknap Press of Harvard University Press: Cambridge MA.

Hart, O. (1995) *Firms, Contracts and Financial Structure*, Oxford University Press: New York.

Hart, O., Shleifer, A. and Vishny, R. (1997) The proper scope of goverment: theory and an application to prisons, *The Quarterly Journal of Economics*, **112** (4), 1127–61.

Henrekson, M. and Jakobsson, U. (2011) *The Swedish Corporate Control Model: Convergence, Persistence or Decline?* IFN Working Paper No. 857.

Herrmann, M. and Franke, G. (2002) Performance and Policy of Foundation-Owned Firms in Germany, *European Financial Management, 8* (3), 261–279.

Hill, C.W. and Jones, T.M. (1992) Stakeholder-agency theory, *Journal of Management Studies*, **29** (2), 131–154.

Högfeldt, P. (2004) *The history and politics of corporate ownership in Sweden*, Cambridge, MA: National Bureau of Research, National Bureau of Economics *Working Paper* 10641.

Holmström, B. (1979) Moral Hazard and Observability, *Bell Journal of Economics*, **10** (1), 74–91.

Holmström, B. (1999) Future of cooperatives: a corporate perspective, *Finnish Journal of Business Economics*, **4**, 404–417.

James, H.S. (1999) Owner as manager, Extended Horizons and the Family Firm, *International Journal of the Economics of Business*, **6** (1), 41–55.

Jensen, M. (1993) The modern industrial revolution, exit and the failure of internal control systems, *Journal of Finance*, **48** (3), 481–531.

Jensen, M. and Meckling W. (1976) Theory of the firm: Managerial Behavior, Agency Costs and Ownership Structure, *Journal of Financial Economics*, **3** (4), 305–360.

Johnson, J.L., Daily, C.M. and Ellstrand, A.E. (1996) Boards of directors: a review and research agenda, *Journal of Management*, **22** (3), 409–438.

Johnson, W.B., Young, S.M. and Welker, M. (1993) Managerial reputation and the informativeness of accounting, *Contemporary Accounting Research*, **10** (1), 305–332.

Jones, T.M. and Goldberg, L.D. (1982) Governing the large corporation: more arguments for public directors, *Academy of Management Review*, **7** (4), 603–612.

Kanter, R.M. (1977) *Men and Women of the Corporation*, Basic Books: New York.

Kay, J. (1995) *Why Firms Succeed*, Oxford University Press: New York.

Kogut, B. and Walker, G. (2001) The small world of Germany and the durability of national networks, *American Sociological Review*, 66 (June), 317–335.

Kreps, D.M. (1990) Corporate culture and economic theory, in J.E. Alt and K. Shepsle (eds) *Perspectives on Positive Political Economy*, Cambridge University Press: Cambridge.

Kronke, H. (1988) *Stiftungstypus und Unternehmensträgerstiftung*, J.C.B. Mohr: Tübingen.

Krüger Andersen, P. (2004) The takeover directive and corporate governance: The Danish experience, *European Business Law Review*, 15 (6), 1461–1475.

Laffont, J.-J. and Tirole, J. (1993) *A Theory of Incentives in Procurement and Regulation*, MIT Press: Cambridge.

La Porta, R., Lopez-de-Silanes, F., Shleifer, A. and Vishny, R. (1997) Legal Determinants of External Finance, *Journal of Finance*, 52 (3), 1131–1150.

La Porta, R., Lopez-de-Silanes, F., Shleifer, A. and Vishny, R. (1998) Law and Finance, *Journal of Political Economy*, 106 (6), 1113–1155.

La Porta, R., Lopez-de-Silanes, F. and Shleifer, A. (1999) Corporate Ownership around the World, *Journal of Finance*, 54 (2), 471–517.

La Porta, R., Lopez-de-Silanes, F. and Shleifer, A. (2002a) Investor protection and corporate governance, *Journal of Financial Economics*, 58 (1–2), 3–27.

La Porta, R., Lopez-de-Silanes, F. and Shleifer, A. (2002b) Government ownership of banks, *Journal of Finance*, 57 (1), 265–301.

Lausten, M. (2002) CEO turnover, firm performance and corporate governance: empirical evidence on Danish firms, *International Journal of Industrial Organization*, 20 (3), 391–414.

Lazear, E.P. (1995) Corporate Culture and the Diffusion of Values, in *Trends in Business Organization*, H. Siebert (ed.), Tübingen, Germany: J.C.B. Mohr, pp. 134–140.

Luoma, P. and Goodstein, J. (1999) Stakeholders and corporate boards: institutional influences on board composition and structure, *Academy of Management Journal*, 42 (5), 553–563.

Malani, A., Philipson, T. and David, G. (2003) Theories of Firm Behavior in the Non-Profit Sector: A Synthesis and Empirical Evaluation, in *The Governance of Not-for-Profit Firms*, E.L. Glaeser (ed.), University of Chicago Press.

Manne, H. (1964) Some Theoretical Aspects of Share Voting, *Columbia Law Review* 64 (8), 1427–1445.

Milbourn, T. T (2003) CEO reputation and stock-based compensation, *Journal of Financial Economics*, 68 (2), 233–262.

Mitchell, R.K., Agle, B.R. and Wood, D.J. (1997) Toward a theory of stakeholder identification and salience, *Academy of Management Review*, 22 (4), 853–886.

Morck, R. and Nakamura, M. (2005) A Frog in a Well Knows Nothing of the Ocean: A History of Corporate Ownership in Japan, in R.K. Morck (ed.) *A History of Corporate Governance around the World: Family Business Groups to Professional Managers*, University of Chicago Press, 367–459.

Morck, R., Stangeland, D. and Yeung, B. (2000) Inherited Wealth, Corporate Control, and Economic Growth?, in R. Morck (ed.) *Concentrated Corporate Ownership, National Bureau of Economic Research Conference Volume*, University of Chicago Press: Chicago.

Nenova, T. (2003) The value of corporate voting rights and control: A cross-country analysis, *Journal of Financial Economics*, 68 (3), 325–351.

Newhouse, J.P. (1970) Toward a Theory of Nonprofit Institutions: An Economic Model of a Hospital, *American Economic Review*, 60 (1), 64–74.

North, D.C. (1991) Institutions, *Journal of Economic Perspectives*, 5 (1), 97–112.

Oxelheim, L. (1998) Regulations, institutions and corporate efforts – The Nordic Environment, in Oxelheim, L. et al. (eds), *Corporate Strategies to Internationalise the Cost of Capital*, Copenhagen: Copenhagen Business School Press.

Pagano, M. and Volpin, P.F. (2005) The political economy of corporate governance, *American Economic Review*, 95 (4), 1005–1030.

Pauly, M. and Redisch, M. (1973) The Not-for-Profit Hospital as a Physician's Cooperative, *American Economic Review*, 63 (1), 87–99.

Pedersen, T. and Thomsen, S. (1997) European Patterns of Corporate Ownership, *Journal of International Business Studies*, 28 (4), 759–779.

Pelled, L.H. (1996) Demographic diversity, conflict, and work group outcomes: An intervening process theory, *Organization Science*, 7 (6), 615–631.

Prendergast, C. (2007) The Motivation and Bias of Bureaucrats, *American Economic Review*, 97 (1), 180–196.

Prowse, S. (1995) Corporate Governance in an International Perspective: A Survey of Corporate Control Mechanism among Large Firms in the U.S., U.K., Japan and Germany, *Financial Markets, Institutions & Instruments*, 4 (1), 1–63.

Putterman, L. (1993) Ownership and the Nature of the Firm, *Journal of Comparative Economics*, 17 (2), 243–263.

Randøy, T. and Nielsen, J. (2002) Company Performance, Corporate Governance, and CEO Compensation in Norway and Sweden, *Journal of Management and Governance*, 6 (1), 57–81.

Roe, M.J. (1991) A Political Theory of American Corporate Finance, *Columbia Law Review*, 91 (1), 10–67.

Roe, M.J. (1994) *Strong Managers, Weak Owners: The Political Roots of American Corporate Finance*, Princeton University Press: Princeton, New York.

Rose, C. and Mejer, C. (2003) The Danish Corporate Governance System: From Stakeholder Orientation Towards Shareholder Value, *Corporate Governance: An International Review*, 11 (4), 335–344.

Rosenstein, S. and Wyatt, J. (1990) Outside Directors, Board Independence and Shareholder Wealth, *Journal of Financial Economics*, 26 (2), 175–191.

Scott, S.G. and Lane, V.L. (2000) A stakeholder approach to organizational identity, *Academy of Management Review*, **25** (1), 43–62.

Sen, A. (1993) Does business ethics make economic sense?, in Minus, P.M. (ed.), *The Ethics of Business in a Global Economy*, Kluwer: Boston, MA.

Shepherd, W.G. (1989) Public enterprise: criteria and cases, in de Jong, H.W. (ed.), *The Structure of European Industry*, Kluwer Academic Publishers: Dordrecht.

Shleifer, A. and Vishny, R.W. (1997) A Survey of Corporate Governance, *Journal of Finance*, **52** (2), 737–783.

Sinani, E., Stafsudd, A., Thomsen, S., Edling, C. and Randøy, T. (2008) Corporate governance in Scandinavia: comparing networks and formal institutions, *European Management Review*, **5** (1), 27–40.

Stein J. (1989) Efficient Capital Markets, Inefficient Firms: A Model of Myopic Corporate Behaviour, *Quarterly Journal of Economics*, **104** (4), 655–669.

Tadelis, S. (1999) What's in a Name? Reputation as a Tradable Asset, *American Economic Review*, **89** (3), 548–563.

Thomsen, S. (1996) Foundation Ownership and Economic Performance, *Corporate Governance: An International Review*, **4** (4), 212–221.

Thomsen, S. (1999) Corporate Ownership by Industrial Foundations, *European Journal of Law and Economics*, **7** (2), 117–137.

Thomsen, S. (2004) Corporate values and corporate governance, *Corporate Governance*, **4** (4), 29–46.

Thomsen, S. (2005a) Foundation Ownership, Corporate Reputation and Economic Performance. Paper presented to the Workshop on Corporate Governance of Closely Held Firms, Center for Corporate Governance and Center for Economics and Business Research, Copenhagen, June 2005.

Thomsen, S. (2005b) Corporate governance as a determinant of corporate values, *Corporate Governance – The International Journal of Effective Board Performance*, **5** (4), 10–27.

Thomsen, S. and Rose, C. (2004) Foundation Ownership and Financial Performance, *European Journal of Law and Economics*, **18** (3), 343–364.

Tirole, J. (2001) Corporate governance, *Econometrica*, **69** (1), 1–35.

Villalonga, B. and Amit, R. (2006) How do family ownership, control, and management affect firm value?, *Journal of Financial Economics*, **80** (2), 385–341.

Vives, X. (2000) Corporate governance: Does it matter?, in X. Vives (ed.) *Corporate Governance*, Cambridge University Press: Cambridge, UK, 1–15.

Weiss, Y. and Fershtmanm, C. (1998) Social status and economic preference: A survey, *European Economic Review*, **42** (3–5), 801–820.

Williamson, O.E. (1975) *Markets and Hierarchies*, Free Press: New York.

Williamson, O.E. (1996) *The Mechanisms of Governance*, Oxford University Press: Oxford.

World Bank Development Indicators (2007)–04–01. www.worldbank.org

Zander, A. (1979) The psychology of group processes, *Annual Review of Psychology*, **30**, 417–451.

Zingales, L. (2001) Corporate governance, National Bureau of Economic Research, Working paper 6309, Published in the *New Palgrave Dictionary of Economics and the Law*.

Chapter 17

Family Business with Examples from East Asia

Chapter contents

17.1 Introduction

In this chapter, we analyse the governance of family business, which is the most common corporate governance model around the world. We take a look at what family ownership is, outline its strengths and weaknesses, summarize what is known about its economic performance, and describe the means of keeping control.

As an example, we use family business in East Asia. We could have chosen examples from many countries around the world. Family business is the predominant, private governance mode in all emerging economies and even in quite a few developed economies. Government ownership is also quite widespread, particularly of course in communist or socialist countries, but unusual for small and medium-sized companies, which normally constitute the vast majority of all companies.

Firm size distributions are invariably skewed with many small firms, much fewer medium-size ones and very few large firms. This holds for firm size distributions within countries, and even for most industries (Figure 17.1).

Company size can be measured by employment, assets, sales or other measures. The skewed distribution is probably the result of random growth processes without economies of scale. Given that most firms are also founded by single individuals and inherited or acquired by other individuals, they come to dominate the economy in terms of number of firms.

In terms of volume (percentages of total sales, value added or assets), large firms are obviously much more important, but in most cases small and medium-sized firms account for a majority of employment and even overall activity. In recent decades they also appear to have accounted for the bulk of job creation and firm size may have dropped in many countries. The small and medium-size firms are farms, shops, window cleaners, restaurants and other basic businesses, but also a growing number of professional service firms. Very often they have only one employee: the owner.

17.2 Family business defined

A **privately-held firm** is simply a firm whose shares are not publicly listed. A **closely held firm** is a firm owned by a few shareholders. Most privately held firms are closely held.

Founder ownership means that the firm is currently owned by its founder. Founder ownership may be called first-generation family ownership, but most first-generation firms never make it to the second generation. In some cases, like Bill Gates in Microsoft, the founders themselves regard it as a bad idea for the family to take over, and of course most firms do not live that long anyway.

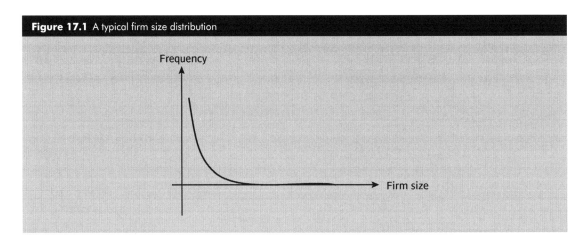

Figure 17.1 A typical firm size distribution

Second-generation ownership means that a firm is owned by one or more of the founder's children. Third-generation ownership firms are owned by the grandchildren. In fourth-generation firms, we sometimes talk of 'cousin ownership'. To add to the confusion, we sometimes talk about family ownership as including founder ownership and sometimes excluding first-generation ownership.

Personal ownership means that a company is owned by a single person. This person need not be the founder, for example a restaurant may be personally owned, without having been inherited. Most small shops are believed to be acquired, not inherited. Even in large companies you sometimes see management buy-outs.

Families can play a continuum of roles in their companies. In Table 17.1 we classify some of them in a matrix.

- In an **owner-managed** company, the owner (acquirer, founder or family) manages the company. This is the company with no separation of ownership and control and therefore minimal agency problems.
- The family may choose a professional manager, in which case we can talk about **family-governed** companies. In many cases, family members will retain seats on the board and thereby specialize in corporate governance.
- If the founder/family sells its shares, but continues to manage the company, we talk about a **family-managed company.**
- If the founder/family sells its shares to outside investors and steps down from management and board positions, we get an **investor-owned** (i.e. professionally managed) company.

The different roles are important because, as we shall see, they may have very different implications for company performance.

Above and beyond the business relations, families have other characteristics which add to the complexity of family firms. It is customary to illustrate this by drawing a three-sphere diagram (Figure 17.2).

Table 17.1 Family roles in business firms

		Management	
		Professional	Family
Ownership	Dispersed (outsiders)	Investor governance	Family management
	Family (insiders)	Family governance	Owner management

Source: Burkart, Panunzi and Shleifer (2003).

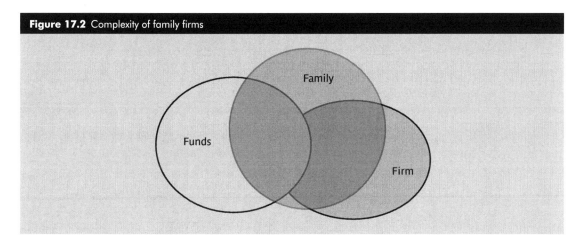

Figure 17.2 Complexity of family firms

There are the family, the firm, and the funds. Some members of the family may work in the firm, while others do not. Some of the family's funds may be invested in the firm, while others are not. For business families, the three spheres are connected, so what happens in one sphere influences the others.

For example, illness or death of family members may lead the family to sell the firm even though family managers are not directly affected. The presence or absence of offspring will influence whether the family wishes to continue the business.

The family's non-firm funds will also influence the firm. Succession, i.e. continuation of family ownership, is more likely if siblings outside the firm can remain independently wealthy. Large families may put pressure on the firm to pay high dividends even though the firm has profitable investment opportunities.

17.3   The costs and benefits of family ownership

Personal ownership (first generation, founder ownership) has many attractive characteristics. From an agency theory viewpoint, it provides a solution to the moral hazard problem because the owner has both the power and the incentives to make efficient decisions. It's her money, after all. It also solves the adverse selection problem because the owner has an incentive to sell if she is not the 'best owner'. If others can run the business more profitably, or 'better' all things included from the viewpoint of the owner, she will be better off selling the company to others who can make more money with it.

Founder-managers in particular are self-selected to be good owners. They could choose to sell out, but choose not to, which implies that they are particularly committed to the business. Moreover, among many start-ups which failed, they have succeeded. It is no surprise, therefore, that founder-owned companies tend to be high performers.

From a management point of view, personal ownership may be particularly competitive because it involves a clear allocation of responsibility with a single individual. Ideologically and philosophically, many people value personal ownership because they associate it with freedom.

But there are also costs which need to be weighed against the benefits. **Risk aversion** is a result of having a large ownership stake (e.g. 100%) in a single firm. Given the trade-off between risk and return, risk aversion will in many cases lower company performance because there are profitable projects which are not implemented. **Capital constraints** are closely connected to risk aversion. Unlike joint stock companies, personally owned companies cannot issue an unlimited number of shares to the public (if they want to remain personally owned). **Entrenchment** means that it may be difficult to replace owner managers who do not realize that they are not the best managers. Entrenchment effects will often be combined with age effects.

Family ownership (second generation and so on) has many of the advantages of personal ownership, i.e. continuing personal ownership. Family-owned businesses may benefit from loyalty among family members and employees, and large families may act as a source of insurance (if a family member is in trouble or needs start-up capital, they may help financially).

Family ties are no doubt conducive to trust, and in the absence of formal institutions, i.e. justice, law, and enforcement, family business may be the only effective way of doing business. For example, the Medicis of Florence or the Jewish merchant families used family members in different countries and locations as an infrastructure for financial transactions and transportation of goods during the Middle Ages.

However, there are also costs of family ownership. The selection mechanism is different from that of personally owned companies since inheritance is no guarantee of ability. In general, in the average firm, we must expect to see regression towards the mean in the next generation (Figure 17.3).

The founder-owners are self-selected to be better than average in terms of business ability (IQ, initiative, and other characteristics necessary to succeed in business). But their sons and daughters will probably be no different from the mean, and even if they are genetically slightly 'better equipped' they will statistically be worse than their founder parent (whose genes are mixed with the other parent's).

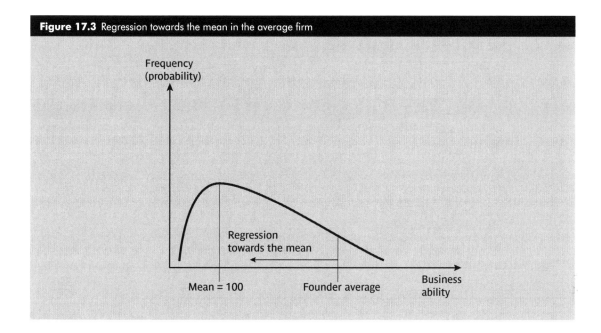

Figure 17.3 Regression towards the mean in the average firm

We will therefore see 'regression towards the mean' (as observed by Sir Francis Galton among the British nobility). Theoretically, therefore, we cannot expect second generation owners to do as well as their parents, but there seems to be no reason that they cannot do just as well as other businesses.

Moreover, there are special problems in family firms which are very much part of this mode of governance. While family ties can be a source of competitive advantage, the mirror image, **nepotism,** implies that family members are sometimes given jobs which they are not capable of and therefore mismanage the firm more or less. An added consideration is **family conflict**, which can be more emotional and therefore more difficult to resolve than conflicts among rational, professional managers. There are many examples of family feuds taking even large firms down.

17.4 Family ownership and economic performance

Family business has a bad press. There are many politicians, journalists, and researchers who are ideologically opposed to it. Nevertheless, several studies have found that family firms perform well compared with professionally managed, investor-owned firms. Some results by Anderson and Reeb (2003) from the largest US firms (S&P 500 index) are reproduced in Table 17.2.

The first surprise in this table is that family business is fairly common even among large listed US firms. One-third of the S&P 500 can be characterized as family firms, either because they are managed by members of the founding family (family management), or because the family owns a controlling share (family ownership), or both. Of the family firms, 55% are managed by an outside CEO, 15% are managed by the founder, and 30% are managed by a descendant.

The second surprise is that the family firms perform better than the investor-owned firms. Firm value (q) – a measure of market valuation – is 25% higher and so are profit rates. Apparently, they must be doing something right despite their critics.

Table 17.3, adapted from Villalonga and Amit (2006), on a similar but larger sample of large listed US firms, examines differences between founders and heirs. According to this table, the best of all worlds would be to have a founder CEO with a mean firm value of 3.14 compared with an average of 2.17 for the

Table 17.2   Family ownership in large US firms – Standard and Poor's 500 industrials

	Family firms	Others
Number of firms	141	262
Family ownership %	18	0
Board independence %	43.6	61.1
Founder-managed %	14.5	0
Heir-managed %	30.4	0
Outside CEO (%)	55.0	100.0
Firm value	1.6	1.3
ROA %	6.1	4.7

Source: *Anderson and Reeb (2003).*

Table 17.3   Firm value (no. of firms) in large listed US firms

	Founder CEO	Heir CEO	Outside CEO	Total
Founder chair	3.14 (215)	1.61 (10)	2.81 (73)	3.0 (298)
Heir chair	– (0)	1.74 (306)	1.81 (78)	1.76 (384)
Outside chair	– (0)	– (0)	1.94 (359)	1.94 (359)
Total	3.14 (215)	1.74 (316)	2.04 (510)	2.17 (1041)

Source: *Villalonga and Amit (2006).*

entire sample. In contrast, heir CEOs do substantially worse than average (average $q = 1.74$) depending whether or not their father continues as chairman of the board. Companies with a professional CEO do much better than heir-managed firms, particularly if the founder stays as CEO. However, the difference between an heir chair/CEO (1.74) and a professional chair/CEO (1.94) is insignificant.

Altogether, this evidence indicates that founder ownership is a blessing associated with superior performance whereas there is not much of a difference between family-managed and professionally managed firms. Certainly the second generation family firms do not do better than those which are professionally managed. This is consistent with agency theory, as argued above, and with regression towards the mean.

17.5   Family CEOs

Succession is clearly a difficult issue in family businesses. Bennedsen et al. (2007) examine the effect of succession to professional outside managers compared with succession within the family business, e.g. when a son takes over as CEO after his father. In a sample of closely held Danish firms they find that succession to professional managers is associated with significantly superior subsequent profitability. In general, studies of family business suffer from endogeneity problems: does family ownership lead to good performance, or does good performance lead to family ownership (e.g. does good performance make families maintain their ownership and executive positions)? To isolate the effect of family CEOs on company performance, researchers need an exogenous source of variation in the frequency of family CEOs, which they can get if they can find a variable (an instrument) which influences the probability of succession within the family without at the same time influencing company performance. Bennedsen et al. (2007) ingeniously used the gender of the first-born child as their instrument, since a male son is known to enhance the probability of family succession, but is unlikely to be influenced by corporate performance since, for example, it was determined many years ago.

The underperformance of family CEOs indicates that too many heirs take over the family business. However, in many firms, particularly those which are very small, it may be difficult or too costly to hire qualified professional managers. In fact in quite a few cases the successor is not the son, but the widow, who tries to pick up the pieces.

Another problem in family business is **entrenchment**. Given their strong position in the firm, family managers may hang on for too long even when they perform badly. This may be partly attributable to psychological biases such as confirmation bias which leads people to search for evidence confirming their preconceived ideas. Hillier and McColgan (2009) find that family CEOs are less likely to depart and that stock prices and profitability increase when family CEOs leave.

In contrast Hansson, Liljeblom and Martikainen (2011) find a positive effect of family CEOs, but this effect is tempered by a tendency for family CEOs to hire other family members, which may have a negative effect on company performance. They use lagged company performance as an instrument for family CEOs. While hiring qualified family members may well be an advantage for family businesses, nepotism is obviously a potential weakness, which needs to be checked if they are to achieve their full potential.

17.6 Family control mechanisms

Families can retain control of their firms by several direct and indirect means. First, they may choose not to share ownership by issuing shares to the public. Alternatively, they may sell shares but retain control by various control mechanisms, which all involve deviations from the proportionality principle (one share – one vote): dual class shares, pyramids, shareholder agreements, etc.

Dual class shares, or more precisely, differential voting rights, usually signify the existence of more than one class of shares of which one class has more voting rights than the others, while they have the same dividends, or cash flow, rights.

In Table 17.4 we provide an example. A founding family decides to split its shares into two classes (before listing, as long as the family holds 100% of the shares, there is no problem with this): 1000 A shares with 1 vote per share and 10,000 B shares with one-tenth of a vote per share. The B shares are then listed on a stock exchange and sold to the public. The public now holds 90% of the shares (or more precisely 90.9%) and has a right to a similar portion of the dividends, but only 50% of the votes. With one B share in addition to the A shares the family has a majority of the votes and the ability to win most votes at a shareholder meeting. This gives rise to some agency problems: for example, the family can refuse to pay dividends and instead elect family members to sit on the board and pay them high fees.

We can calculate the disproportionality between vote and cash flow rights as a difference:

Control rights – cash flow rights of the family = 50% – 9% = 41%
Control rights – cash flow rights of outside investors = 50% – 91% = –41%

Or we can calculate it as a ratio:

Table 17.4 Dual class shares: an example

	A-shares	B-shares
Voting rights	1	0.1
Number issued	1000	10,000
Held by	Family	Outsiders
Number of votes	1000	1000
Share of vote (control)	50%	50%
Share of dividend (cash flow)	1000/11,000 = 9%	10,000/11,000 = 91%
Ratio control/cash flow	50/9 = 5.6	50/91 = 0.55
Difference control – cash flow	41%	–41%

The family has a vote to cash flow rights ratio of 50%/9% = 5.5
Outside investors have a vote to cash flow rights ratio of 50%/91% = 0.55

Dual class shares are widely used in most countries around the world. They were banned from US exchanges for a while, but are currently allowed again. Note that there may be more than two classes of shares, so we might have A, B, and C shares.

Pyramids are another control mechanism in which the family maintains the majority of the shares in a company, which owns the majority of the shares in another company, which owns the majority of the shares in a third company, etc. An example is given in Figure 17.4.

If the family holds 51%, we can then calculate its share of the total capital invested as a function of the number of levels in the pyramid (Table 17.5).

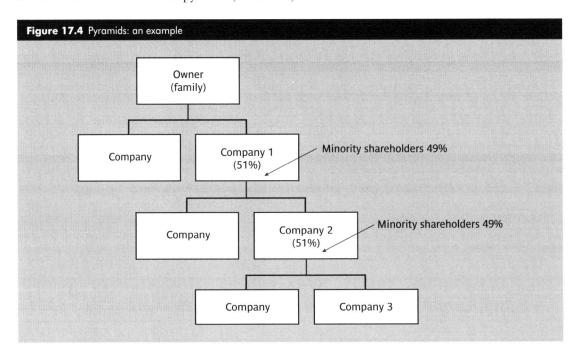

Figure 17.4 Pyramids: an example

Table 17.5 Control and capital investment in a pyramid structure (example)

Companies in pyramid	Family's share of capital	Board members appointed by family	Outsiders' share of total capital invested
1	51%	100%	49%
2	26%	100%	74%
3	13%	100%	87%
4	7%	100%	93%

Thus, with four companies in the pyramid, the family can control the entire structure, e.g. appoint all board members in all four companies, with only 7% of the capital. Again, this may give rise to type II agency problems between majority and minority owners: for example if the family refuses to pay dividends.

As an example, if the bottom company (4) sells a piece of property worth 200 million for 100 to its closest parent company (no 3), which resells it to company 2 for 50 which resells the privately held family company for 25, the family makes 200 – 25 = 175 million at the expense of the minority investors who have no power to prevent it. The minority investors, therefore, depend completely on the legal system for the protection of their interests.

Other kinds of control mechanisms include shareholder agreements, cross holdings, and voting caps. **Shareholder agreements** can, in principle, specify anything legal, so that dual class shares for example are a special kind of shareholder agreement.

Cross holdings can also help maintain control. A family can control two companies with 20% of shares in each company if they both hold 30% in the other company.

Voting caps limit the voting rights of any single owner to a certain maximum (e.g. 10%). This makes it more difficult for an outsider to challenge family control even though the family has sold its shares.

17.7 Should dual class shares be prohibited?

The critics of family enterprise often argue that dual class shares should be prohibited. So do eager European bureaucrats and politicians who would rather that the smaller companies of small countries were taken over by the large companies in the large countries (called 'restructuring' and 'efficiency' in the jargon). Another argument, more politically correct and therefore more widely used, is that common standards are necessary to create a common European capital market which can be competitive with the USA. A third, very understandable, argument is reciprocity: if they can take over our firms, why can we not take over theirs? A fourth argument is that managers of pension funds believe that the value of their shares will increase (which would benefit just about everyone these days).

However, there are a few important counterarguments. First, where is the externality? Nobody forces people to buy dual class shares. Government intervention requires an argument. Second, some companies with dual class shares are well managed and value their ability to make long-term decisions or to be socially responsible (e.g. Google, Novo Nordisk, Nike, the Wallenberg Group, Nestlé). Should they be punished just because some people do not like dual class shares? Third, prohibiting dual class shares may lead to delistings and fewer new listings because families value control. This would lead to fewer listed companies.

A large recent study for the European Commission concluded that there is no case against dual class shares (Burkhart and Lee, 2007). Subsequently, the Commission dropped plans to take action in this area.

17.8 **Ownership and control in East Asia**

In two seminal papers, Claessens et al. (2000, 2002) study ownership and control in listed East Asian firms. They find that family ownership is the most common ownership model in eight East Asian countries with Japan as a clear exception. Half of the listed companies, often more, are family-owned (only 10% in Japan where family ownership of the largest companies was abolished after the Second World War). Government ownership is fairly important in Singapore (24% of companies) but this is also an exception.

The typically Chinese business families in East Asia use various mechanisms to maintain control: direct minority ownership, pyramids, cross holdings, etc. In this way they have been able to establish big business groups. On average, the value of the assets controlled by the 15 most important families account for 40–50% of the gross domestic product on average and much more in Hong Kong (84%) and Malaysia (74%).

The average cash flow to voting rights ratio of the largest owner is 80%, i.e. the owners vote 20% more shares than they have dividend rights to (Table 17.6).

In an estimate of the effect of ownership structure, Claessens et al. (2000) find an overall positive relationship between cash flow rights and firm value (Figure 17.5). This is consistent with classic agency logic: a larger share of cash flow rights will give the largest owner a larger incentive to maximize value in the absence of risk aversion and capital constraints. After all, it is their own money. However, the authors also find that disproportionality has a negative effect on firm value (see Figure 17.6).

So while family ownership appears to have a positive effect on family business, this may be attributable to the beneficial effects of economic incentives rather than to family control in excess of shareholdings. A high degree of disproportionality between ownership and control invites type II agency problems and investors react by discounting the value of the company's shares. Cronqvist and Nilsson (2003) find similar results in Sweden.

An example of a family business in East Asia is the Li Ka-Shing group which was named after the Hong Kong billionaire Li Ka-Shing. Li Ka-Shing controls one of the oldest British trading houses from the 19th century (or 'hongs' of Hong Kong) known as Hutchison Whampoa. The group is involved

Table 17.6 Votes and cash flow rights of the largest owner

Country	Cash flow	Voting	Ratio
Hong Kong	24.3	28.1	86.5%
Indonesia	25.6	33.7	76.0%
Japan	6.9	10.3	66.8%
Korea	14.0	17.8	78.5%
Malaysia	23.9	28.3	84.4%
Philippines	21.3	24.4	87.6%
Singapore	20.2	27.5	73.4%
Taiwan	16.0	19.0	84.3%
Thailand	32.8	32.3	101.7%
East Asia	15.7	19.8	79.4%

Source: Claessens et al. (2000).

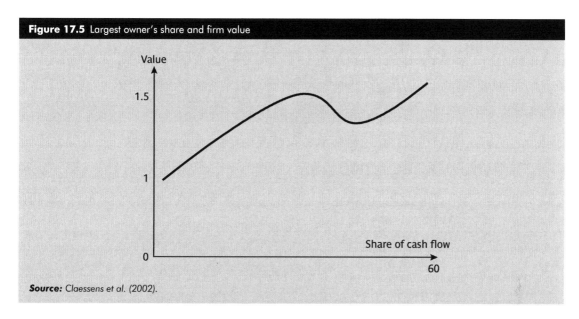

Figure 17.5 Largest owner's share and firm value

Source: Claessens et al. (2002).

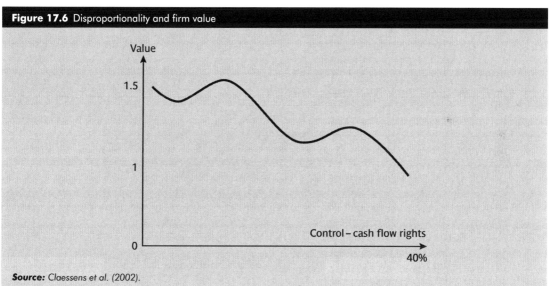

Figure 17.6 Disproportionality and firm value

Source: Claessens et al. (2002).

in trading, cargo and container operations, logistics, warehousing, engineering, and retail sales. With an estimated net worth of $13 billion, Mr Ka-Shing is one of the richest men in the world.

The Li Ka-Shing conglomerate consists of 25 companies, including Hutchison Whampoa. Cheung Kong is the sixth largest, Hong Kong Electric Dai Heng Bank is the 22nd largest: all are very large listed companies in Hong Kong. For example, the Li Ka-Shing family controls 34% of the vote in Hong Kong Electric with 2.5% of the cash-flow rights to the pyramid chain: Cheung Kong – Hutchison Whampoa – Cavendish International – Hong Kong Electric.

As an outside investor, you may wonder what you are actually investing in if you buy stock in one of these entities, for example Hutchison Whampoa. First, each company is diversified. Second, ownership ties within the business group mean that you are also investing partly in the other

companies. Transactions between company group members complicate the business even further. Moreover, as part of a communist country the borderline between government and private may be hazy. The one common denominator is the controlling owner and his family. The reputation of Mr Li Ka-Shing as a shrewd businessman is no doubt one reason to have confidence. But is it realistic to expect the same results in the future as in the past? Will the next generation be as successful as the first? It is no surprise that business groups like these often trade at a discount to compensate for the uncertainty.

17.9 Family business in India

India is a good example of an emerging economy where family business is very important (Khanna and Palepu, 2005; Chakrabarti et al., 2008).

Partly because of its size and its common law heritage India has many listed companies. In fact Bombay Stock Exchange (BSE) is the largest exchange in the world in terms of listed companies with close to 5000 firms in 2008. There are almost as many listed Indian as US companies. Trading volume is also very high (Chakrabarti et al., 2008). It does not take much imagination to see it will become many times larger as the Indian economy continues to develop.

However, the vast majority of these companies have concentrated ownership so that only a minority of the shares are actually sold. Half of them are business groups, in some cases with many listed companies. Many of the others are controlled by the government. Though never communist India has a strong socialist tradition, and it was held that the government should occupy 'the commanding heights' of the economy. This led to a 'licence raj' in which many firms were nationalized and most were highly regulated. However during the 1980s the government started deregulating, which has contributed to the strong performance of the Indian economy during the past three decades.

The business groups are often owned by members of business communities, ethnic minorities, which constitute only a few percent of the total population: the Marwari, the Gujarati, the Parsi and so on. It is estimated that half of the listed companies belong to such groups. The Parsi are members of the Zoroastrian communities, originally from Iran.

Parsi business families include the Tata, Godrej (manufacturing) and the Wadia. The Marwaris (from Rajasthan) have been said to own half of all business assets in India. The Gujarati (from Gujarat, where the Parsi first settled) constitute another important group.

It is perhaps no accident that these large businesses tend to be run by small communities which enable strong social control through ethnic or religious ties, internalization of social norms and reputation effects. Informal governance may substitute for formal governance.

The Tata group, run by the Parsi Tata family, with some 24 listed companies is probably the largest and most famous example. Tata started in textiles (1874), but diversified into steel (1902), power (1910), cement (1912), soap (1917), printing and publishing (1931) (Khanna and Palepu, 2005), aviation (1932), chemicals (1939), consumer electronics (1940), commercial vehicles and locomotives (1945), cosmetics (1952), air conditioning (1954), pharmaceuticals (1958), tea and coffee (1962), information technology (1968), financial services (1984), auto components (1993), telecommunications (1994), passenger cars (1998), retailing (1999), and insurance (2001). In many of these areas the company is very competitive and the industry leader, but some, like aviation, cosmetics and pharmaceuticals, textiles and printing and publishing, had to be exited. The company has recently shown its entrepreneurial spirit by taking over Jaguar and Rover and by developing its new inexpensive Nano car intended to be affordable in India and other emerging economies.

According to the group's website, in 2010/11 total revenue of the Tata Group companies was $83.3 billion and it employed more than 424,000 people worldwide. Interestingly, a majority of the stock of Tata Sons, the main holding company of the group, is held by philanthropic trusts, so the company is a foundation-owned company (cf. Chapter 14). The Aditya Birla Group of Marwari origin is another major group with more than 133,000 employees in mining, cement, mobile phones, life insurance and many other industries.

Business groups can be theorized as a way to overcome institutional failures or simply a lack of institutional development, particularly in emerging economies (Khanna, 2000). For example, they can provide capital in the absence of a well-developed capital market. However, they have also been associated with monopoly and crony capitalism. Close ties to government was doubtlessly an important advantage for older business groups like Tata and Birla. Khanna and Palepu (2005) note that relatively high turnover among the largest Indian groups is a sign of dynamic competition. The significant international expansion of the groups and their continued profitability under deregulation also indicate that they are not, or at least not just, founded on monopoly.

The Indian business groups do not always rest on majority ownership by the founding family. Phani et al. (2005) refer to a 'social ethos which always associates and implicitly accepts that corporate governance belongs to the founding families irrespective of their level of ownership'. Traditionally, reputation effects did much to deter expropriation in family businesses, but it is not clear that they are sufficient in a larger and more open stock market.

Most recently, the growing Indian IT industry has created a new business segment with new governance practices based on international standards. Born global, many software companies have listed their shares on foreign stock exchanges and attracted international investment, not just to attract capital but also to enhance their credibility towards foreign customers. Software was a new and therefore unregulated industry. It was labour and human capital intensive rather than capital intensive and therefore fitted India's comparative advantage of a huge supply of highly skilled and cheap engineers.

Legal reform has done much to improve Indian corporate governance. Voluntary codes of best practice have been adopted. After recommendations by the Birla committee (headed by Kumar Mangalam Birla from the Birla Group) and the Murthy Committee (headed by Narayana Murthy, founder of Infosys) a section 49 was put into the listing requirement at BSE. It is proscribed that independent directors should constitute at least half of the board if the chair is also the CEO and at least a third if not. It also mandates the board committees with specific regulation on how often they should meet etc. It requires increased transparency with regard to related party and transactions and transactions within business group. Given the predominance of family business, it is questionable how much independent directors will matter in practice. But Khanna and Black (2007) find a positive effect of its adoption.

Bank governance has also been modernized with less direct intervention, but banks are still mostly government-owned. This was regarded as an important advantage during the 2008–2009 financial crisis, and it therefore seems unlikely that banks will be privatized anytime soon.

17.10 Governing and managing family firms

The interdependence between the personal and the professional is the distinguishing characteristic of family firms. This creates special challenges for management and governance. It is telling that a large part of the research and professional work on family business is done by psychologists rather than economists or management scholars. De Vries (1993) provides a useful overview of the issues from a psychoanalytical perspective.

Nepotism

The emotional attachment between family members, and especially the love of parents for their children, means that family relations may trump efficiency. So an incompetent, indolent and sometimes unwilling son or nephew may be put in charge of a large business or a function which requires specialist expertise. In some cases family members are employed in the firm because it gives them 'something to do' while their wealth and family ties enable them not to take their job seriously. As de Vries (1993) notes, most firms cannot afford to have too many of these people around for long, not least because of the morale problems they create for other employees.

Managers and board members of family firms have to contend with such problems whether or not they belong to the family. If the business is to succeed it is necessary for them to create a power base that is sufficiently strong to resist meddling by incompetent family members. This may involve negotiating an *ex ante* agreement on the division of labour between the owners, the board and the executives before agreeing to take on a board or management position. It may in some cases be possible to shield the business from damage by assigning family members to ceremonial or peripheral areas. Knowing that a family member is destined to take over a business also creates opportunities for education and personal development in and outside the company.

Founder dominance

De Vries (1993) relates how workaholic founding fathers of family businesses often come to neglect their children emotionally and seek to compensate by spoiling them with toys, sports cars, expensive apartments and allowances. Siblings may come to compete for love and affection, sowing the seeds of future emotional conflicts. When they take over as owners after the founder's death, these immature individuals can come to dominate the lives of thousands of employees and other stakeholders.

Professionals trying to manage such businesses may find themselves spending half their time doing amateur psychotherapy. This takes time from the business so as mentioned the best solution may be to distance the owners from the business with a clear division of labour.

Father–son conflicts

The dominating personality of some founders may make it difficult for their sons to establish their own independence and personal integrity (de Vries 1993). They may have to live with anxiety, inferiority and in severe cases depression, never feeling that they are good enough. Some founders even go out their way to belittle their sons, cutting them down to size or even humiliating them as part of a misguided theory of upbringing. De Vries (1993) describes how Edsel Ford was dominated by his father Henry Ford resulting in stress, ulcers and perhaps even his premature death.

Father–son conflicts are one reason why succession is such a conundrum in family firms. Dominant fathers may unwittingly create weak sons or scare them away from the family business. Advisers therefore stress the value of succession planning so that the company and the family are not suddenly left without leadership when the father dies or has a stroke. However, succession planning also has to overcome psychological barriers. Some founders are reluctant to discuss the subject, and bringing it up may be seen as an impolite reminder of their mortality. One reason may be their strong identification with the business. The founders cannot imagine a life without it. It may also be that they are emotionally reluctant to recognize the ineptitude of their offspring or to make distinctions between their children.

Family conflicts

Successful family businesses will often flourish not just businesswise but also in terms of the growing number of family members. When ownership is shared by many family members there is a potential for conflict which can end up destroying the business. Classic conflicts include wars between siblings with emotional hang-ups, or between different branches of the family, strife between family members which are active in the business and those which are not, between poorer and richer individuals etc. Family business managers and outside family members will for example often have different views on dividend policy, divesting the business to outsiders or going public. Non-managers will often be interested in dividends and shareholder value, while family business managers may want to favour business continuity and growth.

Family councils

A family council is one solution to handling and aggregating the interests of a large family in a consistent way (Jaffe, 2005). The council is composed of members of the founder family including all shareholders regardless of whether or not they are active in running the company. It may also consist of future heirs and other relatives such as spouses. Jaffe (2005) describes how a family council can enable the family to solve conflicts, handle conflicts of interests and speak with one voice to the company. The family council can for example decide on who is to hold what positions in the firm, what the dividend policy should be and so on. Formally, of course, these matters are decided at the annual general meeting of shareholders, but it is difficult to imagine a suitable discussion of family affairs in that forum. The family council may be more or less formal. It may just be the extended family getting together for Christmas with a meeting discussing business affairs. Alternatively it may be a parallel organization with its own board of directors, rules of procedure and so on.

Family trusts

A company founder may decide to set up a trust owning the company with his heirs as beneficiaries and managed by a board of trustees. The trustees then manage the company and other parts of the estate in a hopefully consistent way on behalf of the family as a whole. Trusts may also be a convenient way to handle estate taxes.

Family foundations

A more radical alternative is for the founder to donate her shares in the company to a foundation whose bylaws then determine how the company is to be managed and how to distribute dividends. The founder and the founding family may sit on the foundation board and thus exercise effective control, but it is illegal for them to appropriate the foundation's wealth. It is quite common in Northern Europe for companies to be owned by such industrial foundations (cf. Chapter 13), but for tax and regulatory reasons it is less common in the rest of the world.

Outside board members

A generic decision in family firms is whether or not to elect non-family directors to the board of the company. To allow outsiders to the board can help professionalize the company, but may also challenge the autarchy of the owner-manager (Johannisson and Huse, 2000). However, there is reason to assume that the functions of the board in family firms while formally similar are in fact quite distinct. While dispersed shareholders appoint a board to hire and control the manager, the situation in family businesses is rather the reverse. The owner-manager appoints the board and fires it if he is not satisfied. Moreover it is much less necessary for the board to check for agency problems since the owner-manager has his own money at stake. Consistent with this, van den Heuvel, Van Gils and Voordeckers (2006) find that the advisory role of boards in small and medium-size companies is especially important, but maintain that the control role remains an important part of the job. After all minority shareholders, banks and tax authorities may also have a legitimate interest in the company.

Family firm types

As Leenders and Waarts (2003) argue, family firms are not all the same. Some family firms have a strong business focus while the family is relatively anonymous. Others have a strong family focus which dominates professional considerations. They use this distinction to construct a typology of family firms (Figure 17.7).

Family-first firms exist primarily to service the needs of the family, or in other words to maximize the utility of the family rather than to maximize profits. They are willing to accept lower returns if this is believed to benefit the family. For example, they will want to have a family CEO and will be unwilling to sell the company even if the sales price would more than compensate the loss of future

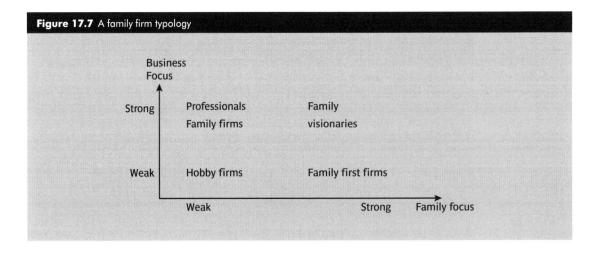

Figure 17.7 A family firm typology

dividends. An example could be the Japanese hotel chain Hoshi Ryokan (founded in 718) or the US department store chain Dillard's.

Professional family firms could also be called 'business first' firms. They are dominated by professional considerations and do not differ much from investor-owned firms except for the presence of a large monitor. They will gladly accept a professional CEO or sell their shares if this turns out to create more value. Examples could be the role of Bill Gates in Microsoft or Warren Buffet in Berkshire Hathaway.

Family visionary firms synthesize family and business. Examples could be the Indian Tata Corporation or the German retailer Aldi Group. These firms believe that the family has a special contribution to make to the business and therefore it is worth continuing.

Hobby firms are firms whose owners do not take them seriously, perhaps because they are very wealthy. An example could perhaps be the role of Paris Hilton in the Hilton hotel group.

17.11 Discussion

It is still debated theoretically and empirically whether being a family business is good or bad for a company, but the discussion is somewhat hypothetical. Family business is here to stay. It is the predominant mode of organizing economic activity around the world. It is not even clear that it will decline over time. In a sample of the 4000 biggest companies in France, Germany, Italy and the UK in 1996–2006, Franks, Mayer, Volpin and Wagner (2009) find evidence of a governance life cycle in the UK in that family businesses tend to diversify ownership over time and eventually become investor owned. However, they find no trend to diversify and so no governance life cycle in continental Europe.

So the most important task at hand is perhaps to understand how family business works and to remedy some of its weaknesses without at the same time undermining its strengths.

The strengths of family businesses include personal ownership and incentives, autonomy and flexibility and identification with the business. Weaknesses include risk aversion, conservatism, succession problems, nepotism and family conflicts. It is important to remember however that family firms differ and that general descriptions like these will in many cases not be appropriate.

For further reading on family business see Bennedsen and Fan (2011).

Sinar Mas Group

Sinar Mas Group is one of the largest conglomerates in Indonesia. The group is active in palm oil, pulp and paper, agribusiness, telecommunications and financial services. Its companies are listed in Djakarta and Singapore. Founded by a refugee from China, Eka Tjipta Widjaja, the company is now managed by his sons and grandsons.

The palm oil business PT Sinar Smart is a listed subsidiary of Golden Agri Resources (GAR), which is a listed subsidiary of a family holding company.

GAR's board is composed as follows:

- Franky Oesman Widjaja (Executive)
- Muktar Widjaja (Non-executive, Non-independent)
- Frankle (Djafar) Widjaja (Non-executive, Non-independent)
- Simon Lim (Executive)
- Rafael Buhay Concepcion, Jr. (Executive)
- Hong Pian Tee (Non-executive, Independent)
- Lew Syn Pau (Non-executive, Independent)
- Kaneyalall Hawabhay (Non-executive, Independent)
- Jacques Desire Laval Elliah (Non-executive, Independent)
- William Chung Nien Chin (Non-executive, Independent).

Mr. Franky Oesman Widjaja, Mr. Muktar Widjaja and Mr. Frankle (Djafar) Widjaja are brothers.

Franky Oesman Widjaja was paid around €2 million in 2010, two-thirds of which was bonus. The other executives were paid one-third of that, while the non-executives got a fixed director's fee of roughly €150,000.

PT Sinar Smart has a Board of Commissioners (Supervisory Board) consisting of eight members, three of which are said to be independent, and a management board (board of directors) of seven members.

In 2010 the members of the BoC (supervisory board) were as follows:

- President Commissioner: Franky Oesman Widjaja
- Vice President Commissioner: Muktar Widjaja
- Vice President Commissioner: Simon Lim
- Commissioner: Rachmad Gobel
- Commissioner: Rafael Buhay Concepcion, Jr.
- Independent Commissioner: Prof. Dr. Teddy Pawitra
- Independent Commissioner: Dr. Susiyati B. Hirawan
- Independent Commissioner: hj. Ryani Soedirman.

The members of the BoD (management board) were as follows:

- President Director: J. Daud Dhar ono
- Vice President Director: Budi Wijana
- Vice President Director: Edy Saputra Suradja
- Director: H. Uminto
- Director: Dr. Ir. Gianto Widjaja
- Director: Jimmy Pramono
- Director: Djanadi Bimo Prakoso.

Both GAR and Smart are financially healthy with average return on equity above 20% over the last five years, sales growth over 30% and increasing stock prices. Generally, group companies

appear to have been doing very well over the past years because of strong global demand for raw materials.

Sinar Mas has been targeted by Greenpeace for contributing to deforestation of Indonesian rain forests. As a result Unilever, Nestlé, Carrefour and Burger King have suspended Sinar Mas as a supplier, and HSBC has sold its shares in group companies. The company's annual report emphasizes its commitment to sustainability.

Sources: http://www.goldenagri.com.sg/pdfs/Annual%20Report/GAR_AnnualReport2010.pdf, http://www.sinarmas.com/en/, http://en.wikipedia.org/wiki/Sinar_Mas_Group, http://www.smart-tbk.com/pdfs/Annual%20Report/AR%20SMART%202010.pdf, http://www.gt.com/intl/cms/s/0/ce71bf4e-c731-11df-aeb1-00144feab49a.html ax221iPcRy

Discussion questions

1 Are there any pertinent agency problems in Sinar Mas?
2 What do you think of the ownership structure? Is it appropriate for the company?
3 What do you think of the board composition?
4 Is the incentive system appropriate?
5 Overall, how would you rate governance at Sinar Mas?
6 Do you expect to see more or less of this governance style over time?

Summary (learning points)

- Family business (including personal ownership) is the most common ownership structure around the world, particularly for smaller companies.
- The reason for the high frequency of family firms is probably that personal ownership is a relatively efficient solution to agency problems.
- Families can play different roles in firms: as owner managers, board members, managers or outside investors.
- Compared with investor-owned companies, founder-owned companies appear to overperform, while second-generation family firms appear to perform on par.
- Families can exercise control through business groups, dual class shares and other control-enhancing mechanisms.
- Statistically, firm value tends to decline when control rights exceed cash flow rights, presumably because of agency problems.
- Family firms face a number of special problems such as succession, conflicts between family members or nepotism. Family firms can seek to address such problems by family councils, succession plans and common governance principles.

 # References and further reading

Anderson, R. and Reeb, D. (2003) Founding-Family Ownership and Firm Performance: Evidence from the S&P 500, *Journal of Finance*, **58** (3), 1301–1328.

Bennedsen, M. and Fan, J. (2011), *Governing the Family Business*, Unpublished Book Manuscript.

Bennedsen, M., Nielsen, K.M., Pérez-González, F. and Wolfenzon, D. (2007) Inside the Family Firm: the Role of Families in Succession Decisions and Performance, *Quarterly Journal of Economics*, **122** (2), 647–691.

Bertrand, M. and Schoar, A. (2006) The Role of the Family in Family Firms, *Journal of Economic Perspectives*, **20** (2), 73–96.

Burkart, M. and Lee, S. (2007) *The One Share – One Vote Debate: A Theoretical Perspective*, ECGI. Finance Working Paper No. 176/2007.

Burkart, M., Panunzi, F. and Shleifer, A. (2003) Family Firms, *Journal of Finance*, **58** (5), 2167–2202.

Chakrabarti, R., Megginson, W.L. and Yadav, P.K. (2008) Corporate Governance in India, *Journal of Applied Corporate Finance*, **20** (1), 59–72. Available at SSRN: http://ssrn.com/abstract=1115534.

Claessens, S., Djankov, S., Fan, J.P.H. and Lang, L.H.P. (2002) Disentangling the Incentive and Entrenchment Effects of Large Shareholdings, *Journal of Finance*, **57** (6), 2741–2771.

Claessens, S., Djankov, S. and Lang, L.H.P. (2000) The separation of ownership and control in East Asian corporations, *Journal of Financial Economics*, **58** (1–2), 81–112.

Cronqvist H., and Nilsson, M. (2003) Agency Costs of Controlling Minority Shareholders. *Journal of Financial and Quantitative Analysis*, **38** (4), 695–719.

de Vries, M. (1993) The Dynamics of Family Controlled Firms: The Good and the Bad News, *Organizational Dynamics*, **21** (3), 59–71.

Franks, J.R., Mayer, C., Volpin, P.F. and Wagner, H.F. (2009) *The Life Cycle of Family Ownership: International Evidence* (October 1). AFA 2009 San Francisco Meetings Paper; EFA 2009 Bergen Meetings Paper. Available at SSRN: http://ssrn.com/abstract=1102475.

Hansson, M., Liljeblom, E. and Martikainen, M. (2009) Corporate Governance and Profitability in Family SMEs (December 14). Available at SSRN: http://ssrn.com/abstract=1531638.

Hansson, M., Liljeblom, E. and Martikainen, M. (2011) Corporate governance and profitability in family SMEs, *European Journal of Finance*, **17** (5–6), 391–408.

Hillier, D. and McColgan, P. (2009) Firm Performance and Managerial Succession in Family Managed Firms, *Journal of Business Finance and Accounting*, **36** (3–4), 461–484.

Jaffe, D.T. (2005). Strategic Planning for the Family in Business, *Journal of Financial Planning*, **18** (3), 50–56.

Johannisson, B. and Huse, M. (2000) Recruiting outside board members in the small family business: an ideological challenge, *Entrepreneurship & Regional Development*, **12** (4), 353–378.

Khanna, T. (2000) Business groups and social welfare in emerging markets: Existing evidence and unanswered questions, *European Economic Review*, Elsevier, **44** (4–6), 748–761.

Khanna, T. and Krishna P. (2005) The Evolution of Concentrated Ownership in India: Broad Patterns and a History of the Indian Software Industry, in *The History of Corporate Governance around the World: Family Business Groups to Professional Managers*, R. Morck (ed) University of Chicago Press.

Khanna, V.S. and Black, B.S. (2007) Can Corporate Governance Reforms Increase Firms' Market Values? Evidence from India, *Journal of Empirical Legal Studies*, **4**, ECGI – Finance Working Paper No. 159/2007.

Leenders, M. and Waarts, E. (2003) Competitiveness and Evolution of Family Businesses: The Role of Family and Business Orientation, *European Management Journal*, **21** (6), 686–697.

Molly, V., Laveren, E. and Deloof, M. (2010) Family Business Succession and Its Impact on Financial Structure and Performance, *Family Business Review*, **23** (2), 131–147.

Phani, B.V., Reddy, V.N., Nagi, R.N. and Bhattacharyya, A.K. (2005) *Insider Ownership, Corporate Governance and Corporate Performance*, NSE Research Initiative Proposal No. 89.

Sharma, P., Chrisman, J.J. and Chua, J.H. (2003) Predictors of satisfaction with the succession process in family firms, *Journal of Business Venturing*, **18** (5), 667–687.

van den Heuvel, J., Van Gils, A. and Voordeckers, W. (2006) Board Roles in Small and Medium-Sized Family Businesses: performance and importance, *Corporate Governance: An International Review*, **14** (5), 467–485.

Venanzi, D. and Morresi, O. (2010) Is Family Business Beautiful? Evidence from Italian Stock Market (February 8). Available at SSRN: http://ssrn.com/abstract=1549535.

Villalonga, B. and Amit. R. (2006) How Do Family Ownership, Control, and Management Affect Firm Value? *Journal of Financial Economics*, **80** (2), 385–417.

PART 4

Practice

Chapter 18

Corporate Governance in Practice

Chapter contents

18.1 Introduction

Corporate governance has grown to be more than an academic subject. It is a field of practice. Investors, board members, lawyers and consultants are increasingly occupied by governance. Some specialize in it. In this final chapter we examine how corporate governance is evolving as a field of practice. Though this topic is by nature less academic than previous chapters, we nevertheless deem it important that students should know some of the issues that practitioners grapple with. True to form we structure the discussion by corporate governance mechanism. We examine how people practise governance working with law, ownership, boards and incentive systems.

18.2 Law and governance

Usually companies cannot make law. They may be able to influence new laws through lobbying but most of the time they have to take the law for granted. However, they can opt in and out of legal regimes by changing their legal status, moving their headquarters or listing their shares on a foreign stock exchange.

A change of legal regime can occur if a company (or more accurately its owners) decides to delist from a stock exchange or change from a joint format to another legal form. Since the law is more restrictive in some areas than others, this can sometimes reduce costs and increase flexibility. However there are also advantages to incorporation or being a listed company, for example investors, banks or other stakeholders may have greater confidence in a more regulated legal entity.

Companies can also change legal regime by moving their headquarters from one state to another. In the USA there has been a lengthy discussion about companies choosing to incorporate in Delaware where company law is said to protect incumbent managers. It has been suggested that legal arbitrage might result in a 'race to the bottom' in which companies opportunistically select legal regimes which protect them against shareholders (Cary, 1974). However, because of regulation benefits as mentioned above it is not clear that companies will always seek to minimize regulation or to entrench managers. It may be that they opt for higher legal status, i.e. a race for the top (Winter, 1977), if their business opportunities improve because of higher investor and stakeholder confidence.

Companies can even move their headquarters to different nations or have their shares listed on a foreign stock exchange. For example by having its shares listed in the USA a foreign company becomes liable under US company law. In the literature such moves have commonly been regarded as a way to bind the company to higher legal standards which could make it easier to attract capital (Coffee, 2002) because investors feel better protected against self-dealing and other agency problems. Foreign listing may also help enhance the reputation and legitimacy of a company which can open new business opportunities, for example by making it easier to get approval for M&A or win government contracts.

18.3 Compliance

Within a given legal regime companies have to decide how they want to comply with the law and best practice codes. Do they want to be best in class or is some ambiguity acceptable? Complete certainty can be very costly. Moreover, should they comply with best practice codes or is it acceptable to explain why they do not? What constitutes a good explanation? Compliance is ultimately the responsibility of the board, but many firms (particularly in the financial sector) now employ compliance officers because regulation has become so complex. Lawyers and auditors are also willing to help carry the burden.

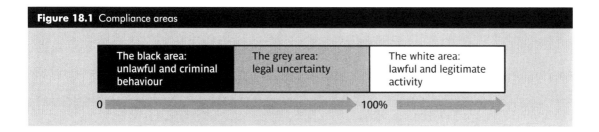

Figure 18.1 Compliance areas

| The black area: unlawful and criminal behaviour | The grey area: legal uncertainty | The white area: lawful and legitimate activity |

0   100%

While compliance is simple in principle, it is difficult in practice because the law is not always clear. Any given activity may in principle be rated by its compliance with the law (Figure 18.1) from 0% to 100% or more.

Some activities with 100% compliance (or more) are clearly lawful and considered legitimate by the general public. This we call the white area. This is where most companies want to be. Others are clearly unlawful or even criminal. This is the black area. Very few companies go there voluntarily. Between these two extremes there is always a range of activities characterized by legal uncertainty. It is not clear whether or not they are legal because the law is not always clear.

Alternatively, the law may be clear but not enforced. For example it may be that there is a speed limit of 70 miles per hour, but since it is difficult to measure the speed of a moving vehicle, the traffic police will only fine you if they are sure that you have exceeded the limit, i.e. if their equipment measures a speed at least 10% above the speed limit. Many drivers take this to mean that they can lawfully drive at 77 miles per hour. Since the speed limit is only enforced above 77 miles per hour, it may be said that prevailing or effective law is a speed limit of 77 miles per hour. Since there is presumably some uncertainty in the equipment this may mean that drivers are occasionally fined anyway.

A company's compliance policy defines how and to what extent it complies with the law. Does it want to be in the white area? Or is it okay to have some activities in the grey area? If so, how close does it want to be to the black area? How closely will it monitor its activities? How many compliance officers? 1, 2 or 100? 1000? Will the board step back if one employee is found to be criminal? A department? The CFO? The CEO? Even if the company insists on a policy of full compliance, how close does it want to be to the grey area? In many cases it is costly to comply and overcompliance may lower the company's accounting returns and market value. Since company management has a legal duty of loyalty towards the shareholders, it may well be that a policy of overcompliance conflicts with other legal duties.

Effectively, this means that companies weigh the costs and benefits of compliance and find a compromise which suits them. The compliance level will depend on the costs of non-compliance including the fines and reputational damage of being found unlawful. Often the reputational damage is more important. Some regulators use this by naming and shaming practices which ensure a much higher level of compliance.

Compliance work may differ according to what policies are monitored: corporate governance, corporate social responsibility, financial regulation, competition policy, tax or other policies. Tax governance has grown to be a topic in its own right.

Compliance takes many forms from economic control or internal auditing to corruption squads checking the practices of foreign subsidiaries. One of the more interesting forms is '**whistleblowing**': evidence supplied by internal informants, who can report anonymously to a mailbox monitored not by company officers, but by a board member or a regulator.

The governance of the compliance function itself is subject to the same trade-offs that you find elsewhere in corporate governance. If compliance officers are part of a functional organization, for example finance, accounting or production, the risk is that they will end up trying to please their bosses and certify that their own functions at least are fully compliant. If on the other hand they are isolated and report to the top level of the organization, ultimately to the board, the risk is that they will be insufficiently informed about what is going on and will make demands that are impractical.

Since compliance officers are presumably no less self-serving than others, the compliance function can grow to enormous proportions with very little value added for the organization. As always the sensible choice is likely to try to strike a balance.

Comply or explain

Authorities such as stock exchanges typically mandate that best practice corporate governance codes are adopted by companies on a 'comply or explain basis', i.e. companies must either comply with a specific recommendation or they must explain why they choose not to. It is then up to investors to react, for example to sell shares if they are not satisfied with the explanation.

The most transparent way of responding is probably to list, in a spreadsheet format, how the company relates to the individual provisions of the code (e.g. see Table 18.1). If there are 86 recommendations in the relevant national code, there are 86 responses with either compliance or non-compliance and explanations documented. Another approach is to explain only if the company does not comply.

A study on company practices for the European Commission revealed that 86% of 233 companies disclosed information on their comply/explain reactions to the relevant national governance code (EU 2009). However, only 39% disclosed provision-by-provision as indicated above; most companies disclosed more general information. Only 23% of all the companies reported compliance with all code provisions while 77% deviated from at least one of the relevant code provisions. In some important areas like director independence or use of board committees compliance was found to be higher and explanations more detailed, while there was less compliance and less explanation with regard to executive pay.

It is debatable what constitutes a satisfactory explanation. In the above-mentioned EU study 26% of all explanations were found to be 'limited', 16% were 'invalid' and 10% were 'general'. Simply responding 'we do not comply' or 'we do not comply with these recommendations because we do not think that it makes sense in our company' does not provide much information to investors. For the most part, however, companies have been able to get away with quite superficial explanations. Many companies have chosen 'general' explanations, i.e. not to respond to the individual recommendations but simply to state that they are in compliance with the relevant national code except the recommendation such and such and then give more or less satisfactory explanations for that. This is less transparent, especially since closer inspection often reveals that they are not really in compliance with some code provisions and that this is not mentioned. Moreover, explanations of compliance are often at least as important as explanations for non-compliance. If for example there is a recommendation that the board oversees major risks, investors may not be satisfied with a simple statement of compliance but may want to know *how* the board chooses to oversee the risks and what risks they focus on.

Table 18.1   Comply or explain in provision-by-provision format

Recommendation no.	Compliance
1	We comply with this recommendation (documentation)
2	We comply with this recommendation (documentation)
3	We do not comply with this recommendation because ... (documentation)
4	We do not comply with this recommendation because ... (documentation)
5	We comply with this recommendation (documentation)
...	...

The best practice codes have led to much 'box checking'. Company boards or compliance officers go through the formalities of providing just sufficient compliance and documentation to be able to check the box. This sometimes substitutes for attention to the content of the recommendations. However, board discussions of how to respond to best practice codes also have a beneficial effect by making board members more aware of governance issues.

18.4 Best owner

Though few people think of ownership as a choice variable, businessmen are increasingly considering who is the best owner of a company or a business unit (Dobbs, Huyett and Koller, 2010). In a sense this is what the entire M&A market is about. Private equity funds certainly make a living by buying and selling companies. Governments decide whether or not to privatize. Entrepreneurs decide whether or not to take their company public. Conglomerates may decide to break up or to spin off business units. Companies decide whether to make or buy a given product or service, i.e. whether or not to outsource.

What guidance can theory give to practice in this area? One view is that the 'best owner' of a company is the one which can maximize its value. This is relatively straightforward, if not easy, if the goal is to maximize shareholder value.

Acquisition: To sell or not to sell?[1]

Should the company continue as a stand-alone entity or accept a takeover offer from another company? For the incumbent shareholders this will depend on the offer price compared with its 'fair value', for example what value the company would be expected to create if it continues on its own. The current stock price is one estimate of the company's value, but for various reasons the market may under- or overestimate it. Alternatively, the company's fair value may be estimated by a discounted cash flow valuation. So, for example, if you can estimate the company's equilibrium cash flow you can divide by its estimated costs of capital to obtain a fair value, which reflects what the company would be expected to create with the existing ownership and management team. Valuation books will tell you how to do this more precisely. A third approach is to compare with market valuations of benchmark companies or recent transactions of a similar nature. There are various reasons why an acquirer may be able to bid higher than the fair value. Synergies with other businesses, lower costs of capital or a better business plan, and many other factors may provide a rationale. Owners differ, and some owners will provide a better match with a given company. Industrial buyers may be able to exploit economies of scale or scope. Private equity funds can work the balance sheet to lower the cost of capital, or they may be better able to identify and implement a value-creating business plan. A management buy-out may completely change the incentives of the management team. In addition there are obviously many reasons (such as empire building or hubris) why acquirers overpay and destroy value in the process.

Fission or spin-off

Sometimes companies face the reverse decision, e.g. whether the company should be broken up or a business unit should be spun off from a larger entity. One of the main reasons is focus: the top management of the new entity can focus on one business. In addition investors can invest in a more clearly defined entity. Finally, the whole entity can much more easily be sold off if it is set up on a stand-alone basis. The spin-off decision will weigh these benefits against synergy losses such as added administrative costs.

---

[1] M&A is obviously a subject area in itself. For an overview and further reading, see Sudarsanam (2010).

Going public

Going public is another fundamental ownership transformation, which may, for example, create value for owners who want to diversify their portfolios. For a comprehensive empirical study see Chemmanur, He and Nandy (2010). It typically involves a change of concentrated ownership of some sort (e.g. family) to institutional investor ownership and a broader set of minority investors. This change will (if successful) lower the company's costs of capital since large institutional investors are well equipped to carry risk. In addition there are benefits for both managers and owners of having a stock price, which continuously tracks a company's value. Managers get immediate feedback on their publicly announced decisions. Owners can reduce (or increase) their shareholdings without having to go through complicated transactions. Listing comes at a price, of course. The market may systematically undervalue a company, particularly if it is a small one with a relatively illiquid share. There are also listing costs of red tape, compliance with codes etc. Moreover, by selling out ownership becomes dispersed and the familiar agency costs between owners and managers or between majority and minority owners will appear.

The going-public decision will weigh the benefits of listing against added administrative and agency costs. Typically, going public will be recommended for large, profitable companies with good growth prospects. Since investors buy into future profits, it is difficult to list loss-making businesses. Large companies can better carry the administrative costs, and the benefits of diversification are higher (corresponding to higher risks of concentration). It is also beneficial to have a track record which investors can examine before they buy (as larger companies will typically have). Smaller (e.g. high tech) companies may also list successfully if they are believed to have particularly good growth prospects. In principle, riskier companies should also be more likely to list, but higher risk will often be associated with greater uncertainty and information (i.e. agency) problems which make investors less likely to invest. Investors would like to understand the businesses they invest in, i.e. to be presented with a convincing business plan. A trade-off between transparency and risk is no doubt why we see many examples of listed low-risk firms such as public utilities.

Going private

Going private is the mirror decision of going public just like spin-off is the mirror decision of acquisition (Bharath and Dittmar, 2006). In some cases listed companies will find that the cost of being listed exceeds the benefits. For example, their stock may be very infrequently traded at a large discount to their fair value, growth prospects are modest, and it is difficult to get investors interested. Private equity funds spot such companies and make money by delisting them. But there are also other solutions like a management buy-out or acquisition by industrial buyers (which often end up buying from private equity funds anyway).

Succession

Most companies begin with ownership by a single entrepreneur, but what happens after that? Acquisition? Go public? Alternatively, continuation as a private stand-alone entity will often involve family ownership. This choice can be made as a valuation exercise, but the company's amenity value for the family needs to be added to the equation (and will often be decisive). Succession from founder ownership is known to be costly, so on average a drop in performance is to be expected (Bennedsen et al., 2007), although there are of course exceptions. For the family successor the need to pay inheritance tax will put an extra drain on liquidity. Depending on their severity and the willingness of banks to provide bridging finance, this can be more or less costly, sometimes prohibitively so. Succession plans well ahead of time can greatly facilitate this process (as well as selling the company), but it is known that few companies have them, presumably because founders are reluctant to admit their own mortality. Hence a high failure rate, because the company's processes are not sufficiently well documented for others to take over from the founder, and because banks are unwilling to provide large amounts of bridging finance at short notice when estate taxes have to be paid. In Northern Europe, **foundation ownership** is a widely used solution to these problems. The founder donates his

shares to a charitable foundation, which exercises ownership after his death. Family members may continue to exercise control through the foundation board, but no longer own the company.

Privatization

Privatization (Megginson 2005, 2010) involves listing a government-owned enterprise or selling it to private owners. In general this tends to improve shareholder performance measures like profit rates or firm value. However, government owners may have objectives other than shareholder value, and in fact these alternative objectives provide the only rationale for government ownership in the first place. For example, during the 2007–2009 crisis a number of banks were nationalized because it was thought to be unacceptable to let them go bankrupt as almost all banks around the world would have if the market had been given free rein. Subsequently bank managers were criticized for taking excessive risk in trying to maximize shareholder value (it is doubtful whether they actually did so because bank shareholders were generally wiped out during the crisis). Social objectives like financial stability, availability and universal, low price service may conflict with shareholder value. To some extent governments can accomplish these social goals by regulation, such as concession or competition policies, while leaving the rest to private enterprise. But as the financial crisis has shown, it may occasionally be necessary for governments to step in and impose objectives other than shareholder value maximization. Despite this, value considerations still play some role in privatization decisions. For example, despite the warning of efficient market theorists, governments may try to time their privatizations to a favourable stock market climate. Moreover, not all government businesses have sufficient profit potential to warrant private investment. Finally, recent research has shown that the long-run gains to privatization may be more elusive than was previously assumed (Megginson, 2010).

18.5 Board work

In current practice, board work can be said to consist of getting the right team together (choosing and replacing board members), leading it to deliver (board leadership) and evaluating the results (board evaluation).

Choosing board members

Board members can be chosen more or less systematically. A nomination committee can come up with a competence profile: a list of competencies which would be advantageous to have represented. Typical desired competencies include industry and top management experience, financial expertise, international experience and knowledge of issues which are deemed to be particularly important to the company's future. The board can then commission a headhunter to find candidates who fit the desired profile. The nomination committee proposes a new board among the candidates.

Typically boards will choose a soft approach and not replace all members at once, but wait for members to retire voluntarily or for election periods to expire. There are some sound reasons for this. Board members get to know the company as they serve and it is therefore advantageous to have some continuity on the board. But patience also means that some underperforming board members get to stay on for longer than they should.

In addition to competencies, independence is also important and sometimes there is a trade-off between the two. Major owners, past employees or executives, and board members with high seniority are usually well informed and competent, but not deemed independent according to most best practice codes. There is a tendency for boards to use formal independence definitions because these are easy to communicate to outside investors. But what matters is obviously real independence, e.g. the ability and integrity to challenge a well-prepared management team when this is necessary.

Very frequently shareholders will have ideas and demands for new board members, for example directors who emphasize shareholder value creation. Since they are ultimately in charge, they will

get their way, if they insist. But if they trust the people they have previously elected, they are often willing to listen to proposals from the incumbent board.

Board leadership

The chair is responsible for making the best possible use of board's human resources. This is difficult because the board needs to work together as a team and at the same time tolerate dissenting voice. The best board is not necessarily the board whose members all agree. This calls for a leadership style which inspires trust and open discussions but draws clear conclusions.

It also means stimulating active participation by non-executive directors. Historically board meetings have been characterized by long presentations by executives, interrupted occasionally by polite questions from non-executives. While this may have been quite satisfactory for mostly ceremonial purposes, it makes little sense to ask highly qualified individuals to sit on the board if they do not get to voice their opinions. By leading the discussion, the chair can do quite a lot to get them involved in a real dialogue.

A board probably approves management proposals 95% of the time (McNulty and Pettigrew, 1999). Active board leadership means saying no to management proposals more often instead of rubber stamping them. This needs to be done in a diplomatic way in order not to insult the executives. For example, the board may demand to be involved earlier in the corporate decision processes rather than being presented with a fully fledged decision proposal. At an earlier stage of the strategic planning process (for example when brainstorming) there will often be more options open, and decisions will be less specific.

Even when the board ends up accepting decision proposals, it can set the tone for future decisions through the discussion, which can for example indicate what proposals would not have been acceptable, and thus warn executives not to make such proposals in the future (McNulty and Pettigrew, 1999). The board may also through its discussion indicate what directions it would like to see the company go in the future. It may also approve management suggestions more or less enthusiastically, holding managers more personally responsible for decision proposals which it only reluctantly accepts.

Instead of reducing risks by rejecting decision proposals, boards may sometimes want to challenge companies to become more ambitious (and thus take more risk). This can be done by setting (and raising) growth targets in budgets and strategy plans. For example the management team may propose a budget which involves 3% growth, but the board may ask for 5%.

From the board's viewpoint risk management will not necessarily be concerned with taking less risk, but rather with an understanding of the risks involved in the company's budget and strategy plans. When company performance falls significantly short of expectation, the board would like to have been prepared for this eventuality beforehand (and for the management to have drawn up a contingency plan) if the event was within the predictable, for example having to do with the company's own market or business model. In contrast the board will not ask risk managers to draw up contingency plans for less predictable macro events such as perhaps a sudden alien invasion. As a rule of thumb the board members will ask risk managers to prepare for risks which could get them fired (i.e. risks for which shareholders will hold them responsible).

Ultimately, a dissatisfied board will have to replace the management team. This can be done abruptly following unexpectedly poor performance or more gradually by 'strengthening the management team' through for example the appointment of a new chief financial officer. To keep their options open, many boards insist on contact with potential future candidates who can be groomed for top jobs. A succession plan is important in case of sudden executive death, but also quite convenient if the CEO decides to get another job, or if they need to be fired.

Board evaluation

There are various ways of evaluating the board (Daily and Dalton, 2003; Minichilli et al., 2007). In corporate governance we examine who is the agent, what their incentives are and how they are held

accountable. In this case we ask who evaluates, what the incentives of the evaluator are and how they are held accountable.

One way is for the chair to evaluate, e.g. to have an annual talk with the individual board members to assess how they are doing, for example their attendance, activity level at board meetings and interaction with other board members. She can then make recommendations to the shareholders or the nomination committee concerning replacements. While this may be a good exercise if both parties desire to improve, it does raise a few questions. First, who evaluates the chair? If a board is malfunctioning, this will often be attributable to a bad chair. Second, chair-led evaluations can create an authority relationship in which the board members try to please the chair, for example by suppressing unpleasant opinions. This may be contrary to good board work. In conclusion, if the chair is in charge, the risk is that the evaluation will tend to reinforce the chair.

Another way is to call in a consultant who conducts individual interviews with the board members, perhaps assisted by a questionnaire. Again this can be a useful exercise, particularly since board members are more likely to say unpleasant things in an anonymous questionnaire or a one-to-one talk. But it does raise the question of who the consultant is working for, since consultants will want to please their customer. If the board or the chairman of the board is perceived as the customer, consultants may come up with a positive evaluation or precisely emphasize the points which the chair or the board would like to emphasize. Secondly, consultants may be tempted to complicate the evaluation process to justify higher fees. They will also want to make frequent evaluations, but while shareholders should continually assess whether the board creates sufficient value, it is far from certain that a formal board evaluation is necessary every year, given how infrequently boards meet and how long it takes before their decisions influence company performance. An evaluation every three years may be fully sufficient.

Major shareholders may also be in charge of the evaluation. In listed companies this may create potential problems of inside information, but it is feasible and practised in private equity. Since private equity fund managers are often on the boards of the companies they own, other managers in the private equity firm may be asked to be in charge. The advantage of involving the owners is that their incentives are correct, since they will presumably be interested in value maximization.

Another way to get the owners 'on board' is found in the Swedish system which makes use of nomination committees elected at the annual general meeting. Such nomination committees are typically composed mainly of shareholder representatives, i.e. representative of the largest shareholders and perhaps a member of the shareholder association to represent minority shareholders. The dilemma is that shareholders may have the right incentives, but since they do not participate in board meetings they have little sense of how the board actually works. They may in fact feel that they are making their recommendations 'out of the blue'. To handle this problem a board member (e.g. the chair) is usually asked to sit in on the nomination committee.

18.6 Designing an incentive programme

CEO compensation has become a science in itself. It typically involves a basic salary, a bonus based on operational performance, a stock option grant, restricted stock (which cannot be sold right away), benefits such as pension or health insurance, terms of employment and dismissal clauses such as a 'golden parachute'. Since this can be quite complicated most boards will in practice ask a pay consultant to come up with a compensation package which is considered to be attractive for the position in question. The package will typically be based on an average level of pay and an average pay mix for similar jobs, with a little extra to make the job attractive. This little extra is probably one of the factors which has led to a relentless growth of executive pay in the past four decades. Not everyone can pay their executives better than average.

A more thoughtful board may try to match executive pay to the job at hand and to the candidate. All else equal a high level of fixed pay will make the CEO more risk averse, since she will not be paid more for good performance, but will lose her attractive salary in case of bad performance. Paying managers like bureaucrats may tend to make them behave like bureaucrats. In contrast a stock options package will make the executive more risk seeking and less risk averse, particularly to downside risk.

Restricted stock programmes (in which executives are asked to invest part of their salary in the company's stock and keep it until for example two years after they retire) sensitizes managers both to downside and upside risk. Since restricted stock is simple and involves a high degree of alignment with stockholders, it is perhaps the most practical way to incentivize managers. It is also a way to avoid public outrage. In some cases, however, restricted stock is not a practical solution. Stock options may for example be favoured for tax reasons. It is also more difficult, though not quite impossible, in closely held firms whose stock is illiquid or not traded at all. It is possible to apply an automatic valuation formula and commit the majority shareholders to repurchasing the stock, but this is then effectively a bonus scheme based on the factors in the valuation formula.

Bonus is paid based on operational performance measures, e.g. a percentage of profits or achievement of a threshold (target) value of sales or costs. It can also be based on a share of shareholder value (for example economic profits: profits after capital costs). Since bonus is often calculated on accounting figures, the standard criticisms against accounting figures apply: accounting returns deviate substantially from economic returns, they may to some extent be manipulated by managers and they fail to correct for risk. After the financial crisis it has become fashionable to recommend that bonus programmes are stretched over 3–5 years rather than paid annually. A bonus in one year is paid into an account, from which a 'malus' may be deducted the following year to reflect any underperformance. It is also recommended that variable pay is adjusted for risk, which makes sense theoretically, but is very difficult in practice. The only practical way to adjust for risk may be to lower the ratio of variable to total pay, perhaps by raising total pay.

It is also possible to make executive pay more holistic by incorporating a larger set of performance measures, including balanced scorecard measures of customer satisfaction, employee satisfaction, innovation, sustainability and social responsibility. However, complicating executive pay comes at a cost: more random (and non-random) noise is introduced into the manager's pay, and the incentive effect may be dissipated. A better alternative may be to rely on a subjective bonus to capture these complicated effects (i.e. boards may simply grant managers an extraordinary bonus at the end of the year).

18.7 Discussion

Corporate governance has evolved from a set of demands or principles to a field of practice, in which companies all over the world are continuously experimenting with finding the best solutions. Rather than imposing standard solutions on companies, their shareholders are devising their own tailor-made solutions to fit the individual company. The consensus view seems to be that corporate governance has in fact improved markedly (EU 2009), most of all perhaps because of the increased attention given to the subject.

Corporate governance is likely to continue to evolve in response to demands by investors and governments. Transparency and disclosure have increased rapidly during the past decade, and the trend seems likely to continue. We expect to see more accurate information on corporate ownership, board structures and board behaviour as well as executive compensation. Compliance with corporate governance codes is expected to improve, and companies are likely to be pressured to provide better (provision by provision) explanations if they choose not to comply.

The balance between soft and hard law may also change, for example some code provisions could be made mandatory by being included as hard law. The efficiency of the European 'soft touch' regulation has been criticized, but so far the consensus view seems to be that soft law works and should be continued (EU 2009).

With regard to ownership structures, most governance thinking has so far been directed at listed companies, but corporate governance is increasingly spreading to other organizations such as state-owned enterprises, mutuals and cooperatives, family businesses or non-profits. It is clear that these entities face different governance issues so that practices from listed companies cannot be directly transferred. Nevertheless, central issues like independence and transparency are also important for entities other than public corporations. Codes of best practice directed at their specific characteristics are emerging, and this is likely to continue for many years.

Board work has already increased in terms of remit and time commitment. We expect to see this trend continue with boards being responsible for an increasing number of issues. With the lessons of the financial crisis, issues like risk management are sure to remain high on the agenda. Separate risk committees are already widely used in the financial sector and could spread to other companies. Other areas like corporate social responsibility are also likely to become more important.

Executive pay will almost certainly remain a focus area. Correcting for risk so that pay for performance does not lead to excessive risk taking is one of the major lessons of the financial crisis. While the idea is simple, it is going to be difficult to operationalize because of the multifaceted nature of risk.

Minicase

Google

Google Inc. is a US-based IT company focusing on internet searching, online advertising and operating systems (Android), but diversifying into other business like the recent acquisition of Motorola's mobile phone business. The company generates revenue primarily by delivering online advertising.

The company was founded by Larry Page and Sergey Brin, PhD students at Stanford University. Larry Page is currently CEO while Brin is an executive and a member of the board. The founders continue to exercise effective control through large shareholdings and dual class shares.

The board consists of Larry Page, Sergey Brin, executive chairman Eric E. Schmidt (CEO 2001–2011, formerly CEO of Novel and chief technology officer at Sun Microsystems), L. John Doerr (a venture capitalist), John L. Hennessy (an engineering professor at Stanford University), Ann Mather (an executive with experience from the media industry), Paul S. Otellini (executive at Intel Corporation), K. Ram Shriram (a venture capitalist), and Shirley M. Tilghman (President, Princeton University).

Former CEO Eric E Schmidt was paid $0.03 million in 2010, but owns 2.9% of the company worth almost $5 billion. He has cashed in some of his shares. Google uses 5% of its revenue on stock-based compensation for other employees.

The company has high growth and profit rates although both have come down since the company was listed. It share price skyrocketed until 2007, took a tumble during the 2008 crisis and is now back around the same level.

Google's is a CSR sensitive company with the slogan 'first, do no evil'. It was criticized for accepting censorship in the Chinese market, but has now withdrawn.

Sources:
http://money.cnn.com/2011/01/24/technology/google schmidt payday/index.htm
http://people.forbes.com/profile/eric-e-schmidt/37783
http://www.forbes.com/lists/2010/12/boss-10 Eric-E-Schmidt OYW6.html

Discussion questions

1 Google is at risk of a lot of law suits in the USA. Would it make sense to move headquarters to another country? Why not?
2 What do you think about the company's ownership structure? Does concentrated founder ownership make sense? How about dual class shares?
3 Is the board appropriate for the company? Is there enough general business experience?
4 Are the incentives appropriate?
5 Could there be unresolved agency problems at Google? If so, what kind?
6 Does the company's diversification strategy make sense or is it an expression of empire building?

Summary (learning points)

- A growing industry of corporate governance specialists are working on corporate governance in practice.

- Boards, compliance officers, CFOs and company secretaries must decide how to comply with company law, tax law and best practice codes.

- Private equity funds, investment banks and others seek to determine best ownership and how value can be created by changing ownership.

- Nomination committees and shareholders work on recruiting the best board members.

- Board chairs try to lead the board to maximize its contribution.

- Incentive programmes need to be designed to enhance performance while avoiding excessive risk taking.

- The governance industry is likely to continue to develop new solutions to changing demands by shareholders, legislators and the rest of society.

References and further reading

Beaumier, C.M. (2006) Should Your Board Have a Compliance Committee?, *Bank Accounting & Finance* (08943958), **19** (3), 35–38.

Becht, M., Bolton, P., and Roell, A. (2003) Corporate Governance and Control, in *Handbook of Economics and Finance*, Constantinides, M., Harris, M., Stulz, R.M. (eds), North Holland: Amsterdam. 4–109.

Bennedsen, M., Nielsen, K., Pérez-González, F. and Wolfenzon, D. (2007) Inside the family firm: the role of families in succession decisions and performance, *Quarterly Journal of Economics*, **122** (2), 647–691.

Bharath, S.T. and Dittmar, A.K. (2006) *To Be or Not to Be (Public). Using going private transactions to examine why firms go public*, University of Michigan, Ross School of Business Research Paper.

Brickley, J.A. and Zimmerman, J.L. (2010) Corporate governance myths: Comments on Armstrong, Guay, and Weber, *Journal of Accounting & Economics*, **50** (2/3), 235–245.

Cadbury Commission (1992). *Code of best practice: Report of the committee on the financial aspects of corporate governance*, Gee and Co.: London.

Cary, W. (1974) Federalism and corporate law: reflections upon Delaware, *Yale Law Journal*, **83** (4), 663–705.

Chemmanur, T.J., He, S. and Nandy, D. (2010) The going public decision and the product market, *Review of Financial Studies*, **23** (5), 1855–1908.

Chong, A. and Gradstein, M. (2011) Is the World Flat? Country- and Firm-Level Determinants of Law Compliance, *Journal of Law, Economics & Organization*, **27** (2), 272–300.

Coffee Jr., J.C. (2002) Racing Towards The Top?: The Impact of Cross-Listings and Stock Market Competition on International Corporate Governance, *Columbia Law Review*, **102** (7), 1757.

Daily, C.M. and Dalton, D.R. (2003) Looking in the mirror: board evaluation, *Journal of Business Strategy*, **24** (6), 8–9.

Dobbs, R., Huyett, B. and Koller, T. (2010) Are you still the best owner of your assets?, *McKinsey Quarterly*, **1**, 107–111.

EU (2009) http://ec.europa.eu/internal_market/company/docs/ecgforum/studies/comply-or-explain-090923_en.pdf

McNulty, T. and Pettigrew, A. (1999) Strategists on the Board, *Organization Studies*, **20** (1), 47–74.

Megginson, W.L. (2005) *The Financial Economics of Privatization*, Oxford University Press: New York.

Megginson, W.L. (2010) *Privatization and Finance* (January 30). Available at SSRN: http://ssrn.com/abstract=1544889.

Minichilli, A., Gabrielsson, J. and Huse, M. (2007) Board Evaluations: making a fit between the purpose and the system, *Corporate Governance: An International Review*, **15** (4), 609–622.

Organisation for Economic Cooperation and Development (1999) Principles of Corporate Governance, Paris: OECD. Available at www.oecd.org/dataoecd/47/50/4347646.pdf.

Sudarsanam, S. (2010) *Creating Value from Mergers and Acquisitions*, Prentice Hall.

Thomsen, S. (2009) Corporate Governance and The Financial Crisis, in S.Thomsen, C.Rose, O.Risager (eds), *Understanding the Financial Crisis: Investment, Risk and Governance*, Simcorp, August 2009.

Van der Bauwhede, H. (2009) On the relation between corporate governance compliance and operating performance, *Accounting & Business Research*, **39** (5), 497–513.

Winter, R.K. (1977) State law, shareholder protection, and the theory of the corporation, *Journal of Legal Studies*, **6**, 251–292.

Wolfenzon (2007) Inside the Family Firm: The Role of Families in Succession Decisions and Performance, *Quarterly Journal of Economics*, **122** (2), 647–691.

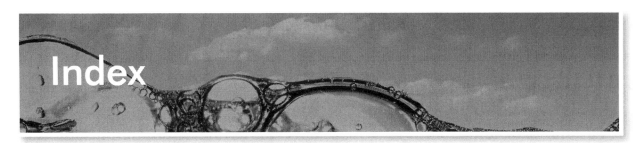

Index